MW01011993

Handbook of
PUBLIC ECONOMICS

VOLUME 5

Edited by

ALAN J. AUERBACH

RAJ CHETTY

MARTIN FELDSTEIN

EMMANUEL SAEZ

ELSEVIER

Amsterdam • Boston • Heidelberg • London • New York • Oxford
Paris • San Diego • San Francisco • Singapore • Sydney • Tokyo
North Holland is an imprint of Elsevier

North Holland is an imprint of Elsevier
Radarweg 29, PO Box 211, 1000 AE Amsterdam, The Netherlands
The Boulevard, Langford Lane, Kidlington, Oxford, OX5 1GB, UK

Notices
Knowledge and best practice in this field are constantly changing. As new research and experience broaden our understanding, changes in research methods, professional practices, or medical treatment may become necessary.

Practitioners and researchers must always rely on their own experience and knowledge in evaluating and using any information, methods, compounds, or experiments described herein. In using such information or methods they should be mindful of their own safety and the safety of others, including parties for whom they have a professional responsibility.

To the fullest extent of the law, neither the Publisher nor the authors, contributors, or editors, assume any liability for any injury and/or damage to persons or property as a matter of products liability, negligence or otherwise, or from any use or operation of any methods, products, instructions, or ideas contained in the material herein.

Library of Congress Cataloging-in-Publication Data

A catalog record for this book is available from the Library of Congress

British Library Cataloguing-in-Publication Data

A catalogue record for this book is available from the British Library.

ISBN: 978-0-444-53759-1

For information on all North Holland publications
visit our website at http://store.elsevier.com

Working together
to grow libraries in
developing countries

www.elsevier.com • www.bookaid.org

Transferred to Digital Printing in 2013

CONTENTS

The aim of the *Handbooks in Economics* series is to produce Handbooks for various branches of economics, each of which is a definitive source, reference, and teaching supplement for use by professional researchers and advanced graduate students. Each Handbook provides self-contained surveys of the current state of a branch of economics in the form of chapters prepared by leading specialists on various aspects of this branch of economics. These surveys summarize not only received results but also newer developments, from recent journal articles and discussion papers. Some original material is also included, but the main goal is to provide comprehensive and accessible surveys. The Handbooks are intended to provide not only useful reference volumes for professional collections but also possible supplementary readings for advanced courses for graduate students in economics.

Kenneth J. Arrow and Michael D. Intriligator

More than a decade has passed since the publication of the last volume of the Handbook of Public Economics, and with the evolution of the field and appearance of many important contributions there are many worthwhile topics to include in Volume 5.

The first chapter, by James Andreoni and Abigail Payne, considers the determinants of charitable giving. These include, of course, the tax price familiar from the classic public finance literature on the subject, but the more recent literature considers many novel issues to help us understand what gives rise to such potentially altruistic behavior.

In Chapter 2, Timothy Besley and Torsten Persson evaluate the role of taxation in economic development. A backdrop is the fact that mature developed countries have much larger public sectors and very different tax systems than developing countries. With this frame of reference, the chapter explores the interplay between economic development and the evolution of tax systems, with political institutions playing an important role in determining the process.

Raj Chetty and Amy Finkelstein present and discuss important strands in the literature on social insurance in Chapter 3, emphasizing empirical work aimed at evaluating theoretical predictions. The chapter consists of two parts, developing theoretical models of selection in insurance markets and the impact of government intervention and then describing work aimed at empirical testing of the predictions of theory.

Urban public finance is the subject of Chapter 4, by Edward Glaeser. Distinct from the areas of fiscal federalism and local public finance (as considered in the chapters by Rubinfeld, v. 2, and Scotchmer, v. 4), which focus on intergovernmental relations and the sorting of individuals among communities but devote relatively less attention to what happens within cities, the research this chapter reviews focuses more on the special role played by large urban areas, bringing together work in public finance and urban economics.

Earlier volumes of this Handbook have included chapters on taxation in open economies (Dixit, v.1 and Gordon and Hines, v.4), but not specifically on the phenomenon of international tax competition, analyzed by Michael Keen and Kai Konrad in Chapter 5, which arises as governments seek to attract productive economic activity and tax bases. With increasing cross-border economic activity and factor mobility and the rise of multinational companies serving as motivation, an active literature has developed on both the positive and normative aspects of tax competition, including the potential for policy coordination.

The transmission of wealth to successive generations is of considerable interest to economists because of the various factors that may determine the bequest motive and the potential impacts on the behavior of individuals on both sides of the bequest. Wealth transfers are also of considerable policy interest because of the role that wealth concentration may play in economic inequality. Chapter 6, by Wojciech Kopcuzk, considers the role that taxation in general and the taxation of wealth transfers in particular plays in influencing the size and timing of bequests.

In the final chapter of the volume, Thomas Piketty and Emmanuel Saez present and discuss developments in the optimal income tax literature, focusing primarily on work since that discussed in the chapters in earlier Handbooks by Stiglitz (v. 2) and Auerbach and Hines (v. 3). A question of particular importance is the optimal tax rate on high income individuals, and the chapter offers an in-depth analysis of this question under a variety of modeling assumptions.

Earlier versions of the chapters in this volume were presented at a conference held in Berkeley in December, 2011, sponsored by the Robert D. Burch Center for Tax Policy and Public Finance. We are grateful to discussants at that conference for their helpful contributions and to Camille Fernandez of the Burch Center for organizing the conference and helping us to shepherd the papers into publishable form.

Chapter 1
James Andreoni
University of California, San Diego, CA
A.Abigail Payne
McMaster University, Hamilton, Ontario, Canada

Chapter 2
Timothy Besley
London School of Economics, London, WC
Torsten Persson
Stockholm University, Stockholm, Sweden

Chapter 3
Raj Chetty
Harvard University, Cambridge, MA
Amy Finkelstein
MIT, Cambridge, MA

Chapter 4
Edward L. Glaeser
Harvard University, Cambridge, MA

Chapter 5
Michael Keen
International Monetary Fund, Washington, DC
Kai A. Konrad
Max Plank Institute of Tax Law and Public Finance, Munich, Germany

Chapter 6
Wojciech Kopczuk
Columbia University, New York, NY

Chapter 7
Thomas Piketty
Paris School of Economics, Paris, France
Emmanuel Saez
University of California, Berkeley, CA

CHAPTER 1

Charitable Giving

James Andreoni[*] and A. Abigail Payne[†]

*University of California, San Diego, USA
†McMaster University, Hamilton, Ontario, Canada

Contents

Handbook of Public Economics, Volume 5
ISSN 1573-4420, http://dx.doi.org/10.1016/B978-0-444-53759-1.00001-7

1. INTRODUCTION

Charitable giving has remained an active and important area within Public Economics since researchers like Martin Feldstein and coauthors published some of the first policy studies on the topic in the 1970s.[1] Today, our knowledge on charitable giving draws from important research in applied econometrics, economic theory, game theory, and experimental and behavioral economics.

The applied econometrician, looking either at individual tax returns, survey data, or tax returns of the charities themselves, is interested in how economic variables influence or are correlated with giving. Do givers respond to tax incentives? How does giving change with income? How do receipts of charities vary with dollars spent on fundraising? Do government grants to charities affect the dollars raised by charities and through what mechanism?

The economic theorist is confronted with the issue of what form preferences take. Since charities have primary properties that are similar to public goods, a natural model of charities is as a privately provided public good. However, free riding provides a strong incentive in these models, leading to predictions of very little giving. But most households give something to charity each year, and in many countries average giving is a significant fraction of income—nearly 2% in the US, for instance. This would indicate that motives other than a pure interest in charitable output itself are involved in the decision to give. Unfortunately, these other motives are difficult to detect in survey or tax return data.

With this quandary as a backdrop, much of the recent theoretical, experimental, and behavioral research on giving has focused on identifying the underlying motives. Careful thinking on the theoretical side is necessary to generate hypotheses that can be confronted with data. Since naturally occurring data often lacks the specificity to test theories, data must at times be collected under some experimental control, either in the laboratory or in the field. This branch of the literature on charitable giving is the source of some of the greatest insights and the greatest promise and, in recent years, greatest growth in research.

Once one has a better handle on the underlying preferences for giving, the theorist can begin to tackle broader issues regarding policy toward charitable giving. How does the charitable sector overcome the free rider problem? What are the strategic responses in the market for giving among all the players? Does competition among charities spark efficient innovation or wasteful fundraising? What is the optimal tax policy toward charitable giving, and how can it take advantage of these naturally occurring preferences and institutions to maximize efficiency?

The importance and popularity of research on charitable giving is evidenced by a number of recent review articles. Andreoni (2006b) provides a lengthy summary of research from the prior 25 years of study. List (2011) gives a cogent account of innovations in the study of charity markets since 2006, and in between numerous other chapters and

---

[1] See Feldstein and Clotfelter (1976), Feldstein and Taylor (1976), and the important book by Clotfelter (1985).

reviews have also appeared.[2] Given the availability of other summaries of findings in the literature, this *Handbook* chapter will be more thematic, programmatic, and prescriptive than what is common for chapters of its type. Certainly we will highlight the main contributions since 2006, but we will use these to construct a lattice for how we think future work in the area would be most informative and productive, highlighting unpublished as well as published works. We hope to provide the new reader with a perspective on the current state of the literature, and for the experienced reader, we hope to point to new and important questions that remain unanswered.

The next section will give a brief summary of the overall facts about charitable giving, in the US and internationally. This will lay out the main facts to be explained or captured in the research. We will then discuss four main approaches one could take to research on charitable giving, highlighting the primary questions and limitations of each approach. Of course, all approaches have value and none in isolation can answer every question.

The first approach is to look at giving as a simple *individual economic decision*, where a quantity of gifts to supply is determined by maximizing a utility function subject to a budget constraint. This is a natural place to begin and allows an easy framework for approaching simple survey data from individuals, and for identifying simple and important policy goals.

The second approach is to think of giving as a *strategic interaction*, with many actors involved. This market view of giving suggests that donors are choosing gifts, charities are choosing fundraising efforts and mechanisms, and if the government is involved it is choosing grants to charities and subsidies to donors.[3] A fourth player may also be at work: charitable foundations. Foundations are a kind of charitable intermediary. They collect contributions, often qualifying the donor for a tax benefit, and only later spend these dollars on the "end producer" of the charitable goods and services. All four of these types of participants can be acting in response to the choices of the others. We will discuss new theoretical and empirical studies that take account of these interdependencies.

Recently scholars have added a third and potentially very fruitful approach based on giving as a *social exchange*. In particular, a charitable contribution is rarely made in the absence of an overt request to give. The request may come from a friend, a co-worker, a door-to-door solicitor, a phone call from a fund drive, an on-air campaign from public broadcasting, a television commercial with an emotional appeal, or even from a news report during a time of a disaster. Moreover, when giving is to some degree visible by others, it complicates the social interaction with a league of new influences. What, for example, will someone watching infer about a giver's character? The important thing

---

[2] See, for example, Vesterlund (2006), Andreoni (2001), Andreoni, Harbaugh, and Vesterlund (2008), Bekkers (2008), Bekkers and Wiepking (2011), Wiepking and Bekkers (2012), or the special issue of the Journal of Public Economics, edited by Andreoni and List (2011).

[3] The idea of charities as markets was first introduced in Andreoni and Payne (2003) and later developed in Andreoni (2006b) and List (2011).

about social interactions is that they are likely to be central to understanding *changes* in giving. While once one becomes a giver, simply answering annual appeals may be a way of "planning" responsible degrees of altruism, if we are to discuss what affects a *change* in giving, we will need to address the question, "What makes one become a giver in the first place?" The inherent sociality of giving, we conjecture, will be a part of this answer.

This leads naturally to the fourth and newest approach: giving as a response to conscious, or perhaps even unconscious, *empathic, moral, or cultural urges.* These are the kinds of urges that psychologists, biologists, and anthropologists tell us distinguish humans from most other animals. We tend to have heightened senses of empathy, we are governed more by internal—yet socially agreed upon—notions of justice, and we are concerned with the moral impressions we leave with neighbors and acquaintances. These are all true even though, as a species, we are far removed from the environments that likely implanted these values in our psyche: competing for survival in small communities of clan and kin. Understanding how these pressures are presented today, we conjecture, will be key to the next generation of research on altruism, giving, fundraising, and markets for charity.

How does all this research feed into prescriptions for policy? Historically, there have been two main policy questions regarding charity: What is the price elasticity of giving, and do government grants crowd out private donations? While these questions remain relevant today, recent work has broadened the kinds of policy issues economists face. Most central to these are issues related to fundraising and institutional design. For instance, scientific research can be supported through government taxation and grants to scientists by institutions like the National Science Foundation, or through private foundations that mimic the NSF but are funded through tax-deductible donations. One requires distortionary taxes to fund, while the other may create deadweight loss through the costs of fundraising. The incidence of the two is also quite different—those with high demand pay more under private provision, but their preferences are also more heavily weighted than low demanders. The more we understand these social and financial costs of fundraising, the more we can say about how best to organize society to provide needed social goods.

A related pedagogical issue arises about fundraising. Many studies and experiments help us to understand why people give and what triggers a gift. While this helps us understand foundational economic questions, such as the psychic costs of saying "no" to a fundraiser, it also often yields information that can help fundraisers increase donations. There are two delicate issues here that economic research has yet to debate. First, one must resist the inference that anything that increases donations is good for society. The role of the public economist has always been to find the greatest good for the greatest number, and fundraising for charity is just one of many institutional forms for supporting these goods that are available to society. Second, do we as economists have an obligation or even an interest in uncovering new methods that help charities raise more dollars? We don't study how for-profits could improve revenues, so if the objective of a study is to find better fundraising methods for non-profits then it is incumbent upon the scientist to argue that it is in the social interest to do so.

2. BACKGROUND: FACTS AND FIGURES ON CHARITABLE GIVING

Here we summarize the within and between country differences in charitable giving. This seemingly straightforward task is, unfortunately, difficult to accomplish, as data sources vary in the frequency and methods of their collection, and in the fidelity of the reports. Nonetheless we make our best attempt to characterize the general facts about giving.[4]

Looking at giving as a percent of GDP in 2005, Charities Aid Foundation (2006) ranked the US highest (1.67%), followed by the UK (0.73%), Canada (0.72%), Australia (0.69%), and South Africa (0.64%).[5] At the lower end of the scale were France (0.14%), Germany (0.22%), and Turkey (0.23%). These numbers, however, are based on values of reported donations by individuals. This is but a partial picture of philanthropy. Philanthropy also encompasses donating time, helping a stranger, participating in a community event, and even helping one's family members. Creating measures that compare giving across countries is difficult if countries and/or cultures value these types of giving differently. Depending on the method used to measure giving, which country is more generous will vary. For example, consider the World Giving Index developed by the UK Charities Aid Foundation (CAF) using world survey data collected by the Gallup organization. The index is based on surveys of 150,000 individuals from 153 countries. The following three questions formed the basis of the index: In the month prior to the survey being complete[6]: (i) Have you donated money to a charity? (ii) Have you volunteered your time to an organization? (iii) Have you helped a stranger or someone you did not know who needed help?

Based on the responses to these questions, CAF assigned to each country a number to reflect their level of giving behavior for 2010 and 2011. As with any survey, however, there are many possible avenues for inaccuracies, and indeed there is a great variation in the index across these 2 years. For example, in 2010 the US ranked fifth in overall giving; in 2011, the US ranked first. The top countries for giving money include Thailand, the UK, Ireland, the Netherlands, Hong Kong, Indonesia, Morocco, Australia, Iceland, and Malta (the US in 2011 was tied for tenth place). Georgia, Russia, Madagascar, and Cote d'Ivoire are at the bottom. The top countries for volunteering are Turkmenistan, Liberia, Sri Lanka, Tajikistan, the US (fifth place), Guinea, Nigeria, Philippines, Uzbekistan, and Myanmar. Greece, Serbia, Croatia, and China are at the bottom. And the top countries for helping a stranger include Liberia, the US (2nd), Ghana, Sierra Leone, Nigeria, Senegal, Sudan, New Zealand, Qatar, and Australia. Madagascar, Rwanda, Burundi, Albania, Indonesia, and Japan are at the bottom.

[4] Bekkers (2012) provides additional information on regional differences in philanthropy.
[5] International comparisons of charitable giving, November 2006, Charities Aid Foundation briefing paper.
[6] World Giving Index 2011: A global view of giving trends, Charities Aid Foundation, 2011.

These statistics illustrate that giving and perceptions about giving vary across the world. They also illustrate that there is no single measure that fully captures generosity or giving.

Next we ask, how has giving changed over time? Let us start by looking at data for the United States. Our numbers are drawn from the annual publication, Giving USA 2012. The analysts for this publication draw their data from several sources and then apply an econometric model to estimate how the general population behaves. This is necessary because there is no single source for identifying either individual donations to charity or the recipients of the donations. For example, reported giving on tax returns only identifies the giving of those with taxable income who itemize. Charity tax returns are only required by organizations that meet a minimum threshold for income and are not religious. Given there is no single source that allows us to measure giving and the charity recipients of the gifts in the US, the figures in the Giving USA 2012 publication represent the best guesses of trained analysts.

In 2010, total contributions to charity by individuals, corporations, foundations, and through bequests were estimated at nearly $296 billion in the US, an increase of approximately 2% over the previous year after adjusting for inflation. The increase in 2010 over 2009, however, came after a 2-year decline in giving. Over the last four decades (1970–2010) the biggest increase in real growth occurred in the late 1990s and again around 2007. These patterns are shown in Figure 1. Giving by individuals as a share of their disposable income has varied over the period but for the most part has hovered around 2% (minimum of 1.7% in the early 1990s; maximum of 2.4% in the mid-2000s). While a high percentage of individuals give to charity today, there is great variance in the levels

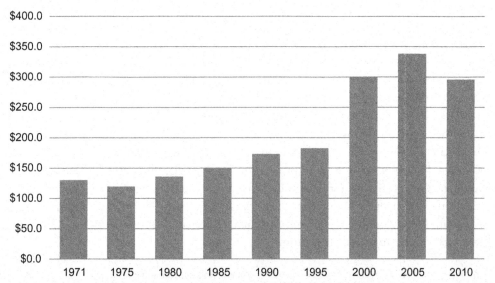

Figure 1 Annual giving by private sources, 1970–2010 $ billions (real, base year 2011). (*Source*: Giving USA 2012: The annual report on Philanthropy, giving USA.)

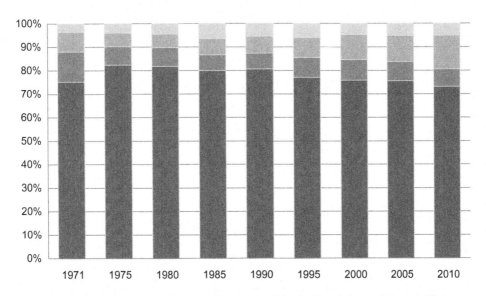

Figure 2 Share of private giving, by type of donor, 1970–2010. (*Source*: Giving USA 2012: The annual report on Philanthropy, giving USA.)

of giving. Many people give a small amount and a few people give a large amount. There is also variation in the types of charities to which individuals give. For example, as will be shown below, the largest recipient of charitable donations are religious organizations. These gifts come largely from lower income individuals. If one studies individuals that gave more than $1 million, their gifts go mostly to education and health-related organizations.[7]

In Figure 2, we show the share of private giving by type across four groups: individual giving, giving through bequests, giving by foundations, and corporate giving. The striking phenomenon is that the share of giving from private individuals has declined and the share of giving by foundations has increased over time. While the data currently available make it difficult to understand this trend, there is a sense that the growth in foundation giving may be attributable to a growth in giving by higher wealth individuals who choose to first direct their giving to a foundation and then to use the foundation as a vehicle for giving to charities.

The above figures are similar to those observed in other countries, especially Canada and the UK. Using tax returns filed in Canada by individuals that reside in urban areas,

---

[7] In addition to there being differences in giving based on measures of family income, other observed differences include: donors that believe the most in the afterlife are less sensitive to changes in economic conditions; women are more likely to donate than men, and, conditioning on income, will give more; higher wealth families are less sensitive than lower wealth families to economic conditions in their giving; the decline in giving through a bequest is mostly attributable to a decline in giving by those estates valued at less than $2 million. See Giving USA 2011 and 2012 for details on these findings.

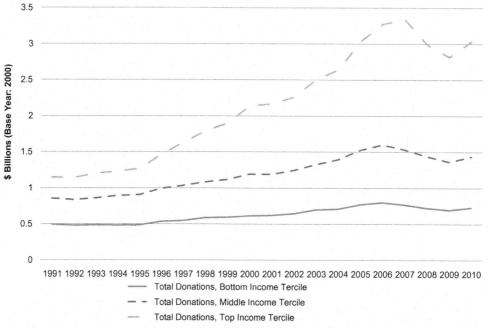

Figure 3 Reported tax receipted gifts in Canada by neighborhood income grouping. (*Source*: Data at neighborhood level for reported giving on individual tax returns, statistics Canada, as modified by public economics data analysis laboratory, McMaster University, 2012.)

we can depict the level of giving across neighborhood types defined by the average household income for the neighborhood (defining a neighborhood as a postal code area that covers approximately 5000–8000 households). Figure 3 depicts the total reported charitable giving by individuals for neighborhoods broken down into income terciles. Giving by those living in higher income neighborhoods has grown much faster in the 1990s and early 2000s than for the other two groups.

Notice that Figures 2 and 3 are pointing to an interesting pattern. Giving is becoming increasingly concentrated with the wealthy, either through individual giving or from foundations. In the US, the number of foundations increased by 54% between 1999 and 2009, to over 120,000 (National Center for Charitable Statistics, 2011, *Nonprofit Sector in Brief: Public Charities, Giving, and Volunteering*). In Canada, foundations grew by 74% between 1992 and 2008, from 5400 to 9400. This raises interesting questions about the influence of foundations on giving by others and in promoting the stability of the charitable sector.

While tax laws impose some requirements around the distribution of funding, foundations are able to harbor their endowments well into the future. They have flexibility in how they use their funds intertemporally, and in how they target funding to support certain types of charitable activities. Increasingly, however, we are observing foundations taking on a bigger policy role in that they can influence charity activity and can use their funds to leverage donor behavior. One example of this leverage is the lead that has been taken by the Gates Foundation to focus on big issues (e.g., eradication of polio, fixing the public educational system) and to encourage others to match their funding. For example, the Gates Foundation teamed up with Rotary International and encouraged Rotary groups all over the world to raise funds in support of eradicating polio.

In a broader context, foundations and well-positioned individuals can influence charitable giving. An example of the dynamics of using wealth and/or prestige to influence giving is found in the activities being undertaken by the Clinton Global Initiative (CGI). While CGI is not an organization to which individuals can donate, it views itself at the "eBay of philanthropy, bringing together buyers and sellers in the world of giving." ("How Clinton Changed Philanthropy," *Time Magazine*, October 1, 2012, page 32). The CGI seeks to influence giving by promoting philanthropic policies and raising awareness of issues that can affect the decisions of donors about what causes to support. The CGI is an example of how social networking by influential individuals (versus direct donations) can affect the growth of certain charities and the direction of charitable giving in a significant way.

If wealth that supports charities is held in the hands of a few, this can create a greater divide between charities with significant assets and those with virtually none. Despite the large numbers of charities in the US and elsewhere, most charities operate on very small budgets and have few if any assets. In 2010, for instance, 16.5% of charities reported total expenditures greater than $1 million; 45% of charities reported expenditures less than $100,000. These statistics exclude the very small charities (Urban Institute, *The Nonprofit Sector in Brief: Public Charities, Giving, and Volunteering*, 2012). If tax policy promotes giving by those with higher incomes and greater wealth, then it is important to understand how these policies affect charity operations. For instance, if donors with greater wealth support bigger charities, then we will observe a greater divide between charities with and without sufficient capital to operate. This hypothesis would hold up if there is a strong correlation between the wealth of the benefactors and charity size.

While most charities would not begrudge funding from any donor, if charities are reliant on a few major donors, this places them in a vulnerable position. For example, if the few donors change preferences or change their behavior with external events (like changes in the economy, or natural disasters) this could cause gifts to swing across charities, making the charities too vulnerable in the whims of their financiers.

Who are the recipients of these contributions? In 2010 there were close to 1.3 million 501(c)(3) organizations in the US—this excludes churches, nonprofits, and social enterprises. In the last decade, the number of charities has grown by close to 59% (from 632,000 in 1999). Other types of nonprofits, those classified as 501(c) but not 501(c)(3),

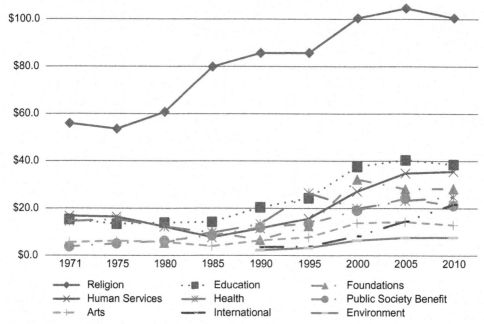

Figure 4 Total private giving by charity classification, $ billions (2011 base year). (*Source*: Giving USA 2012: The annual report on Philanthropy, giving USA.)

experienced very little growth (approximately 3%).[8] The types of nonprofits that benefit the most from private giving are those in the area of religion, which accounts for 35% of the total contributions. Educational organizations are the second biggest recipient (14%), followed by foundations (11%), human services (9%), health (8%), and public-society (8%). Contributions to other types of charities (arts, international affairs, environment, and animal-related organizations) accounted for less than 5% of private giving. Figure 4 illustrates these differences and the growth in giving by charity type for US charities between 1970 and 2010.

Figure 4 illustrates that religious giving dominates other forms and, perhaps, should be analyzed separately from other types of giving. For example, do individual donations to churches respond to tax incentives the same as other forms of giving? The figure also illustrates difference in the contributions and growth (or lack thereof) in contributions across sectors, demonstrating that one might want to explore these sectors separately when studying the impacts of tax and other policies. Second is the growth foundation giving. In 1980 this was the smallest of the categories, but by 2010 it was the third largest category, just below gifts to education-based charities.[9] We will return to these and other issues throughout the discussion below.

[8] Examples of other 501(c) nonprofits include civic leagues, business leagues, fraternal societies, social clubs, and agricultural organizations.

[9] One might also add a third observation: the languishing of giving to the arts.

3. APPROACH 1: INDIVIDUALS

We begin this section by briefly reviewing what we have learned through controlled experiments and how this helps to better frame a characterization of preferences. We then turn to econometric applications of this approach to data on individuals.

3.1. Preferences for Giving

Consider an individual i with post-tax income m_i who consumes a composite private numeraire good x_i and gives g_i dollars to charity. With n individuals, let $G = \sum_{i=1}^{n} g_i$ be the total contributions to the charity. If individuals gain utility from only the final output of the charity, sometimes called *pure altruism* (Andreoni 1989), then G is a public good. The natural first model, therefore, is to assume preferences $U_i = u_i(x_i, G)$. As shown by Bergstrom, Blume, and Varian (1986) and Andreoni (1988), such a model leads to many absurd conclusions, including that only a sliver of the population should be contributors to the charity. Hence, any model that is going to capture the empirical findings is likely going to require that individuals, through some means, experience greater utility from their own contributions than those of others, that is, $U_i = u_i(x_i, G, g_i)$, where utility is increasing in the third argument.[10] This impure altruism was (somewhat pejoratively) dubbed *warm-glow giving* by Andreoni (1989, 1990).[11]

   Evidence for a warm-glow has come from many quarters. Laboratory experiments find responses to manipulations that most often support a basic "joy of giving" explanation. A laboratory experiment by Crumpler and Grossman (2008) showed that 57% of subjects made a contribution to charity, even though the contribution had no impact on the dollars received by the charity, but only on the composition of the dollars given—the subjects' contributions completely displaced the experimenter's contribution. This strongly supports a warm-glow. Tonin and Vlassopoulos (2010) look for a warm-glow in a real-effort field experiment on pro-social behavior. Using a manipulation similar to that of Crumpler and Grossman, these authors tell subjects that a charity will get £15 regardless of the subject's actions, but that the more effort the subject chooses the more of this £15 will be credited to the subject. They find that this manipulation creates a significant increase in effort. Many other laboratory tests find similar patterns in which own and others' contributions are not perfect substitutes, as the warm-glow hypothesis requires.[12] Konow (2010) develops a model of warm-glow that is founded on affective (emotional) states. He shows in theory and experiments that not all giving is the same—those gifts

[10] Also see Ribar and Wilhelm (2002) for a limit result arguing that for large n, only the warm-glow component of utility is going to have any significant influence on the margin of any person's decision.
[11] See also Cornes and Sandler (1984) and Steinberg (1987). The pejorative nature of the term is deliberate, and meant to remind the reader that the notion of a warm-glow is something of a black box. That is, there are many notions—sympathy, guilt, norm adherence, social approval—that could fall under the umbrella of impure altruism, the essential feature is that, once the model is reduced to its barest form, own and others' contributions.
[12] See Andreoni (1993), Bolton and Katok (1998), Konow (2010), Eckel, Grossman, and Johnson (2005), Palfrey and Prisbey (1997), Goeree, Holt, and Laury (2002), and Andreoni and Miller (2002).

connected with a greater sense of need or deservingness also create more warm feelings. In a theme we will return to when discussing the fourth approach, giving and the utility of the warm-glow depends critically on the context, the need, and the impact of one's donation. That is, the utility of the warm-glow is not separate from the altruistic concern one has for the recipient.

Perhaps the most convincing and provocative evidence for warm-glow comes from the neuroeconomics experiments done by Harbaugh, Mayr, and Burghart, published in *Science* in 2007. Subjects were told that some of their payment fee of $100 would be donated to charity involuntarily in some cases, as in the case for taxation, or only if they approved in other cases. Even though the outcome for the charity was the same in both scenarios, the subjects' brains reflected significantly greater pleasure when the choice was made voluntarily. The effect was shown within subjects. A surprising finding, however, is that subjects preferred larger donations to smaller ones, even when they were made involuntarily. That is, people enjoy giving through taxation or voluntarily, but they enjoy the latter the most. This is precisely the foundational assumption of the model of warm-glow giving.

3.2. Analysis of Data on Individual Givers

One way of encouraging giving is to lower its price. Many countries provide some form of an income tax credit or deduction for giving. In the United States, for example, tax filers who itemize deductions may claim charitable donations as a deduction against taxable income. With a marginal tax rate of t, this creates a price of $1-t$, that is, a gift g only costs the giver $(1-t)g$ out-of-pocket. This has led to a surfeit of research measuring the compensated elasticity of giving, effectively asking the question, if there is a 1% change in price, $1-t$, how responsive is giving, g. Bakija and Heim (2011) summarize this research and provide the most recent estimates of the price elasticity using a panel data set of individual tax returns spanning the period 1979–2006. Much of the research they report suggests the elasticity of giving, ε, is close to -1. A few find an inelastic response, $|\varepsilon| < 1$, and Bakija and Heim suggest giving may most likely be elastic, $|\varepsilon| > 1$.

There is more to understanding how tax policies affect giving than simply trying to measure a price elasticity for giving. Across countries, there are a variety of schemes in place to provide individuals incentives to donate. In some countries (e.g., Denmark, Finland, Germany, Italy, Switzerland) some or all individuals are obligated to donate as the laws require a fixed percentage of individual taxes be allocated to churches or other charities.[13] With respect to voluntary donations, some countries provide direct incentives to all taxpayers (e.g., the US, Canada, the UK, Germany, Australia, India, Indonesia), others only to those with high incomes or high levels of donations, some strictly limit how much

---

[13] The US International Grantmaking website, http://www.usig.org/index.asp, provides details on differential treatments of donations across countries.

one can offset tax liability with her donation (e.g., Argentina [limited to 5% of taxable base], China [up to 30% of taxable income], Czech Republic [limit of 10% of income if at least 2% is donated], France [limit of 20% of taxable income], Russia [limit of 25% of taxable income], South Africa [limit of 10% of taxable income]), and others provide no incentives (e.g., Afghanistan, Brazil, Croatia, Israel [incentives given only for donations to public institutions]).

In recent decades, many of the changes in tax policies related to charitable giving provide greater incentives for wealthier individuals to donate. For example, in Australia donations of more than $5000 (AUD) receive a more advantageous tax treatment than donations of lesser amounts. In Germany, while donations are limited to 20% of income, an individual can deduct up to $1 million Euros if the donation is for the endowment of a foundation. In the US and Canada, donations of publicly traded securities and other property such as ecologically sensitive land have a lower effective price of giving than a cash donation of the same value. The reason for this is that the donor is allowed to take a charitable deduction against taxable earned income for the fair market value and *not* incur any capital gains on the difference between the fair market value and the basis of the securities or property. These changes may help to explain the growth in donations to foundations and faster growth in giving by individuals in higher income tax brackets. In Canada, for instance, a high proportion of foundations report receiving gifts of publicly traded securities. An extremely low proportion of registered charities, by contrast, report gifts of publicly traded securities. Very little work, however, has been done to explore the impacts of these policies on the price elasticity of giving, on the substitution between donations of cash and publicly traded securities, or the growing divergences in giving between higher and lower income individuals.

What if tax policy did not benefit the taxpayer but benefited the charity? For most taxpayers this is exactly what happens in the United Kingdom. Taxpayers receive neither a tax credit nor a deduction, unless they are high earners. Instead a system called "Gift Aid" is used. When an individual donates to a charity and identifies herself as a UK taxpayer, the charity can receive from the UK government the equivalent of the credit that the taxpayer would receive. For every pound donated, a charity can claim from the UK government a match that is based on the lowest tax rate for individuals (20%). Effectively this means that the charity can receive £1.25 for every £1 donated (tax price is £0.80). The exception to this system is for high income taxpayers. If they complete a form, they can receive a tax credit for their donations. Effectively this means that for every pound donated by a high rate taxpayer the price is £0.60. Scharf and Smith (2010) explore whether high rate taxpayers giving differs across the scheme whereby the charity receives an amount equivalent to the credit and the scheme whereby the taxpayer receives the credit. If individuals understand the relationship, the government disbursement of revenues (in the system where charities receive the credit) is equivalent to receiving a tax credit on a reported donation to the government, then both systems should yield the same results.

In the context of a survey of known high rate taxpayers that are donors, they randomly assigned questions about an increase in tax incentives (in the form of gift aid or in the form of a direct tax credit) to the donors. They find, despite the equivalence financially, that donors are likely to respond more positively to an increase in the gift aid amount than to an increase in the direct tax credit.

3.3. Households as Decision Makers

The analysis to this point has made the simplifying assumption that charitable decisions are made by individuals. In many cases, however, giving will be made by households. If men and women have different tastes about giving—or about the opportunity costs of giving—this presents a more complex and interesting question about how households resolve this conflict.

One could imagine a number of scenarios about how couples treat giving differently than individuals. For instance, if the couple shares the same tastes, then charitable giving could be seen as an enjoyable joint activity that couples do together. This could make couples give more to charity than individuals, and do so together. However, suppose that the couple disagrees either about the size or type of gifts. For example, one wants to support the homeless while the other prefers the opera. This might result in the couples bargaining with each other but making donation decisions jointly that effectively monitors or reins in each other's spending. Another alternative is that one spouse may have stronger feelings about charity, better information, stronger social reasons (like giving at work), or lower transactions costs (like payroll deductions) that lead spouses to a delegate giving to one spouse. Finally, imagine a household where spouses keep separate finances. These spouses are likely to make independent decisions on giving.[14]

Two papers have explored these questions and come to many similar, but several importantly different conclusions. Andreoni, Brown, and Richall (2003) use a question on the 1992 and 1994 Survey of Giving and Volunteering (SGV) in the United States that asked, "Who in your household is considered most involved in deciding which charities your household will give to?" The answers could be the respondent, spouse, or both. Yörük (2010) replicates this study, instead using the 2002 wave of the Center on Philanthropy Panel Study (COPPS), the Philanthropy Module of the PSID. This survey asks, "Who in your family was involved in decisions about how much support to give individual charities in 2002?" The answer could be the husband, wife, decide together, or decide separately. Thus the category, "both" from the SGV is more finely separated into "decide together" and "decide separately." The two surveys differ in other important

---

[14] Besides having differing tastes about charity, spouses have another reason to bargain. As noted in a recent paper by Jackson and Yariv (unpublished), if spouses have differing discount rates, then the tastes of the spouse who is most impatient will be dominant in the decisions made about the present. The more impatient spouse will trade consumption in the future for preferred consumption today, and the more patient spouse will agree. The studies we discuss here are purely cross-sectional so they cannot address relative discounting, but this part of the bargaining process could be interesting if data on discount rates could be combined with data on choices of giving.

ways. While respondents have similar mean ages, the COPPS survey was taken 8–10 years later than the SGV survey, thus shifting the mix of marital cohorts. This shows up in other areas. The COPPS respondents have more education; there are about 7.7% points greater likelihood of being a college graduate among men, and about 6% points among women. Perhaps the biggest difference is that in the SGV data the likelihood that the husband is the primary earner is about 90%, while in the COPPS data the partnerships show more parity, with only about 60% of households having male as primary earners. If households are bargaining, therefore, one would expect more equal bargaining power in the COPPS than the SGV. This is exactly what is observed.

Adjusting for observables, both studies show little to no differences in amounts given by single males and females, but both show significant differences in the number of causes supported. Women appear to prefer giving less to more causes, while men prefer to specialize in one or two causes. Male deciders were also more sensitive to price in both data sets, especially when the price was low.[15] In the SGV data, when both spouses decide (which could include both deciding together and independently), the analysis shows that households give about 6% less than had they each decided unilaterally and, moreover, the husband was estimated to have the dominant bargaining power, with his preferences getting more than twice the weight given to hers.[16] COPPS data, by contrast, showed that couples deciding jointly (but not independently) actually gave 7% more than one would predict if they acted unilaterally. Moreover, bargaining power was nearly identical between spouses, with the wives estimated to actually have a bit more leverage than their husbands.

The degree of similarity between the two studies of Andreoni, Brown, and Rischall (2003) and Yörük (2010) tends to make the differences between the two all the more fascinating.[17] Could it be that the differences in household bargaining could be due to cohort effects as more progressive values are represented in the newer data, and that these households are more likely to have female earners with good salaries and thus greater bargaining power? If so, does this parity among spouses actually create a more harmonious attitude toward giving, making it an enjoyable shared activity rather than a contentious case of spousal monitoring? These and other questions remain fascinating and important areas for understanding not simply charitable giving, but also for uncovering how households make decisions in general.

---

[15] This mimics lab data from dictator games in which male subjects showed greater price elasticity. See Andreoni and Vesterlund (2001).

[16] More detailed analysis revealed that the strong presence of religious giving, which men prefer to specialize in, was largely responsible for the strong male bargaining power. Separating religious from other giving, males and females had much more equal bargaining power, although still showed more "conflict" than in Yörük's (2010) analysis.

[17] Contributing to the intrigue, Wiepking & Bekkers (2010) examine data on couples in the Netherlands and find that the household choices depend heavily on the "marital capital" and commitment, for which the Dutch collect more specific data (they code for cohabitants, committed couples who live apart, and married couples who live together). For instance, males were more likely to decide in heavily religious households, and relative education, not relative income was the more powerful determinant of bargaining power.

3.4. Experiments on Individual Givers: Price

An individual with consumption c, giving g, income y, and a marginal tax rate t, faces a budget constraint of $c + g = y - t(y - g)$, or

$$c + (1 - t)g = (1 - t)y \quad \text{[tax subsidy]} \tag{1}$$

Letting $p_1 = 1 - t$ then we see that the tax deduction lowers the price of giving, resulting in an out-of-pocket donation of $d = (1 - t)g$. A difficulty with estimating the effects of p_1 and y on g is that t and y are determined jointly. One way to break the link between price and income is to look for an unanticipated change in the relationship, such as from a tax reform. Another way to get identification is through laboratory or field experiments that independently vary p or y.

A popular avenue for manipulating price both in actual fundraising and in experiments is from matching contributions. Suppose a rich philanthropist offers to match every dollar donated, d, with m dollars of his own. An out-of-pocket donation of d results in the charity receiving a gift of $g = d(1 + m)$. Then when the charity receives g dollars, it only costs the giver $1/(1 + m)$, that is $p_2 = 1/(1 + m)$. For instance, under a 2-for-1 match it costs the donor \$1 to give \$3, so $p = 0.33$. This results in a budget

$$c + [1/(1 + m)] g = (1 - t)y \quad \text{[matching gift]} \tag{2}$$

Notice that Eqs. (1) and (2) are quite similar. If $m = t/(1 - t)$ then the two are the same.

A significant side issue is that, in practice, matching contributions typically have a limit. For instance, a philanthropist may pledge to match the first \$100,000 donated. Then if donations exceed \$100,000, the philanthropist's "match" becomes equivalent to a direct contribution to the charity—no individual is being subsidized on the margin. If the limit is likely to be exceeded or, equivalently, the philanthropist cannot credibly commit to *not* giving the full limit pledged even if the match limit is not reached, then it is rational for givers to treat the match as simply a single unconditional grant. If this is the case, then the "matching grant" could in theory be expected to *reduce* individual donations d through an income effect. Since most matches do have limits that are exceeded,[18] there is a question of whether donors suffer from a "matching illusion," that is, whether they perceive that their contributions will actually result in more donations from the rich philanthropist, resulting in a substitution effect (encouraging giving) and an income effect (discouraging giving), or whether there is no matching illusion and a match results in only the income effect on d.

A second manipulation on price may be to offer a rebate. Suppose an individual gives g to the charity, and then shortly thereafter receives a rebate of r per dollar donated. The rebate could come from the government, a philanthropist, or the experimenter. This rebate now means that to give an additional dollar to the charity costs only $p_3 = 1 - r$ to

---

[18] If the matching grant is not fully utilized on one fund drive, it is often the case that the remainder will be recycled and used as a match for later fundraising campaigns. That is, in practice most "matching grants" are equivalent to unconditional cash gifts.

the donor, that is a gift g to the charity costs $d = (1-r)g$ out-of-pocket. Thus the budget is

$$c + (1 - r)g = (1 - t)y \qquad \text{[rebate]} \qquad (3)$$

Equations (1) and (3) are identical as long as $r = t$. In fact, this point makes it clear that the tax deduction is in fact a rebate—only when one's taxes are finally reconciled is the benefit of the deduction realized in a higher tax refund or lower tax bill. Looking at (1)–(3), modulo the "matching illusion" problem, if $r = t = m/(1 + m)$ then the prediction from simple economic theory would be that the outcomes are the same.

Experimental research on rebates and matches began with a provocative of experiment by Eckel and Grossman (2003). Endowing laboratory subjects with cash, they allowed subjects to give some of the money to a favored charity at set rebate rates r of $0, 0.2, 0.25$, and 0.5. Another group of subjects faced the equivalent tasks but framed as a match, with m of $0, 0.25, 0.33$, and 1. They found matching significantly dominated subsidies, with the charity receiving 27–88% more with matching. They also found an interesting pattern that we will return to later. Under the matching scheme, the out-of-pocket cost to the subject, that is $d = p_2 g = g/(1 + m)$, is a nearly identical fraction of the endowment on average for every value of p_2, ranging only between 47 and 52%. In other words, when one looks at the out-of-pocket donation $d = g/(1 + m)$, subjects allocated about the same d as fraction of their endowment to the charity, regardless of m. This could lead one to infer that the match does not matter. However, when looked at as the gift received, $g = (1 + m)d$, it would lead one to infer that matches are hugely influential. In fact, if utility depends on the gift g, then the match has an income effect that should suppress d: a 1-to-1 match can reach the same g at half the d. But it also creates a substitution effect that should increase d. Thus, only if g is elastic with respect to $p, \varepsilon \leq -1$, will d not *fall* in response to an increased match. Eckel and Grossman confirm this by estimating an elasticity of g with respect to p of about -1.1. If instead they had looked at the effects of m on d, the inference would have been that, after accounting for the endowment, m and d are virtually unrelated.[19]

A series of field experiments on matching grants finds results that in many ways parallel the laboratory studies. Karlan and List (2007) team with an actual nonprofit to send fundraising letters to over 50,000 potential donors, one third of whom acted as a control group. The letters to those treated varied in ways that are intended to capture the issues raised above. Letters included either no match, a 1-to-1, 2-to-1, or 3-to-1 match, that is, $p = 1, 0.5, 0.33$, or 0.25, respectively. They also addressed the "matching illusion" by claiming in the letter that matches would go up to $25,000, $50,000, or $100,000, thus increasing the likelihood that a giver would feel their contribution would truly be subsidized (assuming they see any unmatched portion of the limit as credibly not given).

The mailing received a response rate of 2%, which is not atypical for charitable solicitations of this type. Of the 50,083 mailings, they received 300 control responses, and 735

---

[19] Begin with the measurement $\ln(g) = -1.1 \ln(p)$. Substitute to find $\ln(d(1 + m)) = -1.1 \ln(1/(1 + m))$. Rearrange to see $\ln(d) = 0.1 \ln(1 + m)$, which indicates an elasticity of d with respect to m of virtually zero.

treatment responses (roughly 245 per match level). While individual characteristics of the donors were not observable, the authors could control for census-level characteristics based on the zip codes of potential donors. Note also, there is no way to know that the envelopes were opened and, thus, who was treated. The authors would ideally wish to control who was treated and examine the effect of the treatment on the treated. Since this is impossible, the authors' analysis uses either all 50,000 mailings as observations, or simply the 1035 who responded.[20]

The presence of any match had a significant impact on the likelihood of giving (0.018 for the control and 0.022 for the treatment), increasing the propensity by 22% (that is, 0.022/0.18−1). It also increased the donation d per solicitation by 19%, from $0.81 to $0.97. However, as the match increased from 1 to 2 to 3-to-1, out-of-pocket donations d per mailing remained flat at $0.94, $1.03, and $0.94, respectively, which is not a significant difference. However, if one looks at the total gift including the match, $g = (1 + m)d$, one would conclude the match greatly increases generosity, going from $1.87 in the 1-to-1 match up to $3.75 per mailing in the 3:1 match.[21]

Interestingly, Karlan and List found no effect of the ceiling on the dollars to be matched. This would indicate that either donors did not suffer from a matching illusion, other than to perhaps change the timing of donations to fall under the period of the match, or that they all suffered similarly from marginal-illusion *and* the elasticity of g is roughly $\varepsilon \approx -1$, which implies a constant d. Harkening back to the parallels with the laboratory study of Eckel and Grossman, who also found d independent of m, there is something yet to be understood about how individuals see a match as affecting the price.[22] We return to this in the next section when we discuss leadership giving.

3.5. Experiments on Individual Givers: Leadership Gifts

A rule of thumb that fundraisers use when launching a fundraising campaign is that about one third of the announced goal should be committed prior to the announcement of the public campaign. That is, pledges made from a small group of donors to provide

---

[20] If the propensity to open envelopes is independent of the vulnerability to matching, then this will lead to unbiased estimates of the effect of matching, conditional on self-selecting into being treated. If opening the envelopes is itself a uncorrelated with a willingness to give, once treated, then the estimates will be unbiased measures of the effect of the treatment on the treated. Later sections on self-selection into treatment suggest that this assumption may not be met. The authors are interested in the more practical issue of the effect of mailings on giving, and thus welcome the influences of self-selection into treatment. The point of this footnote is to alert the reader to be cautious in generalizing these results.

[21] The experiment used a left-wing political organization and ran the experiment shortly after the election of George W. Bush as President in 2004. Further analysis on voter trends found the effects of the match were only significant in counties that one would expect to have felt most bitter about the tightly contested election, such as those living in a Republican leaning county or state. This feature diminishes the generalizability of the results to other charitable organizations.

[22] In an effort to shed more light on this issue, Karlan, List, and Shafir (2011) conducted a field experiment on 20,000 prior donors to a particular charity, looking at 1-to-1 and 3-to-1 matches. The sample includes both recent and "lapsed" donors who may not have given for over a decade. This experiment found a small positive effect of the match m on d, but only for those donors who are active givers.

seed money—called "leadership gifts" by fundraisers—are seen as an essential part of fundraising.[23]

Andreoni (1998) presented a theory of seed money based on the charity having fixed costs (or equivalently, a range of increasing returns) associated with its operations. The consequence of the fixed costs is that even if there is an equilibrium that would allow the charity to reach its goal, there will also be an equilibrium in which no donations are received as long as the fixed costs exceed what any donor is willing to pay alone. The way the charity can eliminate the undesirable equilibrium is to get enough pledges to (almost) fully cover the fixed costs.[24] Vesterlund (2003) and Andreoni (2006a) provide alternative explanations of seed money as conveying information. In both models there is a first mover (or movers) who are given or endogenously acquire superior information about the quality of the charity. Only by making large gifts can these informed players credibly convey that the charity is worth supporting at a high level.[25]

Bracha, Menietti, and Vesterlund (2011) provide a direct test of the fixed-costs model in a laboratory setting. The experiment has an elegant 2×2 design. Groups play a public goods game where giving is either simultaneous (no lead giver) or sequential (a designated lead giver), interacted with the presence or absence of a fixed cost. In the presence of fixed costs that are binding on subjects (that is, they exceed the equilibrium with no fixed costs) the combination of high fixed costs and sequential play significantly increases the level of donations and the likelihood that the threshold is met. The experiment neatly supports the model's predictions.

List and Lucking-Reiley (2002) provide a direct test of the effect of seed money in a field study. They contact donors to give to small public goods ($2000 computer work stations) with varying degrees of seed money provided. As in the laboratory, those solicitations that included the highest seed money gained the greatest likelihood of giving and the largest donations.

A recent field study by Huck and Rasul (2011) combines the reasoning about leadership givers with that of matching grants described above. They note that the very existence of a matching contribution is itself meaningful in the same way that a leadership gift can provide credibility that a fundraising goal will be met. Huck and Rasul test these ideas in a field experiment to raise money for disadvantaged families in Germany. The fund drive was sponsored by the Bavarian State Opera House, whose patrons served as the subjects in the field experiment.

---

[23] See Greenfield, *The Nonprofit Handbook: Fundraising (2001)* as well as the discussion in Andreoni (1998) on the support for this observation.

[24] The technical condition is that leadership gifts must be large enough that best replies by other givers will cover the fixed costs, thus eliminating the inferior equilibrium.

[25] The problem for the lead givers is that they are better off if they can convince others that the quality of the charity is higher than it truly is. The reason is that this will counteract the free riding problem, get more donations, and make the lead giver better off. Thus the lead gift must be large enough that the leader would only make such a large gift if the charity truly had high quality.

The opera house mailed 14,000 solicitation letters to individuals who had purchased tickets to operas or ballets. This likely means the sample will be weighted toward more educated and higher income individuals. A control group did not receive any mention of a lead giver or a match. Treatment group 1 was simply told of a €60,000 leadership gift. In two additional treatment groups the €60,000 leadership gift was mentioned, but it was framed as a limit on matching contributions. Treatment group 2 was told the match was 0.5-to-1, for an effective price of giving g of $p_2 = 0.66$ in, while in treatment group 3 the match 1-to-1, yielding a $p_2 = 0.50$. The inclusion of treatment group 1 distinguishes this study from Karlan and List and allows one to identify the effect of the match independent of the mere presence of a lead donor. That is, comparing the control to group 1 captures the effect of a lead donor, then comparing group 1 to groups 2 and 3 allows isolation of the effect of a match.

Huck and Rasul found the biggest effect of the experiment was announcing the lead gift itself. Control group giving averaged €74.3, which increased to €132 in group 1. That is, simply announcing the lead gift, without any match, raises giving by 78%. Adding the 0.5-to-1 match raised giving to €151, a 14% increase over group 1, and the 1-to-1 match raised giving to €185, a 40% increase over group 1. While these averages indicate that the gift g responds to reductions in price, the response is inelastic. This means that the match actually causes the out-of-pocket donation to *fall* in response to the match. Relative to group 1 there $g = d = €132$, in group 2 $d = €101$, and in group 3 $d = €92.3$.

Huck and Rasul have two important conclusions. First, using a control group that received a solicitation that has no mention of the lead gift, then one would find a very small effect of the match on out-of-pocket donations, as was found by Karlan and List. Second, and most importantly, they find that the largest effect of a match is in announcing the leadership gift, not in lowering the price. In fact, the charity in this experiment is best off by simply announcing a leadership donation and *not* including a match at all. This can explain why Karlan and List report that the existence of a match and not the size of the match is what matters. Huck and Rasul allow an even stronger statement: for the population of opera patrons in the study, giving g is mildly responsive to the match but is inelastic with respect to price. However, giving is highly responsive to the announcement of the lead gift, meaning that leadership gifts can encourage giving by others, but converting leadership giving into matching grants is counterproductive for the charity.

3.6. Experiments on Individual Givers: Give more Tomorrow

Thaler and Benartzi (2004) made famous a simple device that is successful at getting people to save in retirement funds. The program, called Save More Tomorrow (SMT), allows workers to commit in the present to save more at a date sufficiently far into the future. Compared to asking them to commit to save more immediately, the SMT program increases savings over the long run.

Breman (2011) uses the same logic to motivate an intervention she calls Give More Tomorrow (GMT). She works with a charity in Sweden that allows donors to sign up for automated monthly donations that are made electronically. In the control group, the charity calls donors with a request to increase their monthly donation starting at the next billing date, as is typical for charity operations. In two treatment groups, an identical script is used by the solicitor, except that they offer to begin the increased donation in 1 month or 2 months past the next billing date. She finds that a delay of 2 months, but not 1 month, had a significant positive effect on the increase in donations. Moreover, a year after the intervention, individuals who were treated with GMT continued to have higher donations and, compared to asking people to give more today, GMT increases the total receipts of the charity. This effect could be due to present-bias or planning constraints, or simply because it is harder to say "no" to requests for obligations far off into the future.[26]

3.7. The Salience of Incentives to Give

All of this analysis of the effect of tax incentives, matching grants, on individuals is, of course, built on the assumption that individuals understand the financial consequences of their donations on both themselves and the charities. A recent paper on the salience of "tax expenditures" by Goldin and Listokin (2012) uses a survey of US taxpayers to show that, while 72% of all tax filers correctly identify their eligibility to benefit from a charitable deduction, people systematically underestimate the value of the deduction. For instance, only 18% of those with a marginal tax rate of 0.28 correctly identified the subsidy on giving as "20–40%," and 78% stated that the subsidy was below "20%." As other findings of a lack of awareness of sales taxes and EITC benefits have led to a discussion of the impact and incidence of these policies (Chetty and Saez, 2013; Chetty, Looney, and Kroft, 2009), the lack of salience about the charitable deduction could generate similar conversations among academics and policy makers. Moreover, some of the differences discussed above could be explained through salience. For instance, do matching grants during fundraising campaigns make the consequences and costs of a gift more salient, and that is why they can be more effective? Are men more aware of marginal tax rates, and could this explain why households in which men decide on giving are more price sensitive? These and other effects of salience are, it would appear, promising and important areas of future research.

4. APPROACH 2: THE CHARITABLE SECTOR AS A MARKET

The machine of charitable giving has many moving parts. Charities receive grants from the government, gifts from foundations, donations from individuals, and raise money through ordinary appeals like mailings, phone banks, and advertising, but also through fundraising events, like galas, walkathons, charity auctions, sponsorships, and in some cases

---

[26] This technique is well known, and is often applied by editors of Handbooks to encourage authors to agree to prepare chapters with distant due dates.

by charging fees for services. The use, intensity, and effectiveness of each channel is likely affected by the use, intensity, and effectiveness of the other channels. This interdependence is clearly important and, obviously, presents a tremendous challenge for researchers. With charities as demanders of funds, donors as suppliers, and the government providing policy interventions that are dependent on choices made by donors and charities, identifying the "equilibrium" in this market becomes a delicate and difficult issue. This section looks at new theoretical and econometric studies that try to understand charitable giving from this more holistic approach.

4.1. Theories of Charity from the Supply Side

Early thinkers in the area of nonprofits, such as Weisbroad (1991) and Rose-Ackerman (1996), deserve credit for identifying and advocating a broad approach to charitable giving, and since then the research that takes both demand and supply aspects into account has grown tremendously. Most recently, an elegant theoretical model by Correa and Yildirim (2013) combines and generalizes models by Rose-Ackerman (1982), Andreoni (1998), Andreoni and McGuire (1993), and Andreoni and Payne (2003) to describe the equilibrium among donors and fundraisers, and to explore the impacts of government policies. In the model, fundraising is costly, individuals give only if they are solicited by the charity, each potential "target" donor has a different propensity to give based on heterogeneity across givers.[27] Correa and Yildirim provide a solution in which the charity determines the set of potential donors for whom the "profits" are the highest, that is, for whom the marginal donation most greatly exceeds the margin cost of solicitation. Since the charity chooses the set of donors, and commits to a total fundraising cost C, it forces the donors into a subgame with fixed costs. In this subgame the set of donors who are solicited must contribute at least C or the charity will provide no net services. This non-convexity effectively creates a threshold, which in turn creates an equilibrium at giving zero (Andreoni, 1998). Correa and Yildirim show that if there also exists an equilibrium among some set of donors where this equilibrium at zero can be overcome, then a clever charity can select the set of donors that guarantee it will be overcome and the charity will have a successful fundraising campaign.

The Correa-Yildirim model also has interesting and important policy predictions. Foremost among these is the prediction about crowding out of private donations by government grants to charities. The classic model of charity coming from purely altruistic motives indicates that individuals should be indifferent to giving directly or through their taxes, thus grants should crowd out donations dollar-for-dollar. Since crowding out is often measured as incomplete, one reason could be that preferences are not purely

---

[27] The model attributes heterogeneity to income alone, for ease of analysis. However, it is also possible to interpret heterogeneity to preferences as well as incomes. The main aspect is to identify the best reply function of each donor, and to apply the Andreoni and McGuire (1993) algorithm for identifying donors for a given level of fundraising effort. Any heterogeneity can be subsumed into this solution, regardless of its source.

altruistic but include a warm-glow, as discussed in the prior section. This is a *supply side* explanation. The Correa-Yildirim model, maintaining altruistic preferences, provides a *demand side* explanation instead (while the proofs are provided under an assumption of pure altruism, the results are made only stronger by including a warm-glow). Because of the strategically active charity, and the endogeneity of the set of donors through fundraising, the model prediction is that grants will only be partially crowded out, and that some of this crowding out will be attributable to reductions in fundraising efforts by the charity in addition to classic direct crowding out of donors. As we see below, this is fully in line with the results from recent econometric analyses of charitable organizations.

4.2. Econometric Evidence

The most natural policy question applying the market approach to charities is crowding out. Testing theories of crowding out, however, has been a challenge. For instance, how does one pair private giving to public funding for the same type of good, and should the analysis constrain coefficients that measure crowding out to be the same across different types of charitable goods? What about donors who may give to multiple goods—can government grants to one charity affect giving to another? And could the government actually crowd in giving by providing a signal of quality, and should this vary depending on how easily quality can be publicly verified?

What is the best methodology for pairing private and public funding?[28] Kingma (1989) was the first to match private giving and public funding directly by focusing on giving to local public radio stations.[29] Schiff and Weisbrod (1991) gathered measures of private giving from non-profit tax returns but then matched these measures to aggregated measures of government funding. Hungerman (2005) and Gruber and Hungerman (2007) match church spending on charitable goods with aggregate measures of government spending. Khanna, Posnett, and Sandler (1995) and Payne (1998) were among the first to match both private and public giving to specific charities and for a large sample of charities. Another approach, taken by Andreoni and Payne (2011a), is to look at crowding out by different categories of donations, that is, tax receipted versus non-tax receipted giving by individuals, and transfers from foundations and from other charities.

An underlying econometric issue when seeking to measure the relationship between private and public funding is how best to control for dynamic changes in giving. Primary estimation issues revolve around concerns of heterogeneity in the charities due to size, scope, mission, and location. One means to help control for this heterogeneity is in the use of panel data (e.g., Khanna, Posnett and Sandler, 1995; Payne 1998, 2001; Gruber

---

[28] The first studies relied on individual tax return data and/or survey data for measures of individual giving. However, it is difficult to identify the types of charitable goods to which the individuals are giving and the locations of the charities that are receiving these donations, making this accurate pairing impossible. See, e.g., Abrams and Schmitz (1978, 1984), and Schiff (1985).

[29] Although, see Manzoor and Straub (2005) for a challenge to Kingma's results.

and Hungerman, 2007; Hungerman, 2005; Okten and Weisbrod, 2000; Ribar and Wilhelm, 2002; Andreoni and Payne 2003, 2011a, 2011b). With panel data, one can include organizational fixed effects to help control for time-invariant differences across charities.

A second key concern in estimation is the potential omitted variable bias due to time-varying events that could drive both the government and private donors to simultaneously change giving. For example, a natural disaster (Haiti earthquake, Hurricanes Katrina and Sandy) is likely to increase both private and public funding. Failing to control for these positive correlations in demands will lead to a biased understatement of the degree of crowding out, and could erroneously even suggest crowding *in*.

There is likely a similar downward bias associated with the endogeneity in public funding, the third main concern. As pointed out by Payne (1998), donors are also voters. If voters' preferences are reflected in both public policy and in private donations, it will create a biased impression that crowding out is low. Hence, even with panel data estimation, one must be concerned about the exogeneity of government funding in a specification that has private giving as a dependent variable.

Estimations of crowding out, thus, should control for the heterogeneity among charities and take into account potential omitted variable and endogeneity biases. This suggests that unless one has conducted a field experiment or has a strong natural experiment, an OLS type of regression will underestimate (bias toward a more positive coefficient) the effect of government funding on private donations. Most of the current research has relied on two-stage least squares ("2SLS") framework to address issues of endogeneity and omitted variable bias. This requires that one find measures that directly explain variations in government funding but only indirectly (through the government funding channel) explain private giving. Although 2SLS is a popular and useful technique, it has its limitations. The biggest concern is weak instruments (see, Bound et al., 1995; Choa & Swanson, 2005; Cruz & Moreira, 2005). If one uses instruments that only weakly identify the level of government funding, the estimates of crowd out will still be biased. In any 2SLS estimation, therefore, the researcher should ensure that the instruments work, that there is a good story to explain how the instruments affect government funding, and that the instruments do not directly explain private giving.

The literature that employs a 2SLS technique, generally finds that government funding crowds out private giving. Hungerman (2005) suggests that public social welfare funding crowds out revenues by faith-based organizations on the order of 67 cents for every dollar of public funding. Andreoni and Payne (2011a) find an overall crowd out of 70 cents for every dollar of government grants when studying charities involved in the provision of goods related to social welfare and community development. These use data from the United States. Andreoni and Payne (2011b) use data on Canadian charities and measure crowding out at close to dollar-for-dollar.

Is the measure of crowding out usually the same across different types of charities? While crowding out seems large for social welfare organizations, there is no evidence of crowd out for health organizations or for overseas and relief organizations.[30] Borgonovi (2006) studies the effects of changes in government funding on private giving to American non-profit theaters. He presents evidence to suggest that small levels of government funding crowd in private donations but large levels of funding crowd out donations. However, Borgnovi only studies a small sample of charities. In the context of education, the analysis of both Connolly (1997) and Payne (2001) suggests that donors may not be as informed about the goods and services provided by universities, potentially allowing the government grants to serve as a signal of quality to private donors, especially when the signal relates to grants associated with research activity. Both empirical analyses support this conjecture. Recent work by Blume-Kohout (2012) also suggests that government research grants provide a signal of quality to private donors.

Overall, however, while there are numerous studies that explore crowd out as it relates to the provision of social services, there are too few studies that examine crowding out in other charity sectors, such as environmental, health, education, and the arts.

If crowding out ranges from 70 cents to 1 dollar, is this mostly attributable to a change in donor behavior? There are several things to consider in answering this. First, donors may be latent givers, that is, they must be encouraged to give through fundraising and marketing campaigns. Second, charities are likely more concerned about service provision than revenue growth. That is, as non-profits, charities may not be net revenue maximizers and instead may view fundraising as a "necessary evil." Third, it is important to control heterogeneity among charities when analyzing the interaction between private and public funding. In short, it is important, yet delicate, to treat charities as active players when it comes to the collection of private donations.

Andreoni and Payne (2003, 2011a) shed light in the role of charity fundraising on crowding out using US data. In 2003 they demonstrate that for both arts and social welfare charities, increases in government funding to an organization significantly decrease fundraising efforts by the organization. In 2011 they study a panel of more than 8000 charities operating in the United States. They measure an overall level of crowding out on the order of 75%. This crowding out can be decomposed into the portion that is attributable to donors independently changing their contributions and the portion attributable to a change in fundraising behavior. Their research suggests the bulk of the crowding out is due to a change in charity fundraising. Depending on the specification, in fact, donors may be slightly crowded in by government grants. The maximum level of crowd out attributable to a direct change in donors' giving is 30%. Thus, the portion of crowding out attributable to a change in the charity's behavior ranges between 70% and 100%.

Andreoni and Payne (2011b) expand upon these findings with a rich data set of more than 13,000 charities involved in the provision of social welfare and community services

---

[30] For both of these types of organizations the effects are imprecisely measured. Health organizations can be difficult to study because these organizations exist in the private, public, and charitable sectors, making it difficult to understand the incentives and the organizational structures of the institutions that qualify as a charity. Relief organizations can also be difficult to study because in many cases the funds collected in one community are used in another community.

in Canada over more than 15 years. For overall private giving, they measure crowding out of close to 100%. Similar to the US data, approximately 77% of this crowding out is attributable to change in charity fundraising. Unlike the US data, however, Andreoni and Payne can examine whether crowding out is similar across different types of private givers to the charity: individuals that give directly, individuals that give through participation in fundraising events (such as gala dinners or other non-tax receipted revenues), and donations from other charities and charitable foundations. The analysis suggests that individuals that give directly do not reduce their giving when the charity receives a government grant – instead they increase their giving, suggesting a crowding in effect as would occur if individuals use government funding as a signal. The crowding out is attributable to a decline in revenues from fundraising events (likely because the charities reduce their fundraising efforts) and a decline in revenues from other charities and foundations. These other charities and foundations are likely better informed about the activities of the charities under study and, thus, more likely to change their funding levels when the charity receives government funding.

Despite the great attention to crowding out, there remain many open questions. Crowding out clearly differs across the types charitable good or service being provided, and it differs across each source of private revenue, in ways that are not yet understood. Moreover, if giving is crowded out, where does the giving go? Do donors give it to another cause or use it for private consumption. Conversely, if a fundraiser succeeds in attracting a new donor, is that money simply moved from another charity, or is the new donor also giving new dollars to the charitable sector.[31] One thing that is clear, however, is that viewing organizations as active players in the market for donations has brought rich new insights to questions of crowding out and the effectiveness of government policy.

4.3. Evidence from Field Experiments

The main models of fundraising discussed above are built on the assumption that there are some latent transaction costs to giving. Contacting donors with a request to give, perhaps providing a return envelope and information about the organization, can lower the transaction costs and hence trigger a gift. We start this section by discussing a paper by Huck and Rasul (2010) that attempts to measure the selection into giving based on a model of transaction costs.

Notice that if an individual faces random transaction costs—one's day could be particularly busy or unusually slow—this effect cannot be captured in a single request to give. Thus, one needs at least two requests to identify a model of selection into the set of donors. Huck and Rasul conduct a study using the same fund drive described above. Potential donors received a detailed solicitation letter that varied across donors with respect to

---

[31] Reinstein (2011) discusses a framework for thinking about displaced giving, while Rose-Ackerman (1982) discusses the potential for fundraising to only reallocate givers without actually raising more funds for the charitable sector as a whole. Both papers raise important issues that seem worthy of additional research.

whether a leadership gift was mentioned and potential matching rates for donations. Six weeks later these donors received a brief reminder of the earlier mailing but carried no new information. Let r_1 be the response rate on the first mailing and r_2 be the response rate on the second mailing. Let s stand for the share of donors who would like to give if transaction costs were sufficiently low and let t be the probability that an individual draws a transaction cost that is at or below the threshold at which they will find the time to consider the solicitation and mail a check. Assuming s and t are the same across solicitations (the authors provide cogent arguments about why the data support this assumption), then with two mailings the response rates would be defined as $r_1 = st$, and $r_2 = s(1-t)t$. These two equations can be solved for s and t. The authors do this for both a control group that was not told of a lead giver, and for a treatment group that was. Solving for the control group, s is 0.069 and t is 0.54, while for the treatment group, s is 0.061 and t is 0.57. The fact that these numbers are so similar, despite the fact that the treatment group gives higher amounts at both the initial and reminder solicitations, is supportive evidence for an underlying model of fundraising built on notions of transaction costs of givers.[32]

An important implication and lesson of field experiments using mailings that is worth emphasizing is clarified in this multiple-solicitation technique. The reminder letter mentioned nothing about the leadership gift or matching rates. Yet, those who gave after the second solicitation but had gotten letters mentioning the lead gift in the first solicitation gave more. This leads one to ask whether the differential propensity to be treated—that is, opening the envelope on the first solicitation—is interacting with the willingness to give in the second mailing. Backing up one more stage, one could also imagine that those willing to open envelopes from charities in the first mailing are also hopeful to have something to support, which in turn may select themselves into being treated based on an openness to being influenced by, say, a leadership giver. This self-selection into being treated, along with the low response rates, means that these experiments are not informing us about a general population, but a self-selected and potentially extreme subset of potential givers. Charities that offer matches over a telephone solicitation, radio advertising, or using a social network, for instance, may find entirely different patterns of responses.

4.4. Further Evidence from Experiments

Here we discuss other laboratory and field experiments that consider charities as participants in a complex strategic game among several players. We highlight two issues: crowding out and sequential giving.

---

[32] Huck and Rasul (2010) argue convincingly that other explanations of choice cannot explain the data. For instance, the fact that the second mailing gets any response is evidence that either preferences or transaction costs of giving have some random element. A random utility model, however, is contradicted by the fact that response rates fall by half in the reminder. This leaves randomness in transaction costs as a likely explanation. The simple two equation approach is, obviously and necessarily overly simple—it is the most one can do with two solicitations.

Early experiments on crowding out focused on abstract public goods provided in the laboratory (Andreoni (1993); Bolton and Katok (1998); Chan, Godby, Mestelman, and Muller, 2002). These found incomplete crowding out, suggesting that subjects' preferences included some imperfect willingness to substitute own giving for forced giving through "taxation." The strength of this approach is that it clearly identifies the role of preferences apart from any context brought into the experiment from the real world, or any value placed on being a "donor," either through conscience, identity, audience effects, or other elements that may account for the warm-glow. However, this narrowness is also a weakness. What if context (that is, giving to an actual public good in the world) interacts with warm-glow to change its impact?

In a simple and clever manipulation by Eckel, Grossman, and Johnson (2005), laboratory subjects play a dictator game[33] with an actual charity.[34] Using the setup of Bolton and Katok (1998), both the individual and the charity were endowed with an initial split of $20, either $18 for the subject and $2 for the charity, or $15 for the subject and $5 for the charity. Subjects could then "top up" the small forced donation. The hypothesis of complete crowding out is the final allocation should be independent of this initial allocation. The interesting twist here was a further manipulation in how the initial endowment was framed. If it was stated simply as a starting allocation, crowding out was seen as essentially zero—giving did not depend on the starting allocation. However, if subjects were told that they had $20 to start with and that $2 (or $5) had been "taxed" away from them, this tax was incorporated into the contribution leading to 100% crowding out.

What accounts for this difference in framing? Obviously it cannot be that subjects have utility functions over the final provision of the charitable good, since otherwise giving would have been zero in all conditions.[35] Instead, it is likely that the frame affects how subjects perceive themselves or how they feel they are perceived by others. It would appear that publicly framing the initial allocation as a tax served to create the mutual knowledge

---

[33] People often ask about the validity of an experimental dictator game to explain behavior outside the laboratory, pointing to potential experimenter demand effects as a possible confound (List, 2007; Bardsley, 2008). Recently, Franzen and Pointner (2013) correlate behavior in the laboratory with real choices made many weeks later with a real solicitation for a charity, and found laboratory and field choices were significantly correlated. One way to reconcile the intuition of demand effects with this result is that in the field there are "fundraiser demand effects" that are similar to those in the laboratory, and affect similar people. This would then turn the argument upside down—dictator games are excellent games for studying giving in the field precisely because they contain demand effects.

[34] The authors offer each subject a choice from a menu of charities. The idea is to increase the likelihood that subjects are paired with a charity they support. One could imagine, however, using this selection as a commitment device: choose a charity that one dislikes so as to make it easier to say no in the giving stage. While the authors found no evidence of the strategic use of choice, the hypothesis was not given a clear test; all charities offered were likely to be supported by some degree by all subjects.

[35] A closely related paper by Crumpler and Grossman (2008), discussed earlier, makes this point clearly. In a similar set up, lab subjects can play a dictator game with a charity. However, the experimenter has already guaranteed the charity a large donation. Any gifts from subjects will be deducted from the experimenter's guarantee. Thus, subjects' gifts will have no marginal effect on total giving, but will have a compositional effect of including more money from the subject. Despite the strong incentives to give zero, the authors find 57% of subjects donate, and about 20% of endowments go to charity. This is striking evidence in favor of a warm-glow motive.

that subjects would get credit for this contribution.[36] Li, Eckel, Grossman, and Brown (2011) show this must be the case. In another "real donation" setup, subjects can give to private charities, or to government agencies that would appear to be providing a near-perfect substitute (such as disaster relief, or cancer research). Individuals made similar levels of donations to the government or private sector provider, although the 22% going to the government was smaller than the 27% going to the private alternative.[37] Nonetheless, this study shows that people are not opposed to taxation, but will *voluntarily* pay a tax, as long as it is clear to all sides, and perhaps especially the subject herself, that the "gift" includes the dollars going to the government.

Next we turn to sequential giving. Much of the intuition for markets for giving is based on static models in which all givers move simultaneously. In life, as has already been noted in the discussion of leadership giving, giving is often sequential. Often these "leadership gifts" will come from a small set of large donors. It is believed, however, that this way of organizing donations is the best way to guarantee the success of the fund drive.[38] Several theoretical papers have suggested that the leadership giver may have an incentive to become better informed than other donors, thus the lead gift conveys useful information (Andreoni, 2006a; Vesterlund, 2003). Another hypothesis is that leadership givers are instrumentally giving to promote reciprocal gift exchange. A clever experiment by Potters, Sefton, and Vesterlund (2007) shows that when leadership givers reveal private information using a credible signal, leadership giving is effective. This supports the model of signaling over reciprocity.

Another feature of real-world giving is that it unravels slowly over time. In an important paper by Marx and Matthews (2000), giving is modeled as an iterative mechanism. Building off of Schelling's (1960) intuition, giving little-by-little can help solve the free rider problem since each giver only risks a small amount of money and reveals only a small bit of information about his willingness to pay. Marx and Matthews show formally, however, that for this to be true there must be a discontinuous "completion benefit." If there is, and if players are sufficiently patient, iterative giving can have the effect suggested by Schelling. Duffy, Ochs, and Vesterlund (2007) find iterative giving is indeed more successful but, in contrast to the formal model, the success does not depend on the existence of a discontinuous completion bonus.

A final way sequential giving could be important in the real world is that it helps givers form beliefs about what size gift is "appropriate." Giving, as we have argued, has many

---

[36] It is amusing how this also mirrors the political debates. Those who favor smaller government tend to discuss the government in terms of "your taxes," while those wanting a larger presence for government discuss policy in terms of "your schools" or "your highways."

[37] This set of results is also striking in line with the results of a neuro-economics study by Harbaugh, Mayr, and Burghart (2007), which showed that people enjoyed giving to charity, even if it was a forced versus a voluntary gift, but the joy of voluntary giving (as measured by neural activity in the pleasure centers of the brain) was higher than for involuntary giving.

[38] See Andreoni (1998) for a discussion of these practices and a theory of seed money as signals for charitable giving, and see List and Lucking-Reiley (2002) for a field experiment supporting this model.

components of a purely social good, such as audience effects, identity, and status, and as such how much a person wants to give could be a *positive* function of what others give. Sequential giving allows people to learn from those who came before. In an experiment using public radio donors, Shang and Croson (2009) manipulated information given to donors calling into a station to make a pledge. When they announced the largest of recent donations, this indeed had a positive effect on giving.

5. APPROACH 3: GIVING AS A SOCIAL ACT

Markets, as economists have idealized them, are impersonal. Supply meets demand. There is no courtship, no flattery, no salesmanship—just exchange. Thinking of charity as existing in a market with many players is a necessary step toward understanding how the different participants respond to each other. But the extremely personal nature of charitable giving, the fundamentally human aspect of giving and helping, suggests that perhaps this idealized analog of a market is missing some fundamental aspects of the giving dynamic that could be critical to understanding why people give, and why we rely on charity to provide so many social goods and services. Understanding giving as a social act will allow us to ask whether this structure is efficient or whether, as is often the case in textbook markets, the exchanges are fraught with "market" imperfections.

To make the point starkly, as researchers in the area of giving and altruism will surely affirm, a perennial question asked of us is, "Why do people give?" Why is this question asked in the first place? Do labor economists get asked, "Why do people work?" Do newspapers print headlines asking, "Why do people buy food?" Giving, altruism, charitable feelings, and behaviors are as common to everyone's personal experience as getting a job or eating a meal, yet charitable behavior remains something that has escaped an easy explanation and remains a topic of great fascination, both in and out of academia.

One reason economists have, perhaps, struggled to provide a simple answer to the question is that the answer goes beyond the borders of mainstream economics. Sociology and psychology may be needed as well. Scientists from these areas will tell us that giving typically involves at least two steps. First is an intellectual recognition of a need. But this is clearly in itself not enough. For nearly everyone on the planet there is someone they know (or know of) who is in much greater need than themselves, or is aware that there are causes whose social benefit greatly exceeds one's own private benefit of the last dollar of consumption. Awareness is not enough. So what else is needed to move awareness into action?

This section will explore several answers to what could be part of that "what else." All of these will revolve around the inherent sociality of giving.

Begin with the trivial observation: giving requires a recipient. Giving is rarely anonymous and even more rarely is it unnoticed or unknown. That is, someone is typically watching and the fact of an audience may influence giving. But even when no one truly knows about a gift, the giver herself knows.[39] Are we, as Adam Smith wrote in *The Theory of Moral Sentiments*, our own audience?

Another feature common in the giving exchange is a request to give. It is a fair approximation to say that virtually all giving is accompanied by a direct request, a fundraising solicitation, a phone number or web address on a television screen, or an extended hand. Rarely does a donor get "hungry" for more giving, instead the recipient tends to come seeking the donor. People may be more or less willing to put themselves on life paths to do good deeds, such as the person who becomes an overworked and underpaid teacher or nurse rather than an accountant or statistician. On a day-to-day scale, a willingness to give will often be correlated with a willingness to let oneself be asked. And when being asked is truly exogenous, a willingness to give may be correlated with a weakness of will to say no.

If asking is so powerful, this leads us to imagine what hold asking has on people. Why does asking work? Economists are just beginning to examine these questions, but the answer, we will conjecture, lies in another key ingredient to the chain of mental states that leads to giving. In particular, once one intellectually acknowledges the needs of another, an emotional experience of those needs is most often present in those who give. That is, humans feel great empathy.

5.1. Audience Effects

Public Broadcasting fundraisers read names aloud on the air, the symphony lists donors in the program, and after class reunions the names of those who gave will be printed in the annual college newsletters.

These tactics apparently work to increase donations, but why? One hypothesis is that, for whatever accident of evolution—biological or cultural—individuals form judgments about others and, more to the point, people care that they themselves are judged positively. Two papers published in the same year discussed the importance of such audience effects, Ariely, Bracha, and Mier (2009) and Andreoni and Bernheim (2009). Here we discuss the second of these, though each had a similar intent.

The paper by Andreoni and Bernheim uses a simple dictator game in which the dictator has $20 to share with a recipient. It seems obvious that most people will agree that the socially acceptable—some would say normative—choice in this dictator game is a 50-50 split. People, however, may have heterogeneous values for how much they personally care about adhering to this 50-50 norm. The key innovation in this analysis is to assume that in addition to caring about others and about adhering to the norm, people also care their "social image." That is, people care that others *perceive* that they are altruistic.

---

[39] Adam Smith famously discussed this self-monitoring in the *Theory of Moral Sentiments* as the notion that inside our minds is an "impartial spectator" who evaluates the moral value of our choices, and whose opinion of us matters greatly. Smith did not speculate as to whether this spectator, while impartial, was also naïve. That is, are we capable of hiding our true intentions from the impartial spectator? Stated differently, do we benefit from signaling our true types to the spectator (or perhaps hiding our true types by pooling), or is the spectator, who, after all lives in the same neighborhood as our consciousness, smart enough to know our true types, but simply judges us by our choices.

Suppose that with no audience Alice would most prefer to give Bob a 45% share of the pie, keeping 55% for herself. Notice, that with an audience it will cost just 5% more of the pie for Alice can appear just as generous as those who care infinitely about conforming to the 50-50 norm. By giving 45%, conversely, she reveals her true type. Here the audience makes her behave more generously.

Instead, suppose Alice would, without an audience, be willing to give Bob 2% of the pie. With an audience Alice will be seen almost as poorly as those others who are taking everything. To gain an extra 2% of the pie Alice relinquishes almost nothing in her social image and, depending on the distribution of the preferences for conforming to the norm, could find the trade-off makes her better off. That is, an audience makes her behave more selfishly.

Combining these two effects, the audience can create a "double pooling equilibrium," and this outcome exactly captures the specific data from experiments.

Andreoni and Bernheim follow this theory with a new experiment. They do this by adding noise to a Dictator Game choice. For instance, regardless of what the dictator chooses, there could be a 50% chance that her choice will be substituted with "give nothing." Thus, when a recipient gets nothing it is unclear whether the dictator or the experimenter is responsible. The theory neatly shows, as this likelihood of being "forced" to be selfish grows, the pool at giving 50:50 should shrink and the pool at "give nothing" should grow. This is precisely what happens in the experiment.[40]

The model and experiment of Andreoni and Bernheim, while not about charitable giving per se (although Ariely et al. do contain elements of charitable giving), provides a structure and a backing for understanding the social aspects of an audience that may bring richness to future studies of giving.

5.2. The Power of the Ask

Fundraisers are fond of saying that there are two kinds of mistakes to make in a fund drive: asking for too little and asking for too much. Ask for too much, they say, and you get nothing. Ask for too little and you get what you asked for. A recent experiment by Andreoni and Rao (2011) illustrates this wisdom, but with a twist about how giving is activated.

Again, a laboratory Dictator Game is the backdrop. In a baseline game there was no communication between dictators and recipients. In the *Ask* condition, recipients could make a request of dictators, including a short written statement. In the *Explain* condition, the dictators could include a short explanation along with their choice. Both of these allow only one-way communication. In *Ask-Explain* and *Explain-Ask* conditions, communication goes two ways, but who speaks first is switched in the two conditions.

---

[40] In a complementary condition, the random device instead forced dictators to "give 1". Even though no subjects ever gave just one in the first condition, as the likelihood of this forced choice grew, the pool at give 1 did as well.

As is common, the baseline resulted in about 16% given. Asking improved this. Most recipients asked for 50%, said something about fairness, and this boosted giving to 24%. With explaining came the first big surprise: giving dropped to 6% and dictators most commonly said, "I'm sorry." However, combining asking and explaining does not result in an averaging of the result. Recipients again ask for a 50-50 split, but now both dictators and recipients tend to mention fairness, regardless of which player moved first, and giving surges to almost 29%, with significantly more 50-50 splits—the highest among all conditions.

Andreoni and Rao added one more manipulation. They re-ran the two one-way communication conditions, but before subjects made their choices they actively engaged in imagining themselves in the other's shoes. That is, they engaged in empathic thinking about the other player. The result was that one-way communication with induced empathic thinking looked indistinguishable from that in two-way communication.

What does this teach us? While the mental processes are not measured, the behavior is consistent with a simple story that linguists, sociologists, and language specialists would tend to support. Communication—a fundamental feature of any social interaction such as giving—requires empathic reasoning. Without communication we can maintain an intellectual awareness of a need yet still maintain a "willful indifference" to the emotions that an "empathic awareness" might then ignite. Perhaps, it is conjectured, asking is powerful because it forces people beyond an intellectual awareness into an empathic awareness, and it is the latter that is necessary for an altruist to become a giver.[41]

5.3. Diversity and the Socio-economics of Giving

In urban centers across North America and Europe, neighborhood diversity is increasingly common. This diversity is often lauded as a virtue in and of itself. From a public economics perspective, however, public good provision often decreases in the presence of diversity. The observed decrease in public goods includes spending less on schools, roads, and hospitals (Alesina et al., 1999, 2004; Poterba, 1997; Goldin & Katz, 1999). What is less clear is how diversity affects the support for *privately* provided public goods such as charities. Standard economic models suggest the predictive effect of diversity on privately provided public goods is unclear. If individuals sort into groups that are distinct based on characteristics such as ethnicity, religion, or income, then increased diversity may foster greater participation in organizations that allow for this sorting, resulting in an increase in giving to these types of groups. But if charities are perceived to benefit individuals that are outside of one's group, then we might observe a decrease in giving.

---

[41] Recent neurological studies back this up. Jack, Dawson, Begany, Leckie, Barry, Ciccia, and Snyder (2013) show that the cool intellectual aspects of reasoning suppress the impulsive empathic parts of the brain, and vice versa. This suggests a physiological reason to avoid a fundraiser—an awareness that being asked will stimulate your empathy and thus make it harder to engage your intellect when making a giving decision.

Andreoni, Payne, Smith, and Karp (2011), using data from Canadian tax-filers, begin to shed light on this issue. Their data is at a neighborhood level (approximately 5000 households per neighborhood) spanning up to four censuses (15 years) and using over 17,000 neighborhood-year observations. They use an empirical methodology adapted from Vigdor (2002, 2004). By using shares of the population as a measure for group affiliation, one can develop a Fragmentation Index to measure the level of diversity in the neighborhood. This index is widely used in the literature and is easily interpreted as the probability that any two randomly selected individuals in the community belong to different groups. The authors observe that while the average adult donates approximately \$200/year, an increase of 10% points in the Fragmentation Index for ethnic diversity implies a decrease in giving of \$27, approximately a 14% reduction. The decline is attributable to the intensive (amount of giving) and not on the extensive (number of givers) margin. That is, increased diversity appears to make givers give less.

The research suggests that different ethnic groups respond differently to diversity. For a 10% point increase in the share of the identified group, giving by whites is higher by \$92, by blacks is higher by \$390, by east Asians is lower by \$111. Moreover, there are strong effects of diversity based on the educational background of the neighborhoods. For a 10% point increase in the share of the identified religious grouping, Catholics' donations increase by \$69 but there is no statistically significant change in the level of giving by those affiliated with other religious groups.

Other work has also found that race and religion matter to givers. Hungerman (2008) found that charitable spending by all-white church congregations is more sensitive to increases in the shares of blacks in the county than more diverse congregations. He did not find a similar sensitivity, however, to changes in shares of other races (e.g., Hispanics). Hungerman (2009) also provides evidence to suggest that the effect of changes in government spending on church spending varies across communities that is tied to measures of racial diversity. Experimental work by Fong and Luttmer (2009, 2011) shows that racial composition affects perceptions about giving. This literature suggests there is more to understand about the impacts of diversity on charitable giving and the provision of charitable goods. If governments are looking to transfer more of their services to charities, then we should consider more how diversity affects charity operations and how these effects could affect the delivery of public goods by charities and other private groups.

6. APPROACH 4: THE GIVER'S MIND

Recently, decision scientists and economists have conducted experiments that have had an eye-opening effect on the study of giving. Dana, Cain, and Dawes (2006) showed that, rather than enter a \$10 dictator game with an anonymous partner, many people would accept \$9 and be allowed to leave with the potential recipient not being made aware of the choice to exit. This would seem to violate revealed preference—entering and taking

$10 is optimal for a selfish person, and entering and giving $1 and keeping $9 would seem to be preferred by an altruist. So why would people prefer to exit? A second study, with Dana, Weber, and Kuang (2007), hid from people the consequences of their own actions on another subject—a maximizing choice for oneself either harmed or helped another. Subjects could find out whether their interests were aligned or opposed simply by clicking a box on the computer screen before making their choices. A surprising fraction refused the free information and made the choice that maximized their own payoff, willfully remaining ignorant of the consequences. Subjects were, the authors argue, preserving "moral wiggle room" that allowed them to escape the guilt of creating a negative externality by preserving a belief that maybe the externality was actually positive.[42]

This led people to ask, do people actually dislike giving? Are fundraisers, by putting people in the social situation that creates an expectation of meeting some norm or standard of generosity, actually making people worse off? Should we care about this from a public policy perspective?

These observations and arguments are reminiscent of a recent but important question raised about the efficient subsidies to the provision of public goods through private charities. Most notably, Diamond (2006) asked whether the warm-glow of giving is something that those concerned with social welfare should take into account. Andreoni (2006b) summarizes and amplifies these arguments. While the institutions themselves may manipulate warm-glow as an impulse or incentive to give, these authors argue that it is the final allocations of actual public good that should be what enters the welfare calculus. In contrast to this question, there is no debate about whether we should change welfare calculus to include the delight one might feel at getting a new sweater at a bargain price, nor the remorse one feels buying the sweater the day *before* the price was discounted. There is common agreement that welfare should depend on the allocation of sweaters and prices paid. What makes markets for giving different? Should social welfare calculations consider the means to an end in charity markets? Obviously, if the state has a compelling interest in the institutions per se then institution itself becomes a public good whose utility should be counted, but this is not the argument being made. This line of reasoning suggests that the answer to the question of how to calculate costs and benefits of giving—physical and social—should not lie solely in uncovering what is in the minds or hearts of donors, but include the consequences for the set of public goods that are provided by them and the deadweight cost of acquiring them. Moreover, the calculation must depend on the value relative to the next best alternative, which would appear to be government provision.

There is also a further question about what one can infer from an individual who shows reluctance to give, or a desire to avoid a solicitation. Obviously, one cannot and should not give on all occasions, just like one cannot and should not eat whenever food is available. A resistance to give may not indicate a lack of altruism, but could be a sign of discipline,

---

[42] See also Lazear, Malmendier, and Weber, R. (2012).

restraint, and adherence to careful spending plans. What about an unwillingness to even be asked to give? Just as the smell of freshly baked cookies may make it difficult to be disciplined when on a diet, being asked to give may trigger psychologically uncomfortable feelings—feelings that exist in our minds because of natural instincts to be benevolent when it is helpful and when we can afford it—and avoiding temptation helps maintain our self-discipline.

In the next two subsections we summarize two recent papers that examine, in different contexts, the willingness of individuals to be solicited to give. Both provide evidence of individuals who appear to be very aware, perhaps at a subconscious level, of the need to exert control over how intensely they are solicited to give.

6.1. Social Costs of Social Pressure

DellaVigna et al. (2012) present an ambitious and important study on the "social pressure" costs of fundraising.[43] They conducted a door-to-door fundraising field experiment that visited over 7600 homes in 2009. The baseline experiment was a standard cold call, where the fundraiser arrives at the door unexpectedly. A second condition announced the potential visit by leaving a flier on the front door of the home, indicating that a fundraiser would visit the home the next day at a specified time. A third condition used the fliers again, but this time the resident could check a box on the flier asking not to be disturbed. Finally, in a separate manipulation to estimate the opportunity cost of time, the fundraiser offered to pay the resident a small fee to take a short survey, with rates of pay and lengths of the survey varying. The study explored two key questions. First, do people avoid fundraisers, yet give because of some social pressure? Second, what is the social cost of fundraising, including the cost of social pressure?

Key to their analysis is the structural estimation of the utility equation

$$U = w_i - g_{ij} + a_{ij} \ln (\Gamma_j + g_{ij}) - S_j * \mathrm{I}(g_{ij} < \$10),$$

where w_i is income, g_{ij} is the gift to the charity, a_{ij} is a utility parameter for the warm-glow of giving, Γ_j is a utility shift parameter, S_j is an estimated parameter for the social pressure cost, and $\mathrm{I}(\cdot)$ is a function equal to 1 if the gift was under $10, that is, the authors assume that social cost is felt most severely when giving nominal amounts. Notice, the a_{ij} and S_j parameters are identified from the random assignment to the "do not disturb" conditions, from the willingness to accept payment for answering a short survey, that is, to be inconvenienced in the service of a good cause, and by assuming the a_{ij} are normally distributed across individuals.[44]

---

[43] See also Meer (2011) who shows the additional effect of peer pressure over and above any social pressure. When a college roommate calls to ask for a donation to the alma mater, both the likelihood and amount of giving rise significantly. Fong and Luttmer (2011) show as well that similarity among potential recipients and the donors also matters.

[44] While the "i" dimension refers to individuals, the "j" dimension refers to the fact that there were two charities under consideration in this field experiment. One was local and well known, and the other was conspicuously not local and likely unfamiliar.

Estimating this utility function through iterated method of moments, the authors are able to estimate the desire to avoid and, by estimating the a_{ij} and S_j, gain a sense of the net social pressure cost of fundraising. They are able to find evidence for both warm-glow altruism and social pressure. About half of donors they sample would prefer not to be contacted by the fundraiser. Moreover, the parameter estimates suggest refusing a request for a $1 donation has a social pressure cost of around $4, indicating that, in this study, the social costs of door-to-door fundraising are likely negative at the individual (although not necessarily societal) level.[45]

6.2. Avoiding the Ask

The second study complements the DellaVigna et al., results by approaching a different venue. Andreoni, Rao, and Trachtman (2012) teamed with the Salvation Army for 4 days in December 2009 to perform a natural field experiment at a suburban Boston supermarket. The supermarket was chosen to be typical in that it faced a large parking lot and had two main entrances facing the lot. In a 2×2 design, college aged women stood in Salvation Army aprons and rang bells at one door or both doors, and either simply rang or rang and said, "Merry Christmas, please give today." Thus, a quarter of the patrons had an indirect ask that was easy to avoid (one door, just ringing), another quarter had an indirect ask that was difficult to avoid (both doors covered), a third quarter had direct asks that were easy to avoid (one door and "please give"), while a final quarter were directly asked to give and were difficult to avoid (two doors of "please give").

The four conditions were randomized into 16 blocks over four consecutive days, the "kettles" were swapped out 64 times to count donations, helpers counted the number of passings through each door, and the number of givers. In all, over 17,000 entrances and exits were counted. The randomization allowed the authors to account for those wishing to avoid, those seeking an opportunity to give, the gifts of those opting to pass by the bell ringer and to forecast the lost contributions of those who avoided the bell ringer.

Notice the experimental manipulations here were very minor, as were the costs to avoid—a person may need to spend 45 s walking farther through the parking lot to avoid a simple "please give today."

The findings were that shoppers did almost nothing to avoid the simple bell ringing. However, when the ringing was accompanied by a direct ask, about 30% of shoppers used an alternative entrance when they could. Only about 1.5% actively sought an opportunity to give. Surprisingly, however, those who were captured by the coverage of two doors gave, on average, just as frequently and just as much as those shoppers who did not avoid being asked, a result similar to that found in field data (Meer & Rosen, 2010). In other words, there appeared to be virtually no sorting on the magnitude or propensity to donate.

---

[45] When the charity was the unfamiliar out-of-state charity, the cost appeared far higher–$37 cost of declining a $1 request. In other words, the benefit to society would need to be 37 times the value of the $1 to the individual in order to make the request a net positive for the world.

People, it seemed, were not avoiding giving a small amount or saying "no," but instead appeared to be avoiding saying "yes." Much like the self-control or present-bias literature, people appeared to be using the tactic of avoiding being asked as a means to control their impulse to give when directly asked by a human to give to a worthy cause.

6.3. Is Fundraising Bad for Society?

The last two sections indicate that many, if not most, people dislike being asked to give. Does that mean that fundraising is bad for society? The only way to answer this is with another question: compared to what? There are many ways to organize a society to achieve certain social goals, and each leads to a different set of burdens and distortions. For instance, most people dislike paying taxes but like a rich set of public services. Their efforts at avoiding taxes are what we call deadweight loss of taxation, and the consequence of taxes on the distribution of consumption is what we call the incidence of taxation. If instead of mandated giving through taxes we opt for voluntary giving through charities, we create another type of distortion and incidence. One distortion is that people must tolerate saying "no" or avoid saying "yes" to many worthy causes. A question of incidence is that the "tax" of charitable fundraising falls disproportionately on those who are the most "charitable," that is, those who are most willing to give. Moreover, compared to government provision, where preferences are represented by votes, with private giving the preferences of people are expressed by their donations. Hence, the distribution of goods provided through giving is likely to focus more on goods enjoyed by the wealthy, such as operas, art museums, and elite colleges, rather than on goods favored by the poor, such as parks, crime prevention, and primary education.

The question of whether fundraising is bad, therefore, relies on how one feels about the efficiency and incidence of different systems of providing social goods. For instance, how costly is it for givers to decline requests to give? Is the cost ephemeral and easily forgotten, or long lasting? Can givers adopt cognitive strategies that make dealing with fundraisers less stressful, such as planning annual giving budgets and sticking to them? Or is asking the donor with the big heart for a gift like asking the chronic overeater if he would like to see the desert menu—is it cruelly preying on the vulnerable? Is it inequitable for a society to let those with the greatest wealth also have the greatest say in what kinds of goods are provided, or is it efficiency enhancing to let wealthy donors build self-named monuments (think of Andrew Carnegie) for their own and society's benefit?

These questions about how to organize institutions, examining the distortions and incidence of each institutional framework, are deep, difficult, important, and largely unexplored within economics.[46] Breaking the issue down, starting with attempting an estimate

---

[46] Samuel Bowles (1998) argues for similar interactions between preferences, institutions, and welfare in a wide-ranging survey article including, among other things, institutions that shape social preferences.

of the deadweight loss of fundraising, would open up a much-needed discussion in the literature on public policy toward charitable giving.[47]

7. FUNDRAISING AND THE GIVER'S MIND

In the prior sections we have taken the perspective of the social planner by asking what are the impacts on welfare of certain institutions, such as tax deductions for donations, and the relative costs of fundraising versus government taxation. Here we take the perspective of the charity that, with a fundraising goal, is looking for the most efficient and effective way to reach it. This literature, which is blossoming quickly, is often built on the assumption that, since fundraising is a reality in our society, economists can use what we know about incentives and equilibria to help build better fundraising mechanisms.

Before proceeding with this section, it is worth placing a few questions in the backs of readers' minds. First, is this a topic for economics, or is it better thought of as marketing? The pragmatic answer could be that, given that a society has chosen fundraising and charity as the means to, for instance, subsidize education, it implies that economists can be helpful in making this successful in the most efficient way. But this answer begs an important question: how is efficiency defined within the context of fundraising schemes that may prey on primal desires for empathy, conformity, and social approval, among other "social distortions?" Certainly not every fundraising scheme that raises more money is also a scheme that improves efficiency. This literature, which is of great intrinsic and practical interest, is presented here along with a notice that there remain many unanswered questions about the impacts of these ideas on social welfare.

7.1. Charity Auctions

John Morgan (2000) first asked why so many charities raise money through lotteries. The charity offers a prize P, itself paid for through donations, and sells raffle tickets for a chance to win P. If they sell n raffle tickets, each ticket has a $1/n$ chance of winning. The remarkable thing that Morgan shows is that such a raffle can actually increase donations. If each dollar donated buys one ticket, then in expectation a donation of d costs only $d - (d/n)P = d(1 - P/n) = d(1 - P/\sum d)$. Hence, the lottery mechanism has qualities similar to a subsidy and in theory should increase donations. The brilliant innovation, however, is that this subsidy requires no government and no taxation. Morgan and Sefton (2000) confirm in a laboratory study that lotteries do indeed increase giving.

This work inspired others to consider new auction or prized-based mechanisms for raising funds. One such mechanism is an all-pay auction: people bid for the prize, the highest bidder wins it, but all bids—even the losing bids—must be paid. Theoretically,

---

[47] An important consideration here is how to infer preferences if indeed people are avoiding being asked as a means of self-control. Masatlioglu, Nakajima, and Ozbay (2012) discuss the difficulties of inference about preferences when individuals selectively pay attention to only a portion of the entire choice set.

the all-pay auction should be superior to an auction in which just the winner pays. The reason is intuitive. Without the donation aspect of bids, all-pay and winner-pay should yield identical revenue. Now add in that profits go to charity and imagine the second highest bidder in a winner-pays auction. By becoming the top bidder the person gains the object, but loses the other person's donation to the public good, making winning less sweet. The incentive in the charity auction, therefore, is to bid less aggressively. This same effect is not present in all-pay auctions, since all bids are paid, win or lose.[48]

Despite the clear theoretical predictions, evidence on the relative performance of lotteries, winner-pay, and all-pay auctions is mixed. Schram and Onderstal (2009) confirm the prediction, while Corazzini, Faravelli, and Stanca (2009) show that all-pay fares worse than the other two. An important field experiment by Carpenter, Holmes, and Matthews (2008) again shows that all-pay auctions fare relatively poorly, but because of the setting they are able to offer an additional concern about all-pay auctions: people appear not to like them–many people in the field experiment chose not to participate in the auction.

Carpenter, Holmes, and Matthews (2010, 2011) recently add a variation to all-pay that shares elements of the giving little-by-little mechanisms presented earlier. They call it a bucket auction. Imagine donors sitting in a circle. One donor begins by placing a dollar in a bucket and passing it left. The next donor puts in another dollar then passes the bucket left, and so on. If a donor passes the bucket without adding a dollar, the donor loses all prior contributions *and* any chance at winning the prize. The winner of the prize is the last one to contribute. Carpenter et al. show that the bucket auction raises more money than any prize-based fundraising device considered. Why? One can think of the bucket auction as a modification of a Dutch clock auction. These are known to be easy to explain, easy to understand, and to extract great surplus from bidders. So, even though it also has elements in common with all-pay auctions, the bucket auction is both successful and, apparently, revealed preferred by the donors in the authors' field experiments.

7.2. Motivational Crowding

In a famous study by Titmus (1970), he argued that paying for blood donations might actually make people less likely to supply blood than if it is accepted as a pure donation. The reason, he conjectured, is that by paying for blood one is denying the individual the joy of acting unselfishly. In modern terms, reducing the cost of giving blood in turn diminishes the (possibly self-) signaling value of being a blood donor, "crowding out" this incentive to give.

Although Titmus' book was heavily scrutinized and often dismissed by scholars, there have been mounds of evidence that all manner of moral choices are subject to such "motivational crowding out."[49] Recently Mellstrom and Johannesson (2008), using a

---

[48] See Goeree et al. (2005), and Engers and McManus (2007). Extending this to endogenous participation, see Carpenter et al. (2009).

[49] See Bowles and Hwang (2008) for an application to giving.

very clever field experiment, revisited Titmus' conjectures. They explored whether intro-ducing compensation for donations of blood reduces the number of donors willing to donate blood. The researchers divided their subjects into three groups: those asked to donate blood with no compensation, those asked to donate blood with compensation, and those asked to donate blood with compensation but an opportunity to donate that compensation to a charity. The authors found little difference in behavior by men across the three treatments, but found the cash payment appeared to crowd out the willingness to contribute by women. However, the motivational crowding by women was undone when they were given an opportunity to donate the payment to a charity. That is, by restoring the signaling value, the motivation to give was restored as well.

7.3. Peer Pressure

If, as argued earlier, individuals are sensitive to an audience when making charitable choices, should not the response be especially strong when that audience is a true peer? Meer and Rosen (2011) examine this using data on a lengthy panel of alumni donations to an anonymous university. See also Apinunmahakul and Devlin (2008). The data is rich with personal information, including not only one's year of matriculation, but also major, extracurricular activities, SAT score, grade point average, and, most importantly, a person's randomly assigned freshman roommate. The development office offered one more key piece of data: did an alumnus who volunteered as a fundraiser for the university attempt to contact their freshman roommate to seek a solicitation?

Meer and Rosen take great care to address issues of selection into volunteering and other potential confounding correlates with willingness to give. In the end the data show something surprising about the power of being asked by a peer, rather than by an unknown other alumnus. Peers increase the likelihood of a donation by 8.5%, increasing total donation by about 10.2%. Interestingly, these numbers are very close. This is because the peer solicitation has only a small and insignificant impact on the amount given, conditional on giving. That is, the marginal donors lured in by peer pressure give about the same as those lured in simply by an unknown alumnus, and so the predominant effect of peer pressure is on the likelihood of giving, rather than the amount given.

7.4. The Giving Habit

Can charitable values be taught? Can the habit of giving be acquired? The popular belief is that the answer to both questions is yes. Parents are encouraged to provide a good example so that children will adopt the giving practices they see in their parents, and charities believe that if they can get a donor to start giving, that not only will they continue to give as a habit but that as they become more wealthy they will give more and more.

The question of whether charitable giving can be taught was explored by Wilhelm, Brown, Rooney, and Steinberg (2008). Using the charitable giving supplement to the PSID, they found a strong positive correlation between the religious giving of adult children and their parents—the correlation matched that of the two households' incomes. Non-religious giving was significantly correlated too, although the correlation was smaller. This parallels findings in the psychology literature that suggest charitable values can be "inherited" by the example set by parents.

Do adults gain a habit of giving? Meer (2013) looks at alumni of a university who become givers—typically very small givers—directly after graduation. He forms a somewhat mixed view of the giving habit. Those who begin giving right after graduation are more likely to be givers several years later, as the fundraisers believe. However, contrasting that, they do not appear to become more generous givers with time. Thus, the habit is formed on the extensive rather than the intensive margin.

7.5. Giving to Disasters

Imagine a hurricane or tsunami that causes immediate and great harm and, moreover, is intensively covered by the news. If, as conjectured earlier, empathy is an important step, how does this very emotional situation affect giving to help the victims, and does helping during disasters reduce other forms of giving?

Eckel, De Oliveira, and Grossman (2007) find interesting evidence of overstimulated empathy causing a reduction in giving. When people in Texas were primed with emotionally moving stimuli about hurricane Katrina victims shortly after the disaster, their giving fell, while those in Minnesota, with presumably less exposure, gave more when primed.[50]

This effect is reminiscent of the well-known "identifiable victim" problem of Thomas Schelling (1968), and studied more recently by Loewenstein, Slovic, and colleagues.[51] A single flood victim pulls at one's heart strings, and to deal with empathic feelings one can give. But thousands of victims present an emotionally overwhelming problem and instead, the hypothesis goes, our minds treat them as "statistical victims" in order to regulate our overwhelming empathy. More information on the depths of the disaster, in other words, can reduce giving.

The question often asked about giving during disasters is, does this giving draw donations away from other charities? Systematic evidence on this is difficult to find. Anecdotally, charities unrelated to the disaster report drops in giving in the midst of the disaster, but only small or imperceptible effects over the longer horizon. Brown, Harris, and Taylor (2012) study donations made in 2004 and 2006 to explore the effects of the 2004 Indian Ocean tsunami on donations to natural disasters. Backing up the consensus view, they find little evidence to suggest that donations given to support the tsunami relief efforts divert donations away from future donations to other charitable causes.

---

[50] Fong and Luttmer (2009) study individual reactions to the characteristics of individual victims. They found that potential donors who report feeling affinity for those of their own ethnic or racial group tend to give more if the victims they see are from this group. Those who don't express this affinity show no racial preference in giving.

[51] See Jenni and Loewenstein (1997), Small and Loewenstein (2003), and Small, Loewenstein, and Slovic (2007), to name a few.

7.6. Giving Bundled with Consuming

When a for-profit company promises to give a share of its sales or profits to a charitable cause, is it because the firm has a heart? Perhaps, but it also has keen business sense according to McManus and Bennet (2011). In a field experiment run in collaboration with an online store, they found that shoppers paid little attention to the details of this bundled donation and consumption, but instead showed particularly strong preferences for the bundled good versus a good without the bundled donation, even though providing a donation directly to the charity and purchasing the good separately would have saved the consumer considerable sums.

Gneezy, Gneezy, Nelson, and Brown (2010) ran a field experiment showing further the large effect bundling a good with a charitable donation has on the willingness to pay for the bundle. Subjects were told that they could pay any price they wished to for a good, and that half the price would go to charity. Compared to a posted price, this "pay-what-you-want" pricing strategy created greater revenue and higher profits for the firm, despite the fact that the posted price was available for consumers to choose in pay-what-you-want.

These results show how savvy marketers can exploit the giver's weakness for their own profit and, arguably, for society's gain as well.

8. CONCLUSION

This chapter's goals were to summarize and integrate the main contributions since the last large survey written in 2006 and to present and discuss the themes and questions that we think will carry the field forward.

A fresh look at the data revealed several interesting trends in giving. First, while giving has remained high in the US, the composition of those gifts is shifting. Individuals, who made up about 80% of the giving dollars from 1970 to 1990, now only comprise about 72%. Bequests, which were about 12% in 1970, had fallen to 8% by 2010. Corporate giving was constant at about 2% of all giving. Foundations, however, grew from about 6% of all giving in the 1970s and 1980s to about 14% of donations by 2010. Part of this shift to foundations could be for tax reasons—reductions in estate taxes may have led people to give while alive in order to take deductions against income. Another reason could be the rapid concentration of wealth in the US over the past 20 years. This means that both the demographics of who gives, and the means by which they give, has changed in ways economists have yet to adequately study.

These changes are reflected in the data when it is broken down by the average household giving in the postal code. Since 1990 the gap in dollars given by those in the top income tercile and those in the low and middle terciles has exploded. This confirms that high income and high wealth donors are taking a larger role in the charitable sector. Giving by this economic class has been difficult for economists to study, largely because of data restrictions, but should be an increasingly important focus for policy analysis.

In addition to, or perhaps because of, the shift in the economic class of donors, the composition of donations has changed too. Religious giving in some countries (such as the US) has grown far faster than most other types of giving, followed by giving to educational institutions. Economists are only just beginning to take seriously the fact that religious giving may respond differently to taxation and fundraising incentives, and now that its dominance has become so much greater, the urgency and interest in understanding the special nature of religious giving has grown too.

A number of other themes have become apparent in preparing this survey. First is that interest in fundraising has reached a fever pitch. While we see this as a healthy recognition of reality and a powerful way for economists to use their tools of experimental analysis, econometric rigor, and theory of mechanism design in a purposeful way, we also think that time has come to step back and ask what purpose we are serving. As public economists, our first concern is to ask what does the greatest good for the greatest number. Selecting an institution of private philanthropy and fundraising rather than, for instance, government provision and taxation, is to swap one social aggregator with its incumbent distortions for another. Private provision means people vote with their dollars rather than their ballots, and pay the distortionary costs of avoiding fundraisers and saying no rather than the distortionary costs of avoiding taxation. Explicit recognition that each institutional form offers its own costs, benefits, and incidence is, we think, essential to moving forward to understanding how to improve the world we inhabit. Moreover, economists should avoid the automatic assumption that just because a charity raises money it also raises welfare or affects social equity. There are many poorly understood costs and benefits of the charitable sector that need to be accounted for when thinking of charitable giving from the standpoint of welfare.

Another main lesson of this review is that asking for donations is essential to understanding the strategic relationship between a charity and its donors, and understanding this relationship more clearly will help both fundraisers and policy makers.

Another key next step in understanding the strategic forces in charity markets is to look at how charities compete with each other. Here there are a number of open areas for research. First, when one charity gains a new donation, does another charity lose one? That is, is fundraising socially wasteful by simply moving donations among charities? Second, do the competitive forces among charities lead to innovations in fundraising which rise or fall under competitive pressures? Just as competition brought us technical innovations with private goods, does it bring us better charitable goods, better fundraising mechanisms, and more efficient private provision of charitable goods?

The next area that seems ripe for investigation is the effect of the Internet on the relationship between donors and the charity. Reducing donations to a few quick clicks is a dramatic reduction in transaction costs, which should increase giving, but also a severe depersonalization of donation experience, which undercuts some of the key motivators of giving. Which effect dominates? Is Internet fundraising better for society?

A closely related topic is the role of social networks in giving. We learned that being asked by a friend is even more powerful than being asked by a stranger, even if it is a distant friend. With the pervasiveness of social media websites, are there new frontiers for fundraising as well, or new perils?

Finally, collecting charity is just one side of the social welfare equation, and the other side has gone virtually unstudied. That is, what is the effect of a charity on the recipients of that charity? Does receiving food, shelter, education, a cure for cancer, comfort and refuge, esthetic beauty, or a safe place for children to play make for a stronger, more sympathetic, and more tolerant society? Or does giving donations to private schools that benefit one's own children, or to churches, synagogues, mosques that benefit one's own faith, or to operas and museums that benefit one's own class create a more segregated world, isolated from the needs of others, and thus tearing at the fabric of society?

We have presented a number of important and valuable findings about charity and have issued a number of challenges as well. All is meant in the spirit of inspiring research and encouraging a broader view of the kinds of questions economists can and should ask about giving, fundraising, and consuming charitable goods and services.

REFERENCES

Abrams, B. A., & Schmitz, M. A. (1978). The crowding out effect of government transfers on private charitable contributions. *Public Choice, 33*, 29–39.

Abrams, B. A., & Schmitz, M. A. (1984). The crowding out effect of government transfers on private charitable contributions: Cross sectional evidence. *National Tax Journal, 37*, 563–568.

Alesina, A., Baqir, R., & Easterly, W. (1999). Public goods and ethnic divisions. *The Quarterly Journal of Economics, 114*(4), 1243–1284.

Alesina, Alberto, Baqir, R., & Hoxby, C. (2004). Political jurisdictions in heterogeneous communities. *Journal of Political Economy, 112*, 348–396.

Andreoni, J. (1988). Privately provided public goods in a large economy: the limits of altruism. *Journal of Public Economics, 35*(1), 57–73.

Andreoni, J. (1989). Giving with impure altruism: Applications to charity and Ricardian equivalence. *The Journal of Political Economy, 97*(6), 1447–1458.

Andreoni, J. (1990). Impure altruism and donations to public goods: A theory of warm-glow giving. *The Economic Journal, 100*(401), 464–477.

Andreoni, J. (1993). An experimental test of the public-goods crowding-out hypothesis. *American Economic Review, 83*, 1317–1327.

Andreoni, J. (1998). Toward a theory of charitable fundraising. *Journal of Political Economy, 106*, 1186–1213 [December].

Andreoni, J. (2006a). Leadership giving in charitable fund-raising. *Journal of Public Economic Theory, 8*, 1–22.

Andreoni, J. (2006b). Philanthropy. In Kolm, S.-C., Mercier Ythier, J. (Eds.), *Handbook of Giving, Reciprocity and Altruism* (pp. 1201–1269). Amsterdam: North Holland.

Andreoni, J. & Bernheim, B. D. (2009). Social Image and the 50-50 Norm: A Theoretical and Experimental Analysis of Audience Effects. *Econometrica, 77*(5), 1607–1636.

Andreoni, J. & List, J. A. (2011). Special issue on charitable giving and fundraising, *Journal of Public Economics*, *95*.

Andreoni, J., & McGuire, M. C. (1993). Identifying the free riders: A simple algorithm for determining who will contribute to a public good. *Journal of Public Economics*, *51*, 447–454.

Andreoni, J., & Miller, J. H. (2002). Giving according to GARP: An experimental test of the consistency of preferences for altruism, *Econometrica*, *70*(2), 737–753.

Andreoni, J., & Payne, A. A. (2003). Do government grants to private charities crowd out giving or fundraising? *American Economic Review*, *93*, 792–812.

Andreoni, J., & Payne, A. A. (2011a). Is crowding out due entirely to fundraising? Evidence from a panel of charities. *Journal of Public Economics*, *95*(5–6), 334–343.

Andreoni, J., & Payne, A. A. (2011b). Crowding-out charitable contributions in Canada: New knowledge from the north. *No. w17635*. National Bureau of Economic Research. Cambridge, MA.

Andreoni, J., & Rao. J. (2011). The power of asking: How communication affects selfishness, empathy, and altruism. *Journal of Public Economics*, *95*, 513–520.

Andreoni, J., Brown, E., & Rischall, I. (2003). Charitable giving by married couples: Who decides and why does it matter? *Journal of Human Resources*, *38*, 111–133.

Andreoni, Harbaugh, & Vesterlund (2008). *Altruism in experiments in the new palgrave dictionary of economics* (2nd ed.).

Andreoni, J., Payne, A., Smith, J. D., & Karp, D. (2011). Diversity and donations: The effect of religious and ethnic diversity on charitable giving. *No. w17618*. National Bureau of Economic Research. Cambridge, MA.

Andreoni, J., Rao, J. M. & Trachtman, H. (2012). Avoiding the ask: A field experiment on altruism, empathy, and charitable giving. *No. w17648*. National Bureau of Economic Research. Cambridge, MA.

Andreoni, J., & Vesterlund, L. (2001). Which is the fair sex? Gender difference in altruism. *Quarterly Journal of Economics*, *116*(1), 293–312.

Apinunmahakul, A., & Devlin, R. A. (2008). Social networks and private philanthropy. *Journal of Public Economics*, *92*(1), 309–328.

Ariely, D., Bracha, A., & Meier S. (2009). Doing good or doing well? Image motivation and monetary incentives in behaving prosocially. *American Economic Review*, *99*(1), 544–555.

Bakija, J., & Heim, B. T. (2011). How does charitable giving respond to incentives and income? New estimates from panel data. *National Tax Journal*, *64*(2), 615–650.

Bardsley, N. (2008). Dictator game giving: Altruism or artefact? *Experimental Economics*, *11*(2), 122–133.

Bekkers, R. H. F. P. (2008). Volunteerism. In W. A. Darity Jr (Ed.), *International encyclopedia of the social sciences* (2nd ed.) (pp. 641–643). Detroit: Macmillan Reference USA.

Bekkers, R., & Wiepking, P. (2011). A literature review of empirical studies of philanthropy. *Nonprofit and Voluntary Sector Quarterly*, *40*(5), 924–973.

Bergstrom, T., Blume, L., & Varian, H. (1986). On the private provision of public goods. *Journal of Public Economics*, *29*(1), 25–49.

Blume-Kohout, M. E. (2012). Does targeted, disease-specific public research funding influence pharmaceutical innovation? *Journal of Policy Analysis and Management*, *31*, 641–660.

Bolton, G. E., & Katok, E. (1998). An experimental test of the crowding out hypothesis: The nature of beneficent behavior. *Journal of Economic Behavior and Organization*, *37*(3), 315–331.

Borgonovi, F. (2006). Do public grants to American theatres crowd-out private donations? *Public Choice*, *126*(3), 429–451.

Bound, J., Jaeger, D. A., & Baker, R. M. (1995). Problems with instrumental variables estimation when the correlation between the instruments and the endogenous explanatory variable is weak. *Journal of the American Statistical Association*, *90*(430), 443–450.

Bowles, S. (1998). Endogenous preferences: The cultural consequences of markets and other economic institutions. *Journal of Economic Literature*, *36*(1), 75–111.

Bowles, S., & Hwang, S.-H. (2008). Social preferences and public economics: Mechanism design when social preferences depend on incentives. *Journal of Public Economics*, *92*(8–9), 1811–1820.

Bracha, A., Menietti, M., & Vesterlund, L. (2011). Seeds to succeed?: Sequential giving to public projects. *Journal of Public Economics*, *95*(5), 416–427.

Breman, A. (2011). Give more tomorrow: Two field experiments on altruism and intertemporal choice. *Journal of Public Economics, 95*(11), 1349–1357.

Brown, S., Harris, M. N., & Taylor, K. (2012). Modelling charitable donations to an unexpected natural disaster: Evidence from the US panel study of income dynamics. *Journal of Economic Behavior and Organization, 84*(1), 97–110.

Carpenter, J., Holmes, J., & Matthews, P. (2008). Charity auctions: A field experiment. *Economic Journal, 118,* 92–113.

Carpenter, J., Holmes, J., & Matthews, P. H. (2010). Endogenous participation in charity auctions. *Journal of Public Economics, 94*(11–12), 921–935.

Carpenter, J., Holmes, J., & Matthews, P. H. (2011). Jumping and sniping at the silents: Does it matter for charities? *Journal of Public Economics, 95*(5–6), 395–402.

Chan, K. S., Godby, R., Mestelman, S., & Andrew Muller, R. (2002). Crowding-out voluntary contributions to public goods. *Journal of Economic Behavior and Organization, 48*(3), 305–317.

Chao, J. C., & Swanson, N. R. (2005). Consistent estimation with a large number of weak instruments. *Econometrica, 73*(5), 1673–1692.

Chetty, R. (2009). Bounds on elasticities with optimization frictions: A synthesis of micro and macro evidence on labor supply. *No. w15616.* National Bureau of Economic Research. Cambridge, MA.

Chetty, R., Looney, A. & Kroft, K. (2009). Salience and taxation: Theory and evidence. *American Economic Review, 99*(4), 1145–1177.

Chetty, R. & Saez, E. (2013). Teaching the tax code: Earnings responses to an experiment with EITC recipients, *American Economic Journal: Applied Economics, 5*(1), 1–31.

Connolly, (1997). Does external funding of academic research crowd out institutional support? *Journal of Public Economics, 64*(3), 390–406.

Corazzini, L., Faravelli, M., & Stanca, L. (2009). Royal economic society. *The Economic Journal, 120*(547), 544–555.

Cornes, R., & Sandler, T. (1984). The theory of public goods: non-Nash behaviour. *Journal of Public Economics, 23*(3), 367–379.

Correa, A., & Yildirim, H. (2013). A theory of charitable fundraising with costly solicitations. *American Economic Review, 103*(2), 1091–1107.

Crumpler, H., & Grossman, P. J. (2008). An experimental test of warm glow giving. *Journal of Public Economics, 92,* 1011–1021.

Cruz, L. M., & Moreira, M. J. (2005). On the validity of econometric techniques with weak instruments inference on returns to education using compulsory school attendance laws. *Journal of Human Resources, 40*(2), 393–410.

Dana, J., Cain, D. M., & Dawes, R. M. (2006). What you don't know won't hurt me: Costly (but quiet) exit in dictator games. *Organizational Behavior and Human Decision Processes, 100*(2), 193–201.

Dana, J., Weber, R. A., & Kuang, J. X. (2007). Exploiting moral wiggle room: Experiments demonstrating an illusory preference for fairness. *Economic Theory, 33*(1), 67–80.

DellaVigna, S. List, J. A., & Malmendier, U. (2012). Testing for altruism, and social pressure in charitable giving. *Quarterly Journal of Economics, 127*(1), 1–56.

Diamond, P. (2006). Optimal tax treatment for private contribution for public goods with and without warm glow preferences. *Journal of Public Economics, 90*(4–5), 897–919.

Duffy, J., Ochs, J., & Vesterlund, L. (2007). Giving little by little: Dynamic voluntary contribution games. *Journal of Public Economics, 91*(9), 1708–1730.

Eckel, C. C., & Grossman, P. J. (2003). Rebate versus matching: Does how we subsidize charitable contributions matter? *Journal of Public Economics, 87*(3), 681–701.

Eckel, C. C., Grossman, P. J., & Johnston, R. M. (2005). An experimental test of the crowding out hypothesis. *Journal of Public Economics, 89*(8), 1543–1560.

Eckel, C., De Oliveira, A., & Grossman, P. (2007). Is more information always better? An experimental study of charitable giving and Hurricane Katrina. *Southern Economic Journal, 74*(2).

Engers, M., & McManus, B. (2007). Charity auctions. *International Economic Review, 48*(3), 953–994.

Feldstein, M. S., & Clotfelter, C. (1976). Tax incentives and charitable contributions in the United States: A microeconometric analysis. *Journal of Public Economics, 5*(1–2), 1–26.

Feldstein, M. S., & Taylor, A. (1976). The income tax and charitable contributions. *Econometrica, 44*(6), 1201–1222.

Fong, C. M., & Luttmer, E. F. (2009). What determines giving to Hurricane Katrina victims? Experimental evidence on racial group loyalty. *American Economic Journal: Applied Economics, 1*(2), 64–87.

Fong, C. M., & Luttmer, E. F. (2011). Do fairness and race matter in generosity? Evidence from a nationally representative charity experiment. *Journal of Public Economics, 95*(5), 372–394.

Franzen, A., & Pointner, S. (2013). The external validity of giving in the dictator game: A field experiment using the misdirected letter technique. *Experiment Economics, 16*(2), 155–169.

Gneezy, A., Gneezy, U., Nelson, L. D., & Brown, A. (2010). Shared social responsibility: A field experiment in pay-what-you-want pricing and charitable giving. *Science, 329*(5989), 325–327.

Goeree, J., Holt, C., & Gomez, R. (2002). Private costs and public benefits: Unraveling the effects of altruism and noisy behavior. *Journal of Public Economics, 83*(2), 257–278.

Goeree, J. K., Maasland, E., Onderstal, S., & Turner V, J. L. (2005). How (not) to raise money. *Journal of Political Economy, 113*(4), 897–926.

Goldin C & Katz, L.F. (1999). The Shaping of higher education: The formative years in the United States, 1890–1940. *Journal of Economic Perspectives, American Economic Association, 13*(1), 37–62 [Winter].

Goldin, J., & Listokin, Y., (2012), Tax expenditure salience. In *7th annual conference on empirical legal studies paper*.

Gruber, J., & Hungerman, D.M., (2007). Faith-based charity and crowd-out during the great depression. *Journal of Public Economics, 91*(5), 1043–1069.

Harbaugh, W. T., Mayr, U., & Burghart, D. R. (2007). Neural responses to taxation and voluntary giving reveal motives for charitable donations. *Science, 316*(5831), 1622–1625.

Huck, S., & Rasul, I. (2010). Transactions costs in charitable giving: Evidence from two field experiments. *The BE Journal of Economic Analysis and Policy, 10*(1), Article 1.

Huck, S., & Rasul, I. (2011). Matched fundraising: Evidence from a natural field experiment. *Journal of Public Economics, 95*(5), 351–362.

Hungerman, D. M. (2005). Are church and state substitutes? Evidence from the 1996 welfare reform. *Journal of Public Economics, 89*(11), 2245–2267.

Hungerman, D. M. (2008). Race and charitable church activity. *Economic Inquiry, 46*, 380–400.

Hungerman, D. M. (2009). Crowd-out and diversity. *Journal of Public Economics, 93*(5), 729–740.

Jackson & Yariv (unpublished). Collective dynamic choice: The necessity of time inconsistency. unpublished.

Jack, A. I., Dawson, A. J., Begany, K. L., Leckie, R. L., Barry, K. P., Ciccia, A. H., & Snyder, A. Z. (2013). fMRI reveals reciprocal inhibition between social and physical cognitive domains. *Neurolmage, 66*, 385–401.

Jenni, K. E., & Loewenstein, G. (1997). Explaining the "identifiable victim effect." *Journal of Risk and Uncertainty, 14*(3), 235–257.

Karlan, D., & List, J. A. (2007). Does price matter in charitable giving? Evidence from a large-scale natural field experiment. *The American Economic Review, 97*(5), 1774–1793.

Karlan, D., List, J. A., & Shafir, E. (2011). Small matches and charitable giving: Evidence from a natural field experiment. *Journal of Public Economics, 95*(5–6), 344–350.

Khanna, J., Posnett, J., & Sandler, T. (1995). Charity donations in the UK: New evidence based on panel data. *Journal of Public Economics, 56*, 257–272.

Kingma, B. R. (1989). An accurate measurement of the crowd-out effect, income effect, and price effect for charitable contributions. *Journal of Political Economy, 97*, 1197–1207.

Konow, J. (2010). Mixed feelings: Theories of and evidence on giving. *Journal of Public Economics, 94*(3), 279–297.

Lazear, E., Malmendier, U., & Weber, R. (2012). Sorting in experiments with application to social preferences. *American Economic Journal: Applied Economics, 4*(1), 136–163.

Li, S. X., Eckel, C. C., Grossman, P. J., & Brown, T. L. (2011). Giving to government: Voluntary taxation in the lab. *Journal of Public Economics, 95*(9), 1190–1201.

List, J. A. (2007). On the interpretation of giving in dictator games. *Journal of Political Economy, 115*, 482–493.

List, J. A. (2011). The market for charitable giving. *The Journal of Economic Perspectives, 25*(2), 157–180.

List, J. A., & Lucking-Reiley, D. (2002). The effects of seed money and refunds on charitable giving: Experimental evidence from a university capital campaign. *Journal of Political Economy, 110*(1), 215–233.

Manzoor, S. H., & Straub, J. D. (2005). The robustness of Kingma's crowd-out evidence: Evidence from new data on contributions to public radio. *Public Choice, 123*, 463–476.

Marx, L. M., & Matthews, S. (2000). Dynamic voluntary contribution to a public project. *Review of Economic Studies, 67*(2), 327–358.

Masatlioglu, Y., Nakajima, D., & Ozbay, E. Y. (2012). Revealed attention. *The American Economic Review, 102*(5), 2183–2205.

McManus, B., & Bennet, R. (2011). The demand for products linked to public goods: Evidence from an online field experiment. *Journal of Public Economics, 95*(5), 403–415.

Meer, J. (2011). Brother, can you spare a dime? Peer pressure in charitable solicitation. *Journal of Public Economics, 95*(7), 926–941.

Meer, Jonathan (2013). The habit of giving, economic inquiry. http://dx.doi.org/10.1111/ecin.12010.

Meer, J., & Rosen, H. S. (2010). Family bonding with universities. *Research in Higher Education, 51*(7), 641–658.

Meer, J., & Rosen, H. S. (2011). The ABCs of charitable solicitation. *Journal of Public Economics, 95*(5), 363–371.

Mellström, C., & Johannesson, M. (2008). Crowding out in blood donation: Was Titmuss right? *Journal of the European Economic Association, 6*(4), 845–863.

Morgan, J. (2000). Financing public goods by means of lotteries. *Review of Economic Studies, 67*(4), 761–784.

Morgan, J., & Sefton, M. (2000). Funding public goods with lotteries: Experimental evidence. *The Review of Economic Studies, 67*(4), 785–810.

Okten, C., & Weisbrod, B. A. (2000). Determinants of donations in private nonprofit markets. *Journal of Public Economics, 75*, 255–272.

Palfrey, T. R., & Prisbrey, J. E. (1997). Anomalous behavior in public goods experiments: How much and why? *American Economic Review, 87*(5), 829-846.

Payne, A. A. (1998). Does the government crowd-out private donations? New evidence from a sample of non-profit firms. *Journal of Public Economics, 69*, 323–345.

Payne, A. A. (2001). Measuring the effect of federal research funding on private donations at research universities: is federal research funding more than a substitute for private donations? *International Tax and Public Finance, 8*, 731–751.

Poterba, J. (1997). The estate tax and after-tax investment returns. *No. w6337*. National Bureau of Economic Research. Cambridge, MA.

Potters, J., Sefton, M., & Vesterlund, L. (2007). Leading-by-example and signaling in voluntary contribution games: An experimental study. *Economic Theory, 33*(1), 169–182.

Ribar, D. C., & Wilhelm, M. O. (2002). Altruistic and joy-of-giving motivations in charitable behavior. *Journal of Political Economy, 110*, 425–457.

Rose-Ackerman, S. (1982). Charitable giving and excessive fund-raising. *Quarterly Journal of Economics, 97*, 193–212.

Rose-Ackerman, S. (1996). Altruism, nonprofits, and economic theory. *Journal of Economic Literature, 34*(2), 701–728.

Scharf, K., & Smith, S. (2010). The price elasticity of charitable giving: Does the form of tax relief matter? IFS Working Papers W10/07. Institute for Fiscal Studies.

Schelling, T. C. (1960). *The strategy of conflict*. Cambridge Massachusetts: Harvard University Press.

Schelling, T. C. (1968). The life you save may be your own. *Problems in Public Expenditure Analysis, 127*, 129–30.

Schiff, J. (1985). Does government spending crowd out charitable contributions? *National Tax Journal, 38*, 535–546.

Schiff, J., & Weisbrod, B. A. (1991). Competition between for-profit and nonprofit organizations in commercial markets. *Annals of Public and Cooperative Economics, 62*(4), 619–40.

Schram, A. J., & Onderstal, S. (2009). Bidding to give: An experimental comparison of auctions for charity. *International Economic Review, 50*(2), 431–457.

Shang, J., & Croson, R. (2009). A field experiment in charitable contribution: The impact of social information on the voluntary provision of public goods. *The Economic Journal, 119*(540), 1422–1439.

Small, D., & Loewenstein, G. (2003). Helping a victim or helping the victim: Altruism and identifiability. *Journal of Risk and Uncertainty, 26*(1), 5–16.

Small, D., Loewenstein, G., & Slovic, P. (2007). Sympathy and callousness: The impact of deliberative thought on donations to identifiable and statistical victims. *Organizational Behavior and Human Decision Process, 102*(2), 143–153.

Steinberg, R. (1987). Voluntary donations and public expenditures in a federal system. *American Economic Review, 77*(1), 24–36.

Thaler, R.H., & Benartzi, S. (2004). Save more tomorrow[TM]: Using behavioral economics to increase employee saving. *Journal of political Economy, 112*(S1), S164–S187.

Titmuss, R. (1970). *The gift relationship: From human blood to social policy*. London: Allen & Unwin.

Tonin, M., & Vlassopoulos, M. (2010). Disentangling the sources of pro-socially motivated effort: A field experiment. *Journal of Public Economics, 94*(11), 1086–1092.

Vesterlund, L. D. (2003). The informational value of sequential fund-raising. *Journal of Public Economics, 87*, 627–657.

Vesterlund, L. (2006). Why do people give? In R. Steinberg & W. W. Powell (Eds.), *The nonprofit sector* (2nd ed.). Yale Press.

Vigdor, J.L. (2002). Locations, outcomes, and selective migration. *Review of Economics and Statistics, 84*(4), 751–755.

Vigdor, J. L. (2004). Community composition and collective action: Analyzing initial mail response to the 2000 census. *Review of Economics and Statistics, 86*(1), 303–312.

Weisbrod, B.A. (1991). *The nonprofit economy*. Cambridge Massachusetts: Harvard University Press.

Wiepking, P., & Bekkers, R. (2010). Does who decides really matter? Causes and consequences of personal financial management in the case of larger and structural charitable donations. *Voluntas: International Journal of Voluntary and Nonprofit Organizations, 21*(2), 240–263.

Wiepking, P., & Bekkers, R. H. F. P. (2012). Who gives? A literature review of predictors of charitable giving. Part two: Gender, marital status, income, and wealth. *Voluntary Sector Review, 3*(2), 217–245.

Wilhelm, M. O., Brown, E., Rooney, P. M., & Steinberg, R. (2008). The intergenerational transmission of generosity. *Journal of Public Economics, 92*(10), 2146–2156.

Yörük, B. K. (2010). Charitable giving by married couples revisited. *Journal of Human Resources, 45*(2), 497–516.

CHAPTER 2

Taxation and Development

Timothy Besley[*] and Torsten Persson[†]

[*]LSE and CIFAR
[†]IIES, Stockholm University and CIFAR

Contents

> It is shortage of resources, and not inadequate incentives, which limits the pace of economic development. Indeed the importance of public revenue from the point of view of accelerated economic development could hardly be exaggerated.
>
> **Nicholas Kaldor, "Taxation for Economic Development," Journal of Modern African Studies, 1963, p. 7.**

1. INTRODUCTION

Perhaps more than any other economist in the post-war generation, Nicholas Kaldor appreciated the centrality of public finance to development. Following his lead, we believe that the power to tax lies at the heart of state development. A moment's reflection on the history of today's developed countries and the current situation of today's developing nations suggests that the acquisition of that power cannot be taken for granted. The central question in taxation and development is: "how does a government go from raising around 10% of GDP in taxes to raising around 40%?"

In the process of development, states not only increase the *levels* of taxation, but also undergo pronounced changes in *patterns* of taxation, with increasing emphasis on broader tax bases, i.e., with fewer exemptions. Some taxes—notably trade taxes—tend to diminish

Handbook of Public Economics, Volume 5
ISSN 1573-4420, http://dx.doi.org/10.1016/B978-0-444-53759-1.00002-9

51

in importance. Thus, in the developed world taxes on income and value added do the heavy lifting in raising sufficient revenue to support the productive and redistributive functions of the state.

The power to tax is taken for granted in most of mainstream public finance. Traditional research focuses on limits imposed by incentive constraints tied to asymmetric information, or sometimes political motives, rather than the administrative capabilities of the state. Thus, public finance and taxation remains a relatively unexplored field. However, this is now changing with a better understanding of the issues at a macro level and a range of efforts to collect micro data, some of it based on policy experiments. In part, this reflects a growing insight among policymakers that a better working tax system helps the state to support economic development.

Governments in all parts of the world and at all points in history have faced similar challenges when it comes to funding their ambitions. We do not believe that governments in the past or in today's developing world are any less rational or farsighted compared to those in today's developed world. But they may face incentives and constraints shaped by weakly institutionalized political environments. A key challenge for the study of taxation and development is to understand how these incentives and constraints work, and how—if at all—the situation might be improved for the citizens in today's developing nations.

Against this background, we take the view that governments in poor countries do their best in raising taxes, *given* the administrative structures in place and the political incentives they face. The real question then becomes why the supporting administrative structures remain so weak in many places. To answer it requires an analysis of endogenous *fiscal capacity* which is sometimes in the literature referred to simply as state capacity. Crudely, this concept captures how much tax a government could potentially raise given the structure of the tax system and its available powers of enforcement. But as a government need not always operate at or near the level of fiscal capacity, its capacity may not be directly observable.

We view the creation of fiscal capacity as a product of investments in state structures—including monitoring, administration and compliance through e.g., well-trained tax inspectors and an efficient revenue service. Our approach gets away from the false juxtaposition between positive and normative analyses of optimal taxes on the one hand, and studies of tax administration and political economy on the other.[1]

Economists who have studied taxation and development have tended to see the evolving economy as the driving force behind the government's approach to taxation. However, we will argue that this standard economic view needs to be augmented by an understanding of how political incentives shape the evolution of the tax system. This argument is in line with Schumpeter (1918), who saw the development of the tax system as intrinsically intertwined with the nature of the state and its history. Moreover, we will

[1] See Slemrod (1990) for a related perspective which puts compliance at center stage.

draw on the modern approach to development, which puts political motives (and the role of institutions) at the heart of understanding economic change.[2] Without invoking political motives as shaped by institutions, it is difficult to explain why some countries are rich and others are poor in the first place.[3]

The remainder of this chapter is organized as follows. In Section 2, we briefly discuss different perspectives on taxation and development, and outline our own perspective in more detail. Section 3 presents some background facts on levels and patterns of taxes in rich and poor countries and countries with strong and weak political institutions. Section 4 presents our analytical framework to study the equilibrium choices of taxation and investments in fiscal capacity. In Section 5, we use this framework to identify different determinants of taxation and fiscal capacity: economic development, political institutions, social structures, the value of public spending, non-tax revenues like aid and resource rents, and tax administration. Section 6 concludes.

2. PERSPECTIVES ON TAXATION AND DEVELOPMENT

There can be little doubt that the nature of the economy, and its structural characteristics, influence the ability to tax and the types of taxes that can be imposed. The standard economic approach to taxation and development focuses on how economic change influences the evolution of the tax system. In this approach, changes to the tax system reflect structural change. For example, a declining informal sector widens the tax net, the growth of larger firms creates a vehicle for compliance, and expansion of the financial sector encourages transparent accounting procedures which facilitate taxation. Such structural approaches have been emphasized in the influential commentaries of Tanzi (1987, 1992) and the review of the issues by Burgess and Stern (1993). Important recent contributions, focusing on specific economic channels, include Gordon and Li (2009), who emphasize the link between taxation and formal finance, and Kleven, Kreiner, and Saez (2009) who emphasize third-party reporting through firms.

Of course, the standard economic approach also studies the influence of the tax system on the economy. Well-designed tax systems can minimize the efficiency losses imposed by taxes and even raise the growth rate in endogenous-growth models, as in Barro and Sala-i-Martin (1992). Tax revenues can be spent on public goods and investments that make the economy more productive, as in Barro (1990). Tax design in a developing country context has to take into account the information about behavioral responses needed by governments, as in the papers collected in Gordon (2010) and Newbery and Stern (1987).

---

[2] See, for example, Engerman and Sokoloff (2002), Hall and Jones (1999), and Acemoglu, Johnson, and Robinson (2001).
[3] Of course, that is not to say that institutions are *all* that matter. Other long lived factors such as factor endowments, geography and culture, and the interplay between them, could also play an important role.

Figure 1 Standard approach.

The standard economic view has also dealt with the issues of administration and compliance—see Slemrod and Yitzhaki (2002) for an overview. These issues also take center stage in the influential writings of Richard Bird (see, e.g., Bird & Oldman, 1980).[4] Looking at the recent experience through the lens of effective administration, Bird (2004) observes that "the best tax policy in the world is worth little if it cannot be implemented effectively". The greater reliance on trade taxes (and seigniorage) than income taxes in poor economies, which we discuss further below, has been noted and discussed by many authors—see Burgess and Stern (1993), Hinrichs (1966), and Tanzi (1992), for early contributions.

But important as it is, economic development does not mechanically translate into increases in the tax take. Even in fast-growing economies, such as India and China, decisions by the state are needed to yield a dividend in the form of a higher tax share in GDP. For example, Piketty and Qian (2009) argue that increases in exemptions have meant that income tax revenues in India have stagnated at around 0.5% of GDP since 1986. Widening the scope of taxation to broad bases as income and value added is only feasible if accompanied by investments in compliance structures.

In summary, the standard economic approach views low levels of revenue and disproportionate reliance on narrow tax bases as important constraints on the tax take. This standard economic view is summarized schematically in Figure 1.

Whether or not administration, and compliance is given a central role, most of the work in the standard economic approach has little room for endogenous government behavior. By contrast, historical accounts of how tax systems have evolved, such as Brewer (1989) and Dincecco (2011), put a great deal of emphasis on government behavior and motives for raising taxes.[5] These accounts suggest that it is essential for the study of taxation and development to focus on conscious efforts to build fiscal capacity.

A first feature of our approach in this chapter is to augment the standard approach by giving not only economic factors but political factors as well key roles in the analysis of taxation and development.[6] This is in tune with the thrust of modern research on development, which sees political motives as central to understanding how development proceeds and to explain why some countries languish while others prosper. In keeping with this approach, we highlight the structure of political *institutions* and the degree of political *instability* as key drivers of investments in fiscal capacity. Changes in the power to

---

[4] See also Aizenman and Jinjarak (2008) on VAT and Zolt and Bird (2005) on the personal income tax.

[5] See also Bräutigam, Fjeldstad, and Moore (2008) for a perspective where politics is important.

[6] See Persson and Tabellini (2002, chap. 24, 2003) for previous overviews of relevant theoretical and empirical issues in the political economics of public finance and government spending.

tax may also reflect *circumstances*—e.g., threats of foreign conflicts—that forge common political interests in building a strong state.

A second feature of our approach is to point to a further endogenous feedback loop *from* taxation *to* development which has not featured in most discussions to date. When the government has a larger stake in the economy through a developed tax system, it has stronger motives to play a productive role in the economy, as a complement to its extractive role. Obvious examples include building high-return infrastructure projects and developing the legal system to reduce the extent of informality in the economy. Such *complementarity* can create a virtuous circle between taxation and development that goes beyond the standard technocratic view of government.

Both of these features are incorporated in the analysis of this chapter, as illustrated schematically in Figure 2.

The approach that we adopt sees tax compliance as something more than a technical issue. Observed compliance also reflects the underlying incentives of policymakers to improve the tax system and ensure that taxes are paid. This contrasts with the purely economic approach in thinking about better compliance structures and broader tax bases as a result of purposive, forward-looking activity by politically motivated incumbents. In this sense, our approach is related to earlier theoretical and empirical work by Cukierman, Edwards, and Tabellini (1992) on how the use of seigniorage depends on the efficiency of the tax system, and how the strategic choice of the latter depends on factors like political stability and polarization.

A focus on political economics also rhymes well with the extensive work by political and economic historians on how a state's fiscal capacity evolves. Scholars of history have emphasized the key role of government motives to build fiscal capacity, and especially the centrality of warfare in stimulating demands for fiscal capacity. This research has yielded many interesting case studies, such as Bonney (1999), Brewer (1989), and O'Brien (2001, 2005). But there are also attempts at broader generalizations, as in the work by Hoffman and Rosenthal (1997), Levi (1988), Schumpeter (1918), and Tilly (1985). Tilly, in particular, aims at explaining European exceptionalism, although his work appears greatly inspired by the encyclopedic scholarship of German historian Hintze (1906). Much debate still remains about whether the fiscal state necessarily follows a pattern of

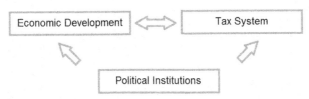

Figure 2 Our approach.

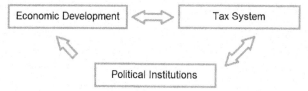

Figure 3 Extended approach.

war, with Centeno (1997) arguing that Latin America may be an exception to the Tilly hypothesis of war as a major motive for building fiscal capacity.

The fact that many states remain unable to levy broad-based taxes is often seen as key to the persistence of weak states in many poor countries, by development scholars like Migdal (1988). Others, such as Herbst (2000), have ventured the hypothesis that some countries in Africa might have been able to strengthen their weak states if external wars had been more frequent on the continent. By picking up similar themes, our approach thus parallels the approach taken by scholars in other branches of social sciences as well as the humanities.

Political scientists and sociologists sometimes push the role of taxation in development even further, by arguing that taxation can be a catalyst for political and economic change. This view is illustrated in Figure 3, where political institutions respond to an expanding tax domain. The old American adage of "no taxation without representation" is a vivid instance of such thinking, whereby demands for transparency and representation are built as part of the need to build a strong fiscal state in a "fiscal contract" between the citizens and the state.

In the remainder of the chapter, we first present some useful background facts on taxation and development. We then develop our approach, beginning with an exclusive focus on economic factors, as in Figure 1. Next, we consider how political incentives affect the arguments and give a well-defined role for political institutions in determining how tax systems develop, as in Figure 2. Endogenous political institutions as in Figure 3, however, lie beyond the scope of this chapter, although we briefly return to this possibility in the concluding remarks.

3. BACKGROUND FACTS

The growth of the state and its capacity to extract significant revenues from citizens is a striking economic feature of the last two centuries. For example, Madisson (2001) documents that, on average, France, Germany, the Netherlands, and the UK raised around 12% of GDP in tax revenue around 1910 and around 46% by the turn of the Millennium. The corresponding US figures are 8% and 30%. Underpinning these hikes in revenue are a number of tax innovations, including the extension of the income tax to a wide population. For example, large-scale compliance with the income tax required states

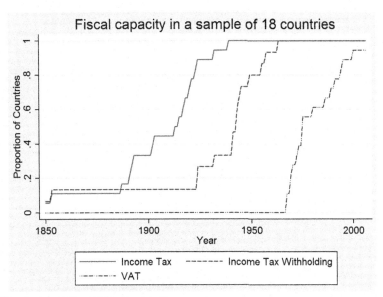

Figure 4 Historical evolution of fiscal capacity.

to build a tax administration and implement withholding at source. Such investments in fiscal capacity have enabled the kind of mass taxation now considered normal throughout the developed world.[7]

Figure 4 gives a partial picture of how fiscal capacity has evolved *over time* based on a sample of 18 countries using data from Mitchell (2007a,b,c). We will use this sample for time-series comparisons throughout this section.[8] The figure plots the distribution of three kinds of changes in tax systems since 1850 which can be thought of as fiscal-capacity investments. The solid line shows the proportion of countries that have introduced an income tax, the dashed line shows the proportion that have implemented income-tax withholding, and the line with a mixture of dots and dashes shows the proportion that have adopted a VAT. Although a useful illustration for a limited sample of countries, the reader should bear in mind that looking at dates for these significant discrete changes almost certainly understates the extent of change since, over time, the reach of the income tax, withholding, and VAT have all increased. The graph shows that income taxes began appearing in the mid-nineteenth century, direct withholding follows somewhat later with

---

[7] See Keen (2010), Kenny and Winer (2006), and Tanzi (1987, 1992) for general discussions of features of tax systems and their evolution.

[8] The countries in the sample are Argentina, Australia, Brazil, Canada, Chile, Colombia, Denmark, Finland, Ireland, Japan, Mexico, the Netherlands, New Zealand, Norway, Sweden, Switzerland, the United Kingdom, and the United States. The sample is selected, as we are reasonably confident that the data are comparable across countries and time in Mitchell (2007a,b,c).

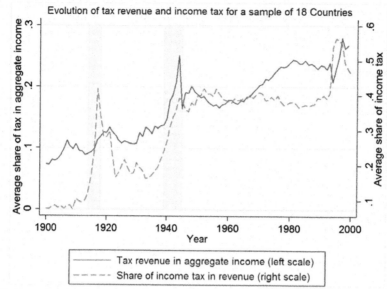

Figure 5 Taxes and share of income tax over time.

both being found in the full sample by around 1950.[9] VAT adoption lagged behind the income tax and with only the USA not having adopted a VAT in our sample of 18 countries by the end of the year 2000.

The model developed in Section 3 below will be used to explain the forces that shape such changes in the tax system. The changes illustrated in Figure 4 are all associated with investments in administrative structures that support tax collection.[10] Figure 5 looks in more detail at the historical picture *over time* during the last 100 years for the 18 countries in our sample. The figure illustrates how the average tax take has increased over time from around 10% in national income to around 25% in the sample as a whole. Equally striking is the increasing reliance on income taxation which only made up about 5% of revenues in 1900 but about 50% by the end of the last century. These hikes in the income tax share during the two world wars, and the ratchet effect associated with them, also stand out in Figure 5.

However, the narrow sample in Figures 4 and 5 ignores many of the poorer countries in the world. We would also like to use the model in this chapter to understand how fiscal capacity varies *over countries*. A first salient feature of the data is that richer countries tend to raise more tax revenue as a share of national income than poorer countries. This is illustrated in Figure 6. The left panel plots the overall tax take as a share of GDP from

---

[9] We have been unable to verify the dates in which income tax withholding was introduced in Finland, New Zealand, and Norway so this line represents the proportion of the 15 countries for which we have data. This explains why the dashed line lies above the solid line in the very early years of the data.

[10] Aidt and Jensen (2009a,b) study the factors, such as spending pressures and extensions of the franchise, behind the introduction of the income tax in panel data for 17 countries from 1815 to 1939.

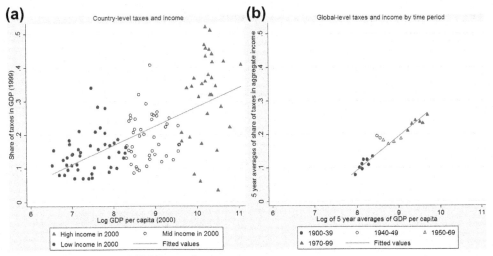

Figure 6 Tax revenue and GDP per capita.

Baunsgaard and Keen (2005) against the log of GDP per capita from the Penn World Tables, both measured around the year 2000, and distinguishes observations by income. The right panel looks at the same relationship instead using the time-series data on our sample of 18 countries from Mitchell (2007a,b,c) to plot 5-year averages of the tax share over the 20th century against national income from Maddison's data, and distinguishing observations by time period. The cross-section and time-series patterns are strikingly similar. Higher-income countries today raise much higher taxes than poorer countries, indicating that they have made larger investments in fiscal capacity. Moreover, the tax share in GDP of today's developing countries does not look very different from the tax take 100 years ago in the now developed countries.

To probe further into tax differences across countries, it is interesting to look at the relative uses of different types of taxes, differentiated by the investments that they require to be collected. Arguably, trade taxes and income taxes are the two polar cases. To collect trade taxes just requires being able to observe trade flows at major shipping ports. Although trade taxes may encourage smuggling, this is a much easier proposition than collecting income taxes, which requires major investments in enforcement and compliance structures throughout the entire economy. We can thus obtain an interesting indication of fiscal-capacity investments by holding constant total tax revenue, and ask how large a share of it is collected from trade taxes and income taxes, respectively.

These shares are plotted against each other in Figure 7.[11] Again, we report the cross-sectional pattern for the year 2000, based on contemporaneous data from Baunsgaard and Keen (2005), as well as the time-series pattern over the last 100 years based on historical

---

[11] Other taxes not included in either trade or income taxes include indirect taxes such as VAT, property and corporate taxes.

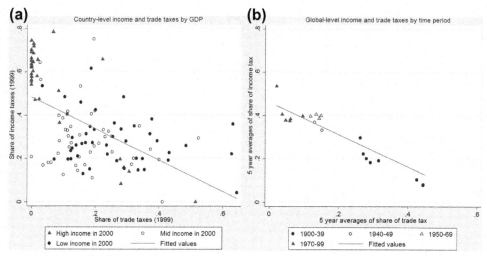

Figure 7 Income taxes and trade taxes.

data from Mitchell (2007a,b,c). The income-tax share is displayed on the vertical axis, and the trade-tax share on the horizontal axis. We observe a clear negative correlation: countries that rely more on income rely less on trade taxes. The left panel also shows a striking pattern by income: high-income countries depend more on income taxes, while middle-income and, especially, low-income countries depend more on trade taxes. The right panel of Figure 7 shows that the move from trade to income taxes is also reflected in the historical development of tax systems, as all countries have become richer. Again, the cross-sectional and time-series patterns look conspicuously alike with a similar slope of the regression lines.

Figure 8 homes in on the income tax, plotting the relationship between the share of income taxes in total taxes and income per capita, in the current cross-section as well as the historical time series. The left panel separates the observations into three groups by tax take: countries that raise more than 25% of taxes in GDP, countries that raise 15–25% of taxes in GDP, and countries that raise less than 15%. The countries in the high-tax group again look markedly different, raising much more of their tax revenues in the form of income taxes. The right panel again differentiates observations by time period. The historical trend in this sample of older nations and the pattern in the world today is again very similar.

Another indicator of fiscal capacity is the relation between statutory tax rates and actual tax take. Figure 9 plots the top statutory income-tax rates in 1990s for the 67-country sample in Gordon and Lee (2005) against the share of income taxes in GDP from Baunsgaard and Keen (2005). The figure shows that the distribution of the top statutory rate is about the same among high-income and low-income countries. Obviously, the figure does not take aspects such as coverage and progressivity into account.

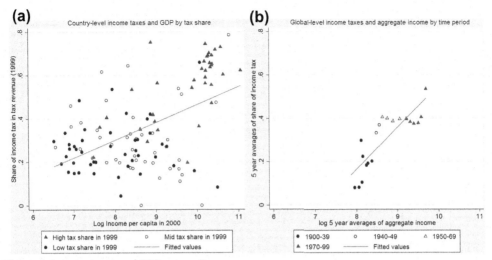

Figure 8 Income taxes and GDP per capita.

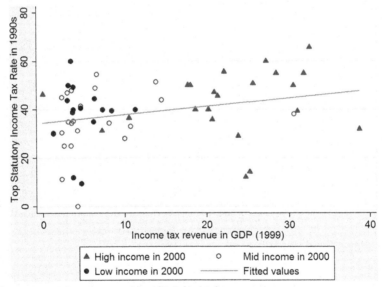

Figure 9 Top statutory income tax rate and total tax take.

With this qualification, the fact that high-income countries raise much more income-tax revenue than low-income countries suggests that a narrow tax base driven by compliance difficulties is a much bigger issue among low-income countries. This reinforces the earlier observation that fiscal capacity is considerably less developed in poor countries.

Finally, we turn to some facts relating tax structure and politics. As our core measure of political institutions, we use an indicator of executive constraints from the well-known

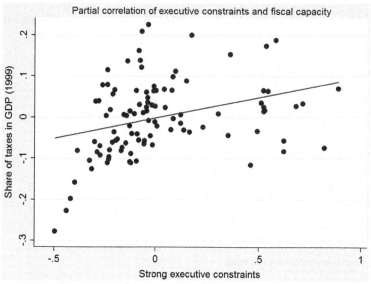

Figure 10 Tax revenue and executive constraints.

Polity IV database (see Marshal and Jaggers, 2010). We use the highest coding of such constraints (the variable x-const is equal to 7 on a 1–7 scale) to measure the proportion of years since independence (or since 1800 if independence is earlier) that a country had strong constraints on the executive. To highlight that this political dimension captures something different than country heterogeneity in income, we control for current income before plotting the *partial* correlation of high executive constraints and two of our fiscal-capacity measures: total tax share in GDP (Figure 10) and the income tax share in total income (Figure 11). In both cases, we see a clear positive correlation between this measure of political institutions and fiscal capacity, taking the level of economic development into consideration—in Figure 10 the correlation hinges mainly on the countries with very low executive constraints (relative to income). The facts illustrated in these figures illustrate the need to adopt an approach where political factors help shape the level and evolution of fiscal capacity.

Taken together, the cross-sectional and time-series data suggest the following seven facts:

Fact 1: *Rich countries have made successive investments in their fiscal capacities over time.*

Fact 2: *Rich countries collect a much larger share of their income in taxes than do poor countries.*

Fact 3: *Rich countries rely to a much larger extent on income taxes as opposed to trade taxes than do poor countries.*

Fact 4: *High-tax countries rely to a much larger extent on income taxes as opposed to trade taxes than do low-tax countries.*

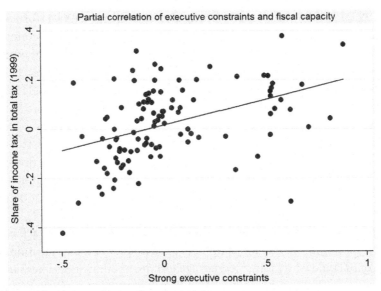

Partial correlation of executive constraints and fiscal capacity

Figure 11 Income tax share and executive constraints.

Fact 5: *Rich countries collect much higher tax revenue than poor countries despite comparable statutory rates.*

Fact 6: *Countries with strong executive constraints collect higher tax revenues, when income per capita is held constant, than do countries with weak executive constraints.*

Fact 7: *Countries with strong executive constraints rely on a higher share of income taxes in total taxes, when income per capita is held constant, than do countries with weak executive constraints.*

Together, these seven facts suggest strongly that rich, high-tax, and executive-constrained states have made considerably larger investments in fiscal capacity than have poorer, low-tax, and non-executive-constrained states.

Given these clear patterns in the data, it is indeed surprising that economists have not devoted much attention to dynamic models of economic and political determinants of fiscal capacity. As discussed in Section 2, most normative and positive theories of taxation hardly ever touch upon lacking administrative infrastructure as an important constraint on the taxes that governments can raise.

4. FRAMEWORK

The framework that we develop in this section is a generalization of the models studied by Besley and Persson (2009a,b, 2011a,b,c). Our specific approach in this chapter also builds on the recent literature on how taxable income responds to taxes, allowing for a wider range of responses than the traditional view based on labor-supply elasticities—see

Feldstein (1995, 1999) for the original contributions and Slemrod (2001) for a formulation close to the one we adopt.[12] This makes particular sense in a developing country context, where non-compliance and decisions to earn or spend in the informal (untaxed) sector are such important issues. We build a framework to help us understand the forces behind the decisions to build a more effective tax system, where such decisions are made by a forward-looking government. In keeping with the stylized facts, we model larger fiscal capacity as increasing the yield on statutory taxes by reducing the extent of non-compliance.

The core focus is on the taxation of labor income and of goods and services which fall directly on households. This neglects the important issue of taxation of firms. Nor does the framework deal explicitly with taxation of capital income. We also limit attention to a centralized tax system, ignoring the complications created by local taxation and federal structures.

Basic Set-Up: Consider a population with $\mathcal{J}$ distinct groups, denoted by $J = 1, \ldots, \mathcal{J}$, where group J is homogeneous and comprises a fraction ξ^J of the population. In principle, these groups could be regions, income/age groups, or ethnicities. There are two time periods: $s = 1, 2$. The economy has $N + 1$ consumption goods, indexed by $n \in \{0, 1, \ldots, N\}$. Consumption of these goods by group J in period s is denoted by $x_{n,s}^J$. There is also a traditional (non-rival and non-excludable) public good g_s. Individuals in group J supply labor, L_s^J, and choose how to allocate their income across consumption goods. This is a small open economy with given pre-tax prices of $p_{n,s}$. Wage rates ω_s^J are potentially group-specific and may vary over time.

Taxation and tax compliance: The government may levy taxes on labor income and all goods except the untaxed numeraire, good 0. The post-tax price of each good is:

$$p_{n,s}(1 + t_{n,s}), \quad n = 1, 2, \ldots, N,$$

while the net wage is:

$$\omega_s^J(1 - t_{L,s}),$$

where $\{t_{1,s}, \ldots, t_{N,s}, t_{L,s}\}$ is the vector of tax rates.

As in the standard model, statutory tax policy is a vector of tax rates for commodities and labor supply. However, to allow for non-compliance, we suppose that tax payments can be reduced by actions by those who are obliged to remit taxes to authorities. If the costs of non-compliance were large enough, then this would not happen and we would be back in the standard model. But we suppose this may not be the case and allow the cost of non-compliance to depend on investments in fiscal capacity.

To capture these ideas simply, we assume that tax payments to the government from group J in period s, associated with the commodity tax imposed on good n, are:

$$t_{n,s}\left[p_{n,s}x_{n,s}^J - e_{n,s}\right],$$

[12] See Piketty, Saez, and Stantcheva (2011) and Saez, Slemrod, and Giertz (2009) for reviews of the research on taxable income elasticities.

which we assume to be non-negative. Thus, $e_{n,s}$ (denominated in the units of the numeraire good) is the amount of the statutory tax which is not paid—think about $e_{n,s}$ as purchases from the informal sector. The cost function for such non-compliance is the same for all groups J, namely $c(e_{n,s}, \tau_{n,s})$ with c increasing and convex in $e_{n,s}$. The parallel expression for labor taxes is

$$t_{L,s}\left[\omega_s^J L_s - e_{L,s}\right]$$

with cost $c(e_{L,s}, \tau_{L,s})$. Analogously, one can interpret $e_{L,s}$ as the amount of work undertaken in the informal sector.

The vector $\boldsymbol{\tau}_s = \{\tau_{1,s}, \ldots, \tau_{N,s}, \tau_{L,s}\}$ represents investments in fiscal capacity which affect non-compliance costs. For each tax base, $k = 1, \ldots, N, L$, we assume:

$$\frac{\partial c(e_{k,s}, \tau_{k,s})}{\partial \tau_{k,s}} > 0 \quad \text{and} \quad \frac{\partial^2 c(e_{k,s}, \tau_{k,s})}{\partial e_{k,s} \partial \tau_{k,s}} \geq 0,$$

such that greater fiscal capacity makes avoiding taxes more difficult.[13] Moreover, we postulate that $c(e_{k,s}, 0) = 0$, i.e., for a tax base where the government has made no investments in fiscal capacity, the cost of evading taxes is negligible. If citizens evade taxes fully when it is costless to do so, no tax revenue is raised from that base.

For simplicity, we have assumed that fiscal capacity has a common effect on all individuals' abilities to avoid paying statutory taxes. As a consequence, every consumer in the model adjusts their non-compliance on the intensive margin. An alternative way of modeling non-compliance would be to introduce heterogeneity in the cost or in the stigma of being caught not complying. This alternative formulation would introduce an extensive margin in tax evasion—i.e., whether to use the informal sector or not—but would lead to generally similar results. Of course, the most general approach would consider both margins and allow for heterogeneous effects according to economic circumstance, e.g., greater difficulties in measuring the value of labor earnings by owner-cultivators, the values of own production, or the value of bartered exchange in some sectors of the economy.[14]

Costs of fiscal-capacity investments: There is a *given* period-1 level of fiscal capacity relevant to sector k denoted by $\tau_{k,1}$ and a level for period 2 denoted by $\tau_{k,2}$ which is endogenously determined by costly investments. The investment costs across the $N+1$ tax bases $k = 1, \ldots, N, L$ are:

$$\mathcal{F}^k(\tau_{k,2} - \tau_{k,1}) + f^k(\tau_{k,2}, \tau_{k,1}) \quad \text{for} \quad k = 1, \ldots, N, L.$$

---

[13] See Kopczuk and Slemrod (2002) for a related model, where governments can affect the elasticity of taxable income through decisions about the extent of compliance.

[14] We are modeling all costs of non-compliance as resource costs. If they represent fines paid to the government, they are purely a transfer cost. This difference matters when considering optimal taxation and determining which elasticities should be considered.

We assume that the first part of the investment-cost function $\mathcal{F}^k(\cdot)$ is convex with $\frac{\partial \mathcal{F}^k(0)}{\partial \tau_{k,2}} = 0$, i.e., the marginal cost at zero is negligible. There may or may not be a fixed-cost component, depending on whether the period-1 government inherits a fiscal capacity of zero for tax base k

$$f^k(\tau_{k,2}, \tau_{k,1}) = \begin{cases} f^k \geq 0 & \text{if} \quad \tau_{k,1} = 0 \ \& \ \tau_{k,2} > 0, \\ 0 & \text{if} \quad \tau_{k,1} > 0. \end{cases}$$

Let

$$\mathcal{F}(\boldsymbol{\tau}_2, \boldsymbol{\tau}_1) = \sum_{k=1}^{L} \mathcal{F}^k(\tau_{k,2} - \tau_{k,1}) + f^k(\tau_{k,2}, \tau_{k,1})$$

be the total costs of investing in fiscal capacity. The separability of the cost function across tax bases is made for analytical convenience. Another feature of the technology is that it does not depend on the wage rate, even though it could be that investing in fiscal capacity costs more in a more productive economy.

In practical terms, the costs of fiscal-capacity investment are more obvious for some tax bases than others. For example, levying an effective income tax requires a collection system with trained inspectors, some kind of record keeping, and the ability to cross check. We would thus expect a relatively large fixed-cost component, i.e., $f^k > 0$ for $k = L$. Equally, a VAT system requires an ability to monitor and verify the use of inputs and the value of sales for *all* goods simultaneously (but the VAT does not directly fit the framework above). Levying border taxes usually takes place by monitoring ports and airports to measure trade flows. For such taxes, we would expect the fixed-cost component to be small or absent. Moreover, inspecting trade flows is easier for volumes than values, which might explain why so many border taxes are specific rather than ad valorem.

However, in all these cases, public resources need to be devoted to monitoring and compliance. Below, we will discuss in greater detail different options for introducing new technologies to improve compliance.

Household decisions: Preferences are quasi-linear and given by:

$$x_{0,s}^J + u(x_{1,s}^J, \ldots, x_{N,s}^J) - \phi\left(L_s^J\right) + \alpha_s^J H(g_s),$$

where u is a concave utility function and ϕ is the convex disutility of labor. The utility of public goods is partly described by concave function H. We use α_s^J to parametrize the value of public goods, which we allow to be group and time specific. The individual budget constraint is:

$$x_{0,s}^J + \sum_{n=1}^{N} p_{n,s}\left(1 + t_{n,s}\right) x_{n,s}^J \leq \omega_s^J\left(1 - t_{L,s}\right) L_s^J + r_s^J + \sum_{k=1}^{L}\left[t_{k,s} e_{k,s} - c\left(e_{k,s}, \tau_{k,s}\right)\right].$$

In this expression, r_s^J is a group-specific cash transfer.[15] The only non-standard feature is the last term, namely the total "profit" from reducing tax payments. What makes this formulation of the household problem simple is the fact that tax incidence and behavior are still governed by the statutory tax rates as long as $e_{k,s} < p_{k,s} x_{k,s}^J$.

Maximizing the consumers' utility yields a vector of commodity demands and labor supply which is quite conventional. Commodity demands are the same for all groups $x_{n,s}^J = x_{n,s}$. This is because preferences for private goods are the same and there are no income effects on taxed commodities.

For the tax bases where the government has some fiscal capacity, $\tau_{k,s} > 0$, the decisions to reduce the tax burden, which we assume have an interior solution,[16] are also equal across groups, and implicitly defined by

$$t_{k,s} = c_e\left(e_{k,s}^*, \tau_{k,s}\right) \quad \text{for } k = 1, \ldots, N, L \quad \text{if } \tau_{k,s} > 0. \tag{1}$$

It is straightforward to see that the convexity of the cost function makes equilibrium evasion $e_{k,s}^*(t_{k,s}, \tau_{k,s})$ decreasing in the fiscal capacity investment, tax base by tax base. The household profits from such activities are:

$$q(t_{k,s}, \tau_{k,s}) = t_{k,s} e_{k,s} - c(e_{k,s}, \tau_{k,s}),$$

which are increasing in $t_{k,s}$ and decreasing in $\tau_{k,s}$.[17]

When there is no fiscal capacity, $\tau_{k,s} = 0$, any positive tax rate $t_{k,s}$ would give us a corner solution with $e_{k,s}^* = p_{k,s} x_{k,s}$ or $e_{L,s}^* = \omega_s^J L_s^J$. This is a case where all consumption could be sheltered from taxation in the informal sector where the individual has no tax liability. Thus, no tax income is raised at whatever level the statutory rate is set. We assume that in such cases the government sets the statutory tax rate at zero.

Indirect utility: Let

$$Q(\mathbf{t}_s, \boldsymbol{\tau}_s) = \sum_{k=1}^{L} q(t_{k,s}, \tau_{k,s})$$

---

[15] We allow this to be targetable across groups. But clearly there are limits on this in many systems due to administrative costs. Although we do not consider it, the model/approach could also be used to consider investments which make it easier to target transfers to specific groups.

[16] One special case of the model is where

$$c(e, \tau) = ec(\tau).$$

In this case $t \leq c(\tau)$ otherwise evasion is complete and we essentially go back to the formulation of fiscal capacity in Besley and Persson (2009a,b) who model it as an upper bound on the feasible tax rate.

[17] While we have formulated the model in terms of household decisions not to comply with taxes, it should now be clear that we could have formulated this as a series of firm-level decisions, where consumers pay their taxes faithfully and firms decide whether to remit taxes to tax authorities. Profits of non-compliance would still appear as individual income for owners of firms. Our key assumption is that these non-compliance profits are distributed equally across the population with each individual getting his own per capita share. But it would be straightforward to generalize the model to allow for any sharing rule for these profits.

be the aggregate (equilibrium) per-capita profit from efforts devoted to tax-reducing activities where $\mathbf{t}_s = \{t_{1,s}, \ldots, t_{N,s}, t_{L,s}\}$ is the vector of tax rates.

The indirect utility function for group J becomes:

$$V^J\left(\mathbf{t}_s, \boldsymbol{\tau}_s, g_s, \omega_s^J, r_s^J\right) = v(p_{1,s}(1 + t_{1,s}), \ldots, p_{N,s}(1 + t_{N,s})) + v^L\left(\omega_s^J(1 - t_{L,s})\right)$$
$$+ Q(\mathbf{t}_s, \boldsymbol{\tau}_s) + \alpha_s^J H(g_s) + r_s^J. \tag{2}$$

The first term on the right-hand side is the private surplus from the consumption of goods $n = 1, \ldots, N$. The separable, quasi-linear preferences make the private surplus additively separable in goods and labor—hence the second term. A convenient, but special, feature of the setup is that the gains from tax reduction are not group specific—hence the third term is not indexed by group. These features help make the analysis much simpler but do not compromise the economic insights. They could all be relaxed, albeit with increased complexity.

The policy problem: Governments choose tax rates on all goods and labor and a spending policy, dividing the tax proceeds between public goods, transfers, and investments in fiscal capacity. Let

$$B\left(\mathbf{t}_s, \boldsymbol{\tau}_s\right) = \sum_{n=1}^{N} t_{n,s}(p_{n,s}x_{n,s} - e_{n,s}) + \sum_{J=1}^{\mathcal{J}} \xi^J t_{L,s}\left(\omega_s^J L_s^J - e_{L,s}\right)$$

be the tax revenue from goods and labor, where the expression in the first sum relies on the fact that all groups choose the same consumption vector for non-numeraire goods. This is not true for labor supply, however, if different groups have different wage rates. The government budget constraint becomes

$$B(\mathbf{t}_s, \boldsymbol{\tau}_s) + R_s \geq g_s + \sum_{J=1}^{\mathcal{J}} \xi^J r_s^J + m_s, \tag{3}$$

where

$$m_s = \begin{cases} \mathcal{F}(\boldsymbol{\tau}_2, \boldsymbol{\tau}_1) & \text{if } s = 1 \\ 0 & \text{if } s = 2 \end{cases}$$

is the amount invested in fiscal capacity (relevant only in period 1) and R_s is any (net) revenue from borrowing, aid, or natural resources.

We now go on to consider, first, how a government will set taxes and spending and, then, how it will choose to invest in fiscal capacity. Thus, we begin by studying the static (within-period) problem taking fiscal capacity as given.

The social objective of the government has fixed weights μ^J, one for each group, which are normalized so that $\sum_{J=1}^{\mathcal{J}} \mu^J \xi^J = 1$. Then the government maximizes:

$$\sum_{J=1}^{\mathcal{J}} \mu^J \xi^J V^J\left(\mathbf{t}_s, \boldsymbol{\tau}_s, g_s, \omega_s^J, r_s^J\right)$$

subject to (3). This is a more or less standard optimal-tax *cum* public-goods problem, along the lines first studied in Diamond and Mirrlees (1971). It is special only in that we have assumed quasi-linear utility and added the possibility of tax evasion.

Optimal taxation: Taxes will follow a standard Ramsey-tax rule, except for the fact that taxes affect non-compliance decisions, as well as consumption and labor supply decisions. To state the tax rules, define the effective tax bases:

$$Z_{n,s}(\mathbf{t}_s, \boldsymbol{\tau}_s) = p_{n,s}x_{n,s} - e_{n,s} \quad \text{and} \quad Z_{L,s}(t_{L,s}, \tau_{L,s}) = \sum_{J=1}^{\mathcal{J}} \xi^J \omega_s^J L_s^J - e_{L,s}, \qquad (4)$$

where $x_{n,s}$ and L_s^J are per-capita commodity demands and (group-specific) labor supplies. The additive separability of the utility function makes the effective income tax base a function of the income tax alone. With this notation, the Ramsey-tax rule for commodities is

$$(\lambda_s - 1)Z_{n,s}(\mathbf{t}_s, \boldsymbol{\tau}_s) + \lambda_s \sum_{n=1}^{N} t_{n,s}\frac{\partial Z_{n,s}(\mathbf{t}_s, \boldsymbol{\tau}_s)}{\partial t_{n,s}} = 0 \quad \text{for } n = 1, \ldots, N \quad \text{if } \tau_{n,s} > 0,$$

$$t_{n,s} = 0 \quad \text{if } \tau_{n,s} = 0,$$

where λ_s is the value of public funds. Given the possibility of reducing the tax burden, it is the demands net of avoidance $p_{n,s}x_{n,s} - e_{n,s}$ and the behavioral response of these taxable net demands that shape the tax rates.

For those goods where there is no fiscal capacity, the government (by assumption) sets taxes at zero. Moreover, we focus on the natural case where $e_{k,s}^* < p_{k,s}x_{k,s}$ whenever $\tau_{k,s} > 0$. This says that, if the government has any fiscal capacity in some tax base, there is a non-trivial level of non-compliance. In this case, we also expect that the optimal-tax rate will be positive for any tax base where $\tau_{k,s} > 0$.

The optimal income tax solves:

$$-\tilde{Z}_{L,s} + \lambda_s \left[Z_{L,s}(t_{L,s}, \tau_{L,s}) + t_{L,s}\frac{\partial Z_{L,s}(t_{L,s}, \tau_{L,s})}{\partial t_{L,s}} \right] = 0 \quad \text{if } \tau_{L,s} > 0,$$

$$t_{L,s} = 0 \quad \text{if } \tau_{L,s} = 0,$$

where $\tilde{Z}_{L,s} = \sum_{J=1}^{\mathcal{J}} \mu^J \xi^J \omega_s^J L_s^J - e_{L,s}$ is weighted net taxable labor income allowing for heterogeneous wages. The optimal-tax expression is similar to the optimal commodity tax in that it involves the total behavioral response of the tax base $Z_{L,s}$. However, the income transferred from citizens to government (the first term) is weighted by the social objective. In general, this term depends on the correlation between the group weights μ^J and wages ω_s^J across groups.

To illustrate how the lack of fiscal capacity to enforce income taxes affects choices, let us assume that wages are the same for all groups, $\omega_s^J = \omega_s$. In this case, the optimal income tax rate solves:

$$\frac{t_{L,s}^*}{1 - t_{L,s}^*} = \frac{(\lambda_s - 1) - \lambda_s(\kappa - 1)\varepsilon}{\lambda_s \kappa \eta}, \tag{5}$$

where

$$\eta = \frac{\partial(\omega_s L_s)}{\partial(1 - t_{L,s})} \cdot \frac{1 - t_{L,s}}{\omega_s L_s}$$

is the elasticity of labor supply with respect to the (net of tax) after-tax wage,

$$\varepsilon = \frac{\partial e_{L,s}}{\partial t_{L,s}} \cdot \frac{t_{L,s}}{e_{L,s}}$$

is the elasticity of evasion with respect to the income tax rate and

$$\kappa = \frac{\omega_s L_s}{(\omega_s L_s - e_{L,s})} > 1$$

reflects the extent of non-compliance. The standard optimal income tax formula has $\kappa = 1$ so only the labor-supply elasticity η and the value of public funds λ_s, to be spent on public goods or transfers, determine the optimal tax. In that case, λ_s above 1 is sufficient for the optimal-tax rate to be positive.

With non-compliance, however, the optimal-tax rate is lower all else equal. To see this, observe that, using Eq. (5),

$$\frac{\partial t_{L,s}^*}{\partial \varepsilon} < 0 \quad \text{and} \quad \frac{\partial t_{L,s}^*}{\partial \kappa} < 0.$$

So any factor which makes it easier to avoid paying taxes or increases the extent of avoidance depresses the incentive to use the income tax. Thus, we would expect lower rates of taxation, as well as lower collection of taxes for a given rate, in jurisdictions, and times with little investment in fiscal capacity for tax collection (insofar as fiscal capacity decreases ε and κ).

The optimal-tax formulas above reflect that, when citizens can reduce their tax liability, taxes raise less revenue than otherwise. The total behavioral response to taxation can, in principle, be larger or smaller than in the absence of tax avoidance, depending on the sensitivity of such activity to a higher tax rate. And these responses will be influenced by investments in fiscal capacity.

There is a direct link here to the literature on taxable income elasticities and which elasticity is the right sufficient statistic for welfare-relevant behavioral responses—see Chetty (2009). Define

$$\hat{\eta} = \frac{\partial(\omega_s L_s - e_{L,s})}{\partial(1 - t_{L,s})} \cdot \frac{1 - t_{L,s}}{\omega_s L_s - e_{L,s}}$$

as the taxable income elasticity with respect to the after-tax rate. Then, (5) can be written as

$$\frac{t^*_{L,s}}{1 - t^*_{L,s}} = \frac{(\lambda_s - 1)}{\lambda_s \hat{\eta}}.$$

Thus, the taxable income tax elasticity is the right sufficient statistic for all behavioral responses for the model that we are using.[18] These considerations should be applied to all tax bases, not just to labor income. In many countries' compliance with the VAT is a big issue and the taxable demand elasticity would be relevant to understanding tax policy.

As things stand, the collection of evidence regarding the total response of tax revenues to tax rates, and the sources of these effects, is only in its infancy for developing countries. This is true even for income taxes, the area where most progress has been made in the developed country literature. An important exception are the findings of Kleven and Mazhar (in press), who estimate taxable income elasticities for Pakistan using detailed administrative data, and find these elasticities to be quite small, at least among those who are already registered to pay income taxes. To collect more micro-data, and use administrative records where they exist, to improve knowledge of behavioral responses to income taxation in developing countries, and to understand how the responses relate to alternative compliance structures, is a very important topic for future research.

The analysis in this section suggests that to understand the fiscal facts about developing countries laid out in Section 3, we may be able to appeal to the fiscal-capacity investments that shape total behavioral responses to taxation through standard consumption and labor-supply distortions but also through compliance decisions. The observed structure of taxes reflects that low or non-existing fiscal capacity makes it difficult to collect statutory taxes for some tax bases. This is particularly true when we compare income taxes to trade taxes, with the latter being less demanding in terms of fiscal-capacity investments. A low tax take may thus not reflect large distortions in consumption and labor supply, for any given tax system, but large opportunities for non-compliance. Hence, our emphasis on fiscal-capacity investments is given below.

Optimal public spending: Before turning to fiscal capacity, we briefly deal with public spending. In this dimension, the government decides how much revenue to allocate to transfers and public goods, respectively. With quasi-linear utility, an unconstrained government will direct all transfer spending, if any, to the group with the highest "welfare weight", μ^J. This is, of course, a stark and unrealistic prediction (but in Section 5.2 we

---

[18] We are grateful to Anders Jensen for this observation. He also pointed out that in the case where all of the non-compliance cost is a transfer, due to fines being paid, the equivalent of (5) becomes

$$\frac{t^*_{L,s}}{1 - t^*_{L,s}} = \frac{(\lambda_s - 1)}{\lambda_s \kappa \eta}.$$

Now, the sufficient statistic for behavioral responses is the elasticity of labor supply with respect to taxes. More generally, when there is a mixture of transfer costs and resource costs, this sufficient statistic obeys a weighted-average formula between η and $\hat{\eta}$.

introduce political constraints that potentially bring about more equal sharing). In the special Utilitarian case, where $\mu^J = 1$ for all J, we can assume without loss of generality that any transfer spending is spent equally. Let $\mu^{\max} = \max_J \{\mu^J; J = 1, \ldots, \mathcal{J}\}$.

To define the optimal level of public spending, let $B\left(\mathbf{t}_s^*(\lambda), \boldsymbol{\tau}_s\right)$ be total tax revenue when taxes are set optimally and the marginal value of public funds is λ. There are two cases. If

$$\sum_{J=1}^{\mathcal{J}} \mu^J \xi^J \alpha_s^J H_g \left(B\left(\mathbf{t}_s^*\left(\mu^{\max}\right), \boldsymbol{\tau}_s\right) + R_s - m_s\right) > \mu^{\max}$$

then all spending will be allocated to public goods, i.e.,

$$\lambda_s = \sum_{J=1}^{\mathcal{J}} \mu^J \xi^J \alpha_s^J H_g \left(B\left(\mathbf{t}_s^*(\lambda_s), \boldsymbol{\tau}_s\right) + R_s - m_s\right).$$

This is a case where public goods are very valuable and/or tax revenue is scarce.

In the other case, the marginal value of public funds is $\lambda_s = \mu^{\max}$, tax revenues are $B\left(\mathbf{t}_s^*\left(\mu^{\max}\right), \boldsymbol{\tau}_s\right)$, public goods have an interior solution, and the remaining revenue is spent on transfers to the group defining $\mu^{\max}$.

Investments in fiscal capacity: The main novelty in our approach to taxation and development is to study purposeful and forward-looking decisions by government to invest in alternative forms of fiscal capacity, i.e., in vector $\boldsymbol{\tau}_2$. We now study this investment decision when $\boldsymbol{\tau}_2$ is endogenous and chosen by the government in period 1. The next section will then use the results to evaluate which forces drive the creation of fiscal capacity and how these relate to economic, political, and social development.

Let

$$W\left(\boldsymbol{\tau}_s, R_s - m_s; \{\mu^J\}\right) = \max_{g_s, \mathbf{t}_s, r_s^1, \ldots, r_s^J} \left\{\sum_{J=1}^{\mathcal{J}} \mu^J \xi^J V^J\left(\mathbf{t}_s, \boldsymbol{\tau}_s, g_s, \omega_s^J, r_s^J\right) \quad \text{subject to (3)}\right\}$$

(6)

be the maximized value of the government's payoff. Implicit in this payoff are the optimal tax and spending vectors for each level of the fiscal-capacity constraints.

The fiscal-capacity investment decision amounts to choosing $\boldsymbol{\tau}_2$ to maximize:

$$W\left(\boldsymbol{\tau}_1, R_1 - \mathcal{F}\left(\boldsymbol{\tau}_2, \boldsymbol{\tau}_1\right); \{\mu^J\}\right) + W\left(\boldsymbol{\tau}_2, R_2; \{\mu^J\}\right).$$

(7)

This yields a series of conditions for creating fiscal capacity, or investing in it once it has been created.

For fiscal capacity already in existence, i.e., $\tau_{k,1} > 0$, we have standard first-order conditions in a convenient and readily interpretable form. Using the envelope theorem to eliminate terms in optimal government (and private) choices, these first-order conditions can be written as:

$$\lambda_2 \frac{\partial B\left(\mathbf{t}_2^*, \boldsymbol{\tau}_2\right)}{\partial \tau_{k,2}} + \frac{\partial Q\left(\mathbf{t}_2^*, \boldsymbol{\tau}_2\right)}{\partial \tau_{k,2}} - \lambda_1 \frac{\partial \mathcal{F}(\boldsymbol{\tau}_1, \boldsymbol{\tau}_2)}{\partial \tau_{k,2}} \leqslant 0 \quad \text{for } k = 1, 2, \ldots, N, L, \quad (8)$$

$$\text{c.s. } \tau_{k,2} \geqslant \tau_{k,1} > 0.$$

Three terms govern the investment decisions. The first is the added revenue from better fiscal capacity, weighted by the period-2 marginal value of public funds. The second term in (8) is the marginal cost imposed on citizens by higher fiscal capacity—essentially due to higher tax payments, as the profits from non-compliance fall when fiscal capacity is higher. The third term is the marginal cost of investing, weighted by the period-1 marginal value of public funds.

The three terms in Eq. (8) nicely encapsulate the forces that shape fiscal-capacity decisions. First, some factors make future revenue more valuable (cost of public funds λ_2 and the revenue function B)—these will have a disproportionate effect on investment in tax bases, which are not very elastic. Second, some circumstances shape the utility cost of taxation, which depend on the lengths governments have to go to increase compliance (the profit function Q). Third, some features of the economy make it more or less expensive to invest—including a high current marginal cost (the cost function $\mathcal{F}$ and value of public funds λ_1). The investment cost could be quite specific to some kinds of tax bases.

For the case where the government is thinking about introducing a new tax base, the reasoning is inherently non-marginal. Discrete gains or losses have to be weighed against the fixed cost of the investment. So consider a decision by a government to add a tax base k where initially $\tau_{k,1} = 0$. This will give a discrete (non-marginal) change in indirect utility, which comes from changes in the use of existing tax bases as well as increased spending on public goods. It will also imply discrete changes in the profits from non-compliance with new tax base as the optimal taxes change. Together, these yield a discrete change in $W\left(\boldsymbol{\tau}_2, R_2; \{\mu^J\}\right)$—evaluated at the level $\tau_{k,2}$ which solves (8)—that must be weighed against the cost of the investment $\lambda_1\left[\mathcal{F}^k(\tau_{k,2}) + f^k\right]$. In general, this kind of non-marginal analysis is quite complicated. That said, the main economic forces identified in our discussion of (8) remain the salient forces to shape the decision to invest in new tax bases. In Section 5, we illustrate this for the specific case of introducing an income tax.

Next steps: Having built an approach for studying investments in fiscal capacity, we will exploit it to gain insights into differences between different societies at a point in time and the same society at different points in time.

More specifically, Section 5 brings up six sets of factors pinpointed by our modeling approach. First, we study the effect of purely economic factors on the incentive to build a tax system. Second, we turn to the role of politics, asking how political instability and the structure of political institutions affect the choice of fiscal capacity. Third, we look at social structure, including inequality, heterogeneity, and polarization. Fourth, we study the demand side for revenue and the factors that determine the value of public spending. Fifth, observing that many poor states rely heavily on aid or natural resource rents, we explore how these non-tax income flows affect the incentives to build other kinds of fiscal capacity. Finally, we go into more detail on the technology for increasing tax compliance.

In all cases, we use the model developed in this section as a starting point. However, in each case it will prove convenient to specialize some features to home in on a particular issue.

5. DRIVERS OF CHANGE

5.1. Economic Development

In this subsection, we discuss how economic change affects choices of fiscal capacity and the implications for observed taxation. Against the background of the stark time-series and cross-sectional facts in Section 3, we focus on the role of economic development for the introduction and expansion of the income tax. As discussed at the outset, this has also been the standard focus in the taxation and development literature. We begin by discussing exogenous differences in the economy across countries or time, turning then to changes that are endogenous to the government's investment in fiscal capacity.

Exogenous economic differences: We noted in Section 3 (recall Figure 4) the typical path of change involves the two discrete steps of introducing the income tax and upgrading its reach via direct withholding. In a contemporary cross-section, we also saw (recall Figures 7 and 8) that rich and high-taxing states rely much more on the income tax than poor and low-taxing states. Through which channels does our framework explain such patterns in the data?

To answer this question, we specialize the model to include only one consumption good, in addition to the numeraire good and labor—i.e., we set $N = 1$. Moreover, there is no fixed cost in building fiscal capacity for the taxable consumption good, whereas a fixed cost may exist for the income tax—i.e., we have $f^1 = 0$ and $f^L \geq 0$. Of course, this stark difference is for illustrative purposes only. To keep things simple and pin down the value of public funds, we specialize the utility function to be linear in public goods, i.e., $H(g_s) = g_s$, and the value of public goods to be equal across groups exceeding the value of transfers, i.e., $\alpha_s^J = \alpha_s = \lambda_s > \mu^{max}$. These assumptions are relaxed in later subsections on politics and the value of public spending. For now, they allow us to focus on a government that spends only on public goods with a constant marginal value of funds.

We start by assuming that wages are given by the simple expression

$$\omega_s^J = \Lambda_s \omega,$$

i.e., every group J has the same wage. Different values of Λ_s could represent natural exogenous income differences across countries, or across time, due to, say, geography or total factor productivity.

In this specialized framework, the *marginal* first-order conditions (8) associated with the two tax bases are

$$\alpha_2 \frac{t_{k,2} \partial Z_{k,2}(t_{k,2}, \tau_{k,2})}{\partial \tau_{k,2}} + \frac{\partial q(t_{k,2}, \tau_{k,2})}{\partial \tau_{k,2}} - \alpha_1 \frac{\partial \mathcal{F}^k(\tau_{k,2} - \tau_{k,1})}{\partial \tau_{k,2}} \lessgtr 0 \quad \text{for } k = 1, L, \quad (9)$$

$$\text{c.s. } \tau_{k,2} \gtrless \tau_{k,1}.$$

If there were no fixed costs, this expression would tell us that the government invests more in the tax base that raises more revenue on the margin at the future value of public funds (the first term), induces a lower utility cost for consumers via the cost of tax evasion (the second term), or has a lower marginal cost of investing at the current value of public funds (the third term). Provided the positive first term outweighs the negative second term, for $k = 1, L$, we observe positive investments in both types of fiscal capacity since $\frac{\partial \mathcal{F}^k(0)}{\partial \tau_{k,2}} = 0$.

We now revisit the question of when an income tax is worth levying at all and why economic growth might typically induce the introduction of an income tax, as we have seen historically. Suppose fiscal-capacity building for the income tax has a fixed cost and the period-1 level of this capacity is zero, $\tau_{L,1} = 0$. Recall that the government raises no revenue at zero fiscal capacity. In order for the income tax to be introduced, the perceived welfare gains from doing so, by bringing fiscal capacity up to locally optimal level $\tau_{L,2} > 0$ given by (9), have to be large enough to outweigh the effective fixed cost $\mathcal{F}^L(\tau_{L,2}) + f^L > 0$ associated with setting up a compliance and monitoring system. Using the definitions and additive separability of the government payoff (6), the net tax bases (4), and the indirect utility function (2), and recalling that when $\tau_{L,2} = 0$ we have $c(\cdot, \tau_{L,2}) = t_{L,2}^* = 0$ (private evasion cost and taxes are zero), we can write the formal condition as follows:

$$\Lambda_2 \omega \int_0^{t_{L,2}^*} \left[\alpha_2 L^* \left(\Lambda_2 \omega \left(1 - t_{L,2}^* \right) \right) - L^* \left(\Lambda_2 \omega (1 - t) \right) \right] dt$$

$$+ \left[q \left(t_{L,2}^*, \tau_{L,2}^* \right) - (\alpha_2 - 1) t_{L,2}^* e^* \left(t_{L,2}^*, \tau_{L,2}^* \right) \right] \geq \alpha_1 \left[\mathcal{F}^L \left(\tau_{L,2}^* \right) + f^L \right], \quad (10)$$

where $\tau_{L,2}^*$ solves (9).

There are three main considerations. The term on the first line reflects the value of transferring funds from private incomes to public spending, recognizing that lower labor supply induces a deadweight loss. This expression is positive only if α_2 is sufficiently high (above one).[19] Also, the first-line term is proportional to exogenous productivity Λ_2, as this determines how lucrative the income tax base is. The second term on the left-hand side reflects the possibility of non-compliance. It has two parts, the first reflecting the gain from a new source of profits from tax avoidance. However, this is offset by the fact that greater avoidance reduces valuable public spending. If there was full compliance at $\tau^*_{L,2}$, then this expression would be zero. Finally, the term on the right-hand side reflects the costs of introducing a new tax base—fixed costs and the cost of the investment in fiscal capacity up to $\tau^*_{L,2}$.

Notice that the tax base in the first term of (10) is increasing in the productivity factor Λ_2. Moreover, the optimal income tax rate $t^*_{L,2}$ associated with a given level of fiscal capacity will generally be higher if income is higher. To see this, recall the Ramsey-tax formula (5), where $t^*_{L,s}$ is decreasing in $\kappa = \omega_s L_s / (\omega_s L_s - e_{L,s})$, and hence increasing in ω_s (since κ is decreasing in ω_s).

If Λ_2 captures income growth over time, this can naturally explain the eventual introduction of an income tax, as in Figure 4, by reference to (10). If Λ_2 instead captures differences across countries, at a given point in time, this can explain the higher reliance of the income tax in rich and high-tax countries, as in Figures 7 and 8. To explicitly link up with the data on income taxes vs. trade taxes discussed in Section 3, the argument would have to be recast in a setting where trade rather than consumption is the alternative tax base (see Besley & Persson, 2011c, chap. 2 for such a model).

Endogenous economic differences: In this section, we make the level of fiscal capacity endogenous to other government decisions. The general modeling follows the analysis in Besley and Persson (2011c).

Let wages be given by $\omega_s^J = \Lambda_s \omega(\pi_s)$, where scalar π_s represents endogenous government investment to increase productivity and where $\omega(\pi_s)$ is an increasing concave function. As Besley and Persson (2011c, chap. 3) show, one can microfound such a formulation if π_s represents the capacity to carry out legal support to the private sector concerning contract enforcement or, alternatively, protection of property rights. In this interpretation, which we will maintain in this subsection, π_s captures the legal capacity of the government: its courts, its supply of educated judges, or its registers for credit or property. An alternative interpretation would be to think of π_s as government infrastructure

---

[19] To see this, observe that this expression can be written as:

$$\Lambda_2 \omega [\alpha_2 - 1] t^*_{L,2} L^* \left(\Lambda_2 \omega (1 - t^*_{L,2}) \right) +$$

$$\Lambda_2 \omega \int_0^{t^*_{L,2}} \left[L^* \left(\Lambda_2 \omega (1 - t^*_{L,2}) \right) - L^* \left(\Lambda_2 \omega (1 - t) \right) \right] dt,$$

where the first term is positive and the second term is negative if there is any labor supply response to taxation. To a first-order approximation this is

$$\Lambda_2 \omega \left[[\alpha_2 - 1] t^*_{L,2} L^* (\Lambda_2 \omega) - \left(t^*_{L,2} \right)^2 \alpha_2 L^{*'} (\Lambda_2 \omega) \right].$$

that raises the productivity in the private sector. We could also let π_s be a vector of productive capacities, rather than a scalar.

Analogous to fiscal capacity, we assume that legal capacity in period 2 can be augmented by investment in period 1 at cost $\mathcal{L}(\pi_2 - \pi_1)$. We assume that legal-capacity investments have no fixed costs, for simplicity, and that $\mathcal{L}$ is a convex function with $\frac{\partial \mathcal{L}(0)}{\partial \pi} = 0$. As a consequence, the total investment costs for the period-1 government are now given by

$$
m_s = \begin{cases} \mathcal{F}(\boldsymbol{\tau}_2, \boldsymbol{\tau}_1) + \mathcal{L}(\pi_2 - \pi_1) & \text{if} \quad s = 1, \\ 0 & \text{if} \quad s = 2. \end{cases}
$$

What happens to the investment in fiscal capacity in the specialized model that we just studied, when we replace exogenous wages $\omega_s^J = \Lambda_s \omega$ with endogenous wages $\omega_s^J = \Lambda_s \omega(\pi_s)$? The marginal investment conditions in (9) are not affected, because neither $\frac{\partial Z_{k,2}}{\partial \tau_{k,2}} = -\frac{\partial e_{k,2}}{\partial \tau_{k,2}} > 0$ nor $\frac{\partial q_{k,2}}{\partial \tau_{k,2}} = -\frac{\partial c}{\partial \tau_{k,2}} < 0$ depend on legal-capacity investments π_2. However, the condition for incurring the fixed costs of the income tax now becomes:

$$
\Lambda_2 \omega(\pi_2) \int_0^{t_{L,2}^*} \left[\alpha_2 L^* \left(\Lambda_2 \omega(\pi_2)(1 - t_{L,2}^*) \right) - L^* \left(\Lambda_2 \omega(\pi_2)(1 - t) \right) \right] dt
$$
$$
+ q \left(t_{L,2}^*, \tau_{L,2}^* \right) - [\alpha_2 - 1] t_{L,2}^* e^* \left(t_{L,2}^*, \tau_{L,2}^* \right) \geq \alpha_1 [\mathcal{F}^L \left(\tau_{L,2}^* \right) + f^L]. \tag{11}
$$

Only the first term from (10) is affected with higher legal capacity increasing wages. There are good reasons to expect that this key expression is increasing in Λ_2 and $\omega(\pi_2)$. For example, in the case of a constant elasticity of labor supply, η, the first expression in (11) becomes:

$$
[\Lambda_2 \omega(\pi_2)]^{1+\eta} \int_0^{t_{L,2}^*} \left[\alpha_2 (1 - t_{L,2}^*)^\eta - (1 - t)^\eta \right] dt
$$

which is clearly increasing in π_2. Thus, a country with higher legal capacity and endogenously higher income is more likely to have an income tax than one with low legal capacity.

Of course, this raises the question what drives investments in legal capacity. Maximizing the investment objective (7) with regard to π_2, under the assumptions of the specialized model and using Roy's identity, we obtain the first-order condition

$$
[1 + (\alpha_2 - 1) t_{L,2}^* L_2^* \Lambda_2] \frac{\partial \omega}{\partial \pi_2} - \alpha_1 \frac{\partial \mathcal{L}(\pi_2 - \pi_1)}{\partial \pi_2} = 0. \tag{12}
$$

Since the two terms in the first bracket, the net benefit of legal capacity, are both nonnegative and since $\frac{\partial \mathcal{L}(0)}{\partial \pi_2} = 0$, there are always positive investments in legal capacity. Moreover, a higher level of fiscal capacity in the income tax $\tau_{L,2}$ raises the equilibrium tax rate $t_{L,2}^*$. This way, a higher value of $\tau_{L,2}$ raises the net benefit of investing in legal capacity, by raising the private marginal surplus from higher wages as well as boosting the fiscal benefits of the income tax through a higher tax base.

This result and the earlier result, that a higher π_2 makes (11) more likely to hold, make the investment in legal capacity and the investment in fiscal capacity necessary to introduce the income tax *complementary* decisions. This is a close relative to the complementarity discussed in Besley and Persson (2009a,b, 2011a,b,c). Thus, the endogenous growth of income triggered by investments in the productive side of the state makes it more likely that a country at some point in time will incur the fixed costs necessary to put an income tax in place.

As discussed at length in this earlier work, measures of fiscal capacity—like a high share of total tax income collected by the income tax—and measures of legal capacity are strongly positively correlated across countries in the data, and both of these capacities indeed have a strong positive correlation with income.

This point is illustrated in Figure 12 which plots the share of income tax in total tax revenue in 1999 against the ICRG measure of property-rights protection. Countries that raise more in income tax (have more fiscal capacity) also tend to enforce property rights in a better way (have more legal capacity).

Structural change: Development is about a lot more than raising income per capita. The process of rising incomes typically goes hand in hand with structural change toward a more urbanized and non-agriculturally based economy. As a consequence, more economic activity operates in the open, particularly in the formal sector where transactions and employment relations are recorded. To some extent, informality in production is just the flip side of tax avoidance. But it is more than that. Firms also choose not to become part of the formal sector in order to avoid an array of regulations. But this has a cost: such

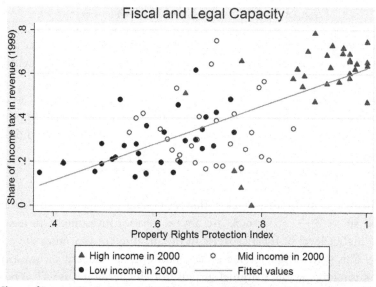

Figure 12 Share of income tax in revenue and protection of property rights.

firms are not able to take advantage of formal legal protection and contract disputes have to be resolved informally, often placing trust between parties at a premium. This limits the scope of business, which often becomes restricted to social networks.

The move toward formality tends to facilitate tax compliance. More employment takes place in legally registered firms rather than self-employment, as stressed by Kleven et al. (2009), and more financial transactions take place via formal intermediaries (such as banks), as stressed by Gordon and Li (2009). Both of these make transactions more visible to tax authorities and enable tax authorities to obtain corroborating evidence from cross-reported transactions. Falsifying these requires collusion rather than unilateral secrecy. Such changes result from transformations in the nature of economic activity whereby larger firms take advantage of scale economies in production. To the extent that this is reflected in higher wages, the arguments from the last section apply and we expect investments in fiscal capacity to occur.

The typical discussion of development and taxation couches structural change as an exogenous feature of economic development with causality running from economic development to fiscal capacity. This can be captured in our model either by allowing the function $c(e_{k,s}, \tau_{k,s})$ to depend on the sector of the economy in which an individual is operating. Suppose we exogenously assign individuals to the formal and informal sectors denoted by $\delta \in \{f, n\}$ where f stands for "formal" and n for "informal" with evasion functions $c(e_{k,s}, \tau_{k,s}, \delta)$. We may then reasonably suppose that

$$-\frac{c_{\tau e}(e_{k,s}, \tau_{k,s}, f)}{c_{ee}(e_{k,s}, \tau_{k,s}, f)} > -\frac{c_{\tau e}(e_{k,s}, \tau_{k,s}, n)}{c_{ee}(e_{k,s}, \tau_{k,s}, n)},$$

i.e., the marginal impact of an investment in fiscal capacity is more effective in deterring evasion for those operating in the formal sector. In this event, more formality would boost the revenues that can be generated from fiscal-capacity investments, all else equal. This is consistent with the observation that countries with smaller informal sectors also raise more taxes. This is illustrated in Figure 13 which plots a measure of the size of the informal economy in 1999/2000 from Schneider (2002) against the share of income taxes in total tax revenue in 1999 from Baunsgaard and Keen (2005). The downward sloping relationship is extremely clear.

The literature has paid less attention to the possibility that the size of the informal sector and the structural development of the economy evolve endogenously with the development of fiscal capacity, as in our discussion of legal capacity above. However, we may also take a further step and think of legal capacity as affecting the returns to being formal. It is very hard for an individual to simultaneously be largely invisible to the tax system and take full advantage of the formal legal system. This creates a further complementarity between the legal and fiscal capacities of the state. A state which invests in the infrastructure to support formal financial intermediation will overcome some of the barriers to formality and enhance the ability to raise more taxes. A good example

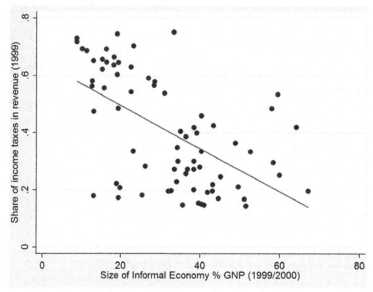

Figure 13 Share of income taxes and informal economy.

are efforts to build credit and land registries in the process of development, to increase property rights and contract enforcement. Such registries bring the patterns of ownership and credit contracts into the daylight for tax authorities. To study these issues explicitly, we would have to extend the model with an endogenous decision to choose the sector δ based on costs and benefits. While a higher cost of tax evasion is a cost of choosing the formal sector, there may be benefits in the form of a better trading environment.[20]

5.2. Politics

No account of the development process can be complete without considering the political forces that shape policy selection. It is widely held that the failure of states to build strong institutions might reflect weak motives embedded in political institutions. In this section, we explore the implications of introducing a government which operates under institutional constraints and faces the possibility of political turnover. The specific framework that we use is based on Besley and Persson (2010a,b, 2011a,b,c). This belongs to a wider body of work and thinking in dynamic political economics which is reviewed in Acemoglu (2006). As we shall see, this adds new issues to the analysis of fiscal-capacity building and allows us to uncover additional forces which can explain high or low investments.

Cohesive institutions: Suppose the government in power acts on behalf of a specific group in the spirit of the citizen-candidate approach to politics—see Besley and Coate

---

[20] Similar spillovers arise when, as in many countries, receiving certain transfer benefits—e.g., social security—are linked to paying taxes and working in the formal sector.

(1997) and Osborne and Slivinsky (1996). There is no agency problem within groups: whoever holds power on behalf of a group cares only about the average welfare of its members.

We model how political institutions constrain the incumbent's allocation of transfers in a very simple way. Specifically, the incumbent group in period s, called I_s, must give (at least) a fixed share θ to all non-incumbent groups J for any unit of transfers awarded to its own group. That is to say, we impose the restriction

$$r_s^J \geq \theta r_s^I, \quad \text{for } J \neq I.$$

The parameter $\theta \in [0, 1]$ represents the "cohesiveness" of institutions with θ closer to 1 representing greater cohesiveness.

This is an extremely simple and tractable, but reduced-form, way of looking at politics and is used extensively in Besley and Persson (2011a,b,c). We can interpret a higher value of θ in one of two broad ways. One real-world counterpart might be minority protection by constraints on the executive, due to some constitutional separation of powers. In practice, we expect democracies to impose greater constraints on the executive than autocracies. An alternative real-world counterpart might be stronger political representation of the interests of political losers in policy decisions through proportional representation elections or parliamentary democracy. The literature on the policy effects of constitutional rules suggests that both of these institutional arrangements make policymakers to internalize the preferences of a larger share of the population—see, e.g., Aghion, Alesina, and Trebbi (2004), Persson, Roland, and Tabellini (2000), and Persson and Tabellini (2000).

In this representation of political institutions, we can solve for transfers allocated to the incumbent group and all the groups in opposition $J = O$. In the model of Section 4, these are

$$r_s^I = \beta^I(\xi^I, \theta)[B(\mathbf{t}_s, \boldsymbol{\tau}_s) + R_s - g_s - m_s], \quad \text{and}$$
$$r_s^O = \beta^O(\xi^I, \theta)[B(\mathbf{t}_s, \boldsymbol{\tau}_s) + R_s - g_s - m_s],$$

where

$$\beta^I(\xi^I, \theta) = \frac{1}{\theta + (1 - \theta)\xi^I} \quad \text{and} \quad \beta^O(\xi^I, \theta) = \frac{\theta}{\theta + (1 - \theta)\xi^I}. \tag{13}$$

For $\theta = 1$, any residual tax revenue is equally divided in transfers to all groups. Otherwise, the incumbent group receives a higher per-capita share of transfer spending.

We maintain the simplifying assumption of a linear utility function for public goods, but allow the valuation of public goods to differ across groups. The shadow value of public revenue now compares the incumbent's value of transfers $\beta^I(\xi^I, \theta)$ to spending on public goods α_s^I. As in the general model, we have two cases. If $\alpha_s^I > \beta^I(\xi^I, \theta)$, all spending is allocated to public goods, i.e., $\lambda_s^I = \alpha_s^I$, else the marginal value of public funds is $\lambda_s^I = \beta^I(\xi^I, \theta)$.[21] Suppose now that a single group is in power in period 1 as well as period 2, i.e., there is a natural political elite and no political turnover for sure. In this case, the preferences of the elite determine policy and investment in fiscal capacity. For simplicity, we assume away any fixed costs in investment (or alternatively $\tau_{k,1} > 0$ for all k so that the fixed costs have already been incurred). Then, we get the following first-order conditions for investment in fiscal capacity:

$$\lambda_2^I \frac{\partial B\left(\mathbf{t}_2^*, \boldsymbol{\tau}_2\right)}{\partial \tau_{k,2}} + \frac{\partial Q\left(\mathbf{t}_2^*, \boldsymbol{\tau}_2\right)}{\partial \tau_{k,2}} - \lambda_1^I \frac{\partial \mathcal{F}(\boldsymbol{\tau}_1, \boldsymbol{\tau}_2)}{\partial \tau_{k,2}} \lessgtr 0, \tag{14}$$

$$\text{c.s. } \tau_{k,2} \geqslant \tau_{k,1}.$$

The analysis requires only a modest modification of the benchmark model, where we recognize that the driving force behind the decision to build fiscal capacity is now the preference of the ruling elite for tax revenue, rather than society as a whole. Clearly, an elite that greatly values public goods is more likely to spend on public goods compared to one that does not. Spending on public goods rather than transfers is more likely as institutions become more cohesive, $\theta \to 1$ and the ability of the incumbent group to extract transfers diminishes. However, an elite can also be motivated to build capacity to collect tax revenue as a means of increasing transfers for itself when $\lambda_s^I = \beta^I(\xi^I, \theta)$, because the elite faces few constraints on its power to pursue group interests (i.e., θ is low which makes $\beta^I(\xi^I, \theta)$ high).

Political turnover: The model becomes more interesting when we introduce the possibility of political turnover, i.e., the identity of the incumbent group may shift over time. To home in on this issue, we specialize the model to the case of only two groups each comprising half the population, $\xi^J = 1/2$. Let $\gamma \in [0, 1]$ be the probability that the incumbent group is replaced between the two time periods. Clearly, γ is a natural measure of political (in) stability. This new feature adds new and important dimensions to the analysis of policy and investments in fiscal capacity.

Let the period-s payoff of being either the incumbent or the opposition, $J = I_s, O_s$, be:

$$W^J(\boldsymbol{\tau}_s, R_s - m_s) = V_s^J\left(\mathbf{t}_s^*\left(\lambda_s^{I_s}, \boldsymbol{\tau}_s\right), \boldsymbol{\tau}_s, g_s^*\left(\lambda_s^{I_s}, \boldsymbol{\tau}_s\right), \omega_s^J, \beta^J(\theta)\, b_s\left(\lambda_s^{I_s}, \boldsymbol{\tau}_s\right)\right),$$

where

$$b_s\left(\lambda_s^{I_s}, \boldsymbol{\tau}_s\right) = \left[B\left(\mathbf{t}_s^*\left(\lambda_s^{I_s}, \boldsymbol{\tau}_s\right), \boldsymbol{\tau}_s\right) + R_s - m_s - g_s^*\left(\lambda_s^{I_s}, \boldsymbol{\tau}_s\right)\right]$$

is the total budget available for transfers, and $\beta^I(\theta) = \beta^I\left(\frac{1}{2}, \theta\right)$ and $\beta^O(\theta) = \beta^O\left(\frac{1}{2}, \theta\right)$ are the shares of transfers going to the incumbent and opposition groups. Now the level of fiscal capacity will be chosen to maximize

$$W^I(\boldsymbol{\tau}_1, R_1 - \mathcal{F}(\boldsymbol{\tau}_1, \boldsymbol{\tau}_2)) + (1 - \gamma)W^I(\boldsymbol{\tau}_2, R_2) + \gamma\, W^O(\boldsymbol{\tau}_2, R_2). \tag{15}$$

---

[21] Here, we abstract away from corruption and within-group agency problems, which are introduced below.

The effect of political turnover follows from the fact that γ enters this expected payoff. The optimization of the incumbent over the vector of fiscal capacity yields:

$$(1-\gamma)\frac{\partial W^I(\boldsymbol{\tau}_2, R_2)}{\partial \tau_{k,2}} + \gamma\frac{\partial W^O(\boldsymbol{\tau}_2, R_2)}{\partial \tau_{k,2}} - \lambda_1^{I_1}\frac{\partial \mathcal{F}(\boldsymbol{\tau}_1, \boldsymbol{\tau}_2)}{\partial \tau_{k,2}} \leqslant 0, \tag{16}$$
$$\text{c.s. } \tau_{k,2} \geqslant \tau_{k,1},$$

which, of course, just says that marginal costs and benefits are equated (at an interior solution). The third marginal cost term in (16) is by now familiar. However, some additional considerations go into computing the marginal benefit represented by the first and second terms.

After some simple algebra, we can rewrite (16) as:

$$[\lambda_2^I - \gamma(\lambda_2^I - \lambda_2^O)]\frac{\partial B\left(t_2^*, \boldsymbol{\tau}_2\right)}{\partial \tau_{k,2}} + \Delta_2^O + \frac{\partial Q\left(t_2^*, \boldsymbol{\tau}_2\right)}{\partial \tau_{k,2}} - \lambda_1^I\frac{\partial \mathcal{F}(\boldsymbol{\tau}_1, \boldsymbol{\tau}_2)}{\partial \tau_{k,2}} \leqslant 0, \tag{17}$$
$$\text{c.s. } \tau_{k,2} \geqslant \tau_{k,1},$$

where

$$\Delta_2^O \equiv \gamma\frac{\partial V_2^O\left(t_2^*\left(\lambda_2^{I_2}, \boldsymbol{\tau}_2\right), \boldsymbol{\tau}_2, g_2^*\left(\lambda_2^{I_2}, \boldsymbol{\tau}_2\right), \omega_2^J, \beta^J(\theta) b_s\left(\lambda_s^{I_s}, \boldsymbol{\tau}_s\right)\right)}{\partial t_2^*\left(\lambda_2^{I_2}, \boldsymbol{\tau}_2\right)} \cdot \frac{\partial t_2^*\left(\lambda_2^{I_2}, \boldsymbol{\tau}_2\right)}{\partial \tau_{k,2}} \tag{18}$$

and

$$\lambda_2^O = \begin{cases} \alpha_2^{I_1} & \text{if } \alpha_2^{I_1} \geq \beta^I(\theta), \\ \beta^O(\theta) & \text{otherwise}. \end{cases}$$

The third and fourth terms in (17) are the same as in earlier cases, capturing the utility costs of greater compliance and the marginal costs of investment in fiscal capacity. As before, the first term represents the value of extra revenue. However, the weight on this is now more complicated since the value of future public revenue to the current incumbent is different when a marginal future dollar is spent by a future incumbent different than herself, especially when the spending is on transfers rather than public goods. Unless there is agreement on the valuation of public goods $\alpha_2^{I_1} = \alpha_2^{O_1}$ and/or institutions are fully cohesive $\theta = 1$, we would expect $\lambda_2^O < \lambda_2^I$, so this effect will tend to diminish the incentive to invest in fiscal capacity, and more so the higher is the probability of turnover γ.

The second term Δ_2^O is entirely new. It represents an effect familiar from the work on strategic policy making in dynamic models of politics, which began with Alesina and Tabellini (1990) and Persson and Svensson (1989). The fact that the current incumbent and opposition may differ in their views about optimal period-2 taxes, means that the period-1 incumbent should structure investments in fiscal capacity to influence those decisions. For example, she may overinvest (underinvest) in the income tax if she likes the income tax more (less) than the opposition, so as to encourage (discourage) the opposition in using the income tax in the future, and the more so the higher the likelihood that the opposition takes over.

The size of this effect and whether it is positive or negative cannot be determined without going into details. A specific example that may lead to underinvestments is the case of a period-1 high-wage incumbent, who might be unlikely to invest heavily in income tax compliance if she anticipates being replaced by a period-2 low-wage incumbent (see Section 5.3 for more details) who would like to engage in more redistribution.

On balance, we may therefore expect higher political turnover to diminish investments in fiscal capacity, especially if there are few executive constraints so that θ is low and transfers are unequally shared.

Three types of states: Following Besley and Persson (2011a,b,c), the political model of the previous section allows us to think about three types of fiscal states that can emerge, depending on the combination of political cohesiveness and turnover. For simplicity, and to focus on a specific set of issues, we will work through the case where $\alpha_s^{I_1} = \alpha_s^{O_1} = \alpha_s$ and $\omega_s^I = \omega_s^O$, so the valuations of public goods as well as earnings opportunities are identical across the two groups.

A common-interest state: As long as α_2 is high enough relative to the value of transfers, we have:

$$\lambda_2^I = \lambda_2^O = \lambda_2 = \alpha_2 > \beta^I(\theta). \tag{19}$$

In this case, all incremental tax revenue is spent on public goods and there is agreement about the future value of public funds. We will refer to this as a case of common interests, as both groups agree that the state should be for a common purpose, either because public goods are valuable (so that α_2 is high), or political institutions are very cohesive (so that $\beta^I(\theta)$ is low). In this case, we have a common-interest state, where the level of investment is driven entirely by the motive to invest in tax revenue to provide public goods. Moreover, both groups agree on the level and structure of taxation. The Euler equations for investing in fiscal capacity become identical to the benchmark model in Section 3, namely:

$$\lambda_2 \frac{\partial B(t_2^*, \tau_2)}{\partial \tau_{k,2}} + \frac{\partial Q(t_2^*, \tau_2)}{\partial \tau_{k,2}} - \lambda_1 \frac{\partial \mathcal{F}(\tau_1, \tau_2)}{\partial \tau_{k,2}} \leqslant 0,$$

$$\text{c.s. } \tau_{k,2} \geqslant \tau_{k,1}.$$

Political institutions do not affect these decisions since the two groups agree on policy, and the state is run with a common purpose, no matter who is in charge. Although somewhat stylized, the nearest real-world example might be what happens in a state of war, or a common external threat where common interests are paramount. We return to this theme in Section 5.3 on the value of public spending.

A redistributive state: Now consider what happens when

$$\alpha_2 < \beta^I(\theta). \tag{20}$$

In this case, the marginal dollar is spent on transfers, i.e., $\lambda_2^I = \beta^I(\theta)$. Moreover, the value of public funds to the opposition is $\beta^O(\theta)$. Now each group values public revenues differently and the period-1 incumbent cares about whether his group will remain in power to reap the rewards from investing in fiscal capacity which will accrue to the incumbent. The expected value of public revenues in period-2 to the period-1 incumbent is now:

$$\lambda_2^{I_1} = (1 - \gamma)\beta^I(\theta) + \beta^O(\theta)$$

which is decreasing in γ for all $\theta < 1$. Indeed, this value is maximized at 2, when $\theta = \gamma = 0$. This is the case, when an incumbent faces no threat of removal and no executive constraints. The desire to build a revenue base is then based on the desire to redistribute resources toward the incumbent group.

Besley and Persson (2011a,b,c) refer to the case where a strong group-based motive to redistribute is the driving force for state building as a redistributive state. Such states thrive on low turnover and low cohesion. In the limiting case of $\lambda_2^I = 2$, the Euler equations are:

$$2\frac{\partial B\left(t_2^*, \tau_2\right)}{\partial \tau_{k,2}} + \frac{\partial Q\left(t_2^*, \tau_2\right)}{\partial \tau_{k,2}} - 2\frac{\partial \mathcal{F}(\tau_1, \tau_2)}{\partial \tau_{k,2}} \leqslant 0,$$
$$\text{c.s. } \tau_{k,2} \geqslant \tau_{k,1}.$$

Since the incumbent is guaranteed to remain in power, the strategic effect disappears.

A weak state: A weak state combines non-cohesive institutions so that (20) holds with high political instability. To illustrate this, consider what happens if an incumbent expects to lose power for sure and his successor faces no meaningful executive constraints, i.e., $\gamma = 1$ and $\theta = 0$. Then, the expected value of public revenues created by investments in fiscal capacity is zero! The future incumbent, i.e., the current opposition is the residual claimant on all revenue created by fiscal-capacity investments. In this special case, the fiscal-capacity Euler equations are:

$$\Delta_2^O + \frac{\partial Q\left(t_2^*, \tau_2\right)}{\partial \tau_{k,2}} - \lambda_1 \frac{\partial \mathcal{F}(\tau_1, \tau_2)}{\partial \tau_{k,2}} \leqslant 0,$$
$$\text{c.s. } \tau_{k,2} \geqslant \tau_{k,1}.$$

Since the second and the third terms are both negative, the only potential argument for building fiscal capacity would be to influence strategically the decisions over taxation of a future incumbent, according to the first term. However, this term is negative too: because $\lambda_2^I > \lambda_2^O = 0$, the future incumbent (the current opposition) wants (much) higher taxation than the current incumbent. Hence, the strategic motive makes the current incumbent not want to invest at all, perhaps even destroy fiscal capacity if that is a feasible option.

While we have illustrated this mechanism for an extreme case, the logic is much more general. Political instability and little political cohesion (weak executive constraints) generally mean that the incentives to invest in fiscal capacity are very weak, so we expect tax compliance and hence tax revenues to stay poorly developed under these conditions.

One bottom line of this discussion is that we should expect countries that have operated on more cohesive institutions in the past to have a higher stock of fiscal capacity today. Besley and Persson (2011c, chaps. 2 and 3) show that this is indeed the case, when fiscal capacity is measured in different ways and cohesive political institutions are measured by executive constraints. Political instability is harder to measure in a convincing way, but there seems to be some evidence that more stability is correlated with higher fiscal capacity.[22]

Figure 14 illustrates the relationship between current fiscal capacity and past cohesive political institutions using a partial correlation plot. As a measure of cohesiveness, we use the history of the strength of a country's executive constraints from 1800, or its year of creation, up to 2000. As in Section 3, the data come from the Polity IV database, specifically the variable *executive constraints* measuring various checks and balances on the executive. Following the theory outlined above, the underlying regression controls for the value of public spending, through measures of ethnic fractionalization and (past) external wars, and the degree of political instability, through measures of openness and competition in the selection of the executive. We see a very clear upward slope in the regression line, consistent with the argument in this section—countries with a history of more cohesive institutions appear to have built more fiscal capacity.[23]

Social Structure: The two-group model with common valuations of public goods and identical wages has served well to illustrate some key points. But clearly, it misses a lot in terms of social structure which may affect the struggle for power. Indeed political struggle often has different values concerning public spending and/or an unequal distribution of resources at its heart. We now briefly explore these issues and their implications for investing in fiscal capacity.

Group size and elite rule: Suppose the two groups in the specialized model have different size but face the same institutions, as represented by θ, when in office. Observe that $\beta^I(\xi^I, \theta)$, as defined in (13), is larger for the minority group than for the majority group, meaning that transfer behavior becomes more cohesive when larger groups are in office, as their value of extracting a dollar in transfers is much lower than for a small group. A lower value of $\beta^I(\xi^I, \theta)$ means that the condition

$$\alpha_s^I > \beta^I(\xi^I, \theta)$$

[22] See Besley and Persson (2011c, chap. 2) and Besley, Ilzetzki, and Persson (in press).
[23] The upward sloping relationship is also found if we control for GDP per capita in addition to the specified controls.

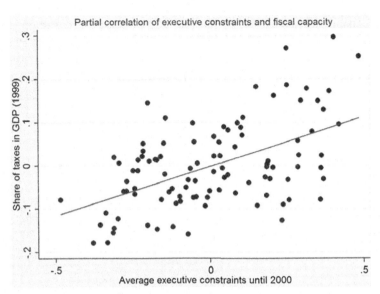

Figure 14 Share of tax revenue and executive constraints.

for all spending to be on public goods is more easily fulfilled. Thus, there is a greater chance the state pursues a policy in the common interest when large groups hold power. In view of this, majority rule is more likely to stimulate the build-up of fiscal capacity than minority rule. Indeed, if a country is governed by a small elite, it seems rather unlikely that a common-interest state will emerge—instead the state will become redistributive or weak.

The same basic effect emerges when a leader rules on behalf of a small elite rather than on behalf of her group as a whole. When such narrow elites alternate in power, it is difficult to create common interests in the use of public resources. Therefore, the value of political reform that raises θ toward 1 can be particularly strong in such countries. Similarly, measures which reduce the agency problem between elites and rank and file group members could also push a country toward a common-interest state.

Income inequality: The discussion in Section 5.2, abstracted from heterogeneity in earnings. To focus on this, we now look exclusively at income taxation and assume away all other forms of heterogeneity, e.g., in group size or preferences for public spending. Using the standard logic from Romer (1975), Roberts (1977), and Meltzer and Richards (1981), we would expect a low-income group to prefer a higher rate of income taxation than the high-income group, due to the redistributive effect of income taxation whether it is spent on public goods or transfers. We might also expect these policy preferences to translate into different incentives to invest in fiscal capacity to increase income taxation.[24]

---

[24] Cárdenas and Tuzemen (2010) use a similar model, allowing for income inequality between two groups, called Elites and Citizens. When the (richer) Elites are in power, in the presence of political instability, both income and political inequality lead to lower investment in state capacity. Conversely, if the (poorer) Citizens rule, high political and income inequality result in higher state capacity.

These mechanisms are most simply illustrated in the case of a common-interest state where (19) holds. Suppose we specialize the model to two groups, $J = P, R$, where P stands for "poor" and R for "rich" with $\omega^R > \omega^P$. By dropping the time subscripts, we are assuming that the wages of the rich and the poor stay constant over periods 1 and 2. In the case with constant elasticity of labor supply, the income tax preferred by group J (assuming an interior solution) becomes:

$$\frac{t_{L,s}^{*J}}{1 - t_{L,s}^{*J}} = \frac{(\lambda_s - \nu^J) + (1 - \kappa)\varepsilon}{\kappa\eta}, \tag{21}$$

where $\nu^J = \omega^J L^J / \sum \xi_K \omega^K L^K$ is the ratio of group J's labor income to average labor income. For the rich to want a positive income tax, the value of public spending as represented by λ_s has to be great enough. Clearly, we have

$$t_{L,s}^{*P} > t_{L,s}^{*R}$$

in general. We can now say something concrete about the strategic effect in Eq. (18) provided we assume, as the discussion following Eq. (5) suggests, that

$$\frac{dt_{L,s}^{*I_s}}{d\tau_{L,s}} > 0 \quad \text{for} \quad I_s \in \{P, R\}.$$

This says that an incumbent of any type would wish to implement a higher rate of income taxation if there is greater fiscal capacity in the income tax. Recall that this effect arises because greater fiscal capacity in the form of income tax enforcement raises the marginal yield from any given statutory income tax rate. The strategic effects become:

$$\Delta_2^P > 0 > \Delta_2^R.$$

To see why, take the case of a rich incumbent. If the poor group takes over in the future, then it will tax too much from the viewpoint of the rich, so a rich group contemplating being in future opposition would gain a strategic advantage by lowering fiscal capacity. In the same way, a poor incumbent contemplating being in future opposition would gain a strategic advantage by pushing investment in income tax capacity further. These incentives are larger the higher is income inequality and the larger is political instability. The logic is the same as the one that makes a right-wing group want to impose a larger debt on a left-wing successor, and a left-wing group to impose a smaller debt on a right-wing successor, in Persson and Svensson (1989).

It is perhaps unsurprising that inequality creates a conflict of interest over investing in fiscal capacity, which mirrors the conflict of interest over the tax base itself. However, the patterns of political control also matter to whether income tax capacity gets built. If the rich have a secure hold on power, they will invest in fiscal capacity to support public spending. However, if they fear losing power, they will invest less as their investment would encourage the poor to use income taxation more intensively in the future making the rich pay for an even larger share of public spending. If the poor are securely in power, this should encourage investment in income tax capacity. To the extent that transitions to more democratic rule lead to lower-income citizens being in political ascendancy, we should observe a tendency to build income tax capacity. This would be spurred on even further if the poor are more fearful of a reversion to elite rule. Generally, the poor have a strategic incentive to overinvest.

While we have applied this argument to income tax capacity, the same argument applies to any tax base which generates a strong conflict of interest between groups that could hold power. We have made the argument in the case of a common-interest state, where there is agreement over the disbursement of public resources. But the basic logic could equally well be applied to a redistributive or weak state.

The bottom line from this discussion is that we may expect income inequality to play an important role in the development of fiscal capacity. Given that a high level of income inequality particularly curtails the investment incentives for a rich incumbent, this conclusion is strengthened if we are willing to assume that economic power and political power tend to go hand in hand. Cárdenas (2010) considers the question empirically, using cross-sectional data for $100 +$ countries, and finds that political and (especially) economic inequality appears to be associated with lower incentives to invest in state capacity. In fact, he uses income inequality to explain Latin America's generally underdeveloped fiscal capacity.

Polarization: In the political models above, we have assumed that there is a *common* way of valuing public goods across the two groups. However, this need not be the case. Alesina, Baqir, and Easterly (1999), e.g., have forcefully argued that ethnic conflicts may lead to polarized preferences that diminish society's spending on public goods.[25] Differences in valuation may reflect, e.g., ethnic, linguistic, or religious cleavages in society. We now briefly consider the implications of such divergent views, which we think about in two different ways. First, we consider what happens when groups inherently differ in their value of public goods in a way unrelated to whether they are incumbents. Second, we consider the possibility that differences arise according to whether a group is an incumbent, since an important dimension of policy choice may be the type of public goods that are chosen.

To illustrate the first case, we suppose that $\alpha_2^J \in \{\alpha_L, \alpha_H\}$ with $\alpha_H > \alpha_L$. For simplicity, we focus on the common-interest case where all public spending is allocated to public goods. Now it is clear that the marginal value of public spending depends on which group is in office. Any group for whom $\alpha_2^J = \alpha_H$ has a higher value of future public funds $\lambda_2^I = \alpha_H$ than the low-valuation group, and will therefore invest more in

---

[25] See Esteban and Ray (1994) for a discussion of how to measure polarization.

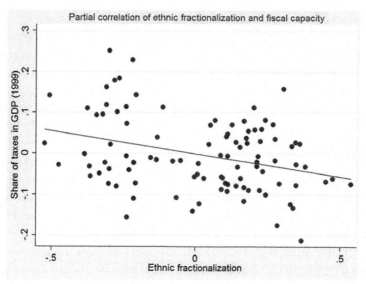

Figure 15 Share of taxes and ethnic fractionalization.

fiscal capacity of all types, everything else equal. For such groups, securely holding power will encourage investing. One interpretation of such heterogeneity in values may be that certain groups have stronger social capital and hence can provide public goods on their own, e.g., through ethnic or family networks. Then, arranging the public-goods provision through the state will be of lesser interest. For example, authors such as Esping-Andersen (1999) and, more recently, Alesina and Guiliano (2010) have argued that countries with strong family ties invest less in the welfare state.

To illustrate the second case, where the decision rights of being in power affects the mix of public goods when in office, we suppose that $\alpha_2^I = \alpha_H > \alpha_L = \alpha_2^O$.[26] In this case, $\alpha_H - \alpha_L$ becomes a natural measure of the polarization in preferences. The expected value of future public revenues to an incumbent becomes

$$\lambda_2^I = [(1-\gamma)\alpha_H + \gamma\alpha_L].$$

It follows from the expressions above that more polarization and higher political instability both reduce the incentive to invest in fiscal capacity of all types. Figure 15 illustrates the partial correlation (controlling for political stability, executive constraints, and external wars) between ethnic fractionalization and the share of taxes in GDP.[27] There is a clear negative relationship between the two.[28]

[26] A more involved case would explicitly introduce different types of public goods, with different groups having a preference bias toward certain types, as in Alesina and Tabellini (1990).

[27] The ethnic fractionalization measure is from Fearon (2003).

[28] This negative relationship is also found if we control for GDP per capita in addition to the specified controls.

5.3. Value of Public Spending

Our approach gives the value of collective goods a central place among the motives to build fiscal capacity. Formally, parameter α_s^J affects the value of public revenues in the eyes of group J. In this section, we discuss some factors that go into determining this value. Of course, in the standard interpretation, these are just fixed preference parameters. But there are strong reasons to think that they depend on factors which can be shaped by history as well as policy.

Common-interest spending and war finance: As discussed in the introduction, war has played a central role in the history of public finance. In terms of the model, external threats can help determine the structure of preferences $\{\alpha_2^J\}_{J=1}^{\mathcal{J}}$. The threat of war may also act like a common-interest shock that moves a society close to a common-interest state, or from the status of a weak to a redistributive state (at least during a period where the threat is felt). In our approach, the mechanism is to raise the value of public revenues and make it incentive compatible to spend these revenues on public goods rather than redistribution. This allows our framework to capture the arguments made by Hintze (1906), Tilly (1985, 1990), and others. Dincecco and Prado (2010) use pre-modern war causalities to explain fiscal capacity today (measured as direct taxes as a share of total taxes), and relate GDP per capita to fiscal capacity. Gennaioli and Voth (2011) build a two-country model, where endogenous external conflict interacts with the fragmentation of political institutions and the cost of war to shape state-building motives. They then apply the insights of the model to explain the divergent paths of taxation of European states in the years between 1500 and 1800. Feldman and Slemrod (2009) link tax compliance to episodes of war. Figure 16 illustrates the partial correlation between the share of years in war from 1800 (or year of independence) and the share of taxes in GDP in 1999.

War may have other effects which are more non-standard to the extent that war actually shapes social preferences. One interpretation may be that it diminishes polarization, as citizens forge a clearer sense of national identity—see Shayo (2009) on the endogenous formation of national identity. This might translate a transitory shock to a permanent effect. Thus, war may have lasting effects in a dynamic model where fiscal capacity investments are long-lived. The fact that a country built a strong tax system during a past war may raise its long-term tax take to the extent that such investments are permanent. This could be true, for example, in countries that introduced collection of income taxes at source as a means to help finance their war expenditures.[29]

An important aspect of income tax compliance is direct withholding of taxes from wage packets. So its introduction is an interesting discrete investment in income tax capacity. Figure 17 illustrates the introduction of withholding over time, for a sample of 76 countries for which we have been able to find data. We compare the 19 countries in this sample that participated in the second world war (WWII) with the 57 that did not. The

---

[29] An upward sloping line is also found if we additionally control for GDP per capita.

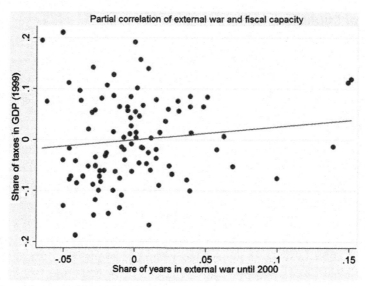

Figure 16 Share of taxes in GDP and external war.

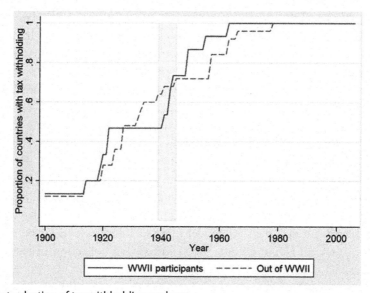

Figure 17 Introduction of tax withholding and war.

significant increase in the proportion of countries with direct withholding among the war participants is striking, especially when compared to the non-perceptible effect among the non-participants. Although this figure represents no more than casual empiricism, it is consistent with the arguments in this section.

Identifying public projects: We could also see $\{\alpha_2^J\}_{J=1}^{\mathcal{J}}$ as reflecting the ability of governments to identify good projects. An important line of development research in recent years has been instrumental in using Randomized Controlled Trials (RCTs) to identify the value of public interventions. These can be thought of as trying to find ways of better allocating resources to public goods by identifying high-benefit interventions. (See Duflo, Glennerster & Kremer, 2007 and Banerjee & Duflo (2009) for a discussion of the methodology.)

In our framework, we can represent an RCT as a particular form of experiment to evaluate project effectiveness. To model this, suppose there is a continuum of possible public projects indexed by $p \in [0, 1]$ where some have high returns and other low returns. Preferences for public goods are now:

$$\int_0^1 \alpha(p) h(g(p)) dp,$$

where $g(p)$ is spending on projects of type p. In the absence of discriminating information, we assume that the expected return on each project is the same, such that $\alpha(p) = \overline{\alpha}$. In this case, spending will be identical on all projects. For the sake of illustration, let us suppose that utility from public goods is quadratic, i.e., $h(g) = g - \frac{1}{2}g^2$.

Suppose now that RCTs have been conducted on a subset of projects, which we assign to the interval $[0, \iota]$, to establish which have high and low returns. For simplicity, suppose all projects are equally likely to be high return, α_H or low return α_L and that

$$\frac{\alpha_H + \alpha_L}{2} = \overline{\alpha}.$$

Given the outcomes of the trials and a given level of public spending, g_s, the government chooses three numbers—g_H, g_L, and $\overline{g}$—to maximize:

$$\iota \frac{[\alpha_H h(g_H) + \alpha_L h(g_L)]}{2} + (1 - \iota)\overline{\alpha}h(\overline{g})$$

subject to

$$\frac{\iota}{2}(g_H + g_L) + (1 - \iota)\overline{g} = g_s.$$

This will lead to governments spending more on projects that have value α_H, and less on those with value α_L. Denote the solution by $H(g_s; \iota)$. Solving this for the quadratic case, the marginal value of public goods spending is

$$H_g(g_s; \iota) = \frac{1 - g_s}{\left(\frac{\iota}{2}\left(\frac{1}{\alpha_H} + \frac{1}{\alpha_L}\right) + \frac{1-\iota}{\overline{\alpha}}\right)},$$

an expression which is increasing in ι, the fraction of spending in which the government is informed about returns. In words, better information about worthwhile projects raises the value of public spending. Moreover, this information effect is larger the greater is the difference between high and low returns, $\alpha_H - \alpha_L$.

This illustrates how public interventions found through randomized-controlled trials—provided they could be scaled up to achieve large aggregate returns—might assist the creation of common-interest states. Arguably, the argument may also illustrate why Western welfare states have gradually become the engine of state development during times of peace. Creating effective public health-care systems seems like an especially important example. Such systems persist essentially because the returns are perceived as common-interest spending with high returns.

One could develop a related argument regarding improvements in cost efficiency in the delivery of public spending. In that case, there could be a role for using knowledge about best practice to enhance the value of public spending. This could include innovations in the mode of delivery or lower cost forms of delivery, such as making better use of information and communication technologies. Our modeling approach links such efficiency enhancement to the scale of demand for public goods at the expense of transfer payments.

The key point here is to point to a complementarity between creating fiscal capacity and finding better and more efficient ways of spending public resources.

Corruption: Our model assumes that all resources that are spent on public projects find their way into actual spending on public goods. But in many countries, this is a poor assumption due to high levels of corruption. Many studies, following the pioneering work by Reinikka and Svensson (2008), have shown the value of interventions which reduce corruption and increase the effective flow of spending benefiting the end users.

This argument is especially poignant when fiscal capacity is endogenous. Suppose that only a fraction φ of the intended spending on public goods actually finds its way into actual spending on the ground. If so, the value of public goods is

$$\alpha_s^J H((1 - \varphi_s)g_s).$$

In terms of accounting, a share of the spending, $\varphi_s g_s$, ends up in the hands of citizens who earn corruption rents. Indeed, if $\varphi_s g_s$ is a pure transfer, then corruption is also a pure transfer. In practice, corruption in this or other forms creates constituencies in favor of maintaining the status quo. In terms of our approach, if the corruption rents flow disproportionately to ruling groups, this can affect the decisions to build fiscal capacity.

To understand the implications for public finance, we ask how the parameter φ_s affects incentives to build fiscal capacity. Two broad effects need to be understood. First, we have an effect on the marginal value of spending on public goods. This depends on how

$$(1 - \varphi_s)H_g((1 - \varphi_s)g_s)$$

depends on φ_s. As long as the elasticity $-H_{gg}\, g(1 - \varphi)/H_g$ is less than unity, greater corruption reduces the marginal value of spending on public goods.

The second effect comes from the distribution of rents from corruption $g_s\varphi_s$. If these accrue exclusively to the incumbent group, this will enhance the value of holding power—in effect, there is a blur between spending on transfers and on public goods since:

$$r_s^I = \beta^I(\xi^I, \theta)[B(\mathbf{t}_s, \boldsymbol{\tau}_s) + R_s - g_s - m_s] + g_s\varphi_s.$$

With low political turnover γ, corruption tends to enhance motives for building fiscal capacity, as in the case of a redistributive state above. But this effect is weakened by turnover, as in the case of the redistributive state. Moreover, even as $\theta \to 1$, a redistributive motive for building fiscal capacity remains due to extra-budget transfers accruing to incumbents through corruption. To the extent that corruption rents are widely held, i.e., are not distributed toward incumbent status, these motives will be weakened.

In summary, the first effect, via the marginal value of public goods, likely cuts the value of public funds and thus reduces the motives for investing in fiscal capacity. The second effect, via corruption rents, may go the other way—at least when incumbent groups capture a large share of the rents from corruption.

Summary: The discussion in this section ties together the taxation and spending sides of the state. A requirement for building a state run on common-interest grounds is that public revenues are spent on goods valued by a wide group of citizens. In history, war has arguably been an important source of such common interests and provides a key motive for creating fiscal capacity. Our framework suggests that states which lack common interests will have fiscally weak states, all else equal. One way to foster such interests might be to improve project evaluation and to identify which public interventions work in practice. This may not only improve the use of a given budget, but may also foster endogenous increases in fiscal capacity. As we have seen, combatting corruption in public spending is also linked to the motives for building an effective tax system.

5.4. Non-Tax Revenues

Our model framework permits states to have a source of non-tax revenues, denoted R_s, in the form of aid or natural resources. How this affects incentives to invest is clear in the first-order conditions for fiscal capacity (8). The conditions show that non-tax income matters for investments in the state through changing the marginal value of tax revenue, as represented by λ_1 and λ_2.

Aid and development finance: Anticipated period-2 aid, embodied in R_2, reduces the incentive to invest, whenever marginal spending is allocated to public goods. However, current non-tax income, R_1, reduces costs of investing in the short term, when marginal spending is on public goods, thus boosting the incentives to invest. When the transfer motive for investing in the state is dominant, we would expect aid and resources to go into transfers having no effect on the incentive to build fiscal capacity. As a result, political institutions matter—in the way we have already discussed—by governing the likelihood that a common-interest, rather than special-interest, motives dominate politics.

This discussion justifies the standard focus of development finance on lending to government rather than handing out cash grants. Lending promotes the incentives to build an effective tax system. When public goods are valuable, a period-1 grant or loan should increase investment in fiscal capacity. Forcing repayment of the loan, thereby increasing λ_2, further reinforces the investment effect. But the incentives would be reversed in a Samaritan's dilemma, where a period-1 failure to invest in fiscal capacity elicits more aid to be paid in period 2. This dilemma seems relevant to some debates about the situation in aid-dependent countries where part of the gain from building indigenous fiscal capacity would be taxed away in the form of lower aid.

Figure 18 looks at the relationship between fiscal capacity, measured by the total tax take, and aid receipts as a share of gross national income from the World Development Indicators database. The graph shows that the partial correlation (controlling for political stability, executive constraints, external war, and ethnic fractionalization) is negative, in line with what we would expect within the framework presented here. Of course, the direction of causality implied by a picture like this is far from clear. One justification of aid is often the difficulty that poor countries have in raising revenue domestically. Therefore, aid is unlikely to be exogenous to the process of fiscal-capacity investment.

Resource revenues: The model also gives insights into why natural resource discoveries can stifle the efforts to build fiscal capacity. A government that discovers oil in period 1 with anticipated revenues in period 2 will reduce their investment in fiscal capacity. Of course, such resource revenues may be beneficial but may necessitate a catch-up period

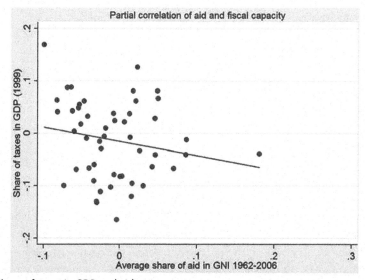

Figure 18 Share of taxes in GDP and aid.

of fiscal-capacity building and leave country vulnerable to negative commodity-price shocks.

Some data support the prediction that fiscal-capacity building is related to resource dependence. Jensen (2011) presents econometric evidence, using panel data with country-specific price indexes constructed for natural gas and oil and weighted by respective shares in total national energy production. He finds that a 1% increase in the share of natural resource rents in total government income is associated with a 1.4% decrease in the fiscal capacity of a country.

Informal taxation: The previous subsection discussed the role of corruption on the spending side of the state and touched upon the revenues generated by corruption. But corruption may also work as a direct, non-tax revenue-raising device for governments or government bureaucrats. Like explicit taxation, such informal means of extracting revenue through corruption imposes static and dynamic distortions on the business of the private sector. Here, we briefly discuss how such considerations can be brought into the approach.

Suppose that there are now two kinds of taxation on activity k in period s, the formal tax rate $t_{k,s}$ studied above and informal taxation at rate $T_{k,s}$. Unlike formal taxation, we suppose that returns to corruption accrue directly as transfers to the ruling group, rather than being funneled through the public budget and subject to any checks and balances in place to constrain government spending. Moreover, we suppose that the governing group has some "informal fiscal capacity" and that it is impossible to avoid corruption. This may be extreme, but will serve us well to make a few important points. It is clear that we could extend the treatment and make informal and formal fiscal capacity more alike.

The individual budget constraint is now:

$$x_{0,s}^J + \sum_{n=1}^{N} p_{n,s} \left(1 + t_{n,s} + T_{n,s}\right) x_{n,s}^J \leq \omega_s^J \left(1 - t_{L,s} - T_{L,s}\right) L_s^J + r_s^J$$

$$+ \sum_{k=1}^{L} \left[t_{k,s} e_{k,s} - c\left(e_{k,s}, \tau_{k,s}\right)\right]$$

and the earnings from informal taxation are

$$B^I\left(\mathbf{T}\right) = \sum_{n=1}^{N} T_{n,s} p_{n,s} x_{n,s} + \sum_{J=1}^{\mathcal{J}} \xi^J T_{L,s} \omega_s^J L_s^J.$$

The existence of such informal taxation affects optimal formal tax rates, as formal and informal tax rates interact for each tax base.

An increase in $T_{k,s}$ has a static effect in that it cuts available formal tax revenue by reducing goods demand or labor supply. This is a negative externality for formal taxation.

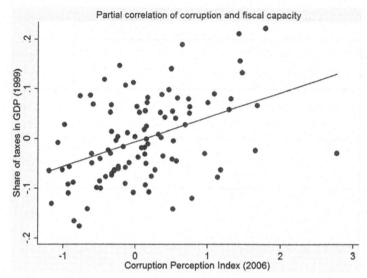

Figure 19 Share of taxes in GDP and corruption.

If the motive for informal taxation is purely redistributive, as here, it also reduces the resources available to spend on public goods. There are no constraints on raising such revenues except any informal controls that may exist within a group. Incentives for informal taxation are particularly high when the revenues accrue to a small subset, an "elite," within the ruling group. In addition to this static effect, however, informal taxation through corruption can also have a dynamic effect. Specifically, it may undermine the incentive to invest in the formal tax base, since the latter shrinks in response to informal taxation. The lower tax base therefore diminishes investments in formal fiscal capacity, paralleling the effect of a lower level of development in Section 5.1.

Unlike corruption on the spending side, we would thus expect higher corruption on the revenue side to be associated with less tax collection, everything else equal. This is confirmed in Figure 19, which plots the partial correlation between fiscal capacity (measured by total tax take) and corruption, measured by a perceptions index from Transparency International (a higher score denotes less corruption).[30] Countries with a higher share of taxes in GDP are also the least corrupt. Of course, as with our other correlations, this should not be interpreted as a causal relationship.

5.5. Compliance Technologies

So far, we have basically left the technology for evading taxes and for increasing compliance as a black box. In this section, we will open this black box a little to see how this can enrich the analysis. We begin with a simple model of the forces that may shape the costs

[30] The controls are the same as for Figure 18.

of non-compliance, and then extend it in a few ways to motivate interventions to increase compliance.

A simple micro-foundation for the costs of non-compliance: The simplest micro-foundation for the evasion cost function $c(e, \tau)$, which plays a crucial role for tax compliance, is a variant of the classic analysis of detection and punishment. Let $\zeta(e)$ be a non-pecuniary punishment for non-compliance with the tax code, which is increasing and convex in the amount of evasion e and let $\upsilon(\tau)$ be the probability of detection, which is increasing in τ.[31] Then

$$c(e, \tau) = \upsilon(\tau)\zeta(e).$$

This is the classic Allingham and Sandmo (1972) model of evasion, except that we have supposed that punishments are non-pecuniary. To the extent that $\zeta(e)$ is pecuniary, it adds directly to tax revenue and would have to be added to the government budget constraint. However, this would be a fairly minor difference with little effect on the main insights and we therefore stick to the non-pecuniary punishment case.

The other important part of the compliance technology is $\upsilon(\tau)$—factors shaping the probability of being caught and facing a sanction. A raft of measures based on technological improvements in record keeping and the competence of tax authorities belongs here. It is questionable whether low-income countries generally use best-practice procedures, so there might be scope for technology transfer. At least, this seems to be a presumption motivating extensive technical development assistance, in the form of capacity building in the area of taxation.

The function $\upsilon(\tau)$ also depends on the production structure, as we discussed in Section 5.1, with some kinds of economic activities intrinsically easier to monitor than others depending on the degree of formality, the need for transparent record keeping, and the use of the formal financial system.

Social norms and tax morale: The model can be used to consider the role of social norms in affecting tax compliance. Suppose that shame or stigma from non-compliance in a particular tax base depends on the average amount of non-compliance in the population as a whole, which we denote by $\bar{e}$. Thus

$$c(e, \tau; \bar{e}) = \upsilon(\tau)\zeta(e; \bar{e}),$$

with $\zeta_{\bar{e}}(e; \bar{e}) < 0$, i.e., an increasing amount of evasion in the population as a whole lowers the stigma/shame from cheating. In this simple case, evasion decisions, corresponding to (1) in Section 4, will form a Nash equilibrium where:

$$t_{k,s} = \upsilon\left(\tau_{k,s}\right)\zeta_e\left(e_{k,s}^*; e_{k,s}^*\right) \quad \text{for} \quad k = 1, \ldots, N, L \quad \text{if} \quad \tau_{k,s} > 0.$$

With $\zeta_{e\bar{e}} < 0$, we get the possibility of multiple Pareto-ranked, tax-evasion equilibria, since the reaction functions for evasion slope upwards.

---

[31] It would be straightforward to allow $\upsilon(\tau)$ to depend on e so that larger transgressions are more likely to be detected.

This opens the door for tax culture to affect compliance. Countries with a strong culture of compliance may find it much cheaper to achieve a similar level of fiscal capacity compared to one where the norm is unfavorable. Such issues have been discussed by political scientists, e.g., Levi (1998), Rothstein (2000), and Torgler (2007).

Obviously, the simple model considered here could be modified in different directions. For instance, there could be spillover effects between different tax bases, so that common cheating on some tax base spreads by contagion and erodes compliance with other taxes. Also, the relevant reference group for the social norm espoused by some particular individual may be more local than the entire set of tax payers. Local reference groups of this sort might help explain local pockets with widespread tax evasion, like the favelas at the outskirts of large Brazilian cities in which whole communities function largely outside the formal sector.

If tax morale is important, then interventions that increase the stigma from non-compliance may be an important form of intervention to improve compliance. It may even make sense to increase the visibility of compliers and to associate compliance with social approval—see Chetty, Moborak, and Singhal (in press). But the real and fundamental question here, about which we know preciously little, is how legal and administrative interventions interact with social norms—see, however, Benabou and Tirole (2011) for a recent interesting theoretical analysis.

Our discussion of tax morale has been speculative and sketchy. But the issue is certainly important and it is plausible that different tax cultures in, say, Sweden and Greece contribute to the large differences in their tax take. The idea of tax morale also goes to the heart of debates about state legitimacy, a concept we have not dealt with at all. However, the interactions between social norms of compliance, state legitimacy, fiscal capacity, and institutions are an interesting and important topic for further research. There is, in particular, scope for more experimental interventions which can change behavior along the lines studied in Chetty et al. (in press).

Incentives for tax inspectors: In many countries, a major problem in collecting tax revenues is the weak motivation of tax inspectors. These could reflect either low incentives to detect tax evasion or a willingness to take bribes from non-compliers if caught. Our simple model allows us to think about both issues.

Suppose that detection of evasion requires that inspectors put in effort χ. Such effort increases the chances of catching a non-complier, but is privately costly to the tax inspector. Denote the probability that an evader is caught by $\upsilon(\tau, \chi)$ with $\upsilon_\chi(\tau, \chi) > 0$. For any given tax base and level of fiscal capacity, let equilibrium non-compliance be

$$e^*(t, \tau; \chi) = \arg\max_e \{et - \upsilon(\tau, \chi)\zeta(e)\}.$$

It is easy to see that $e^*(t, \tau; \chi)$ is decreasing in χ. Let $q(t, \tau, \chi)$ now be the private profit per capita from non-compliance when tax inspectors put in effort χ.

An important question, on which much tax administration has tripped up, is what motivates inspectors to put in such costly monitoring. A traditional view is that this is taken care of by some kind of pro-social motivation, i.e., inspectors are intrinsically honest. But as governments have learned to their cost, this cannot be taken for granted.

Assuming that inspectors have to be compensated for their disutility of labor in a competitive labor market, the socially optimal level of tax-raising effort is:

$$\chi^* \left(t_{k,s}, \tau_{k,s} \right) = \arg \max_{\chi} \left\{ q \left(t_{k,s}, \tau_{k,s}, \chi \right) + \lambda_s \left[t_{k,s} e^* \left(t_{k,s}, \tau_{k,s}; \chi \right) - \chi \right] \right\}, \qquad (22)$$

where λ_s, as above, is the marginal value of public revenues. The maximand includes two terms—the private non-compliance profits and the value of tax revenues net of effort cost. Higher effort χ will reduce the first term and increase the second term and the balance between the two will define the optimum.

The main question is how the government can implement such an optimal effort level. If χ is not observed, inspectors face a potential moral-hazard problem—see Mookherjee and Png (1995) and Besley and McLaren (1993) for studies along these lines. If the tax inspector were offered a fixed wage and is not strongly intrinsically motivated, he would set $\chi = 0$. In this case, there would be no point in employing inspectors at all. In this framework, we can think of changes in fiscal capacity as corresponding to alternative ways of organizing the tax-collection service to avoid this outcome.

One regime would be to focus on recruiting tax inspectors who set $\chi = \chi^*(t_{k,s}, \tau_{k,s})$ by establishing some kind of rigorous recruiting and training regime. Such merit-based professionalization of the bureaucracy is certainly a feature of fiscal history.

Another possibility would be to contemplate tax farming, a popular solution in historic times where tax inspectors are sold a franchise to collect taxes on a particular tax base, in exchange for becoming a residual claimant. In this case, we would expect:

$$\hat{\chi} \left(t_{k,s}, \tau_{k,s} \right) = \arg \max \left\{ t_{k,s} e^* \left(t_{k,s}, \tau_{k,s}; \chi \right) - \chi \right\}.$$

Comparing this to the expression in (22), we see that tax farming would never be optimal in our framework, for reasons that make sense given its somewhat checkered history. Specifically, tax farming would lead to too much effort in extracting taxes, as tax farmers would fail to internalize the utility costs they impose on the public. In practice, tax farmers would have tended to use brutal methods of collecting taxes, ignoring most of the costs to the populations from whom they were collecting.

Another option would be to pay tax inspectors efficiency wages, as discussed in Besley and McLaren (1993). To see how this might work, assume inspectors are themselves subject to inspection in a hierarchical structure. Suppose that inspectors are asked to put in effort χ and that the probability a tax inspector is monitored and caught is $\varrho \left(\tau \right)$. Finally, assume that if inspectors are caught, they are fired without being paid. Now, an inspector will put in effort at a wage of $\tilde{w}$ if:

$$\tilde{w} - \chi \geq (1 - \varrho(\tau)) \tilde{w}.$$

Solving this inequality says that the wage needed to elicit effort χ is an increasing function:

$$\tilde{w} = \frac{\chi}{\varrho(\tau)} > \chi.$$

Compared to a benchmark model with observable and contractible effort, getting effort is more expensive, meaning that the level of non-compliance will be higher for any $\varrho(\tau) < 1$. However, compared to a world which relies entirely on public spiritedness, or a world where $\chi = 0$, this could be a worthwhile proposition.

There is little work to date that has explored empirically how changing incentives for tax inspectors can change revenue collection. However, recent ongoing work by Khan, Khwaja, and Olken (2013) is exploring such issues using experimental interventions for wage and incentive schemes for property tax collectors in Pakistan. This is an area where there is future innovative work to be done.

Corrupt tax inspectors: Now consider how the possibility of corruption affects these arguments. Suppose for the moment that the level of effort put into detection is fixed. After detection, however, a bribe of b can be paid by an evader to the inspector, which exempts the evader from suffering the punishment $\zeta(e)$. Assume that the inspector and the evader engage in Nash bargaining, so that the bribe paid is:

$$b^* = \arg\max \{b(te - b + \zeta(e))\} = \frac{te + \zeta(e)}{2}.$$

In this case, higher penalties for non-compliance are partly transferred to tax inspectors since they grant the ability to tax inspectors to extort money from non-complying taxpayers.

Somewhat paradoxically, bribery can motivate inspectors to put in greater detection effort since their payoff is:

$$\upsilon(\tau, \chi) \left[\frac{te + \zeta(e)}{2} \right] - \chi.$$

Moreover, this effort is sensitive to tax rates, with greater taxes actually motivating tax inspectors to put in greater effort. This suggests the possibility that efforts to reduce bribery in a world with a great deal of unobserved effort need not necessarily increase tax compliance. This is not to say that bribery should be condoned, but that we need to consider the full set of incentives in a second-best world. Note also that if some component of fiscal capacity is independent of the incentive scheme for the inspectors' own efforts (such as income tax withholding), then higher independent capacity raises equilibrium effort by complementing the inspector's own efforts.

Exploiting local information: How far should local information be harnessed in improving tax compliance? Focusing on the formal inspection process underestimates the scope for schemes, which fall under the heading of "cross reporting". This has become very important in the development literature on peer monitoring in micro-finance but has received less attention in the taxation literature. It has been brought to the fore in a recent paper by Kleven et al. (2009). Moreover, Kleven, Knudsen, Kreiner, Pedersen and Saez (2011) show that, even in a country like Denmark with large fiscal capacity, income that is not reported using third-party enforcement is susceptible to underreporting.

The main idea exploits something well known in mechanism design, namely that once more than one person is informed about something then a variety of means can be used to illicit that information (see Maskin, 1999 and Moore & Repullo, 1988, among others). This has an obvious counterpart in taxation.

The following canonical model illustrates the idea. Suppose that evasion activity e is observed by two parties—whom we can call a purchaser (denoted by a subscript p) and a vendor (denoted by a subscript v). Suppose that the vendor is asked first to declare e_v and then the purchaser either agrees or disagrees. If there is disagreement, the government audits the transaction and the honest party is given a small reward and the dishonest party has to pay $\zeta(e)$.

In the unique subgame perfect equilibrium of this game, there is full compliance as long as $\zeta(e) > te$. In other words, it is as if there is complete and costless auditing of transactions—the gamble in the traditional Allingham and Sandmo (1972) model goes away. This simple "mechanism" is simply an illustration of the potential power of cross-reporting. However, it only works under two key assumptions. First, there is no scope for collusion between the vendor and purchaser. Second, both parties to a given transaction can be observed and verified. The latter is true when there exist formal contracts of employment or purchase, or where a receipt or record of the transaction is kept.

The evidence on informal taxation in Olken and Singhal (2011) suggests that traditional societies have developed ways of mutually raising revenues using local information and enforcement. In modern economies, firms have taken on this role as argued by Kleven et al. (2009).

Tax remittance by firms: Our model of compliance has focused exclusively on individual decisions. But in reality much of the onus for compliance is on firms and the gains from non-compliance accrue to firm owners.[32] Substantively, this makes a difference when the size of the firm affects its non-compliance costs due to the visibility of its operations. It is straightforward to incorporate this feature into our model if we introduce some factor which affects the size distribution of firms. Consumers are assumed to face the same post-tax price but decisions not to comply are now only made at the firm level.

For simplicity, we focus only on commodity taxes and suppose that each industry comprises M firms indexed by m. At each date, we suppose that firms service demands (expressed in per-capita terms) of $\hat{x}_{n,s}^m$ from consumers for good n at date s, where

---

[32] See Kopczuk and Slemrod (2006) for discussion of these issues in general.

$\sum_{m=1}^{M} \hat{x}_{n,s}^m = x_{n,s}$, i.e., the firms exhaust the market. We further suppose that all firms have identical costs of production denoted by u_n. Now let $c^m \left(E_{n,s}^m, \hat{x}_{n,s}^m, \tau_{n,s} \right)$ be the firm's cost of non-compliance which we denote by $E_{n,s}^m$. We allow this cost to depend on the firm's sales because this makes evasion more visible.

Now, a firm's profits are:

$$\left[p_n \left(1 + t_{n,s} \right) - u_n \right] \hat{x}_{n,s}^m - t_{n,s} \left[p_n \hat{x}_{n,s}^m - E_{n,s}^m \right] - c^m \left(E_{n,s}^m, \hat{x}_{n,s}^m, \tau_{n,s} \right)$$
$$= \left[p_n - u_n \right] \hat{x}_{n,s}^m + t_{n,s} E_{n,s}^m - c^m \left(E_{n,s}^m, \hat{x}_{n,s}^m, \tau_{n,s} \right).$$

This is the sum of profits from sales and profits from evasion. Such pure profits have to be distributed across citizens in proportion to their ownership of firms. If we assume competitive pricing, i.e., $p_n = u_n$, then the only pure profits are from tax non-compliance. However, notice that nothing essential is changed from the basic model if we define:

$$\hat{Q} \left(\mathbf{t}_s, \boldsymbol{\tau}_s \right) = \sum_{n=1}^{N} \sum_{m=1}^{M} \left[\arg \max_{E_{n,s}^m \leq p_n \hat{x}_{n,s}^m} \left\{ t_{n,s} E_{n,s}^m - c^m \left(E_{n,s}^m, \hat{x}_{n,s}^m, \tau_{n,s} \right) \right\} \right]$$

to be the total profits from evasion in firms. Note, however, that we have put the value of sales to be an upper bound on evasion, so firms cannot evade more tax than they could in principle collect from final consumers. It is clear that the size distribution of firms can now make a difference to compliance.[33] A firm with small sales could find it worthwhile not to comply at all if

$$t_{n,s} \geq \frac{\partial c^m \left(p_n \hat{x}_{n,s}^m, \hat{x}_{n,s}^m, \tau_{n,s} \right)}{\partial E}.$$

This condition would endogenously create informal-sector firms in our framework. If there are some large firms, these would tend to comply more with taxes as they are more visible to tax authorities. And we might even have firms who deliberately reduce their sales to a point they benefit from reduced compliance, in the spirit of Dharmapala, Slemrod, and Wilson (in press).

This extension shows why changes in the economy that make it optimal for firms to grow will also change the structure of compliance. For example, in an oligopoly model with m firms producing a good $u_n^1 < u_n^2 = u_n^3 = \cdots u_n^m$, firm 1 would normally decide to price a shade below the others and take the entire market. However, with endogenous tax compliance, it may prefer to divide the market with other firms in order to remain less visible.

Firm-to-firm transactions provide a further interesting issue and are central to adoption of a VAT. This could be incorporated by supposing that some fraction of the cost

---

[33] To give this a proper micro-foundation, we would have to underpin the reasons why some firms are larger or smaller than others for a homogeneous good. Very small elements of product differentiation such as location would be an example.

u_n is based on purchased inputs that carry a tax but which are deductible against taxation of final goods. This gives the firm an incentive to comply in order to claim back input taxation. It also increases the scope for cross-reporting as we discussed above. We could then suppose that the cost of evasion depends on the extent to which a firm is claiming a rebate on taxes on inputs which raises the marginal cost of non-compliance of taxation on final goods. The evidence from a clever field experiment, in cooperation with the Chilean tax administration reported in Pomeranz (2011), suggests that cross-reporting in the value-added chain indeed helps enforce payments of the VAT except when the majority of transactions do not have firms but consumers (who cannot deduct) on the other side. There is much that could be done using administrative and other kinds of data to further explore compliance with VAT at the firm level in developing countries.[34]

More generally, and as argued by Gordon and Li (2009), when firms start to use formal financial markets, their costs of non-compliance rise and this increases the feasible array of tax bases. In the simple model above, suppose firms have to publish accounts to inform outside investors. When these accounts declare profits, $[p_n - u_n] \, \hat{x}^m_{n,s}$, this is a useful piece of information to tax authorities who care about estimating $p_n \hat{x}^m_{n,s}$ for tax purposes. It is a short step from this to having accountants serve as agents of revenue authorities, and to report data needed for VAT and income tax compliance. Of course, there would be difficulties in preventing collusion between firms and accountants. But it is clear that the need to raise external funds will put pressure to limit such collusion. This example further highlights how economic development may support compliance. But it also illustrates the complementarity between legal and fiscal capacity. Building legal structures to protect outside investors and to demand transparent dealings in financial markets creates positive spillover effects on fiscal-capacity building.

Summary: Many factors shape the costs of non-compliance with statutory taxes. A wider range of micro-studies should investigate these issues. Revenue authorities interested in reducing non-compliance have strong incentives to work with researchers to increase knowledge as means of improving policy. The nascent movement toward field experiments and data collection that we have mentioned is likely to become an important research field, which should eventually provide a better understanding of how to more effectively raise broad-based income taxes and the VAT.

6. CONCLUSION

As a state moves from collecting a low level of public revenue of around 10% of national income toward collecting around 40%, tax bases typically shift from trade taxes and excises

---

[34] For further discussion, see Keen and Lockwood (2010).

toward labor income and other broad bases such as value added. To study this process is a challenge of appreciating incentives and constraints. Incentives are shaped by political institutions, existing power structures, and societal demands that the state perform certain functions. Constraints are imposed by a society's economic environment, social cleavages, and political interests. Over time, these constraints can be shifted and governments play a key role for such shifts. They may invest to improve the working of the economy and the efficiency of public-goods provision. They may also try to create a sense of national identity and propose reforms to political institutions. Analyzing such issues requires a dynamic framework and this chapter has sketched an approach.

Throughout the chapter, we have taken political institutions as given. But it is questionable whether the forces that shape the development of the tax system can be separated from those that lead to institutional change. States that raise significant revenues will find themselves facing strong demands for accountability and representation, creating a two-way relationship between political development and the growth of the tax system. Little is yet known about this relationship. But it seems far from coincidental that states that are able to appropriate nearly half of national income in the form of taxation have also evolved strong political institutions, particularly those that constrain the use of such resources. This further underlines the close links between taxation and state development suggested long ago by Schumpeter, namely:

"The fiscal history of a people is above all an essential part of its general history. An enormous influence on the fate of nations emanates from the economic bleeding which the needs of the state necessitates, and from the use to which the results are put."

(Joseph Schumpeter, The Crisis of the Tax State, 1918).

This quote underlines the importance of combining economic, political, and social factors when studying the development of tax systems at the macro level. The tools of modern political economics can augment traditional explanations, based on economic factors alone. This lesson is now widely accepted in development economics and has a wider resonance for public finance.

We have also stressed the gains that can be made by innovative micro-level studies of tax compliance in developing countries. Research based on collaboration between tax-collection authorities and academics is still in its infancy. But expanding this into new areas—particularly with policy experiments in the field—is an exciting agenda for the future.

For developing countries to support their citizens at a level now taken for granted by citizens in developed countries, they have to undertake a series of investments, making the state more effective and responsive. Discovering the preconditions for such investments and what works on the ground are central tasks for future research on taxation and development.

ACKNOWLEDGMENTS

We are grateful to Mohammad Vesal for superb research assistance. We also thank Alan Auerbach, Roger Gordon, Anders Jensen, Henrik Kleven, Laszlo Sandor, Joel Slemrod, and participants at the Berkeley Conference in December 2011 for comments. Financial support from CIFAR, Martin Newson, the ESRC, the ERC and the Torsten and Ragnar Söderberg Foundation is gratefully acknowledged.

REFERENCES

Acemoglu, D. (2006). Modeling inefficient institutions. In R. Blundell, W. Newey, & T. Persson (Eds.), *Advances in economic theory and econometrics: Proceedings of the nineth world congress of the econometric society.* Cambridge UK: Cambridge University Press.

Acemoglu, D., Johnson, S., & Robinson, J. A. (2001). The colonial origins of comparative development: An empirical investigation. *American Economic Review, 91,* 1369–1401.

Aghion, P., Alesina, A., & Trebbi, F. (2004). Endogenous political institutions. *Quarterly Journal of Economics, 119,* 565–612.

Aidt, T. S., & Jensen, P. S. (2009a). The taxman tools up: An event history study of the introduction of the personal income tax. *Journal of Public Economics, 93,* 160–175.

Aidt, T., & Jensen, P. S. (2009b). Tax structure, size of government, and the extension of the voting franchise in Western Europe, 1860–1938. *International Tax Public Finance, 16,* 362–394.

Aizenman, J., & Jinjarak, Y. (2008). The collection efficiency of the value added tax: Theory and international evidence. *Journal of International Trade and Economic Development, 17,* 391–410.

Alesina, A., & Guiliano, P. (2010). The power of the family. *Journal of Economic Growth, 15,* 93–125.

Alesina, A., & Tabellini, G. (1990). A positive theory of fiscal deficits and government debt. *Review of Economic Studies, 57,* 403–414.

Alesina, A., Baqir, R., & Easterly, W. (1999). Public goods and ethnic divisions. *Quarterly Journal of Economics, 114,* 1243–1284.

Allingham, M. G., & Sandmo, A. (1972). Income tax evasion: A theoretical analysis. *Journal of Public Economics, 1,* 323–338.

Banerjee, A., & Duflo, E. (2009), The experimental approach to development economics. *NBER working paper,* No. 14467.

Barro, R. J. (1990). Government spending in a simple model of endogeneous growth. *Journal of Political Economy, 98,* 103–125.

Barro, R. J., & Sala-i-Martin, X. (1992). Public finance models of economic growth. *Review of Economic Studies, 59,* 645–661.

Baunsgaard, T., & Keen, M. (2005). *Tax revenue and (or?) trade liberalization.* IMF: Mimeo.

Benabou, R., & Tirole, J. (2011). Laws and norms. *NBER working paper.* No. 17579.

Besley, T., & Coate, S. (1997). An economic model of representative democracy. *Quarterly Journal of Economics, 112,* 85–114.

Besley, T., & McLaren, J. (1993). Taxes and bribery: The role of wage incentives. *Economic Journal, 103,* 119–141.

Besley, T., & Persson, T. (2009a). Repression or civil war? *American Economic Review, Papers and Proceedings, 99,* 292–297.

Besley, T., & Persson, T. (2009b). The origins of state capacity: Property rights, taxation and politics. *American Economic Review, 99,* 1218–1244.

Besley, T., & Persson, T. (2010a). State capacity, Conflict and development. *Econometrica, 78,* 1–34.

Besley, T., & Persson, T. (2010b). *From trade taxes to income taxes: Theory and evidence on economic development and state capacity.* LSE: Mimeo.

Besley, T., & Persson, T. (2011a). Fragile states and development policy. *Journal of the European Economic Association, 9,* 371–398.

Besley, T., & Persson, T. (2011b). The logic of political violence. *Quarterly Journal of Economics, 126,* 1411–1445.

Besley, T., & Persson, T. (2011c). *Pillars of prosperity: The political economics of development clusters.* Princeton: Princeton University Press.

Besley, T., Ilzetzki, E., & Persson, T. (in press). Weak states, strong states and steady states: The dynamics of fiscal capacity. *American Economic Journal: Macroeconomics.*

Bird, R. (2004). Administrative dimensions of tax reform. *Asia-Pacific Tax Bulletin, 10,* 134–150.

Bird, R., & Oldman, O. (Eds.). (1980). *Readings on taxation in developing countries* (3rd ed.). Baltimore: Johns Hopkins University Press.

Bonney, R. (Ed.). (1999). *The rise of the fiscal state in Europe c1200–1815.* Oxford: Oxford University Press.

Bräutigam, D., Fjeldstad, O.-H., & Moore, M. (2008). *Taxation and state-building in developing countries.* Cambridge: Cambridge University Press.

Brewer, J. (1989). *The sinews of power: War, money and the english state, 1688–1783.* New York: Knopf.

Burgess, R., & Stern, N. (1993). Taxation and development. *Journal of Economic Literature, 31,* 762–830.

Cárdenas, M. (2010). State capacity in Latin America. *Economía, 10,* 1–45.

Cárdenas, M., & Tuzemen, D. (2010). *Under-investment in state capacity: The role of inequality and political instability.* The Brookings Institution: Mimeo.

Centeno, M. A. (1997). Blood and debt: War and taxation in Latin America. *American Journal of Sociology, 102,* 1565–1605.

Chetty, R. (2009). Sufficient statistics for welfare analysis: A bridge between structural and reduced-form methods. *Annual Review of Economics, 1,* 451–488.

Chetty, R., Mobarak, M., & Singhal, M. (in press). Can social incentives and taxpayer recognition improve tax compliance? manuscript. See http://faculty.som.yale.edu/mushfiqmobarak/Taxation.htm.

Cukierman, A., Edwards, S., & Tabellini, G. (1992). Seignorage and political instability. *American Economic Review, 82,* 537–555.

Dharmapala, D., Slemrod, J., & Wilson, J. D. (in press). Tax policy and the missing middle: Optimal tax remittances with firm-level administrative costs. *Journal of Public Economics.*

Diamond, P., & Mirrlees, J. (1971). Optimal taxation and public production: I production efficiency. *American Economic Review, 61,* 8–27.

Dincecco, M. (2011). *Political transformations and public finances: Europe, 1650–1913.* Cambridge: Cambridge University Press.

Dincecco, M., & Prado, J. M., Jr. (2010). *Warfare, fiscal capacity, and performance.* IMT Lucca Institute for Advanced Studies: Mimeo.

Duflo, E., Glennerster, R., & Kremer, M. (2007). Using randomization in development economics research: A toolkit. In T. P. Schultz & A. S. John (Eds.). *Handbook of development economics. Vol. 4.* Amsterdam: Elsevier.

Engerman, S. L., & Sokoloff, K. L. (2002). Factor endowments, inequality, and paths of development among new world economies. *Economia, 3,* 41–88.

Esping-Andersen, G. (1999). *Social foundation of post-industrial economies.* Oxford: Oxford University Press.

Esteban, J., & Ray, D. (1994). On the measurement of polarization. *Econometrica, 62,* 819–851.

Fearon, J. (2003). Ethnic and cultural diversity by country. *Journal of Economic Growth, 8,* 195–222.

Feldman, N., & Slemrod, J. (2009). War and taxation: When does patriotism overcome the free-rider impulse? In I. W. Martin, A. K. Mehrotra & M. Prasad (Eds.), *The new fiscal sociology: Taxation in comparative and historical perspective.* Cambridge: Cambridge University Press.

Feldstein, M. (1995). Behavioral responses to tax rates: Evidence from the tax reform act of 1986. *American Economic Review, 85,* 170–174.

Feldstein, M. (1999). Tax avoidance and the deadweight loss of the income tax. *The Review of Economics and Statistics, 81,* 674–680.

Gennaioli, N., & Voth, H.-J. (2011). State capacity and military conflict, *working paper,* UPF.

Gordon, R. (Ed.). (2010). *Taxation in developing countries: Six case studies and policy implications.* New York: Columbia University Press.

Gordon, R., & Lee, Y. (2005). Tax structure and economic growth. *Journal of Public Economics, 89,* 1027–1043.

Gordon, R., & Li, W. (2009). Tax structures in developing countries: Many puzzles and a possible explanation. *Journal of Public Economics, 93,* 855–866.

Hall, R., & Jones, C. O. (1999). Why do some countries produce so much more output per worker than others? *Quarterly Journal of Economics, 114,* 83–116.

Herbst, J. I. (2000). *States and power in Africa: Comparative lessons in authority and control*. Princeton, NJ: Princeton University Press.

Hinrichs, H. H. (1966). *A general theory of tax structure change during economic development*. Cambridge, MA: The Law School of Harvard University.

Hintze, O. (1906). Military organization and the organization of the state. In F. Gilbert (Eds.), (1970). *The historical essays of otto hintze*. New York: Oxford University Press [reprinted].

Hoffman, P., & Rosenthal, J.-L. (1997). Political economy of warfare and taxation in early modern Europe: Historical lessons for economic development. In J. Drobak & J. Nye (Eds.). *The frontiers of the new institutional economics*. San Diego: Academic Press.

Jensen, A. (2011). State-building in resource-rich economies. *Atlantic Journal of Economics, 39*, 171–193.

Kaldor, N. (1963). Taxation for economic development. *Journal of Modern African Studies, 1*, 7–23.

Keen, M. (2010). *Taxation and development again*. IMF: Mimeo.

Keen, M., & Lockwood, B. (2010). The value added tax: Its causes and consequences. *Journal of Development Economics, 92*, 138–151.

Kenny, L., & Winer, S. (2006). Tax systems in the world: An empirical investigation into the importance of tax bases, administrative costs, scale and political regime. *International Tax and Public Finance, 13*, 181–215.

Khan, A., Khawaja, A., & Olken, B. (2013). Property tax experiment in Punjab, Pakistan: Testing the role of wages, incentives and audit on tax inspectors' behaviour. Details at http://www.theigc.org/publications/igc-project/property-tax-experiment-punjab.

Kleven, H., &, Mazhar, W. (in press). Tax notches in Pakistan: Tax evasion, real responses, and income shifting. *Quarterly Journal of Economics*.

Kleven, H., Kreiner, C. T., & Saez, E. (2009). Why can modern governments tax so much? An agency model of firms as fiscal intermediaries. *NBER working paper*, No. 15218.

Kleven, H., Knudsen, M., Kreiner, C. T., Pedersen, S., & Saez, E. (2011). Unwilling or unable to cheat? Evidence from a tax audit experiment in Denmark. *Econometrica, 79*, 651–692.

Kopczuk, W., & Slemrod, J. (2002). The optimal elasticity of taxable income. *Journal of Public Economics, 84*(1), 91–112.

Kopczuk, W., & Slemrod, J. (2006). Putting firms into optimal tax theory. *American Economic Review* (Papers and Proceedings), *96*(2), 130–134.

Levi, M. (1988). *Of rule and revenue*. Berkeley: University of California Press.

Levi, M. (1998). A state of trust. In V. Braithwaite & M. Levi (Eds.), *Trust & Governance*. New York: Russell Sage Foundation.

Madisson, A. (2001). *The world economy: A millennial perspective*. Paris: Organisation for Economic Co-operation and Development.

Marshall, M. G., & Jaggers, K. (2010). Polity IV project: Political regime characteristics and transitions, 1800–2010, version p4v2010. College Park, MD: Center for Systemic Peace [Computer File].

Maskin, E. (1999). Nash equilibrium and welfare optimality. *Review of Economic Studies, 66*, 23–38.

Meltzer, A., & Richards, S. (1981). A rational theory of the size of government. *Journal of Political Economy, 89*, 914–927.

Migdal, J. S. (1988). *Strong societies and weak states: State-society relations and state capabilities in the third world*. Princeton NJ: Princeton University Press.

Mitchell, B. R. (2007a). *International historical statistics: Africa, Asia, and Oceania, 1750–2005*. Palgrave Macmillan.

Mitchell, B. R. (2007b). *International historical statistics: The americas, 1750–2005*. Palgrave Macmillan.

Mitchell, B. R. (2007c). *International historical statistics: Europe, 1750–2005*. Palgrave Macmillan.

Mookherjee, D., & Png, I. (1995). Corruptible law enforcers: How should they be compensated? *Economic Journal, 105*, 145–159.

Moore, J., & Repullo, R. (1988). Subgame perfect implementation. *Econometrica, 56*, 1191–1220.

Newbery, D., & Stern, N. (Eds.). (1987). *The theory of taxation for developing countries*. Oxford: Oxford University Press for the World Bank.

O'Brien, P. (2001). Fiscal exceptionalism: Great Britain and its European rivals from civil war to triumph at trafalgar and waterloo. Mimeo. Available at http://www2.lse.ac.uk/economicHistory/pdf/WP6501.pdf.

O'Brien, P. (2005). *Fiscal and financial preconditions for the rise of British naval hegemony: 1485–1815.* London School of Economics: Mimeo.

Olken, B. A., & Singhal, M. (2011). Informal taxation. *American Economic Journal: Applied Economics, 3,* 1–28.

Osborne, M. J., & Slivinsky, A. (1996). A model of political competition with citizen-candidates. *Quarterly Journal of Economics, 111,* 65–96.

Persson, T., & Svensson, L. E. O. (1989). Why a stubborn conservative would run a deficit: Policy with time-inconsistent preferences. *Quarterly Journal of Economics, 104,* 325–345.

Persson, T., & Tabellini, G. (2000). *Political economics: Explaining economic policy.* Cambridge, MA: MIT Press.

Persson, T., & Tabellini, G. (2002). Political economics and public finance. In A. Auerbach & M. Feldstein (Eds.), *Handbook of public economics. Vol. 3.* Amsterdam: Elsevier.

Persson, T., & Tabellini, G. (2003). *The economic effects of constitutions.* Cambridge MA: MIT Press.

Persson, T., Roland, G., & Tabellini, G. (2000). Comparative politics and public finance. *Journal of Political Economy, 108,* 1121–1161.

Piketty, T., & Qian, N. (2009). Income inequality and progressive income taxation in China and India, 1986–2015. *American Economic Journal: Applied Economics, 1,* 53–63.

Piketty, T., Saez, E., & Stantcheva, S. (2011). Optimal taxation of top labor incomes: A tale of three elasticities. *NBER working paper,* No. 17616.

Pomeranz, D. (2011). *No taxation without information: Deterrence and self-enforcement in the value added tax.* Department of Economics: Harvard University: Mimeo.

Reinikka, R., & Svensson, J. (2008). Working for god? Evaluating service delivery of religious not-for-profit health care providers in Uganda. *Policy research working paper,* WPS3058. World Bank.

Roberts, K. (1977). Voting over income tax schedules. *Journal of Public Economics, 8,* 329–340.

Romer, T. (1975). Individual welfare, majority voting, and the properties of a linear income tax. *Journal of Public Economics, 4,* 163–185.

Rothstein, B. (2000). Trust, social dilemmas and collective memories. *Journal of Theoretical Politics, 12,* 477–501.

Saez, E., Slemrod, J., & Giertz, S. H. (2009). The elasticity of taxable income with respect to marginal tax rates: A critical review. *NBER working paper,* No. 15012.

Schneider, F. (2002). Size and measurement of the informal economy in 110 countries around the world. Mimeo.

Schumpeter, J. A. (1918). The crisis of the tax state. *International Economic Papers, 4,* 5–38.

Shayo, M. (2009). A model of social identity with an application to political economy: Nation, class, and redistribution. *American Political Science Review, 103,* 147–174.

Slemrod, J. (1990). Optimal taxation and optimal tax systems. *Journal of Economic Perspectives, 4*(1), 157–178.

Slemrod, J. (2001). A general model of the behavioral response to taxation. *International Tax and Public Finance, 8,* 119–128.

Slemrod, J., & Yitzhaki, S. (2002). Tax avoidance, evasion, and administration. In A. Auerbach & M. Feldstein (Eds.), *Handbook of public economics. Vol. 3.* Amsterdam: Elsevier.

Tanzi, V. (1987). Quantitative characteristics of the tax systems of developing countries. In D. Newbery & N. Stern (Eds.), *The theory of taxation for developing countries.* Oxford: Oxford University Press for the World Bank.

Tanzi, V. (1992). Structural factors and tax revenue in developing countries: A decade of evidence. In G. Ian & L. A. Winters (Eds.), *Open economies: Structural adjustment and agriculture.* Cambridge: Cambridge University Press.

Tilly, C. (1985). Warmaking and state making as organized crime. In P. Evans, D. Rueschemeyer & T. Skocpol (Eds.), *Bringing the state back.* Cambridge: Cambridge University Press.

Tilly, C. (1990). *Coercion, capital and European states, AD 990–1992.* Oxford: Blackwells.

Torgler, B. (2007). *Tax morale and tax compliance: A theoretical and empirical analysis.* Cheltenham UK: Edward Elgar.

Zolt, E. M., & Bird, R. M. (2005). Redistribution via taxation: The limited role of the personal income tax in developing countries. *UCLA law review, 52,* 1627–1695.

CHAPTER 3

Social Insurance: Connecting Theory to Data

Raj Chetty[*,†] and Amy Finkelstein[†,‡]

[*]Harvard University
[†]NBER
[‡]MIT

Contents

Handbook of Public Economics, Volume 5
ISSN 1573-4420, http://dx.doi.org/10.1016/B978-0-444-53759-1.00003-0

1. INTRODUCTION

Over the last century, social insurance—government intervention in providing insurance against adverse shocks to individuals—has emerged as one of the major functions of government in developed countries.[1] Social insurance programs began by providing limited coverage for risks such as injury at work and unemployment (Baicker, Goldin, & Katz, 1998; Fishback & Kantor, 1998). Today, governments provide substantial insurance for a broad range of risks, including health (Medicare and Medicaid in the US), disability and retirement (the Old Age, Survivors, and Disability insurance program), work injury (Worker's Compensation), and unemployment (Unemployment Insurance).[2] In the United States, expenditures on social insurance have risen from less than 10% of the federal government's budget in the early 1950s to almost 60% today and continue to grow rapidly (Gruber, 2009). Social insurance expenditures are now a defining characteristic of modern developed economies. The fraction of GDP devoted to social insurance increases sharply with GDP per capita (Figure 1).

Academic research on social insurance policies has grown alongside the expansion of these programs. Research on social insurance has addressed two broad questions. First, when should the government intervene in private insurance markets? The standard set of rationales includes private market failures, income redistribution, and paternalism. More recently, a growing empirical literature has sought to quantify the importance of these motives for government intervention. Much of this literature has focused on one particular market failure that can provide a rationale for social insurance: adverse selection due to asymmetric information. Second, if the government chooses to intervene, what is the optimal way to do so? The key issue here is that expanding social insurance creates moral hazard by distorting incentives. The literature on optimal policies seeks to identify the policies that maximize welfare, trading off the distortionary costs of social insurance programs with the benefits they provide in reducing exposure to risk. This literature has analyzed several dimensions of social insurance policies, ranging from the optimal level of benefits to whether the optimal tools are provision of liquidity (e.g., via loans) or state-contingent transfers.

Research on each of these two questions has traditionally been divided into two distinct methodological strands: a normative theoretical literature that focuses on welfare analysis and a positive empirical literature that documents the workings of private insurance markets or the impacts of social insurance programs. The limitation of this

---

[1] We use the term "social insurance" to refer to government programs that transfer resources across states of nature after an individual is born rather than transfers of resources across individuals (e.g., through redistributive taxation). Transfers of resources across individuals—which effectively provide insurance behind the veil of ignorance—are discussed in the chapters on optimal taxation in this volume.

[2] See Social Security Administration (1997) for an excellent overview of modern social insurance programs in the United States. Krueger and Meyer (2002) also provide a description of many social insurance programs in the US, as well as a review of the empirical literature on their labor supply impacts.

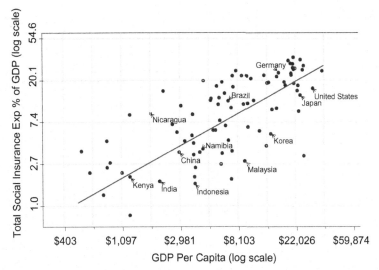

Figure 1 Social insurance vs. GDP per capita in 1996. *Notes*: Social insurance statistics are from International Labor Organization (2000). Social insurance is defined as total expenditures on social security, disability insurance, unemployment insurance, insurance against work-related injuries, and government provided health insurance. GDP statistics are from the Penn World tables. GDP is measured in PPP-adjusted 1996 US dollars.

two-pronged approach is that the theoretical models do not by themselves offer quantitative answers to the key policy questions, while the descriptive empirical literature often has little to say about the welfare implications of its findings. For example, the rich theoretical literature on adverse selection has shown that private markets may provide too little insurance in the presence of asymmetric information. A more recent empirical literature has documented that adverse selection does in fact exist in many private insurance markets. However, the empirical techniques developed to identify the existence of selection do not, by themselves, permit even qualitative comparisons of the welfare costs of selection across markets, let alone quantitative welfare statements. Similarly, a large theoretical literature has characterized the properties of optimal insurance contracts in the presence of moral hazard. In parallel, empirical work has documented the causal impacts of social insurance programs on a broad range of behaviors, ranging from job search to health expenditures. Again, however, the implications of estimates of parameters such as the elasticity of unemployment durations with respect to benefits for optimal policy were unclear from the initial empirical literature.

Over the past two decades, researchers have made considerable progress in connecting theoretical and empirical work on social insurance to make empirically grounded statements about welfare and optimal policy. For instance, recent work has shown how data on selection patterns in insurance markets can be used to quantify the welfare costs of adverse selection in models of asymmetric information. Similarly, researchers have developed new methods of mapping estimates of behavioral elasticities to statements about the optimal level of social insurance benefits.

In this survey, we provide an overview of some of the key advances in connecting theory to data in analyzing the welfare consequences of social insurance. In focusing on this goal, we deliberately do not provide a comprehensive survey of the literature on social insurance. We cover only a selected subset of the many theoretical studies that have advanced the literature. We also discuss only a small subset of the numerous empirical studies that have estimated relevant empirical parameters. Readers seeking a more detailed discussion of empirical evidence on behavioral responses to social insurance may refer to Krueger and Meyer (2002) and Cutler (2002).

We divide our review of the literature into two sections, corresponding to the two major questions discussed above. In Section 2, we discuss motives for government intervention in insurance markets. In Section 3, we discuss optimal policy design once the government has decided to intervene. This literature on optimal design of social insurance has proceeded mostly independently from the work on the economic motivations for social insurance. As a result, the two sections of the paper draw on fairly distinct literatures. Indeed, one limitation of existing work on optimal government policy is that it typically assumes away the existence of formal private insurance markets rather than considering optimal policy design in an environment with endogenous market failures. We conclude in Section 4 by discussing this as well as some of the other broad challenges that remain in going from the work we review here to statements about optimal policy design.

2. MOTIVATIONS FOR SOCIAL INSURANCE

Research in public economics usually begins with the question of why the government might have a reason to intervene in a particular private market transaction. Only then can one move forward to consider potential forms of intervention and their consequences. Standard economic rationales for social insurance include redistribution, paternalism, and market failures (Diamond, 1977). Within this relatively broad limit, our focus here is quite narrow. Following much of the recent literature, we concentrate on the potential role for social insurance in ameliorating one particular type of private market failure, namely selection. We return at the end of this section to briefly comment on other potential rationales for social insurance and some of the existing empirical work on them.

Modern theoretical work on adverse selection in insurance markets dates to the seminal work of Akerlof (1970) and Rothschild and Stiglitz (1976), which introduced a key motivation for social insurance: the competitive private equilibrium may under-provide insurance, creating scope for welfare-improving government intervention. Relative to the rich theoretical literature, empirical work on adverse selection in insurance markets lagged decidedly behind for many years. Indeed, in awarding the 2001 Nobel Prize for the pioneering theoretical work on asymmetric information, the Nobel committee noted this paucity of empirical work (Bank of Sweden, 2001).

Over the last decade or so, empirical research had made considerable progress in developing tools to identify whether asymmetric information exists in a given insurance market, as well as to begin to quantify the welfare costs of this asymmetric information and the welfare consequences of alternative public policy interventions. Some of the findings of this empirical work have suggested important refinements to the initial theory. In particular, a growing body of evidence suggests that in addition to heterogeneity in risk type, heterogeneity in preferences can be a quantitatively important determinant of demand for insurance. This is in contrast to the original theoretical literature on asymmetric information which focused on the potential for (unobserved) heterogeneity in risk type and assumed away the possibility of heterogeneity in preferences. Once one allows for heterogeneity in preferences in addition to risk type, the competitive equilibrium may look very different and the optimal policy intervention is no longer a priori obvious.

To summarize and discuss this empirical literature, we begin by presenting a highly stylized model and graphical framework that allow us to review the basic results of the standard theory and to describe their sensitivity to incorporating several "real world" features of insurance markets. The graphical framework provides a lens through which we discuss empirical work detecting whether selection exists and quantifying its welfare costs. Finally, we discuss some of the limitations of the work to date and some directions for further work.

2.1. Adverse Selection: Review of the Basic Theory

We structure our analysis using a simplified model of selection based on that presented in Einav, Finkelstein, and Cullen (2010a), and discussed further in Einav and Finkelstein (2011). We begin with the "textbook model" in which the qualitative results are unambiguous: adverse selection creates a welfare loss from underprovision of insurance, and public policy such as mandates can reach the efficient allocation and improve welfare. Even in this textbook case, however, the magnitudes of the welfare costs of adverse selection and the welfare gains from government intervention remain empirical questions. Moreover, these qualitative results can be reversed with the introduction of two important features of actual insurance markets: loads and preference heterogeneity. With loads, it is no longer necessarily efficient for all individuals to be insured in equilibrium, and mandates can therefore reduce welfare in some cases. With preference heterogeneity, the market equilibrium may lead to over insurance rather than underinsurance. Given the qualitative as well as quantitative uncertainty of the impact of selection and of government intervention, these naturally become empirical questions.

2.1.1. A Stylized Model

Setup and Notation. A population of individuals chooses from two insurance contracts, one that offers high coverage (contract H) and one that offers less coverage (contract L). To further simplify the exposition, assume that contract L is no insurance and is available for free, and that contract H is full insurance. These are merely normalizations and it is straightforward to extend the analysis to partial coverage contracts or to more than two contracts (Einav et al., 2010a).

The key simplification we make is to fix the contract space, but allow the price of insurance to be determined endogenously. In other words, the set of contracts that insurance companies offer is determined exogenously, and the focus of the model is on how selection distorts the pricing of these existing contracts. The analysis is therefore in the spirit of Akerlof (1970) rather than Rothschild and Stiglitz (1976), who endogenize the level of coverage as well. This assumption greatly simplifies the analytical framework and makes it easier to both allow for multiple sources of heterogeneity across consumers and to illustrate some of the key insights and implications of selection models. However, it means that the analysis of the welfare consequences of selection or alternative possible government interventions is limited to the cost associated with inefficient pricing of a fixed set of contracts; it does not capture welfare loss that selection may create by distorting the set of contracts offered, which may be large in some settings. We return to this central issue below.

Define the population by a distribution $G(\zeta)$, where ζ is a vector of consumer characteristics. For our initial discussion of the "textbook case," we will assume that these consumer characteristics ζ include only characteristics relating to their risk factors; later, we will relax this assumption and explore the implications of allowing for preference heterogeneity.

Denote the (relative) price of contract H by p, and denote by $v^H(\zeta_i, p)$ and $v^L(\zeta_i)$ consumer i's (with characteristics ζ_i) utility from buying contracts H and L, respectively. Although not essential, it is natural to assume that $v^H(\zeta_i, p)$ is strictly decreasing in p and that $v^H(\zeta_i, p = 0) > v^L(\zeta_i)$. Finally, denote the expected monetary cost to the insurer associated with the insurable risk for individual i by $c(\zeta_i)$. For ease of exposition, we discuss the benchmark case in which there is no moral hazard; the cost c of insuring an individual does not depend on the contract chosen. Allowing for moral hazard does not fundamentally change the analysis, although it does complicate the presentation (Einav et al., 2010a). Of course, as we will discuss at length when we turn to the empirical work on selection in insurance markets, the potential presence of moral hazard as well as selection does pose important empirical challenges to the analysis of either one.

Demand for Insurance. Assume that each individual makes a discrete choice of whether to buy insurance or not. Since there are only two available contracts and their associated coverages, demand is only a function of the (relative) price p. Assume that firms cannot offer different prices to different individuals. To the extent that firms can make prices depend on observed characteristics, one should think of the foregoing analysis as applied to a set of individuals that only vary in unobserved (or unpriced) characteristics. Assume that if individuals choose to buy insurance they buy it at the lowest price offered, so it is sufficient to characterize demand for insurance as a function of the lowest price p.

Given the above assumptions, individual i chooses to buy insurance if and only if $v^H(\zeta_i, p) \geq v^L(\zeta_i)$. We can define $\pi(\zeta_i) \equiv \max\left\{p : v^H(\zeta_i, p) \geq v^L(\zeta_i)\right\}$, which is the highest price at which individual i is willing to buy insurance. Aggregate demand for insurance is therefore given by

$$D(p) = \int 1(\pi(\zeta) \geq p) dG(\zeta) = \Pr(\pi(\zeta_i) \geq p), \qquad (1)$$

and we assume that the underlying primitives imply that $D(p)$ is strictly decreasing and differentiable.

Supply and Equilibrium. We consider $N \geq 2$ identical risk neutral insurance providers, who set prices in a Nash Equilibrium (a-la Bertrand). We further assume that when multiple firms set the same price, individuals who decide to purchase insurance at this price choose a firm randomly. In the "textbook case," we assume that the only costs of providing contract H to individual i are the direct insurer claims $c(\zeta_i)$ that are paid out; later we will explore the implications of allowing for the possibility of loading factors, such as other administrative (production) costs of the insurance company.

The foregoing assumptions imply that the average (expected) cost curve in the market is given by

$$AC(p) = \frac{1}{D(p)} \int c(\zeta) 1(\pi(\zeta) \geq p) dG(\zeta) = E(c(\zeta)|\pi(\zeta) \geq p). \qquad (2)$$

Note that the average cost curve is determined by the costs of the sample of individuals who endogenously choose contract H. The marginal (expected) cost curve in the market is given by

$$MC(p) = E(c(\zeta)|\pi(\zeta) = p). \qquad (3)$$

In order to straightforwardly characterize equilibrium, we make two further simplifying assumptions. First, we assume that there exists a price $\bar{p}$ such that $D(\bar{p}) > 0$ and $MC(p) < p$ for every $p > \bar{p}$. In words, we assume that it is profitable (and efficient, as we will see soon) to provide insurance to those with the highest willingness to pay for it. Second, we assume that if there exists $\underline{p}$ such that $MC(\underline{p}) > \underline{p}$ then $MC(p) > p$ for all $p < \underline{p}$. That is, we assume that $MC(p)$ crosses the demand curve at most once. These assumptions guarantee the existence and uniqueness of an equilibrium. In particular, the equilibrium is characterized by the lowest break-even price, that is:

$$p^* = \min\left\{p : p = AC(p)\right\}. \qquad (4)$$

Measuring Welfare. We measure consumer surplus by the certainty equivalent. The certainty equivalent of an uncertain outcome is the amount that would make an individual indifferent between obtaining this amount for sure and obtaining the uncertain outcome. This is an attractive measure of welfare because it is a money metric. Total surplus in the market is the sum of certainty equivalents for consumers and profits of firms. We ignore income effects associated with price changes. Note that price changes have no income effects if the utility function exhibits constant absolute risk aversion (CARA).

Denote by $e^H(\zeta_i)$ and $e^L(\zeta_i)$ the certainty equivalent of consumer i from an allocation of contract H and L, respectively. Under the assumption that all individuals are risk averse, the willingness to pay for insurance is given by $\pi(\zeta_i) = e^H(\zeta_i) - e^L(\zeta_i) > 0$. We can write consumer welfare as

$$CS = \int \left[\left(e^H(\zeta) - p \right) 1 \left(\pi(\zeta) \geq p \right) + e^L(\zeta) 1 \left(\pi(\zeta) < p \right) \right] dG(\zeta) \tag{5}$$

and producer welfare as

$$PS = \int \left(p - c(\zeta) \right) 1 \left(\pi(\zeta) \geq p \right) dG(\zeta). \tag{6}$$

Total welfare is

$$TS = CS + PS = \int \left[\left(e^H(\zeta) - c(\zeta) \right) 1 \left(\pi(\zeta) \geq p \right) + e^L(\zeta) 1 \left(\pi(\zeta) < p \right) \right] dG(\zeta). \tag{7}$$

It is now easy to see that it is socially efficient for individual i to purchase insurance if and only if

$$\pi(\zeta_i) \geq c(\zeta_i). \tag{8}$$

In other words, in a first best allocation individual i purchases insurance if and only if his willingness to pay is at least as great as the expected social cost of providing to him the insurance.

2.1.2. The Textbook Case
2.1.2.1. Adverse Selection Equilibrium

Figure 2 provides a graphical representation of the adverse selection insurance equilibrium for the "textbook case" we have just outlined. The relative price (or cost) of contract H is on the vertical axis. Quantity (i.e., share of individuals in the market with contract H) is on the horizontal axis; the maximum possible quantity is denoted by Q_{max}. The demand curve denotes the relative demand for contract H. Likewise, the average cost (*AC*) curve and marginal cost (*MC*) curve denote the average and marginal *incremental* costs to the insurer from coverage with contract H relative to contract L.

Because agents can only choose whether to purchase the contract or not, the market demand curve simply reflects the cumulative distribution of individuals' willingness to

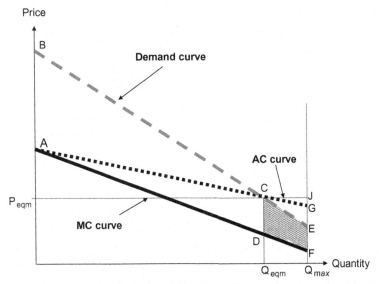

Figure 2 Adverse selection in the textbook setting. *Notes*: Figure 2 shows the demand (willingness-to-pay) for a high coverage *H* relative to a lower coverage contract *L*, and the associated marginal and average incremental cost (i.e., expected insurance claims) curves. The downward sloping marginal cost curve indicates adverse selection. The efficient allocation is for everyone to be covered by *H* (since willingness to pay is always above marginal cost) but the equilibrium allocation covers only those whose willingness to pay is above average costs, creating the classic under insurance result of adverse selection. The welfare loss from this under insurance is given by the trapezoid *CDEF*, representing the excess of demand above marginal cost for those who are not covered by *H* in equilibrium. *(Source: Einav and Finkelstein (2011)).*

pay for the contract. The difference between willingness to pay $\pi(\zeta)$ and $MC(\zeta)$ is the risk premium, and is positive for risk averse individuals.

Because of the "textbook" assumption that individuals are homogeneous in all features of their utility function—i.e., ζ_i includes only characteristics relating to one's expected claims c_i—willingness to pay for insurance is increasing in risk type. This is the key feature of adverse selection: individuals who have the highest willingness to pay for insurance are those who, on average, have the highest expected costs. This is represented in Figure 2 by drawing a downward sloping *MC* curve. That is, marginal cost is increasing in price and decreasing in quantity. As the price falls, the marginal individuals who select contract *H* have lower expected cost than infra-marginal individuals, leading to lower average costs.

The link between the demand and cost curve is arguably the most important distinction of insurance markets (or selection markets more generally) from traditional product markets. The shape of the cost curve is driven by the demand-side consumer selection. In most other contexts, the demand curve and the cost curve are independent objects; demand is determined by preferences and costs by the production technology.

!

The distinguishing feature of selection markets is that the demand and cost curves are tightly linked since the individual's risk type not only affects demand but also directly determines cost.

As noted, the efficient allocation is to insure all individuals whose willingness to pay is at least as great as their expected cost of insuring them. In the textbook case, the risk premium is always positive, since by assumption all individuals are risk averse and there are no other market frictions. As a result, the demand curve is always above the MC curve and, as shown in Figure 2, it is therefore efficient for all individuals to be insured ($Q_{eff} = Q_{max}$). The welfare loss from not insuring a given individual is simply the risk premium of that individual, or the vertical difference between the demand and MC curves.

The essence of the private information problem is that firms cannot charge individuals based on their (privately known) marginal cost, but are instead restricted to charging a uniform price, which in equilibrium implies average cost pricing. Since average costs are always higher than marginal costs, adverse selection creates underinsurance, a familiar result first pointed out by Akerlof (1970). This underinsurance is illustrated in Figure 2. The equilibrium share of individuals who buy contract H is Q_{eqm} (where the AC curve intersects the demand curve), while the efficient number is $Q_{eff} > Q_{eqm}$; in general, the efficient allocation Q_{eff} is determined where the MC curve intersects the demand curve, which in the textbook case is never (unless there are people with risk probability of zero or who are risk neutral). The fundamental inefficiency created by adverse selection arises because the efficient allocation is determined by the relationship between *marginal* cost and demand, but the equilibrium allocation is determined by the relationship between *average* cost and demand.

The welfare loss due to adverse selection arises from the lost consumer surplus (the risk premium) of those individuals who remain inefficiently uninsured in the competitive equilibrium. In Figure 2, these are the individuals whose willingness to pay is less than the average cost of the insured population, P_{eqm}. Integrating over all these individuals' risk premia, the welfare loss from adverse selection is given by the area of the "dead-weight loss" trapezoid $CDEF$.

The amount of underinsurance generated by adverse selection, and its associated welfare loss, can vary greatly in this environment. As illustrated graphically in Einav and Finkelstein (2011), the efficient allocation can be achieved despite a downward sloping marginal cost curve if average costs always lie below demand. In contrast, if average costs always lie above demand, the private market will unravel completely, with no insurance in equilibrium.

2.1.2.2. Public Policy in the Textbook Case

One can use the graphical framework in Figure 2 to evaluate the welfare consequences of common public policy interventions in insurance markets that alter the insurance allocation. The comparative advantage of the public sector over the private sector is that it can directly manipulate either the equilibrium quantity of insurance (through mandates) or the equilibrium price of insurance (through either tax/subsidy policy or regulation of insurance company pricing). We briefly discuss each in turn.

Mandates. The canonical solution to the inefficiency created by adverse selection is to mandate that everyone purchase insurance, a solution emphasized as early as Akerlof (1970). In the textbook setting, mandates produce the efficient outcome in which everyone has insurance. However, the magnitude of the welfare benefit produced by an insurance purchase requirement varies depending on the specifics of the market since, as noted, the amount of underinsurance produced by adverse selection in equilibrium can itself vary greatly.

Tax subsidies. Another commonly discussed policy remedy for adverse selection is to subsidize insurance coverage. Indeed, adverse selection in private health insurance markets is often cited as an economic rationale for the tax subsidy to employer provided health insurance, which is the single largest federal tax expenditure. We can again use Figure 2 to illustrate. Consider, for example, a subsidy toward the price of coverage. This would shift demand out, leading to a higher equilibrium quantity and less underinsurance. The gross welfare loss would still be associated with the area between the original (pre-subsidy) demand curve and the *MC* curve, and would therefore unambiguously decline with any positive subsidy. A large enough subsidy (greater than the line segment *GE* in Figure 2) would lead to the efficient outcome, with everybody insured.

Of course, the net welfare gain from public insurance subsidies will be lower than the gross welfare gain due to the marginal cost of the public funds that must be raised to finance the subsidy; this may be quite large since the subsidy must be paid on all the infra-marginal consumers as well as the marginal ones. Given a non-zero deadweight cost of public funds, the welfare maximizing subsidy would not attempt to achieve the efficient allocation. It is possible that the welfare maximizing subsidy could be zero. That is, starting from the competitive allocation (point *C*), a marginal dollar of subsidy may not be welfare enhancing. Although given the equilibrium distortion the welfare gain will be first order, the welfare cost of raising funds to cover the subsidy is first order as well. Hence, the benefits of subsidies are again an empirical question.

Restrictions on characteristic-based pricing. A final common form of public policy intervention is regulation that imposes restrictions on the characteristics of consumers over which firms can price discriminate. Some regulations require "community rates" that are uniform across all individuals, while others prohibit insurance companies from making prices contingent on certain observable risk factors, such as race or gender. For concreteness, consider the case of a regulation that prohibits pricing on the basis of gender. Recall that Figure 2 can be interpreted as applying to a group of individuals who must be given the same price by the insurance company. When pricing based on gender is prohibited, males and females are pooled into the same market, with a variant of Figure 2 describing that market. When pricing on gender is allowed, there are now two distinct insurance markets—described by two distinct versions of Figure 2—one for women and one for men, each of which can be analyzed separately. A central issue for welfare analysis is whether, when insurance companies are allowed to price on gender, consumers still have residual private information about their expected costs. If they do not, then the insurance market within each gender-specific segment of the market will exhibit a constant (flat) MC curve, and the equilibrium in each market will be efficient. In this case, policies that restrict pricing on gender unambiguously reduce welfare because they create adverse selection where none existed before. However, in the more likely case that individuals have some residual private information about their risk that is not captured by their gender, each gender-specific market segment would look qualitatively the same as Figure 2 (with downward sloping MC and AC curves). In such cases, the welfare implications of restricting pricing on gender could go in either direction. Depending on the shape and position of the gender-specific demand and cost curves relative to the gender-pooled ones, the sum of the areas of the deadweight loss trapezoids in the gender-specific markets could be larger or smaller than the area of the single deadweight loss trapezoid in the gender-pooled market.[3] See Einav and Finkelstein (2011) for a numerical illustrative example.

Comment: Pareto improvements. It is important to note that while various policies may be able to increase efficiency or even produce the efficient outcome—such as mandates—they are not, in this environment, Pareto improving. Consider for concreteness the case of mandates. The insurance provider (be it the government or the private market) must break even in equilibrium, and therefore the cost of providing the insurance must be recouped. The total cost is equal to the market size (Q_{max}) times the average cost of insurance provision to Q_{max} individuals, which is given by point G. Suppose the government uses average cost pricing, effectively issuing a lump sum tax on individuals equal to the average cost of insuring all individuals (given by the vertical distance at point G). While this policy achieves the efficient allocation, those whose willingness to pay is less than the price level at point G are made strictly worse off. Other financing mechanisms may generate welfare gains for a larger set of individuals, but assuming that the government does not observe the private information about individuals' costs, the government—like the private sector—cannot price insurance to individuals based on their (privately known) marginal cost.

The inability for mandates to produce a Pareto improvement are a direct consequence of the Akerlovian modeling framework which has fixed the contract space. Some models that endogenize the contract offers generate Pareto improving mandates (e.g., Wilson, 1977) or Pareto improving tax-transfer schemes (Rothschild & Stiglitz, 1976). Crocker

---

[3] This analysis focuses only on static welfare considerations and ignores the issue of insurance against reclassification risk (e.g., being a sick type, or—behind the veil of ignorance—being born a particular gender), which restrictions on characteristic-based pricing can provide. Bundorf, Levin, and Mahoney (2012) investigate empirically the reclassification risk created by characteristic-based pricing of employer-provided health insurance. Hendel and Lizzeri (2003) examine issues of reclassification risk in the context of life insurance.

and Snow (1985) discuss the assumptions under which the decentralized equilibrium is constrained Pareto efficient in models with endogenous contracts.[4]

2.1.3. Departures from the Textbook Environment: Loads and Preference Heterogeneity

The qualitative findings of the textbook model are unambiguous: private information about risk always produces underinsurance relative to the efficient outcome, and mandating insurance always improves welfare. We now discuss two empirically relevant departures from the textbook environment that change these qualitative findings.

2.1.3.1. Production Costs (Loads)

Consider first the supply-side assumption we made above that the only costs of providing insurance to an individual are the direct insurer claims that are paid out. Many insurance markets show evidence of non-trivial loading factors, including long-term care insurance (Brown & Finkelstein, 2007), annuity markets (Friedman & Warshawsky, 1990; Mitchell, Poterba, Warshawsky, & Brown, 1999; Finkelstein & Poterba, 2002), health insurance (Newhouse, 2002), and automobile insurance (Chiappori, Jullien, Salanié, & Salanié, 2006). While these papers lack the data to distinguish between loading factors arising from administrative costs to the insurance company and those arising from market power (insurance company profits), it seems a reasonable assumption that it is not costless to "produce" insurance and run an insurance company.

We therefore relax the textbook assumption to allow for a loading factor on insurance, for example in the form of administrative costs associated with selling and servicing insurance. In the presence of such loads, it is not necessarily efficient to allocate insurance coverage to all individuals. Even if all individuals are risk averse, the additional cost of providing an individual with insurance may be greater than the risk premium for certain individuals, making it socially efficient to leave such individuals uninsured. This case is illustrated in Figure 3, which is similar to Figure 2, except that the cost curves are shifted upward reflecting the additional cost of insurance provision.

In Figure 3, the MC curve crosses the demand curve at point E, which depicts the socially efficient insurance allocation. It is efficient to insure everyone to the left of point E (since demand exceeds marginal cost), but socially inefficient to insure anyone to the right of point E (since demand is less than marginal cost).

2.1.3.2. Implications for Policy Analysis

The introduction of loads does not affect the basic analysis of adverse selection but it does have important implications for standard public policy remedies. The competitive equilibrium is still determined by the zero profit condition, or the intersection of the

---

[4] All of the models discussed by Crocker and Snow (1985) assume that individuals differ only in their risk type. Allowing for preference heterogeneity as well presumably makes the potential for Pareto improvements more limited.

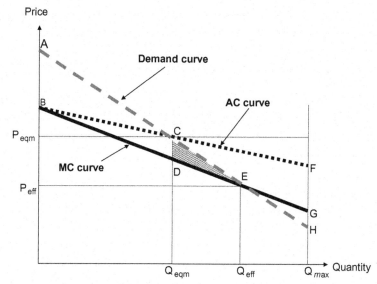

Figure 3 Adverse selection with additional costs of providing insurance. *Notes:* In this departure from the textbook case, we allow for the possibility of a loading factor on the insurance contract *H*. As a result, the marginal cost curve may now intersect the demand curve internally, in which case it is not efficient to cover all individuals with *H*. The efficient allocation is given by point *E* (where demand intersects the marginal cost curve) and the equilibrium allocation is given by point *C* (where demand intersects the average cost curve). Once again there is under insurance due to adverse selection ($Q_{eqm} < Q_{eff}$) and the welfare loss from this under insurance is given by the triangle *CDE*. *(Source: Einav et al. (2010a)).*

demand curve and the AC curve (point C in Figure 3), and in the presence of adverse selection (downward sloping MC curve) this leads to underinsurance relative to the social optimum ($Q_{eqm} < Q_{eff}$), and to a familiar deadweight loss triangle CDE.

However, with insurance loads, the qualitative result in the textbook environment of an unambiguous welfare gain from mandatory coverage no longer obtains. As Figure 3 shows, while a mandate that everyone be insured recoups the welfare loss associated with underinsurance (triangle CDE), it also leads to overinsurance by covering individuals whom it is socially inefficient to insure (that is, whose expected costs are above their willingness to pay). This latter effect leads to a welfare loss given by the area EGH in Figure 3. Therefore whether a mandate improves welfare over the competitive allocation depends on the relative sizes of triangles CDE and EGH. These areas in turn depend on the specific market's demand and cost curves, making the welfare gain of a mandate an empirical question. It may also depend on factors outside of our model—such as the administrative costs of (publicly provided) mandatory insurance relative to private sector competition. Naturally, if government-mandated or provided insurance has lower loads—e.g., because of less spending on marketing—then the welfare gains of a mandate could be larger.

2.1.3.3. Preference Heterogeneity and Advantageous Selection

Our "textbook environment"—like the original seminal papers of Akerlof (1970) and Rothschild and Stiglitz (1976)—assumed that individuals varied only in their risk type. In practice, however, consumers of course may also vary in their preferences. Thus the vector of consumer characteristics ζ_i that affects both willingness to pay $\pi(\zeta_i)$ and expected costs $c(\zeta_i)$ may include consumer preferences as well as risk factors.

Recent empirical work has documented not only the existence of substantial preference heterogeneity over various types of insurance, but the substantively important role of this preference heterogeneity in determining demand. Standard expected utility theory suggests that risk aversion will be important for insurance demand. And indeed, recent empirical evidence suggests that heterogeneity in risk aversion may be as or more important than heterogeneity in risk type in explaining patterns of insurance demand in automobile insurance (Cohen & Einav, 2007) and in long-term care insurance (Finkelstein & McGarry, 2006). In other markets, there is evidence of a role for other types of preferences. For example, in the Medigap market, heterogeneity in cognitive ability appears to be an important determinant of insurance demand (Fang, Keane, & Silverman, 2008); in choosing annuity contracts, preferences for having wealth after death play an important role (Einav, Finkelstein, & Schrimpf, 2010c); in annual health insurance markets, heterogeneity in switching costs can also play an important role in contract demand (Handel, 2011).

Such heterogeneity in preferences can have very important implications for analysis of selection markets. In particular, if preferences are sufficiently important determinants of demand for insurance and sufficiently negatively correlated with risk type, the market can exhibit what has come to be called "advantageous selection."

2.1.3.4. Equilibrium and Public Policy with Advantageous Selection

In our graphical framework, advantageous selection can be characterized by an *upward sloping* marginal cost curve, as shown in Figure 4. This is in contrast to adverse selection, which is defined by a *downward sloping* marginal cost curve.[5] When selection is advantageous, as price is lowered and more individuals opt into the market, the marginal individual opting in has higher expected cost than infra-marginal individuals. Note that preference

---

[5] Allowing for preference heterogeneity can complicate the notion of efficiency since the mapping from expected cost to willingness to pay need no longer be unique. In what follows, when we discuss the "efficient allocation" under preference heterogeneity we are referring to the constrained efficient allocation which is the one that maximizes social welfare subject to the constraint that price is the only instrument available for screening (see Einav et al., 2010a for further discussion).

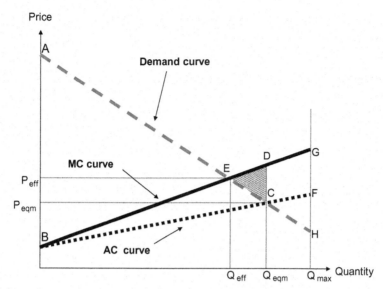

Figure 4 Advantageous selection. *Notes:* Advantageous selection is characterized by an upward slop-ing marginal cost curve. the average cost curve therefore lies below the marginal cost curve, resulting in over insurance relative to the efficient allocation ($Q_{eff} < Q_{eqm}$). The welfare loses from over insur-ance is given by the shaded area *CDE* and represents the excess of marginal cost over willingness to pay for people whose willingness to pay exceed the average costs of those covered by *H*. *(Source: Einav et al. (2010a)).*

heterogeneity is essential for generating these upward sloping cost curves. Without it, willingness to pay must be higher for higher expected cost individuals. Marginal costs must be upward sloping because the individuals with the highest willingness to pay are highest cost.[6]

Since the *MC* curve is upward sloping, the *AC* curve lies everywhere below it. If there were no insurance loads (as in the textbook situation), advantageous selection would not lead to any inefficiency; the *MC* and *AC* curves would always lie below the demand curve, and in equilibrium all individuals in the market would be covered, which would be efficient.

With insurance loads, however, advantageous selection generates the mirror image of the adverse selection case; it also leads to inefficiency, but this time due to *overinsurance* rather than *underinsurance*. This can be seen in Figure 4. The efficient allocation calls for providing insurance to all individuals whose expected cost is lower than their willingness to pay—that is, all those who are to the left of point *E* (where the *MC* curve intersects the demand curve) in Figure 4. Competitive equilibrium, as before, is determined by the intersection of the *AC* curve and the demand curve (point *C* in Figure 4). But since the

---

[6] Once one allows for preference heterogeneity, the marginal cost curve need not be monotone. However for simplicity and clarity we focus on montone cases here.

AC curve now lies below the *MC* curve, equilibrium implies that too many individuals are provided insurance, leading to overinsurance: there are $Q_{eqm} - Q_{eff}$ individuals who are inefficiently provided insurance in equilibrium. These individuals value the insurance at less than their expected costs, but competitive forces make firms reduce the price in order to attract these individuals, simultaneously attracting more profitable infra-marginal individuals. Intuitively, insurance providers have an additional incentive to reduce price, as the infra-marginal customers whom they acquire as a result are relatively good risks. As we discuss below, such advantageous selection is quite important empirically. Cutler, Finkelstein and McGarry (2008) summarize some of the findings regarding the presence of adverse compared to advantageous selection in different insurance markets.

We can characterize the welfare loss from overinsurance due to advantageous selection as above. The resultant welfare loss is given by the shaded area *CDE*, and represents the excess of *MC* over willingness to pay for individuals whose willingness to pay exceeds the average costs of the insured population. Once again, the source of market inefficiency is that consumers vary in their marginal cost, but firms are restricted to uniform pricing.

From a public policy perspective, advantageous selection calls for the opposite solutions relative to the tools used to combat adverse selection. For example, given that advantageous selection produces "too much" insurance relative to the efficient outcome, public policies that tax existing insurance policies (and therefore raise P_{eqm} toward P_{eff}) or outlaw insurance coverage (mandate no coverage) could be welfare improving. Although there are certainly taxes levied on insurance policies, to our knowledge advantageous selection has not yet been invoked as a rationale in public policy discourse, perhaps reflecting the relative newness of both the theoretical work and empirical evidence. To our knowledge, advantageous selection was first discussed by Hemenway (1990), who termed it "propitious" selection. de Meza and Webb (2001) provide a theoretical treatment of advantageous selection and its implications for insurance coverage and public policy.

Advantageous selection provides a nice example of the interplay between theory and empirical work in the selection literature. Motivated by the seminal theoretical papers on adverse selection, empirical researchers set about developing ways to test whether or not adverse selection exists. Some of this empirical work in turn turned up examples of advantageous selection, which the original theory had precluded. This in turn suggested the need for important extensions to the theory.

2.2. Empirical Evidence on Selection

Over the last decade, empirical work on selection in insurance markets has gained considerable momentum, and a fairly extensive and active empirical literature on the topic has emerged. We discuss this literature using the graphical framework described in the previous section. We begin with work designed to test whether or not selection exists in a particular insurance market. Existence of selection is a natural and necessary condition for investigation of its welfare consequences and, not surprisingly, where empirical work started first. We then discuss more recent work designed to empirically quantify the welfare consequences of adverse selection or public policy interventions.

2.2.1. Testing for Selection

As is evident from our graphical framework, adverse selection is defined by a downward sloping marginal cost curve. Testing for adverse selection essentially requires testing whether the marginal cost curve is downward sloping. But making inferences about marginal individuals is difficult. Not surprisingly, initial empirical approaches focused on cases under which one could make inferences simply by comparing average rather than marginal individuals. We begin by discussing these "positive correlation tests." We then move onto a "cost curve test," which has the advantage of being able to make inferences about marginal individuals, but requires more data.

2.2.1.1. Positive Correlation Test for Asymmetric Information

The graphical depiction of adverse selection in Figures 2 and 3 suggests one natural way to test for selection: compare the expected cost of those with insurance to the expected cost of those without. More generally, one can compare the costs of those with more insurance to those with less insurance. If adverse selection is present, the expected costs of those who select more insurance should be larger than the expected costs of those who select less insurance.

Figure 5 illustrates the basic intuition behind the test. Here we start with the adverse selection situation already depicted in Figure 3, denoting the AC curve shown in previous figures by AC^H to reflect the fact that it averages over those individuals with the higher coverage contract, H. We have also added one more line: the AC^L curve. The AC^L curve represents the average expected cost of those individuals who have the lower coverage contract L. That is, the AC^H curve is derived by averaging over the expected costs of those with H coverage (integrating from $Q = 0$ to a given quantity Q) while the AC^L curve is produced by averaging over the expected costs of those with L coverage (integrating from the given quantity to $Q = Q_{\max}$).

A downward sloping MC curve—i.e., the existence of adverse selection—implies that AC^H is always above AC^L. Thus, at any given insurance price, and in particular at the equilibrium price, adverse selection implies that the average cost of individuals with more insurance is higher than the average cost of those with less insurance. The difference in these averages is given by line segment CF in Figure 5 (the thick arrowed line in the figure). This basic insight underlies the widely used "positive correlation" test for asymmetric information. The positive correlation test amounts to testing if point C (average costs of those who in equilibrium are insured) is significantly above point F (average costs of those who in equilibrium are not insured).

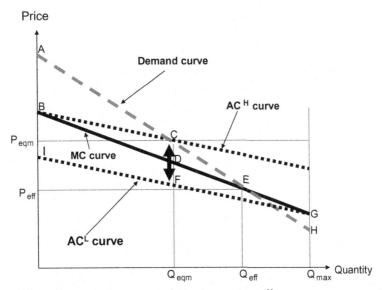

Figure 5 The "positive correlation" test for selection. *Notes: AC^H* denotes the *AC* curve shown in previous figures (i.e., average costs of those with the higher coverage contract *H*. The *AC^L* curve represents the average costs of those with the lower coverage contract *L*. The difference in the average costs of those with more and less insurance in equilibrium is given by the line segment *CF*. The positive correlation test for asymmetric information tests whether average costs of those who in equilibrium have more insurance (point *C*) are above average costs of those who in equilibrium have less insurance (point *F*). *(Source: Einav and Finkelstein (2011))*.

   Chiappori and Salanie (2000) formalized this intuition and emphasized that the basic approach requires some refinement because it does not clearly differentiate between individual characteristics that are observable and those that are not.[7] In particular, one must stratify on the consumer characteristics that determine the contract menu offered to each individual. Implementing the positive correlation test requires that we examine whether, among a set of individuals who are offered the same coverage options at identical prices, those who buy more insurance have higher expected costs than those who do not. In the absence of such conditioning, it is impossible to know whether a correlation arises due to demand (different individuals self select into different contracts) or supply (different individuals are offered the contracts at different prices by the insurance company). Only the former is evidence of selection. As a result, some of the most convincing tests are those carried out using insurance company data, where the researcher knows the full set of characteristics that the insurance company uses for pricing. Absent data on individually

---

[7] Variants of this idea have been discussed in earlier work as well. For instance, Glied (2000) and Cutler and Zeckhauser (2000) summarize attempts to identify risk-based sorting in health insurance choice, where instead of directly comparing claims or "accidents" across individuals with different insurance coverage, the comparison is made over a particular individual characteristic thought to be associated with higher claims, such as age or chronic illness.

customized prices, which are sometimes difficult to obtain, one may instead try to flexibly control for all individual characteristics that affect pricing.

Chiappori and Salanie's work has led to a large literature studying how average costs vary across different coverage options in several insurance markets, including health, life, automobile, and homeowners insurance. The widespread application of the test in part reflects its relatively minimal data requirements. The test requires that one observe the average expected costs of individuals (who are observationally identical to the firm) with different amounts of insurance coverage.

A central limitation in interpreting the results of the positive correlation test is that it is a joint test of the presence of either adverse selection or moral hazard. Even in the absence of selection (i.e., a flat marginal cost curve), moral hazard (loosely, an impact of the insurance contract on expected claims) can produce the same "positive correlation" property of those with more insurance having higher claims than those without. Intuitively, individuals with more generous insurance coverage may choose to utilize more services simply because their marginal out-of-pocket cost is lower. These two very different forms of asymmetric information have very different public policy implications. In particular, in contrast to the selection case where government intervention could potentially raise welfare, the social planner generally has no comparative advantage over the private sector in ameliorating moral hazard (i.e., in encouraging individuals to choose socially optimal behavior). Thus distinguishing between adverse selection and moral hazard is crucial.[8]

2.2.1.2. Cost Curve Test of Selection

Faced with the challenge of how to interpret the results of the correlation test, researchers have taken a variety of approaches. One is to test for selection in insurance markets where moral hazard is arguably less of a concern, such as annuity markets. More generally, researchers have used experimental or quasi-experimental variation in prices that consumers face to try to separate selection from moral hazard (see e.g., Abbring, Chiappori, & Pinquet, 2003a; Abbring, Heckman, Chiappori, & Pinquet, 2003b; Adams, Einav, & Levin, 2009; Cutler & Reber, 1998; Einav et al. (2010a); Karlan & Zinman, 2009).

---

[8] If one finds convincing evidence of a negative correlation between insurance coverage and expected claims, this is arguably more informative, as it is consistent with advantageous selection, even in the presence of moral hazard. This is the approach taken by Fang et al. (2008) who document a negative correlation between insurance and claims in the Medigap market, thus pointing to the existence of *advantageous selection* in this market. When a positive correlation is found however—as is the case in many of the papers reviewed by Cohen and Siegelman (2010)—further work is needed to determine whether the results are driven by adverse selection, or by moral hazard (perhaps combined even with advantageous selection). Another vexing case occurs when one is unable to reject the null of no correlation between insurance coverage and expected claims in the market, as in Chiappori and Salanie (2000) or Finkelstein and McGarry (2006). Such a finding is consistent with symmetric information or with the presence of offsetting advantageous selection and moral hazard. Even if moral hazard is ruled out, the inability to reject the null of no correlation could reflect the presence of multiple forms of private information acting in offsetting directions, as Finkelstein and McGarry (2006) find to be the case in the US market for long-term care insurance.

The intuition for how pricing variation that is exogenous to demand (and hence by definition to costs since demand depends on expected costs) allows one to separate selection from moral hazard is easily seen in our simple graphical framework. Consider an experiment that randomly varies the relative price at which the H contract is offered (relative to the L contract) to large pools of otherwise identical individuals. For each relative price, we observe the fraction of individuals who bought contract H and the average realized costs of the individuals who bought contract H.[9] We thus can trace out the demand curve as well as the average cost curve in Figure 3. From these two curves, the marginal cost curve is easily derived. Total costs are the product of average costs and demand (quantity), and marginal costs are the derivative of total cost with respect to quantity. The features of the marginal cost curve then provide direct evidence on selection. Specifically, rejecting the null hypothesis of a constant marginal cost curve is equivalent to rejecting the null of no selection. Moreover, the sign of the slope of the estimated marginal cost curve informs us of the nature of any selection. A downward sloping marginal cost curve (i.e., a cost curve declining in quantity and increasing in price) indicates adverse selection, while an upward sloping curve indicates advantageous selection. Einav et al. (2010a) develop and discuss in more detail this "cost curve" test of selection.

Crucially, this "cost curve" test of selection is unaffected by moral hazard. Conceptually, variation in prices for a fixed contract allows us to distinguish selection from moral hazard. To see this, recall that the AC curve is estimated using the sample of individuals who choose to buy contract H at a given price. As prices change, the sample changes, but everyone always has the same coverage. Because the coverage of individuals in the sample is fixed, the estimate of the slope of the cost curve is not affected by moral hazard, which only affects costs when coverage changes.[10]

2.2.2. Evidence on Selection

There is now a large body of empirical work testing for selection in many different insurance markets. The results of this empirical literature have been mixed. In some markets, researchers have found evidence consistent with adverse selection—that is, higher average costs for individuals with greater insurance coverage—while in others they have found evidence of advantageous selection—defined by a negative relationship between insurance coverage and average costs—or have been unable to reject the null of symmetric

---

[9] When the L contract is no coverage, the average realized costs of individuals who bought contract H are simply the average claims paid out for people who have contract H. When the L contract involves some (lower) coverage amount, then we measure the average *incremental* claims for those with policy H, or, in other words, the average additional claims that insurance policy H would have to pay out beyond what policy L would pay out, for the accident occurrences of those who have policy H.

[10] Of course, it is possible that the moral hazard effect of insurance is greater for some individuals than others and that, anticipating this, individuals whose behavior is more responsive to insurance may be more likely to buy insurance. We should still view this as selection, however, in the sense that individuals are selecting insurance on the basis of their anticipated behavioral response to it. Einav, Finkelstein, Ryan, Schrimpf and Cullen (2011) provide empirical evidence of such "selection on moral hazard."

information, meaning no difference in average costs. Cohen and Siegelman (2010) provide a comprehensive review of this work. We focus instead on characterizing the literature as it pertains to markets with significant social insurance, such as old age assistance and health insurance. Our reading of the evidence for these two markets is that there is very clear evidence of selection in these markets.

2.2.2.1. Annuities

In return for an up-front lump sum premium, annuities provide an individual with a survival-contingent income stream. They therefore offer a way for a retiree facing stochastic mortality to increase welfare by spreading an accumulated stock of resources over a retirement period of uncertain length (Davidoff, Brown, & Diamond, 2005; Yaari, 1965). Yet private annuity markets remain quite small. As a result, annuities have attracted a great deal of interest in discussions involving the design and reform of public pensions. Many of these public pension systems, including the current US Social Security System, provide benefits in the form of mandatory, publicly provided annuities. A major economic rationale for this form of benefit provision is the potential for adverse selection to undermine the functioning of private annuity markets, making it important to determine whether selection actually exists in these markets.

Several studies have implemented variants of the positive correlation test for selection in annuity markets. In the context of annuities, higher risk (i.e., higher expected claim) individuals are the ones who are longer lived than expected; adverse selection therefore is expected to generate a positive correlation between annuitization and survival. Results from a number of studies all point to evidence of a positive correlation in annuity markets on both the extensive margin—individuals who purchase annuities tend to be longer lived than those who do not—and on the intensive (i.e., contract feature) margin—individuals who purchase annuity contracts with shorter gaurantee periods tend to be longer lived than those who purchase less. These findings obtain conditional on the characteristics of individuals used to price annuities, namely age and gender. The positive correlation has been documented in several countries including the United States (Mitchell et al., 1999), the United Kingdom (Finkelstein & Poterba, 2002, 2004, 2006), and in Japan (McCarthy & Mitchell, 2003).

In the case of annuities, it may be reasonable to assume that annuitization does not induce large behavioral effects. Indeed, work in this literature tends to assume that moral hazard—an impact of income in the form of an annuity on the length of life—is likely to be quantitatively negligible even though theoretically possible (see Philipson & Becker, 1998). As a result, evidence of a positive correlation between annuitization and survival can be interpreted as clear evidence of adverse selection in this market (Finkelstein & Poterba, 2004). Finkelstein and Poterba's (2004) empirical findings also illustrate how selection may occur not only along the dimension of the amount of payment in the event the insured risk occurs, but also in the form of selection on different insurance instruments, such as the length of a guarantee period during which payments are not survival-contingent; see Sheshinski (2008) for a theoretical discussion of this point.

2.2.2.2. Health Insurance

Cutler and Zeckhauser (2000) review a large literature that tends to find a positive correlation between insurance coverage and risk occurrence in health insurance. Conditional on the menu of contracts offered to them, individuals with more health insurance tend to have higher medical spending than individuals with less insurance. This literature provides a nice example of the substantive importance of conditioning on the observable characteristics of the individual that determine the menu of contracts offered to him, as emphasized by Chiappori and Salanie (2000). In particular, since employer offering of health insurance is such a major determinant of coverage, some of the most convincing implementations of the positive correlation test compare health insurance coverage and medical spending among individuals within the same employer, who therefore all face the same option set. Indeed, without such conditioning, one can get the opposite result suggesting that the insured have lower medical spending than the uninsured, driven by the difference in who is offered health insurance.

In the case of health insurance, the potential moral hazard effects are non-negligible. There is compelling evidence—including results from randomized trials (Finkelstein et al., 2011; Newhouse & RAND Corporation, 1996)—that health insurance has a causal effect on medical spending. As a result, the large body of evidence on the "positive correlation" property in health insurance suggests that asymmetric information exists in health insurance, but does not itself provide direct evidence of selection.

The task of trying to separate selection from treatment effects is greatly aided by the availability of variation in the offered contracts that is uncorrelated with demand. Arguably the most compelling evidence of adverse selection in health insurance markets comes from observing "death spirals" brought about by changes in the contract set. For example, Cutler and Reber (1998) examine the response to a change in health insurance pricing at Harvard University that required employees to pay more on the margin for more comprehensive coverage. The introduction of this pricing change was staggered over time across different employees. They document a death spiral dynamic whereby the pricing change produced a decline in enrollment in the more comprehensive plan that was particularly concentrated among lower cost (specifically, younger) employees. This prompted a further price increase in the more comprehensive plan to prevent it from losing money, which in turn prompted further exit by disproportionately younger individuals. More recently, Einav et al. (2010a) implemented the "cost curve" test for selection using data from a large firm and variation across employees within the firm in the relative price they faced for more comprehensive coverage. They estimate a downward sloping marginal cost curve, providing direct evidence of selection distinct from moral hazard.

We conclude that in the market for acute medical insurance in the United States, there seems to be compelling evidence of the presence of adverse selection. The findings in two other health insurance markets—specifically Medigap and long-term care insurance—are more mixed. While there is compelling evidence of private information in these markets, the evidence suggests that the resulting selection is advantageous rather than adverse (Fang et al., 2008; Finkelstein & McGarry, 2006; Oster, Shoulson, Quaid, & Dorsey, 2010).

2.2.2.3. Disability Insurance, Unemployment Insurance, and Worker's Compensation

In contrast to the study of selection in annuity and health insurance markets there is, to our knowledge, a dearth of work on adverse selection in several settings where there are important social insurance programs including disability insurance, unemployment insurance, and worker's compensation.[11] It would be interesting to test for selection in these markets, although the lack of a robust private market for these risks makes it much more challenging to implement the tests described above. To make progress, one would need to develop tests that—unlike the existing positive correlation or cost curve tests—do not require observing individual choices. In this respect, Hendren's (2012) development of a method for characterizing the distribution of private information in a market where trade is not observed likely represents an important step forward for empirically based estimates of private information in non-existent or virtually non-existent markets. He develops a method to infer agents' private information based on subjective probability elicitations which he models as noisy measures of their beliefs. His results provide, among other things, the first evidence of private information about risk type in the disability insurance setting.

2.2.3. Welfare Consequences

The tests for asymmetric information described above are relatively uninformative about the welfare impacts of interventions. Markets that appear to be "more adversely selected" by the positive correlation metric—i.e., in which there are larger differences between the expected costs of the insured and uninsured—are not necessarily ones in which there is a greater welfare cost imposed by that selection. Einav and Finkelstein (2011) provide a graphical illustration of this point. Intuitively, the degree of positive correlation is a statement about the shape of the cost curves in e.g., Figure 3 or 5. However, the welfare cost of adverse selection—i.e., the magnitude of the "deadweight loss triangle" CDE depends not only on the shape of the cost curve but also on that of the demand curve.

This problem has motivated recent empirical work that quantifies the welfare losses from asymmetric information and the potential impact of government policies such as mandates, pricing restrictions, and taxes. Conceptually, one must estimate both the

---

[11] Hendren (2011) is a notable exception that tests for and detects evidence of private information in disability and unemployment insurance markets.

demand and marginal cost curve to pin down the welfare cost of adverse selection. Once these have been estimated, one can identify the efficient allocation and compare it to alternative allocations induced by various government policies.

Abstractly, there are two approaches one can take to recovering the demand and marginal cost curves. The first is to estimate these curves directly without estimating the underlying primitives that generated these curves. It might be usefully called a "plan valuation" approach and is similar in approach to traditional discrete choice demand analysis. Einav et al. (2010a) develop and implement such an approach to estimating the welfare cost of selection. They show that the demand and cost curves shown in the prior figures are sufficient statistics for welfare analysis of equilibrium and non-equilibrium pricing of existing contracts. That is, different underlying primitives (i.e., preferences and private information as summarized by ζ) have the same welfare implications if they generate the same demand and cost curves. As a result, the identifying variation used to trace out the demand and cost curves for the "cost curve" test of selection provides the estimates needed to estimate the welfare cost of adverse selection (triangle CDE in Figure 3).

Einav, Finkelstein, and Cullen's approach to estimating welfare is attractive for its transparency and its reduced reliance on assumptions about consumer preferences or the nature of their ex-ante information. Moreover, it is relatively straightforward to implement in terms of data requirements. Data on costs and quantities in insurance markets are relatively easy to obtain—as evidenced by the widespread application of the "positive correlation" test which requires both of these data elements. The key additional data requirement is exogenous price variation. While naturally more challenging to obtain, the near-ubiquitous regulation of insurance markets offers many potential opportunities to isolate such variation.

A major limitation of this approach, however, is that the analysis of the welfare cost of adverse selection is limited to the cost associated with inefficient pricing of a fixed (and observed) set of contracts. It does not capture the welfare loss that adverse selection may create by distorting the set of contracts offered, which in many settings could be the primary welfare cost of adverse selection. Intuitively, in order to analyze the welfare effects of introducing contracts not observed in the data, one needs a model of the deeper primitives (ζ_i).

This limitation partly motivates the second approach that researchers have taken to estimating the welfare costs of selection, which is to directly estimate these primitives and then simulate the welfare cost of alternative policies. For example, Einav et al. (2010c) estimate a model of demand for annuities in which the utility from different annuity contracts depends on underlying consumer primitives (ζ_i). Specifically, they examine the semi-compulsory market for annuities in the United Kingdom in which individuals who have saved for retirement through certain tax preferred retirement vehicles are required to annuitize their savings but face a choice over some of the contract features. They focus on the choice of "gaurantee period," the number of years in which the annuity is guaranteed to pay out even if one has already died. The demand for guarantees depends on both indivdiuals' unobserved risk type (i.e., survival probability) and unobserved preferences (i.e., for wealth when alive relative to wealth after death). All else equal, longer guarantee periods are more attractive both to individuals who believe they have high mortality and to individuals who have a greater value for wealth after death. Using the model, together with individual-level data on annuity choices and ex-post survival length, they recover the joint distribution of survival types and preferences for wealth after death. Unlike the plan valuation approach, this realized utility approach allows recovery of the underlying consumer primitives (ζ_i).

Einav, Finkelstein, and Levin (2010b) provide more discussion of these two different approaches and their relative attractions. Broadly speaking, the choice between the realized utility approach and plan valuation approaches involves a standard tradeoff. The realized utility approach requires stronger assumptions about how consumers derive value from insurance, but allows the researcher to use the resulting estimates to (at least in principle) examine counterfactual allocations that are much further from the observed data.[12] For instance, papers that model realized utility directly as a function of individual primitives such as risk aversion and beliefs about risk type are able in principle to analyze choice and welfare over contracts that vary over dimensions over which one observes no heterogeneity in the data. The papers by Cardon and Hendel (2001), Cohen and Einav (2007), Einav et al. (2010c), and Einav et al. (2011) are examples in this vein.

The plan valuation approach requires weaker assumptions but commensurately limits the type of analysis one can do. At one extreme, the approach taken by Einav et al. (2010a) recovers the willingness to pay for one health plan over another, but provides no information on the characteristics of the plan determining that valuation. With this approach, inferences about contracts that are not observed in the data are not feasible. Other papers in this literature analyze valuation of contracts as a function of plan and individual characteristics, making it feasible to extrapolate to contracts not observed provided that the model's assumptions are accurate outside the estimation sample. Examples in this vein include Carlin and Town (2010) and Lustig (2011).

2.2.3.1. Estimates of Welfare Costs of Selection

Relative to the literature discussed earlier that tests for the existence of selection, there has been substantially less empirical work attempting to estimate the welfare costs of selection. The work that has been done to date has focused on the welfare cost of selection in the health insurance market for acute medical expenses or the market for annuities. The empirical estimates of the welfare cost of selection have consistently tended to be a few percent of premia, bounding the potential welfare gains from policy interventions that

---

[12] An additional attraction of this approach is that it recovers primitives that may be of inherent interest for other reasons, such as estimates of the distribution of risk aversion in the population.

aim to address selection at relatively low levels. This is true both in the insurance markets for acute medical expenses (see e.g., Cutler & Reber, 1998; Carlin & Town, 2010; Einav et al., 2010a, 2011; Handel, 2011; Lustig, 2011) as well as annuity markets (Einav et al., 2010c). However, as emphasized above and as we return to below, virtually all of these papers have studied only the welfare cost of selection arising from inefficient pricing of a given set of contracts, and have not investigated the potentially much larger welfare losses arising from selection limiting the set of contracts offered or, in the extreme, causing a market to unravel completely.

2.2.3.2. Welfare Consequences of Public Policy Interventions

Beyond estimating the welfare cost of selection, several papers have analyzed the welfare consequences of alternative public policy interventions. A recurring theme of this empirical work is that—as indicated by the stylized model we began with—the welfare consequences of "textbook" public policy interventions are not as straightforward as the simple theory suggests.

For example, recent work on mandatory insurance—perhaps the canonical public policy response to selection—has failed to find welfare improvements from the set of mandates considered (Einav et al., 2010a). Other work has concluded that while the optimal mandate would be welfare improving, it is difficult to determine which mandate would raise welfare with preference heterogeneity and some types of mandates may actually reduce welfare (Einav et al., 2010c).

Another focus of the literature has been on the welfare consequences of regulating the characteristics of consumers that can be used in pricing insurance contracts. Bundorf et al. (2012) emphasize that in the presence of heterogeneity in preferences for coverage that is not perfectly correlated with risk, uniform pricing of contracts across consumers of different risk types cannot induce efficient consumer choice. This creates scope for welfare improvements through characteristic-based pricing, often known as "risk adjustment." In their empirical application, which uses data on employer-provided health insurance at several firms, they estimate that the welfare gains from feasible risk adjustment turn out to be relatively modest. In a similar spirit, Geruso (2011) empirically explores the potential welfare gains from age-adjusted pricing in a different employer-provided health insurance context. Focusing instead on distributional impacts, Finkelstein, Poterba, and Rothschild (2009b) calibrate a stylized equilibrium screening model of annuities to investigate the impact of banning gender-based pricing in a compulsory annuity market; they find that the redistribution inherent in requiring unisex pricing can be greatly undone by equilibrium adjustment of annuity contracts to the restricted pricing regime.

Other work, focusing once again on health insurance, has examined the implications of pricing restrictions for insurance coverage and government expenditures. Empirical examinations of restrictions on characteristic-based pricing, such as community rating in the small group and non-group health insurance markets have shown that such regulations can reduce coverage among lower risk individuals (e.g., Buchmueller & DiNardo, 2002; Bundorf & Simon, 2006; Simon, 2005). Examining risk adjustment in Medicare Advantage plans, where the government is the insurer, Brown, Duggan, Kuziemko, and Woolston (2011) conclude that more detailed pricing on consumer characteristics can exacerbate, rather than ameliorate, the selection problem as defined with respect to government expenditures. The intuition stems from the fact that the variance of medical spending is increasing with its mean. More detailed risk adjustment—which puts consumers into finer pricing "bins" on the basis of their expected health care costs—results in higher dispersion in the high expected spending bins than in the overall pool, increasing the incentives for an insurer to invest in cream skimming within the finer risk classifications.[13]

2.2.3.3. Welfare Consequences with Multiple Imperfections

Another interesting vein of this literature has investigated how adverse selection impacts welfare in the presence of other market imperfections. When selection is the only departure from the perfectly competitive neoclassical benchmark, eliminating private information is always welfare improving. This need not be the case when there are multiple frictions. For example, Starc (2011) discusses how, when firms have market power, moving from symmetric information to asymmetric information can improve consumer welfare. Intuitively, when firms have market power, prices are inefficiently high. Adverse selection reduces the incentive for firms to mark up prices because the marginal consumers they lose when they raise prices have lower costs (and thus are higher profits) than the infra-marginal ones that they retain. In a similar spirit, Handel (2011) demonstrates how in the presence of adverse selection, switching costs that reduce consumer response to changes in plan pricing can be welfare increasing by blunting the selection pressures that would otherwise operate.

Measuring the welfare costs of selection is also more complicated in models with additional imperfections. Spinnewijn (2012) shows that calculations based on revealed preference—as in Einav et al. (2010a)—may understate the welfare costs of adverse selection in the presence of frictions such as misperception of risks or adjustment costs. Intuitively, such frictions create a wedge between the revealed demand for insurance via the demand curve and the actual value of insurance. As a result, the demand curve overstates the surplus from insurance for those who buy insurance (because some who purchased do not truly value insurance above cost) and understates it for those who do not (because some who do not purchase should have purchased).

---

[13] Brown et al. (2011) provide a helpful example to illustrate this intuition: "pre-risk adjustment, Hispanics were roughly $800 cheaper than their (non-risk adjusted) capitation payments; after risk adjustment, Hispanics with a history of congestive heart failure (one of the most common conditions included in the risk formula) are $4000 cheaper than their (risk adjusted) capitation payment" (page 3). As a result, the incentive of the insurer to try to recruit Hispanics into plans is much higher when plans are reimbursed differently on the basis of whether the individual has a history of congestive heart failure."

More generally, though the graphical framework developed above assumes perfect competition among insurers, one can generalize the welfare analysis to any other *given* model of the insurance market as long as one can solve for the equilibrium allocation. Lustig (2011), for example, examines the welfare cost of adverse selection in Medicare Advantage, allowing for imperfect competition on the supply side.

2.2.4. Directions for Future Work

Most of the empirical papers to date on welfare in insurance markets have taken the relatively narrow (albeit practical) approach of focusing on the welfare costs associated with the pricing distortions selection induces in insurance markets. In general, these papers have concluded that, defined in this way, the welfare costs of selection are relatively small. One limitation to this work, discussed above, is that it analyzes adverse selection in the absence of other potential frictions, which can be important for both the sign and magnitude of the welfare costs of selection. In addition, in at least two important respects, the existing work may be missing important potential welfare consequences of selection or of government intervention. These omissions highlight both the challenges and opportunities for further empirical work.

First, most of the existing empirical welfare analysis has abstracted from a potentially more significant welfare cost of selection that could arise from distortions in the set of contracts offered. Selection may result in certain types of coverage not being available, as in the classic Akerlof (1970) unraveling of a market, and the welfare costs of the disappearance of certain contracts is potentially much larger than the welfare costs of pricing distortions of the contracts that do exist. The ability to make empirically based estimates of the welfare cost of selection via selection's effect on the set of contracts offered remains a very important area for future work.

There are several challenges inherent in any such attempts. One is that although in principle estimates from realized utility models can use the recovered primitives to say something about the welfare consequences of offering contracts not observed in the data, researchers have been (reasonably) wary of using the estimates of such models to say much about contracts that are too far from the observed contracts. Another challenge stems from the supply side task of trying to characterize the counterfactual equilibrium for unobserved contracts; as discussed by Einav et al. (2010b), this can be particularly challenging when allowing for realistic consumer heterogeneity as well as imperfect competition.

Even more challenging is empirical work in markets that have almost or completely unraveled, yet it may be that these markets are precisely where the welfare costs of selection are largest; in other words, the "lamp post problem" of empirical work gravitating to markets for which there are data and dimensions of coverage along which there is observed variation may be one reason that existing papers have found relatively small welfare losses.

A few recent papers have used calibration exercises to try to investigate the value of insurance in markets that are virtually non-existent; examples include the market for annuities (Hosseini, 2010), long-term care insurance (Brown & Finkelstein, 2008), and high deductible health insurance (Mahoney, 2012). Such exercises require that the researchers make assumptions about the population distribution of certain primitives such as risk aversion and risk type, which are often based on estimates made in other, thicker markets. As noted, Hendren (2011) makes important progress in empirically characterizing the distribution of private information in markets where trade does not occur. More work is needed in this area so that researchers may be equipped to examine the counterfactual functioning of private insurance markets that currently do not exist but where we have important social insurance programs such as unemployment insurance, worker's compensation, and disability insurance.

Second, existing empirical work has focused on testing for the presence of selection and examining its welfare consequences *given the existing public policies,* such as tax subsidies to employer-provided health insurance or publicly provided annuities through Social Security. This raises the question of whether selection would exist—and what its welfare consequences would be—in the absence of these public programs or under very different public programs than we currently have. Theoretically, it is not clear whether or when government intervention mitigates or exacerbates selection. For example, as discussed earlier, regulatory restrictions on the consumer characteristics insurance companies may use in setting pricing may potentially increase or decrease the welfare costs of selection in the private market. As another example, the impact of mandatory, partial social insurance (such as Medicare which covers some but not all medical expenses or Social Security which provides partial annuitization) on adverse selection in the residual private market for insurance is theoretically ambiguous. Under different assumptions regarding the ability to offer exclusive contracts, Abel (1986) finds that partial public annuities provided by Social Security exacerbates adverse selection pressures in the residual private market while Eckstein, Eichenbaum, and Peled (1985) document a potential welfare enhancing role for partial public annuities. Empirically, we know little about whether the existing partial public insurance programs such as Medicare and Social Security have exacerbated or ameliorated adverse selection problems in the residual private markets for the elderly for health insurance (Medigap) and annuities. Finkelstein (2004) attempts to try to begin to examine such questions empirically. The recent introduction of Medicare Part D, which covers some but not all prescription drug expenses, may provide a fruitful opportunity for empirical work on this question.

2.3. Other Motivations

Following much of the recent literature, we have concentrated our discussion above on asymmetric information as a motive for social insurance.[14] This recent focus should not

---

[14] We focused on adverse selection and not moral hazard since, as previously noted, moral hazard is in general not an area where the public sector has a comparative advantage over the private sector in redressing market failure.

be interpreted as a reflection of a conclusion that selection is the important rationale for social insurance. Here, we briefly summarize several other potential rationales for social insurance. Many of these are ripe for empirical work quantifying their importance.

Incomplete Contracts. Private insurance contracts can only insure risks which are realized after birth, as one cannot write contracts behind the Rawlsian veil of ignorance. Social insurance programs can address this problem by redistributing across individuals born with different endowments (e.g., of skills or health). The ability of social insurance to insure risks realized at or before birth might explain why most developed countries—including the United States in the near future—provide or mandate universal health insurance. Social insurance for risks behind the veil of ignorance is formally analogous to optimal taxation and hence we do not treat it further here; see the chapter by Piketty and Saez in this volume for a review of this literature.

Aggregate Risks. Some risks represent aggregate shocks for which the private insurance market's ability to diversify the risk cross-sectionally may be impaired. By contrast, the government may be able to spread such risk intergenerationally. This may suggest a welfare-improving role for social insurance against such correlated risks as aggregate unemployment shocks, natural disasters, changes in population life expectancy, or technological change in medicine.

An interesting vein of this literature has investigated why such aggregate shocks cannot instead be effectively diversified—and thus insured—intertemporally through private capital markets. In the context of catastrophe risk (e.g., hurricanes and earthquakes), Froot (2001) discusses a variety of possible demand-side and supply-side explanations for why in practice the role of capital markets in reinsuring these risks appears to be limited and prices appear to be high. He also reviews the available evidence for each hypothesis. Demand-side explanations include agency issues with insurance company managers who do not value protection for policyholders against extremely high losses if the protection does not avoid default by the firm, ex-post intervention by third parties such as the Federal Emergency Management Agency (FEMA) that substitute for insurance, and optimization failures. Supply side explanations include potential market failures such as adverse selection and moral hazard, firm market power, capital market imperfections that restrict the supply of reinsurance, and high transaction costs.

A related set of issues for private insurance concerns aggregate uncertainty. On the supply-side, it may be difficult for would be providers to offer insurance against risks with considerable parameter uncertainty; terrorism risk insurance is an example of where this issue may be important (e.g., Brown, Kroszner, & Jenn, 2002). On the demand-side, aggregate uncertainty may reduce demand for long-term insurance contracts against future risk. For example, Brown and Finkelstein (2011) conjecture that aggregate uncertainty regarding future policy and the survivorship of private insurance companies may depress demand among prime age adults for long-term care insurance that would cover nursing and home health costs in old age.

Externalities. Externalities from insurance constitute another potential rationale for government intervention. One possibility is physical externalities, particularly in the case of health insurance, which subsidizes the treatment or prevention of infectious disease.[15] Another is the possibility of fiscal externalities stemming from the Samaritan's dilemma (Buchanan, 1975). If an altruistic society will provide charitable assistance to those experiencing adverse events ex-post, this can reduce individuals' incentives to purchase insurance ex-ante. Coate (1995) demonstrates that the optimal transfer policy therefore involves in-kind transfers of insurance to address the inefficient underinsurance that arises in response to unconditional transfers. Ex-post unconditional public transfers are frequently observed in the context of health, natural disasters, and terrorism and thus may deter ex-ante insurance purchases in these markets to some extent. In health insurance, researchers have documented the relationship between charity care and private insurance coverage (e.g., Herring, 2005) and the role of bankruptcy protection in reducing demand for high deductible health insurance (Mahoney, 2012). However, we have little evidence on the overall importance of the Samaritan's dilemma effects as a motive for social insurance.

Optimization Failures. Another class of motivations for social insurance is a paternalistic motive premised on imperfect optimization in individual insurance purchases. There is considerable evidence that individuals do not adhere to the lifecycle expected utility model underlying traditional models of risk and insurance. For instance, demand for insurance that covers very small risks with high loads—such as toaster warranties, flight insurance, or homeowners insurance deductibles (e.g., Sydnor, 2010)—implies levels of risk aversion that are inconsistent with expected utility theory (Rabin, 2000). Barseghyan, Molinari, O'Donoghue, and Teitelbaum (2012) argue that this excess demand for low deductibles is explained by misperceptions of loss probabilities. The lack of demand for other types of insurance such as annuities is also difficult to explain in neoclassical models (e.g., Davidoff et al., 2005).

In the context of Medicare Part D—the 2006 addition to the Medicare program that allows individuals to choose a subsidized prescription drug plan—there is also evidence that individuals make suboptimal choices in choosing not just the level but also the characteristics of insurance coverage. Abaluck and Gruber (2011) argue that many individuals choose suboptimal drug insurance plans in the Medicare Part D program given the risks they face. Kling, Mullainathan, Shafir, Vermeulen, and Wrobel (2012) implement a field experiment which suggests that these suboptimal choices in drug insurance plans are due to "comparison frictions"—difficulty for consumers in using available information about plan features to make choices. These are just some examples from a vast literature in psychology and economics that has documented that individuals are prone to various biases such as impatience, loss aversion, overconfidence, and inattention.

---

[15] Physical externalities may be substantial in some cases; in a developing country context, recent work has documented the enormous social returns in both the short and longer run to the subsidized de-worming of children (Baird, Hicks, Kremer, & Miguel, 2011; Kremer & Miguel, 2004).

The need to account for such biases is especially evident in dynamic models of temporary shocks such as unemployment. As we discuss below, unemployment shocks are quite costly as judged by ex-post measures of consumption smoothing or liquidity effects. Given these costs, rational agents would build up buffer stocks to help cushion temporary shocks (Carroll, 1997; Deaton, 1991). But in practice, most individuals build very limited buffer stocks. The median job loser has less than $200 in liquid assets at the beginning of his unemployment spell (Chetty, 2008).[16] Thus, it is difficult to reconcile the ex-post costs of shocks with optimizing behavior even in an environment without any private insurance markets, because self insurance would be adequate to smooth most temporary shocks.[17] Indeed, Lucas (1987) calculates that optimizing agents would pay less than 1% of lifetime consumption to entirely eliminate business cycle fluctuations even without any private insurance. Hence, the role for social insurance against temporary shocks is quite limited in optimizing models. This suggests that imperfect optimization must be an important motive for social insurance programs in practice. We briefly discuss recent work on optimal social insurance with agents who do not optimize perfectly in Section 3.3.5.

3. DESIGN OF PUBLIC INSURANCE PROGRAMS

A large literature has analyzed the optimal government response to the failures in private insurance markets discussed above. The goal of this literature is to find the optimal system in terms of trading off protection against risk with minimizing moral hazard. In practice, this problem has several dimensions. Conditional on deciding to insure a risk such as unemployment, there are several policy choices to be made. What level of benefits should be paid? Should benefits rise or fall over an unemployment spell? Should the insurance plan be financed by taxing firms or workers?

The traditional approach to answering such policy questions is to identify a model's structural primitives and conduct welfare analysis by simulating alternative policies. In social insurance, Wolpin (1987), Hansen and Imrohoroglu (1992), Wang and Williamson (1996), and Hopenhayn and Nicolini (1997) are influential examples of such work. Lentz (2009) and Huggett and Parra (2010) provide recent state-of-the-art applications. While the structural approach is in principle the ideal method of analyzing policy, in practice it is difficult to fully identify all the primitives of complex dynamic models.

Because of this problem, recent studies have instead tackled the optimal policy problem using a "sufficient statistic" approach, which we focus on here. This approach seeks

---

[16] One potential explanation for low asset holdings is that individuals would save much more in the absence of government-provided social insurance. However, empirical estimates of the impact of unemployment benefit levels on savings are relatively modest in magnitude (Engen & Gruber, 2001) and increases in unemployment benefits appear to substantially relax liquidity constraints in practice (Card, Chetty, & Weber, 2007a, 2007b; Chetty, 2008). These findings indicate that individuals would not accumulate substantial buffer stocks even if social insurance benefits were lower.

[17] The lack of such buffer stock savings is even more difficult to explain given that shocks such as unemployment generate long-lasting, possibly permanent earnings losses (von Wachter, Song, & Manchester, 2009).

formulas for optimal policy that are a function of high-level empirically estimable elasticities and are relatively robust to changes in the underlying model of behavior. The advantage of this approach is that it offers results about optimal policy that do not rely on the strong assumptions made in structural studies for tractability and identification. The cost is that it can only be used to analyze marginal changes in policy, e.g., the impact of changing the level of benefits incrementally from its current observed level. See Chetty (2009) for a more detailed discussion of the advantages and disadvantages of the sufficient statistic approach.

Research on social insurance has focused primarily on identifying the optimal level of benefits. We organize our discussion of the optimal level of benefits into three subsections. First, we analyze a static model of insurance in which individuals live for a single period and face one risk. In this static model, it is straightforward to derive an intuitive condition for the optimal level of benefits that trades off the moral hazard costs with the benefits of smaller consumption fluctuations.

Second, we show that this condition for the optimal level of benefits can be written in terms of various empirically estimable parameters. We derive three representations of the formula discussed in recent work: consumption-smoothing benefits, moral hazard vs. liquidity effects, and changes in reservation wages. We discuss empirical evidence on each of these parameters and their implications for the optimal level of benefits.

Third, we analyze the implications of relaxing the assumptions made in the static model. Some of the assumptions are inconsequential. For instance, the formulas obtained from the static model carry over with minor modifications to more realistic dynamic models with endogenous savings, borrowing constraints, and persistent uncertainty. But other extensions to the model—in particular, introducing features such that total private surplus is not maximized by agents' choices—have significant consequences. For example, if private markets provide insurance that also generates moral hazard, the simple formulas no longer apply because of "multiple dealing" externalities. Similarly, if agents do not maximize their expected utilities because of behavioral failures, the formulas again require modification.

After discussing the literature on the optimal level of benefits, we review recent work on three other aspects of optimal social insurance. First, we discuss work on using mandated savings accounts instead of tax-and-transfer systems to help agents smooth consumption when they face shocks. Next, we discuss imperfect take up of social insurance programs and its implications for optimal policy. Finally, we review recent work on the optimal path of benefits in dynamic models. Unlike the work on the optimal level of benefits, this literature is primarily theoretical. We therefore present brief summaries of some of the key results in this literature and discuss ways in which theory could be connected to data to make further progress on these questions.

Most recent work on connecting theory to data in optimal social insurance has focused on the case of unemployment insurance. Formal models of unemployment translate readily to most other insurance programs such as worker's compensation, disability, and catastrophic risks. One exception is the analysis of social security. The models we consider below focus on redistribution across states of nature for a given individual. Social security programs do insure against longevity risk by providing annuities, but also have important effects on the path of individuals' consumption profiles over their lifecycle. As a result, models of optimal social security typically focus on other factors—such as discount rates and wealth accumulation for retirement—independent of risk reduction. We do not consider models of optimal social security design here; see the chapter by Feldstein and Liebman (2002) for a survey of these models. Gruber and Wise (1999) and Krueger and Meyer (2002) summarize the existing evidence on the impacts of social security programs on retirement behavior. Unlike other social insurance programs, the evidence on social security has not been integrated as tightly with theoretical models to make quantitative statements about welfare and optimal policy. We view this as a fertile area for future research and return to this issue in the concluding section.

3.1. Optimal Benefit Level in a Static Model

Setup. The simplest model of insurance is static and has two states, high (h) and low (l). These states could reflect the risk of job loss (unemployment insurance), injury at work (Worker's Compensation), or natural disasters (home insurance). Let w_h denote the individual's income in the high state and $w_l < w_h$ income in the low state. Individuals enter the model with exogenously determined assets A. The government pays a benefit b in the low state that is financed by an actuarially fair tax $\tau(b) = \frac{1-e}{e}b$ in the high state. Let $c_h = A + w_h - \tau(b)$ denote consumption in the high state and $c_l = A + w_l + b$ denote consumption in the low state. Let $v(c)$ denote the agent's utility as a function of consumption in the high state and $u(c)$ utility in the low state. This allows for the possibility that utility is state-dependent, e.g., agents may value consumption more when healthy. We assume that both u and v are smooth and strictly concave.

A critical feature of the optimal social insurance problem is moral hazard. If individuals' behaviors were not distorted by the provision of insurance, the planner would achieve the first best by setting b to perfectly smooth marginal utilities, $v'(c_h) = u'(c_l)$. We model moral hazard by assuming that the agent can control the probability of being in the bad state by exerting effort e at a cost $\psi(e)$. For instance, "effort" could reflect spending time to search for a job, taking precautions to avoid injury, or locating a house away from areas prone to natural disasters. We choose units of e so that the probability of being in the high state is given by $e \in [0, 1]$.

Agent's Problem. The agent chooses effort e to maximize his expected utility:

$$\max_e V(e) = ev(c_h) + (1-e)u(c_l) - \psi(e). \tag{9}$$

Importantly, we assume that the agent takes the tax and benefit levels offered by the government ($\tau(b), b$) as fixed when solving this maximization problem. This assumption is a convenient analytical approximation to capture behavior in an economy with a large number of agents, in which the impact of any single agent's choice of e on the tax rate $\tau(b)$ is negligible.[18] The first-order condition for the maximization problem in (9) is:

$$v(c_h) - u(c_l) = \psi'(e). \tag{10}$$

Intuitively, the level of e that maximizes $V(e)$ equates the marginal benefit of an extra unit of effort, given by the difference in utilities in the low and high states, with the marginal cost of exerting an extra unit of effort. Let $e(b)$ denote the agent's optimal choice of effort given a benefit level b.

Planner's Problem. The social planner's objective is to choose the benefit level b that maximizes the agent's expected utility, taking into account the agent's endogenous choice of effort:

$$\max_b W(b) = ev(A + w_h - \tau(b)) + (1-e)u(A + w_l + b) - \psi(e) \tag{11}$$

$$\text{s.t. } e = e(b).$$

Differentiating (11) and using the first-order condition for e in (10) gives

$$\frac{dW(b)}{db} = (1-e)u'(c_l) - \frac{d\tau}{db}ev'(c_h) \tag{12}$$

$$= (1-e)\{u'(c_l) - (1 + \frac{\varepsilon_{1-e,b}}{e})v'(c_h)\},$$

where $\varepsilon_{1-e,b} = \frac{d(1-e)}{db}\frac{b}{1-e}$ denotes the elasticity of the probability of being in the bad state (which can be measured as the unemployment rate, rate of health insurance claims, etc.) with respect to the benefit level.[19] Notice that in this expression, the behavioral response $\varepsilon_{1-e,b}$ enters only via its impact on the government budget constraint $t(b)$. The direct impact of changes in e on the agent's private welfare is second order because the agent has already set e at the optimum that maximizes his private welfare ($\frac{\partial W}{\partial e}(e(b)) = 0$). This envelope condition plays a critical role in generalizing (12) to richer, more realistic models, as we discuss in Section 3.3.1.

Equation (12) does not have a cardinal interpretation because it is scaled in utils. One natural cardinal metric is to normalize the welfare gain from a $1 (balanced budget) increase in the size of the government insurance program by the welfare gain from raising

[18] Formally, consider an economy with $i = 1, \ldots, N$ identical agents solving (9) and facing idiosyncratic risks. For each agent, the impact of changes in his own effort on $t(b)$ are proportional to $\frac{de}{db}\frac{1}{N}$. For the planner, the aggregate impact of changes in effort is $\sum_{i=1}^{N}\frac{1}{N}\frac{de}{db} = \frac{de}{db}$. As N grows large, the impact of agent i's effort on $t(b)$ approaches 0 and can therefore be ignored when solving the private optimization problem in (9). However, the impact of changes in effort on the planner's problem in (11) are unaffected by N.

[19] This elasticity measures the *total* effect of an increase in benefits on e, taking into account the tax increase needed to finance the higher level of benefits.

the wage bill in the high state by \$1:

$$M_W(b) = \frac{\frac{dW}{db}(b)/(1-e)}{\frac{dW}{dw_h}(b)/e}$$

$$= \frac{u'(c_l) - v'(c_h)}{v'(c_h)} - \frac{\varepsilon_{1-e,b}}{e}. \tag{13}$$

The first term in (13) measures the gap in marginal utilities between the high and low states, which quantifies the welfare gain from transferring an additional dollar from the high to low state. The second term measures the net cost to the government of transferring this \$1 across states due to behavioral responses. The second term arises because the agent does not internalize the fiscal externality that he imposes on the government budget when changing his level of effort. This creates a wedge between the private return to effort and the social return to effort, generating a welfare loss.

At the optimal benefit level b^*, $M_W(b) = 0$ and hence

$$\frac{u'(c_l) - v'(c_h)}{v'(c_h)} = \frac{\varepsilon_{1-e,b}}{e}. \tag{14}$$

This expression is a simple variant of Baily's (1978) classic formula for the optimal level of social insurance. It captures a simple—and, as we show below, quite robust—intuition about optimal policy: the optimal benefit level equates the marginal gains from a smoother consumption path with the marginal cost, measured by the behavioral response in effort. Note that (14) is a condition that must hold at the optimal benefit level b^* but is *not* an explicit formula for the level of benefits because all the parameters in (14) are endogenous to b.

Another way to write (14) is in terms of the replacement rate, $r = b/w_h$:

$$\frac{r}{1-r} = -\frac{u'(c_l) - v'(c_h)}{v'(c_h)} \frac{e}{\varepsilon_{1-e,w_h-b}}, \tag{15}$$

where $\varepsilon_{1-e,w_h-b} = -\frac{d(1-e)}{db}\frac{w_h-b}{1-e}$ denotes the elasticity of the probability of being in the bad state with respect to the net wage $w_h - b$. This formula bears a close resemblance to the inverse elasticity rules that are familiar from the literature on optimal commodity taxation (Auerbach, 1985). Indeed, the optimal social insurance problem is formally identical to an optimal Ramsey taxation problem (Chetty & Saez, 2010).

It is important to note that Eq. (15) is not an explicit formula for the optimal replacement rate r^*. The reason is again that the parameters on the right hand side are all functions of r. The very purpose of raising r is to reduce $\frac{u'(c_l)-v'(c_h)}{u'(c_h)}$. Moreover, the elasticity ε_{1-e,w_h-b} may also vary with r because of liquidity effects (Chetty, 2008), as we explain below.

Even in this simple static model, calculating the marginal welfare gain (13) empirically requires some work. The challenge is estimating the gap in marginal utilities $\frac{u'(c_l)-v'(c_h)}{v'(c_h)}$, which requires knowledge of the utility function as well as assets A and wage rates, which may be unobserved by the econometrician. We now discuss recent approaches to tackling this problem.

3.2. Sufficient Statistics Implementation

The modern literature on social insurance has developed three approaches to recover the marginal utility gap in (13): studying consumption fluctuations (Gruber, 1997), liquidity and substitution effects in effort (Chetty, 2008), and reservation wages (Shimer & Werning, 2007). We present simple derivations of each approach here and review empirical evidence in each context.

3.2.1. Consumption Smoothing

Gruber (1997) implements (13) under the assumption that utility is state independent, i.e., $v = u$. We first present Gruber's approach under this assumption and then show how it can be extended to allow for state-dependent utility. Taking a quadratic approximation to the utility function yields:

$$\frac{u'(c_l) - u'(c_h)}{u'(c_h)} = \gamma \frac{\Delta c}{c_h}(b), \qquad (16)$$

where $\gamma = -\frac{u''(c_h)}{u'(c_h)} c_h$ is the coefficient of relative risk aversion evaluated at c_h and $\Delta c = c_h - c_l$. Plugging this expression into (13), one obtains the following expression for the marginal welfare gain of raising b:

$$M_W(b) = \gamma \frac{\Delta c}{c_h}(b) - \frac{\varepsilon_{1-e,b}}{e}.$$

This equation shows that risk aversion γ, the observed consumption drop from the high to low state $\frac{\Delta c}{c_h}$, and the elasticity $\varepsilon_{1-e,b}$ are together sufficient to calculate the marginal welfare consequences of changing benefits from the current level. It follows that estimating these statistics is adequate to determine whether the current benefit level is too high or low if the welfare function is concave. To go further and calculate the optimal level of benefits, Gruber estimates the relationship between the size of the consumption drop $\frac{\Delta c}{c_h}(b)$ and the level of benefits b. He posits that the effect of benefits on consumption is a linear function of the replacement rate $r = b/w_h$:

$$\frac{\Delta c}{c_h}(b) \simeq \Delta \log c = \alpha + \beta r. \qquad (17)$$

In this specification, α measures the drop in consumption that would occur absent government intervention while β measures the slope of the consumption function with respect to the benefit level. Putting this equation together with (16) and (13) yields the following expression for the marginal welfare gain from increasing the benefit level:

$$M_W(b) = (\alpha + \beta r)\gamma - \frac{\varepsilon_{1-e,b}}{e}. \tag{18}$$

Gruber solves for the level of r that sets (18) equal to zero to identify the optimal replacement rate.[20] Implementing this formula empirically requires estimates of how consumption fluctuates around shocks as a function of benefit levels (α, β), the curvature of the utility function γ, and the elasticity that measures distortions in behavior $\varepsilon_{1-e,b}$. There are now several studies estimating each of these parameters for various social insurance programs; we briefly review some illustrative examples of quasi-experimental studies from this literature here.

Evidence on Consumption Smoothing. An early study by Hamermesh (1982) investigates the impacts of unemployment insurance on consumption using cross-sectional consumption data from the Consumer Expenditure Survey. Because Hamermesh does not have panel data, he cannot study changes in consumption around unemployment shocks. Instead, he compares individuals who are currently unemployed and receiving UI with those who are employed. He finds evidence that the marginal propensity to consume out of UI benefits is significantly higher than out of other sources of income, which he interprets as evidence supporting a consumption-smoothing role of UI.

Cochrane (1991) improves upon the analysis in Hamermesh (1982) by using panel data from the Panel Study of Income Dynamics (PSID). Using panel data, he studies how unemployment shocks affect within-household food consumption fluctuations. This is a significant advance over cross-household comparisons, which are likely to be plagued by omitted variable bias. Cochrane finds that unemployment shocks are imperfectly insured—i.e., $\alpha > 0$ in (17)—implying that there is a potential role for government intervention via unemployment insurance. However, Cochrane does not estimate the extent to which providing insurance through a UI system would affect consumption.[21]

Gruber (1997) exploits variation in UI benefit levels that is driven by state law changes to identify β using data on food consumption from the PSID. By controlling flexibly for cross-sectional determinants of the level of UI benefits (such as prior wage rates) and simulating UI benefits based on state laws, Gruber isolates variation in UI benefits that is plausibly orthogonal to other determinants of consumption. Gruber's point estimates of (17) are $\alpha = 0.24$ and $\beta = -0.28$. These estimates imply that consumption drops

---

[20] This approach assumes that the other parameters in (18)—namely γ and $\varepsilon_{1-e,b}$—do not vary with b. In practice, these parameters are likely to vary with b. For example, the liquidity effects documented e.g., in Chetty (2008) imply that $\varepsilon_{1-e,b}$ is likely to fall as b rises, as liquidity constraints bind more tightly when b is low. Hence, one should ideally estimate *all* the sufficient statistics in (18) as a function of b to calculate the optimal benefit level.

[21] Cochrane's conclusion that insurance markets for unemployment are incomplete rests on the assumption that utility is not state-dependent. If utility is state-dependent, consumption may fall during unemployment spells simply because the marginal utility of consumption is lower when not working. Gruber's (1997) approach provides more definitive evidence of incomplete insurance by using variation in UI benefit amounts rather than simply quantifying the size of consumption drops during unemployment.

on average by 10% given existing UI replacement rates, which are approximately 50% of wages. In the absence of UI, consumption would drop by 24%. Hence, UI plays a significant role in smoothing consumption. However, a 10% increase in UI replacement rates generates only a 2.8% point reduction in the consumption drop. This implies that part of the increase in UI benefits is crowded out by other responses, such as reductions in savings (Engen & Gruber, 2001) and changes in spousal labor supply (Cullen & Gruber, 2000).[22]

Gruber's approach has since become the benchmark quasi-experimental strategy for analyzing how social insurance affects consumption.[23] For instance, Browning and Crossley (2001) implement a similar analysis using data on a broader set of consumption goods from Canada. They find that the average impact of increases in UI benefits on consumption is quite modest, but the impacts are especially large among a subset of households that are likely to be liquidity constrained. Gertler and Gruber (2002) show that severe health shocks have large effects on consumption using panel data from Indonesia and that buffering these shocks by reducing income fluctuations would significantly reduce consumption fluctuations. Bronchetti (2012) implements an approach analogous to Gruber (1997) to the Worker's Compensation program in the US and again finds evidence that increases in Worker's Compensation benefits significantly increase consumption levels while individuals are out of work due to injury.

While the evidence that has been accumulated clearly demonstrates that insurance markets are incomplete—i.e., consumption does fall when individuals are hit with shocks—the consumption-smoothing role of social insurance programs is less clear. We can be confident given available evidence that $\alpha > 0$ for at least a subset of households, but we have very imprecise estimates of β. For instance, the estimates of β from Gruber (1997) have a confidence interval spanning $\beta = 0.08\text{--}0.48$. The imprecision and instability of estimates arise from the fact that consumption is very difficult to measure accurately due to noise and recall errors and is typically available for relatively small samples. Obtaining a more precise understanding of the consumption-smoothing benefits of insurance will likely require administrative data on consumption, e.g., from credit-card databases, scanner data, or value-added tax registers.

Empirical studies of consumption smoothing have focused on the short-run drop in consumption from employment to unemployment. We show below that this short-run consumption drop is what matters for calculating optimal unemployment benefit levels using (18) irrespective of how consumption evolves after the individual finds a new job. However, it is important to recognize that long-term impacts of temporary shocks on consumption are also significant. von Wachter et al. (2009) show that unemployment

---

[22] If $c_h \simeq w_h$, as we would expect with low unemployment risk, then a 10% point increase in the replacement rate would lead to a 10% point reduction in the consumption drop absent crowd out.

[23] Another prominent approach is to analyze the impacts of income fluctuations on consumption using statistical decompositions of the income process into permanent and transitory components and examining the covariances of these components with consumption (see e.g., Blundell, Pistaferri, & Preston, 2008). Jappelli and Pistaferri (2010) provide a comprehensive review of this work.

shocks due to mass layoffs have large, permanent impacts on earnings. Given that consumption must converge to income in the long run for all workers except the few with substantial wealth before job loss, this result strongly suggests that even temporary unemployment shocks have long-lasting effects. If shocks have persistent impacts on consumption, the optimal insurance policy may not be just to provide benefits while agents are out of work, but rather a wage insurance system that insures long-lasting earnings losses, as proposed e.g., by LaLonde (2007).[24] An interesting direction for further work would be to apply the methods reviewed here to analyze optimal wage insurance policies.

Evidence on Distortions in Behavior. The literature on measuring behavioral responses to social insurance programs—the impacts of unemployment insurance on unemployment durations, health insurance on health expenditures, disability insurance on labor force participation rates—has a long tradition that predates the theoretical work on social insurance discussed here. We have much more evidence on the distortions created by insurance programs than their consumption-smoothing benefits because of data availability. For instance, administrative data on unemployment durations must be collected in order to make UI payments, making it much easier to study the impacts of UI on durations than on consumption.

There are many excellent surveys of the literature on how social insurance affects behavior; see e.g., Krueger and Meyer (2002) for a review of work on how UI, DI, and Worker's Compensation affect labor supply and Cutler and Zeckhauser (2000) or Cutler (2002) for a review on how health insurance affects the demand for medical care. Here, we briefly discuss selected findings from the literature that have been used to inform theoretical calculations of optimal benefit levels using sufficient statistic formulas.

In the context of unemployment, most studies have focused on measuring the impacts of increases in UI benefits on the duration of unemployment. The probability of being laid off could also respond to the level of benefits. The literature has focused less on this issue because UI benefits are typically at least partially experience rated, meaning that firms bear the unemployment insurance cost of laying off workers. In a perfectly experience rated system, changes in the level of benefits do not distort incentives to lay off workers. However, with imperfect experience rating, changes in the level of UI benefits can also affect unemployment rates by distorting firms' layoff decisions (Blanchard & Tirole, 2008; Feldstein, 1978). While studies such as Topel (1983) and Anderson and Meyer (1993) have documented significant effects of experience rating on firm layoffs, there is relatively little recent work on this issue. Analyzing whether social insurance programs affect the rate at which firms hire and lay off workers using modern quasi-experimental designs is a very promising area for further research.

---

[24] To be clear, persistent wage shocks do not invalidate the use of temporary consumption drops to analyze optimal UI, because the observed consumption drop incorporates all future changes in income in an optimizing model (see Section 3.3.1). However, persistent wage shocks raise the possibility that the optimal insurance policy is not merely to provide benefits while the agent is out of work but also after he is reemployed.

The modern literature estimating the impact of UI on durations has adopted the hazard model specifications used by Meyer (1990). Meyer estimates semi-parametric models for the hazard of exiting unemployment as a function of UI benefits and other variables using administrative data on the duration of UI claims. He exploits variation in UI benefits coming from differential changes in benefits over time across states, as in Gruber (1997). Meyer finds that higher UI benefits reduce the hazard of exiting unemployment significantly, with an implied elasticity above 0.8 in most specifications.

Subsequent studies have obtained qualitatively similar results using a variety of different data sources. For instance, Lalive, van Ours, and Zweimüller (2006) use a regression-discontinuity design in administrative data from Austria and find that UI benefit increases significantly raise unemployment durations, although to a lesser extent than suggested by Meyer's estimates. Chetty (2008) estimates elasticities of approximately 0.5 using survey data from the Survey of Income and Program Participation. Landais (2012) replicates Meyer's analysis using a regression-kink design and estimates smaller elasticities, around 0.3. In general, the literature has settled on a consensus estimate of $\varepsilon_{1-e,b}$ for UI and unemployment durations of about 0.5 (Krueger & Meyer, 2002).

Meyer (1990) and Katz and Meyer (1990) document a spike in hazard rates when unemployment benefits expire. This is typically viewed as prima facie evidence that UI distorts search behavior, as it suggests that people time their unemployment exits to coincide with the expiry of social assistance. This spike in unemployment exit hazards in the weeks prior to benefit exhaustion is now a well-established empirical regularity; see Card et al. (2007a) for a review of this literature.

However, Card et al. (2007a) use data from Austria to show that the spike in *job finding* rates when UI benefits expire is far smaller than the spike in unemployment exit rates. In Austria, as in most other European countries, individuals can stay on the UI system to receive job finding assistance and other benefits even after their benefits expire, but the majority of individuals choose to drop out of the UI system when their benefits end. Most of these individuals, however, remain unemployed even after they leave the UI system. In the US, individuals may choose not to collect their last unemployment check because it is often a small leftover amount, which would create the appearance of a surge in hazard rates in the weeks before benefits expire. Because the margin relevant for calculating the efficiency costs of the UI system are time spent working rather than time spent on the UI system, this evidence suggests that the original sharp spikes documented in the literature likely overstate the degree of moral hazard created by UI. The more general lesson is that it is crucial to measure distortions in real economic choices rather than simply use measures that are well recorded in administrative databases.

Analogous behavioral responses have been documented for other social insurance programs beyond unemployment insurance. Meyer, Viscusi, and Durbin (1995) use differential changes in worker's compensation benefits across states to show that higher benefit levels induce injured workers to stay out of work longer before returning to work. Gruber (2000) analyzes a disability insurance expansion in Canada that raised benefit levels for individuals in all provinces except Quebec. He finds that this benefit increase significantly reduced labor force participation rates for males ages 45–59, implying an elasticity of the non-participation rate with respect to DI benefits of 0.25. Maestas, Mullen, and Strand (forthcoming) use random variation in assignment to disability insurance examiners to estimate that eligibility for DI reduces labor force participation rates for the marginal entrant to DI by approximately 20% points, with significantly smaller effects for those with more severe impairments. In the context of health insurance, the RAND health insurance experiment (Manning, Newhouse, Duan, Keeler, & Leibowitz, 1987) and Oregon health insurance lotteries (Finkelstein et al., 2011) have demonstrated that increases in consumer cost-sharing significantly reduce health care expenditures.

Evidence on Risk Aversion. Economists have estimated risk aversion using a broad array of techniques. The most direct and widely used method of estimating risk aversion is to assess preferences over gambles. Using empirical estimates of the distribution of risk and an expected utility model with a specific functional form for utility such as constant relative risk aversion, one can back out the value of γ implied by individuals' choices over risky streams of income. Early work in asset pricing inferred risk aversion from portfolio choice and asset returns in standard asset pricing models (e.g., Kocherlakota, 1996; Mehra & Prescott, 1985). More recent work has used responses to hypothetical large-stake gambles (Barsky, Juster, Kimball, & Shapiro, 1997), automobile insurance choices (Cohen & Einav, 2007), risk taking in game shows (Metrick, 1995), and home insurance deductible choices (Sydnor, 2010) to infer risk aversion. There is little consensus on the value of γ from this literature: the estimates range from 1 to well above 10 in the case of deductible choices and asset prices. One explanation of this discrepancy in estimates is that they reflect the behavior of different subgroups of the population. Barseghyan, Prince, and Teitelbaum (2011) and Einav, Finkelstein, Pascu, and Cullen (forthcoming) test this explanation by examining the risk preferences of the same individuals in different domains of choice, such as health insurance deductibles and 401(k) portfolio allocations. While individuals' risk preferences are correlated across the domains, there is substantial heterogeneity in estimated risk aversion from each choice.

All of these estimates of risk aversion are based on ex-ante choices, which requires that individuals' subjective assessment of risks (e.g., the probability of a large fluctuation in stock prices) and other parameters are consistent with the model assumed by the researcher as well as the maintained assumptions of expected utility theory. Chetty (2006a) proposes a different method of estimating γ that does not rely on subjective probabilities. He shows that expected utility models imply a direct connection between the curvature of the utility function over consumption and the impacts of wage changes on labor supply. Intuitively, if the utility function is very curved, individuals should become sated with goods as their income rises, and should choose to work *less* as their wages rise. The fact that uncompensated wage increases almost always raise labor supply in practice implies an upper bound on the coefficient of relative risk aversion of approximately 1 without any assumptions about the structure of the utility function.[25] Because this method of estimating risk aversion uses the same types of ex-post data used to measure $\varepsilon_{1-e,b}$ and $\frac{\Delta c}{c}$, it offers a more direct estimate of the curvature of utility that matters for evaluating the welfare cost of shocks.[26]

Unfortunately, even this ex-post measure of risk aversion varies significantly across contexts. Chetty and Szeidl (2007) develop a theoretical model of risk preferences in which individuals have "consumption commitments"—goods such as housing or fixed service contracts which can only be adjusted by paying fixed transaction costs. In this environment, individuals have amplified risk aversion over moderate-stake shocks because of their commitments. To understand the intuition, consider a two good model in which the agent spends half his income on housing (which can only be adjusted by paying a transaction cost) and half on food (which is freely adjustable). When facing a shock such as temporary job loss that forces them to reduce expenditure by say 10%, most individuals will rationally choose to bear the shock by cutting food consumption by 20% in order to avoid having to move out of their house. This concentrated reduction in food expenditures raises marginal utility sharply, amplifying risk aversion. Chetty and Szeidl confirm this prediction of the model in the PSID data used by Cochrane and Gruber: homeowners who become unemployed do not change housing consumption but cut back on food consumption significantly, while renters (who face lower adjustment costs) diversify the shocks more broadly by reducing consumption of both food and housing. Chetty and Szeidl's analysis suggests that the value of γ relevant for shocks such as unemployment could be as high as $\gamma = 4$ because of fixed commitments. However, for large shocks such as permanent disability that induce households to abandon commitments, the relevant value of γ could be closer to 1.

Because of the tremendous uncertainty about the appropriate value of γ, researchers typically report welfare calculations for a range of values of γ. Gruber implements the formula in (18) using his own estimates of the consumption smoothing response and estimates of $\varepsilon_{1-e,b}$ from Meyer (1990). He finds that with a coefficient of relative risk aversion $\gamma < 2$, increasing the UI benefit level above the levels observed in his data (roughly 50% of the wage) would lead to substantial welfare losses. Extrapolating out-of-sample based on the assumption that $\varepsilon_{1-e,b}$ remains constant and the consumption function is given by (17), Gruber shows that it is difficult to justify having a positive level of UI benefits ($b^* > 0$) with risk aversion $\gamma < 2$ given his estimates of the consumption-smoothing benefit of UI. With $\gamma = 4$, however, the optimal benefit level could be as large as 50%. Bronchetti (2012) presents estimates of the optimal level of Worker's

---

[25] If utility is non-separable, one must bound the degree of complementarity between consumption and leisure in order to bound risk aversion using this method. Chetty uses the estimates of Cochrane (1991) and Gruber (1997) to place an upper bound on this complementarity parameter and shows that even at this upper bound, $\gamma < 1.25$.

[26] Conversely, however, this approach is less likely to yield accurate predictions about ex-ante choices in risky environments.

Compensation benefits based on a range of values for γ using the formula in (18). She concludes that the optimal level of worker's compensation benefits is likely to be below the current level of 68%, but her estimates of the optimal replacement rate range from 26% to 61% as risk aversion varies from $\gamma = 1$ to $\gamma = 4$. Bound, Cullen, Nichols and Schmidt (2004) calculate the welfare gains from the current Disability Insurance program under varying degrees of risk aversion taking account of heterogeneity across individuals. Based on simulations of the benefits of DI, they conclude that the optimal level of benefits is likely somewhat lower than current levels, but the optimal level of benefits again is quite sensitive to assumptions about γ.

Estimating risk aversion accurately is particularly important because the size of the consumption drop $\frac{\Delta c}{c}$ is inversely related to γ, as shown by Chetty and Looney (2006). As a result, the welfare gains from insurance could be large even if consumption drops are small, as documented by Townsend (1994) and others in developing economies. Intuitively, highly risk averse households—e.g., those facing subsistence constraints—are likely to have very smooth consumption paths because they will go to any effort (e.g., by taking their children out of school in developing countries) in order to subsist. But these efforts to smooth consumption are very costly—i.e., $\psi(e)$ is highly convex. Chetty and Looney show that the marginal gains from insurance, given by $\gamma \frac{\Delta c}{c}$, could actually be larger in economies with smoother consumption paths if that smoothness is driven by greater risk aversion.

State-Dependent Utility. When utility is state-dependent, the consumption-smoothing approach requires estimation of an additional parameter that measures the degree to which marginal utilities vary across states. With state-dependent utility, the quadratic approximation used above yields

$$\frac{u'(c_l) - v'(c_h)}{v'(c_h)} = \gamma_v \frac{\Delta c}{c} + \theta,$$

where $\gamma_v = -\frac{v''(c_h)c_h}{v'(c_h)}$ denotes the coefficient of relative risk aversion in the employed state and $\theta = \frac{u'(c_l)-v'(c_l)}{v'(c_h)}$ measures the degree of state dependence in marginal utilities. The parameter θ answers the question, "starting from equal consumption in the low and high states, how much would the agent pay to reallocate \$1 of consumption from the high state to the low state?" If utility is not state-dependent, the answer to this question would be $\theta = 0$. If the marginal utility of consumption is higher when the agent is in the low state, the willingness to pay is $\theta > 0$.[27] The parameter θ directly enters the formula for $M_W(b)$ in (18) as an additive term. If $\theta > 0$, insurance has greater value because it is transferring resources to a state where money has more value at any given level of consumption.

---

[27] Technically, one must measure the willingness to pay in the high state, as $v'(c_h)$ appears in the denominator of θ.

Finkelstein, Luttmer, and Notowidigdo (2009) describe some approaches to estimating θ. Broadly speaking, θ can be estimated based on either choice data that reveals individuals' demand for moving resources across states or based on observed utility changes as states change. For example, the extent to which agents voluntarily choose to have more or less consumption in high vs. low states reveals θ in an environment with perfect insurance. Unfortunately, most individuals are not perfectly insured in practice—if they were, there would be no reason for social insurance to begin with!—and it is rare to be able to observe consumption across state changes in data (e.g., health shocks or unemployment spells). Absent perfect insurance, one can try to focus on subgroups that are better insured. This requires assumptions about the degree of insurance one has. Moreover, since the life cycle budget constraint must be satisfied, inferring state dependence from the consumption fluctuations of individuals who experience different unexpected shocks (such as health events) requires strong assumptions about the nature of bequest motives. For example, Lillard and Weiss (1997) estimate a structural model of health shocks and use data on consumption trajectories to identify θ under the assumption that the marginal utility of bequests does not depend on health. They estimate $\theta > 0$, i.e., positive state dependence for health and disability.[28]

An alternative approach to identify state dependence that does not require choice data from environments with full insurance is to use data on subjective well being. Intuitively, by estimating whether a cash grant has a larger impact on happiness in the low vs. high state, one can learn about θ. The challenge in implementing this approach is that subjective well-being measures have no inherent cardinal interpretation, whereas θ is a cardinal parameter.[29] One must therefore choose a cardinal scale for happiness to estimate θ using data on subjective well being. One approach is to scale happiness so that one obtains estimates of the coefficient of relative risk aversion γ that match estimates from choice data. Finkelstein, Luttmer, and Notowidigdo (2008) implement such an approach and conclude based on survey data that $\theta < 0$, i.e., the marginal utility of consumption is higher when individuals are healthy. In sum, there is currently little consensus in the literature on the sign of θ for shocks such as unemployment, disability, and sickness, let alone its magnitude in these contexts. We view this as an important but challenging area for future work.

Because optimal benefit calculations are highly sensitive to the assumed value of γ and θ, more recent studies have sought alternative techniques for recovering the gap in marginal utilities that do not require estimates of these parameters. We now turn to these alternative approaches.

---

[28] In a different context, Browning and Crossley's (2001) finding that unemployment shocks have little impact on consumption for individuals with high levels of assets suggests that θ may be 0 for unemployment (i.e., no state dependence for leisure).

[29] For instance, suppose giving an agent $1000 increases his reported happiness from 2 to 3 in the low state and 7 to 9 in the high state. One cannot identify θ without knowing whether an increase in happiness from 2 to 3 translates into a smaller or larger welfare gain than an increase in happiness from 7 to 9.

3.2.2. Liquidity vs. Moral Hazard

Chetty (2008) shows that the gap in marginal utilities in (13) can be inferred from the comparative statics of effort choice, yielding a formula for optimal benefits that does not require any data on consumption or risk preferences. Recall that the first order condition for effort in our static model is $\psi'(e) = v(c_h) - u(c_l)$. Now consider the effect of an exogenous cash grant (such as a severance payment to job losers) on effort, holding fixed the tax τ:

$$\partial e/\partial A = \{v'(c_h) - u'(c_l)\}/\psi''(e) \leq 0. \tag{19}$$

The effect of increasing the benefit level on effort (again holding τ fixed) is:

$$\partial e/\partial b = -u'(c_l)/\psi''(e). \tag{20}$$

Finally, the effect of increasing the wage in the high state on effort is:

$$\partial e/\partial w_h = v'(c_h)/\psi''(e). \tag{21}$$

Combining (19) and (20), we see that the ratio of the "liquidity" effect ($\partial e/\partial A$) to the "substitution" effect ($\partial e/\partial w_h = \partial e/\partial A - \partial e/\partial b$) recovers the gap in marginal utilities:

$$\frac{u'(c_l) - v'(c_h)}{v'(c_h)} = \frac{-\partial e/\partial A}{\partial e/\partial A - \partial e/\partial b}.$$

Plugging this expression into (13) yields the following expression for the welfare gain from increasing the benefit level:

$$M_W(b) = \frac{-\partial e/\partial A}{\partial e/\partial A - \partial e/\partial b} - \frac{\varepsilon_{1-e,b}}{e}. \tag{22}$$

In this formula, the degree to which marginal utilities fluctuate across states is identified from the relative size of liquidity and moral hazard effects in the impact of benefit levels on effort.[30] In a model with perfect consumption smoothing, the liquidity effect $\partial e/\partial A = 0$, because a cash grant raises $v(c_h)$ and $u(c_l)$ by the same amount. Note that unlike the consumption-smoothing method above, this approach does not require estimation of the degree of risk aversion or state dependence in utility.[31]

---

[30] A technical issue which arises in empirical implementation of (22) is that $\frac{\partial e}{\partial b}$ must be measured holding the tax τ fixed, whereas the elasticity $\varepsilon_{1-e,b}$ must be measured while permitting τ to vary. Instead of attempting to estimate both parameters, Chetty uses numerical simulations to show that the effect of a UI benefit increase on job finding rates is virtually identical whether or not UI taxes are held fixed. This is because the fraction of unemployed individuals is quite small, making UI tax rates very low.

[31] If utility is not state dependent, one could infer the agent's degree of risk aversion γ from the size of moral hazard vs. liquidity effects and the consumption drop: $\gamma = \frac{-\partial e/\partial A}{\partial e/\partial A - \partial e/\partial b}/(\Delta c/c)$. This restriction, which is closely related to the formula for risk aversion in Chetty (2006a), could be evaluated empirically in future work.

One intuition for the liquidity vs. moral hazard formula comes from familiar results from price theory. The impact of an increase in b on e can be decomposed into two terms, analogous to a Slutsky decomposition: $\partial e/\partial b = \partial e/\partial A - \partial e/\partial w_h$. The first term is analogous to an income effect, and reflects the fact that higher benefits also raise agents' cash-on-hand and thus reduce the supply of effort. The second term is a pure substitution (price) effect and arises from the distortion in marginal incentives created by the social insurance program. The substitution effect is efficiency reducing because it reflects second-best behavior arising from the wedge between private and social incentives. In contrast, the liquidity effect is efficiency *enhancing* because it allows the agent to choose a level of e that is closer to what he would choose with complete markets. The size of the liquidity effect measures the extent to which insurance markets are incomplete. The ratio of the liquidity effect to the distortionary substitution effect thus captures the marginal benefit of social insurance.

Another way to understand (22) is that it uses revealed preference to value the benefits of insurance. Consider an application to health insurance. The effect of a lump-sum cash grant on health care consumption reveals the extent to which health insurance permits the agent to attain a more socially desirable allocation. If the agent chooses to spend a lump-sum grant on buying a new car instead of purchasing more health care, we infer that the agent only spends more on health care when health insurance benefits are increased because of the price subsidy for doing so. In this case, health insurance simply creates inefficiency by distorting the private cost of health care below the social cost, implying $\frac{dW}{db} < 0$. In contrast, if the agent raises his health expenditures substantially even when he receives a non-distortionary lump-sum cash grant, we infer that insurance permits him to make a more (socially) optimal choice, i.e., the choice he would make if insurance market failures could be alleviated without distorting incentives. The liquidity vs. moral hazard approach in (22) thus identifies the policy that is best from the libertarian criterion of correcting market failures as revealed by individual choice.

It follows from Eq. (22) that larger elasticities $\varepsilon_{1-e,b}$ do not necessarily mean that social insurance is less desirable, a point emphasized by Nyman (2003) in the context of health insurance. It matters whether a higher value of $\varepsilon_{1-e,b}$ comes from a larger liquidity $(-\frac{\partial e}{\partial A})$ or moral hazard $(\frac{\partial e}{\partial w_h})$ component. To the extent that comes from a liquidity effect, insurance reduces the need for agents to make suboptimal choices driven by insufficient ability to smooth consumption. In contrast, if $\varepsilon_{1-e,b}$ is large primarily because of a moral hazard effect, insurance is distorting incentives. For instance, the reductions in labor force participation caused by disability insurance documented by Maestas, Mullen, and Strand (2011) may not be undesirable. If DI helps individuals whose marginal product is lower than their disutility of work, this behavioral response is welfare improving.

Evidence on Liquidity vs. Moral Hazard. The advantage of this formula relative to (18) is that it can be implemented purely using data on e (e.g., unemployment durations or health expenditures). Chetty (2008) implements (22) using survey data from the US. He estimates $\frac{\partial e}{\partial b}$ using data from the Survey of Income and Program Participation, following the specifications in Meyer (1990). Using the SIPP data, Chetty shows that individuals who have low levels of assets prior to job loss exhibit much higher levels of $\frac{\partial e}{\partial b}$ than those with higher levels of assets. This suggests that a significant part of the impact of UI benefits on durations may be driven by a liquidity effect. Chetty then estimates $\frac{\partial e}{\partial A}$ by studying the effects of lump sum severance payments on unemployment durations using data from a survey of UI exhaustees conducted by Mathematica in collaboration with the Department of Labor. He finds that individuals who receive lump sum severance payments have significantly longer unemployment durations, especially if they have low levels of assets prior to job loss. Using his estimates, Chetty calculates the welfare gain of raising the UI benefit level from the current replacement rate of approximately 50% of wages. He finds that the welfare gains from raising b are small but positive, suggesting that the current benefit level is slightly below but near the optimum.

Chetty's (2008) analysis relies on cross-sectional variation across individuals in severance pay, and therefore rests on the strong identification assumption that severance recipients and non-recipients are comparable. More recent studies have documented similar results using research designs that make weaker assumptions. Card et al. (2007b) use a regression-discontinuity design that exploits a universal cutoff for severance pay eligibility based on job tenure in Austria. Using administrative data for the universe of job losers in Austria, they show that individuals laid off just after the tenure cutoff—who receive 2 months of wages as a lump sum severance payment as a result—have unemployment durations that are about 10 days longer than individuals laid off just before the cutoff. They compare these liquidity effects to the impacts of UI benefit extensions using a similar RD design and show that the size of liquidity effects is large relative to the impact of benefit extensions, implying that many unemployed individuals are liquidity constrained. Centeno and Novo (2009) present evidence that liquidity constrained households are more sensitive to UI benefit changes using a regression-discontinuity design in Portugal. LaLumia (2011) shows that individuals who happen to be laid off after they receive a tax refund (and have more cash-on-hand) have longer unemployment durations relative to individuals laid off at other times of the year.

There is less evidence on liquidity effects in other insurance programs because of the relatively recent development of these formulas and because researchers have not yet formulated quasi-experimental designs to estimate liquidity effects $\frac{\partial e}{\partial A}$ for many programs. One exception is Nyman (2003), who presents considerable anecdotal evidence and theoretical arguments suggesting that liquidity effects play a very important role in health insurance. The benefits of health insurance are extremely difficult to quantify, making the liquidity-based revealed preference approach particularly attractive in that context. Finding research designs to identify liquidity effects in health and other insurance programs is thus a very promising area for further work.

3.2.3. Reservation Wages

Shimer and Werning (2007) show that the gap in marginal utilities can be recovered from the comparative statics of reservation wages in a standard model of job search. They analyze a model in which the probability of finding a job, e, is determined by the agent's decision to accept or reject a wage offer rather than by search effort. Wage offers are drawn from a distribution $F(w)$. If the agent rejects the job offer, he receives income of $w_l + b$ as in the baseline model above.[32]

The agent rejects any net-of-tax wage offer $w - \tau$ below his outside option $w_l + b$, i.e., his reservation wage once searching for a job is $w_l + b + \tau$. Therefore, $e = 1 - F(w_l + b + \tau)$ and the agent's expected utility when searching for a job is

$$W(b) = e\mathbb{E}[v(A + w - \tau)|w - \tau > w_l + b] + (1 - e)u(A + w_l + b).$$

Now suppose we ask the agent what wage he would be willing to accept with certainty *before* the start of job search. Define the agent's reservation wage prior to job search as the wage $\overline{w}_0$ that would make the agent indifferent between accepting a job immediately vs. starting the process of job search, which yields expected utility of $W(b)$. This pre-job-search reservation wage $\overline{w}_0$ satisfies

$$v(A + \overline{w}_0 - \tau) = W(b)$$

The government's problem is to

$$\max W(b) = \max v(A + \overline{w}_0 - \tau)$$
$$\Rightarrow \max \overline{w}_0 - \tau. \tag{23}$$

Differentiating (23) gives the following formula for the marginal welfare gain of raising b:[33]

$$M_W(b) = \frac{d\overline{w}_0}{db} - \frac{d\tau}{db} = \frac{d\overline{w}_0}{db} - \frac{1 - e}{e}(1 + \frac{1}{e}\varepsilon_{1-e,b}). \tag{24}$$

In this formula, $\frac{d\overline{w}_0}{db}$ encodes the marginal value of insurance because the agent's reservation wage directly measures his expected value when unemployed. Intuitively, if agents can smooth marginal utilities perfectly across states, their reservation wage will depend purely on their expected income, and the marginal value of raising b by \$1 (holding fixed τ) is simply $(1 - e)$. But this marginal gain is outweighed by the cost of financing the extra dollar of benefits, which exceeds $1 - e$ because of the behavioral response $\varepsilon_{1-e,b}$. When marginal utilities fluctuate across states, agents value an increase in b at more than its actuarial cost, increasing the marginal value of public insurance. The extent to which agents value insurance can be captured by asking them how their valuation of being in the unemployed state varies with b, which is the parameter $\frac{d\overline{w}_0}{db}$. Like the liquidity vs. moral

---

[32] Both formulas derived above continue to hold in this model with stochastic wages. Conversely, the Shimer and Werning formula also holds in a model with variable search intensity.

[33] This corresponds to Eq. (12) in Shimer and Werning (2007), where the unemployment rate is $u = 1 - e$. The slight difference between the formulas (the $\frac{1}{1-u}$ factor in the denominator) arises because Shimer and Werning write the formula in terms of a partial-derivative-based elasticity. Here, $\varepsilon_{1-e,b}$ is the elasticity including the UI tax response needed to balance the budget; in Shimer and Werning's notation, it is holding the tax fixed.

hazard method, this approach also does not require identification of state dependence in utility or risk aversion.

An interesting implication of this result is that a higher sensitivity of reservation wages to benefits implies a *larger* value of social insurance, contrary to the intuition embodied in earlier empirical studies (e.g., Feldstein & Poterba, 1984), which view the sensitivity of reservation wages to UI benefits as a distortion. This point, like the moral hazard vs. liquidity decomposition above, illustrates the importance of connecting empirical estimates to models in order to fully understand the implications of empirical findings for policy.

Evidence on Reservation Wages. A long literature has sought to measure unemployed workers' reservation wages; see Devine and Kiefer (1991) for a review of early work and Krueger and Mueller (2011) for recent evidence. While these studies have shown that reservation wages have predictive power for unemployment durations and the types of offers that workers accept, they have also documented significant problems with self-reported reservation wage measures. For instance, a large fraction of workers end up accepting jobs that pay below their reported reservation wage. Moreover, most jobs have many characteristics that matter beyond the wage rate, such as the nature of the work or commuting distance. A one-dimensional reservation wage measure does not incorporate these other dimensions. When jobs have multiple characteristics, in order to implement (24), one would ideally like to measure how reservation *utilities* for jobs vary with the benefit rate. Because such reservation utilities cannot be easily measured, it is difficult to estimate $\frac{d\bar{w}_0}{db}$ accurately.

Perhaps because of these measurement issues, there is relatively little evidence on the impact of UI benefits on reservation wages. Feldstein and Poterba (1984) use survey data from the Current Population Survey to estimate $\frac{d\bar{w}_0}{db}$ by studying how changes in UI benefit levels affect reported reservation wages. Their point estimates imply a substantial correlation between UI benefit levels and reservation wages. However, their specification does not isolate purely exogenous variation in UI benefits due to law changes, as in more recent work, which raises concerns about omitted variable bias. Shimer and Werning implement (23) using an estimate of $\frac{d\bar{w}_0}{db}$ from Feldstein and Poterba (1984) and find a large, positive value for $M_W(b)$ at current benefit levels. They caution, however, that their exercise must be viewed as purely illustrative given the uncertainty in estimates of $\frac{d\bar{w}_0}{db}$ and call for further work on estimating this parameter using alternative methods.

One alternative approach is to use data on actual wages obtained at the next job and back out the implied distribution of reservation wages. There are now a large set of studies using administrative panel data that study whether increasing UI benefits raises subsequent wage rates. Card et al. (2007b) use a regression-discontinuity design in data from Austria to show that individuals eligible for 10 additional weeks of UI benefits take more time to find a job but do not have higher wages at their next job. Their estimates are sufficiently precise to rule out even a 1% increase in the wage rate at the upper bound of the 95% confidence interval. They also show that there are no detectable impacts on other observable job characteristics or on the number of years the worker spends at his next job, a summary measure of job match quality. Subsequent studies using similar RD designs have reached very similar conclusions. For instance, Lalive (2007) studies a 170 week benefit extension in Austria and shows that it has no impact on subsequent wages. van Ours and Vodopivec (2008) use a difference-in-difference approach using data from Slovenia and find that changes in benefit duration from 6 months to 3 months had no impact on subsequent earnings. These findings that ex-post observed wages are unaffected by benefit levels imply that reservation wages must be unaffected by benefit levels, i.e., $\frac{d\bar{w}_0}{db} = 0$.

How can UI have significant consumption smoothing and liquidity benefits but little effect on ex-post wages? Lentz and Tranas (2005), Chetty (2008), and Card et al. (2007b) develop pure search intensity models with borrowing constraints that generate these patterns. We present a stylized version of this model in Section 3.3.1 below. In these models, workers can control the amount of effort they spend searching for a job, but have a fixed wage rate. Such models can be viewed as an approximation to an environment in which the arrival rate of suitable job offers is relatively low, so the option value of waiting for a better offer is small and most workers take the first offer they receive. One puzzling feature of the data given this explanation is that there is tremendous heterogeneity in observed wage changes from the previous job to the new job across unemployed workers. Understanding how the variance of job offers can be reconciled with the lack of mean impacts of UI benefits on reservation wages is an open question for future research.[34]

In summary, there are now a variety of methods of calculating the welfare gains from increasing benefit levels in social insurance programs, but each of the methods yields different results because empirical evidence on many of the key parameters remains inadequate. Moreover, the three formulas discussed above are not an exhaustive list of potential approaches for connecting theory to data in analyzing optimal benefit levels for social insurance. There could be many other representations of the optimality condition in (13) that could be useful for applied work. The multiplicity of formulas for $M_W(b)$ is a general property of the sufficient statistic approach (Chetty, 2009). Because the positive model is not fully identified by the inputs to the formula, there are generally several representations of the formula for welfare gains. This flexibility allows researchers to use the representation most suitable for their applications given the available variation and data.

---

[34] One possibility is a model with impatient workers who wait to search for a job until they have no cash-on-hand. Such a model would generate significant liquidity effects but no impacts on ex-post wages, and would have very different welfare implications.

3.3. Generalizing the Static Model

The analysis above rests on a static model that makes several strong assumptions that are unlikely to hold in practice. Many of these assumptions turn out to have little impact on the formulas for optimal social insurance derived above, which is why these formulas have been widely applied. However, there are some assumptions that are more consequential and raise issues that remain unresolved. In this section, we consider the consequences of each of the main assumptions in turn. The general principle is that if agents' choices in the private sector maximize private surplus, then the formulas derived above continue to hold irrespective of the structure of the model. However, as soon as choices do not maximize private surplus—either because of externalities or imperfect optimization—the formulas no longer hold.

One important assumption that we do not relax below—not because it is inconsequential but rather because there is very limited normative work on this issue—is that wage rates and all other prices are fixed. That is, we do not consider the possibility that changes in social insurance policies will affect market clearing prices in general equilibrium. Acemoglu and Shimer (1999) analyze optimal unemployment insurance in an equilibrium search model with endogenous occupation choice and show that expanding UI can improve efficiency in this environment by encouraging more workers to take high-wage, high-risk jobs. There is no empirical evidence to date on the magnitude of such effects.[35] Perhaps an even greater challenge is that there are no results to date on how such empirical estimates could be connected to equilibrium models to make quantitative statements about optimal policy.

3.3.1. Dynamics: Endogenous Savings and Borrowing Constraints

The most important limitation of the model analyzed above is that it does not incorporate dynamics. In dynamic models, agents can smooth consumption across periods and thus "self insure" part of the income fluctuations they face, potentially reducing the value of social insurance. In addition, social insurance distorts not just agents' effort choices but also their consumption and savings decisions. Hubbard, Skinner, and Zeldes (1995) present simulation evidence suggesting that social insurance and means-tested transfer programs can substantially reduce savings rates. Engen and Gruber (2001) show that increases in UI benefits have small but significant effects on wealth accumulation prior to job loss among workers at risk of layoff. These intertemporal consumption-smoothing and savings responses may be further complicated by borrowing constraints, generating buffer stock behavior as in Deaton (1991) or Carroll (1997).

---

[35] Rothstein (2010) and Chetty, Friedman, Olsen, and Pistaferri (2011) present evidence that tax and transfer policies affect wage rates and the distribution of jobs in equilibrium. Rothstein shows that expansions of the Earned Income Tax Credit (EITC) depress wages for workers who are ineligible for the EITC, while Chetty et al. show that the tax schedule in Denmark affects even the earnings of workers unaffected by the tax incentives because of firm responses. The effects of social insurance on equilibrium outcomes could potentially be uncovered using a similar research design that focuses on groups whose incentives are not directly affected by the program.

Models that incorporate all of these features have been widely studied and are complex and difficult to solve analytically. Surprisingly, however, the three simple formulas for the marginal welfare gain from raising social insurance benefits derived above continue to hold in such models with small modifications. Because this result underpins much of the modern literature on connecting theory to data in analyzing optimal social insurance, we provide a simple proof here.

We analyze the optimal level of unemployment benefits in a dynamic job search model with borrowing constraints, following Lentz and Tranas (2005) and Chetty (2008). For instructive purposes, we structure the analysis to parallel the steps for the static case in Section 3.1: (1) model setup, (2) characterizing the agent's problem, (3) the planner's problem, (4) deriving a condition for optimal benefits by exploiting envelope conditions, and (5) deriving empirically implementable sufficient statistic formulas.

Setup. The agent lives for T periods $\{0, \ldots, T-1\}$. The interest rate and the agent's time discount rate are set to zero to simplify notation. The agent becomes (exogenously) unemployed at $t = 0$. An agent who enters a period t without a job first chooses search effort e_t. As in the static case, we normalize e_t to equal the probability of finding a job in the current period. Let $\psi(e_t)$ denote the cost of search effort, which is strictly increasing and convex. If search is successful, the agent begins working immediately in period t. All jobs last indefinitely once found.

We make two assumptions to simplify exposition: (1) the agent earns a fixed pre-tax wage of w when employed, eliminating reservation wage choices and (2) assets prior to job loss (A_0) are exogenous, eliminating effects of UI benefits on savings behavior prior to job loss. Neither assumption affects the results below (Chetty, 2008).

If the worker is unemployed in period t, he receives an unemployment benefit $b < w$. If the worker is employed in period t, he pays a tax τ. Let c_t^e denote the agent's consumption in period t if a job is found in that period. Note that the agent will optimally set consumption at c_t^e for all $t' > t$ as well because he faces no uncertainty once he finds a job and therefore smooth consumption perfectly. If the agent fails to find a job in period t, he sets consumption to c_t^u. The agent then enters period $t + 1$ unemployed and the problem repeats. Let $u(c_t)$ denote flow consumption utility when unemployed and $v(c_t)$ denote flow utility when employed.

Agent's Problem. We characterize the solution to the agent's problem using discrete-time dynamic programming. The value function for an individual who finds a job at the beginning of period t, conditional on beginning the period with assets A_t is

$$V_t(A_t) = \max_{A_{t+1} \geq L} v(A_t - A_{t+1} + w_t - \tau) + V_{t+1}(A_{t+1}), \qquad (25)$$

where L is the borrowing constraint. The value function for an individual who fails to find a job at the beginning of period t and remains unemployed is

$$U_t(A_t) = \max_{A_{t+1} \geq L} u(A_t - A_{t+1} + b_t) + J_{t+1}(A_{t+1}), \qquad (26)$$

where

$$J_t(A_t) = \max_{e_t} e_t V_t(A_t) + (1 - e_t)U_t(A_t) - \psi(e_t) \tag{27}$$

is the value of entering period t without a job with assets A_t.[36]

An unemployed agent chooses e_t to maximize expected utility at the beginning of period t, given by (27). Optimal search intensity is determined by the first-order condition

$$\psi'(e_t) = V_t(A_t) - U_t(A_t). \tag{28}$$

The condition parallels (10) in the static model, except that the marginal value of search effort is given by the difference between the optimized present values of employment and unemployment in the dynamic model rather than the difference in flow utilities.

Planner's Problem. The social planner's objective is to choose the unemployment benefit level b that maximizes the agent's expected utility at time 0, $J_0(A_0; b, \tau)$, subject to balancing the government's budget. Let $D = \sum_{t=0}^{T-1} \prod_{j=0}^{t} (1 - e_j)$ denote the agent's expected unemployment duration. The planner's problem is:

$$\max_{b, \tau} J_0(A_0; b, \tau) \text{ s.t. } Db = (T - D)\tau. \tag{29}$$

Differentiating J_0 w.r.t. b yields:

$$\frac{dJ_0}{db} = e_0 \frac{\partial V_0}{\partial b} + (1 - e_0) \frac{\partial U_0}{\partial b} - \left(e_0 \frac{\partial V_0}{\partial \tau} + (1 - e_0) \frac{\partial U_0}{\partial \tau} \right) \frac{d\tau}{db}. \tag{30}$$

The key step in obtaining an empirically implementable representation of (30) is to exploit the envelope conditions for e_t, c_t^u, and c_t^e. These variables are all chosen to maximize the agent's expected utility at each stage of his dynamic program. Because changes in these variables do not have a first-order impact on utility, one can ignore the impacts of changes in b and τ on these choices when calculating the derivatives in (30). Hence, the only terms that appear in the derivatives are the marginal utilities in which b and τ directly appear. To characterize these terms, define the average marginal utility of consumption while unemployed as

$$\mathbb{E}u'(c_t^u) = \frac{1}{D} \sum_{t=0}^{T-1} \prod_{i=0}^{t} (1 - e_i)u'(c_t^u))$$

and the average marginal utility of consumption while employed as

$$\mathbb{E}v'(c_t^e) = \frac{1}{T - D} (e_0 T v'(c_0^e) + \sum_{t=1}^{T-1} [\prod_{i=1}^{t} (1 - e_{i-1})]e_t(T - t)v'(c_t^e)).$$

---

[36] It is easy to show that V_t is concave because there is no uncertainty following reemployment; however, U_t could be convex. Lentz and Tranas (2005) and Chetty (2008) report that non-concavity never arises in their simulations for a broad range of plausible parameters. Therefore, we assume that U_t is globally concave in the parameter space of interest and use first-order conditions to identify the optimal level of benefits.

Some algebra yields:

$$e_0 \frac{\partial V_0}{\partial b} + (1 - e_0) \frac{\partial U_0}{\partial b} = D \mathbb{E} u'(c_t^u),$$

$$e_0 \frac{\partial V_0}{\partial \tau} + (1 - e_0) \frac{\partial U_0}{\partial \tau} = (T - D) \mathbb{E} v'(c_t^e).$$

The government's budget constraint implies that $\frac{d\tau}{db} = \frac{D}{T-D}\left(1 + \frac{T}{T-D}\varepsilon_{D,b}\right)$. Combining these expressions, it follows that

$$\frac{dJ_0}{db} = D \mathbb{E} u'(c_t^u) - D \mathbb{E} v'(c_t^e)\left(1 + \frac{T}{T-D}\varepsilon_{D,b}\right).$$

As in the static model, we normalize the welfare gain from a $1 increase in the size of the government insurance program by the welfare gain from raising the wage bill in the high state by $1 to obtain

$$
\begin{aligned}
M_W(b) &= \frac{\frac{dJ_0}{db}(b)/D}{\frac{dJ_0}{dw}(b)/(T-D)} \\
&= \frac{1}{\mathbb{E} u'(c_t^e)}\left\{\mathbb{E} u'(c_t^u) - \mathbb{E} v'(c_t^e)\left(1 + \frac{T}{T-D}\varepsilon_{D,b}\right)\right\} \\
&= \frac{\mathbb{E} u'(c_t^u) - \mathbb{E} v'(c_t^e)}{\mathbb{E} v'(c_t^e)} - \frac{1}{1 - D/T}\varepsilon_{D,b}.
\end{aligned}
\tag{31}
$$

This expression coincides with the formula for $M_W(b)$ from the static model in (13) with two changes. First, the fraction of time spent unemployed is measured over the entire life of the agent (D/T) instead of in a single period. Correspondingly, the relevant elasticity is $\varepsilon_{D,b}$ rather than $\varepsilon_{1-e,b}$. Second, and more importantly, the gap in marginal utilities that enters the formula is the difference between the *average* marginal utility when employed and unemployed. This is because the average value of a marginal dollar of UI benefits depends upon the mean marginal utility across all the periods over which the agent is unemployed during his life. Similarly, the average cost of raising the UI tax depends upon the cost of losing $1 during all the periods over which the agent is employed.

Sufficient Statistics Implementation. Equation (31) can be implemented using each of the three approaches described above with modifications to account for the fact that one must measure the gap in average marginal utilities. To implement the consumption-smoothing approach, one must estimate the *mean* consumption drop between periods when the agent is employed and unemployed, $\frac{\Delta \bar{c}}{\bar{c}^e} = \frac{\mathbb{E} c_t^u - \mathbb{E} c_t^e}{\mathbb{E} c_t^e}$, as the gap in expected marginal utilities when utility is not state-dependent is $\frac{\mathbb{E} u'(c_t^u) - \mathbb{E} u'(c_t^e)}{\mathbb{E} u'(c_t^e)} = \gamma \frac{\Delta \bar{c}}{\bar{c}^e}$. Identifying $\frac{\Delta \bar{c}}{\bar{c}^e}$ is conceptually analogous to identifying $\frac{\Delta c}{c}$ in the static model. However, it may not directly correspond to the difference between consumption immediately before and after unemployment, as measured by Gruber (1997) and others, if consumption trends substantially over the lifecycle. The extent to which $\frac{\Delta \bar{z}}{\bar{c}^e}$ differs from estimates using Gruber's approach has not yet been investigated empirically and requires further work.

Similarly, to implement the liquidity vs. moral hazard approach, one must estimate the impacts of *annuities* to recover expected marginal utilities over the unemployment spell in a dynamic model. Again, this is conceptually no different than estimating the impact of lump sum cash grants, but may be harder to implement empirically. In practice, Chetty (2008) translates his estimates of the impacts of cash grants on unemployment durations into the impacts of annuities by making assumptions about discount rates. Finally, Shimer and Werning (2007) show that their reservation wage approach goes through in a dynamic model provided that utility has a CARA specification that eliminates income effects.

The general lesson from the analysis of the dynamic model is that one does not need to fully characterize all the margins through which agents may respond to shocks to calculate the marginal welfare gains of social insurance. Even in complex dynamic models, the calculation of welfare gains can be distilled to two parameters: the gap in average marginal utilities and the elasticity that enters the government's budget constraint $\varepsilon_{D,b}$. There is no need to identify additional structural parameters such as the tightness of the borrowing constraint (L) or the cost of job search ψ to calculate $\frac{dW}{db}$. Similarly, one can show that the formula in (31) is robust to a variety of other extensions as well. For example, Kaplan (2012) shows that many young unemployed workers move back in with their parents as a method of consumption smoothing. He shows that incorporating this margin of adjustment into a structural model has significant effects on consumption fluctuations and the benefits of unemployment insurance. However, this margin is automatically accounted for in the formulas derived above. Mathematically, the option to move back home is simply another choice variable for agents and thus has no impact on (31). Intuitively, optimizing agents account for the option to move back home in all their choices. Thus, empirically observed consumption patterns, liquidity effects, and reservation wages all already incorporate this margin.

Chetty (2006b) establishes the validity of (31) at its most general level by analyzing a dynamic model where transitions from the good state to the bad state follow an arbitrary stochastic process. Agents make an arbitrary number of choices and are subject to arbitrary constraints. The choices could include variables such as reservation wages, savings behavior, spousal labor supply, or human capital investments. Chetty shows that (31) holds in this environment as long as agents' choices maximize private welfare.[37] This

---

[37] A related point is that the same formula also holds in the context of other social insurance programs where the structure of the positive model differs. For instance, in the context of health insurance, one may choose the intensity of care *after* getting sick rather than controlling ex-ante effort. The formula in (31) holds in such a model with an appropriate redefinition of the average marginal utilities and the elasticity that enters the planner's budget constraint. Chetty (2006b) considers an example of "tenure review" that is formally analogous to this case.

is the critical assumption underlying (31). In the rest of this section, we discuss a series of important externalities that violate this assumption.

3.3.2. Externalities on Private Insurers

Public insurance is motivated by market failures of the types discussed in Section 2. However, most of the literature on optimal public insurance simply assumes that private markets do not provide any insurance against risks rather than modeling the underlying sources of the market failure. This assumption—which we made when deriving (31) above—is a convenient technical simplification but has important consequences for optimal social insurance.[38] If there is a formal market for private insurance, agents' choices will no longer maximize *total* private surplus (including the agent and private insurer) because the private insurance contract will distort choices. As a result, marginal changes in agents' choices will have fiscal externalities on private insurers. For example, suppose that part of health expenditures are covered by public insurance and part by private insurance. When the government raises health insurance benefits, agents will spend more on health care, and this increased expenditure will raise costs for *both* the government and the private insurer. This added fiscal externality on the private insurer is a first-order effect that reduces the marginal value of insurance and is not accounted for in (31).

Before discussing how these fiscal externalities affect optimal benefits, it is worth emphasizing that only private insurance contracts that generate moral hazard alter the formulas for optimal public insurance. Private insurance that does not generate moral hazard—such as informal insurance between relatives that is well monitored—has no impact on the original formula in (31). To see this, suppose that the agent can transfer b_p between states at a cost $q(b_p)$, so that increasing consumption by b_p in the low state requires payment of a premium $\frac{1-e}{e}b_p + q(b_p)$ in the high state. As long as the level of b_p is chosen to maximize utility, it is simply another choice variable in Chetty's (2006b) framework, and thus has no impact on the optimal social insurance formula. The effects of any such insurance arrangement are automatically embedded in the empirically observed consumption drop and other parameters that enter the formula.

There is relatively little work analyzing optimal social insurance with private insurance that induces moral hazard. Golosov and Tsyvinski (2007) analyze optimal government policy in a model in which agents can purchase insurance from multiple private providers. They rule out market failures due to adverse selection by assuming that agents can sign contracts before private information is revealed. However, the private market still does not achieve an efficient outcome because of a "multiple dealing" externality across firms, originally discussed by Pauly (1974). Intuitively, each firm does not take into account the

---

[38] One potential rationale for this approach is that private markets are essentially at a corner of providing zero insurance against certain risks (e.g., unemployment), and thus marginal changes in public insurance can be evaluated under the assumption that there is no private insurance. Unfortunately, this is not an accurate description of insurance markets in many important applications such as health.

fact that its provision of insurance distorts the agent's behavior, thereby affecting other insurers' budgets and leading to overprovision of insurance in the decentralized private market equilibrium. Golosov and Tsyvinski show that the government can raise welfare by imposing a corrective tax that countervails the multiple dealing externality. They also show that the provision of public insurance partially crowds out private insurance and may reduce welfare because it leads to further overprovision of insurance. Using numerical calibrations, they demonstrate that these effects could be quite large quantitatively. While these results demonstrate that endogenous private insurance could reduce the scope for government intervention in insurance markets, the implications of their analysis for optimal benefit levels in practice are less clear. Golosov and Tsyvinski rule out many of the rationales for publicly provided insurance we discussed above, such as adverse selection, by assumption. In addition, their numerical calibrations rest on strong assumptions about the structure of the underlying model that are not directly grounded in empirical evidence.

Chetty and Saez (2010) attempt to connect the theory to the data more explicitly by deriving formulas for optimal benefits in terms of empirically estimable parameters with endogenous private insurance. They first analyze a case in which agents are homogeneous and purchase insurance from a private firm. Because there is no market failure in this model, if agents in the private sector optimize perfectly, the marginal gain from government intervention is strictly negative (Kaplow, 1991). When the private sector does not offer the optimal level of insurance—e.g., because of behavioral biases of the types discussed in Section 3.3.5 below—there is a potential role for government intervention. Chetty and Saez assume that the planner maximizes the agent's true expected utility (which they assume is not state-dependent) and show that the marginal welfare gain from public insurance b can be expressed as

$$M_W(b) = (1-r)\left[\frac{u'(c_l) - u'(c_h)}{u'(c_h)} - \frac{\varepsilon_{1-e,b}}{e}\frac{1 + b_p/b}{1 - r}\right], \tag{32}$$

where b_p is the private insurance benefit level in equilibrium and $r = -\frac{db_p}{db}$ measures the extent to which private insurance is crowded out by public insurance. When $b_p = 0$, this formula reduces to (13) with state-independent utility. When $b_p > 0$, two additional terms enter the formula. First, the marginal welfare gain is scaled down by $(1-r)$ because \$1 more of public insurance raises total insurance $(b + b_p)$ by only \$$(1 - r)$. This effect rescales but does not change the sign of $M_W(b)$ and thus does not affect the optimal public benefit level b^*. The second and more important effect of endogenous private insurance is captured by the added term $\frac{1+b_p/b}{1-r}$ that amplifies the elasticity. This term reflects the fiscal externality that expanding public insurance has on private insurers. When the agent reduces e in response to a \$1 increase in b, it not only has a cost to the government proportional to $\varepsilon_{1-e,b}$ but also a cost to the private insurer proportional to $\varepsilon_{1-e,b}b_p/b$. This externality effect reduces the optimal benefit level beyond what one would have calculated based on the formula in (31) that ignored private insurance.

Chetty and Saez implement (32) in the context of unemployment insurance and health insurance to illustrate their approach. For unemployment—where the only form of private insurance is severance pay—Chetty and Saez estimate $\frac{b_p}{b} = 0.2$ and $r = 0.14$ using cross-state variation in UI benefits. Because the share of private UI benefits and crowd-out effects are small, endogenous private insurance has small effects on the optimal UI benefit level with plausible elasticities. For health, the share of private insurance is much larger ($\frac{b_p}{b} = 0.89$), as is the degree of crowd out. Cutler and Gruber (1996) estimate that a \$1 increase in public health insurance benefits reduces private insurance benefit levels by 50 cents, implying $r = 0.5$. As a result, accounting for endogenous private insurance reduces the marginal welfare gains of an aggregate health insurance expansion by more than an order of magnitude according to (32).

The shortcoming of the formula in (32) is that it is sensitive to the sources of private market failures. For instance, Chetty and Saez extend their baseline analysis to a case where there are heterogeneous agents who have private information about their risk types. This generates adverse selection and partial private insurance provision by the market. In this setting, the formula for $M_W(b)$ has additional terms relative to (32) because it has the added benefit of pooling risks across individuals of different types through a mandate. Hence, (32) is not a robust "sufficient statistic" formula because it is sensitive to the structure of the positive model. Developing formulas that are robust to the underlying sources of private market failures and can be implemented empirically is among the most important priorities for future research on social insurance.

3.3.3. Externalities on Government Budgets

Fiscal externalities can also arise when the government itself provides multiple types of social insurance or levies taxes. For instance, expansions in disability insurance may reduce the probability that a worker with a high disutility of work chooses to search for a job and claim unemployment insurance. A more general source of fiscal externalities is taxation. Any reduction in labor supply induced by social insurance programs will have a negative fiscal externality on the government by reducing income tax revenue.

It is useful to divide fiscal externalities into two categories. The first are mechanical externalities that arise because the choice insured by the program (e) directly affects other parts of the government's budget, such as tax revenue. The second are indirect fiscal externalities that arise because of *other* behavioral responses unrelated to e itself. For instance, an increase in UI benefits may induce agents to save less, which could reduce revenue from capital gains taxes.

To see how such fiscal externalities affect (31), let us return to the static model and add an initial period, $t = 0$, in which the agent chooses how much to save, which we denote by A, before he faces the risk of unemployment. Let Z denote the agent's wealth at the beginning of period 0, which we take as fixed. In period 0, consumption is given by $c_0 = Z - A$. Let τ_A denote the tax levied on savings A (e.g., a capital gains tax) and

τ_e denote an income tax levied on employed individuals. Tax revenue $R = \tau_A A + \tau_e e$ is rebated to the agent as a lump sum in the high state, so that $c_h = A + w_h - \tau(b) + R$.

The agent chooses effort e to maximize his expected utility taking the parameters of the tax system as fixed:

$$\max_{e,A} V(e, A) = v(Z - A) + ev(A + w_h - \tau(b) + R) + (1 - e)u(A + w_l + b) - \psi(e)$$

The social planner's objective is to choose the benefit level b that maximizes the agent's expected utility:

$$\max_{b} W(b) = v(Z - A) + ev(A + w_h - \tau(b) + R) + (1 - e)u(A + w_l + b) - \psi(e)$$

$$\text{s.t. } e = e(b) \text{ and } A = A(b) \text{ and } R = \tau_A A + \tau_e e.$$

Algebra analogous to that above yields:

$$M_W(b) = \frac{u'(c_l) - v'(c_h)}{v'(c_h)} - \frac{\varepsilon_{1-e,b}}{e}\left(1 + \frac{\tau_e}{b}\right) + \frac{1}{1-e}\frac{A}{b}\tau_A \varepsilon_{A,b}.$$

This equation differs from the original formula in (13) in two ways. The first new term, $\frac{\tau_e}{b}$, reflects the mechanical externality arising from the fact that reductions in e reduce income tax revenue. The magnitude of this effect is proportional to $\frac{\varepsilon_{1-e,b}}{e}$. Accounting for this mechanical externality does not require estimating any additional parameters; one must simply take the income tax rate into account when calculating the impact of changes in e on the government budget. The second new term is proportional to $\tau_A \varepsilon_{A,b}$. This term reflects the indirect fiscal externality imposed by distorting the choice of savings A. Accounting for this indirect externality requires estimation of the additional elasticity $\varepsilon_{A,b}$, e.g., as in Engen and Gruber (2001).[39]

Empirically, an important source of indirect fiscal externalities are behavioral responses that affect takeup of other social insurance programs. Autor and Duggan (2003) provide empirical evidence on the interaction between unemployment and disability insurance in the US. Using local employment shocks instrumented by industry shares, they show that more individuals exit the labor force and apply for DI when they are laid off when DI benefits are raised. As a result, unemployment rates rise less when disability insurance is expanded and, correspondingly, one would expect UI benefit payments to fall. Of course, the government also loses revenue by collecting fewer taxes from individuals who would have worked if the DI benefit level were lower.

Borghans, Gielen, and Luttmer (2010) quantify the magnitude of such fiscal externalities using administrative data from the Netherlands. They use a regression-discontinuity design to show that reducing the generosity of DI benefits increases reliance on other

---

[39] Consistent with the results in Section 3.3.1, the distortion in A has no impact on the formula if $\tau_A = 0$; it is only because savings are taxed that this behavioral response matters.

forms of social insurance. They estimate that every \$1 saved in DI benefits via a benefit cut leads to approximately 50 cents of additional expenditure on other social insurance programs. Part of this cost is offset by increased tax revenue, but it is clear that accounting for such fiscal externalities is critical in designing optimal social insurance policy. More generally, one should ideally analyze social insurance and tax policies in a unified framework rather than optimizing each program (UI, DI, health insurance, etc.) separately.

3.3.4. Other Externalities

Agents in the private sector may have direct non-pecuniary externalities on each other independent of the fiscal channels discussed above. In Section 2.3, we discussed how such externalities—such as the spread of contagious diseases—could provide a motivation for social insurance. In this section, we discuss how such externalities affect the optimal design of social insurance policies.

While any externality would affect (31), the literature on optimal social insurance has focused on two types of externalities in particular. The first are social multiplier effects, which refer to the idea that one individual's choices may affect the choices of those around him. For instance, an increase in disability benefits may induce some agents to stop working, which in turn may increase the value of leisure for their peers. The second are congestion externalities, which arise because of constraints that make one agent's behavior change the returns to effort for another agent. For instance, in the context of unemployment, agents compete for a limited number of positions when jobs are rationed. In this setting, changes in UI benefits can have different effects at the macroeconomic level relative to the microeconomic level.

Theoretical work on social multipliers effects and social insurance has shown that the aggregate effects of insurance on behavior could be significantly larger than microeconomic estimates of a single individual's behavioral responses to a change in his marginal incentives. For instance, Lindbeck, Nyberg, and Weibull (1999) present a benchmark model of how social norms about labor supply change the impacts of the welfare state on the economy. In their model, individuals' taste for work depends not only upon their private disutility of work but also the fraction of individuals who rely on social support rather than work to make a living. They demonstrate that in this environment, small changes in policy can lead to dramatic, discontinuous changes in the size of the welfare state by shifting the equilibrium. For instance, the macroeconomic effect of an increase in disability benefits on labor supply, ε^M, could be much larger than the microeconomic elasticity ε for any single individual. Intuitively, when social insurance benefits are increased, the direct effect on each agent's behavior is amplified by the feedback mechanism of the change in the norm. Lindbeck, Nyberg, and Weibull argue that these non-linear responses could explain why some developed countries (e.g., Scandinavia) have much larger social insurance systems than others (such as the US).

How do such social multipliers affect the formula for optimal benefits in (31)? If social multipliers affect behavioral responses but do not directly affect utility, (31) holds, but ε must be replaced by the macro elasticity ε^M. This is because the aggregate response ε^M is what determines how an increase in benefits affects the government budget. If the social externalities enter utility directly—e.g., if one agent not working increases the utility of leisure for others agents—then an additional term enters (31) to capture the impact of this externality on welfare, as the envelope conditions used to derive (31) do not take account of this effect.[40]

Empirical evidence lends support to the presence of such social multipliers. For instance, Lalive (2003) presents evidence that an extension of unemployment benefits to workers over age 50 in Austria affected the labor supply of their peers below age 50, although his results rely on relatively strong identification assumptions. Clark (2003) uses data on subjective well being from a panel of households in the United Kingdom and shows that unemployed individuals report higher levels of happiness when the local unemployment rate is higher, while employed individuals report lower levels of satisfaction. Bertrand, Luttmer, and Mullainathan (2000) show that individuals are more likely to take up welfare when living in neighborhoods with a large population of residents who speak their own language, suggesting that there are network effects in welfare takeup. A limitation of this analysis is that it relies purely on cross-neighborhood comparisons and thus rests on relatively strong identification assumptions. Chetty, Friedman and Saez (2012) present evidence of social spillovers via learning using panel data. They show that individuals are more likely to *change* their earnings behavior in response to the incentives created by the Earned Income Tax Credit in the US when they move to a neighborhood where other individuals respond to the program. Unfortunately, none of these studies provide estimates of how the micro impacts of policy (ε) changes differ from their macro impacts (ε^M).

While social multiplier effects amplify elasticities and potentially reduce the optimal level of social insurance, congestion externalities have the opposite effect. Landais, Michaillat, and Saez (2012) analyze optimal unemployment insurance in a job search model with rationing. A standard matching function maps the number of vacancies and job openings to the equilibrium level of unemployment. They assume that wages are rigid, so that when the economy is hit by a negative productivity shock, jobs are rationed in the sense that the labor market does not clear even if workers exert arbitrarily high search effort. In this environment, job seekers have a negative search externality on each other: each individual tries to outrun his peers to find a job, leading to excess search effort via a standard rat-race mechanism. Landais, Michaillat, and Saez demonstrate that this externality has two effects on (31). First, it reduces the macro elasticity of unemployment with respect to the benefit rate relative to the micro elasticity. Again, it is the

---

[40] See Kroft (2008) for an analysis of optimal UI with social spillovers in takeup decisions.

macro elasticity that enters (31) for the reasons described above. Second, the negative job search externality creates an added benefit from raising UI benefits, because when each individual searches less, he has a positive spillover effect on other job seekers. Because job rationing is more severe in recessions, Landais, Michaillat, and Saez conclude that the optimal level of UI benefits should be countercyclical. They show that the micro and macro elasticities along with the other parameters in (31) are sufficient statistics to calculate the optimal level of benefits in a relatively general environment.[41]

Motivated by the question of whether unemployment benefits should vary over the business cycle, a recent empirical literature has investigated whether elasticities of unemployment durations with respect to benefit levels vary with labor market conditions. Most of the existing evidence uses identification strategies that are more likely to recover partial-equilibrium micro elasticities rather than general-equilibrium macro elasticities. This is because the need for a control group often makes it easier to identify partial equilibrium effects using quasi-experimental methods. Schmieder, Wachter, and Bender (2012) show that UI benefit extensions have smaller effects on unemployment exit hazards in recessions than in booms using data for Germany, implying that the moral hazard effect of UI is smaller at the micro level in recessions. Landais (2011) uses a regression kink design to show that changes in UI benefit levels have similar effects on unemployment durations in recessions and booms in the United States. Kroft and Notowidigdo (2011) present evidence that the moral hazard effects of changes in UI benefits are smaller in recessions, while the consumption-smoothing benefits are roughly constant, although their estimates are somewhat imprecise due to a lack of power.

Crépon, Duflo, Gurgand, Rathelot, and Zamora (2012) present evidence that the macro elasticity ε^M is much smaller than the micro elasticity ε in weak labor markets because of congestion effects. They run a randomized experiment that provides job placement assistance to a large group of individuals in a given labor market. They find that the individuals who did *not* receive assistance have significantly *lower* probabilities of finding a job in weak labor markets when many of their peers receive job placement assistance. This constitutes direct evidence of congestion effects in the labor market and, based on the models discussed above, suggests that the optimal UI benefit level is higher when labor markets are weak.

3.3.5. Imperfect Optimization

Another important reason that agents' choices may not maximize total private surplus is failures of optimization. As we noted in Section 2.3 above, if agents optimized perfectly, we would observe very small consumption fluctuations $\frac{\Delta c}{c}$ for temporary shocks such as unemployment. Hence, (31) would imply that the welfare gains of social insurance are

---

[41] Landais, Michaillat, and Saez focus on benefits levels rather than the duration of benefits. However, the typical policy response to a recession is an extension in the duration of benefits rather than an increase in the level of benefits. Understanding why this is the case is an interesting open area for further work.

small. It is tempting to simply plug in a statistic such as the observed (large) values of $\frac{\Delta c}{c}$ and calculate the welfare gains of social insurance by applying (31) even if agents do not optimize. Unfortunately, (31) is not a valid formula for optimal benefits when agents do not optimize. This formula is valid only if agents optimize, and we know that if they optimized $\frac{\Delta c}{c}$ would not be large. Because a biased agent's choices do not maximize his own utility, the envelope conditions exploited to derive (31) no longer hold. Hence, one must modify the formulas to allow for imperfect optimization to obtain an internally consistent understanding of optimal social insurance.[42]

At a broad level, there are two conceptual challenges in accounting for imperfect optimization. First, conducting welfare analysis requires recovering the individuals' true preferences, which is challenging when one cannot rely on the standard tools of revealed preference used above. One approach to solving this problem is to posit a structural model of behavioral failures, such as hyperbolic discounting (Laibson, 1997), and estimate the parameters of that model to analyze optimal policy. Another approach, which is closer in spirit to the sufficient statistic methods we have focused on here, is to derive formulas for the welfare consequences of social insurance that do not rest on a specific positive model of optimization failures (Bernheim & Rangel, 2009; Chetty, Looney, & Kroft, 2009). The chapter by Bernehim in this volume discusses welfare analysis in behavioral models in greater detail. Second, from an empirical perspective, it is unclear how to systematically distinguish mistakes from unobserved attributes such as risk aversion or private information about expected losses under an insurance contract. While we are able to identify specific examples where we can reject the null of perfect optimization, it is less clear how we can quantify the degree to which individuals are biased, which is necessary for implementing corrective policies.

There is relatively little work on social insurance in behavioral models. DellaVigna and Paserman (2005) estimate a model of job search with impatient agents and show empirically that agents who are more impatient—as measured by variables that quantify tradeoffs between immediate and delayed payoffs—search less for jobs. In their model, increasing UI benefits would have additional costs because it would further reduce effort below the optimum. Fang and Silverman (2009) estimate a similar model of time inconsistency in the context of welfare program participation and estimate the model's structural parameters. They then use their model to show that policies that limit the number of months for which individuals are eligible for social transfers could raise welfare. These papers are examples of the first approach to welfare analysis in behavioral models described above— positing a structural model and using it to analyze the welfare consequences of policy changes.

---

[42] This point illustrates a general weakness of the sufficient statistic approach, which is that the assumptions used to derive the formula are never explicitly tested because the parameters of the model are never fully identified. See Chetty (2009) for further discussion of these issues.

Spinnewijn (2010) is an example of the second approach to behavioral welfare analysis. He generalizes the sufficient statistic formulas for optimal benefit levels derived above to an environment in which agents are overoptimistic about their probability of finding a job. Spinnewijn shows that it is crucial to distinguish between two types of biases in beliefs: baseline bias, which is misestimating the probability of finding a job holding search effort fixed, and control bias, which is misestimating the impact of increased search effort on the probability of finding a job. Baseline bias has no impact on the formula in (31) because it does not affect the agent's behavioral responses to benefit changes or his utility. In contrast, control bias introduces a new term in the formula that arises from the fact that the agent does not set e at its true optimum. As a result, changes in b have a first-order effect on utility by inducing changes in e. For instance, an agent who is control pessimistic will undersupply effort in equilibrium, and increases in benefits will lower welfare by distorting e downward even further. Spinnewijn presents empirical evidence that agents are indeed control pessimistic in practice, suggesting that calculations of optimal benefits based on the traditional formula in (31) will overstate the welfare gains of insurance.

The limitation of these papers is that each one characterizes the implications of a specific type of bias for policies. The challenge for research on social insurance in behavioral models is finding a framework that incorporates a broad set of biases yet offers empirically implementable results for optimal policy. Further work along these lines is a challenging but promising direction for future research.

3.4. Other Dimensions of Policy

While much of the literature connecting theory to data has focused on identifying the optimal level of social insurance benefits, there are many other important questions in the design of insurance programs. In this section, we briefly review three areas that have received attention in recent work: mandated savings accounts, increasing program takeup rates, and changing the path or duration of benefits.

3.4.1. Liquidity Provision and Mandated Savings Accounts

Our analysis thus far has focused exclusively on a social insurance system that transfers money from individuals in the high state to those in the low state via taxes and transfers. However, as we discussed above, there would be little need for social insurance against temporary shocks such as unemployment if individuals had access to sufficient liquidity while unemployed. Recent research has therefore analyzed policies that provide liquidity to unemployed individuals or force them to build a buffer stock via mandated savings accounts rather than transferring resources across individuals. Intuitively, if the motive for social insurance benefits is a lack of liquidity, the optimal tool to correct this problem may be to directly provide liquidity rather than to provide state–contingent transfers.

Shimer and Werning (2008) analyze optimal unemployment insurance in a model where agents can freely save and borrow using a riskless asset while unemployed. Under constant absolute risk aversion preferences, they demonstrate that the optimal policy provides free access to liquidity and a relatively low level of unemployment benefits. Chetty (2008) numerically compares the welfare gains from the provision of zero-interest loans with the welfare gains of increasing unemployment benefits in a search model calibrated to match empirical estimates of liquidity and moral hazard effects. Consistent with Shimer and Werning's intuition, Chetty's simulations show that the provision of loans yields large welfare gains and greatly reduces the gains from raising unemployment benefit levels. While these results highlight the potential value of liquidity provision as a policy tool, the costs of providing liquidity (e.g., due to default risk) are not modeled in these studies. Hence, these studies do not shed light on the optimal combination of loans and unemployment insurance benefits. Identifying the optimal combination of these two policies in an environment where both policies have social costs is an important open question.

An alternative approach to providing liquidity is to directly address agents' failure to build buffer stocks by mandating savings prior to unemployment. Feldstein and Altman (2007) propose a system of UI savings accounts in which individuals are required to save a fraction of their wages in accounts designated to be used only in the event of unemployment spells. If they become unemployed, individuals would draw upon these accounts at standard benefit rates. If individuals run out of money in their savings account, they would automatically draw benefits from the state UI system, which would continue to be financed by a (smaller) payroll tax. Any remaining balance at the point of retirement would be refunded to the individual. The benefit of such a system is that individuals' incentives to search for a job while unemployed are not distorted by the provision of UI benefits, because each extra $1 they use in UI benefits leaves them with $1 less of wealth in retirement, provided that they do not fully deplete their savings account balance. Using data from the Panel Study of Income Dynamics, Feldstein and Altman show that less than half of UI benefits would be paid to individuals who hit the corner of a zero account balance, implying that incentives could potentially be improved for many people. Orszag and Snower (2002) present calibrations showing that the impacts of such a system on unemployment durations could be quite large.

Stiglitz and Yun (2005) present a more formal argument for the optimality of UI savings accounts. They analyze a model in which individuals pay money into a pension system that is taken as exogenous. They prove that permitting individuals to draw down these pension assets in the event of adverse shocks raises welfare if individuals are borrowing constrained. The intuition is that allowing individuals to borrow against retirement savings relaxes borrowing constraints and permits better consumption smoothing at a lower efficiency cost than state-contingent transfers.

An important limitation of existing theoretical work on optimal liquidity provision and mandated savings accounts is that they all analyze models with agents who optimize perfectly. Mandated savings can only be justified if agents suffer from biases such as impatience, as the government is simply restricting the choice set available to agents. However, if agents are impatient, it is not clear that they will fully internalize the benefits of having more wealth in retirement if they draw less UI benefits when they are young. Hence, in a model that justifies mandated savings, such policies could well have efficiency costs similar to traditional social insurance systems. Countervailing this effect, there may be other biases—such as the increased salience of UI savings accounts relative to eligibility for UI benefits—that may reduce distortions when agents do not optimize perfectly. These intuitions illustrate that imperfect optimization should be a central element of future work on optimal liquidity and insurance policies.

Empirical evidence on the impacts of UI savings accounts is scarce because few governments have implemented such systems. Hartley, van Ours, and Vodopivec (2011) present suggestive evidence that a UI savings account program introduced in Chile reduced unemployment durations. Their analysis uses individuals who endogenously choose to opt into a traditional unemployment insurance program as a comparison group. Their conclusions therefore rest on stronger identification assumptions than most of the empirical studies discussed above. Further work using quasi-experimental designs to study the impacts of mandated savings accounts in needed to fully understand their impacts.

3.4.2. Imperfect Takeup

Another important dimension of social insurance policy is program participation. In the analysis above, we assumed that all individuals who are eligible for a social insurance program automatically participate in the program. In practice, takeup rates for most programs are often well below 100% (Currie, 2006). For instance, only 75% of individuals eligible for UI actually receive UI benefits when laid off. Incomplete takeup raises two questions for optimal program design. First, should the government seek to increase takeup rates, and if so what methods should be used to do so? Second, is the optimal level of benefits different when only some agents take up the benefit?

The social value of raising takeup rates—e.g., by reducing the costs of applying for a program—depends upon the value agents who choose not to participate get from the program relative to the takeup utility cost incurred by all agents. Imperfect takeup could in principle be socially desirable if the agents who choose not to takeup value the program significantly below its social cost. For example, Nichols and Zeckhauser (1982) propose a stylized model in which implementing a hurdle to claim benefits raises social welfare by removing individuals who do not value the program highly from the pool of recipients. In this model, the costs of taking up a program can serve as a screening mechanism, allowing public funds to be targeted at the subgroups who are in greatest need of assistance (e.g., those with the least liquidity).[43] However, the screening induced by hurdles to take up need not necessarily operate in this beneficial manner. For instance, suppose individuals who do not participate are uninformed about the program's existence or make optimization errors. In this environment, policies that increase takeup rates could raise welfare, because they may bring the individuals who would value social support most highly into the system. The nature of the marginal agents who do not take-up social insurance is ultimately an empirical question, and the answer could vary across programs and environments.

Empirical evidence on the determinants of takeup shows that imperfect takeup is driven by a mix of factors. Anderson and Meyer (1993) present evidence that individuals are more likely to take up UI benefits when net benefit levels are higher. Black, Smith, Berger, and Noel (2003) present experimental evidence that individuals are more likely to drop out of the UI system when they receive a mailing announcing that they must attend a training program in order to remain eligible for benefits. These results suggest that takeup is based on a rational cost-benefit conclusion and imply that the individuals who do not take up may be those who value the benefit the least. In contrast, Ebenstein and Stange (2010) show that the shift from in-person to telephone registration for UI benefits, which significantly reduced the time costs of takeup, had no impact on UI takeup rates. Bhargava and Manoli (2011) present experimental evidence showing that simplifying tax forms increases takeup of the Earned Income Tax Credit. These results raise the possibility that some individuals who do not take up may actually benefit significantly from the program despite getting screened out under the current program design. What remains unclear is the average valuation of benefits for those who do not take up, which is a key parameter for determining whether resources should be invested in increasing takeup rates. Developing methods to estimate this parameter and calculate the marginal welfare gains from increasing takeup is a promising area for future research.

How does incomplete takeup affect the optimal design of other parameters of the social insurance system? Kroft (2008) analyzes the optimal UI benefit level in a model with imperfect takeup. He generalizes the sufficient statistic formulas derived above to a model with heterogeneous takeup costs and rational agents. The formula in (31) changes in two ways in this setting. First, $\mathbb{E}u'(c_t^u)$ must be computed for the subgroup of individuals who takes up benefits rather than all individuals in the low state. Second, the elasticity parameter that is relevant is the sum of the behavioral elasticity $\varepsilon_{1-e,b}$ and the takeup elasticity, as increases in benefit rates raise expenditures both through traditional margins and by raising the number of individuals claiming benefits. In general, accounting for

[43] Such screening through costly ordeals is only desirable if the ordeal is highly effective at separating agents with high vs. low valuations of the program. If the screening mechanism is not powerful, simply reducing benefit levels by an equivalent amount may yield larger welfare gains. See the chapter by Piketty and Saez in this volume for a discussion of related issues in the context of "workfare" models of taxation.

endogenous takeup lowers the optimal benefit rate relative to computations that apply (31) to the subsample of individuals who take up benefits.

3.4.3. Path of Benefits

Most shocks have a variable time span. For instance, spells of work injury, disability, and unemployment all have uncertain durations. Although many health shocks are one-time events, there are some chronic conditions that generate expenditures over longer periods. In such settings, the social planner can choose not just the level of benefits but also its path. At an abstract level, one can choose a different benefit level b_t in each period t during which the individual is in the low state. In practice, many social insurance systems have one- or two-tiered benefit systems, in which benefits are provided at a constant level for a finite duration and then reduced or completely eliminated (e.g., the termination of UI benefits at 6 months in the US). Our preceding analysis has focused on identifying the optimal level of b under the assumption that $b_t = b$ for all t. In this section, we discuss the small but growing body of work that has sought to characterize the optimal path of benefits.

The fundamental tradeoff in setting the path of benefits, originally described by Shavell and Weiss (1979), is again between consumption smoothing and moral hazard. Increasing benefits over time is desirable from a consumption smoothing perspective, as it provides the largest benefits to the agents who need it most. Intuitively, those who suffered from long unemployment spells are likely to have depleted their assets and have a very high marginal utility of consumption. But increasing benefits over time is costly from an efficiency perspective, as it creates an incentive to "hold out" for higher benefits by prolonging one's duration in the low state. Unfortunately, deriving formulas that map the relative magnitude of these two effects to quantitative predictions about the optimal path of b_t is challenging. The literature on the optimal path of benefits has thus been less successful in connecting theory to data because of the complexity of dynamic models and the high-dimensional nature of the problem. We therefore briefly describe some of the main theoretical and empirical results that bear on this problem, highlighting the scope for further work deriving sufficient statistic formulas in this area.

Shavell and Weiss (1979) characterize the optimal path of a benefits in a discrete-time model in which agents make consumption and search effort choices in each period. When agents cannot save or borrow, the optimal path of benefits is declining because an upward sloping benefit path does not provide a smoother consumption path but creates moral hazard. When agents can save or borrow, Shavell and Weiss show that the optimal path could be upward or downward sloping depending upon the structural parameters of the model. Hopenhayn and Nicolini (1997) extend Shavell and Weiss' analysis to allow for a wage tax after reemployment, but focus on the case with no saving or borrowing. They show that the optimal path of benefits is again declining in this environment, but that there is a significant welfare gain from levying a substantial tax upon reemployment.

Werning (2002) generalizes Hopenhayn and Nicolini's analysis to a case with hidden savings, i.e., a more realistic environment where the planner can set benefit levels but cannot directly control consumption. Werning (2002) shows that when agents can save or borrow, optimal benefit levels may increase over time and are much lower in levels than those predicted by Hopenhayn and Nicolini's analysis.[44] Shavell and Weiss, Hopenhayn and Nicolini, and Werning all study models where agents have fixed wages and only choose search effort. Shimer and Werning (2008) analyze a standard reservation-wage model in which agents draw stochastic wage offers. They prove that the optimal path of benefits is constant ($b_t = b$) in a setting without liquidity constraints and CARA utility. Intuitively, under these assumptions, the agent's problem while unemployed is stationary because his attitudes toward risk and incentives to find a job do not change as he depletes his assets. As a result, the moral hazard costs and consumption-smoothing benefits of a steeper benefit profile perfectly cancel out, yielding a constant optimal benefit path. Shimer and Werning argue that in cases where agents do not have access to perfect capital markets, the optimal government policy is to provide loans and constant benefits.

While this result is a useful benchmark, the optimal path of benefits could differ substantially under alternative assumptions about the structure of the positive model. In practice, agents are highly liquidity constrained while unemployed and governments tend not to offer loans to such agents, perhaps because of moral hazard problems in debt repayment. Moreover, there could be significant non-stationarities in responses to incentives over a spell, due both to selection in an environment with heterogeneity and changes in the cost of effort. For instance, individuals who remain unemployed after 6 months could be relatively elastic types but may also have a hard time controlling the arrival rate of offers, driving $\varepsilon_{1-e,b}$ down over the course of an unemployment spell. Such forces eliminate the stationarity that drives Shimer and Werning's constant benefit result, as discussed in Shimer and Werning (2006). The quantitative magnitude of such effects is ultimately an empirical question whose answer could vary across environments and social insurance programs.

The empirical literature, which also focuses primarily on unemployment insurance, shows that the path of benefits has significant effects on agents' behavior in a manner that is consistent with forward-looking decisions. Card and Levine (2000) analyze the impacts of a 13 week extension in UI benefits in New Jersey on unemployment durations. Their estimates imply that this extension would have raised durations on the UI system by 1 week had individuals been eligible for the extension from the start of their spells. Card et al. (2007b) analyze a discontinuity in the Austrian UI benefit system based on work history that makes some individuals eligible for 20 weeks of benefits and others eligible for 30 weeks of benefits. Individuals eligible for 30 weeks of benefits have significantly lower job finding hazards even in the first five weeks of their unemployment spell, suggesting

---

[44] The very high optimal replacement rates predicted by Hopenhayn and Nicolini's model should essentially be interpreted as optimal *consumption* levels over the unemployment spell rather than optimal benefit levels.

that the "holding out" moral hazard effect identified by Shavell and Weiss is indeed operative in the data. Lalive (2008) finds similar impacts of an age-based discontinuity in the Austrian unemployment system that varies eligibility much more dramatically, from 30 weeks to 209 weeks.

There is no evidence to date on the consumption smoothing of extending benefits for a longer period due to the lack of high-frequency data on consumption. One approach to this problem may be to estimate liquidity effects at different points of a spell using variation in cash-on-hand from tax credits or other sources, as in LaLumia (2011). Investigating the path of asset decumulation and borrowing over the course of shocks would also shed light on the dynamic benefits of social insurance.

One approach for connecting the empirical evidence to theoretical models that make weaker assumptions may be to limit the set of benefit schedules that one considers. For instance, one could analyze two-parameter systems in which benefits are paid at a constant rate b and then terminated at some date T or systems in which benefits follow a linear path $b_t = \alpha + \beta t$. It may be possible to derive analytic formulas in terms of the elasticities estimated in the empirical literature for the optimal two-parameter system. Given that governments are unlikely to implement highly variable benefits over time, such simplifications of the problem might not be very restrictive from a practical perspective.

4. CHALLENGES FOR FUTURE WORK

Our review of the literature indicates that modern methods of connecting theory to data have proven to be quite fruitful, but much remains to be learned before one can draw strong conclusions about social insurance policy from this work. We conclude by summarizing some of the main outstanding challenges and open areas for future research.

First, there is a lack of empirical evidence on key parameters for many programs. Table 1 summarizes the current state of the literature for five major social insurance programs. For each program, we mark areas where we are aware of existing work on five topics: testing for selection (e.g., using positive correlation or cost curve tests), quantifying its welfare costs, estimating the benefits of social insurance (e.g., consumption smoothing or liquidity effects), estimating moral hazard costs (e.g., by studying behavioral responses to the program), and calculating optimal benefit levels (e.g., using sufficient statistic formulas). As discussed earlier, most empirical work to date on selection in insurance markets, and particularly its welfare costs, has concentrated on health insurance, with a few papers on annuities; noticeably missing is work on selection in unemployment insurance, disability insurance, or worker's compensation.[45] Research on government-provided insurance has focused primarily on measuring moral hazard costs rather than benefits. Unemployment

---

[45] The literature may have developed in this way because it is most natural study selection in markets where there is some private provision of insurance. In the US, which has been the primary focus on empirical work because of data availability, private insurance has been much more important in the health care market than the other markets.

insurance is one of the few programs in which both the benefits and costs of insurance have been studied extensively, with a corresponding well-developed literature on optimal policy.

A natural and quite valuable direction for further work is to fill in the empty boxes in Table 1 by applying the approaches surveyed here to these other important areas of social insurance. One particularly important program that has received relatively little attention in terms of measuring benefits and welfare consequences is disability insurance. Social insurance programs for health care—Medicaid and Medicare—are another area ripe for welfare analysis of optimal benefit levels. These programs have been the subject of a rich empirical literature examining their moral hazard impacts on health spending, and their benefits in terms of health and (to a more limited extent) consumption smoothing (see for Medicare e.g., Card, Dobkin, and Maestas (2008, 2009), Finkelstein (2007), or Finkelstein and McKnight (2008) or for Medicaid e.g., Currie and Gruber (1996a, 1996b), Finkelstein et al. (2011) or Gross and Notowidigdo (2011)). Yet there have been virtually no attempts to translate these policy estimates into statements about welfare or optimal policy (Finkelstein and McKnight (2008) is a notable, although highly stylized, exception). Another area in which modern tools connecting theory to data have not yet been applied is the analysis of social security programs. While there is a wealth of evidence of the reduced-form impacts of social security programs and a rich theoretical literature on optimal social security design, there is little work deriving robust formulas for optimal social security design in terms of empirically estimable parameters.

Second, the majority of the research we reviewed has focused on models with perfectly optimizing agents. However, as we argued above, it is difficult to rationalize some social insurance programs such as unemployment insurance in an environment with forward-looking agents because intertemporal consumption smoothing ("self insurance") is quantitatively a very good substitute for insurance against temporary shocks. An important challenge for future work is to understand the consequences of behavioral economics for optimal insurance. For instance, if large liquidity and consumption-smoothing effects of unemployment insurance are driven by the fact that impatient workers postpone job search until they run out of cash, the gains from insurance may be much smaller than existing calculations suggest. Similarly, the optimal tools to correct behavioral biases may be very different from traditional insurance programs, which make state-contingent income transfers.

Third, most methods of connecting theory to data make restrictive assumptions that do not permit a full spectrum of general equilibrium responses. Results on measuring the welfare cost of selection have usually treated the offered contracts as fixed, and focused primarily on the distortions in prices created by selection. Likewise, formulas for optimal social insurance based on reduced-form elasticities all require that wage rates and other prices are unaffected by government policies. In practice, large-scale social insurance policies are likely to induce substantial supply-side responses, making it crucial to develop methods to account for such general equilibrium effects.

Table 1 Social Insurance: A Summary of Existing Applied Work

	(1) Testing for Selection	(2) Quantifying Welfare Costs of Selection	(3) Estimation of Benefits	(4) Estimation of Moral Hazard Costs	(5) Calculating Optimal Benefit Levels
Medicare/Medicaid	X	X	X	X	
Disability insurance				X	
Unemp. insurance	X		X	X	X
Workers' comp.	X		X	X	X

Notes: This table lists areas where we are aware of empirical work on the topic listed in each column for five major social insurance programs. Selected examples of this work would include the following. Column 1: Cutler and Reber (1998) on Medicare/Medicaid (more accurately: private health insurance markets). Column 2: Einav et al. (2010a) on health insurance markets. Column 3: Card et al. (2009) on Medicare and Finkelstein et al. (2012) on Medicaid; Gruber (1997) and Chetty (2008) on unemployment insurance, and Bronchetti (2012) on workers compensation. Column 4: Card et al. (2009) on Medicare and Finkelstein et al. (2012) on Medicaid; Gruber (2001) and Maestas, Mullen, and Strand (2012) on disability insurance, Meyer (1990) and Card et al. (2007a, 2007b) on unemployment insurance, and Meyer et al. (1995) on workers' compensation. Column 5: Gruber (1997) and Chetty (2008) on unemployment insurance and Bronchetti (2012) on workers compensation.

Fourth, and relatedly, the literature on optimal social insurance design we have reviewed has tended to focus on relatively specific design questions within the structure of existing programs, such as the optimal level of benefits given the existing time path of benefits or the optimal financing of benefits. It is generally silent on more global optimal design questions, such as those that would alter several features of a program simultaneously. One relatively understudied design question is the choice of instrument used for government intervention. Governments can intervene in private insurance markets in at least three ways: direct public provision (e.g., Medicare, Social Security, and Unemployment Insurance), mandates on firms to provide insurance (e.g., Worker's Compensation), and direct intervention in or regulation of private insurance markets (e.g., tax subsidies for employer provided health insurance or regulation of the allowable contracts and prices in the individual health insurance markets). The optimal choice of these instruments has not been well explored.[46]

Fifth, the literature on motivations for social insurance and the optimal policy response are not yet well integrated. Existing empirical work on adverse selection analyzes selection and its consequences *given the existing public policies,* such as tax subsidies to employer provided health insurance or publicly provided annuities through Social Security. This raises the question of whether selection would exist—and what its welfare consequences would be—in the absence of these public programs or under very different public programs than we currently have. Understanding, both theoretically and empirically, how public insurance programs or policies affect the existence and nature of adverse selection in the residual private markets is therefore an important area for further work. Similarly, in the optimal policy literature, fiscal externalities on private insurers and other parts of the government budget such as tax revenue could significantly reduce the gains from social insurance. Characterizing optimal public insurance in models that incorporate endogenous private market insurance failures is therefore essential to obtain a more precise understanding of the welfare consequences of social insurance.

Finally, a general conceptual challenge for the approaches we have discussed in this paper is that they are less informative about fundamental policy reforms, such as implementing universal health insurance, than local changes, such as changing copayment rates by 10%. This is because the reduced-form empirical estimates that the literature uses to make quantitative welfare predictions are identified using local variation around the currently observed environment. This makes it difficult to extrapolate out-of-sample to impacts of policies that have not been observed. The questions discussed above of how private markets would function in the absence of public insurance are one example of this problem. More generally, informing policy makers about significant reforms to social insurance programs will require a more global understanding of how these policies affect

---

[46] One exception is Summers (1989), who compares the effects of mandates and taxes in a static model without uncertainty. Extending Summers' analysis to insurance markets would be an interesting direction for future research.

the economy. These issues are a fundamental challenge not just for the literature on social insurance but for empirical work more generally.

ACKNOWLEDGMENTS

We are grateful to Alan Auerbach, Liran Einav, Hilary Hoynes, Emmanuel Saez, and participants at the Handbook of Public Economics conference held at UC-Berkeley for helpful comments. Shelby Lin, Heather Sarsons, and Michael Stepner provided excellent research assistance. We gratefully acknowledge support from the NIA R01 AG032449 (Finkelstein) and the National Science Foundation SES 0645396 (Chetty).

REFERENCES

Abaluck, J., & Gruber, J. (2011). Choice inconsistencies among the elderly: Evidence from plan choice in the medicare Part D program. *American Economic Review, 101*(4), 1180–1210.

Abbring, J. H., Chiappori, P.-A., & Pinquet, J. (2003a). Moral hazard and dynamic insurance data. *Journal of the European Economic Association, 1*(4), 767–820.

Abbring, J. H., Heckman, J. J., Chiappori, P.-A., & Pinquet, J. (2003b). Adverse selection and moral hazard in insurance: Can dynamic data help to distinguish? *Journal of the European Economic Association, 1*(2–3), 512–521.

Abel, A. B. (1986). Capital accumulation and uncertain lifetimes with adverse selection. *Econometrica, 54*(5), 1079–1097.

Acemoglu, D., & Shimer, R. (1999). Efficient unemployment insurance. *Journal of Political Economy, 107*(5), 893–928.

Adams, W., Einav, L., & Levin, J. (2009). Liquidity constraints and imperfect information in subprime lending. *American Economic Review, 99*(1), 49–84.

Akerlof, G. A. (1970). The market for lemons: Quality uncertainty and the market mechanism. *Quarterly Journal of Economics, 84*(3), 488–500.

Anderson, P. M., & Meyer, B. D. (1993). Unemployment insurance in the United States: Layoff incentives and cross subsidies. *Journal of Labor Economics, 11*(1), 70–95.

Auerbach, A. J. (1985). The theory of excess burden and optimal taxation. In A. J. Auerbach & M. Feldstein (Eds.), *Handbook of public economics* (Vol. 1). (pp. 61–127). Amsterdam, North Holland: Elsevier.

Autor, D. H., & Duggan, M. G. (2003). The rise in the disability rolls and the decline in unemployment. *Quarterly Journal of Economics, 118*(1), 157–205.

Baicker, K., Goldin, C., & Katz, L. F. (1998). A distinctive system: Origins and impact of US unemployment compensation. In M. D. Bordo, C. Goldin & E. N. White (Eds.), *The defining moment: The great depression and the American economy in the twentieth century* (pp. 227–263). Chicago: University of Chicago Press.

Baily, M. N. (1978). Some aspects of optimal unemployment insurance. *Journal of Public Economics, 10*(3), 379–402.

Baird, S., Hicks, J. H., Kremer, M., & Miguel, E. (2011). *Worms at work: Long-run impacts of child health gains.* Mimeo. http://elsa.berkeley.edu/~emiguel/pdfs/miguelwormsatwork.pdf.

Bank of Sweden (2001). *Press release: The 2001 Sveriges Riksbank (Bank of Sweden) prize in economic sciences in memory of Alfred Nobel, advanced information.* http://www.nobelprize.org/nobelprizes/economics/laure ates/2001/advanced-economicsciences2001.pdf.

Barseghyan, L., Prince, J., & Teitelbaum, J. C. (2011). Are risk preferences stable across contexts? Evidence from insurance data. *American Economic Review, 101*(2), 591–631.

Barseghyan, L., Molinari, F., O'Donoghue, T., & Teitelbaum, J. C. (2012). The nature of risk preferences: Evidence from insurance choices. *SSRN working paper,* No 1646520.

Barsky, R. B., Juster, F. T., Kimball, M. S., & Shapiro, M. D. (1997). Preference parameters and behavioral heterogeneity: An experimental approach in the health and retirement study. *Quarterly Journal of Economics, 112*(2), 537–579.

Bernheim, B. D., & Rangel, A. (2009). Beyond revealed preference: Choice-theoretic foundations for behavioral welfare economics. *Quarterly Journal of Economics, 124*(1), 51–104.

Bertrand, M., Luttmer, E. F. P., & Mullainathan, S. (2000). Network effects and welfare cultures. *Quarterly Journal of Economics, 115*(3), 1019–1055.

Bhargava, S., & Manoli, D. (2011). Why are benefits left on the table? Assessing the role of information, complexity, and stigma on take-up with an IRS field experiment. *Working paper.*

Black, D. A., Smith, J. A., Berger, M. C., & Noel, B. J. (2003). Is the threat of reemployment services more effective than the services themselves? Evidence from random assignment in the UI system. *American Economic Review, 93*(4), 1313–1327.

Blanchard, O. J., & Tirole, J. (2008). The joint design of unemployment insurance and employment protection: A first pass. *Journal of the European Economic Association, 6*(1), 45–77.

Blundell, R., Pistaferri, L., & Preston, I. (2008). Consumption Inequality and Partial Insurance. *American Economic Review, 98*(5), 1887–1921.

Borghans, L., Gielen, A. C., & Luttmer, E. F. P. (2010). Social support shopping: Evidence from a regression discontinuity in disability insurance reform. *IZA Discussion Paper*, No. 5412, Institute for the Study of Labor (IZA).

Bound, J., Cullen, J. B., Nichols, A., & Schmidt, L. (2004). The welfare implications of increasing disability insurance benefit generosity. *Journal of Public Economics, 88*(12), 2487–2514.

Bronchetti, E. T. (2012). Workers' compensation and consumption smoothing. *Journal of Public Economics, 96*(5), 495–508.

Brown, J. R., & Finkelstein, A. (2007). Why is the market for long-term care insurance so small? *Journal of Public Economics, 91*(10), 1967–1991.

Brown, J. R., & Finkelstein, A. (2008). The interaction of public and private insurance: Medicaid and the long-term care insurance market. *American Economic Review, 98*(3), 1083–1102.

Brown, J. R., & Finkelstein, A. (2011). Insuring long-term care in the United States. *Journal of Economic Perspectives, 25*(4), 119–142.

Brown, J. R., Kroszner, R. S., & Jenn, B. H. (2002). Federal terrorism risk insurance. *National Tax Journal, 55*(3), 647–657.

Brown, J., Duggan, M., Kuziemko, I., & Woolston, W. (2011). How does risk selection respond to risk adjustment? Evidence from the medicare advantage program. *NBER working paper*, No. 16977, National Bureau of Economic Research.

Browning, M., & Crossley, T. F. (2001). Unemployment insurance benefit levels and consumption changes. *Journal of Public Economics, 80*(1), 1–23.

Buchanan, J. (1975). The samaritan's dilemma. In E. Phelps (Ed.), *Altruism, morality and economic theory* (pp. 71–85). New York: Russell Sage.

Buchmueller, T., & DiNardo, J. (2002). Did community rating induce an adverse selection death spiral? Evidence from New York, Pennsylvania, and Connecticut. *American Economic Review, 92*(1), 280–294.

Bundorf, M. K., & Simon, K. I. (2006). The effects of rate regulation on demand for supplemental health insurance. *American Economic Review, 96*(2), 67–71.

Bundorf, M. K., Levin, J., & Mahoney, N. (2012). Pricing and welfare in health plan choice. *American Economic Review, 102*(7), 3214–3248.

Card, D., & Levine, P. B. (2000). Extended benefits and the duration of UI spells: Evidence from the New Jersey extended benefit program. *Journal of Public Economics, 78*(1–2), 107–138.

Card, D., Chetty, R., & Weber, A. (2007a). The spike at benefit exhaustion: Leaving the unemployment system or starting a new job? *American Economic Review, 97*(2), 113–118.

Card, D., Chetty, R., & Weber, A. (2007b). Cash-on-hand and competing models of intertemporal behavior: New evidence from the labor market. *Quarterly Journal of Economics, 122*(4), 1511–1560.

Card, D., Dobkin, C., & Maestas, N. (2008). The impact of nearly universal insurance coverage on health care utilization: Evidence from medicare. *American Economic Review, 98*(5), 2242–2258.

Card, D., Dobkin, C., & Maestas, N. (2009). Does medicare save lives? *Quarterly Journal of Economics, 124*(2), 597–636.

Cardon, J. H., & Hendel, I. (2001). Asymmetric information in health insurance: Evidence from the national medical expenditure survey. *RAND Journal of Economics, 32*(3), 408–427.

Carlin, C., & Town, R. (2010). Adverse selection: The dog that didn't bite. Mimeo: University of Minnesota.

Carroll, C. D. (1997). Buffer-stock saving and the life cycle/permanent income hypothesis. *Quarterly Journal of Economics, 112*(1), 1–55.

Centeno, M., & Novo, A. (2009). Reemployment wages and UI liquidity effect: A regression discontinuity approach. *Portuguese Economic Journal, 8*(1), 45–52.

Chetty, R. (2006a). A new method of estimating risk aversion. *American Economic Review, 96*(5), 1821–1834.

Chetty, R. (2006b). A general formula for the optimal level of social insurance. *Journal of Public Economics, 90*(10–11), 1879–1901.

Chetty, R. (2008). Moral hazard versus liquidity and optimal unemployment insurance. *Journal of Political Economy, 116*(2), 173–234.

Chetty, R. (2009). Sufficient statistics for welfare analysis: A bridge between structural and reduced-form methods. *Annual Review of Economics, 1*(1), 451–488.

Chetty, R., & Looney, A. (2006). Consumption smoothing and the welfare consequences of social insurance in developing economies. *Journal of Public Economics, 90*(12), 2351–2356.

Chetty, R., & Saez, E. (2010). Optimal taxation and social insurance with endogenous private insurance. *American Economic Journal: Economic Policy, 2*(2), 85–114.

Chetty, R., & Szeidl, A. (2007). Consumption commitments and risk preferences. *Quarterly Journal of Economics, 122*(2), 831–877.

Chetty, R., Looney, A., & Kroft, K. (2009). Salience and taxation: Theory and evidence. *American Economic Review, 99*(4), 1145–1177.

Chetty, R., Friedman, J. N., Olsen, T., & Pistaferri, L. (2011). Adjustment costs, firm responses, and micro vs. macro labor supply elasticities: Evidence from Danish tax records. *The Quarterly Journal of Economics, 126*(2), 749–804.

Chetty, R., Friedman, J. N., & Saez, E. (2012). Using differences in knowledge across neighborhoods to uncover the impacts of the EITC on earnings. *NBER working paper*, No. 18232, National Bureau of Economic Research. Forthcoming, *American Economic Review*.

Chiappori, P.-A., & Salanié, B. (2000). Testing for asymmetric information in insurance markets. *Journal of Political Economy, 108*(1), 56–78.

Chiappori, P.-A., Jullien, B., Salanié, B., & Salanié, F. (2006). Asymmetric information in insurance: General testable implications. *RAND Journal of Economics, 37*(4), 783–798.

Clark, A. E. (2003). Unemployment as a social norm: Psychological evidence from panel data. *Journal of Labor Economics, 21*(2), 289–322.

Coate, S. (1995). Altruism, the samaritan's dilemma, and government transfer policy. *American Economic Review, 85*(1), 46–57.

Cochrane, J. H. (1991). A simple test of consumption insurance. *Journal of Political Economy, 99*(5), 957–976.

Cohen, A., & Einav, L. (2007). Estimating risk preferences from deductible choice. *American Economic Review, 97*(3), 745–788.

Cohen, A., & Siegelman, P. (2010). Testing for adverse selection in insurance markets. *Journal of Risk and Insurance, 77*(1), 39–84.

Crépon, B., Duflo, E., Gurgand, M., Rathelot, R., & Zamora, P. (2012). Do labor market policies have displacement effects? Evidence from a clustered randomized experiment. *CEPR Discussion Papers*, No. 9251 [C.E.P.R. Discussion Papers].

Crocker, K. J., & Snow, A. (1985). The efficiency of competitive equilibria in insurance markets with asymmetric information. *Journal of Public Economics, 26*(2), 207–219.

Cullen, J. B., & Gruber, J. (2000). Does unemployment insurance crowd out spousal labor supply? *Journal of Labor Economics, 18*(3), 546–572.

Currie, J. (2006). The take-up of social benefits. In A. Auerbach, D. Card & J. Quigley (Eds.), *Poverty, the distribution of income, and public policy* (pp. 80–148). New York: Russell Sage.

Currie, J., & Gruber, J. (1996a). Health insurance eligibility, utilization of medical care, and child health. *Quarterly Journal of Economics, 111*(2), 431–466.

Currie, J., & Gruber, J. (1996b). Saving babies: The efficacy and cost of recent changes in the medicaid eligibility of pregnant women. *Journal of Political Economy, 104*(6), 1263–96.

Cutler, D. M. (2002). Health care and the public sector. In A. J. Auerbach & M. Feldstein (Eds.), *Handbook of public economics* (1st ed.). (Vol. 4). (pp. 2143–2243). Amsterdam, North Holland: Elsevier.

Cutler, D. M., & Gruber, J. (1996). Does public insurance crowd out private insurance? *Quarterly Journal of Economics, 111*(2), 391–430.

Cutler, D. M., & Reber, S. J. (1998). Paying for health insurance: The trade-off between competition and adverse selection. *Quarterly Journal of Economics, 113*(2), 433–466.

Cutler, D. M., & Zeckhauser, R. J. (2000). The anatomy of health insurance. In A. J. Culyer & J. P. Newhouse (Eds.), *Handbook of health economics* (1st ed.). (Vol. 1). *Handbook of Health Economics* (pp. 563–643). Amsterdam, North Holland: Elsevier.

Cutler, D. M., Finkelstein, A., & McGarry, K. (2008). Preference heterogeneity and insurance markets: Explaining a puzzle of insurance. *American Economic Review, 98*(2), 157–162.

Davidoff, T., Brown, J. R., & Diamond, P. A. (2005). Annuities and individual welfare. *American Economic Review, 95*(5), 1573–1590.

Deaton, A. (1991). Saving and Liquidity Constraints. *Econometrica, 59*(5), 1221–1248.

DellaVigna, S., & Paserman, M. D. (2005). Job search and impatience. *Journal of Labor Economics, 23*(3), 527–588.

de Meza, D., & Webb, D. C., (2001). Advantageous selection in insurance markets. *RAND Journal of Economics, 32*(2), 249–262.

Devine, T. J., & Kiefer, N. M. (1991). *Empirical labor economics: The search approach.* New York: Oxford University Press.

Diamond, P. A. (1977). A framework for social security analysis. *Journal of Public Economics, 8*(3), 275–298.

Ebenstein, A., & Stange, K. (2010). Does inconvenience explain low take-up? Evidence from unemployment insurance. *Journal of Policy Analysis and Management, 29*(1), 111–136.

Eckstein, Z., Eichenbaum, M., & Peled, D. (1985). Uncertain lifetimes and the welfare enhancing properties of annuity markets and social security. *Journal of Public Economics, 26*(3), 303–326.

Einav, L., & Finkelstein, A. (2011). Selection in insurance markets: Theory and empirics in pictures. *Journal of Economic Perspectives, 25*(1), 115–138.

Einav, L., Finkelstein, A., & Cullen, M. R. (2010a). Estimating welfare in insurance markets using variation in prices. *Quarterly Journal of Economics, 125*(3), 877–921.

Einav, L., Finkelstein, A., & Levin, J. (2010b). Beyond testing: Empirical models of insurance markets. *Annual Review of Economics, 2*(1), 311–336.

Einav, L., Finkelstein, A., & Schrimpf, P. (2010c). Optimal mandates and the welfare cost of asymmetric information: Evidence from the UK annuity market. *Econometrica, 78*(3), 1031–1092.

Einav, L., Finkelstein, A., Ryan, S. P., Schrimpf, P., & Cullen, M. R. (2011). Selection on moral hazard in health insurance. *NBER working paper*, No. 16969, National Bureau of Economic Research.

Einav, L., Finkelstein, A., Pascu, I., & Cullen, M. (forthcoming). How general are risk preferences? Choices under uncertainty in different domains. *American Economic Review.*

Engen, E. M., & Gruber, J. (2001). Unemployment insurance and precautionary saving. *Journal of Monetary Economics, 47*(3), 545–579.

Fang, H., & Silverman, D. (2009). Time-inconsistency and welfare program participation: Evidence from The NLSY. *International Economic Review, 50*(4), 1043–1077.

Fang, H., Keane, M. P., & Silverman, D. (2008). Sources of advantageous selection: Evidence from the medigap insurance market. *Journal of Political Economy, 116*(2), 303–350.

Feldstein, M. (1978). The effect of unemployment insurance on temporary layoff unemployment. *American Economic Review, 68*(5), 834–846.

Feldstein, M., & Altman, D. (2007). Unemployment insurance savings accounts. *In Tax Policy and the Economy* (Vol. 21 of NBER Chapters). (pp. 35–64). National Bureau of Economic Research.

Feldstein, M., & Liebman, J. B. (2002). Social security. In A. J. Auerbach & M. Feldstein (Eds.), *Handbook of public economics* (1st ed) (Vol. 4 of Handbook of Public Economics). (pp. 2245–2324). Amsterdam, North Holland: Elsevier.

Feldstein, M., & Poterba, J. (1984). Unemployment insurance and reservation wages. *Journal of Public Economics, 23*(1–2), 141–167.

Finkelstein, A. (2004). The interaction of partial public insurance programs and residual private insurance markets: Evidence from the US medicare program. *Journal of Health Economics, 23*(1), 1–24.

Finkelstein, A. (2007). The aggregate effects of health insurance: Evidence from the introduction of medicare. *Quarterly Journal of Economics, 122*(1), 1–37.

Finkelstein, A., & McGarry, K. (2006). Multiple dimensions of private information: Evidence from the long-term care insurance market. *American Economic Review, 96*(4), 938–958.

Finkelstein, A., & McKnight, R. (2008). What did medicare do? The initial impact of medicare on mortality and out of pocket medical spending. *Journal of Public Economics, 92*(7), 1644–1668.

Finkelstein, A., & Poterba, J. (2002). Selection effects in the United Kingdom individual annuities market. *Economic Journal, 112*(476), 28–50.

Finkelstein, A., & Poterba, J. (2004). Adverse selection in insurance markets: Policyholder evidence from the UK annuity market. *Journal of Political Economy, 112*(1), 183–208.

Finkelstein, A., & Poterba, J. (2006). Testing for adverse selection with unused observables. *NBER working paper*, No. 12112. National Bureau of Economic Research.

Finkelstein, A., Luttmer, E. F. P., & Notowidigdo, M. J. (2008). What good is wealth without health? The effect of health on the marginal utility of consumption. *NBER working paper*, No. 14089, National Bureau of Economic Research.

Finkelstein, A., Luttmer, E. F. P., & Notowidigdo, M. J. (2009a). Approaches to estimating the health state dependence of the utility function. *American Economic Review, 99*(2), 116–121.

Finkelstein, A., Poterba, J., & Rothschild, C. (2009b). Redistribution by insurance market regulation: Analyzing a ban on gender-based retirement annuities. *Journal of Financial Economics, 91*(1), 38–58.

Finkelstein, A., Taubman, S., Wright, B., Bernstein, M., Gruber, J., Newhouse, J. P., Allen, H., Baicker, K., & Group, T. O. H. S. (2011). The oregon health insurance experiment: Evidence from the first year. *NBER working paper*, No. 17190. National Bureau of Economic Research, Inc.

Fishback, P. V., & Kantor, S. E. (1998). The adoption of workers' compensation in the United States, 1900–1930. *Journal of Law and Economics, 41*(2), 305–341.

Friedman, B. M., & Warshawsky, M. J. (1990). The cost of annuities: Implications for saving behavior and bequests. *Quarterly Journal of Economics, 105*(1), 135–154.

Froot, K. A. (2001). The market for catastrophe risk: a clinical examination. *Journal of Financial Economics, 60*(2–3), 529–571.

Gertler, P., & Gruber, J. (2002). Insuring consumption against illness. *American Economic Review, 92*(1), 51–70.

Geruso, M. (2011). *Selection in employer health plans: Homogeneous prices and heterogeneous preferences.* Mimeo: Princeton University.

Glied, S. (2000). Managed care. In A. J. Culyer & J. P. Newhouse (Eds.), *Handbook of health economics* (Vol. 1). (pp. 707–753). Amsterdam, North Holland: Elsevier.

Golosov, M., & Tsyvinski, A. (2007). Optimal taxation with endogenous insurance markets. *Quarterly Journal of Economics, 122*(2), 487–534.

Gross, T., & Notowidigdo, M. J. (2011). Health insurance and the consumer bankruptcy decision: Evidence from expansions of medicaid. *Journal of Public Economics, 95*(7–8), 767–778.

Gruber, J. (1997). The consumption smoothing benefits of unemployment insurance. *American Economic Review, 87*(1), 192–205.

Gruber, J. (2000). Disability insurance benefits and labor supply. *Journal of Political Economy, 108*(6), 1162–1183.

Gruber, J. (2009). *Public finance and public policy* (3rd ed.). New York: Worth Publishers.

Gruber, J., & Wise, D. A. (Eds.). (1999). Social security and retirement around the world. *NBER Book Series - International Social Security.* Chicago: University of Chicago Press.

Hamermesh, D. S. (1982). Social insurance and consumption: An empirical inquiry. *American Economic Review, 72*(1), 101–113.

Handel, B. R. (2011). Adverse selection and switching costs in health insurance markets: When nudging hurts. *NBER working paper*, No. 17459, National Bureau of Economic Research.

Hansen, G. D., & Imrohoroglu, A. (1992). The role of unemployment insurance in an economy with liquidity constraints and moral hazard. *Journal of Political Economy, 100*(1), 118–142.

Hartley, G. R., van Ours, J. C., & Vodopivec, M. (2011). Incentive effects of unemployment insurance savings accounts: Evidence from Chile. *Labour Economics, 18*(6), 798–809.

Hemenway, D. (1990). Propitious selection. *Quarterly Journal of Economics, 105*(4), 1063–1069.

Hendel, I., & Lizzeri, A. (2003). The role of commitment in dynamic contracts: Evidence from life insurance. *Quarterly Journal of Economics, 118*(1), 299–327.

Hendren, N. (2012). Private information and insurance rejections. *NBER working paper*, No. 18282, National Bureau of Economic Research.

Herring, B. (2005). The effect of the availability of charity care to the uninsured on the demand for private health insurance. *Journal of Health Economics, 24*(2), 225–252.

Hopenhayn, H. A., & Nicolini, J. P. (1997). Optimal unemployment insurance. *Journal of Political Economy, 105*(2), 412–438.

Hosseini, R. (2010). Adverse selection in the annuity market and the role for social security. Mimeo. http://www.public.asu.edu/~rhossein/RoozbehHosseini/Researchfiles/HosseiniAnnuitySSFinal.pdf.

Hubbard, R. G., Skinner, J., & Zeldes, S. P. (1995). Precautionary saving and social insurance. *Journal of Political Economy, 103*(2), 360–399.

Huggett, M., & Parra, J. C. (2010). How well does the US social insurance system provide social insurance? *Journal of Political Economy, 118*(1), 76–112.

Jappelli, T., & Pistaferri, L. (2010). The consumption response to income changes. *Annual Review of Economics, 2*(1), 479–506.

Kaplan, G. (2012). Moving back home: Insurance against labor market risk. *Journal of Political Economy, 120*(3), 446–512.

Kaplow, L. (1991). Incentives and government relief for risk. *Journal of Risk and Uncertainty, 4*(2), 167–75.

Karlan, D., & Zinman, J. (2009). Observing unobservables: Identifying information asymmetries with a consumer credit field experiment. *Econometrica, 77*(6), 1993–2008.

Katz, L. F., & Meyer, B. D. (1990). Unemployment insurance, recall expectations, and unemployment outcomes. *Quarterly Journal of Economics, 105*(4), 973–1002.

Kling, J. R., Mullainathan, S., Shafir, E., Vermeulen, L. C., & Wrobel, M. V. (2012). Comparison friction: Experimental evidence from medicare drug plans. *Quarterly Journal of Economics, 127*(1), 199–235.

Kocherlakota, N. R. (1996). The equity premium: It's still a puzzle. *Journal of Economic Literature, 34*(1), 42–71.

Kremer, M., & Miguel, E. (2004). Worms: Identifying impacts on education and health in the presence of treatment externalities. *Econometrica, 72*(1), 159–217.

Kroft, K. (2008). Takeup, social multipliers and optimal social insurance. *Journal of Public Economics, 92*(3–4), 722–737.

Kroft, K., & Notowidigdo, M. J. (2011). Should unemployment insurance vary with the unemployment rate? Theory and evidence. *NBER working paper*, No. 17173, National Bureau of Economic Research.

Krueger, A. B., & Meyer, B. D. (2002). Labor supply effects of social insurance. In A. J. Auerbach & M. Feldstein (Eds.), *Handbook of public economics* (1st ed.). (Vol. 4). (pp. 2327–2392). Amsterdam, North Holland: Elsevier.

Krueger, A. B., & Mueller, A. I. (2011). Job search and job finding in a period of mass unemployment: Evidence from high-frequency longitudinal data. *IZA Discussion Paper*, No. 5450, Institute for the Study of Labor (IZA).

Laibson, D. (1997). Golden eggs and hyperbolic discounting. *Quarterly Journal of Economics, 112*(2), 443–477.

Lalive, R. (2003). Social interactions in unemployment. *IZA discussion paper*, No. 803, Institute for the Study of Labor (IZA).

Lalive, R. (2007). Unemployment benefits, unemployment duration, and post-unemployment jobs: A regression discontinuity approach. *American Economic Review, 97*(2), 108–112.

Lalive, R. (2008). How do extended benefits affect unemployment duration a regression discontinuity approach. *Journal of Econometrics, 142*(2), 785–806.

Lalive, R., van Ours, J. C., & Zweimüller, J. (2006). How changes in financial incentives affect the duration of unemployment. *Review of Economic Studies, 73*(4), 1009–1038.

LaLonde, R. (2007). The case for wage insurance. *Council special report* 30, Council on Foreign Relations Press.

LaLumia, S. (2011). The EITC, tax refunds, and unemployment spells. *Department of Economics working paper*, No. 2011-09, Department of Economics, Williams College.

Landais, C. (2011). Heterogeneity and behavioral responses to unemployment benefits over the business cycle. *SIEPR working paper*, Stanford Institute for Economic Policy Research.

Landais, C. (2012). Assessing the welfare effects of unemployment benefits using the regression kink design. *PEP working paper*, London School of Economics.

Landais, C., Michaillat, P., & Saez, E. (2012). Optimal unemployment insurance over the business cycle. *NBER working paper*, No. 16526, National Bureau of Economic Research.

Lentz, R. (2009). Optimal unemployment insurance in an estimated job search model with savings. *Review of Economic Dynamics, 12*(1), 37–57.

Lentz, R., & Tranas, T. (2005). Job search and savings: Wealth effects and duration dependence. *Journal of Labor Economics, 23*(3), 467–490.

Lillard, L. A., & Weiss, Y. (1997). Uncertain health and survival: Effects on end-of-life consumption. *Journal of Business & Economic Statistics, 15*(2), 254–268.

Lindbeck, A., Nyberg, S., & Weibull, J. W. (1999). Social norms and economic incentives in the welfare state. *Quarterly Journal of Economics, 114*(1), 1–35.

Lucas, R. (1987). *Models of business cycles.* New York: Basil Blackwell.

Lustig, J. (2011). *The welfare effects of adverse selection in privatized medicare.* Mimeo, Boston University. http://people.bu.edu/jlustig/lustigmarch2011.pdf.

Maestas, N., Mullen, K. J., & Strand, A. (forthcoming). Does disability insurance receipt discourage work? Using examiner assignment to estimate causal effects of SSDI receipt. American Economic Review.

Mahoney, N. (2012). Bankruptcy as implicit health insurance. *NBER working paper*, No. 18105, National Bureau of Economic Research.

Manning, W. G., Newhouse, J. P., Duan, N., Keeler, E. B., & Leibowitz, A. (1987). Health insurance and the demand for medical care: Evidence from a randomized experiment. *The American Economic Review, 77*(3), 251–277.

McCarthy, D., & Mitchell, O. S. (2003). International adverse selection in life insurance and annuities. *NBER working paper*, No. 9975, National Bureau of Economic Research.

Mehra, R., & Prescott, E. C. (1985). The equity premium: A puzzle. *Journal of Monetary Economics, 15*(2), 145–161.

Metrick, A. (1995). A natural experiment in jeopardy! *American Economic Review, 85*(1), 240–253.

Meyer, B. D. (1990). Unemployment insurance and unemployment spells. *Econometrica, 58*(4), 757–782.

Meyer, B. D., Viscusi, W. K., & Durbin, D. L. (1995). Workers' compensation and injury duration: Evidence from a natural experiment. *American Economic Review, 85*(3), 322–340.

Mitchell, O. S., Poterba, J. M., Warshawsky, M. J., & Brown, J. R. (1999). New evidence on the money's worth of individual annuities. *American Economic Review, 89*(5), 1299–1318.

Newhouse, J. P. (2002). *Princing the priceless: A health care conundrum.* Cambridge, Massachusetts: The MIT Press.

Newhouse, J. P. & RAND Corporation Insurance Experiment Group (1996). *Free for all?: Lessons from the RAND health insurance experiment.* Cambridge, Massachusetts: Harvard University Press.

Nichols, A. L., & Zeckhauser, R. J. (1982). Targeting transfers through restrictions on recipients. *American Economic Review, 72*(2), 372–377.

Nyman, J. (2003). *The theory of demand for health insurance.* Stanford, California: Stanford University Press.

Orszag, J. M., & Snower, D. J. (2002). Incapacity benefits and employment policy. *Labour Economics, 9*(5), 631–641.

Oster, E., Shoulson, I., Quaid, K., & Dorsey, E. R. (2010). Genetic adverse selection: Evidence from long-term care insurance and Huntington disease. *Journal of Public Economics, 94*(11–12), 1041–1050.

Pauly, M. V. (1974). Overinsurance and public provision of insurance: The roles of moral hazard and adverse selection. *Quarterly Journal of Economics, 88*(1), 44–62.

Philipson, T. J., & Becker, G. S. (1998). Old-age longevity and mortality-contingent claims. *Journal of Political Economy, 106*(3), 551–573.

Rabin, M. (2000). Risk aversion and expected-utility theory: A calibration theorem. *Econometrica, 68*(5), 1281–1292.

Rothschild, M., & Stiglitz, J. E. (1976). Equilibrium in competitive insurance markets: An essay on the economics of imperfect information. *Quarterly Journal of Economics, 90*(4), 630–49.

Rothstein, J. (2010). Is the EITC as good as an NIT? Conditional cash transfers and tax incidence. *American Economic Journal: Economic Policy, 2*(1), 177–208.

Schmieder, J. F., Wachter, T. v., & Bender, S. (2012). The effects of extended unemployment insurance over the business cycle: Evidence from regression discontinuity estimates over 20 years. *Quarterly Journal of Economics, 127*(2), 701–752.

Shavell, S., & Weiss, L. (1979). The optimal payment of unemployment insurance benefits over time. *Journal of Political Economy, 87*(6), 1347–1362.

Shimer, R. and Werning, I. (2006). On the optimal timing of benefits with heterogeneous workers and human capital depreciation. *NBER working paper*, No. 12230, National Bureau of Economic Research.

Shimer, R., & Werning, I. (2007). Reservation wages and unemployment insurance. *Quarterly Journal of Economics, 122*(3), 1145–1185.

Shimer, R., & Werning, I. (2008). Liquidity and insurance for the unemployed. *American Economic Review, 98*(5), 1922–1942.

Simon, K. I. (2005). Adverse selection in health insurance markets? Evidence from state small group health insurance reforms. *Journal of Public Economics, 89*(9–10), 1865–1877.

Social Security Administration (1997). *Social security programs in the United States.* SSA, Publication 13–11758.

Spinnewijn, J. (2010). Unemployed but optimistic: Optimal insurance design with biased beliefs. *Working paper*, London School of Economics. http://personal.lse.ac.uk/spinnewi/biasedbeliefs.pdf.

Spinnewijn, J. (2012). Heterogeneity, demand for insurance and adverse selection. *Working paper*, London School of Economics. http://personal.lse.ac.uk/spinnewi/perceptionswelfare.pdf.

Starc, A. (2011). Insurer pricing and consumer welfare: Evidence from medigap. Mimeo. http://hcmg.wharton.upenn.edu/documents/research/Astarcpricing.pdf.

Stiglitz, J. E., & Yun, J. (2005). Integration of unemployment insurance with retirement insurance. *Journal of Public Economics, 89*(11–12), 2037–2067.

Summers, L. H. (1989). Some simple economics of mandated benefits. *American Economic Review, 79*(2), 177–183.

Sydnor, J. (2010). (Over)insuring modest risks. *American Economic Journal: Applied Economics, 2*(4), 177–199.

Topel, R. H. (1983). On layoffs and unemployment insurance. *American Economic Review, 73*(4), 541–559.

Townsend, R. M. (1994). Risk and insurance in village india. *Econometrica, 62*(3), 539–591.

van Ours, J. C., & Vodopivec, M. (2008). Does reducing unemployment insurance generosity reduce job match quality? *Journal of Public Economics, 92*(3–4), 684–695.

von Wachter, T., Song, J., & Manchester, J. (2009). Long-term earnings losses due to mass-layoffs during the 1982 recession: An analysis using longitudinal administrative data from 1974 to 2004. *Working paper*, Columbia University.

Wang, C., & Williamson, S. (1996). Unemployment insurance with moral hazard in a dynamic economy. *Carnegie-Rochester Conference Series on Public Policy, 44*(1), 1–41.

Werning, I. (2002). *Optimal unemployment insurance with unobservable savings.* Mimeo: University of Chicago.

Wilson, C. (1977). A model of insurance markets with incomplete information. *Journal of Economic Theory, 16*(2), 167–207.

Wolpin, K. I. (1987). Estimating a structural search model: The transition from school to work. *Econometrica, 55*(4), 801–817.

Yaari, M. E. (1965). Uncertain lifetime, life insurance, and the theory of the consumer. *The Review of Economic Studies, 32*(2), 137–150.

CHAPTER 4

Urban Public Finance

Edward L. Glaeser

Harvard University and National Bureau of Economic Research, Cambridge, MA, USA

Contents

1. INTRODUCTION

More than one-half of the world is urbanized and 84% of Americans live in metropolitan areas, which are typically anchored by significant cities. Urban proximity creates abundant externalities—good and bad—and urban governments expanded, long before their rural counterparts, partially to provide the infrastructure that can mitigate adverse urban externalities, like contagious disease. This essay will review the central tasks of local

Handbook of Public Economics, Volume 5
ISSN 1573-4420, http://dx.doi.org/10.1016/B978-0-444-53759-1.00004-2

governments and how they are financed, primarily within the United States, with only pay limited attention paid to the rest of the world.

As of 2008, America's local governments spent about one-eighth of our national gross domestic product (GDP), one-fourth of total government spending, and employ over 14 million people.[1] Local governments differ from state and national governments because there are vastly more of them and because they specialize in delivering quite tangible services, like public safety and education, to taxpayers who generally pay for them. In the US, there are three central features that make local government finance distinctly different from public finance at the national or even the state level: property taxes are responsible for the majority of local taxes, intergovernmental transfers provide about one-third of local revenues, and localities typically maintain relatively balanced budgets.

These core features of urban public finance are intimately connected with the nature of cities and the functions of urban governments. One essential feature of cities is that people and capital can readily leave them; greater factor mobility is a key feature of urban, as opposed to national, public finance (Wildasin, 1986), and I review the evidence of migration in Section 6. Indeed, the modern economics literature on local public finance begins with Charles Tiebout's classic 1956 article, which argued that local governments provided an ingenious way of embedding choice and competition into the provision of public services. The local government dependence on property taxes reflects, in part, the fact that real estate is fixed in a way that labor income is not, which reduces the distortions that can come from mobility. The large role of intergovernmental transfers enables city governments to be tools for redistribution, especially through schooling, despite the fact that the threat of out-migration limits that natural ability to lower levels of government to redistribute.

The discipline that mobility provides on local governments helps explain why these governments are typically far less ideologically partisan than their national equivalents. Ferreira and Gyourko (2009), for example, use a regression discontinuity approach to test whether Democratic or Republican mayors show significantly different spending patterns, as they do at the national or even state levels. Ferreira and Gyourko find little such urban partisanship, which corroborates the apparently similar approaches followed by mayors like New York's Mayor Bloomberg, who was elected as a Republican, and Chicago's former Mayor Daley, who was and is a Democrat.

Mobility is one of the forces that create severe limits that constrain the action of urban governments; state laws provide another set of limits. Cities, within the US, are creations of state governments. With the sole exception of Washington, DC, they have no independent constitutional status. As a result, states have generally restricted the taxing, borrowing, and functional authority of local governments, usually by legislative action and occasionally by referendum. Typically, cities like states face at least a notional balanced budget requirement.

---

[1] The Source for the employment figure is the *2012 Statistical Abstract of the United States.*

Despite the formal limitations that appear to bind city governments, local leaders have often attempted to bypass those limits with different schemes to get around their budget constraints. Compensating workers with underfunded pension and health care benefits may be the most important example of bypassing the budget constraint, but there are many others. Privatizing city assets, such as selling the right to collect parking meter payments over future decades, recently created a cash windfall for Chicago.

There has also been a steady stream of governmental innovations that often create substitutes for traditional local government. There has been phenomenal growth, for example, in the number of special districts which provide services ranging from education to firefighting to public transit (Berry, 2009). America has also seen an explosion in the number of private and often gated communities (Blakely & Snyder, 1999), where corporations essentially take on the core tasks of local governments, and other nations have also followed this trend (Atkinson, Blandy, & Mostowska, 2007). Large cities have increasingly seen Business Improvement Districts (BIDs) where businesses pay fees for increased policing and improvements in public spaces.

The constraints on local government financing become particularly obvious during cyclical downturns, such as the American recession that began in 2007. In response, the federal government has stepped in providing support both for urban infrastructure, like roads, and basic funding of local government services, like schools. Federally managed revenue smoothing over the business cycle may have advantages relative to huge local spending cutbacks during downturns, but relying on federal support may also have costs, especially if the spending goes to services that have limited value, relative to a more locally managed smoothing process.

The American tradition of decentralized political authority is not unique but it does lie at the end of the global spectrum. At the other end are countries, such as the United Kingdom, where the national government maintains far more responsibility over local services. The mayor of London's power, for example, extends primarily over transportation matters, while the home secretary and the education secretary have greater authority over London's safety and schools. India occupies a middle ground where large state governments control most urban services.

Within the US, there are cross-state differences in the responsibilities allotted to cities and cross metropolitan area differences in the degree of political fragmentation. In some areas, such as Boston, the central city occupies a very small sliver of the metropolitan area and is surrounded by a vast number of smaller communities. In other metropolitan areas, such as Denver, the central city occupies a much larger spatial footprint. The spatial size of the central city can mean that its government essentially enjoys more monopoly power within the region.

The costs and benefits of decentralization and political fragmentation have been debated by economists since Tiebout. Tiebout's core followers emphasize the benefits of diversity and competition. Their intellectual opponents argue that smaller areas cannot coordinate sufficiently to provide region-wide public goods or social services (Rusk,

1993). Empirical attempts to uncover the benefits of local government competition (Hoxby, 2000) have often met with serious debate (Rothstein, 2007).

In this essay, I will begin by reviewing the basics of city services, regulatory powers, and finance in Section 2. I will also include some discussion of the history of American city governments and some discussion with government structures in other parts of the world. Every country's approach to urban government is different, so it would be impossible to meaningfully survey the world's urban governments, but I will add a bit of international perspective mainly to emphasize the range of political options that are, at least in principle, available.

In Section 3, I will turn to the key features of urban governments: decentralized and limited authority, urban externalities, and selective migration. As I have already argued, these elements of urban government interact in important ways. Moreover, they all must be understood if we are to better understand or even improve urban government.

In Section 4, I will present a model of urban taxation and city services. The model takes the existence of a city as given, and then presents the key conditions for optimal taxation and service delivery. In line with standard urban models, maximizing social welfare (globally) occurs when a locality makes choices that either maximize local population or land value.[2] The model delivers the standard result that a land tax is essentially nondistortionary at the local level (although that depends on having no investments that improve the value of land), but that in the absence of a land tax, a modified Ramsey rule holds for taxing property and income. There is also a version of this rule that holds when labor is mobile, where second-best tax formulas change to reflect geographic mobility.

In Section 5, I turn to the provision and financing of core city services, such as policing and education that is motivated by the results of the model. I discuss the ways in which the sources of revenue interact with the nature of service of provision. I will also use this section to discuss intertemporal aspects of city-budgeting.

Section 6 turns to local taxes and redistribution. As the model in Section 4 highlights, redistribution is a particular challenge for local governments because of mobility. Social welfare-related services were historically delivered by cities themselves, but since the New Deal these have been at least typically funded by higher levels of government, even when control over the services remained lodged at the city level. Other core urban services, like education, often have a redistributive component. There are also aspects of redistribution in some local regulations, like rent control and in some local tax systems.

In Section 7, I turn to urban infrastructure. Cities have often built extremely expensive investments such as water and transit systems. These have rarely been financed with direct taxes, but have almost always involved borrowing and occasionally been supported with large transfers from other levels of government. The Transportation Aid Act of 1973, for example, initiated federal financing for local transit systems. User fees or the sale of

---

[2] This result does not hold if the locality is being funded with taxes on the population outside its borders.

impacted land can also help finance the investment. I will discuss, briefly, the literature on cost-benefit analysis and infrastructure.

Section 8 addresses urban politics and institutions. Even within the United States, there is substantial heterogeneity in the forms of city government, between weak mayor systems and strong mayor systems, and areas with city managers. There is far more heterogeneity outside the United States. At one time, political machines dominated many larger cities, but they are considerably rarer today. I will discuss the interplay between political forces and city finances and services. Section 9 concludes.

2. THE FUNCTIONS AND POWERS OF CITY GOVERNMENTS

America has a vast number of local governments—more than 89,000 of them—which is quite close to the 91,000 local governments that existed in 1962.[3] Of those, 19,492 are city governments, a number that is almost unchanged in 50 years. In 1962, there were 18,000 municipal governments. The number of county governments has stuck between 3033 and 3049 for the last fifty years, and the number of town governments is only slightly more volatile. The number of general-purpose governments in the US is quite static.

By contrast, the number of school and special districts—the other two major types of local governments—has shifted enormously. There were over 34,000 school districts in 1962 and consolidation of far-flung districts means that there are only 13,000 today. The number of special districts has increased from 18,323 to 37,381 in 2007. These districts specialize in natural resources, like water, firefighting, and housing. They typically have a single primary purpose, and are often led by appointed, rather than directly elected, boards.

Taken as a whole, local governments, which include special and school districts, and townships spend 235 billion dollars on capital outlays and $1.2 trillion on current operations. About 40% of local governments spending goes toward primary and secondary education, and more than one-half (7.9 million) of local governments' workers. The next largest employment area is policing, which employs 909,000, followed by hospitals (644,000), higher education (606,000), and fire protection (429,000). These functions are also significant sources of local government spending, but local utilities are also a large expenditure category, with 168 billion in local government spending nationwide.

There is considerable heterogeneity, however, in the spending patterns of individual large cities, in part because of the functions of government that are taken on by those cities. Taken as a whole, city spending can be grouped into three large bins: basic city services, many of which were meant to address urban externalities (including fire, policing, and waste management); social welfare spending (including explicit social welfare spending, cities hospitals, and housing); and education, which is a service unto itself. The basic services are almost all provided by city governments themselves. Social welfare spending and education are far less ubiquitous.

---

[3] The source for the figures in this and the next two paragraphs is the *2012 Statistical Abstract of the United States*, where I have used the most recent available numbers. See Table 1: Facts about Local Governments for more detail.

The overwhelming majority of large cities do not have any spending on education, because that function is overseen by an independent, or quasi-independent, school board. Even in some cases where the mayor maintains a fair amount of control over schooling, such as Chicago, the schools are not an official budget item. Only six of the thirty-five largest cities spend more than 2% of their budgets on education. Likewise, public welfare (which is typically not handled at the city level) involves more than 10% of the budget items for only four of the largest thirty-five cities (New York, Philadelphia, San Francisco, and Washington, DC); the majority of large cities spend nothing in this category.

Table 1 Facts About Local Governments

Breakdown of Local Government	1962	2007
Number of local governments	91,237	89,527
Number of city governments	18,000	19,492
Number of county governments	3,043	3,033
Number of town governments	17,142	16,519
Number of school districts	34,678	13,051
Number of special districts	18,323	37,381

From *The Statistical Abstract of the United States*, 2012, Table 428: Number of Governmental Unitsby Type: 1962 to 2007.

Spending by Local Governments (in millions of dollars)	2008
General expenditures	1,375,539
Current operations	1,232,399
Primary and secondary education	557,388
Capital outlay	235,806

From *The Statistical Abstract of the United States*, 2012, Table 436: State and Local Governments— Revenue and Expendituresby Function: 2007 and 2008.

Local Government Workers (thousands)	2008
Primary and secondary education	7970
Police protection	909
Hospitals	644
Higher education	606
Fire protection	429

From *The Statistical Abstract of the United States*, 2012, Table 462: All Governments-Employment and Payroll, by Function: 2008.

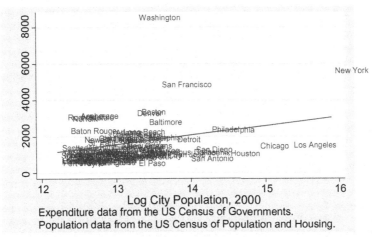

Figure 1 Population vs. Total Expenditure Per Capita, 2000 (for cities with 200,000 or more people).

By contrast, every large city has some spending on police, fire, highways, and "parks and recreation." Almost every city has some spending on "housing and community development," solid waste management, and sewers, and the overwhelming majority spend on health and hospitals. The different tasks assigned to city governments make it extremely difficult to make sense of total city expenditures of tax levels. Figure 1 shows the relationship between the logarithm city population and per capita expenditure levels in 2000 for cities with more than 200,000 people. The relationship is positive, but at this level, it is hard to know if the relationship represents the greater cost of delivering government services at the city level or just the greater range of services typically provided by city governments, relative to other overlapping jurisdictions.

It is somewhat more sensible to discuss differences in spending on particular categories. Figure 2 shows the relationship between per capita spending on police in 2000 and the logarithm of city population for the same sample of larger cities. In this case, the relationship is still potentially troubled by the role that other levels of government often play in policing (e.g., state troopers), but the relationship is closer to have some meaning. Larger cities do typically have higher labor costs and larger crime problems (Glaeser & Sacerdote, 1999) and that combination leads to more police spending.

On the revenue side, local governments as a whole receive the lion's share of their revenues from intergovernmental transfers and local property taxes. Out of the $1.5 trillion of total revenues shared by America's local governments in 2008, $524 billion come from intergovernmental transfers, and $397 billion came from property taxes. Sales taxes produced another $90 billion of revenue, but local governments, taken as a whole, rely very little on income or business taxes. The other two significant sources of revenues are user

202   Edward L. Glaeser

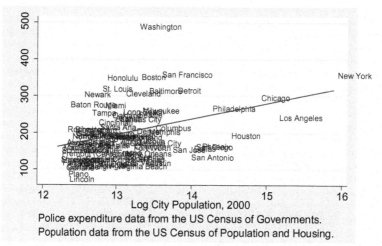

Police expenditure data from the US Census of Governments.
Population data from the US Census of Population and Housing.

Figure 2 Population vs. Police Expenditure Per Capita, 2000 (for cities with 200,000 or more people).

fees for utilities and hospitals, but these revenues fall significantly below the costs of providing these services.

The dominance of the property tax is among the most salient aspects of local government, and this has been the topic of significant amounts of academic research. Property tax rates differ in nominal rates, typical assessment rates (relative to true market values), and overall effective tax rates. For example, Philadelphia and Indianapolis both have quite high effective tax rates of 2.64% and 2.75%, respectively, but Philadelphia's nominal tax rate is 8.24% and Indianapolis' nominal rate is 2.75%. The difference, of course, is that while Indianapolis typically assesses at full market value, Philadelphia typically assess at 30% of market value. New York City has one of the most bizarre systems, and one of the lowest effective tax rates of .62%, which is accomplished with a nominal rate of 16.7% and an average assessment value of 3.7%.

The overall revenue picture for individual large cities can be quite different than the aggregate for local governments. New York City is *sui generis*. With $70 billion in general revenue, New York City's government is approximately 10 times larger than the governments of Los Angeles and Chicago. The transfers the city receives from other levels of government, $26 billion, are 20 times larger than the two next largest cities, reflecting the larger range of services, especially education and social welfare, which are performed by the city of New York.

Property taxes provide less than one-fifth of New York City's revenues, but while that is unusual for local governments as a whole, it is not that unusual for large cities to have less dependence on the property tax, which the model of Section 4 can help explain. Outside of Texas, every one of the 10 largest American cities depends on property tax revenue at less than half the standard 40% level for local governments. The only large cities where property taxes account for anything like that share of revenues are Honolulu (44%), Indianapolis (49%), Boston (40%), and Nashville (37%). Sales taxes are also a significant source of revenues, but general sales taxes are typically less significant than property taxes in all but a few western cities, like Phoenix, Tucson, and Albuquerque. Taxes on utilities, and direct utility revenues, also form a substantial part of big city revenues.

In addition, some cities, like New York and Philadelphia, also have income or wage taxes that generate significant revenues. Typically smaller jurisdictions are not granted the authority to levy these taxes, and many would not want to anyway, given the fears of repelling businesses and wealthier individuals. Indeed, Haughwout, Inman, Craig, & Luce (2004) estimate that the elasticity of earnings in cities with respect to the tax rate is so high that income tax rates quickly become counterproductive for producing revenue.

While there is a great deal of disparity in the revenue sources and spending patterns of local governments, local governments do tend to share a fair amount of authority over the built environment and business formation. The right of localities to regulate structures predates the US constitution. Indeed, Novak (1982) argues that the view of 19th century America as a laissez-faire nation is mistaken, because there was so much regulation going on at the local level. Fire-related building regulations were common in American history for quite understandable reasons.

The Progressive Era saw a great spread of local regulations of both businesses and structures. New York City imposed the first citywide zoning plan in 1916, which was focused largely on preserving light by requiring building setbacks. Zoning that restricted uses of land to commercial, residential, and industrial purposes in different parts of the city became widespread (apart from Houston) after the Supreme Court deemed it legitimate in the Euclid Case (hence Euclidean Zoning). Every city, including Houston, engages in some form of control over land use.

While there are a number of studies that claim that local land use restrictions can severely distort property values and urban growth (e.g., Glaeser, Gyourko, & Saks, 2005), it also seems clear that there is a great deal of heterogeneity in the severity of these restrictions across space. Typically, large cities are less restrictive than their suburbs (Gyourko, Saiz, & Summers, 2008). Cities with less restrictive building environments tend, unsurprisingly, to have more housing and population growth (Glaeser & Gyourko, 2009) and lower housing prices. Only recently have some locations begun to directly monetize their permitting power by charging explicit impact fees for new projects.

Urban governments also typically have the power to restrict new business formation, particularly if that business has any health consequences. Restaurants and bars, for example, usually require licenses, although sometimes the authority to issue those licenses is lodged at the state, rather than the local level. Business owners often complain that individual cities are extremely hard to start a business in, but so far there is little cross-city research comparable to the cross-country work on the ease of starting a new enterprise and this is a pressing area for empirical work.

While the economics literature on local public finance has been considerably less developed in Europe than in the United States, there have been a number of fine survey essays highlighting the key features of local public finance in several European countries. For example, Friedrich, Gwiazda, and Woon Nam (2003) discuss the public finance systems in Germany, Switzerland, Poland, and the United Kingdom, and provide comparisons in the share of spending done by local governments across the developed world. Municipal governments in France, for example, spend only 5.5% of GDP, but in Sweden local government spending accounted for 27.5% of GDP, which reflects both the large role of local governments in Sweden and the relatively large size of the Swedish state.

But the size of local government spending often provides a relatively misleading characterization of the overall importance of local governments, because that spending may be significantly constrained by central government. Ebel and Yilmaz (2003) sagely warn of the difficulties of using simple measures to capture the degree of fiscal decentralization. These empirical difficulties make cross-country work on local public finance (see, e.g., Mello, 2000) extremely complicated.

If anything, local public finance becomes even more difficult in the developing world, where institutional arrangements are often even more opaque. Moreover, these political institutions are notably fluid. For example, China has moved from having an extremely high level of political centralization, during the 1970s and earlier, to allowing considerably more local autonomy. Yet it is hard for outsiders to really understand how much freedom of operation actually exists at the local level in the People's Republic. India, typically, has fairly strong states but quite weak governments within those states.

Latin America has historically had many highly centralized governments, such as Chile (Glaeser & Meyer, 2002), but it also has provided some textbook examples of the problems that can result from fiscal decentralization. Argentina, famously, allowed provincial governments to borrow by issuing obligations that became national government debts (Kruegar, 2002). Brazil's decentralization has also led to significant amounts of subnational debt and a number of other problems (Dillinger & Webb, 1999).

On one level, the dizzying array of local governmental institutions across the world should make international comparative work on fiscal federalism enormously enlightening. However, there are so many ways in which institutions differ that the international literature on local public finance has been slow to mature. Often the best work (like Dillinger & Webb, 1999) focuses on just two countries, so that the authors can acquire the rich institutional detail that is necessary to say anything useful.

Moreover, it is unlikely that institutions have a homogeneous impact throughout the world. More decentralization is likely to be beneficial in some areas, and less so in others. Certainly, the competence of the federal government, the strength of local social institutions, and the advantages that are likely to accrue from local variety will all play into the benefits of localization and these certainly differ internationally. So, while the theory of urban public finance should hold internationally, it is likely to be most commonly used within particular large countries.

3. THE CORE ECONOMICS OF URBAN GOVERNMENT

Before turning to the key empirical findings on urban public finance, this section discusses the core economics of cities and their governments. I begin with discussing why cities exist and then turn to the externalities that are so common in dense communities. Those externalities explain why cities governments emerged early. The final subsection discusses local vs. higher control over public functions in cities.

3.1. The Formation of Cities and their Economies

At their core, cities are the absence of space between people and firms. They are defined by their density. They exist because people either want to be close to each other or close to some fixed geographic characteristic that exists in a place, such as a port, a court, or a coal mine.

Historically, urban theory can be roughly split into agglomeration-based theories of cities and everything else. Agglomeration-based theories, which were clearly described in Marshall (1890) and formalized by Krugman (1991) among others, explain the rise of cities with purely endogenous factors, such as the desire to eliminate the costs of transporting goods, people and ideas. As it is costly to ship products over space, firms cluster in one area. The concentration of potential employers in a place provides a form of insurance for workers who can easily find a new job if their employer has an idiosyncratic shock (see, e.g., Diamond & Simon, 1990)—the resulting matching of worker-to-firm enhances overall productivity. Some recent theories have borrowed from Marshall (1890) and Jacobs (1968) and emphasized the role of spatial proximity in facilitating learning and innovation (Duranton & Puga, 2005; Glaeser, 1999).

While these agglomeration theories now dominate the literature, they are not the only theories of urban concentration. Indeed, the simplest theory of urban density is that an area has an exogenous advantage and people come to be close to that advantage. Those urbanists who claim that geography can explain the location of certain cities have often been derided as geographic determinists, but it is not obvious that they were historically wrong. Waterways played an outsized role in determining the growth of American cities, because shipping was so much cheaper over water than by land. In 1900, every large American city was on a waterway, and Bleakley and Lin (2010) finds that the fall lines of rivers still greatly predict urban density today.

Harbors and agglomeration effects are two economic forces that drive city size, but politics also matters. Cities from ancient Rome to modern Kinshasa have been shaped by powerful central governments that have disproportionately favored residents close to the corridors of power. People cluster around kings and courts, especially when those leaders provide either favors or safety. The tendency of a single mega-city (the capital) to dominate a country's urban form is much stronger in dictatorships than in stable democracies (Ades & Glaeser, 1995) which may reflect the tendency of democratic regimes to check the favoritism shown to the capital city.

Indeed, American political history shows an acute awareness of the potential advantages going to the capital city and repeated attempts to restrain that tendency. For example, many states and the country as a whole located their capitals far away from large, existing urban centers. One reason for that decision was to limit the flow of funds to any existing city. Other British offshoots, but not Great Britain itself, such as Canada and Australia, also chose to locate their capitals away from large cities for similar reasons. In addition, institutions, such as the Senate, explicitly favored less populous areas within the US.

The fact that cities reflect both innate production advantages of a place and agglomeration economies often complicates the task of actually estimating the economic advantages of density. If people move to areas where productivity is innately greater, then regressing productivity on density will yield biased results. The empirical problem is only exacerbated by the fact that more innately able people may sort into higher density locales.

Scholars have attempted to improve on cross-sectional estimates of the density-productivity relationship in three ways. First, they have used historical variables like density or rail networks in the 19th century (Ciccone & Hall, 1996). This approach is valid only if these instruments are themselves uncorrelated with omitted productivity or individual ability levels, which is of course debated. Agglomeration economists argue that harbors may have mattered in the 19th century but are essentially irrelevant today. A similar approach is followed by Rosenthal and Strange (2008) who use geographic variables, such as bedrock, that make it easier or harder to build up as instruments for density and estimate sizable agglomeration effects.

A second approach estimates urban area effects with individual fixed effects looking at the wage changes for migrants (Glaeser & Mare, 2001). These approaches may be able to eliminate some of the impact of omitted individual ability, yet it does little to distinguish between agglomeration economies and omitted area-level productivity variables. Glaeser and Mare do however argue that urban wage pattern for migrants, which shows little immediate wage gain for new migrants but faster wage growth over time, is probably more compatible with a learning-based agglomeration theory than any geographic advantage-based model.

The third approach examines the impact of a seemingly exogenous increase in local employment on the wages and productivity of other works in the city. Greenstone, Hornbeck, and Moretti (2010) use the location decisions of million dollar plants and compare areas that attract these plants with their competitors that just lost. They also estimate sizable agglomeration economies. The natural criticism against this type of work is that winning the plant may not be orthogonal to unobserved area-level characteristics. Kline and Moretti (2011) demonstrate the impact of the Tennessee Valley Authority on manufacturing development and estimate that these effects also suggest significant agglomeration economies. While any one approach is certainly subject to many criticisms, personally, I tend to find the mass of evidence that agglomeration economies exist, taken as a whole, to be fairly compelling, but taking the opposite view is not unreasonable.

Moreover, the selection of people into cities is not obviously a huge confound, at least based on observables, because cities seem to attract a wide variety of residents. In particular, they tend to attract people at both the top and bottom of the human capital distribution (Glaeser, Resseger, & Tobio, 2011). Inequality tends to be higher in denser areas. There has been relatively little written on the attraction that some rich people have for cities. The presumption is that they are there to take advantage of urban agglomeration economies, but it is also quite possible that many of them enjoy the consumption advantages made possible by urban scale, density, and occasionally historic investments (Glaeser, Kolko, & Saiz, 2001). Much more has been written on the urbanization of the poor.

Poverty rates are typically higher inside cities than in suburbs. Glaeser, Kahn, and Rappaport (2008) find a 10% difference in poverty rates in the 2000 Census. Becker (1965) provided one explanation for this tendency. If the income elasticity of demand for land is sufficiently high, then rich people will tend to live where land is cheap outside the urban core and poorer people will live closer to the center. Glaeser et al. (2008) argue that the income elasticity of demand for land is actually pretty modest, and that access to public transit is a dominant force explaining the urbanization of poverty, at least within the United States.

Cities have also traditionally been magnets for immigrants. Public transit may be one reason for the attraction of cities to recent migrants, but there are surely many other factors. Ethnic neighborhoods have traditionally been gateways into a new country. Urban governments have also often been friendlier to immigrants than suburban areas.

These arguments rely on purely economic factors, but social and political forces also help explain the urbanization of poverty. America's system of local schooling, for example, pulls many wealthier parents outside of cities. If there is any local tendency to want to locate near similar people, this will exacerbate the power of public transportation or the demand for land. No matter what the cause, cities will continue to have to struggle with their tendency to attract poorer people. The massing of poverty in cities can exacerbate the great challenge of urban externalities, which are discussed next.

3.2. Urban Externalities

When people locate near one another, externalities become more severe. Human noise and refuse, accidental fire, and bacteria will inflict more damage on people who are close than people who are distant. Transportation becomes more difficult on crowded city streets. Crime becomes easier when there are more targets. Addressing urban externalities is the core function of city government, and historically the fight against blights like contagious disease and fire have consumed much of the public sector's energy in cities.

The most important role of urban government is to provide clean water, for if the water supply becomes polluted death occurs on a large scale. Even the recent history of cities is replete with outbreaks of cholera and yellow fever, which are water-related diseases.[4] Major cities have typically been built on rivers, for transportation purposes, but those rivers may not provide a clean source of water, at least once the city population also starts using the river as a dumping spot for refuse. At low population levels, wells can then supplement rivers and, indeed, Boston's location south of the Charles River owes something to the presence of a usable well. But again, if waste is not properly disposed of, wells can also become easily infected. The signal triumph of modern epidemiology occurred when John Snow traced a London cholera epidemic in 1854 to a water pump that was dispensing disease.

In principle, especially in advanced economies, one could imagine the water problem being essentially handled by private providers. Companies can and do sell clean water and many consumers are willing to pay for water that is not infected. Yet there are three principal reasons why private water provision historically failed to eradicate disease: (1) information asymmetries; (2) contagious disease externalities; and (3) large returns to scale in major infrastructure provision. The quality of water has historically been fairly hard to assess and that means that private providers will often have an incentive to provide dodgy water and claim that it is clean.

In some cases, reputational concerns may be enough to guard against this tendency, but the highly imperfect link between bad water provision and disease limits the power of this reputation mechanism in settings where testing is difficult. In addition, individual consumers do not face the right incentives to buy clean water, since they bear only the costs of disease on themselves, not the costs their illness may impose through contagion on the rest of the city. Finally, the vast scale required for investments, like aqueducts, has been beyond the scope of most private investors historically.

A growing literature is focusing on the impacts of clean water in the US and elsewhere. Troesken and Geddes (2003) have done impressive work showing the health benefits of municipal water provision in early 20th century cities; African-Americans particularly benefitted from the public provision of water. Ferrie and Troesken (2008) document that Chicago's investments in water made a significant impact on that city's mortality transition, causing reduction in a wide range of diseases, even those that are not waterborne. Figure 3 shows the remarkable reductions in mortality within New York City, which have typically been associated with the decline in communicable diseases, many of which are water related. Gamper-Rabindran, Khan, and Timmins (2010) find that piped water significantly reduces infant mortality in modern Brazil.

The large expense of water investments creates a close tie between municipal public finance and clean water. Cutler and Miller (2006) argue that widespread water

---

[4] Yellow Fever is of course mosquito carried, not waterborne, but water vectors are still related to the spread of the disease.

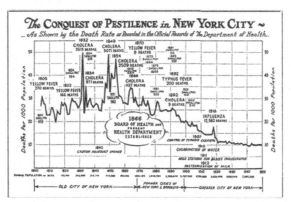

Figure 3 The Reduction in Mortality in New York City Over Time. (*Source: Figure is by courtesy of the New York City Department of Health and Mental Hygiene (http://cjrc.osu.edu/researchprojects/hvd/ usa/nyc/).*)

improvements only became possible as American cities got robust access to credit markets in the early 20th century. They point out that American cities in the early 20th century were spending as much on clean water as the federal government was spending on everything except for the post office and the army.

Cities continue today to be involved with water and sewage by management. Even when these utilities are private, they are highly regulated, both for safety reasons and because they are often seen as natural monopolies. It remains an open question whether private utilities and city governments are spending enough to maintain this infrastructure and certainly some critics allege that they are not.[5]

While city hospitals are also tools for diminishing the negative externalities associated with disease, their origins lie in charity or redistribution rather than fighting urban externalities. In the 18th century, wealthier people received their health care (such as it was) at home, while public hospitals, such as New York City's Bellevue, had their origins as almshouses for the poor. In some cases, city hospitals, such as New York's Riverside Hospital on what is now called Roosevelt Island, were used to isolate the ill and reduce the spread of contagious diseases like typhoid. Nevertheless, I will address city hospitals at greater length when I turn to the topic of cities and redistribution.

Traffic congestion is another primary urban externality and it has existed far longer than automobiles. The provision of public pathways is a classic form of government. Again, in principle, such roads could be provided privately and some private turnpikes have certainly existed. Yet the fragmented nature of land ownership means that hold-up problems can easily occur, such as the classic case of robber barons that extorted travelers on their roads. Moreover, lightly used, unpaved roads are close to being public goods.

---

[5] See http://www.infrastructurereportcard.org/.

They are non-rival, when used lightly, and the cost of charging consumers was high relative to the value of the service.

The public nature of roads meant that cities were closely involved with the private entrepreneurs who initially brought public transportation to cities. America's first omnibus ran in New York City in the 1820s, and at the point it seemed to be a small business that was naturally a private sector activity. Initially, the earliest transit systems had none of the large scale economies that later helped create local monopolies. No one could advocate for subsidizing public transit to reduce the congestion externalities from driving, since the primarily alternative was walking. The early omnibuses seemed like conventional private sector enterprises, except for the fact that they used publicly owned city streets.

Omnibus operators were soon eager to lay down rails to ease the path of their horse drawn carriages. Later in the 19th century, private entrepreneurs, like the Wideners in Philadelphia, Jay Gould in New York City, and Charles Yerkes in Chicago, laid more extensive systems over existing public thoroughfares. While these systems were not typically given overt subsidies, transit operators often managed to appropriate formerly public spaces for nominal costs. Allegations of corruption were ubiquitous.

In the 20th century, these private operations faced tougher fee regulations and lost riders to competing modes of transport. In city after city, transportation became public. Today, public transit systems are typically separate from local government itself, but they still impose significant costs on taxpayers as well as riders. Even the federal government started subsidizing urban transit after the Federal Highway Aid Act of 1973. While these subsidies have been justified as a tool for fighting traffic congestion, Baum-Snow and Kahn (2005) have found that new subway stops typically have had a minimal effect on the share of population commuting by car to work.

While the logic of having free public roads for low density communities is easy to see, the practice of free road use can lead to problems as urban densities increase. Since individuals do not internalize the externalities created by their travel on others, the roads can become overused and slow to a crawl. Rotemberg (1985) provides a classic analysis of the economics of traffic jams.

The most typical means of addressing traffic congestion is to build more roads, yet this approach creates a behavioral response that can easily undo the benefits of new construction. Duranton and Turner (2009) empirically investigate the "fundamental law of road congestion," which says that vehicle miles traveled increase one-for-one with highway miles built. That law suggests that construction on its own is unlikely to eliminate the congestion externality, at least at reasonable levels of construction. Likewise, subsidizing alternative modes of transport is, on theoretical grounds, a highly inefficient means of reducing traffic congestion, and empirically does not seem to solve the problem (Baum-Snow & Kahn, 2005).

Economists since William Vickrey have typically advocated some form of congestion pricing to induce drivers to internalize the costs of these externalities. These schemes can reduce congestion considerably, as seen in Singapore and London. Yet they are often politically unpopular and have met with little success in the United States. New York City's attempt to introduce a congestion charge was stymied by the state legislature.

Instead, cities have turned to alternative tools such as lanes dedicated to cars with more than one or two commuters. Outside the US, cities have used schemes such as allowing cars with odd license plates to drive on some days and cars with even license plates to drive on other days. Rarely have these plans been seen as significant success stories.

Perhaps the most draconian tool that cities have used against congestion is to limit the physical crowding of the city with building regulations. In the 19th century, fire was fought, in cities like St. Louis, by regulations that limited the use of wood in construction. During the Progressive Era, it became more common to require ventilation in buildings to prevent the spread of disease. Euclidean zoning, which restricted industrial uses in residential areas, was also meant to improve urban health. Finally, as land use restrictions became stricter, height requirements became tools that were limiting the overall growth and density of the city.

The limits on building do seem to have had a significant impact on urban growth and pricing. Glaeser et al. (2005) argue that without these restrictions, the cost of an apartment would be close to the physical cost of building up, since higher construction does not typically require any more land in the absence of land use regulations. They estimate that these restrictions have effectively doubled the cost of a Manhattan apartment, which can be seen as the effective "congestion tax" being imposed on people who want to live in the city. They also argue that this "tax" seems far too high relative to the externalities that might occur in the city.

Building heights also relate to crime, as street crime appears to be higher in lower income neighborhoods with taller buildings (Glaeser & Sacerdote, 2000). Crime is not a classic externality, but it has many of the features of congestion and contagious disease. It imposes costs on people who are not criminals and it is typically more severe in cities (Glaeser & Sacerdote, 1999). The maintenance of rule of law is a central role of government, and this remains a significant function for many cities.

The historian Erik Monkonnen provides us with a long time series of murder rates in New York City, which gives us a sense of the changes in that most serious form of crime over time. Figure 4 shows the long time series of murder rates, which experienced tremendous volatility during the 19th century. As the police force became professionalized, murder rates declined in the first decades of the 20th century and then soared again after 1960. Cullen and Levitt (1999) estimate the rising crime levels reduce urban growth, and the dangers in our cities may have been one reason for their post-1960 decline.

While the high crime rates of the 1970s made cities seem ungovernable, there have been significant improvements in safety since then. Levitt (2004) looks at the crime decline in the 1990s and argues that increased expenditures on policing and high incarceration rates help explain the drop. It is possible that improvements in policing techniques

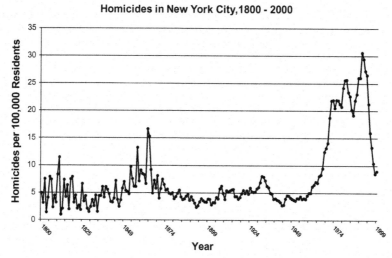

Figure 4 Homicides in New York City,1800–2000. Data from the Homicide in New York City database, assembled by Erik Monkonnen (http://cjrc.osu.edu/researchprojects/hvd/usa/nyc/).

were also helpful. While the decline in big city crime is hardly the only reason why many cities have experienced comebacks, increased spending on safety did help people to see cities as places of pleasure rather than fear.

3.3. Decentralization and Local Government

While the existence of urban externalities means that cities often need government, it is not necessarily obvious that they need local government. Services could be provided by either state or federal governments, and indeed, in many parts of the world higher levels of government manage many of the affairs of their urban areas. Even within the US, particular city services, like policing, have occasionally been run by state governments. In 1857, for example, New York's state legislature abolished the municipal police board and was replaced with a state-appointed metropolitan police board, which led to a pitched battle between the two police forces in front of City Hall. Transit systems have been administered by state-appointed officials. In extreme cases, the fiscal distress of particular cities has led to a complete takeover by state-appointed control boards.

Economists have long actively debated the relative merits of decentralized control; Oates (1999) provides a classic summary. Tiebout, most famously, emphasized the benefits of local diversity which enables citizens to vote with their feet and choose the public services that fit their own needs. Alesina, Baqir, and Easterly (2004) find that more racially and financially heterogeneous counties have split into more school districts. Oberholzer -Gee and Strumpf (2002) provide support for Tiebout by documenting that states with more heterogeneity in local preferences have decentralized control over alcohol policy.

Besley and Coate (2003) emphasize that this argument presupposes some limit to the benevolence, or competence, of a national government. If a national government had the right incentives and abilities, it could produce the same city services that are currently provided by local governments. It could allow the same spatial heterogeneity that now exists in service levels. This work reminds us that incentives and information are crucial ingredients in any theory of decentralized control.

In reality, it is often quite difficult for the federal government to allow all that much local diversity in its programs. One could plausibly argue that higher density areas need more schooling assistance, while lower density areas need more help with roads. Yet legislative realities mean that transportation and other budget items are handled as a bundle, which means that cities received public transit support in an attempt to create more support for national highway spending. Moreover, it would be extremely difficult to have different federal tax rates for different areas in order to finance the different levels of desired government spending.

Given that city governments grew large before the federal government had a major peacetime role, it is perhaps more reasonable to ask about whether it makes sense to centralize authority given that starting point. Before the rise of the federal government, there seemed to be several attractive elements to America's decentralized system. There was certainly considerable heterogeneity in the size of government across space, and local taxpayers typically paid for their government themselves. This created a certain pressure to ensure that funded services delivered meaningful benefits.

Highly localized governments may also have been more in touch with their constituents and their interests. Urban machines catered to the poorer citizenry, and especially the needs of recent immigrants. Reform and good-government groups were more likely to be favored by wealthier citizens. In some cases, relatively localized power structures have made it easier for local groups to influence decision-making. The local nature of government also meant that governments themselves often had relatively good information about local conditions. When he was a police commissioner, Theodore Roosevelt would prowl New York City's streets looking for policemen who were shirking at their jobs.

Despite these seeming advantages, local governments were increasingly seen as inadequate by reformers including abolitionists, populists, progressives, and New Dealers, and there are several arguments that favor centralization. Larger scale governments may attract more talented leaders and enable those leaders to influence a wider range of locations. Boffa, Piolatto, and Ponzetto (2012) present a model where there are decreasing returns to voter information. More informed voters discipline leaders by voting corrupt ones out, as shown in Brazil by Ferraz and Finan (2008), but this has less of an impact as information increases since leaders have fewer rents to forego when they are ousted. If localities have heterogeneous levels of informed voters and the relationship between information and good political behavior is concave, then Jensen's inequality implies that the level of

discipline rises when politicians are elected by larger jurisdictions, since multiple jurisdictions average out local heterogeneity.

Perhaps the most egregious failing of localized authorities is that they are poorly set up
to accomplish redistributive goals. If a locality tries to heavily redistribute, then wealthier
citizens and businesses have an incentive to flee. In a sense, there is a fiscal externality
because the generosity of one jurisdiction attracts beneficiaries from other jurisdictions
thereby reducing the fiscal burden on the taxpayers of those other jurisdictions (Wildasin,
1991). More often, the local government just fails to achieve these redistributive aims.

Likewise, in the 20th century, attempts to redistribute income increasingly involved
the national government. The populists wanted redistribution through bimetallism, but
during the New Deal, the government embraced a more extensive program of social
welfare, which required federal action. One side benefit of this federalization is that an
increasingly bureaucratic system involved more paper work and ultimately less corruption
(Fishback, 2007). When the welfare state expanded during the war on poverty, federal
intervention into local matters, like housing, expanded as well. When Richard Nixon
tried to move away from the welfare state, he championed "New Federalism" meant to
return power to more local governments. If local governments do not want to attract
poorer people, then local control may mean less redistribution, since less generous systems
may be one way to repel the poor.[6]

Today, cities are still entwined in a number of social welfare programs that are federally
funded but that operate at the local level. Cities typically have housing authorities which
interact with the federal government in the operation of housing projects and the administration of Section 8 housing vouchers. Medicaid provides significant funds for city hospitals. These systems are cobbled together to allow local management and federal largesse.

The federal government's role also expanded because of perceived interjurisdictional
externalities often linked to transportation infrastructure. While the Erie Canal was itself
an undertaking of New York State, the federal government itself began funding later canals
and federal support for such infrastructure projects was a major plank of the Whig party.
When the Republicans took over this aspect of Whiggery, the intercontinental railroad
system was subsidized with grants of federal land. Starting in the 1920s, and the expanding
radically in the 1950s, the federal government began to pay for a national highway system.

While these federal interventions are easy to justify as means of solving coordination
problems between jurisdictions, they also remind us that there can be costs of moving
expenditures to the federal level. As the gap between a project's beneficiaries and its
funders increase, it becomes increasingly possible to fund very expensive projects that
yield relatively little benefit. For example, it is impossible to imagine that Detroit would
have funded its People Mover Monorail without federal aid. Given that system's low

---

[6] The switch from AFDC to TANF essentially replaced matching grants with lump-sum grants, following the Nixon-era
move to Community Development Block Grants, and that structure should also decrease the incentive to redistribute,
especially if localities are wary of attracting lower-income individuals.

ridership levels, non-funding would have surely been the right answer. Transportation projects have only rarely been subject to cost-benefit analysis at the federal level which reinforces suspicions about their wastefulness.

The Interstate Highway System, seemingly the poster child for benevolent federal intervention in infrastructure, has itself been subject to heavy criticism. Many urbanists have argued that highways have badly damaged the cities that they were supposed to serve. Baum-Snow (2007) found that a city's population declined on average by 18% when two rays of a highway were built into its center. While the decline of urban population is by no means proof of inefficient infrastructure, the Office of Management Budget relates that highway "funding is not based on need or performance and has been heavily earmarked."[7]

Between 2009 and 2012, spending on local infrastructure has been tightly tied to moves to reduce recession. For economists who believe in Keynesian anti-recessionary spending, there are good reasons to think that localities will be unlikely to perform the right level of stimulus on their own. If generating extra aggregate demand creates nationwide externalities, these are unlikely to be internalized at the local level.[8] This provides one explanation why the federal government's share of total expenditure soared during the Great Depression and has risen during the recent downturn.

The potential cost of these interventions is that the federal government may not spend in ways that deliver social value at the local level. Again, the Besley and Coate (2003) insight remains—a fully capable and benevolent government would not have such problems. But it is certainly possible that a federal government, facing strong incentives to move money quickly, might spend in ways that are not particularly valuable. The willingness of some states to walk away from proposed federal spending for high speed rail is just one example of a federal project that does not seem well matched to local needs.

The problems of inefficient spending may be mitigated if the federal government acts primarily by giving money to localities and letting them spend as they like. Indeed, recent federal largesse has helped states and cities face budget shortfalls created by the downturn. One potential cost of this approach is that it means that local governments have less incentive to budget for the future.

While it may be easy to laud the benefits of local control, one potential cost of decentralization is that segmentation of the population along race or income. Indeed, Tiebout clearly thought that certain types of segregation, based perhaps on the tastes for public services, were highly desirable. But it is less clear that all forms of segregation are so benign. Cutler and Glaeser (1997) show a strong correlation between the degree of political fragmentation and racial segregation across metropolitan areas and find that African-American outcomes are relatively worse in more segregated areas. For equity reasons, it may also not be desirable to have wealthier children segregated from poor

---

[7] http://georgewbush-whitehouse.archives.gov/omb/expectmore/summary/10000412.2007.html.

[8] Moretti (2010) and Serrato and Wingender (2011) both find quite high local multipliers, relative to those found at the national level, which suggests that the interjurisdictional leakages may not be that important.

children because of heterogeneity in local school districts. Local control will inevitably mean some degree of sorting and that surely has both benefits and costs. I now turn to a formal model of the financing and provision of core urban services.

4. A MODEL OF LOCAL GOVERNMENT SPENDING AND FINANCES

I now turn from facts about government finance and spending, and theories about agglomeration economies and negative externalities to a simple benchmark model that nests several of the key results in local public economics. Initially, I assume homogeneous consumers and then extend the model to allow human capital heterogeneity so that I can discuss local redistribution and selective migration across space. In the model, individuals first choose locations and then choose housing quality, effort levels, and an "interactive action" that will impact their neighbors, like driving, which enables me to address local externalities.

Equilibrium in urban models requires three different equilibrium conditions, and the behavior of the local government. Individuals must be indifferent across space or choose to live in one locale only. The costs of supplying housing must equal the price of housing. Finally, the marginal product of labor must equal the wage. I assume that the marginal product of labor per effort unit in the city is fixed at W_j^T for workers of type T in city j and hence that will be the wage per unit of effort. For individuals, gross earnings equal $W_j^T e$, and effort will be chosen by the individual to maximize welfare.

In the housing market, I gloss over differences between renting and owning and assume, in this static situation, that everyone is an owner, and that everyone occupies one unit of housing, although I allow the housing to have different levels of quality. I let $P_j^H(q)$ denote the market price of housing of quality "q" in city j and now turn to the supply decision of developers, whom I assume to be competitive.

The total supply of housing space in the city equals the total amount of land in the area times the average height on that land. Contrary to the Alonso-Muth-Mills model, I assume all land within the metropolitan area is identical, which is a purely simplifying assumption. There is a fixed amount of land available in the area of $\overline{L}_j$.

The total cost of producing a building of height H is $C_j(H)L + (1 + t_j^L)P_j^L L + K_j(q)HL$, where H is the height, $C_j(H)$ denotes convex construction costs, L represents the land area bought by the developer, and P_j^L is the equilibrium price of land in city j. The cost of building also increases with unit quality and that is captured with the $K_j(q)$ function; I have assumed that the cost of quality is independent of height. There is also a land tax, that is paid by the developer, and captured by the term t_j^L.[9] I chose to embed quality in the margin to create a clearer difference between a housing tax (which will also impact the quality choice) and a land tax which, given my other assumptions, will not.

---

[9] In this static model, it would be equivalent to assume that the land tax is paid directly by the final user.

The total amount of housing space produced by the developer is HL. Since I have assumed linearity in L, there are no gains from building larger or smaller developments, which is most compatible with the perfect competition assumption. Developers will choose H, L, and q to maximize $P_j^H(q)HL - C_j(H)L - K_j(q)HL - (1 + t_j^L)P_j^L L$, which implies that $P_j^H(q) = K_j(q) + C_j'H$, $P_j^{H'}(q) = K_j'(q)$, and $C_j'(H)H - C_j(H) = (1 + t_j^L)P_j^L$. Housing prices will equal the marginal cost of building up and land rents will equal the gap between prices and construction costs. All builders will choose the same height, denoted H_j. The convexity in the cost for building up is the force that makes the supply of housing slope upward.

In any locality, the government has the ability to impact the quality of life through spending on police or parks or other public services. I assume that the local amenity level is represented by the function $A_j(S_j, N_j, \hat{a}_j)$, where S_j represents aggregate public spending, and $\hat{a}_j$ represents the average level of the "interactive action" in the community. This amenity level is assumed to be increasing the level of public spending and decreasing in city size, because of congestion.

If there are positive externalities from neighbors, the effect of city size on amenities could also be positive, but I will focus on the downsides of density. The locality is large enough, so that individuals do not internalize the impact of their "interactive action" on the area-level quality of life. The model is somewhat unbalanced, because I allow the possibility of disamenities of city size, which will operate by lowering quality of life, but I exclude the possibility of agglomeration economies, which would cause wages to rise with city size, as they typically do in the real world I made this choice to reduce algebra by allowing only one effect of city size, and I focused on consumption externalities rather than agglomeration economies in production, to tie the model with the externality discussion above and to reduce interactions with the tax on labor income.

The government faces a balanced budget constraint. Revenues come from a tax on labor earnings, t_j^W, a tax on housing that is proportional to total housing spending t_j^H, a tax on land t_j^L, and a tax on the interactive action t_j^A, which should be understood as essentially a Pigouvian tax. Those revenues will be spent on the public amenity and equal S_j.

The utility of residents is separable and quasi-linear and equals:

$$\left(1 - t_j^W\right)W_j^T e - \left(1 + t_j^H\right)P_j^H(q) - t_j^A a + A_j\left(S_j, N_j, \hat{a}_j\right) + U_a(a) + U_q(q) - \theta(e), \quad (1)$$

where π^T represents unearned income for type T, $U_a(a)$ and $U_q(q)$ are the welfare from housing quality and the interactive activity (which are strictly concave), $\theta(e)$ represents the cost of effort (which is strictly convex), and π^T represents unearned income from ownership of land. The separability assumption ensures that housing quality will be independent of changes to the land tax or the earnings tax and that effort levels will be independent of the land or housing taxes.

Three first-order conditions determine the level of effort, housing equality, and amenity-related behavior: $\left(1 - t_j^W\right)W_j^T = \theta'(e)$, $\left(1 + t_j^H\right)P_j^{H'}(q) = U_q'(q)$, and $t_j^A =$

$U'_a(a)$. I denote the optimal effort as $\hat{e}^T(t_j^W)$, and the optimal activity level as $\hat{a}(t_j^A)$. By using the developer's indifference condition, we know that housing quality satisfies $(1+t_j^H)P_j^{H'}(q) = (1+t_j^H)K_j'(q) = U_q'(q)$, which determines a unique value of housing quality denoted $\hat{q}(t_j^H)$. Differentiation tells us that every endogenous choice is strictly decreasing in the tax related to that choice. If N denotes the total population of the city, then $N = H_j\overline{L}_j$, $P_j^H = K_j(\hat{q}(t_j^H)) + C_j'(H_j)$, and $C_j'(H_j)H_j - C_j(H_j) = (1+t_j^L)P_j^L$.

Urban economists have often distinguished between "open city" and "closed city" models, and I will do so here. In closed city models, the population of the city is fixed, which means that the behavior of local governments is typically identical to the behavior of nation-states with the same preferences, tax instruments, and production technology. In open city models, the population adjusts so that welfare in the city equals the reservation utility available elsewhere. The spatial arbitrage condition is crucial in open city models, and absent in closed city models.

In closed city models, Pareto optimality typically involves choosing tax policies to maximize the welfare of residents. In open city models, the welfare of outsiders must also come into normative analysis. Developers compete away any profits in the building industry, so their ownership is irrelevant. I now consider how optimal tax and spending policies differ for closed and open city models, with homogeneous individuals.

In the closed city model I assume that the profits from land sales are shared equally among the residents of the city, so that each resident receives $\frac{C_j'(H_j)-C_j(H_j)/H_j}{1+(t_j^L)}$, which is the gap between marginal cost (which equals price) and average cost. In the closed city model, with homogeneous workers, each person's welfare is identical and equal to:

$$\left(1-t_j^W\right)W_j^T\hat{e}^T(t_j^W) + \frac{C_j'(H_j) - C_j(H_j)/H_j}{1+t_j^L} - \left(1+t_j^H\right)\left(K_j\left(\hat{q}\left(t_j^H\right)\right) + C_j'(H_j)\right)$$
$$- t_j^A\hat{a}\left(t_j^A\right) + A_j\left(S_j, N, \hat{a}\left(t_j^A\right)\right) + U_a\left(\hat{a}\left(t_j^A\right)\right) + U_q\left(\hat{q}\left(t_j^H\right)\right) - \theta\left(\hat{e}^T\left(t_j^W\right)\right).$$

$$(1')$$

Total spending equals total taxes or $S = t_j^L\frac{C_j'(H_j)-C_j(H_j)/H_j}{1+t_j^L} + N(t_j^W W_j^T\hat{e}^T(t_j^W) + t_j^H$ $(K_j(\hat{q}(t_j^H)) + C_j'(H_j)) + t_j^A\hat{a}(t_j^A))$. This leads to the first result.

Claim #1a. *If the city contains a fixed number of homogeneous people, and if the tax rate on land satisfies* $N\dfrac{\partial A_j\left(t_j^L\frac{C_j'(H_j)-C_j(H_j)/H_j}{1+t_j^L} + Nt_j^A\hat{a}(t_j^A),N,\hat{a}(t_j^A)\right)}{\partial S_j} = 1$ *and* $-\dfrac{\partial A_j\left(S_j,N,\hat{a}(t_j^A)\right)}{\partial\hat{a}} = t_j^A$, *then welfare is maximized by setting the other tax rates equal to zero.*

I have specifically omitted formal proofs both to save space and to encourage students to work through the model on their own. When these conditions hold, then the derivative of welfare with respect to the other tax rates is zero, since the benefits of higher taxes (more spending on the public service) are perfectly offset by the cost (less income for private citizens). The second derivative of welfare with respect to all of the taxes is negative, so welfare is maximized when these other taxes are zero.

Claim #1a essentially represents the thinking of Henry George. If a land tax is available, then in a closed city world, then taxing land is the optimal revenue-raising tool since it is non-distortionary. George also thought that the land tax would have desirable redistributive effects, although those are not present here. The result depends on the assumption that no actor has the ability to make investments the increase the market value of land. If developers could build infrastructure that made land more valuable, or even if there were externalities from one development to the value of neighboring land, then a land tax may create distortions.

The amount of the tax should equate the marginal benefit of spending on the public service times the number of people (who all benefit from the spending) with the marginal cost of spending, which here equals 1. Local cost-benefit analysis is essentially about determining whether this equality is satisfied for any particular public project.

The land tax does little to address the externality from social behavior and that is why there needs to be a second tax on that behavior as well. A natural example of the model is urban traffic congestion, where providing an optimal level of road access would require both public spending and a congestion tax. The tax can be negative if the behavior yields a positive spillover.

As the political history of congestion pricing illustrates, political barriers may prevent policies that appear to be desirable. New York City's attempt to introduce congestion pricing in 2007, for example, was stopped by the closed door session of the Democratic leadership of the New York State Assembly, led by Queens Representative Sheldon Silver. Queens has a significant number of middle-income individuals who drive into Manhattan. Taxing other urban externalities, like contagious disease, faces even more formidable obstacles.

If the tax on socially relevant behavior is unavailable, then there is still no use for earnings or housing taxes in this model, since earnings and housing consumption are independent of the externality creating behavior. The condition for the optimal land tax, and optimal spending, becomes: $N\frac{\partial A_j}{\partial S_j} = 1$. If the behavior is harmful, so that the relevant externality tax generates positive revenues, then an inability to tax the externality will push toward higher land taxes to offset the loss in revenue from the externality-reducing tax. The overall impact on spending also depends on the sign of $\frac{\partial^2 A_j}{\partial S_j \partial \hat{a}}$, whether spending complements or substitutes for the social behavior.

If higher levels of the externality-related behavior increase the returns to spending, then the inability to tax the externality will increase the optimal level of overall public spending. If higher levels of the externality reduce the returns to spending, perhaps pollution makes beaches unusable, then an inability to tax the negative externality will reduce the optimal level of public spending. In the case of roads, the sign of the cross effect is unclear. Higher spending on roads may ease traffic congestion, but it also may mean that extra roads bring less benefit, because they are overused.

Land taxes may also be unused for political or administrative reasons, such as the difficulty of evaluating the value of land that sits under structures. As a historical matter, there has been relatively little willingness to tax the urban land underlying buildings, so I now turn to optimal taxation when the land tax is not available.

Claim #2a. *When the land tax is set at zero, then the optimal conditions for the housing and earning taxes satisfy:* $\dfrac{t_j^W \hat{e}^{T'}\left(t_j^W\right)}{\hat{e}^T\left(t_j^W\right)} = \dfrac{t_j^H K_j'(\hat{q})\hat{q}'\left(t_j^H\right)}{P_j^H} = \dfrac{1}{\frac{\partial A_j}{\partial S_j}N} - 1.$

The claim follows from differentiation and it is a slight variation of the classic Ramsey rule. If ε_A denotes $-\dfrac{t_j^A \hat{a}'\left(t_j^A\right)}{\hat{a}\left(t_j^A\right)}$ and ε denotes $\dfrac{t_j^W \hat{e}^{T'}\left(t_j^W\right)}{\hat{e}^T\left(t_j^W\right)}$ $\left(\text{or } \dfrac{t_j^H K_j'(\hat{q})\hat{q}'\left(t_j^H\right)}{P_j^H}\right)$, the condition for the optimal tax on social behavior satisfies $-\dfrac{\partial A_j}{\partial a}\dfrac{\varepsilon_A - \varepsilon_A \varepsilon}{\varepsilon_A - \varepsilon} = t_j^A$. This condition implies that the behavioral response elasticity for the negative social action must be higher than the behavioral response elasticity for the other commodities, since the tax is serving both to raise revenue and internalize an externality. The tax will equal the negative amenity times $\dfrac{\varepsilon_A - \varepsilon_A \varepsilon}{\varepsilon_A - \varepsilon}$ which captures how elastic this behavior is relative to the other goods.

If I assume that $U_q(q) = u_0 q^\alpha$, $\theta(e) = \theta_0 e^\beta$ and that $K_j(q) = kq$, the cost of housing quality is linear just like the cost of leisure (the forgone wage), then: $\dfrac{t_j^W}{1 - t_j^W} = \dfrac{\sigma - 1}{1 - \alpha}\dfrac{kq}{P_j^H}\dfrac{t_j^H}{1 + t_j^H}$. The tax rates depend on the elasticities. Taxes will decline with the elasticity of one of the products (leisure or housing quality). If the two elasticities are equal then $\dfrac{t_j^H}{1 + t_j^H}$ will be higher than $\dfrac{t_j^W}{1 - t_j^W}$ because flexible housing quality only represents a small part of the total cost of housing. The relatively fixed component in housing supply pushes toward greater taxation of that commodity, which may be one reason why localities have typically taxed housing more than income, although this does not explain why localities should use housing taxes more than other levels of government, since this same logic would also operate at the state and federal level.[10]

I now turn to the open city model. In this case, N is a parameter determined by the spatial equilibrium. In the open city model, it is more natural to assume that the profits accrue to individuals whether they move into the city or not. Property revenues should not depend on the migration decision. If the total population sharing in the land profits equals T, then each person receives $\dfrac{N}{T}\dfrac{C_j'(H_j) - C_j(H_j)/H_j}{1 + t_j^L}$, which is denoted by π. Individuals outside the city receive welfare equal $\underline{U} + \pi$, where $\underline{U}$ is an exogenous utility level.

The spatial equilibrium requires that:

---

[10] One potential explanation for this difference is that localities may have better information about housing values than higher levels of government.

$$\left(1 - t_j^W\right) W_j^T \hat{e}^T \left(t_j^W\right) - \left(1 + t_j^H\right) \left(K_j(\hat{q}(t_j^H)) + C_j'\left(\frac{N}{\bar{L}_j}\right)\right) - t_j^A \hat{a}\left(t_j^A\right) \quad (2)$$

$$+ A_j\left(S_j, N, \hat{a}(t_j^A)\right) + U_a\left(\hat{a}(t_j^A)\right) + U_q\left(\hat{q}(t_j^H)\right) - \theta\left(\hat{e}^T(t_j^W)\right) = \underline{U}.$$

Since everyone is identical and all receive the same utility, overall utility in the city will also equal $\underline{U} + \pi$. This fact leads to one of the more curious claims in local public finance:

Claim #3a. *With homogeneous individuals in a spatial equilibrium, maximizing social welfare is equivalent to maximizing total land value.*

This claim is typically associated with Arnott and Stiglitz (1979) who called it the Henry George Theorem. It follows because profits per capita equal total land value divided by T. A second result follows:

Claim #3b. *Socially optimal choices for all taxes, other than the land tax, maximize local population as well as land values.*

This claim follows from the fact that welfare equals the reservation utility plus land values, so maximizing land value is sufficient to maximize welfare. Moreover, as land value equals $\frac{C_j'(H_j)N - C_j(H_j)\bar{L}_j}{1+t_j^L}$, the derivative of land value with respect to any policy parameter, x, other than t_j^L, yields first-order condition $\frac{\partial N}{\partial x} C_j''(H_j)/H_j = 0$, which will be satisfied when $\frac{\partial N}{\partial x} = 0$, or when N is maximized.

This fact will be useful when I turn to policy choices beyond the land tax, but in the case of the open city, there is again a result that is similar to the closed city results about the land tax.

Claim #1b. *In an open city model, if $-\frac{\partial A_j\left(S_j N, \hat{a}\left(t_j^A\right)\right)}{\partial \hat{a}} = t_j^A$ and if $\frac{\partial A_j}{\partial N} = -t_j^A \frac{\hat{a}(t_j^A)}{N}$ then if the land tax is set so that $N\frac{\partial A_j}{\partial S_j} = 1$, then welfare is maximized by setting the other tax rates equal to zero.*

The proof of this claim is similar to the proof of claim #1a. The condition for the optimal externality-related tax is the same as in the closed city model. The condition $N\frac{\partial A_j}{\partial S_j} = 1$ is also the same as in the open city model, but critically now I must assume that $\frac{\partial A_j}{\partial N} = -t_j^A \frac{\hat{a}(t_j^A)}{N}$ for this spending rule to be optimal. That condition means that the tax on the externality creating behavior is also sufficient to eliminate the distortions that come from city size.

One assumption that produces this result is that $A_j\left(S_j, N, \hat{a}(t_j^A)\right) = A_j\left(S_j N \hat{a}(t_j^A)\right)$, so that the size of the externality equals the number of people times the average externality produced by each person. In that case, $\frac{\partial A_j}{\partial N} = \frac{\hat{a}(t_j^A)}{N}\frac{\partial A_j}{\partial \hat{a}}$ and if t_j^A is set at $-\frac{\partial A_j}{\partial \hat{a}}$, then $\frac{\partial A_j}{\partial N} = -t_j^A \frac{\hat{a}(t_j^A)}{N}$. In this case, the externality-related tax handles the population size externality perfectly, and the land tax can pay for the spending on the public amenity without creating distortions. Given these conditions, the derivative with respect to the other taxes is zero, which given our earlier assumptions related to convexity and concavity proves the condition.

If there was an externality associated with city size that was not corrected for by the general tax on externality, then in principle, this externality could be handled with a lump-sum tax or subsidy on city residents. Alternatively, if the externality is negative, then this can be addressed with fixed limitations on city size, such as the growth controls that many communities have adopted. Alternatively, if more people increased the well-being of the city, then the optimal policy would be to subsidize movement into the urban area.

To see this, temporarily assume $A_j(S_j, N, \hat{a}(t_j^A)) = A_j(S_j, N)$, and allow the government to impose a lump sum tax of t_j^{LS} on city dwellers, but assume that the tax revenues from this tax are spread evenly throughout the population. In that case, maximizing social welfare is equivalent to maximizing $\frac{C_j'(H_j)N - C_j(H_j)\overline{L}_j}{1+t_j^L} + t_j^{LS}N$.

Claim #1c. *If $A_j(S_j, N, \hat{a}(t_j^A)) = A_j\left(S_j, N\right)$, then welfare is maximized if the land tax is set so that $\frac{\partial A_j}{\partial S_j}N = 1$ and $-N\frac{\partial A_j}{\partial N} = t_j^{LS}$.*

This claim implies that a local entity cannot reach the right population size on its own if there are positive externalities from in-migration. The subsidy for in-migration would have to come from the city's own coffers, which would mean that there is no way to truly subsidize people who are coming to the city.[11] If the city was too large, the city could, in principle, tax its own residents and transfer the funds to non-residents, but it is hard to imagine that strategy being politically palatable. A more reasonable approach toward negative externalities from in-migration would be to use land use regulations that can be used to limit N. In that case, the optimum could be achieved by just setting N at the optimal quantity and setting the land tax so that $\frac{\partial A_j}{\partial S_j}N = 1$.

The difficulty that cities have in inducing migrants to internalize positive agglomeration effects (in consumption or production) underpins various national place-making policies (Glaeser & Gottlieb, 2008). But while economics can help create a logical role for place-specific subsidies, there are grave difficulties in actually administering such a system since we cannot adequately measure local externalities. Moreover, I have assumed that there are no externalities within the other locales, while there is every reason to expect externalities from every location. As a result, the optimal subsidy weighs the gain from moving to one place from another, and that requires policy-makers to know the relative impact of more residents in each locale.

Before turning to a multitype model, I will drop the assumption that governments have access to land taxes (or lump sum taxes) and focus on the case where revenues must come from either income and taxes that are proportional to housing values. In this case, optimal taxes again will again maximize population size.

---

[11] If there was heterogeneity within the city between marginal residents and fixed residents, then it would be possible to tax the fixed residents to subsidize the marginal residents. While that could, in principle, cause migrants to internalize the social benefits of moving to the city, such a program would be difficult politically.

Claim # 2b. *When the population is homogeneous and mobile and the land tax is set at zero,*

then the optimal housing and earning taxes again satisfy: $\dfrac{t_j^W \hat{e}^{T'}\left(t_j^W\right)}{\hat{e}^{T}\left(t_j^W\right)} = \dfrac{t_j^H K_j'(\hat{q})\hat{q}'\left(t_j^H\right)}{P_j^H} = \dfrac{1}{\frac{\partial A_j}{\partial S_j}N} - 1.$

Claim # 2b implies that the optimal tax on earnings and housing wealth with a mobile population is identical to the optimal tax when the population is immobile. As a result, all of the earlier discussion remains relevant whether people are mobile. This consistency reflects the fact that maximizing the welfare of existing residents in the closed city model is identical to maximizing the size of the city in the open city model, and that is also identical to maximizing the land value and general social welfare in the open city model. Good government in a closed city is identical to good government in an open city, when workers are homogeneous, but this will not be true when there are heterogeneous workers. Just as before, the case for housing taxes, relative to income taxes, must depend on a difference in their elasticities not in anything about migration.

The importance of migration appears once I introduce individual heterogeneity, but heterogeneity must be of a specific type if it is to influence the results. One type of heterogeneity is created by heterogeneity in tastes for the locale, but identical in every other ways. To formalize that case, I assume that everyone in the city receives the baseline welfare from living in the city plus a term μ_i that represents a person-specific benefit from living in the city. This idiosyncratic benefit is distributed with density function f(.) and cumulative distribution F(.). This heterogeneity makes the supply of residents in the city less elastic, but it also complicates the social welfare function.

One simple assumption is that the social planner maximizes expected welfare across the population as a whole. In this case, welfare becomes $1/T$ times: $NB + (T - N)\underline{U} + TR + T\int_{\mu=\mu*}^{\infty} \mu f(\mu)d\mu$, where B represents the baseline welfare in the city, apart from the idiosyncratic taste parameter and any other transfers, such as land earning and payments from a lump sum city-specific tax, which are represented with R. The term $\mu*$ represents the idiosyncratic welfare for the marginal resident of the city. Since the spatial equilibrium equates welfare inside and outside the city, the first derivative of welfare with respect to any policy instrument "X" will set $\frac{dB}{dX} + \frac{dR}{dX} = 0$. If the policy has no direct impact on transfers, but impacts transfers only by changing N, then since N is determined by $\mu*$, the policy instrument will be optimal only if it optimizes baseline welfare.

If the city size externality either doesn't exist, or is multiplicative and is handled through the direct tax on the externality, or is handled through a lump sum tax on locating in the city, then the optimal condition for the land tax is again $\frac{\partial A_j}{\partial S_j}N = 1$, because at that spending level, increases in N have no impact on baseline welfare plus transfers (assuming the externality has been addressed). The direct benefit of the tax on baseline welfare is exactly offset by the reduction in property earnings associated with higher property taxes.

This framework also allows us to consider the impact of different public objective functions. Perhaps the most natural assumption is that the city government only cares about welfare in the city, which would equal: $B + \frac{1}{N}\int_{\mu=\mu*}^{\infty}\mu f(\mu)d\mu + R$, if property is evenly dispersed. The derivative of the expression with respect to any policy variable X would yield: $\frac{dB}{dX} - \frac{dW}{dX}\frac{f(\mu*)}{N}\left(\frac{1}{N}\int_{\mu=\mu*}^{\infty}\mu f(\mu)d\mu - \mu*\right) + \frac{1}{T}\frac{dR}{dX} = 0$. For policy interventions that only impact transfers through N, the total condition becomes: $\frac{dB}{dX}\left(1 + f(\mu*)\frac{dR}{dN} - \frac{f(\mu*)}{N}\left(\frac{1}{N}\int_{\mu=\mu*}^{\infty}\mu f(\mu)d\mu - \mu*\right)\right) = 0$. As long as $1 + f(\mu*)\frac{dR}{dN} > \frac{f(\mu*)}{N}\left(\frac{1}{N}\int_{\mu=\mu*}^{\infty}\mu f(\mu)d\mu - \mu*\right)$, then optimal policy will still maximize baseline welfare and maximize N. This condition means that even though the welfare function creates an incentive to reduce population, which can increase the welfare of the average urban citizen, that effect is not strong enough to overcome the basic incentive to increase well-being in the city.

The basic result on land taxes, however, depends on whether there are absentee owners or not. If property ownership is spread throughout the population evenly, then property taxes will be higher than in the previous results, because the local government doesn't internalize the costs borne by non-residents. If property is held only by inframarginal residents, then the core result returns, where $\frac{\partial A_j}{\partial S_j}N = 1$ (excluding effects related to the externality), because the costs of the tax are born by urban residents.

Results are quite different if the locality can impose a growth control that limits the size of the city. A local government that cares only about the welfare of its citizens has a strong incentive to reduce new growth, as long as the city can achieve that result without lowering welfare in the city. Typically new residents have less welfare in the city than current residents, which means that maximizing average well-being in the city leads to limits of expansion. This provides one of the possible explanations why localities may go too far, from a global perspective, in limiting the amount of construction within their areas.

A more interesting form of heterogeneity is to allow for individuals with more and less human capital. I now assume that there are two types of individuals, labeled S and U, for skilled and unskilled. I continue to assume heterogeneity in the taste for the community within groups, which is categorized by density functions $f_S(\mu)$ and $f_U(\mu)$ and cumulative distribution functions $F_S(\mu)$ and $F_U(\mu)$, for the skilled and unskilled groups respectively.

I assume that $A_j\left(S_j, N, \hat{a}(t_j^A)\right) = A_j\left(S_j, N\hat{a}(t_j^A)\right)$. Following the literature on human capital externalities, I assume that wages in the city for group S equal $W_j^S + \varphi(N_S)$ and wages for U group equal $W_j^U + \varphi(N_S)$, where N_S reflects the number of skilled people in the area. The number of unskilled people in the area is denoted N_U and the total populations of both groups are denoted T_S and T_U. I also assume that the two types have difference reservation utilities of $\underline{U}_S$ and $\underline{U}_U$. I furthermore assume that the taste for housing quality is $K_j(q)$ for the U-types and $\gamma_q K_j(q)$ for the S-types.[12] I assume that welfare from the amenity is A_j for U-types and $\gamma_A A_j$ for S-types. I assume that amenities are only a function of spending and that $W_j^S > W_j^U, \underline{U}_S > \underline{U}_U, \gamma_q > 1$, and

---

[12] It would be more attractive for this difference to come out of declining marginal utility of income among the richer, more skilled residents, but the assumption of quasi-linearity precludes that possibility.

$\gamma_a > 1$. Skilled individuals own $\frac{\gamma_L \overline{L}_j}{T_S + T_U}$ units of land each and unskilled individuals own $\frac{\left(1 - (\gamma_L - 1)\frac{T_S}{T_U}\right)\overline{L}_j}{T_S + T_U}$ units of land each.

The new spatial equilibrium conditions for the skilled are now:

$$\left(1 - t_j^W\right)\left(W_j^z + \varphi(N_S)\right)\hat{e}^S\left(t_j^W\right) - \left(1 + t_j^H\right)\left(\gamma_q K_j\left(\hat{q}\left(t_j^H\right)\right)\right.$$

$$+ C_j'\left(\frac{N}{\overline{L}_j}\right)\bigg) - t_j^A \hat{a}\left(t_j^A\right) + \gamma_a A_j\left(S_j, N\hat{a}\left(t_j^A\right)\right)$$

$$+ U_a\left(\hat{a}\left(t_j^A\right)\right) + U_q\left(\hat{q}\left(t_j^H\right)\right) - \theta\left(\hat{e}^T\left(t_j^W\right)\right) + \mu^{S*} = \underline{U}_S \qquad (2')$$

and the condition for the unskilled is identical except for appropriate subscripts and superscripts.

I assume a linear social welfare with potentially different weights, denoted λ_S and λ_U, for groups S and U respectively. If the baseline utility (excluding the μ terms) in the city are denoted B_j^S and B_j^U and per capita transfers (land taxes and any public payouts) to each group are R_S and R_U, then total welfare can be written:

$$\lambda_S T_S \left(\frac{N_S}{T_S} B_j^S + \frac{T_S - N_S}{T_S} \underline{U}_S + R_S + \int_{\mu = \mu^{S*}}^{\infty} \mu f_S(\mu) d\mu\right)$$

$$+ \lambda_U T_U \left(\frac{N_U}{T_U} B_j^U + \frac{T_U - N_U}{T_U} \underline{U}_U + R_U + \int_{\mu = \mu^{U*}}^{\infty} \mu f_U(\mu) d\mu\right). \qquad (3)$$

Given this welfare function, if $\lambda_S = \lambda_U$, and if the government has access to a land tax, an externality tax, and a lump sum tax/subsidy on skilled and unskilled workers in the city, then the next claim follows:

Claim #1e. *If $\lambda_S = \lambda_U$, then if $\left(N_S \hat{e}^S\left(t_j^W\right) + N_U \hat{e}^U\left(t_j^W\right)\right)\varphi'(N_S) = -\tau^S$, $t_j^A = -(\gamma_a N_S$ $+ N_U)\frac{dA_j}{d(N\hat{a})}$, and if $(\gamma_a N_S + N_U)\frac{dA_j}{dS_j} = 1$, then welfare is maximized with no other taxes.*

In a purely utilitarian setting with multiplicative externalities, three taxes are necessary to maximize welfare. The tax on land must be set so that the value of cash equals $\gamma_a N_S + N_U$ times the value of spending on the public amenity. The tax on the externality must equal $-(\gamma_a N_S + N_U)$ times the welfare cost of the externality. The subsidy to the skilled to live in the community must equal the wage benefits of having the skilled around.

In a more complicated setting with non-utilitarian social welfare function, these basic results would go through, as long as there was some other means of redistributing income between the two groups in the country as a whole. Naturally, the human capital externality only implies a subsidy because it exists within the city and not outside. If human capital externalities were equal everywhere, there would be a case for subsidizing education as a whole, but not for providing incentives for individuals to move across areas.

I now assume that the government only has access to labor and housing taxes, which are spent solely within the city. I also admit the possibility of different welfare weights on the two groups, but eliminate the role of amenity-related externalities, letting

$A_j\left(S_j, N, \hat{a}\big(t_j^A\big)\right) = A_j(S_j)$ and $0 = U_a(a)$. I also assume $\varphi(N_S) = 0$. Skilled individuals own a share, γ_L, of the land (altogether) and unskilled individuals own the remainder.

Claim 2c. *If* $\lambda_S = f_S\left(\mu^{S*}\right)/F_S\left(\mu^{S*}\right)$ *and* $\lambda_U = f_U\left(\mu^{U*}\right)/F_U\left(\mu^{U*}\right)$ *then welfare is maximized when*

$$\frac{\lambda_S \sigma_E^S + \lambda_U(1-\sigma_E^S)}{\frac{\partial A_j}{\partial S_j}\left(\lambda_S N_S \gamma_a + \lambda_U N_U\right)} - 1 = t_j^W\left(\sigma_E^S \frac{\hat{e}^{S'}\left(t_j^W\right)}{\hat{e}^S\left(t_j^W\right)} + (1-\sigma_E^S)\frac{\hat{e}^{U'}\left(t_j^W\right)}{\hat{e}^U\left(t_j^W\right)}\right)$$

$$= t_j^H\left(\sigma_H^S \frac{K_j'\left(\hat{q}_S\left(t_j^H\right)\right)\hat{q}_S'\left(t_j^H\right)}{K_j\left(\hat{q}_S\left(t_j^H\right)\right) + C_j'(H_j)} + (1-\sigma_H^S)\frac{K_j'\left(\hat{q}_U\left(t_j^H\right)\right)\hat{q}_U'\left(t_j^H\right)}{K_j\left(\hat{q}_U\left(t_j^H\right)\right) + C_j'(H_j)}\right),$$

where σ_H^S is the share of housing spending done by the skilled and σ_E^S is the share of earning done by the skilled. This essentially represents a weighted version of the standard elasticity formula. The benefits are weighted by the Pareto weights and the population shares, and the costs and elasticities are similarly weighted. The key condition that generates this formula is that the welfare weights equal the migration elasticity for each group. This condition means that the migration-related reasons for favoring one or the other group are equal to the welfare-related forces favoring one or the other group. There is no particular reason why this condition should hold, as it is quite possible that the skilled are more mobile but the unskilled are valued more in the welfare equation. But this extreme case illustrates one setting where introduction migration of different groups has little impact on the overall results.

The more general formula is considerably more complicated, even with a utilitarian welfare function, which I assume. Using the notation $\theta_U = \frac{f_U(\mu^{U*})}{F_U(\mu^{U*})}C_j''(H_j)H_j$ and $\theta_S = \frac{f_S(\mu^{S*})}{F_S(\mu^{S*})}C_j''(H_j)H_j$, the first-order condition for the optimal earnings tax is that

$$\frac{(\theta_S + 1)N_S W_j^S \hat{e}^S + (\theta_U + 1)N_U W_j^U \hat{e}^U}{N_S W_j^S \hat{e}^S + N_U W_j^U \hat{e}^U}$$

$$= \frac{\partial A_j}{\partial S_j}(\gamma_a(1 + \theta_S)N_S + (1 + \theta_U)N_U)$$

$$\times \left(1 + t_j^W\left(\sigma_E^S \frac{\hat{e}^{S'}\left(t_j^W\right)}{\hat{e}^S\left(t_j^W\right)} + (1-\sigma_E^S)\frac{\hat{e}^{U'}\left(t_j^W\right)}{\hat{e}^U\left(t_j^W\right)}\right)\right)$$

$$+ \frac{\partial A_j}{\partial S_j}\left(\gamma_a N_S\left(1 - \sigma_E^S\right) - N_U \sigma_E^S\right)$$

$$\times \left(\begin{array}{c} \frac{f_S\left(\mu^{S*}\right)}{F_S\left(\mu^{S*}\right)}\left(t_j^W W_j^S \hat{e}^S + t_j^H (K_j(\hat{q}_S) + C_j''(H_j)/\overline{L}_j)\right) \\ -\frac{f_U\left(\mu^{U*}\right)}{F_U\left(\mu^{U*}\right)}\left(t_j^W W_j^U \hat{e}^U + t_j^H\left(K_j(\hat{q}_U) + C_j''(H_j)/\overline{L}_j\right)\right) \end{array}\right).$$

The term before the equal sign reflects the direct cost of raising taxes, where the θ_i terms essentially put more weight on the costs of the more mobile group. The first term after the equality reflects the benefits of spending more, where the benefits are weighted toward the tastes of the more mobile group through the θ_i terms, and there is a variant of the usual effort adjustment in optimal tax terms.

The final term is another mobility-related term. This term will be positive (and therefore raise the effective benefit of taxation) if $\dfrac{W_j^S \hat{e}^S\left(t_j^W\right)}{W_j^U \hat{e}^U\left(t_j^W\right)} < \gamma_a$ and $\dfrac{f_S\left(\mu^{S*}\right)}{F_S\left(\mu^{S*}\right)}\left(t_j^W W_j^S \hat{e}^S\left(t_j^W\right)\right.+$

$\left.t_j^H\left(K_j\left(\hat{q}_S\left(t_j^H\right)\right)\ +\ C_j''\left(N/\overline{L}_j\right)/\overline{L}_j\right)\right)\ >\ \dfrac{f_U\left(\mu^{U*}\right)}{F_U\left(\mu^{U*}\right)}\left(t_j^W W_j^U \hat{e}^U\left(t_j^W\right)\ +\ t_j^H\left(K_j\left(\hat{q}_U\left(t_j^H\right)\right)\ +\right.\right.$

$\left.\left. C_j''\left(N/\overline{L}_j\right)/\overline{L}_j\right)\right)$. The first inequality implies that the ratio of incomes is less than the ratio of the taste for the public good between the two groups. If this inequality holds, then wealthier people actually like taxes more than poor people do, because the taxes are being spent on goods that they prefer. The second inequality gives us that increasing the attractiveness of the community to the wealthy increases total taxable income more than increasing the attractiveness of the community to the poor. This will occur as long as the rich pay more taxes, which should be generally true, and if the number of rich people on the margin of in-migrating isn't too much lower than the density of poorer people on the margin of moving into the community.

If the first inequality fails, but the second inequality holds, then higher taxes will tend to repel the wealthy and this creates a break on local spending. Redistributive spending can be seen as spending on a good that the wealthy do not value at all ($\gamma_a = 0$). In that case, the mobility of the wealthy will act as a break on local spending, and as long as the second condition holds (so the rich pay more and are not dramatically less mobile), then mobility will act as a break on local spending. This last argument provides the strongest explanation of why income taxes are likely to be less attractive at the local level than at the national level. This extra mobility effect, even when there are not human capital spillovers, will make earnings taxation less attractive because it repels the rich and they contribute more to the funding of public goods.

There is an equivalent condition for housing taxes, which finally enables a discussion of the impact of mobility on housing vs. property taxes. The housing tax will have less of an impact on the migration of the wealthy as long as housing expenditures increase less than one for one with income. Overall housing expenditure income elasticities are close to one (Glaeser et al., 2008), but much of this strong relationship reflects the tendency of richer people to live in more expensive communities. If the within-community elasticity is significantly less than 1, then this implies that property taxes will do less to induce out-migration of the rich, which may explain why localities tend to use them more than income taxes.

Using this framework as a starting point, I now turn to discuss the financing and provision of core public services.

5. THE FINANCING AND PROVISION OF CORE URBAN SERVICES

This section addresses the provision and financing of core urban services, including education, police, fire, parks, and the operational expenses of public sewage. These are areas where government intervention is typically justified because of externalities rather than redistribution (with the possible exception of education). These are also areas which typically lack a sizable substantial temporal component to them, except in the area of deferred forms of compensation like pensions, which I will address in Section 6.

I will first discuss the appropriate level of city service and then turn to the public private mix in provision. I will then discuss the financing of these services, whether through property taxes or user fees or other city-specific sources. Finally, I will address intergovernmental transfers from either the state or federal government.

5.1. The Appropriate Level of City Services

Before turning to how the services are to be provided and paid for, it would presumably be desirable to understand both the positive and normative economics of these city services. For education and crime, the normative economics have been well studied even though there is a lack of consensus. In the other areas of municipal service, the economics literature is relatively sparse, although there are certainly accepted standards for appropriate provision of fire safety and sewage. The costs and benefits of parks remain distinctly understudied.

Economists have been engaged in estimating the costs and benefits of education for over half a century (see, e.g., Wiseman, 1965). The literature has become quite sophisticated about general equilibrium effects (see Heckman, Lochner, & Taber (1998)), but there is still uncertainty about the core parameters needed for any serious analysis. There remains a moderate debate about the private returns to schooling, and a far larger debate about the social returns to schooling (Acemoglu & Angrist, 2001; Moretti, 2004). Moreover, it is not all that obvious the more spending alone achieves meaningful increases in test scores (Hanushek, 2000).

Much of the debate has moved instead toward specific institutional reforms, which are then evaluated one-by-one. For example, the remarkable effects of the Perry Pre-School Effects have led many scholars to believe that investments in early education can easily cover their costs (Belfield, Nores, Barnett, & Schweinhart, 2006). While the Tennessee STAR experiment showed that smaller class sizes can improve test scores, the economic benefits of that intervention seem closer to costs (Krueger, 2003). We are, of course, in a golden era of randomized experiments in education and while the economists evaluating these interventions are still focused primarily on what achieves results; cost-benefit analysis will surely follow close behind.

One approach to the optimal level of a public service is to rely on cost-benefit analysis; another is to trust the opinions of voters. There is also a growing literature on how much parents value school quality. For example, Black (1999) looks at property values on two sides of attendance district borders and finds that parents are willing to pay substantially more to live in areas with access to better primary schools. Hilber and Mayer (2009) argue that homeowners without children support public education precisely because it raises the value of their homes.

Overall, it is hard to come to a meaningful conclusion about whether municipalities spend too much or too little on schooling. While it is easy to point to programs, like Perry Pre-School, that have been successes, many scholars doubt the advantages of just increasing total education expenditures (e.g., Hanushek, 2003). At this point, the schooling literature is far more focused on delivering better outcomes at essentially current spending levels rather than changing the overall level of spending.

There is also a robust cost-benefit literature relative to policing and crime prevention (e.g., Welsh & Farrington, 2001). The technologies involved in policing are more transparent than schooling, so it is more straightforward to link spending on police and incarceration levels with crime (e.g., Levitt, 1996, 1997). More recent work has used federal aid for policing to provide exogenous shocks to the level of crime prevention and found significant negative effects on crime (Evans & Owens, 2007). Moreover, we have somewhat more confidence in our estimates of the social costs of crime. Typically, the big costs are associated with murder and these can rely on the extremely rich literature on the value of life. Estimates for lesser crimes are more likely to rely on hedonic estimation (Thaler, 1977) and are understandably contentious.

Cook and Ludwig (2010) present an up-to-date review of the costs and benefits of crime prevention. There take on the evidence is that "providing police departments with more funding has benefits (in terms of crime control) that are a multiple of costs." Donohue and Ludwig (2007) make a similar claim. The advantages of increased prison sentences are far less clear, and many others (such as Donohue and Siegelman, 1998) argue that funding social programs would have more benefit on crime prevention than increased prison sizes.

While the education literature is mixed, the policing literature has a much clearer conclusion that, if anything, we are spending too little on policing. There is, however, far less consensus on incapacitation, and many are profoundly worried about the vast costs of America's large prison population, not just on taxpayers but on the prisoners and their communities (Loury, 2009). There is also a growing literature evaluating the impact of targeted police interventions that shows significant impacts on crime in many cases (see, e.g., Braga, 2010).

There is also an old literature estimating costs of city services, such as refuse collection (Hirsch, 1965), and applying cost-benefit analysis to sewers and water systems planning (Howe, 1971). This area is extremely technical, and economists have had somewhat little to say about this in recent years. Firefighting has received even less attention, and relatively little is known about the relative benefits of adding one more firefighter. Google Scholar produced nothing on this topic, which is somewhat surprising given its importance. By contrast, there is significantly more on cost-benefit analysis of parks (e.g., Ackerman and Heinzerling, 2001–2002), but even in this case, there is relatively little that would be of use to urban planners.

5.2. The Public and Private Provision Mix

Even in cases, where public subsidy is appropriate because of externalities or redistributive reasons, there remains a profound question about whether provision should be undertaken by private or public entities. All of the key service areas have examples of both types of provision. Education is provided by fully private and charter schools, as well as public providers. Policing is provided by private security guards, such as those hired by individual buildings, shopping malls, and Business Improvement Districts. Water and sewers have been in both public and private hands, and volunteer fire departments dot the American countryside, reminding us that there are both for-profit and non-profit options in private provision.

Hart, Shleifer, and Vishny (1997) provide a framework for understanding the costs and benefits of private provision. In their model, private providers are contracted to provide some core public service, like operating a prison. The key difference between private and public providers is that the private providers have incentives to cut costs. That incentive yields the desirable effect of crowding out waste. It also achieves the less desirable effect of lowering quality. The proper role of government, therefore, is to provide those services that are likely to be severely compromised by private provision.

Their work explains the problem of private water supply in the 19th century perfectly. At the end of the 18th century, New York City provided the Manhattan Water Company with a subsidy—the ability to engage in banking activities—in exchange for providing more water for Manhattan. The company provided relatively little water and there were allegations about its quality, but it was quite successful as a bank, which eventually became the Chase Manhattan Bank. Troesken and Geddes (2003) show the water quality seems to have improved dramatically in the move from private to public provision.

Does privatization actually occur when it is efficient? Lopez-de-Silanes, Shleifer, and Vishny (1997) look empirically at privatization within the US and argue that political factors, such as union power, actually explain where privatization does and does not occur. They suggest that politics explains why privatization is rare despite the cost savings that it can bring.

Advocates for privatization argue that cost savings are only a relatively modest benefit from private provision. Private provisions are also allegedly less likely to be encumbered by bureaucratic rules that hinder innovation. In some cases, the rules are restricting the level of service delivery in relatively straightforward ways. The advocates of charter schools argue that they achieve benefits through a combination of innovative methods and longer class hours, which are made difficult because of contracts with teachers' unions.

Glaeser and Shleifer (2001) present a model of not-for-profit firms that draws on Hansmann (1981), Weisbrod (1978), & Hart et al. (1997), and argues that non-profits occupy an intermediate space between governments and the private sector. In this model, non-profits face incentives to cut costs, but these incentives are limited by the non-distribution constraint—the fact that the leaders of non-profits cannot just pocket the profits. This fact makes non-profits an attractive alternative that creates more scope for innovation than direct government provision and less incentive for quality-reducing cost cutting than for-profit providers.

While the literature on water provision in US history showed clear benefits from public provision, many papers have found that at least some charter schools have achieved remarkable successes. The key element in evaluating these schools is that successful schools are typically oversubscribed and admit students based on a lottery, which provides a random sample of treated students. Abdulkadiroglu, Angrist, Dynarski, Kane, and Pathak (2011) and Hoxby and Murarka (2009) are two of the papers documenting significant benefits from charter schools—private providers with public funding. There is also relatively positive evidence on private school provision from the school choice programs in Chile, the Netherlands, and Sweden.

Business Improvement Districts are one of the more radical privatizations of public functions in cities today. They operate within cities and take on responsibility for core urban services, like safety and street quality. They are funded with levies on businesses with the district. While there have been complaints about heavy-handed treatment of street people by BID policemen, the general view of these districts is quite positive. Studies have found that they reduce crime levels (Brooks, 2008) and increase local property values (Ellen, Schwartz, & Voicu, 2007). The fact that businesses voluntarily choose to form them and fund them makes them relatively likely to generate some value.

One concern, however, with the privatization of city services, like policing, is that this reduces the pressure on local governments to improve the general quality of public services. These concerns have been particularly serious in Latin America, where some authors have suggested that the prevalence of private security among the wealthy decreases their incentive to vote for higher taxes for security citywide. While this is a concern, there is little hard evidence that estimates the magnitude of this effect.

5.3. User Fees vs. Property Taxes vs. Alternative Means of Financing

Business districts essentially shift the costs of providing safety for an area from general tax revenues to charges imposed on the businesses that occupy that area. They operate with user fees, and such fees are one source of funding local government services. Utilities, for example, generally rely on user fees, and user fees also help pay for some portion of public transit. As discussed above, property taxes provide the main alternative source of local government funding. Local sales taxes and income taxes are also sometimes used to fund local governments. What determines the optimal mix of financing local public services?

The case for user fees is that they operate like a price and that can be helpful both for efficiency and equity reasons. The efficiency gains from user fees occur in investment, maintenance, and at the point of ultimate use. In the case of standard services, where there is a marginal cost of use (like crowding a city bus or delivering water), user fees generate efficiency at the point of ultimate use because they help deter wasteful overutilization, just like standard prices. If water is costly to provide, then charging people to use water will get them to internalize some of those costs.

One downside of user fees is just the administrative cost of charging people. For example, the London congestion system has operating costs that consume a significant fraction of the system's revenues. We must, however, suspect that technological improvements, such as electronic road pricing, will generally make it easier to charge users at a relatively low administrative cost.

A second downside of using user fees to ration service is that this may be counterproductive if the case for public supply is based on some form of externality. In the case of water, where the externality fundamentally comes from low quality, not quantity, using prices to ration quantity seems natural and efficient. In the case of education, where the externality comes from both quantity and quality, user fees are less natural. Part of the point of public education is to induce people to get more education than they would on their own account. If individuals were charged for the full cost of education, this would eliminate a key advantage of public provision.

In the case of public transportation, theory suggests that user fees should be reduced to account for the externality in driving. It may still make sense to charge bus riders some of the marginal social costs of their transit use, but since governments do not typically charge drivers for the social costs of driving, cross-subsidizing transit is one way of reducing that externality. The subsidy should be proportional to the reduction in external social cost created by taking the bus, i.e., the reduction in the probability that the individual will drive times the social cost of driving.

User fees have value beyond individual choice. By paying providers based on usage, providers have an incentive to maintain quality. This should occur even if the government is paying with a voucher instead of the user paying out of pocket. This is one of the hopes of charter schools. User fees also create a useful discipline on investment within the political process. If projects are to be eventually funded by user fees, then the project must generate enough users to cover its costs. This will tend to cut down on white elephants, as I will discuss later in the section on infrastructure investment.

In some cases, like policing and fire, economic theory suggests that there are less likely to be social gains from user fees. In principle, it might be possible to imagine charging building owners for the firefighting costs associated with addressing a fire, but equity concerns mediate against that course. It would be politically difficult to imagine having a firefighter deliver a bill to a property owner who had just lost a child to a fire. In the case of police, the biggest benefits occur to individuals who are never the victims of a crime. As a result, it is hard to see how a user fee system could be put into operation.

Of course, it is quite possible to set fees on socially harmful behavior. In some cases, businesses are charged for the cost of a fire department visit due to a false alarm. Such fees should, presumably, create an incentive that internalizes the costs to the fire department of making such visits.

If user fees are unable to fund every service, then a tax system is necessary, and then the question becomes whether the current local dependence on the property tax is appropriate. Certainly, it is conceivable to imagine greater dependence on sales or income taxes or to follow Henry George and rely solely on a land tax. Section 4 provides the core theoretical justification for the land tax.

The primary virtue of the property tax that has made it popular for centuries is that historically, property was far more observable to local government than other forms of wealth or income. Sales transactions or earnings were hard to monitor. As such, governments relied on property taxes (or even coarser taxes based only on the number of windows). While incomes and sales have generally become much more observable, property taxes remain dominant in local governments, perhaps partially due to historical path dependence.[13]

But the property tax also has several key virtues for a locality. First, property is considerably less mobile than income or other forms of wealth. Even the tiniest community, like a Business Improvement District, can levy a charge based on the amount of real property in the community. That property will not just get up and walk away, while an attempt to have a neighborhood level income tax would surely lead to considerable out-migration by the wealthy.

The immobility of real property, however, does not mean that property taxes are distortion free. If we tax real estate, we create incentives not to add value by building up. A developer can deduct the price of construction from his income taxes, but property taxes are typically proportional to adjust to the assessed value of the building.

Henry George proposed one approach to this problem—taxing only the value of land, not the value of the structure on the land. In the model above, land taxes consistently produced optimal outcomes. As discussed earlier, George's plan does face an assessment problem—the total value of a building is easier to evaluate than the value of the land under that building. The assessment problem is only increased if the tax is meant to be only on unimproved land values, so that there is no distortion to decisions that might increase the value of a neighborhood and its land. Still, it is somewhat puzzling that pure land taxes have been so rare in the United States.

While property taxes distort the incentive to construct, they do have several advantages beyond mere observability. In some cases, the value of the property may be proportional to the cost of delivering the relevant public services, like police. In that case, the property tax becomes a de facto user fee.

---

[13] The increasing prevalence of internet transactions, however, has pushed in the opposite direction making the enforcement of sales taxes more difficult for local governments (Goolsbee, Lovenheim, and Slemrod, 2010).

Additionally, the property tax makes governments sensitive to the value of local property. This creates an incentive within the government to increase the value of local homes and businesses and that may create desirable incentives (Glaeser, 1996). There is a long-standing result in urban economics that social welfare is maximized, under certain conditions, when local property values (or at least land values) are maximized (Arnott & Stiglitz, 1979; Brueckner, 1990).

The property tax is less redistributive than a progressive income tax, but it is not particularly regressive either. Typically, income elasticity of demand for real estates are estimated to be near 1 (Glaeser et al., 2008). This fact means that, on average at least, the property's tax cost rises proportionally with income.

One key question about property taxes is whether they should have the same rates for commercial and residential real estate. In many cities, such as Boston, commercial real estate is taxed at a higher rate. While the most conventional explanation for this gap is political—votes per dollar of real estate value are higher in residential properties than in commercial properties—there are potential economic justifications for this gap. For example, if commercial real estate creates greater costs for city government than residential government, perhaps by bringing in more commuters per square foot, then the gap would be justifiable. Whatever the reason, the gap does create an incentive to convert from commercial to residential uses, which is appropriate only if the net social benefit of residential space exceeds that of commercial space.

Sales taxes and wage taxes are two other forms of revenue that are used at the local level. One argument for these forms of revenue is that they charge the users of city services, commuters, and tourists, for the costs of their actions. Of course, the users of these services are already implicitly paying some taxes, because the businesses that employ them and the restaurants that serve them are already paying commercial real estate taxes. There is too little written on whether these taxes are already appropriate.

Income taxes, of course, can be far more redistributive than sales taxes and that is one of the reasons for their attraction to many cities. The problem with local income taxes is that they potentially repel wealthier individuals (e.g., Haughwout et al., 2004). That provides one reason why many forms of local redistributive services are actually funded by higher levels of government.

5.4. Intergovernmental Transfers and Basic City Services

As discussed in Section 2, intergovernmental transfers account for about one-third of the total revenues of local governments. Historically, these transfers have been tied to specific local services, such as public housing or transit systems. In recent decades, education has become less local and had more funding from state and local sources. The federal government also began funding local police services during the Clinton Administration.

These funds can either take the form of pure transfers or they can be tied to local performance. Both No Child Left Behind and Race to the Top explicitly aimed at improving local performance by using federal aid to improve incentives. State-initiated school finance equalization schemes also create incentives at the local level that can either increase or decrease the incentives to spend on education (Hoxby, 2000).

There are two core rationales for providing funding for local governments with intergovernmental transfers: redistribution and incentives. Each of these rationales has two different variants as well. The simplest redistribution-related story is that the money is being given for a service that is targeted at the poor and the locality would not provide that service on its own. Housing support is a clear example of this phenomenon.

A second redistribution-related explanation is that intergovernmental transfers are essentially an in-kind transfer to the poor to purchase government services. When state aid to a locality is tied to the number of poor people in a community, it is as if each poor person has a voucher that helps pay for local government. The case for providing aid in this fashion, rather than with direct cash transfers, is the same as for any in-kind transfer. Either there are paternalistic reasons to encourage the poor to consume more government services, or non-poor taxpayers receive positive benefits from seeing the poor consume more government services, as opposed to other forms of consumption.

The first incentive-related explanation is that higher level of government just thinks that, for whatever reason, the locality does not have the right incentives to spend enough on a given service, such as policing. In this case, the optimal strategy would not be to just give cash grants, but to tie grants to increases in local spending. A second incentive-related explanation is that the higher level of government believes that the locality is taking the wrong actions, like retaining below par teachers or making it too hard to open a charter school. Tying aid to performance along these metrics seems to provide one means of improving performance.

The No Child Left Behind Act tied federal aid to education to performance on standardized tests. While the act has been roundly criticized, a number of academic papers have found significant test score improvements, not just on the high stakes tests (Dee and Jacob, 2011) but also on low stakes tests taken by the same students (Ballou and Springer, 2008). Reback, Rockoff, and Schwartz (2011) present a particularly comprehensive analysis of the act and find "either neutral or positive effects on students' enjoyment of learning and their achievement gains on low-stakes exams in reading, math, and science." These results parallel the results found on federal aid for policing found by Evans and Owens (2007).

The Great Recession that started in 2007 represents a particularly radical departure in the federal role in spending for local governments. The federal government structured its recovery support in the form of significant transfers to states and localities that enabled them to sustain existing expenditure levels without significant increases in tax rates. Essentially, the federal government has taken on the role of providing insurance against a downturn, which may be desirable if localities are unable to save or borrow enough to smooth their own spending. Still, this would seem to reduce some of the incentives that do exist for fiscal prudence at the local level. I now turn to city services and redistribution.

6. CITIES, TAXES, AND REDISTRIBUTION

A central difference between cities and national governments is that it is relatively easy to leave a local jurisdiction. This mobility puts significant checks on local welfare systems which should tend to attract the rich and repel the poor. Since there is a redistributive element in many urban services and since the poor are disproportionately drawn to cities, this is an important element in much of urban public finance.

In this section, I will first discuss migration and redistribution, and then turn to local housing policies, and then end with public health and social services, including some redistributive elements in education.

6.1. Migration and Redistribution

How much do the poor and rich respond to financial incentives in making their migration decisions? There is a robust literature on the tendency of the poor to migrate in responses to differences in welfare payments. Before welfare reform, states typically had significant differences in maximum Aid to Families with Dependent Children (AFDC) payments. In some cases, metropolitan areas like St. Louis were split between more and less generous states (Illinois and Missouri), and those welfare gaps seemed to explain the extraordinarily high levels of poverty in higher welfare areas like East St. Louis.

More systematically, a number of papers have examined whether the migrations decisions of the poor respond to the differences in welfare payments. Blank (1988), for example, found that "[t]he probability of a typical female-headed household with little outside income leaving an area with low welfare payments and low wages can be as much as 12% points higher over a four-year period than the probability of leaving a high-welfare area." Borjas (1999) found particularly large impacts on the location decisions of recent immigrants. Conversely, Levine and Zimmerman (1999) find "little evidence indicating that welfare-induced migration is a widespread phenomenon."

There is a similar literature assessing whether the wealthy relocate in response to high local tax rates. Feldstein and Wrobel (1998) take what may be the strongest stance; their data suggests that behavioral responses make local redistribution essentially impossible. It is however unclear whether their findings represent migration or other behavioral responses to higher taxes. Bakija and Slemrod (2004) use income tax records and find that the "rich flee from high tax states," although their estimated effects are modest.

Cohen, Lai, and Stendal (2011) examine Internal Revenue Service data from 1992 to 2008, and find that increases in the state marginal tax rate have "small but significant" impacts on net migration rate. Their estimates suggest that New Jersey's "cumulative losses from increases in average marginal tax rates after 2003 (most importantly the 2004 "millionaires' tax") totaled roughly 20,000 taxpayers and $2.5 billion in annual income." Young and Varner (2011) also examine New Jersey during this period. They find that out-migration of the wealthy increased after the tax increase, but note that out-migration also increased for poorer people, so their estimate of tax migration elasticities using a difference-in-difference (between over and under $500,000 before and after 2003) is tiny.

There is also a literature estimating the impact of local attempts at redistribution on business formation. Holmes (1998) looked at industrial growth in neighboring counties on opposite sides of state borders, where the states had different policies toward businesses, like Right-to-Work rules. He finds quite sizable effects of anti-business rules on industrial growth in post-war America. Carlton (1983) found negative effects of local tax rates on new business formation, and Papke (1991) found similar results for many industries. Hines (1996) and Coughlin, Terza, and Arromdee (1991) find less foreign direct investment in states with higher tax rates.

Taken together, these studies suggest that economic incentives do impact migration decisions of the poor, the wealthy, and businesses, although these migration responses may not be all that large. One reason why migration elasticities can be hard to estimate is that governments typically deliver value as well as taxing, and higher service levels may be correlated with higher tax levels. Another potential empirical confound is that only local governments with sufficient other attraction may take the risk of increasing the local tax burden on the wealthy or on businesses.

Before the New Deal, the redistribution initiated by American governments was often led by the state and local levels. The scale was modest, and urban governments seemingly understood that they had fixed assets, like a thriving harbor, that would keep businesses in the city even with some social welfare spending. Moreover, some of these policies could certainly be justified as a tool for making the city a somewhat more pleasant environment (e.g., moving sick people off the street into almshouses). With the radical transformation of the desired level of social insurance, the federal government took the lead but worked jointly with local governments to administer programs, such as those associated with the Works Progress Administration or the Federal Emergency Relief Administration.

These programs became the nucleus of the larger welfare system that would emerge in the post-war world. Aid to Families with Dependent Children, which was started under the Social Security Act of 1935, became a core means of distributing aid to poorer families, until the 1996 welfare reform. AFDC was always a hybrid federal-state-local program. The federal government set relatively minimal rules and paid for part of the program. The state exercised some oversight, either directly administering or supervising the program, and decided on the benefit level. In states that chose supervision, localities often directly administered the programs. This meant that cities did not have control over the size of the benefits, but they could often control the administrative style and efficiency of the system. As a result, localities had some ability to influence how friendly their jurisdiction was to the poor.

The New Deal also launched the federal government into the housing business in a major way and the Federal Housing Administration was another significant source of funding for urban areas. Fishback, Horrace, and Kantor (2005) claim that this spending was extensive and that it helped shape migration during the New Deal. It is one example of the local housing policies that have some connection to redistribution.

6.2. Local Housing Policies

Localities have long regulated housing, but the purpose of most pre-20th century interventions was the mitigation of externalities, not redistribution. During the 20th century, localities have become more aggressively involved with the production and regulation of housing, often supported by the federal government. There are three primary types of local redistribution-related interventions that have shaped urban housing markets, and often urban finances: rent control; the production of public housing and urban renewal; and the administration of housing vouchers.

Rent control first became common in the US during World War I, as an emergency wartime measure and it reappeared on a large scale during World War II. Price controls were ubiquitous during the wars, partially as an attempt to limit the morale-related costs of obvious producer profits and higher consumer expenditures. Some localities, such as New York City, have kept some form of rent control ever since. The most common form of rent control is a limit on the extent the rents can be increased on an existing tenant, although there can also be limits as well on the extent that rents can be increased between tenants. The alleged benefit of rent control is the redistribution from landlord to tenant, but Arnott (1995) has also argued that rent stabilization serves to minimize a hold-up problem that can occur once tenants have paid the fixed costs of moving into a building.

The economic literature on rent controls is enormous, and since Friedman and Stigler (1946) it has typically been widely criticized. Economists have emphasized the adverse supply consequences of a price control, leading to both underproduction and the conversion of rental units into owner-occupied housing (which appears to have been quite common during the 1940s). Others have emphasized the deterioration of unit quality due to rent control (Frankena, 1975), rent-seeking behavior created by the system (Barzel, 1974), and misallocation of units among renters (Glaeser & Luttmer, 2003). Some have even questioned whether lowering rents is counterproductive from a redistributive perspective, as landlords can be poorer than tenants (Johnson, 1951). Certainly, few economists today would argue that rent control is an efficient means of redistributing wealth.

In an interesting example of restricting local authority, the majority of states have enacted statewide rules preventing localities from imposing rent control. For example, rent control in Cambridge, Massachusetts was ended by the state legislature. An economic explanation for this state intervention is that rent control imposes costs on people outside the jurisdiction, who might want to move to the community but are prevented by the lack of supply of available housing.

Rent control also has possible impacts on municipal finances, which depend heavily on property taxes. By reducing the value of rental properties, rent control would seem to reduce the tax revenues of the community. Of course, the city could offset this with an increase in tax rates, but that may be difficult for institutional or political reasons. The heavily distorted property market in New York City, for example, may have something to do with that city's relatively light reliance on property taxes.

The second primary means in which localities use housing as a means of redistribution is through the direct provision of public housing, which was also initiated as part of the New Deal.[14] The Public Works Administration and later the United States Housing Authority began the federal engagement with public housing projects. More federal funding was made available by the Federal Housing Act of 1949, which helped encourage the process of "urban renewal." These funds typically supported the clearing of existing poorer neighborhoods, often called "slums," and their replacement with newer, often high-rise buildings, frequently for middle-income residents, who would pay below market rate rents.

While these initiatives always had the veneer of redistribution, initially they seemed like redistribution from both taxpayers and the poorest urban residents to people in the middle of the income distribution. Many of these projects had rules that worked to exclude the poorest people from their premises, although explicit racial barriers were met with significant protest (Zipp, 2010). Eventually, however, the projects became far more focused on poorer urbanites.

While state and federal funding provided significant financing for these projects, there were also implications for local budgets. Localities did bear some of the cost of building and maintain public housing. Moreover, public housing meant that large swaths of the city were taken off the tax rolls, and if public housing encouraged poorer people to stay in the city that would lead to larger expenditures on other municipal services.

By the 1960s, there was widespread antipathy to public housing in the United States. Jane Jacobs argued that these projects were poorly designed to meet the human needs of their residents. Cities and taxpayers were increasingly unwillingly to shoulder the costs of these projects. The visible poverty in the projects led many to argue that they actually made things worse for their residents, although that view has been challenged in recent research. Currie and Yelowitz (2000) and Jacob (2004) both provide evidence suggesting that public housing does not have demonstrable negative effects on children's outcomes.

Nevertheless, the Nixon Administration moved away from public housing, embracing instead Section **8** housing vouchers. The Reagan Administration changed its supply focus to the Low Income Housing Tax Credit instead, which provides incentives for developers to construct "affordable" housing for lower income residents. The impact of the Low Income Housing Tax Credit on housing production has been questioned by Sinai and Waldfogel (2005) among others, who present evidence suggesting that these public units significantly crowd out the private production of housing. Glaeser and Gyourko (2009) argue that the Low Income Housing Tax Credit errs by introducing a common housing

---

[14] Zipp (2010) provides a helpful overview of the public projects within New York City.

approach across urban areas with wildly different housing conditions, and that it makes little sense to subsidize housing in areas which are already oversupplied with cheap homes.

Housing vouchers have been typically seen as being a relatively efficient way to provide in-kind housing. Economists of course question whether this aid would not be better distributed in the form of unrestricted cash. Moreover, the somewhat opaque manner in which these vouchers are redistributed has been fairly puzzling to many. By creating a large, lumpy benefit, there is more demand than supply for the vouchers and local authorities typically enjoy significant autonomy over their distribution.

Both the Low Income Housing Tax Credit and Section 8 housing vouchers are administered by local housing authorities, which are important local governmental entities. While these entities typically have independent budgets, they are often controlled by the mayor or other local officials. As such, they remain an arm of local government providing aid that is at least meant to be redistributive in nature and that is largely funded by the federal government.

6.3. Public Hospitals and Health Care in Cities

Cities also engage in the redistribution through public hospitals and other local agencies meant to improve the welfare of the poor. City hospitals have a long history in the United States and they began as tools for addressing illness among the urban poor (Opdycke, 1999). Public hospitals, just like public health insurance, do seem to crowd out private health insurance (Rask & Rask, 2000), but competition from public hospitals, at least in the United Kingdom, appears to increase managerial quality in nearby institutions (Bloom, Propper, Seiler, & Van Reenan, 2010).

Just as the federal government's rising role in paying for redistribution reduced the local role in that area, federal health care interventions have similarly been associated with a reduced local commitment to providing health care for the poor. Medicaid represents a significant shift in the vision for low income health care in America. Historically health care was provided free by public or non-profit hospitals, and was paid for either by local taxpayers, charitable giving, or cross-subsidization from other income. Medicaid meant that the federal government had taken on responsibility for paying for the health needs of the poor. This meant that hospitals of all sort could provide health care to the poor and expect to get it paid for, at least in large part by the federal government.

While public hospitals receive funding from federal Medicaid and state-level support they can also impose costs on local budgets. The combination of fiscal shortfalls at the city level and rising health costs has caused many cities to scale back their commitment to local public hospitals. For example, in response to the fiscal crisis of 1975, New York City cut the payroll of its Health and Hospitals Corporation by 17%, which appears to have led to significantly adverse health outcomes (Freudenberg, Fahs, Galea, & Greenberg, 2006).

More generally, between 1975 and 1995, the number of local government and state-run hospitals declined by 30% and the number of beds in those hospitals declined by 34%.

The rising costs of providing health care have often challenged local budgets, and public hospitals are not particularly nimble in responding to changes in health care compensation. Hansmann, Kessler, and McClellan (2003) show that while for-profit and non-profit hospitals scaled back services to the poor dramatically in response to a reduction in federal reimbursements, public hospitals did not. Duggan (2000) finds that when California increased incentives to care for low income patients, more of these patients ended up at non-profit and for-profit hospitals, while a lower share of them ended up in public hospitals.

Cities, both in their hospitals and in their health care costs more generally, are facing the national challenge of dealing with the expanding costs of providing care. Weak (or non-existent) incentives to ration health care have been cited as a primary problem with the current system. As a result, many of the calls for reform have focused on alternative service models which create stronger incentives to cut costs as well as increase quality.

7. CITIES, INVESTMENT, AND DEFERRED COMPENSATION

To many, urban public finance connotes the intertemporal aspects of municipal spending. Typically, local governments in the US are formally restricted from running operating expenditure deficits. They can, however, borrow to finance infrastructure and indeed their borrowing is implicitly subsidized by the fact that investors often do not have to pay income taxes on interest paid by municipal governments. In this section, I will start with the theory of intertemporal financing decisions by municipalities. I then treat infrastructure and deferred spending on operating expenditures in separate subsections.

7.1. The Timing of Spending by Municipalities

Like US states, cities typically face balanced budget rules that constrain their ability to borrow for operating expenses. While there has been a large literature on the impact of different types of balanced budget rules across US states (Inman, 1998; Poterba, 1994), there has been less investigation of these rules at the city level. Grembi, Nannicini, and Troiano (2011) found that when Italy relaxed its fiscal rules for cities with fewer than 5000 inhabitants, deficits increased from zero to roughly 2% of the city budget, and most of the change occurred because of reductions in tax revenues. Moreover, there are abundant examples of cities that have managed to defer the costs of operational spending either through creative accounting (Gramlich, 1976) or through underfunded pension promises (Novy-Marx & Rauh, 2011).

The economic case for local budget rules trades the costs of limiting financing options with the advantage of imposing discipline on local governments. Certainly, the inability to borrow means that cities may have difficulty responding to revenue shortfalls during a recession. The widespread nature of these rules suggests that voters do see them as necessary to restrain local public excesses, but it is unclear why these rules are more prevalent at the local than at the national level. Perhaps, the national ability to borrow is seen as a critical element in fighting wars or perhaps, local governments are seen as less trustworthy and therefore in need of more fetters.

Importantly, in many states, municipal borrowing is restrained by state law or the state constitution rather than by city charters. One interpretation of these rules is that the state is dealing with an externality related to local borrowing. If the state ultimately feels some obligation to deal with municipal debts, then restricting local borrowing is a means of pushing the city against imposing costs on other municipalities. The extreme example of state interventions in municipal finance occurs when cities have gotten into fiscal trouble and the state actually takes over the administrative function of the city. In some cases, like New York in the 1970s, the outside control board was seen as necessary to persuade investors to continue to buy city debt.

There are also plausible reasons why local public officials might want to engage in too much current spending, relative to voter desires, at least if they do not have to pay for them with current taxes. Certainly, there have been abundant allegations that city mayors have shown a strong desire to do just that in many situations. Perhaps the simplest model of this process is that politicians enjoy spending money, either because it builds political support or because spending is just fun, but they do not enjoy raising taxes, presumably because voters complain. If the costs are put off into the future, the politician faces less current hostility for spending and will overspend.

While this model has the virtue of simplicity and probably also truth, it does run afoul of more sophisticated economic theories. Homeowners, for example, should realize that they will end up paying the cost of extra spending in the future either through higher taxes or because those expected future taxes get compensated into the price of the home. Indeed, on theoretical grounds, we might expect Ricardian equivalence to operate quite strongly at the local level, when revenues are paid for by property taxes.

According to capitalization theory, if the city undertakes a obligation of present value of X dollars, which will be fair by property taxes on a set of N identical homes, then if current tax to pay for the obligation is Y/N, then the value of the homes declines by $(X - Y)/N$ to reflect the future obligations. The assets owned by homeowners decline by Y/N because of the tax payment and $(X - Y)/N$ because of declining property values. The total and immediate loss to homeowner is X/N no matter how the expenditure is financed.

Yet this Ricardian argument is unlikely to hold for renters, who may not expect to pay any future taxes. Rent control will particularly limit the impact that taxes imposed on property owners have on rents, which may reduce the incentive of people in rent-controlled units to oppose taxes, but it may also reduce the preference for current vs. future spending. Moreover, the Ricardian equivalence argument may fail if voters have trouble understanding the size of the expenditures, especially deferred expenditures. Lack of information may mean that voters expect a certain amount of expenditure deferral, but they will not impose extra costs for more deferral and that reduces the costs on politicians who raise total spending beyond revenues.

The cost of these budget restrictions depends on the ability to increase revenues during budget shortfalls or, if revenues cannot be adjusted, the costs of limiting city expenditures during a downturn. Buettner and Wildasin (2006) find that when there are revenue shortfalls, intergovernment grants help provide budgetary stability for larger cities while revenue cuts are more important for smaller cities. Baicker (2004) shows similar results on increasing revenues for county governments using the negative budgetary shock of having a capital crime trial. There has been relatively little work on the impact of local spending cuts on relevant outcomes (e.g., Freudenberg et al., 2006).

The ability of cities to respond to revenue shortfalls also depends on their ability to raise tax rates, which are themselves constrained in some states. For example, California and Massachusetts both passed referenda that severely limit the ability of communities to adjust tax rates. Bradbury, Mayer, and Case (2001) show that Massachusetts Proposition $2\frac{1}{2}$ significantly constrained community spending. Those limits must either be seen as internalizing cross-jurisdictional externalities, or voters perceived inability to restrain their own local governments. Fischel (1989) argued that California's court order restriction on spending differences in schools in *Serrano v. Priest* made Proposition 13 more attractive by limiting the ability to spend more on schooling.

While cities are constrained (at least officially) from running deficits for current expenses, they can borrow to fund infrastructure investments, such as building new schools. In these cases, the logic is that these investments will pay off in the future so it makes sense to charge future residents or homeowners. Moreover, the scale of the investment might overwhelm local budgets if paid for out of current taxes. In some cases, the bond issues will be paid for by user fees on the infrastructure, such as tolls.

The ability of cities to borrow used tax-exempt securities creates potential investment opportunities because municipalities can borrow at lower rates than their taxpayers (Gordon and Slemrod, 1986). This provides an incentive for cities to borrow on behalf of their constituents. Gordon and Metcalf (1991) argue that the tax-exempt borrowing does not so much subsidize municipal investment, which could after all be financed directly by taxes, but it does create incentives for financial rebalancing.

In many cases, municipal bond issues must be approved by voters in an explicit vote. Cellini, Ferreira, and Rothstein (2010) use the need for bond issues to get local votes to estimate the impact of school investment on housing values. Their approach exploits the natural discontinuity in votes when 50% of the population approve. The need for voter approval creates yet another check on the ability to spend for future investments.

Perhaps the most surprising aspect of all the controls on deferring local spending is that things look so different at the local and national level. While the federal government finds it extremely easy to run large deficits, local governments cannot do anything like that. This surely helps explain the increasing role of the federal government. Certainly, this arrangement can be justified because of the federal role in countercyclical spending, but it is still hard to reconcile the ease with which the federal government runs deficits during good periods and the difficulties facing local governments borrowing even during sharp recessions.

7.2. Infrastructure: Cost-Benefit Analysis and Financing

The benefits of infrastructure spending are rarely easy to quantify, and serious cost-benefit analysis has been a significant contribution that economists have made to urban finance debates. Economists have also weighed into the related issue of the financing of infrastructure and the larger place of infrastructure in urban growth and change.

Cost-benefit analysis has progressed through essentially three stages, reflecting the increasing complexity of factors brought into the analysis. The simplest version of cost-benefit analysis essentially values the direct impact of the investment on its users treating current prices as given. For example, a new highway can be evaluated by estimating the time savings for the estimated number of riders who use the highway. A cleaner water system can be evaluated by assessing the health advantage for users of the system.

The second layer of cost-benefit analysis introduces general equilibrium effects and impacts on non-users. For example, a new highway can deliver benefits for users themselves and for drivers on related roads where the congestion has been decreased. Change in wages or prices can also reflect impacts of the investment, although in some cases, there is a risk of double counting. For example, the price impact of a new road on housing should reflect the direct benefit that drivers receive from the infrastructure.

The third layer is to include a wide range of hard-to-measure externalities. For example, the case for Cross Rail investment in London was partially made by emphasizing the positive agglomeration externalities that the added commuters would create (Graham, 2007). Glaeser and Gottlieb (2008) have questioned whether these agglomeration economies are sufficiently well understood to provide a sound basis for public investment.

The vagaries of local situations mean that it is difficult to make any blanket statements about whether there is too much or too little infrastructure investment within the US, despite the claims of the Civil Engineers Report Card and many politicians that America has a dire infrastructure gap. There certainly are papers that find some correlation between infrastructure investments and subsequent growth at least at the national level (e.g., Canning and Pedroni, 2008). But there is reasonable doubt about whether these associations are causal and whether the advantages of infrastructure in developing countries have much to say about the advantages of infrastructure in the developed world.

Duranton and Turner (2009), like Baum-Snow (2007), look at the impact of highway and other transportation investments. They find that highways did tend to increase metropolitan area growth within the US, but this does not actually make the case that highways create benefits that cover the costs. Highways may pull development in one area or another, but that development may well have occurred anyway. Kain (1990) and others have long made the case that subway investments were based on wildly optimistic ridership projections that led to faulty cost-benefit analysis.

The regression discontinuity design of Cellini et al. (2010) does seem to provide a more compelling means of assessing investments, at least in school infrastructure. They find that these investments are significantly valued by local homeowners, who see home prices rise by more than the cost of the infrastructure, but they also see relatively little impact on test scores.

The case for investing in infrastructure is particularly dubious in declining cities, which typically are relatively well endowed with structures and roads, relative to the current state of demand. Glaeser and Gyourko (2005) argue that low-income rustbelt cities remain primarily because of their durable structures. Yet infrastructure for declining areas is often sold as a tool for helping those areas come back. There is little evidence that supports these claims and an abundance of failed projects, such as Detroit's People Mover. Even Bilbao's Guggenheim Museum, which is usually held up as a model of successful urban regeneration, has been found to have costs that are exceeding benefits (Plaza, 2006). Since it is relatively easy to justify white elephant projects with far reaching claims about city-building, it makes sense to be particularly wary about inserting these elements into cost-benefit analysis, especially since moving economic activity from one area to another does not imply any automatic welfare gain.

The financing of infrastructure is also a subject of a considerable economic discussion. The decision about funding infrastructure through user fees or tax revenues goes back to Adam Smith, who argued that user fee-based financing would eliminate unnecessary projects. The case against user fee financing is that the marginal social cost of using the infrastructure may be significantly below the average cost of delivering the infrastructure especially when, as in the case of public transit, the infrastructure's use reduces external costs elsewhere in the system.

If marginal social costs are less than average costs, then the standard argument is that general tax revenues should be used to pay for the infrastructure. Typically, the property tax is seen as handling this problem equitably since property owners will supposedly benefit from the infrastructure as it is capitalized into real estate prices. One argument for using other taxes, such as sales taxes, to pay for infrastructure is that some of the infrastructure's value may be experienced by the tourists or commuters who use the infrastructure to get into the city. Of course, even in those cases, the benefits of the real estate should presumably be capitalized, in part, by commercial real estate prices.

There is also an ongoing debate about private infrastructure provision in the US (Winston, 2010) and throughout the world. The advocates of private provision argue that it can create more scope for innovation, more incentives for maintenance, and a tighter link between costs and benefits. The opponents emphasize the extent to which private-public partnership often ends in the expropriation of either the public or private entity (Engel, Fischer, & Galetovic, 2007).

7.3. Deferred Expenditures for Operating Expenditures

While current tax expenditures are intended to cover current expenses, urban governments have often managed to contrive means of delaying costs. Historically, artful accounting played this role, but today the largest issue appears to be insufficient funding of worker pensions and retiree health care. Novy-Marx and Rauh (2011) present evidence that there is currently a three trillion dollar shortfall in state and local pension plans. They argue that pension plans are usually evaluated using extremely high expected asset returns, which can only be realized by taking on large amounts of risk. Yet pension obligations are essentially fixed, and for that reason, they argue that they should be evaluated essentially using risk-free rates. Even if existing accounting practices are used, many states and municipalities have managed to develop large pension shortfalls.

The fundamental political economy model that explains this behavior is the one discussed above. Politicians seem to have an incentive to obscure the costs of current spending. As such, they strike deals with municipal unions where workers receive relatively low current wages and are compensated with relatively high levels of deferred compensation. One cost of this behavior is that communities may be purchasing more government employee time than would be optimal if voters recognized the true costs of labor.

Another cost is that workers may be provided with suboptimal earnings packages from a standard compensation theory framework. A simple model of optimal compensation would suggest that employers should only defer compensation if workers are more patient than employers. Yet the work of Fitzpatrick (2011) suggests that workers do not value their retirement packages terribly much. She examines an Illinois program that allowed teachers to increase the value of their pensions by making a one-time payment. For younger workers, the cost of the top up was less than one-fifth of its net present value. Yet less than one-half of younger workers typically took the deal. This suggests that the current system is distinctly suboptimal.

If indeed deferred compensation creates social waste by pushing workers to backload compensation and leading communities to have outsized governments, then the natural fix is to ensure more transparency in the cost of pensions and other benefits. One approach would be to require more investment into state pension plans. Another approach is to follow private industry and move from defined benefit to defined contribution plans that would be funded during the year in which the employee works. Facing significant fiscal crises, many municipalities are now considering this sort of move.

8. URBAN POLITICAL ECONOMY

In this final section, I will discuss the political economy of urban governments. I will start by discussing the institutions of local government and how local governments interact with the national political system. I will then turn to the interplay between mobility, sorting, and elections. I will end with a brief discussion of urban political machines.

8.1. The Institutions of Local Government

Typically, cities are endowed with both a legislature, such as a city council, and an executive, typically a mayor in larger governments. A smaller city legislature may employ a professional city manager to serve as its executive, which creates the possibility of benefitting from specialized skills. Allegedly, professional managers might manage to lower costs, but empirically that does not appear to be the case (Chang & Hayes, 1990). Indeed, recent work finds that city spending actually falls when cities switch from managers to mayors, possibly because managers are meant to implement the plans favored by city councils, while mayors can also veto those plans (Coate & Knight, 2011).[15]

Mayors are typically elected by citywide pluralities, but city council members may be elected either from particular districts or at large elections. Large elections essentially allow the entire city to vote on particular candidates and then winning candidates are selected based on some measure of their total support. At-large candidates can sometimes provide one of the rare examples of proportional representation in American politics. The primary literature on at-large elections has focused on their role in promoting diversity (e.g., Welch, 1990), rather than on the functioning of the city.

In many cities, mayors appear to be able to dominate city councils because of their control over patronage and city projects. This essentially means that mayors can reward or punish city councilors as needed. As a result, in some cities, city councils seem to be only a moderate check on the power of the mayor. Indeed, the balance between legislature and executive typically seems far less even than in the federal government. City mayors also typically enjoy far more ability to generate publicity than council members, which gives them an added ability to reward and punish council members.

The advocates of strong city mayors argue that they are the only elected official who is likely to take responsibility for the overall functioning of the city. Since city council members are not really held responsible, they are more likely to be beholden to specific interest groups such as public section unions. The strong power of the mayor is seen as appropriate given the need for a responsible leader to act for the larger interests of the city, but many cities have also introduced term limits to provide some form of limitation on mayoral power. Ferreira and Gyourko (2009) show that mayors typically enjoy strong incumbency advantages and that can also provide an argument for term limits (Glaeser, 1996). Interestingly, however, these limits do not always appear to be all that durable in the face of a strong mayor, as evidenced by the recent rewriting of term limits in New York City.

Of course, mayors and city council members operate in the murky world of urban interest groups. Logan and Molotch (1987) argue that "urban growth machines" are a typical feature of many cities. These growth machines are a combination of real estate, banking, and commercial interests who support the increased expansion of the city and

---

[15] Vlaicu and Whalley (2012) find that cities with managers have fewer police officers per capita, which they interpret as reflecting the greater isolation of managers from popular tastes, but it is unclear whether having fewer police officers is desirable or not.

are able to heavily influence urban policies. The effect of these machines may not be so harmful if without them cities adopt NIMBYist policies that excessively restrict the production of new buildings.

Public sector unions are another important urban interest group that appears to carry sizable weight in local elections. The growth of public sector unions may reflect the fact that in cities, unions influence both the demand and supply of labor (Freeman, 1986). American states differ sharply in the extent to which they allow collective bargaining for municipal services, and research in this area typically finds some positive impact of collective bargaining on labor costs in the relevant sector (e.g., Valletta, 1989).

Cities are, of course, also influenced by political economy factors at the national level. The over-representation of low density states in the Senate and the tendency of cities to vote with the Democratic policy may reduce the political clout of cities in the United States. In other countries, cities have often been more powerful because they are the seats of political power (Ades and Glaeser, 1995).

8.2. Mobility, Sorting, and Elections

The politics of cities is deeply influenced by the fact that people can move across these areas. Ferreira and Gyourko (2009) find little evidence that Democratic and Republican mayors differ in their spending policies. One explanation for this fact is that city mayors are constrained from following their ideological impulses because of the threat of out-migration. The ability to leave cities may also make citizens more tolerant of strong government at the local level than at the national level.

The sorting of people across districts creates the possibility that cities might get caught in political poverty traps. If poorer people vote for more local redistribution, and if local redistribution increases the poverty of an area, then redistribution and poverty might reinforce each other, and lead to a city with high levels of poverty and little effective redistribution.

The tendency of areas to lock themselves into poverty traps will be ameliorated if voters or politicians are forward looking and anticipate that increases in redistribution will lead to more poverty down the road. But this effect will be weakened if mayors draw their electoral support from the poor and therefore welcome the emigration of the wealthy. Glaeser and Shleifer (2005) named this phenomenon the "Curley Effect," after Boston's James Michael Curley, who seemed perfectly happy encouraging wealthier, Protestant Bostonians who opposed his leadership style to leave the city. The administration of Coleman Young in Detroit may provide another example of this phenomenon.

Sorting across cities shapes the demographic composition of cities and this may lead to different political outcomes. Alesina, Baqir, and Easterly (1999) argue that ethnic diversity makes it difficult to agree on public goods and pushes cities instead to focus on public employment that can be spread among ethnicities. Eisinger (1982) finds that

African-American mayors increase the level of African-American employment in city government.

8.3. Urban Political Machines

No discussion of urban political economy could be complete without some mention of the urban political machines that once controlled city governments throughout the country (Steffens, 1904). The basic structure of these machines was that they would provide services to constituents who would then vote for the machine and induce their friends to vote. Critics of machines argued that they led to over-employment of semi-competent workers and corrupt profits for their leaders.

Long-lived modern mayors may create political systems that resemble old style political machines. Mayors still have patronage to dispense and they can still favor their political supporters. Yet the current situation is a shade of past excesses. The level of patronage controlled is far smaller and the legal barriers preventing wholesale expropriation of city property are far more common. Wallis, Fishback, and Kantor (2006) argue that the New Deal was a crucial turning point for the fortunes of political machines that had to obey rules put in place by the federal bureaucracy.

There is a growing literature on the impact of these machines on city costs and employment. Menes (1999), for example, finds that cities with machines typically paid workers more, spent more on government, but also had more public goods.

There were several institutions that progressive reformers put in place to limit the supposedly deleterious effects of local machines. More direct democracy through referendums and recall were meant to be tools against entrenched city government. Civil service reform that limited patronage and often doled out jobs through tests was another measure against patronage politics. Rauch (1995) finds that these reforms had little impact on the overall size of government even though they did shift expenditures from labor to capital. Rauch also found that reform increased manufacturing growth.

Interestingly, while late 20th century privatization was seen as a tool to combat municipal corruption and incompetence, increasing the size of the public force in the 19th century was also seen as a means to combat corruption. Kickback deals between city governments and private providers of services, like street cleaning, were seen as a major problem in cities like New York. Direct public provision of street cleaning, for example, was seen as a means of reducing this problem. The long history suggests that corruption may be fought by changes in either direction—toward more or less private provision—that disturb a cozy and corrupt status quo.

9. CONCLUSION

Cities are an important part of the American economy and increasingly dominate the rest of the world. They need governments to address the externalities that exist in cities and local governments that have often played an important role in addressing perceived national political objectives. Yet the economic literature on urban public finance is still in a relatively early stage.

The most salient aspects of urban political economy are the dependence on property taxes and the important role of intergovernmental transfers. There are good economic arguments for both features of local public finance. Yet we are far from knowing whether the current systems are, in any sense, optimal. The growing dependence of cities on federal largesse is quite understandable, but that change creates distortions and the possibility for spending that is not valued at the local level. These areas are badly in need of future research.

In addition, local governments face important challenges regarding intertemporal tradeoffs. They operate with seemingly strict balanced budget rules, but then often seem to work hard to eliminate the impact of those rules. The political forces that lie behind this process are also an important topic for future research.

While there was a robust urban politics literature during the 1960s, there has been less work in this area in recent years and the positive political economy revolution in political science has produced relatively few papers that are relevant for cities. This is another shortfall that is worth addressing.

ACKNOWLEDGMENTS

I am grateful for financial assistance to the Taubman Center for State and Local Government. Kristina Tobio and Peter Ganong provided helpful research assistance. Alan Auerbach, Patrick Kline, Joel Slemrod, Laszlo Sandor, Ugo Troiano, and David Wildasin provided helpful comments and suggestions.

REFERENCES

Abdulkadiroglu, A., Angrist, J. D., Dynarski, S. M., Kane, T. J., & Pathak, P. A. (2011). Accountability and flexibility in public schools: Evidence from Boston's charters and pilots. *Quarterly Journal of Economics, 126*(2), 699–748.

Ades, A. F., & Glaeser, E. L. (1995). Trade and circuses: Explaining urban giants. *Quarterly Journal of Economics, 110*(1), 195–227.

Acemoglu, D., & Angrist, J. (2001). In B. S. Bernanke & K. Rogoff (Eds.), *How large are human-capital externalities? Evidence from compulsory schooling laws* (Vol. 15). Cambridge, MA and London: MIT Press.

Ackerman, F., & Heinzerling, L. (2001–2002). Pricing the priceless: Cost-benefit analysis of environmental protection. *University of Pennsylvania Law Review, 150*(5), 1553–1584.

Alesina, A., Baqir, R., & Easterly, W. (1999). Public goods and ethnic divisions. *The Quarterly Journal of Economics, 114*(4), 1243–1284.

Alesina, A., Baqir, R., & Easterly, W. (2004). Political jurisdictions in heterogeneous communities. *Journal of Political Economy, 112*(2), 348–396.

Arnott, R. (1995). Time for revisionism on rent control? *Journal of Economic Perspectives, 9*(1), 99–120.

Arnott, R. J., & Stiglitz, J. E. (1979). Aggregate land rents, expenditure on public goods, and optimal city size. *Quarterly Journal of Economics, 93*(4), 471–500.

Atkinson, R., Blandy, S., & Mostowska, M. (2007). Gated communities. *Journal of Housing and the Built Environment, 22*(2), 231–234.

Baicker, K. (2004). The budgetary repercussions of capital convictions. *Advances in Economic Analysis & Policy, 4*(1), 6.

Bakija, J., & Slemrod, J. (2004). Do the rich flee from high state taxes? Evidence from federal estate tax returns. *NBER working paper series.* The National Bureau of Economic Research, Cambridge, MA.

Ballou, D., & Springer, M. G. (2008). *Achievement trade-offs and no child left behind.* Peabody College of Vanderbilt University.

Barzel, Y. (1974). A theory of rationing by waiting. *Journal of Law and Economics, 17*(1), 73–95.

Baum-Snow, N. (2007). Did highways cause suburbanization? *The Quarterly Journal of Economics, 122*(2), 775.

Baum-Snow, N. & Kahn, M. E. (2005). Effects of urban rail transit expansions: Evidence from sixteen cities, 1970–2000. In G. Burtless & J. R. Pack (Eds.), *Brookings-Wharton Papers on Urban Affairs* (pp. 147–197). Washington DC: Institute Press.

Becker, G. S. (1965). A theory of the allocation of time. *Economic Journal, 75*(299), 493–517.

Belfield, C. R., Nores, M., Barnett, S., & Schweinhart, L. (2006). The high/scope perry preschool program: Cost-benefit analysis using data from the age-40 followup. *Journal of Human Resources, 41*(1), 162–190.

Berry, C. R. (2009). *Imperfect union: Representation and taxation in multilevel governments.* Cambridge University Press.

Besley, T., & Coate, S. (2003). Centralized versus decentralized provision of local public goods: A political economy approach. *Journal of Public Economics, 87*(12), 2611–2637.

Black, S. E. (1999). Do better schools matter? Parental valuation of elementary education. *Quarterly Journal of Economics, 114*(2), 577–599.

Blakely, E. J., & Snyder, M. G. (1999). *Fortress america: Gated communities in the United States.* Washington, DC: Brookings Institution Press.

Blank, R. M. (1988). The effect of welfare and wage levels on the location decisions of female-headed households. *Journal of Urban Economics, 24*(2), 86–211.

Bleakley, H. & Lin, J. (2010). Portage: Path dependence and increasing returns in US history. *NBER working papers,* No. 16314. The National Bureau of Economic Research, Cambridge, MA.

Bloom, N., Propper, C., Seiler, S., & Reenan, J.V. (2010). The impact of competition on management quality: Evidence from public hospitals. *NBER working papers,* No. 16032, The National Bureau of Economic Research, Cambridge, MA.

Boffa, F., Piolatto, A., & Ponzetto, G. A. M. (2012). *Centralization and accountability: Theory and evidence from the clean air act.* Mimeograph.

Borjas, G. J. (1999). Immigration and welfare magnets. *Journal of Labor Economics, 17*(4), 607–637.

Bradbury, K. L., Mayer, C. J., & Case, K. E. (2001). Property tax limits, local fiscal behavior, and property values: Evidence from Massachusetts under proposition 2 1/2. *Journal of Public Economics, 80*(2), 287–311.

Braga, A. A. 2010. Setting a higher standard for the evaluation of problem-oriented policing initiatives. *Criminology & Public Policy, 9*(1), 173–182.

Brooks, L. (2008). Volunteering to be taxed: Business improvement districts and the extra-governmental provision of public safety. *Journal of Public Economics, 1–2,* 388–406.

Brueckner, J. K. (1990). Growth controls and land values in an open city. *Land Economics, 66*(3), 237–248.

Buettner, T., & Wildasin, D. E. (2006). The dynamics of municipal fiscal adjustment. *Journal of Public Economics, 90*(6–7), 1115–1132.

Canning, D., & Pedroni, P. (2008). Infrastructure, long-run economic growth and causality tests for cointegrated panels. *Manchester School, 76*(5), 504–527.

Carlton, D. (1983). The location and employment choices of new firms: An econometric model with discrete and continuous endogenous variables. *Review of Economics and Statistics, 65*(3), 440–449.

Cellini, S. R., Ferreira, F., & Rothstein, J. (2010). The value of school facility investments: Evidence from a dynamic regression discontinuity design. *The Quarterly Journal of Economics, 125*(1), 215.

Chang, S., & Hayes, K. (1990). The relative efficiency of city manager and mayor-council forms of government. *Southern Economic Journal, 57*(1), 167–177.

Ciccone, A., & Hall, R. E. (1996). Productivity and the density of economic activity. *American Economic Review, 86*(1), 54–70.

Coate, S., & Knight, B. (2011). Government form and public spending: Theory and evidence from US cities. *American Economic Journal: Economic Policy, 3*(3), 82–112.

Cohen, R., Lai, A., & Steindel, C. (2011). *The effects of marginal tax rates on interstate migration in the US.* New Jersey Department of Revenue. Mimeograph.

Cook, P. J. & Ludwig, J. (2010). Economical crime control. *NBER working paper series*. The National Bureau of Economic Research, Cambridge, MA.

Coughlin, C. C., Terza, J. V., & Arromdee, V. (1991). State characteristics and the location of foreign direct investment within the United States. *Review of Economics and Statistics, 73*(4), 675–683.

Cullen, J. B., & Levitt, S. D. (1999). Crime, urban flight, and the consequences for cities. *Review of Economics and Statistics, 81*(2), 159–169.

Currie, J., & Yelowitz, A. (2000). Are public housing projects good for kids? *Journal of Public Economics, 75*(1), 99–124.

Cutler, D. M., & Glaeser, E. L. (1997). Are ghettos good or bad? *Quarterly Journal of Economics, 112*(3), 827–872.

Cutler, D., & Miller, G. (2006). Water, water everywhere: Municipal finance and water supply in American cities. In E. L. Glaeser & C. Goldin (Eds.), *A national bureau of economic research conference report*. University of Chicago Press: Chicago and London.

Dee, T. S., & Jacob, B. (2011). The impact of no child left behind on student achievement. *Journal of Policy Analysis and Management, 30*(3), 418–446.

de Mello, L. R. Jr., (2000). Fiscal decentralization and intergovernmental fiscal relations: A cross-country analysis. *World Development, 28*(2), 365–380.

Diamond, C. A., & Simon, C. J. (1990). Industrial specialization and the returns to labor. *Journal of Labor Economics, 8*(2), 175–201.

Dillinger, W., & Webb, S. B. (1999). Fiscal management in federal democracies: Argentina and Brazil. *Economica (National University of La Plata), 45*(3), 423–483.

Donohue, J. J. & Ludwig, J. (2007). *More COPS*. Brookings institution policy brief 158. Washington, DC: Brookings Institution.

Donohue, J. J., III, & Siegelman, P. (1998). Allocating resources among prisons and social programs in the battle against crime. *The Journal of Legal Studies, 27*(1), 1–43.

Duggan, M. G. (2000). Hospital ownership and public medical spending. *Quarterly Journal of Economics, 115*(4), 1343–1373.

Duranton, G., & Puga, D. (2005). From sectoral to functional urban specialisation. *Journal of Urban Economics, 57*(2), 343–370.

Duranton, G., & Turner, M. A. (2009). The fundamental law of road congestion: Evidence from US cities. *Working paper*, No. w15376. The National Bureau of Economic Research, Cambridge, MA.

Ebel, R. D., & Yilmaz, S. (2003). On the measurement and impact of fiscal decentralization. In J. Martinez-Vazquez, & J. Alm (Eds.), *Studies in fiscal federalism and state-local finance*. Cheltenham, UK and Northampton, MA: Elgar.

Eisinger, P. K. (1982). Black employment in municipal jobs: The impact of black political power. *American Political Science Review, 76*(2), 380–392.

Ellen, I., Schwartz, A., & Voicu, I. (2007). The impact of business improvement districts on property values: Evidence from New York City. *Brookings-Wharton Papers on Urban Affairs*, 1–39.

Engel, E., Fischer, R., & Galetovic, A. (2007). The basic public finance of public-private partnerships. *NBER Working Paper Series*. The National Bureau of Economic Research, Cambridge, MA.

Evans, W. N., & Owens, E. G. (2007). COPS and crime. *Journal of Public Economics, 91*(1–2), 181–201.

Feldstein, M., & Wrobel, M. V. (1998). Can state taxes redistribute income? *Journal of Public Economics, 68*(3), 369–396.

Ferraz, C., & Finan, F. (2008). Exposing corrupt politicians: The effects of Brazil's publicly released audits on electoral outcomes. *Quarterly Journal of Economics, 123*(2), 703–745.

Ferreira, F., & Gyourko, J. (2009). Do political parties matter? Evidence from US cities. *Quarterly Journal of Economics, 124*(1), 399–422.

Ferrie, J. P., & Troesken, W. (2008). Water and Chicago's mortality transition, 1850–1925. *Explorations in Economic History, 45*(1), 1–16.

Fischel, W. A. (1989). Did serrano cause proposition 13? *National Tax Journal (1986–1998), 42*(4), 465–465.

Fishback, P. V. (2007). The new deal. In *Government and the American economy: A new history*. Chicago: University of Chicago Press.

Fishback, P. V., Horrace, W. C., & Kantor, S. (2005). Did new deal grant programs stimulate local economies? A study of federal grants and retail sales during the great depression. *The Journal of Economic History, 65*(1), 36–71.

Fitzpatrick, M. D. (2011). *How much do public school teachers value their retirement benefits?* Stanford Institute for Economic Policy Research: Mimeo.

Frankena, M. (1975). Alternative models of rent control. *Urban Studies, 12*(3), 303–308.

Freeman, R. B. (1986). Unionism comes to the public sector. *Journal of Economic Literature, 24*(March), 41–86.

Freudenberg, N., Fahs, M., Galea, S., & Greenberg, A. (2006). The impact of New York City's 1975 fiscal crisis on the tuberculosis, HIV, and homicide syndemic. *American Journal of Public Health, 96*(3), 424–434.

Friedman, M., & Stigler G. J. (1946). Roofs or Ceilings: The Current Housing Problem. In *Popular Essays on Current Problems Volume 1, Number 2*. Irvington-on-Hudson, New York: Foundation for Economic Education, Inc.

Friedrich, P., Gwiazda, J., & Nam, C. W. (2003). Development of local public finance in Europe. *CESifo working paper*, No. 1107.

Gamper-Rabindran, S., Khan, S., & Timmins, C. (2010). The impact of piped water provision on infant mortality in Brazil: A quantile panel data approach. *Journal of Development Economics, 92*(2), 188–200.

Glaeser, E. L. (1996). The incentive effects of property taxes on local governments. *Public Choice, 89*(1–2), 93–111.

Glaeser, E. L. (1999). Learning in cities. *Journal of Urban Economics, 46*(2), 254–277.

Glaeser, E. L. & Gottlieb, J. D. (2008). The economics of place-making policies. *Brookings Papers on Economic Activity, 39*(1), 155–253.

Glaeser, E. L., & Gyourko, J. (2009). Arbitrage in housing markets. In E. L. Glaeser & J. M. Quigley (Eds.), *Housing markets and the economy: Risk, regulation, and policy* (pp. 113–146). Cambridge: Lincoln Institute of Land Policy.

Glaeser, E. L., & Gyourko, J. (2005). Urban decline and durable housing. *The Journal of Political Economy, 113*(2), 345–375.

Glaeser, E. L., Gyourko, J., & Saks, R. (2005). Why is Manhattan so expensive? Regulation and the rise in housing prices. *Journal of Law and Economics, 48*(2), 331–369.

Glaeser, E. L., Kahn, M. E., & Rappaport, J. (2008). Why do the poor live in cities? The role of public transportation. *Journal of Urban Economics, 63*(1), 1–24.

Glaeser, E. L., Kolko, J., & Saiz, A. (2001). Consumer city. *Journal of Economic Geography, 1*(1), 27–50.

Glaeser, E. L., Luttmer, E. F. P. (2003). The misallocation of housing under rent control. *The American Economic Review, 93*(4), 1027–1046.

Glaeser, E. L., & Mare, D. C. (2001). Cities and skills. *Journal of Labor Economics, 19*(2), 316–342.

Glaeser, E. L., & Meyer, J. R. (Eds.) (2002). *Chile, political economy of urban development*. Cambridge, MA: Harvard University Press.

Glaeser, E. L., & Sacerdote, B. (2000). The social consequences of housing. *Journal of Housing Economics, 9*(1–2), 1–23.

Glaeser, E. L., & Sacerdote, B. (1999). Why is there more crime in cities? *Journal of Political Economy, 107*(6), S225–S258.

Glaeser, E., & Shleifer, A. (2001). Not-for-profit entrepreneurs. *Journal of Public Economics, 81*(1), 99–115.

Glaeser, E., & Shleifer, A. (2005). The Curley effect: The economics of shaping the electorate. *Journal of Law, Economics, and Organizations, 21*, 1–19.

Glaeser, E. L., Resseger, M., & Tobio, K. (2011). Urban inequality. In N. J. Johnson, & J. H. Svara (Eds.), *Justice for all: Promoting social equity in public administration* (pp. 76–99). Armonk, New York: M.E. Sharpe.

Goolsbee, A., Lovenheim, M. F., & Slemrod, J. (2010). Playing with fire: Cigarettes, taxes, and competition from the internet. *American Economic Journal: Economic Policy, 2*(1), 131–54.

Gordon, R. H. & Metcalf, G. E. (1991). Do tax-exempt bonds really subsidize municipal capital? *National Tax Journal (1986–1998), 44*(4), 71–71.

Gordon, R. H. & Slemrod, J. (1986). An empirical examination of municipal financial policy. In Rosen, H. S. (Ed.), *National bureau of economic research project report series*. Chicago and London: University of Chicago Press.

Graham, D. J. (2007). Agglomeration, productivity and transport investment. *Journal of Transport Economics and Policy, 41*(3), 317–343.

Gramlich, E. M. (1976). The New York City fiscal crisis: What happened and what is to be done? *American Economic Review, 66*(2), 415–29.

Greenstone, M., Hornbeck, R., & Moretti, E. (2010). Identifying agglomeration spillovers: Evidence from winners and losers of large plant openings. *Journal of Political Economy, 118*(3), 536–598.

Grembi, V., Nannicini, T. & Troiano, U. (2011). *Do fiscal rules matter? A difference-in-discontinuities design.* Mimeograph.

Gyourko, J., Saiz, A., & Summers, A. (2008). A new measure of the local regulatory environment for housing markets: The Wharton residential land use regulatory index. *Urban Studies, 45*(3), 693–729.

Hansmann, H. (1981). The rationale for exempting nonprofit organizations from corporate income taxation. *Yale Law Journal, 91*(1), 54–100.

Hansmann, H., Kessler, D., & McClellan, M. (2003). Ownership form and trapped capital in the hospital business. In E. L. Glaeser (Ed.), *The governance of not-for-profit organizations.* Chicago: University of Chicago Press.

Hanushek, E. A. (2003). The failure of input-based schooling policies. *Economic Journal, 113*(485), F64–F98.

Hanushek, E. A. (2000). Rationalizing school spending: Efficiency, externalities and equity, and their connection to rising costs. University of Rochester – Wallis Institute of Political Economy, *Wallis working papers* No. WP2, 2000.

Hart, O., Shleifer, A., & Vishny, R. W. (1997). The proper scope of government: Theory and an application to prisons. *Quarterly Journal of Economics, 112*, 1127–1161.

Haughwout, A., Inman, R., Craig, S., & Luce, T. (2004). Local revenue hills: Evidence from four US cities. *Review of Economics and Statistics 86*(2), 570–585.

Heckman, J. J., Lochner, L., & Taber, C. (1998). General-equilibrium treatment effects: A study of tuition policy. *American Economic Review, 88*(2), 381–386.

Hilber, C. A. L., & Mayer, C. (2009). Why do households without children support local public schools? Linking house price capitalization to school spending. *Journal of Urban Economics, 65*(1), 74–90.

Hines, J. R. (1996). Altered states: Taxes and the location of foreign direct investment in America. *American Economic Review, 86*(6), 1076–1094.

Hirsch, W. Z. (1965). Cost functions of an urban government service: Refuse collection. *Review of Economics and Statistics, 47*(1), 87–92.

Holmes, T. J. (1998). The effect of state policies on the location of manufacturing: Evidence from state borders. *The Journal of Political Economy, 106*(4), 667–705.

Howe, C. W. (1971). *Benefit-cost analysis for water system planning.* Monograph No. 2. Washington, DC: American Geophysical Union.

Hoxby, C. M. (2000). Does competition among public schools benefit students and taxpayers? *American Economic Review, 90*(5), 1209–1238.

Hoxby, C. M., & Murarka, S. (2009). Charter schools in New York City: Who enrolls and how they affect their students' achievement. *Working paper* No. w14852. The National Bureau of Economic Research, Cambridge, MA.

Inman, R. P. (1998). Do balanced budget rules work? US experience and possible lessons for the EMU. *NBER working paper series.* The National Bureau of Economic Research, Cambridge, MA.

Jacob, B. A. (2004). Public housing, housing vouchers, and student achievement: Evidence from public housing demolitions in Chicago. *The American Economic Review, 94*(1), 233–258.

Jacobs, J. (1968). *The economy of cities.* New York: Vintage Books.

Johnson, D. G. (1951). Rent control and the distribution of income. *The American Economic Review, 41*(2), 569–569.

Kain, J. F. (1990). Deception in Dallas: strategic misrepresentation in the promotion and evaluation of rail transit. *Journal of the American Planning Association (Spring)*, 184–196.

Kline, P., & Moretti, E. (2011). *Local economic development, agglomeration economies, and the big push: 100 years of evidence from the Tennessee valley authority.* Mimeographed.

Krueger, A. (2002). *Crisis prevention and resolution: Lessons from Argentina.* International Monetary Fund.

Krueger, A. B. (2003). Economic considerations and class size. *Economic Journal, 113*(485), F34–F63.

Krugman, P. (1991). Increasing returns and economic geography. *The Journal of Political Economy, 99*, 483–499.

Levine, P. B., & Zimmerman, D. J. (1999). An empirical analysis of the welfare magnet debate using the NLSY. *Journal of Population Economics, 12*(3), 391–409.

Levitt, S. D. (1996). The effect of prison population size on crime rates: Evidence from prison overcrowding litigation. *Quarterly Journal of Economics, 111*(2), 319–351.

Levitt, S. D. (2004). Understanding why crime fell in the 1990s: Four factors that explain the decline and six that do not. *Journal of Economic Perspectives, 18*(1), 163–190.

Levitt, S. D. (1997). Using electoral cycles in police hiring to estimate the effect of police on crime. *American Economic Review, 87*(3), 270–290.

Logan, J., & Molotch, H. (1987). *Urban fortunes: The political economy of place*. Los Angeles: University of California Press.

Lopez-de-Silanes, F., Shleifer, A., & Vishny, R. (1997). Privatization in the United States. *RAND Journal of Economics, The RAND Corporation, 28*(3), 447–471.

Loury, G. (2009). A nation of jailers. *Cato unbound*. http://www.cato-unbound.org/2009/03/11/glenn-loury/a-nation-of-jailers/>. Accessed 11.03.09.

Marshall, A. (1890). *Principles of economics*. London: Macmillan and Co.

Menes, R. (1999). The effect of patronage politics on city government in American cities, 1900–1910. *NBER working paper series*. The National Bureau of Economic Research, Cambridge, MA.

Moretti, E. (2004). Estimating the social return to higher education: evidence from longitudinal and repeated cross-sectional data. *Journal of Econometrics, 121*(1–2), 175–212.

Moretti, E. (2010). Local multipliers. *American Economic Review: Papers and Proceedings, 100*(2), 1–7.

Novak, M. (1982). *The spirit of democratic capitalism*. New York: Simon and Schuster.

Novy-Marx, R., & Rauh, J. (2011). Public pension promises: How big are they and what are they worth? *Journal of Finance, 66*(4), 1211–1249.

Oates, W. (1999). An essay on fiscal federalism. *Journal of Economic Literature, 37*, 1120–1149.

Oberholzer-Gee, F., & Strumpf, K. (2002). Endogenous policy decentralization: Testing the central tenet of economic federalism. *Journal of Political Economy, 110*, 1–36.

Opdycke, S. (1999). *No one was turned away: The role of public hospitals in New York City since 1900*. NY: Oxford University Press.

Papke, L. (1991). Interstate business tax differentials and new firm location: Evidence from panel data. *Journal of Public Economics, 41*(1), 47–68.

Plaza, B. (2006). The return on investment of the Guggenheim Museum Bilbao. *International Journal of Urban and Regional Research, 30*(2), 452–467.

Poterba, J. M. (1994). State responses to fiscal crises: The effects of budgetary institutions and politics. *Journal of Political Economy, 102*(4), 799–821.

Rask, K., & Rask, K. (2000). Public insurance substituting for private insurance: New evidence regarding public hospitals, uncompensated care funds and medicaid. *Journal of Health Economics, 19*(1), 1–31.

Rauch, J. E. 1995. Bureaucracy, infrastructure, and economic growth: Evidence from US cities during the progressive era. *The American Economic Review, 85*(4), 968–968.

Reback, R., Rockoff J., & Schwartz, H. L. (2011). Under pressure: Job security, resource allocation, and productivity in schools under NCLB. *NBER working paper series*. The National Bureau of Economic Research, Cambridge, MA.

Rosenthal, S. S., & Strange, W. C. (2008). The attenuation of human capital spillovers. *Journal of Urban Economics, 64*(2), 373–389.

Rotemberg, J. J. (1985). The efficiency of equilibrium traffic flows. *Journal of Public Economics, 26*(2), 191–205.

Rothstein, J. (2007). Does competition among public schools benefit students and taxpayers? Comment. *American Economic Review, 97*(5), 2026–2037.

Rusk, D. (1993). *Cities without suburbs*. Baltimore: Johns Hopkins University Press.

Serrato, J., & Wingender, P. (2011). *Estimating local fiscal multipliers*. Mimeographed.

Sinai, T., & Waldfogel, J. (2005). Do low-income housing subsidies increase the occupied housing stock? *Journal of Public Economics, 89*(11–12), 2137–2164.

Steffens, L. (1904). *The shame of the cities*. New York: Amereon (Reprinted 1957).

Thaler, R. (1977). An econometric analysis of property crime: Interaction between police and criminals. *Journal of Public Economics, 8*(1), 37–51.

Troesken, W., & Geddes, R. (2003). Municipalizing American waterworks, 1897–1915. *Journal of Law, Economics, and Organization, 19*(2), 373–400.

US Government Printing Office (2012). *Statistical Abstract of the United States.*

Valletta, R. G. (1989). The impact of unionism on municipal expenditures and revenues. *Industrial and Labor Relations Review, 42*(3), 430–442.

Vlaicu, R., & Whalley, A. (forthcoming). Hierarchical accountability in government: Theory and evidence. *American Economic Review.*

Wallis, J. J., Fishback, P. V., & Kantor, S. (2006). Politics, relief, and reform: Roosevelt's efforts to control corruption and political manipulation during the new deal. In E. L. Glaeser, & C. Goldin (Eds.), *A national bureau of economic research conference report.* Chicago and London: University of Chicago Press.

Weisbrod, B. (1978). *The voluntary non-profit sector: An economic analysis.* Lexington, MA: Lexington Books, DC Heath.

Welch, S. (1990). The impact of at-large elections on the representation of blacks and Hispanics. *Journal of Politics, 52*(4), 1050–1076.

Welsh, B. C., & Farrington, D. P. (2001). Toward an evidence-based approach to preventing crime. *Annals of the American Academy of Political and Social Science, 578,* 158–173.

Wildasin, D. (1991). Income redistribution in a common labor market. *American Economic Review, 81*(4), 757–774.

Wildasin, D. (1986). *Urban public finance.* Chur, Switzerland: Harwood Academic Press.

Winston, C. (2010). *Last exit: Privatization and deregulation of the US transportation system.* Washington DC: Brookings Institution Press.

Wiseman, J. (1965). Cost-benefit analysis in education. *Southern Economic Journal, 32,* 1–12.

Young, C., & Varner, C. (2011). Millionaire migration and state taxation of top incomes: Evidence from a natural experiment. *National Tax Journal, 64*(2, Part 1), 255–284.

Zipp, S. (2010). *Manhattan projects: The rise and fall of urban renewal in cold war New York.* NY: Oxford University Press.

CHAPTER 5

The Theory of International Tax Competition and Coordination

Michael Keen[*] and Kai A. Konrad[†,‡]

[*]International Monetary Fund, Fiscal Affairs Department, Washington DC 20431, USA
[†]Max Planck Institute for Tax Law and Public Finance, Marstallplatz 1, 80539 Munich, Germany
[‡]Social Science Research Center Berlin, Germany

Contents

Handbook of Public Economics, Volume 5
ISSN 1573-4420, http://dx.doi.org/10.1016/B978-0-444-53759-1.00005-4

1. INTRODUCTION

Awareness that national tax policies can induce economic activity to move across international borders is not new. In 1763 (and there are earlier examples), Catherine the Great gave to "... Foreigners that have settled themselves in Russia [to] erect Fabricks or Works, and manufacture there such Merchandizes as have not yet been made in Russia ..." the right to "sell and export said Merchandizes out of our Empire for 10 years, without paying any inland Tolls, Port Duties or Customs on the Borders ..."[1] It is over the last two decades or so, however, that increased economic integration has made international considerations a central component of tax policy in economies at all levels of development. Like it or not, national tax policy makers are involved in a game with one another. This class of games is what will be meant here by "international tax competition,"[2] and it is the aim of this chapter to provide a reasonably concise account of what is known of such games, the outcomes they may lead to, and the ways in which they might be beneficially reshaped.

The practical policy agenda on these issues is an active one. The constraints that international considerations place on national tax policies are a commonplace of budget (and campaign) speeches, with the downward trend of statutory corporate tax rates— most often remarked upon for advanced economies, but hardly less marked elsewhere[3] (Figure 1)—the paramount *prima facie* example of international tax competition at work. But there are many others. A partial list would include the widespread demise of inheritance and gift taxation; the reduction in top marginal rates of personal taxation on both labor income (reflecting the mobility of high earners and the tax avoidance opportunities created if that rate strays too far from the falling corporate rate) and capital income; and the limits placed on cigarette and alcohol excises in the European Union and some other regional groups by the prospect of cross-border shopping and smuggling from less heavily taxing neighbors.

Concern at the pressures consequently imposed on national tax bases has led to proposals for, and, to a much lesser extent, action on coordinated measures to restrict downward pressures on tax rates. When it removed tax-related controls from its internal frontiers, for instance, the European Union (EU) adopted minimum excise duties in order to curtail expected downward pressure on rates. In the area of corporate income taxation,

---

[1] Weightman (2007, p. 33). She was quite successful, it seems; even James Watt was reportedly tempted.

[2] We will not agonize over a precise definition of "tax competition," but stress that its usage does not imply that taxes are necessarily "too low"—indeed we will see examples of the precise opposite.

[3] Arguably it is actually a greater concern in lower income countries, since they are typically more reliant on the corporate tax as a source of revenue.

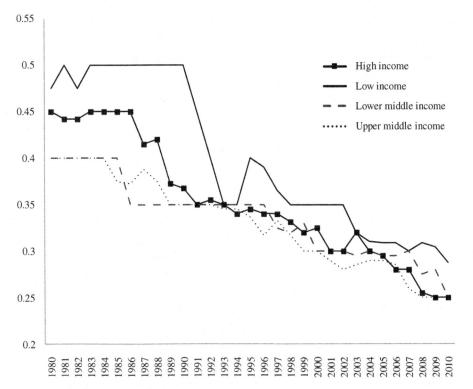

Figure 1 Median statutory corporate tax rates by income group, 1980–2010. *Note*: Tax rates from KPMG tax rates online and IMF compilation. Countries classified by income, at each date, into four equal-sized groups.

the Ruding Committee (1992) proposed for the EU a common minimum tax rate, at the now quaint-looking level of 30%.[4] In the latter 1990s, international efforts focused on identifying forms of "harmful tax competition" (distinguishing this from simply low rates of tax), notably with a landmark report by the OECD (1998) and the adoption by the EU of a Code of Conduct aimed at rolling back and precluding particular forms of tax incentive. The fate of this OECD initiative reflected the difficulty of agreeing on a delineation of harmful tax design, as it came to focus instead on the narrower (but still ambitious) objective of ensuring that countries provide each other with the information needed to enforce their own tax systems. This effort was massively reinforced by leadership from the G20 in the wake of the 2008 crisis. Regional blocs other than the EU—in Central America, Eastern and Southern Africa, and elsewhere—have also sought agreement to limit corporate tax competition among themselves, but, like the EU, have had only limited success. Coordination is more common on commodity taxation and the

---

[4] Assessments of the Ruding Report are in Devereux (1992) and Vanistendael (1992).

VAT—despite the fact, or perhaps because of it, that the lesser mobility of goods (though perhaps not, and increasingly importantly, of some key services) than capital suggests that this is likely to be less important than action on business taxation.

This increased policy focus on international tax competition has been matched, and even to some degree preceded, by a massive expansion of the public economics literature on these issues. This chapter does not aim to provide an exhaustive review of what has become a large and complex body of work, already the subject of several excellent surveys.[5] Instead it focuses on theoretical aspects of strategic interactions in national tax-setting, and possible policy responses, primarily in relation to the taxation of capital income.

This is the area in which tax competition concerns have had the greatest political salience and on which most academic attention has focused. In relation to corporate taxation, Figure 1 goes a long way to explain why. But such much-used figures also raise, and hide, as many questions as they answer. Is it even obvious, for instance, that tax competition implies downward pressure on rates, rather than upward, and is it necessarily the case that downward pressures on statutory tax rates from international tax competition are undesirable? Who gains, who loses? Might the EU have been wise to adopt the Ruding minimum rates, or would that simply have made it even more vulnerable to undercutting by other countries? What exactly are countries trying to attract in competing through their tax systems—productive investments or paper profits shifted by multinationals through a range of avoidance devices—and what difference does that make to the policy advice that might be offered? The figure also conceals the scope for countries to offer special regimes tailored to particular types of investments. Why do they do that—standard tax policy advice being to charge all businesses at the same rate—and does such targeting make tax competition more or less damaging? Not least, the figure also highlights that tax interactions are not a one-shot game, but evolve as a dynamic process in which different countries choose their tax rates repeatedly. How does that affect the nature of the equilibrium and the impact of possible policy interventions?

These are the kind of issues that the literature on international tax competition and coordination seeks to illuminate, and they are at the heart of this review. The focus here is on theoretical perspectives, and especially on the nature and implications of alternative forms of strategic interaction in the setting of taxes on capital and capital income. In this, the chapter emphasizes analogies between the theory of tax competition and competition models in the theory of industrial organization; analogies made evident in some of early and seminal contributions describing tax competition as an oligopoly game (Wildasin, 1988, 1991a; Wilson, 1986; Bucovetsky, 1991).

Doing justice to these issues means that the chapter refers only in passing to important aspects of the broader literature. It does not review econometric work on tax competition, which generally confirms that countries' fiscal policies are indeed interdependent, with

---

[5] These include Wilson (1999), Gresik (2001), Zodrow (2003), Wilson and Wildasin (2004), Fuest, Huber and Mintz (2005), Zodrow (2010), Genschel and Schwarz (2011), and Boadway and Tremblay (2012).

many of the findings in line with the main hypotheses derived from the theory reviewed here.[6] Nor does it consider in any detail the rather different issues that arise in relation to commodity tax competition.[7] And it addresses only briefly the nature of tax competition within and between multileveled federal systems.[8] The models used are a highly stripped down version of a reality that is far more complex in terms of both international tax rules and the avoidance devices that multinationals may use, accounts of which may be found elsewhere.[9] The treatment of profit-shifting by multinationals—in essence, the moving of paper profits between countries without changing the location of any real activity—is thus highly stylized.[10]

A word is also needed on the "international" in our title. Many of the issues raised at the outset also arise in relation to competition between states within federations, and localities within states. Indeed much of the literature reviewed here was developed with precisely such applications in mind. Many of the results reviewed here can thus be thought of as applying to any set of horizontally related jurisdictions, including within nations. Indeed the empirical literature often studies fiscal competition within federations, reflecting better data availability and the potential advantages of dealing with a more homogenous set of jurisdictions.[11] This makes it tempting to speak of "jurisdictions" rather than "countries."[12] But there are important differences. In federal systems, an overarching central government adds an additional level of vertical interaction in tax-setting since, explicitly or implicitly, tax bases are likely to overlap between levels of government. Moreover, the fundamental political context is generally quite different, with greater openness in federations to intergovernmental transfers and some forms of

---

[6] See, notably, Devereux, Lockwood, and Redoano (2008).

[7] There are resonances between the two lines of literature, and the Kanbur-Keen (1993) model discussed in Section 2.1.2, in particular, has applications to both. But tax impacts through final consumption and through factor inputs generally require quite different modeling. Central concerns in the analysis of commodity tax competition, which begins with Mintz and Tulkens (1986), are the characterization of and comparison between non-cooperative equilibria and potential coordination measures under both origin taxation (taxation occurring where commodities are produced) and destination principles (taxation according to where they are consumed). Lockwood (1997) provides an integrated treatment, and a survey (now, however, somewhat outdated) is included in Keen (2001).

[8] See Wilson and Janeba (2005); the survey by Boadway and Tremblay (2012) focuses on fiscal federalism, but includes considerations of tax competition. Zodrow (2010) focuses on the empirical evidence both on the sensitivity of capital flows on taxes and the evidence on the strategic interaction between governments in the context of tax competition.

[9] See Gordon and Hines (2002) on the former and Mintz and Weichenrieder (2010) on the latter. Also relevant here is the literature on double tax agreements, which has been primarily focused on whether these have encouraged capital movements: see for example Blonigen and Davies (2004).

[10] Gresik (2001) covers many of the early contributions on transfer pricing issues. The status of the discussion in the legal and economic literature on transfer pricing and other means of profit-shifting are set out in the collected volume by Schön and Konrad (2012).

[11] An early overview is by Brueckner (2003). More recent empirical contributions are Winner (2005), Carlsen, Langset, and Rattsø (2005), Overesch and Rincke (2009), Parry (2003), Revelli (2003), Boadway and Hayashi (2001), Büttner (2003), Mintz and Smart (2004), Binet (2003), Karkalakos and Kotsogiannis (2007), Gérard, Jayet and Paty (2010), and Jacobs, Ligthart, and Vrijburg (2010). For a recent survey see also Zodrow (2010).

[12] This usage would also have the merit of recognizing that many low tax jurisdictions that are important in practice are not, strictly speaking, independent countries, but overseas territories or dependencies.

coordination by the center. It is the interactions between independent nations, with their distinct powers and objectives, that give rise to the policy concerns above, and which are the primary focus of the chapter; to stress this, we shall speak of "countries" throughout, though other applications will be obvious (and even though many tax havens are dependencies rather than independent nations).

All this leaves a lot of ground to cover. In navigating it, we make extensive use of the two workhorse models that have been most widely used in the literature: those of Zodrow and Mieszkowski (1986) and Wilson (1986)—the "ZMW" model—and that of Kanbur and Keen (1993)—"KK." Both view tax competition as a game between countries played over the choice of a single tax rate, but with different types of interaction in mind: in ZMW (which has been especially prominent), tax differences across countries drive movements in productive capital; in KK (which has been used mainly in relation to commodity taxation, but as will be seen also has application to capital taxation) they affect the country in which tax is paid.

Section 2 starts by setting out and assessing these models, then uses them to explore the features, comparative statics, and welfare properties of noncooperative equilibria. Section 3 considers potential measures of coordination (such as the adoption of minimum tax rates, or coordination among a subset of countries), and Section 4 then takes a broader perspective, addressing a range of issues that are prominent in recent policy debates (including the use of special regimes targeted at particular firms or activities and the impact of tax havens and of the policy responses they might induce) and the political economy of tax competition and coordination. Section 5 concludes.

2. UNCOORDINATED ACTIONS

This section considers the outcomes to which unrestricted international tax competition might lead.

2.1. Workhorse Models

Formal thinking on this, and on many other issues reviewed here, has largely revolved around two, complementary modeling approaches. We start by setting these out.

2.1.1. The Zodrow, Mieszkowski, and Wilson (ZMW) Model

The formal literature on tax competition is largely rooted in an elegant model developed by Zodrow and Mieszkowski (1986) and Wilson (1986), the influence of which pervades the literature and so runs throughout this survey. This "ZMW" model considers a world economy comprised of n "countries," $i = 1, \ldots, n$, each characterized by investment opportunities described by an increasing and strictly concave product-of-capital function $f_i(k_i)$, where k_i denotes the capital-labor ratio, and f_i is to be interpreted as output per unit of labor. (For the most part, one can equally well interpret k_i as aggregate capital and f_i as aggregate output; the difference is material, however, when as later in this section, differences in country size are analyzed.) Behind the scenes there may be other factors of production, such as labor, intangibles, and publicly provided inputs; where these are in variable supply and untaxed, they can be taken to have been concentrated out of the production function; they shape the function $f_i(k_i)$ but for the purposes here need not be considered in the formal analysis. The downward slope of the marginal product of capital, $f_i'(k_i)$, can be explained by the presence of these hidden factors.[13] For clarity, and except where indicated, they are taken throughout to be fixed in supply and immobile across countries. Labor, specifically, is assumed to be supplied in amount unity by each household, so that the aggregate labor supply in country i is simply its population, denoted h_i.

Taxes are levied on a "source" basis, meaning that each country i chooses the per-unit tax $t_i \in [0, 1]$ levied on each unit of capital that is invested within it, generating tax revenue of $t_i k_i$. Since tax treatment depends only on the location of the investment, and investors (those who supply the capital) can invest wherever they choose, all investors (assumed to be price-takers) must achieve, in equilibrium, the same after-tax rate of return on capital, denoted by ρ. Thus

$$f_i'(k_i) - t_i = \rho \text{ for all } i = 1, \ldots, n. \tag{1}$$

In the basic ZMW framework, the aggregate world capital-labor ratio is fixed at some level $\bar{k}$, implying the market clearing condition

$$\sum_{i=1}^{n} \sigma_i k_i = \sum_{i=1}^{n} \sigma_i \bar{k}_i = \bar{k}, \tag{2}$$

where $\sigma_i \equiv h_i / \sum_{s=1}^{n} h_s$ denotes country i's share of the global population (one indicator of its "size"), $\bar{k}_i \geq 0$ the per capita endowment of capital in country i. Attention is confined here, and throughout, to equilibria in which capital is fully employed. Conditions (1) and (2) then characterize the Walrasian equilibrium outcome in the capital market with perfect competition and perfect capital mobility.

Equations (1) and (2) jointly determine both the capital allocated to each country and the common net rate of return as functions $k_i(t_1, \ldots, t_n)$ and $\rho(t_1, \ldots, t_n)$ of tax rates

---

[13] The framework is a special case of a more general model in which output is a function $F(K, N, B)$, with N being an input factor such as labor that is paid a competitive market price (and may be supplied elastically or inelastically) and B representing other fixed factors such as, for instance, national public goods that firms do not have to pay for. The benchmark model is obtained from this, for instance, if B is absent, N completely inelastically supplied, and $F(K, N)$ is homogenous of degree 1; note, however, that the representation in the text does not in itself require constant returns.

in all countries. These, it is dull to show,[14] have the properties that

$$\frac{\partial k_i}{\partial t_j} = \begin{cases} \frac{1}{f_i''} \left(\frac{\sum_{s \neq i}^n \zeta_s}{\sum_{s=1}^n \zeta_s} \right) < 0, & \text{for } i = j \\ -\frac{1}{\sigma_i} \left(\frac{\zeta_i \zeta_j}{\sum_{s=1}^n \zeta_s} \right) > 0, & \text{for } i \neq j \end{cases} \tag{3}$$

where $\zeta_j \equiv \sigma_j / f_j'' < 0$, and $\partial \rho / \partial t_i < 0$ for all i.[15] An increase in the tax rate in any country i thus reduces the capital employed there, increases capital employed in all other countries j—capital moving until the increased scarcity of capital in i has increased the gross marginal product of capital there and reduced the marginal product of capital elsewhere by enough to bring the arbitrage condition back into balance—and reduces the common net rate of return. The magnitude of these effects reflects, as one might expect, shapes of marginal product schedule and the significance in the world capital market of the countries concerned.

On the consumption and welfare side of the model, there is in each country a single representative consumer—immobile across countries—with preferences[16] $W_i(x, r) = x + G_i(r)$ defined over private consumption x and the amount r of some publicly provided good, with G_i strictly increasing, strictly concave, and satisfying an Inada condition which ensures that, in the absence of other sources of revenue, all countries will charge a strictly positive tax rate in equilibrium. Private consumption x is financed by the rents to domestic immobile factors, $f_i(k_i) - f_i'(k_i)k_i$ and the net return to domestically owned capital, of $\rho \bar{k}_i$. Public provision is financed entirely by per capita receipts $t_i k_i$ from capital located domestically, and the relative price of the private and publicly provided goods is taken to be fixed and normalized at unity; so $r_i = t_i k_i$.[17] Welfare of the typical consumer in country i can thus be written as

$$W_i = f_i(k_i) - f_i'(k_i)k_i + \rho \bar{k}_i + G_i(t_i k_i). \tag{4}$$

(where taking the argument of G_i to be per capita rather than total revenue is of course immaterial given a fixed population size). Given their action spaces and payoff functions (4), each government maximizes its objective function by a choice of its tax rate, taking

---

[14] Perturbing the $n - 1$ equations corresponding to (2),

$$f_i'(k_i) - t_i = f_n' \left(\bar{k}/\sigma_{n-1} - \sum_{s=1}^{n-1} (\sigma_s/\sigma_n)k_s \right) - t_n, i = 1, \ldots, n - 1,$$

gives the system $(A + \sigma_n f_n'' \iota \alpha') dk = (dt_1 - dt_n, \ldots, dt_{n-1} - dt_n)'$ where A is the diagonal matrix with jjth element f_{jj}'', ι is the column vector of ones and the typical element of α is σ_j/σ_n. Supposing that only one tax rate changes, (3) follows after using a result on a matrix inversion, found, for instance, in Dhrymes (1978, Proposition 33).

[15] Differentiating (1), for any $j \neq i$, gives $\partial \rho / \partial t_j = f_i'' \partial k_i / \partial t_j$, and the conclusion follows from (3).

[16] Little of substance is lost by the restriction on the functional form of preferences.

[17] Note that this is, in effect, a model of trade in two goods: a final consumption good and capital. Country i's exports, given by the excess of production $f_i(k_i)$ over its aggregate consumption $x_i + r_i$ are equal, given individual and public budget constraints, to its net payments on imported capital $\rho(k_i - \bar{k}_i)$. The elegance of the ZMW model derives largely from its collapsing a model of intertemporal trade into a single period.

the (equilibrium) tax rate choices of all other countries as given, and anticipating the implications of their choice for the allocation of and net return to capital.

Interpretation and Limitations

There are many embellishments of this basic ZMW structure to be found in the literature. Many of these are considered below, though by no means all. One not considered, for instance, is that in which public expenditure enters the production function rather than individuals' preferences, reflecting public spending on some form of infrastructure. In terms of strategic interactions and efficiency considerations, this leads to much the same conclusions as below. Before putting this model through its paces, however, it is important to see where it inherently does and does not connect with practical policy concerns.

One key issue is the interpretation of "capital," k. This is most naturally thought of as physical productive capital. ZMW is not a model of financial investments, since capital flows are taken to lead directly to changes in production: portfolio investments, or direct investments taking the form of acquisitions, need different handling.[18] The interpretation as physical capital requires, of course, some suspension of disbelief in terms of the ease with which factories and the like can be shifted from one country to another—raising issues of sunk and adjustment costs that are taken up later. More generally of course, "capital" here can be read as a metaphor for anything that is mobile internationally and generates real output where it is applied—the ZMW framework has been fruitfully applied, for instance, to issues of labor mobility [as in Wildasin (1991b)]. Note too that, as a first approximation, "capital" is considered as a non-lumpy and homogenous good, with foreign- and domestically-owned variants indistinguishable.[19]

On the tax side, several important elements of reality are abstracted from by specifying tax paid as simply $t_i k_i$.

First, the corporate income tax is in practice levied not on capital itself k_i but on some combination of the rents that capital earns, $f_i(k_i) - f_i'(k_i)k_i$ and the aggregate return to investment, $f_i'(k_i)k_i$. Allowing for a distinct tax on rents that accrue to the domestic citizen is straightforward: being non-distorting, this could be thought of as a preferred source of revenue, with the tax on capital k_i levied only insofar as additional revenue is needed (or to induce a beneficial change in the worldwide net rate of return, akin to an optimal tariff). Since it does not bear directly on rents, the tax rate t_i is best thought of as an indicator of the "marginal effective tax rate" on capital invested in country i—the additional tax paid on a real investment, reflecting both the statutory tax rate and the base of the tax—rather than the statutory tax rate alone. Even this, however, is not precisely right, because tax in the ZMW framework is levied on capital k_i rather than its earnings $f_i'(k_i)k_i$. The distinction here is similar to that between a specific and an ad valorem tax

---

[18] See, for one approach, Becker and Fuest (2010a, 2011).
[19] Mintz and Tulkens (1996) is an important exception on the latter point.

in the context of commodity taxation. In that context, and here too, the distinction is immaterial in terms of the decisions of competitive firms. Lockwood (2004) shows, however, that the distinction does matter in terms of strategic tax-setting, with tax competition likely to be more aggressive in the more realistic case in which it is the return to capital that is taxed. Intuitively, if country i reduces its tax rate, a larger inflow of capital is caused when it is the return to capital that is taxed because the reduction in the marginal return that inflow induces reduces the tax paid per unit of capital and so leads to an inflow in addition to that which would arise if tax per unit of capital were fixed.

Second, the assumption that tax liability follows mechanically from real investment decisions ignores the ability of firms to use a variety of devices—transfer pricing, financial decisions, and organizational structures—to disassociate the two. These issues, at the heart of much international tax debate, cannot be captured in the basic ZMW setting.

Third, the assumption of taxation only by the source country (where the productive capital is located) is apparently at odds with core features of the international tax architecture. Several countries have applied instead the "residence principle" in taxing foreign direct investment (and almost all do so for portfolio investment), by which, while the source (or "host") country has primary taxing rights, the home country (where the parent company is formally resident) also taxes income arising abroad, with a credit (non-refundable in practice) for taxes paid abroad. This is still, most notably, the system applied by the US. Residence taxation and can have profound implications for the strategic issues with which we are concerned here, and for national welfare, since it means that in some circumstances the tax applied by the host country is entirely irrelevant for the foreign investor. A small but long-standing literature aims to understand the choices countries have made as between the residence or source (also known as "exemption" or "territorial") principles (and other possibilities). One prominent puzzle is that of understanding why large capital exporters have historically chosen to give full credit for taxes paid abroad rather than simply allowing them as a deduction (which, as pointed out by Musgrave (1963), would seem preferable from their own perspective, since from their perspective taxes paid to a foreign government are a cost much like any other incurred in the host country). These issues are addressed in Gordon and Hines (2002) and Fuest et al. (2005), and not pursued here. Indeed it may well be that the ZMW assumption of source taxation is a reasonable characterization of reality even where foreign direct investment is subject, notionally, to residence-based taxation: additional taxes payable in the residence country can generally be deferred, for instance, by delaying repatriation of profits (this being a large part of what tax havens enable companies to do). And in some cases—more at the personal level rather than corporate—residence taxes are liable to outright evasion by simply failing to declare taxable income. There has, moreover, been a trend toward territorial systems, with both the UK and Japan having recently moved in this direction. The strong residence elements in the international tax architecture should not, however, be forgotten—there are over 2000 double tax treaties that largely serve to clarify and coordinate taxing rights of residence and source countries.

Equilibrium and Social Optimality

Returning to the model itself, the choice by the typical country i of its own tax rate t_i to maximize its welfare, as in (4), taking the tax rates of all other countries as given, gives the first-order conditions

$$\frac{\partial W_i}{\partial t_i} = -f_i''(k_i)k_i\frac{\partial k_i}{\partial t_i} + G_i'(t_ik_i)\left(k_i + t_i\frac{\partial k_i}{\partial t_i}\right) + \frac{\partial \rho}{\partial t_i}\bar{k}_i = 0, i = 1,\dots,n. \qquad (5)$$

In considering an increase in its tax rate, each government thus weighs the reduction in rents to immobile factors consequent on the capital outflow this would cause, as well as any increase in revenue, against the reduced net income that it would earn on its capital endowment.

For each country i, (5) defines a best response function (or, more generally, correspondence) $t_i(t_{-i})$ relating its maximizing tax rate(s) to the tax rates t_{-i} set by all others (the subscript $-i$ referring to all countries other than i). Of particular importance, in any tax policy game, to understanding the impact of various policy interventions and country characteristics on equilibrium outcomes, is the sign of the slope of best responses: on whether country i's response to a higher tax rate in country j is to raise its own tax rate (in which case tax rates are strategic complements) or to lower it (strategic substitutes).[20] For a game generating some reduced form $W_i(t_i, t_{-i})$ relating welfare directly to tax rate choices, strategic complementarity is equivalent to supermodularity[21] of W_i, and in the differentiable case is equivalent (as a consequence of the implicit function theorem) to

$$\frac{\partial^2 W_i}{\partial t_i \partial t_j} > 0, \qquad (6)$$

with the reverse inequality corresponding to strategic substitutability. Using (5) to construct this cross-derivative in the ZMW model, it is easy to believe from the complex expression which results that, without further restriction, its sign is uncertain. Intuition might suggest, in particular, that the best response to a reduction in some other country's tax rate will be for i to reduce its own rate too; meaning that tax rates are strategic complements. But this is not, in general, assured (even in the case of symmetric countries). A lower tax rate in some other country j, for instance, moves capital out of country i and so reduces its tax revenue and public spending; whether the best response to this is for i to raise or

---

[20] Some care is needed here for a country that may deploy more than one instrument, since the slope of the final response of any one instrument to a change elsewhere will depend not only on the derivative in (4) but also on how it adjusts its other instruments.

[21] See, for instance, Amir (2005), who illustrates the power of supermodularity in a range of areas.

lower its tax rate depends, among other things, on how large an increase in the marginal value of public spending this implies (being more likely the greater is that increase).[22]

A solution to the system (5) is an intersection of the best responses $t_i(t_{-i})$, and characterizes an interior Nash equilibrium in pure strategies where it exists. For present purposes, we simply assume the existence of this equilibrium, $(t_1^N, t_2^N, \ldots, t_n^N)$. The assumption is not trivial, and has received more attention in recent years, sufficient conditions being explored, for instance, by Laussel and Le Breton (1998) and Taugourdeau and Ziad (2011).

A central question of interest is whether such an equilibrium has any social optimality properties. Potential inefficiency arises in a game with objective functions $W_i(t_i, t_{-i})$ when one country j's tax choice has some external effect on the welfare of country i, so that $\frac{\partial W_i}{\partial t_j} \neq 0$, with the sign of this term then shaping whether the expectation is of taxes being "too low" in equilibrium or "too high." If it is the case in equilibrium, for instance, that[23]

$$\frac{\partial W_i}{\partial t_j} > 0, \tag{7}$$

then country j, in ignoring the benefit that an increase would confer on country i, sets a tax rate that, from the perspective of the latter, is too low. For the ZMW model, (4) above implies that

$$\frac{\partial W_i}{\partial t_j} = \{f_i''(\bar{k}_i - k_i) + G_i'(t_i k_i) t_i\} \frac{\partial k_i}{\partial t_j}. \tag{8}$$

Before turning to the implications of this, it is also useful for later purposes to consider the case in which all countries raise their tax rates by some common and small amount $dt_i = dt$. From (1), this simply reduces the common net return ρ by the same amount and leaves the allocation of capital unchanged, so that the welfare impact on country i is $dW_i = -k_i dt + G_i' k_i dt$; evaluating this at the Nash equilibrium (noting from (1) that $\partial \rho / \partial t_i = f_i''(\partial k / \partial t_i)) - 1 = f_j''(\partial k_j / \partial t_i)$ i's first-order condition (5) then implies[24]

$$dW_i = [(k_i - \bar{k}_i) f_i'' - G_i'(t_i k_i) t_i] \frac{\partial k_i}{\partial t_i} dt. \tag{9}$$

With all this in mind, it is helpful to consider first the case in which all countries are identical, before turning to that in which they may differ.

Suppose then that all countries are identical in their production opportunities ($f_i(.) \equiv f(.)$, for all i), capital endowment ($\bar{k}_i = \bar{k}$), and preferences ($G_i(.) = G_j(.) \equiv G(.)$). Then

---

[22] Consistent with this intuition, Rota Graziosi (2013) shows that when the object of policy is simply to maximize tax revenue, log concavity of the production function is sufficient for supermodularity. Vrijburg and de Mooij (2010) argue, however, that it is not hard to find examples of strategic substitutability when the government has a welfarist objective.

[23] More terminology: Eaton (2004) refers to this as the case of plain complementarity and that in which $\frac{\partial W_i}{\partial t_j} < 0$ as plain substitutability.

[24] This can also be seen, more directly but somewhat less instructively, by using (3) in (8).

in the symmetric equilibrium in pure strategies the employment of capital k_i must be the same in all countries, and must equal the endowment of capital in each. Thus $k_i = \bar{k}_i$, and (8) gives

$$dW_i = -G'(t_i k_i) t_i \frac{\partial k_i}{\partial t_i} dt > 0. \tag{10}$$

The Nash equilibrium is thus Pareto inefficient: all countries would benefit from a small, uniform increase in all tax rates. This is the central result in the argument against unconstrained international tax competition.

In this symmetric case, the Nash equilibrium can be very directly compared with the social optimum. With identical countries, the latter is simply the combination of tax rates and transfers between countries that maximizes the sum of all their utilities. A necessary condition for this first-best outcome is the efficient provision of public funds, which, at an interior solution, requires

$$G'(.) = 1 \text{ for all } i = 1, \ldots, n. \tag{11}$$

Since the global capital stock is assumed completely inelastic, taxing its use at the same rate in each country ($t_i = t$ for all $i = 1, \ldots, n$) is entirely non-distorting; production efficiency is maintained, since, recalling (1), this ensures that marginal products of capital are equalized across countries (without which, aggregate output could be increased by reallocating capital between them). From (11), the first-best set of tax rates is given by

$$t_i = \frac{G'^{-1}(1)}{\bar{k}_i}, \text{ for } i = 1, \ldots, n. \tag{12}$$

The Nash equilibrium outcome generically differs from this since, in the symmetric case, the first-order condition (5) implies (substituting for $\partial\rho/\partial t_i$ as before (9))

$$G'(t\bar{k}) = \frac{1}{1 + E_k} < 1, \tag{13}$$

where $E_k \equiv \frac{\partial ln(k_i)}{\partial ln(t_i)} < 0$ denotes the elasticity of capital employed in i with respect to its own tax rate, evaluated at the Nash equilibrium. Relative to the social optimum, there is thus under-provision of the public good, and too low a tax rate, in the Nash equilibrium. The symmetric Nash equilibrium does have production efficiency: all countries charge the same tax rate, so the allocation of capital is first best. But the decentralized tax-setting means that countries fail to properly exploit what is, from the collective perspective, a perfectly inelastic tax base, access to which makes the first best feasible.

The simplicity of the case in which countries are identical, and sharpness of the results to which it leads, has made symmetry a common assumption in the literature. It is, however, highly unrealistic. The implication, for instance, is that there is no capital movement in equilibrium, and no gain from allowing capital to move; indeed there is a loss, given the inefficient tax-setting from allowing capital to move at all. (If borders were closed, each country would recognize the inelasticity of the tax base and achieve the first best.) The asymmetric case is thus inherently more interesting; but it is also much more complex.

The diversity of national interests that can then arise is evident from (9), which shows that country i gains from a small, collective increase in tax rates if and only if $(k_i - \bar{k}_i) f_i'' - G_i'(t_i k_i) t_i < 0$. This is sure to be the case when $k_i > \bar{k}_i$; that is, for a capital importing country. For a capital exporting country, however, the reduction in after-tax capital income may more than outweigh the value of the increased tax revenue.

Social optimality also becomes more complex in the asymmetric case. Consider, for instance, the characterization of Pareto efficient tax structures: ones, that is, from which no country can be made better off without making any other worse off (and from which a selection might then be made if some social welfare function is available). It follows from results of Keen and Wildasin (2004) that if there are three or more countries, then, in the absence of lump sum international transfers, marginal products of capital may differ across countries at a (constrained) Pareto efficient allocation. Constrained Pareto efficient international tax structures, then, may well involve tax rates that vary across countries.

One implication is that the case for the residence principle, sometimes presented as the preferred international tax regime on the grounds that it eliminates the production inefficiency potentially associated with the source principle,[25] is weaker than often thought: it can lead to Pareto inefficient outcomes. The qualification has some policy importance, given the focus of current initiatives—discussed later—on strengthening the enforcement of residence taxation.

Comparative Statics

For the symmetric case, (13) immediately implies that the equilibrium tax rate is lower the larger (in absolute terms) is the elasticity of each country's tax base with respect to its own tax rate. Probing further, this elasticity can be shown, from (3), to be given by

$$E_k = \left(1 - \frac{1}{n}\right)\left(\frac{t}{\bar{k}_i f''}\right). \tag{14}$$

Substituting this into (13), it is straightforward to show that the equilibrium tax rate t is lower the more countries there are and the flatter is the marginal product of capital (the smaller, that is, is $|f''(\bar{k}_i)|$). This is as intuition would suggest: there is no distortion, of course, if $n = 1$; and a flatter marginal product schedule means that small tax differences induce larger capital flows.

In the asymmetric case, however, general results are hard to find. For that one must look to further restrictions on functional form, as for example, assuming a quadratic production function $f_i(k_i)$, as in Wildasin (1991a) and Bucovetsky (2009), giving a linear

---

[25] Under source-based taxation, if $t_i \neq t_j$, the arbitrage condition (2) implies $f_i' \neq f_j'$; under residence-based taxation, tax rates (and net returns) vary by the residence of the investor, so that the arbitrage condition, in obvious notation, becomes $f_j' - t_i = \rho_i$ for all i and j, implying $f_i' = f_j'$.

marginal product in each country i

$$f_i'(k_i) = max\{a_i - k_i, 0\}; \ a_i > 0, \qquad (15)$$

where the constant slope of this relationship is assumed the same in all countries (and normalized to unity), while differing intercepts allow for differing average products. The capital market equilibrium condition (1) then becomes

$$a_i - k_i - t_i = \rho \quad \text{for all } i = 1, \ldots, n. \qquad (16)$$

On the consumption side, $G_i(t_i k_i)$ is assumed to be of the form

$$G_i = \begin{cases} (1 + \lambda_i)t_i k_i & \text{for } t_i k_i \leq \bar{G}, \\ (1 + \lambda_i)\bar{G} & \text{for } t_i k_i > \bar{G}. \end{cases} \qquad (17)$$

so that the private evaluation of the public good is strictly proportional to the cost of its provision up to some level $\bar{G}$, beyond which further increases have no value. This public expenditure generates some surplus, which can be seen as the shadow price of public funds, to the extent of $\lambda_i > 0$. (The upper limit $\bar{G}$ is assumed to be high enough not to affect the tax-competition equilibrium but not so high as to imply that an autarchic government would wish to confiscate all capital.)

To generate the closed forms this structure allows, note first that, since $\sum_{j=1}^{n} \sigma_j = 1$, (16) implies

$$a - \bar{k} - \sum_{j=1}^{n} \sigma_j t_j = \rho, \qquad (18)$$

where $a \equiv \sum_{j=1}^{n} \sigma_j a_j$, and hence

$$\frac{\partial \rho}{\partial t_i} = -\sigma_i. \qquad (19)$$

Substituting (18) in (16) gives

$$k_i = a_i - t_i - a + \bar{k} + \sum_{j=1}^{n} \sigma_j t_j \qquad (20)$$

and so

$$\frac{\partial k_i}{\partial t_i} = -(1 - \sigma_i). \qquad (21)$$

Using (19) and (21), the necessary condition (5) on country i's choice of tax rate gives the best response

$$t_i = \frac{(\lambda_i + \sigma_i)(a_i - a + \bar{k}) - \sigma_i \bar{k}}{(1 - \sigma_i)(1 + 2\lambda_i + \sigma_i)} + \frac{(\lambda_i + \sigma_i)}{(1 - \sigma_i)(1 + 2\lambda_i + \sigma_i)} \left(\sum_{j \neq i}^{n} \sigma_j t_j \right). \qquad (22)$$

Nash equilibrium tax rates follow on solving the system of equation (22) for all n countries. It is straightforward to derive closed forms for the Nash equilibrium tax rates from (22); for present purposes, however, it is enough to focus on these best responses themselves. One immediate implication is that in this special case, country i's tax rate t_i depends only on the weighted average of those set elsewhere; each looks in particular to the tax rates set by the largest countries.

For the two country case, a simple graphical tool proves helpful; the same broad picture can of course be used to thinking about the general case too, but without the same confidence in the structure of the relationships drawn. Introducing this, Figure 2 illustrates the present special case when, moreover, the two countries are identical. It shows the Nash equilibrium N with tax rates (t^N, t^N) where the two reply functions intersect, and the iso-welfare curves $W_1(t^N, t^N)$ and $W_2(t^N, t^N)$ at the Nash equilibrium. The iso-welfare curves for country 1 intersect country 1's reply function $t_1(t_2)$ with a slope of zero: by definition, $t_1(t_2)$ gives the optimal choice of t_1 for the given t_2; so a small deviation in t has only a second-order effect for welfare along the curve $t_1(t_2)$. A similar argument explains the slope of $W_2(t^N, t^N)$ along $t_2(t_1)$. The curves $W_1(t^N, t^N)$ and $W_2(t^N, t^N)$ form a lens (the shaded area in Figure 2) that describes the set of tax rate pairs (t_1, t_2) that, if implemented, yield a strict welfare improvement for both countries relative to the Nash equilibrium even in the absence of any transfers between them.

More particularly, (22) implies that tax rates are in this case strategic complements: country i's best response to an increase in any of the tax rates set abroad is to increase its own tax rate—hence the upward sloping reaction functions in Figure 2. As discussed above, this strategic complementarity of single tax rates cannot be taken for granted.

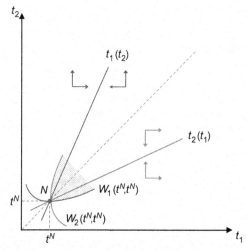

Figure 2 Nash equilibrium as the intersection of best responses in the linear model.

A rich series of comparative statics results follow from (22). Broadly speaking, equilibrium tax rates are lower in countries that are better endowed with capital, have more productive technologies, value public spending less, or are smaller.

To see this, consider first the endowment of capital, per unit of labor, $\bar{k}_i$. From (22), an increase in this endowment affects i's best response only by shifting down the intercept term. This, it is easily seen, leads to a lower equilibrium tax rate. Supposing then that all countries are identical in their shadow price of public goods ($\lambda_i \equiv \lambda$), and local opportunities for production ($a_i = a$), it follows from (22) that country i has a lower tax rate than country j if $\bar{k}_i > \bar{k}_j$. Intuitively, suppose that initially $t_i = t_j$; given identical technologies, (1) implies that capital is allocated so that the capital-labor ratio is the same in all countries. Country i must then be a capital exporter. Increasing its tax rate would reduce the world net rate of return, so that its citizens receive less on their investments both at home and abroad; the former is a matter of indifference, since there is an exactly offsetting increase in domestic revenues—but there is no offset to the loss of private income from investments abroad, which instead manifests itself as increased rents to the foreign citizen. Capital-rich countries will consequently be less aggressive in their tax policies.[26]

Higher productivity, manifested as a higher value of a_i, has an equally straightforward effect: this simply shifts up the intercept in (22), and so—assuming countries to be identical in all other respects—leads to a higher t_i. Intuitively, starting at $t_i = t_j$, (20) implies, given $a_i > a_j$ that $k_i > k_j$, while (21) implies (given equality of size) that $\partial k_i / \partial t_i = \partial k_j / \partial t_j$. The more productive country thus attracts the same amount of capital by lowering its tax rate as does the less productive; but—because it is more productive—this is more than offset by what it loses by taxing less heavily the capital already there.

A stronger taste for public spending over private consumption, corresponding to an increase in λ_i, can be shown (assuming countries to be in all other respects identical) to increase both the intercept in (22) and the slope of the best response function. Both effects point to an unsurprisingly increased tax rate in country i: again taking an initial position in which $t_i = t_j$ and supposing all countries to be otherwise identical, all countries have the same shift from private to public consumption from increasing their tax rate, but country i enjoys a greater benefit than country j.

The effects of country size, parameterized by σ_i, are more complex. Taking the two country case, simply some tedious differentiation and calculation shows (assuming the countries to be otherwise identical, and initially the same size) that both the intercept term and responsiveness to the other country's tax rate are greater in the larger country—the latter perhaps surprising result being a sign of the power of small countries in tax competition games, returned to later. This suggests (and direct calculation of the Nash equilibrium tax rates confirms—in this exercise, both best response functions shift) that the smaller of the two countries will set the lower tax rate in equilibrium. Intuitively, in

[26] More general analyses of tax competition with differences in capital ownership are provided by Wilson (1991) and Peralta and van Ypersele (2006).

considering a tax rate cut, countries must weigh the loss of revenue from their own capital against the benefits of attracting more inward investment; and for a small country, with a narrow domestic capital base and a lot of capital abroad that it might attract, the attractions of a rate cut will be greater. Bucovetsky (2009) further shows, in this same linear case (and assuming it is per capita public spending that matters for welfare, not—as would be the case with a classic Samuelsonian public good—total public spending), that the smaller country is the winner in this tax competition game, in the sense that, in equilibrium, per capita welfare is higher there than in the larger country.

2.1.2. The Kanbur-Keen (KK) Model

As will become abundantly clear, the workhorse ZMW model has proved extremely versatile and informative. In one important respect, however, it is, as noted earlier, inherently limited as an approach to thinking about international tax competition. This is because the tax base over which countries are assumed to compete is mechanically tied to real activity. In practice, both companies and individuals have many ways in which they can rearrange their affairs so as to reduce the total tax they pay with only limited effect on the pre-tax income they receive. Companies can shift paper profits to low tax jurisdictions, for instance, by transfer pricing (that is, manipulating prices charged within the group—for example, by providing highly priced management services to a subsidiary in a high tax country from another located in a low tax country), by financial structuring (such as "thin-capitalization": lending from a subsidiary in a low tax country to subsidiaries in high tax ones, the interest deduction in the latter generating tax savings that exceed additional tax due in the former), or by judicious choice of organizational form (exploiting mismatches in the way different countries view the same entity for tax purposes). Individuals can choose to hold investments through accounts in low tax jurisdictions, and evade or defer taxes due in their home countries. Quantifying these effects is difficult, but there is little doubt that the sums at stake are large.

The aim here is not to review such avoidance or evasion schemes—on the corporate side, an excellent treatment is in Mintz and Weichenrieder (2010)—but rather to consider how profit-shifting activities affect the way in which one should think about strategic aspects of international tax competition. For this, the model of Kanbur and Keen (1993) is a useful start. It was initially exposited as a model of commodity tax competition, and, although that is not the topic of this review, it will be helpful to construct it in the same way and then to reinterpret it as one of profit-shifting.

The framework is a spatial one, with two countries, $i = 1, 2$, each of length unity, located on a line with a border between them in the middle. The population is distributed uniformly in each, but population sizes h_i differ. Consumers buy only one unit of some good, which they can do either where they are located, paying the local tax, or by traveling to the border to buy at the tax-inclusive price of the other country. In the latter case they incur unit transport costs of δ. Suppose then that $t_1 < t_2$, where t_i denotes the unit tax in country i. Then all consumers in low tax country 1 will simply buy at home. In high tax country 2, a consumer living a distance of s from the border will find it worthwhile to purchase abroad if and only if $t_1 + \delta s < t_2$; in aggregate, a proportion

$$s^* \equiv \frac{t_2 - t_1}{\delta} \tag{23}$$

of country 2 consumers will thus shop abroad. Revenues in the two countries are then:

$$r_1 = t_1\left(h_1 + h_2\left(\frac{t_2 - t_1}{\delta}\right)\right); \quad r_2 = t_2 h_2\left(1 - \left(\frac{t_2 - t_1}{\delta}\right)\right) \tag{24}$$

reflecting the revenue gain to the low tax country from sales to a proportion s^* of the h_2 consumers in country 2, and the corresponding loss to the latter. Each government is assumed to maximize its tax revenue, taking as given the tax set of the other. In the region where $t_1 < t_2$, these best responses are readily calculated to be

$$t_1(t_2) = \frac{1}{2}(\delta\eta + t_2); \quad t_2(t_1) = \frac{1}{2}(\delta + t_1), \tag{25}$$

where $\eta \equiv \frac{h_1}{h_2}$, as shown in Figure 3. What the figure also shows, however, is that viewed over the full space of tax rates there is a discontinuity in the best response of (only) the small country.[27] When the larger country sets a low rate, the smaller would have to set such a very low rate to attract shoppers from across the border that the revenue gained thereby would less than offset the revenue lost from its own consumers; as the rate in the larger country increases, however, there comes a point at which the smaller country finds it optimal to shift discontinuously to a strategy of undercutting. While this discontinuity makes existence problematic, Kanbur and Keen (1993) show that there is a unique Nash equilibrium, and, as at E, it is in the region where $t_1 < t_2$. From (25), the Nash equilibrium tax rates are

$$t_1^N = \delta\left(\left(\frac{2}{3}\right)\eta + \frac{1}{3}\right); \quad t_2^N = \delta\left(\left(\frac{1}{3}\right)\eta + \frac{2}{3}\right). \tag{26}$$

The Kanbur-Keen model thus formulates very sharply the idea that smaller countries will set lower tax rates. More generally, such closed form solutions for equilibrium tax rates are rarely available, and generate a series of useful benchmark results.

Several embellishments of this framework are to be found in the commodity tax literature.[28]

[27] Discontinuities are also a prominent feature of the model of commodity tax competition with transport costs in Mintz and Tulkens (1986).
[28] Nielsen (2001), for instance, shows that essentially the same results hold if countries instead have uniform population densities but differ in length. Ohsawa (1999) extends the analysis to the case of three countries located on a line, showing that (in the absence of size differences) tax rates will be higher in the periphery (because the intermediate

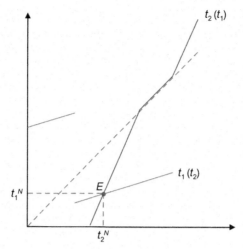

Figure 3 Equilibrium in the Kanbur-Keen model.

To see how a simple model of profit shifting can lead to the same formal structure, consider a multinational that earns "true" profits[29] in each of the two countries
of Π_i, $i = 1, 2$. Profit declared in country i, and taxed there at a proportional rate t_i
differs from true profit, however, to the extent that the company uses transfer pricing
and other devices to shift profit between them. Suppose, as above, that $t_1 < t_2$ so that
the incentive is to shift profits into country 1, and denote by s the fraction of real profit
in country 2 that is shifted. Such shifting is not costless, however, involving some organizational cost, distortion of activities, or risk of penalty. Assuming this cost to take the
form $(1/2)\delta s^2 \Pi_i$ and not to be deductible in either country,[30] the firm's net profit is
then

$$\Pi = \Pi_1 + \Pi_2 - t_1(\Pi_1 + s\Pi_2) - t_2(\Pi_2 - s\Pi_2) - \left(\frac{1}{2}\right)\delta s^2 \Pi_2. \qquad (27)$$

country attracts cross-border shoppers from two countries by setting a lower rate, but the others from just one). Agrawal
(2012) discusses tax competition if countries can choose regionally differentiated tax rates. With a federal structure in
mind, Agrawal (2011) locates states (corresponding to countries in the analysis above) along a circle and allows for tax
differentiation across towns within states. Keen (2002) provides an review of this literature.

[29] The concept of "true" profits being allocable to particular countries is problematic in itself. The centerpiece of
international taxation practice is the principle of valuing intra-group transactions at "arms-length" prices which would
be paid between unrelated parties. Since competitive markets, where such prices can be found, often do not exist
(a fact in itself linked with the existence of the multinationals) this is in practice highly contentious. For present
purposes, however, a broad distinction between profits associated with real activity in particular and those shifted with
the tax-minimizing intention of shifting the distribution rather than the total of group profits is clear enough.

[30] This is for convenience rather than realism. In practice, costs may well be tax-deductible in one country or the other,
and the cost may reflect penalties that in turn depend on the applicable tax rate. The extent of profit-shifting may then
depend on tax rates through more than just the absolute difference between them.

Maximizing with respect to s, the proportion of profits shifted from country 2 to country 1, s^* is exactly as in (23) above and revenues in the two countries are precisely as in (24), with true profit Π_i replacing population size. Conclusions drawn from the commodity tax form of the model can thus be translated directly into results on profit shifting.

Prominent among these is that it is the country which is "smaller," not necessarily (as in the commodity tax variant) in terms of population or geographical size but in the sense of hosting lower aggregate profits from real activities, which sets the lower tax rate in equilibrium. This is a strong prediction that, as will be seen, resonates closely with some features of reality. The intuition underlying it is straightforward: a country that is small in this sense loses little revenue from its own tax base by cutting its tax rate, but can gain a good deal by attracting taxable profit from the rest of the world.

Many of the other implications drawn from the KK model are also broadly similar to those derived earlier for the ZMW model, with the closed forms available enabling particularly sharp expression. These include the finding that setting a uniform rate anywhere between the rates that emerge in the Nash equilibrium always harms the small, low tax country, whereas imposing a minimum tax anywhere in that range is Pareto-improving. There is, though, one important difference: whereas the tax rates in the ZMW model are, as noted, best interpreted as marginal effective rates, capturing the combined impact of tax rates and tax base on the additional liability associated with investing a little more, the relevant tax rates in considering profit shifting are best thought of as corresponding to statutory rates, since the shifting has no impact, for instance, on depreciation allowances claimed. Thus it is quite possible, for instance, that countries might wish to lower the statutory rate in order to manipulate profit-shifting while expanding tax bases so as to protect revenue from real investments.

With this important difference between them, the confluence of results is nonetheless reassuring, in the sense that the insights into equilibrium outcomes and broad policy responses seem reasonably robust to the mix between real and paper shifting of tax bases. But they also point to the importance of asymmetries and the difficulties these create for coordinating beneficial outcomes. It is a general feature of tax competition models that small countries matter a good deal—a sharp contrast, for example, to the literature on tariff wars, in which it is the large countries that are potential winners from trade wars. This has powerful implications for designing feasible reforms in this area, a point taken up in the next section.

2.2. Sequential Decision Making

There is some evidence that countries' tax reforms do not occur simultaneously. The results of Altshuler and Goodspeed (2002), for instance, suggest that sequential choices between the US and European countries have existed since the 1986 US tax reform, with the USA acting as a Stackelberg leader and European countries acting as followers vis-à-vis the USA and moving simultaneously vis-à-vis each other.[31] This raises the question of how the possible sequentiality of choices among governments can change the outcome.

This has been addressed in theoretical contributions by Wang (1999) for indirect taxes (in the setting of the KK model discussed in Section 2.1.2 above) and Kempf and Rota Graziosi (2010), who analyze endogenous timing, using the workhorse ZMW model.

Figure 4 illustrates the Stackelberg leadership case, under the assumption that tax rates are strategic complements. It shows the same best reply functions for the linear variant of the workhorse model as in Figure 2, and the Nash equilibrium that emerges from simultaneous tax-rate choices. Suppose now that, for some reason, country 1 has to choose its tax rate t_1 first while country 2 is the follower who observes this choice and chooses t_2 on the basis of that observation. In this case, country 1 anticipates that, whatever t_1 it selects, country 2 will choose a $t_2(t_1)$ in line with its reply curve. Hence, by choosing t_1 and anticipating subgame perfect play, the country can essentially choose from all combinations $(t_1, t_2(t_1))$ that are graphically described by the reply function $t_2(t_1)$. If country 1 optimizes, it chooses the point along $t_2(t_1)$ that maximizes its objective function. Graphically, such a point is found where an iso-payoff curve for country 1 is tangent to $t_2(t_1)$, as it is drawn in Figure 4. It follows that, in a Stackelberg equilibrium, and given strategic complementarity, both countries choose higher taxes than in the Nash equilibrium. Starting from the latter, there would be no advantage to country 1 from raising its tax rate if country 2 continued to choose the Nash equilibrium tax rate—as would happen in the simultaneous game, because country 2 would have no reason to anticipate this deviation from $t_1 = t^N$. However, if country 1 chooses first and country 2 can observe this choice, country 2 re-optimizes and finds that, given $t_1 > t^N$, its optimal tax rate is also higher. By setting $t_1 > t^N$, country 1 induces a higher t_2, and it is this strategic effect that benefits country 1.

It is clear from the figure that country 2 is also better off than at the Nash equilibrium, being on a higher iso-payoff curve. Indeed in the symmetric country case it may well benefit more than the leader, since the latter charges the higher rate: for both then benefit from the increase in both tax rates to the level that the follower sets in the Stackelberg equilibrium, but the follower then benefits in addition (and the leader suffers) from the further increase in the leader's rate.

While sequential choice is in the interest of all countries here, it requires commitment. In the symmetric case in Figure 4 the Stackelberg follower is seemingly at an advantage, and the commitment problem is one of staying flexible and out-waiting the other country. Procedural rules, the timing of government formation, and so on may yield some differences in the timing in different countries. But the cyclic nature of most of these institutional procedures does not clearly answer the question of who would be expected to move first.

[31] Stackelberg leadership of the federal government is also commonly assumed in the literature that discusses tax competition within a federation (see for instance, Hayashi & Boadway, 2001; Janeba & Osterloh, 2012).

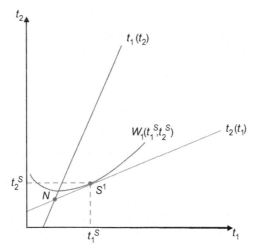

Figure 4 Stackelberg equilibrium.

A solution to this problem comes from the theory of endogenous sequential choices, first developed in the context of duopoly by Hamilton and Slutsky (1990) and applied in the context of tax competition duopolies by Kempf and Rota Graziosi (2010). A Stackelberg leader-follower outcome can typically be obtained as the outcome of a game which is augmented by an earlier stage in which each country first chooses its timing of choice (what Hamilton and Slutsky call "the extended game with observable delay"). Let there be two points of time for tax rate choices: $h \in \{e(arly), l(ate)\}$, with the point $l(ate)$ occurring after the point $e(arly)$ in the time line. First, let each country simultaneously choose whether it would like to choose and fix its tax rate at time e or l. One can then show that there is a subgame perfect equilibrium in which one country, say, country 1, chooses $h_1 = e$ and the other country 2, chooses $h_2 = l$; the Stackelberg game just discussed is the continuation game. To confirm this, we need to show that, assuming subgame perfect play in all possible continuation games, $h_1 = e$ and $h_2 = l$ are mutually optimal replies. Suppose that, for whatever reason, country 1 assumes that country 2 chooses l. Then, country 1 has essentially two options. It can also choose $h_1 = l$. In this case, both countries choose their tax rate at time l and simultaneously. They end up in the Nash equilibrium (t^N, t^N). Alternatively, country 1 can choose $h_1 = e$. In this case they end up in the sequential subgame with country 1 the Stackelberg leader and country 2 the follower, with an equilibrium at S^1 in Figure 5. As just discussed, this outcome is superior to the Nash equilibrium outcome for country 1; hence, $h_1^*(h_2 = l) = e$. Turning now to country 2, it remains to confirm that, given $h_1 = e$, country 2 prefers $h_2 = l$. Supposing that country 2 anticipates $h_1 = e$, it has essentially two options. It can choose $h_2 = e$. This yields simultaneous tax rate choices in the continuation game, and the equilibrium is the Nash equilibrium with tax rates (t^N, t^N). Or country 2 can

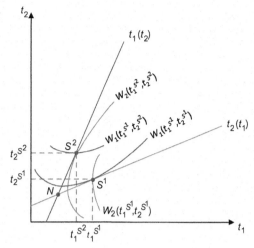

Figure 5 Endogenous sequencing in the tax rate choices.

choose $h_2 = l$ instead. In this case, the subgame is the Stackelberg game discussed above, which country 2 prefers to the Nash equilibrium.

Two difficulties remain with this concept. One is the coordination problem. As was argued in the context of Figure 4 above, both countries prefer the Stackelberg game to the Nash game. But, they typically prefer being in the position of Stackelberg follower (i.e., to be the country that chooses $h = l$) if the other country chooses $h = e$. If the countries cannot coordinate on who becomes follower and who becomes leader, they may randomize independently about their commitment choices. This leads to an equilibrium with mixed strategies at the stage in which they choose timing. In some of the subgames, the mixed strategies result in (e, e) or (l, l), in which case a Nash game follows as the continuation game; in other subgames they manage to end up with (e, l), leading to the Stackelberg equilibrium S^1 or (l, e), leading to the Stackelberg equilibrium S^2 in the continuation game. Kempf and Rota Graziosi (2010) use an equilibrium selection argument (the risk-dominance criterion) to argue that—focusing on country differences in capital productivity—the less productive country is more likely to be the leader. If the countries become sufficiently asymmetric, this order of moves can even become Pareto dominant.[32]

The second problem that remains is to explain what makes the commitment feasible and credible at the stage when countries commit on their timing. In an institutional context in which tax reforms are feasible only in some time windows, within an electoral cycle, for instance, the choice of the timing of elections may induce some sequential ordering of decision making.

---

[32] For further discussion taking into consideration the role of capital ownership and asymmetries between countries, see also Ogawa (2013) and Kempf and Rota Graziosi (2012).

2.3. Pure Profits and International Portfolio Diversification

If aggregate production is a function of internationally mobile capital and other, internationally immobile, factor inputs, and if some of these inputs can be used costlessly, then the ownership of the production facilities in a country may include entitlements in pure profits. The assumption in the ZMW workhorse model above was that any such rents all accrue to domestic residents and are untaxed. Such rents are of course an attractive target for taxation, being non-distorting insofar as these rents are genuinely location-specific. Allowing for such rent taxes adds little when rents all accrue domestically, simply implying that source-based taxes need to be used only insofar as such taxes cannot raise all the revenue required.[33] Foreign ownership, however, raises more substantial issues.

To address these, we consider a simplified version of the ideas outlined in Huizinga and Nielsen (1997, 2002, 2008) and Fuest (2005). Pure profits, it is assumed, cannot be taxed directly but a source tax on capital can be levied—perhaps because paper profits are easier to conceal, or shift across jurisdictions, than productive capital. Production in each country uses capital as the single variable factor in combination with some unpriced fixed factor, which can be thought of as a natural public good. Then $(f_i(k_i) - f_i'(k_i)k_i)$ is the total pure profits that accrue to the owners of the production facilities in country i. Denote by θ_{ij} the share of the production facilities in country j that is owned by the citizens of country i. Then the national welfare function becomes

$$W_i = \sum_{j=1}^{n} \theta_{ij}(f_j(k_j) - f_j'(k_j)k_j) + \rho \bar{k}_i + G_i(t_i k_i) \qquad (28)$$

(with Eq. (4) above being the special case in which $\theta_{ii} = 1$ and $\theta_{ij} = 0$ for $i \neq j$). An assumed interior equilibrium characterized by the first-order conditions can be determined by

$$\frac{\partial W_i}{\partial t_i} = \sum_{j=1}^{n} \theta_{ij}(-f_j''(k_j))k_j \frac{\partial k_j}{\partial t_i} + \frac{\partial \rho}{\partial t_i}\bar{k}_i + G'(t_i k_i)\left(k_i + t_i\frac{\partial k_i}{\partial t_i}\right) = 0, \quad i = 1, \ldots, n.$$

$$(29)$$

Comparing this with Eq. (5) above, the relocation of capital away from the country induced by an increase in its tax rate t_i has different welfare effects in the presence of international portfolio investment. First, country i bears only the share θ_{ii} of any loss in rents $(f_i(k_i) - f_i'(k_i)k_i)$ on domestically employed capital, since its citizens own only a share $\theta_{ii} < 1$ of these rents. This makes an increase in t_i more attractive than when $\theta_{ii} = 1$. Second, the citizens in i benefit from the increase in production rents that accrue

---

[33] The strategic role of an internationally diversified ownership of firms for decision making of a government that maximizes national welfare has been highlighted in other areas of public economics as well. These include strategic trade policy (Dick, 1993, Huck & Konrad (2003, 2004)), competition policy (Haufler & Schulte, 2011), international trade policy (Feeney & Hillman, 2001), and privatization policy (Norbäck & Persson, 2005).

in other countries, in proportion to the shares θ_{ij} which they own in these rents. As an increase in t_i increases these production rents, this effect also makes an increase in t_i more attractive than for $\theta_{ij} = 0$. Starting from the values $(t^N, \ldots, t^N)$ that characterize a Nash equilibrium for $\theta_{ii} = 1$ and $\theta_{ij} = 0$ and fully symmetric countries (including in population size), the first-order welfare effect of an increase in i's own tax rate is

$$\frac{\partial W_i}{\partial t_i} = (\theta_{ii} - 1)\left(-f''\left(\bar{k}\right)\right)\bar{k}\frac{\partial k_j}{\partial t_i} + \sum_{j \neq i} \theta_{ij}\left(-f''\left(\bar{k}\right)\right)\bar{k}\frac{\partial k_j}{\partial t_i}. \qquad (30)$$

This is unambiguously positive for $\theta_{ii} \in (0, 1)$ and $\theta_{ij} \in (0, 1)$. Again assuming strategic complementarity of tax rates, this implies that international portfolio diversification weakens tax competition and leads to higher equilibrium tax rates than in the benchmark case.[34]

This result—that a high degree of international ownership reduces the incentives for a race to the bottom—in turn suggests a potential strategic relationship between the degree of international firm ownership and the intensity of tax competition. If portfolio investors in a country could coordinate on a joint portfolio policy, and if (as seems plausible) they were less interested in the public good than the policy maker (or the median voter), then those investors would have an incentive to reduce their international investment activities in order to induce lower domestic tax rates. Indigenization—encouraging national ownership in national firms and their profits—is a well-known means to reduce the government's incentive to generate tax revenue from them.[35]

This indigenization effect is well-known from other contexts. For instance, it has been argued that indigenization, or joint ventures with host country citizens reduce the incentives of the national government in the host country to expropriate or nationalize foreign direct investment. Konrad and Lommerud (2001) show that the problem of ex-post opportunistic behavior can also be moderated if the host country government has incomplete information about the true profitability of the FDI project and if a large share of the foreign company is owned by citizens of the host country. Key to their argument is that this incomplete information shields an information rent of the firm from being extracted, even if the host government applies the most sophisticated extortionary means to extract as much revenue as possible. Similarly, it has been argued that a country with sovereign debt should be less inclined to default if its debt is held mainly by its own nationals (Broner, Martin, & Ventura, 2010).

---

[34] Huizinga and Nicodème (2006) interpret their empirical findings on the relationship between international ownership and corporate taxes as being in line with this finding.

[35] The trade-off between risk diversification and the incentives for tax revenue extraction in the context of international ownership of fixed resources is developed in Wildasin and Wilson (1998).

2.4. Tax Competition with Multiple Instruments

A common feature of both ZMW and KK is that each country deploys only one tax instrument. Many contributions to the literature relax, in one way or another, this unrealistic assumption.

Even allowing for taxes on immobile factors can make an important difference. In ZMW, a country that could also tax rents to the domestic factors generating the concavity of the production function but was unable to affect the common return ρ would optimally choose not to impose a source-based tax on capital: this is the well-known result that small countries should not tax capital.[36] Bucovetsky and Wilson (1991) show that the same applies when labor supply is variable, and wage income can be taxed directly. The intuition is the same in both cases: with the required return on world markets fixed, the real burden of any tax on capital is passed onto labor—and it is then better to tax labor directly than to distort capital intensity. The fundamental inefficiency remains, however, if the global capital stock is fixed, since a common tax on that base is then lump sum.

The case in which distinct instruments bear directly on the allocation of production and tax bases across countries is of obvious direct interest. One such instance—in which different types of mobile capital can be taxed, in ZMW fashion, at differing rates—is discussed at some length in Section 4.2. Here we consider another. For with ZMW attuned to modeling movements of real capital and KK to the shifting of paper profits—and both important in practice—it is natural to combine the two. This is the essence, for example, of the model set out in Devereux et al. (2008), a stripped down version of which suffices here.

Suppose then that there are two countries, each, in the spirit of ZMW, with a fixed endowment of capital that is freely mobile between them. In each there is a single multinational enterprise, which undertakes real production only there but which, in the spirit of KK, can also, at some increasing and strictly convex cost $c_i(s_i)$, shift an amount of taxable profits s_i to the other country (the assumption being that it has unmodeled taxable income arising there to which it can add or subtract). Country i levies both a source-based tax t_i on the real capital located there and a profit tax T_i on output $f_i(k_i)$ net of profits shifted abroad, financing costs ρk_i, and the source-based tax. With all investment-related costs deductible, T_i is effectively a tax on rents, so that this structure[37] captures two core components of the corporate tax discussed in Section 2.1.1. The after-tax profits of the multinational located in 1 are thus

$$\Pi_1 = (1 - T_1)\{f_1(k_1) - \rho k_1 - t_1 k_1\} + (T_1 - T_2)s_1 - c_1(s_1) \qquad (31)$$

---

[36] A result that is sometimes invoked too loosely: such a country should, if it can, impose a residence-based tax on capital, and will wish to impose a source-based tax if full credit for that payment is given in the residence country of foreign investors (a major consideration, in practice, for many developing countries).

[37] The assumptions that the source-based tax is deductible against the profit tax, and the costs of profit-shifting are not are inessential.

with the net return ρ taken as given by the multinationals but determined in equilibrium, as in ZMW, so as to clear the global capital market; and the tax revenue collected in country 1 is

$$r_1 = T_1\{f_1(k_1) - \rho k_1 - s_1\} + (1 - T_1)t_1 k_1 + T_1 s_2, \tag{32}$$

the final term reflecting revenue raised from profits shifted in by the multinational head-quartered in country 2.

Maximizing in (31), the multinational headquartered in country 1 shifts an amount of profit such that

$$c_1'(s_1) = T_1 - T_2 \tag{33}$$

and invests to the point at which

$$f_1'(k_1) - t_1 = \rho. \tag{34}$$

In terms of behavioral impact, there is thus a simple dichotomy of effects: the extent of profit-shifting depends only on the difference in rates of rent taxation (reminiscent of (23) in the KK case), while the allocation of capital depends only on the difference in effective rates of source-based taxation.

For policy-making, however, there is no such simplifying decoupling of the two tax instruments. In considering acting on profit-shifting by changing the rate of its rent tax, for instance, a country needs to be mindful that although this does not affect the real capital employed there, it does affect the revenue it collects on the earnings generated by that capital. The interactions between the tax instruments, both within and across countries, become complex, and are not discussed here.[38] One lesson worth noting, however, is that it is no longer the case that a small country with access to a rent tax would not wish to impose a source-based tax: it generally will, to provide some safeguard against the erosion of its ability to tax those rents as a consequence of profit-shifting.

2.5. Vertical Externalities and the Strategic Role of Internal Governance Structure

The analysis so far has abstracted from the complex multiplayer decision-making process generating national tax policy choices, treating these decisions as if they were made by single players acting in the interest of their citizens. In fact, many countries have multilayered governance systems, with each layer of government imposing taxes with (explicitly or implicitly)[39] partially overlapping tax bases and, often, systems of intergovernmental grants. This internal architecture can have significant effects on the tax competition games played both within and between countries.

---

[38] Devereux et al. (2008) discuss these, and optimal tax rates, in some detail for symmetric countries.

[39] The overlap is obvious when, for example, central and lower level governments both tax corporate income; but can also arise, for example, when the central government imposes a VAT and lower levels some form of wage tax, since in economic terms the bases of the two taxes are very similar.

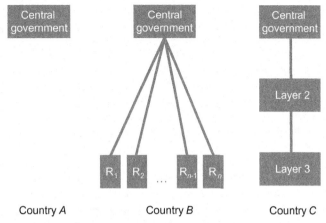

Figure 6 Different prototypes of governance.

To illustrate this, Figure 6 shows three prototype countries with very different federal structures. Country A is fully centralized, all choices about tax rates and the tax system being made at the most central level; it resembles most closely the type of player usually considered in the context of tax competition, as elsewhere in this survey. Country B has one central government and a considerable number of regional governments R_i, with capital horizontally mobile between them. Country C has several vertically related governments, all drawing on the same national tax base, but no horizontal competition between regions inside the country. The "vertical" tax competition induced by these layers of government would generally be expected to lead to inefficiently high tax rates, as more decision makers independently extract tax revenue from the same tax base: in considering an increase in its own tax rate, each level is likely to take account of the consequent contraction of the tax base, but attach relatively little weight to the losses that this also implies for other levels. (The point is especially clear when policy makers at each level are simple revenue-maximizers, in which case, as first noted by Flowers (1988), combined tax rates in the Nash equilibrium may be beyond the peak of the Laffer curve.)

Consider country B more carefully. Suppose the central and local governments each independently choose a unit tax on capital at source. The capital that is applied in region i will then be taxed by both the central and the local government. In each region, these unit taxes add to the total tax burden on capital in the respective region. The tax rate choice of the central government will presumably be guided by the preferences of the citizens in all regions. The regions, however, are likely to focus more narrowly on the well-being of their own citizens. One aspect of the problem they face is the potential for their tax choices to induce capital to move into, or from, other regions: this "horizontal" tax competition is of essentially the same form as discussed above. But there is another set of constraints arising from the vertical relation between regional and central governments. In making their rate decisions, while the regional governments presumably anticipate some tax base deterioration or other distortions that will diminish the revenue accruing to the central level, since they do not receive all the benefit of that revenue they will attribute too low a shadow price to it. Also, the double taxation of the same tax base by the different layers of government may cause an aggregate tax burden in country B that is too high. These effects of vertical tax competition and their interaction with horizontal tax competition between regions and between nations—especially the question of whether tax rates will ultimately be too low or too high—have been quite extensively analyzed (see Keen & Kotsogiannis, 2002, 2004; Wrede, 1999).

Within federations, particularly if regions have some tax autonomy, there are often systems of interregional or vertical intergovernmental transfer systems in place. An analysis of these transfer arrangements can lead to policy conclusions about the disincentive of tax enforcement they can create in the different regions, and to other negative incentive effects of such systems. It is therefore interesting to note that horizontal and vertical transfer systems inside a federal country can and partially do counterbalance the internal forces of vertical and horizontal tax competition inside this federation and can partially correct for the problems caused by interregional or vertical tax competition (see, for instance, Fenge & Wrede, 2007; Kelders & Koethenbuerger, 2010; Kotsogiannis, 2010).

These aspects of domestic fiscal architecture can have strategic implications for international tax competition too. For instance, due to the presence of vertical externalities and absence of horizontal tax externalities, a country of type C with revenue maximizing layers of government has a tendency to choose a higher tax rate on capital than would a country of type A, when competing with each other. This remains the case in a framework with international tax competition between countries of types A and C. The internal governance structure of a country has strategic effects, affecting the tax rate choices in the country. As the internal governance structure of a country affects its tax choices, it can change equilibrium choices in other countries and create further strategic considerations. Wilson and Janeba (2005) and Kessing, Konrad, and Kotsogiannis (2009) highlight this point. Due to this strategic effect, a structure that induces vertical tax competition can be advantageous or disadvantageous. As the choice of governance structure is a long-term decision and cannot be adjusted in the short run as easily as the tax rate, the governance structure could be used as a commitment device by which countries can position themselves in a framework of international tax competition. More independent vertical tiers of governance may lead to higher effective tax rates, the anticipation of which will induce other countries—provided that tax rates are strategic complements—to also choose higher tax rates. This strategic effect is similar to the commitment of a Stackelberg leader and can be a similar source of benefit. However, this advantage becomes small when faced with many competitors, smaller than the negative side effect of deviating from what would have been the tax rate chosen from the perspective of unitary state. Hence, if the number of competitors of the country is sufficiently large, the overall effect will typically work to the disadvantage of this country in the context of capital taxation at source.

3. COORDINATION

It is clear from the analysis above that the tax rate choice of one country can have several external effects on other countries. First, a higher tax rate in one country typically drives capital into other countries. This "tax base" effect benefits these other countries by broadening their capital tax base and so increasing their tax revenues. Second, the inflow of capital abroad leads to an expansion of production there, which may also be to their benefit. Third, an increase in any country's tax rate reduces the net return on capital, imposing a burden on all capital owners, not just its own citizens but those abroad too. Generically, these different external effects do not cancel each other out, and so the tax competition equilibrium can be expected to be inefficient.

In general, there will be a whole range of tax combinations $(t_1, t_2, \ldots, t_n)$ that are Pareto-superior to the non-cooperative equilibrium. If countries could negotiate a cooperative outcome, they would be expected to arrive at one in the core, which will depend, inter alia, on whether or not international transfers are feasible. More generally, if the decentralized solution suffers from externalities between the players, it generically holds that an appropriately chosen central planner's solution exists that yields strictly higher welfare in every country, relative to the decentralized outcome. But the central planner solution is a Nirvana outcome, demanding more than one can reasonably expect. For instance, it requires the absence of problems of asymmetric information and it typically requires full commitment—that is, the ability to write and implement fully binding contracts on all matters of relevance. It also requires that these contracts be written prior to any possible unilateral action by which a single player can tilt the cooperative outcome in their own favor. In an international context, with sovereign countries being the decision makers, full commitment and its enforcement is probably the most serious hurdle—even treaties can be undermined or abrogated—but information problems can also be an obstacle; and transfers between players, though clearly present in international settings, are hard to envisage in the present context (politicians likely finding it hard to explain, for instance, the case for paying another country to increase its tax rate). The question is whether, and if so exactly how, countries may coordinate their tax policies in order to overcome these inefficiencies.

When countries are identical, and can commit over a full range of instruments and time periods, it is straightforward—in principle at least—to identify Pareto-improving forms of coordination. In both the ZMW (as seen) and KK (as readily shown) models, for example, all countries benefit, relative to the Nash equilibrium from a small, common increase in tax rates. Matters are far more complex, however, when—as is manifestly the most relevant practical case—the preconditions at the start of this paragraph fail.

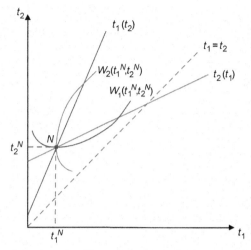

Figure 7 Asymmetries and the dangers of harmonization in the linear model.

3.1. Asymmetries and the Limits of Harmonization

Harmonization, particularly to some average of non-cooperative tax rates, seems to have a natural appeal to policy makers as a response to tax-induced movements of tax base.[40] It is inherently flawed, of course, as a response to problems of tax competition in its neglect of overall levels of taxation: with symmetric countries, tax rates are expected to be spontaneously harmonized, but there are still gains from coordination.

Asymmetries create further difficulties for a strategy of harmonization. Returning to the linear case of the ZMW model in Section 2.1.1 above, for instance, Figure 7 shows the outcome in which country 1 has a higher capital endowment, per unit of labor than country 2, and so sets a lower tax rate in equilibrium. In such a case it may be, as drawn, that there is simply no harmonized tax rate $\tau = t_1 = t_2$ at which both countries are better off than at the Nash equilibrium. The point emerges still more clearly in the KK model. In this case, the smaller country (1, say) is sure to be made worse off by harmonization to any tax rate between those of the Nash equilibrium, because its revenue is then

$$r_1(\tau, \tau) \leq r_1(t_2^N, t_2^N) < r_1(t_1(t_2^N), t_2^N) = r_1(t_1^N, t_2^N), \tag{35}$$

where the first inequality reflects the fixity of the national base and the second the definition of a best response.

3.2. Minimum Tax Rates

As one possible limitation on the amount of cooperation, countries may be unable to harmonize on common tax rates but able to agree on a range within which rates must lie.

---

[40] Harmonization of this kind (both from Nash equilibria and more generally) has been a particular focus of the literature on commodity tax competition: see, for instance, the review in Keen (2001).

One leading example of such type of limited cooperation is agreement on minimum tax rates; as with, for example, the agreement in the West African Economic and Monetary Union of a minimum corporate tax rate of 25% and on minimum rates of excise duty both there and in the EU. Lower (and/or upper) limits for possible tax rate choices leave countries some flexibility to react to structural or macroeconomic developments, or to changes in their shadow price of public funds, which may be more appealing for the countries' decision makers than a fully rigid system of coordinated taxes that can be changed and adjusted to their needs only by renegotiation (especially when, as in the EU, this requires the unanimous approval of all participating countries).

It might seem that the adoption of such minimum taxes must make those countries that are consequently forced to raise their tax rates worse off. This, however, is not the case: lower (or upper) bounds on tax rates can have surprising consequences for welfare in the resulting tax competition equilibrium.

Starting from an asymmetric Nash equilibrium N with (t_1^N, t_2^N) in the fully uncoordinated situation with $t_1^N < t_2^N$, a common lower bound of $t_i = t_0 < t_1^N$ has no impact given simultaneous rate setting (a less trivial observation than it may appear, as will become clear later). A bound t_0 in the interval (t_1^N, t_2^N) between the two Nash equilibrium rates, generally binds country 1 and typically induces it to choose this lower bound. This is illustrated in Figure 8, where the kink in the new best reply function of the low tax country $t_1(t_2)$ reflects the prohibition on setting a rate below t_0. For the same reason, the best response $t_2(t_1)$ for country 2 also acquires a kink, but in a range that is irrelevant for the equilibrium. The change of t_1 from t_1^N to t_0, taken in isolation, would benefit

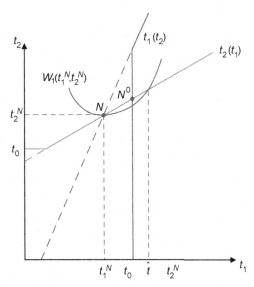

Figure 8 A lower bound on tax rates.

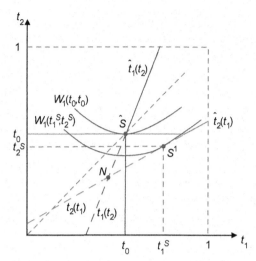

Figure 9 Effects of a binding minimum tax in a Stackelberg equilibrium.

the high tax country 2, but would reduce welfare in the low tax country 1. Country 2, however, will not continue to choose t_2^N in the new equilibrium. Using the Nash equilibrium conjecture $t_1 = t_0$, it will choose its optimal reply $t_2(t_0)$. Assuming strategic complementarity, this means a tax rate higher than t_2^N. This change can be beneficial for both countries. With the new equilibrium at N^0, the overall welfare effect for country 1, compared to the unconstrained Nash equilibrium, is in general unclear.

Consider, though, a marginal increase in t_1 from its level in the unconstrained Nash equilibrium, t_1^N, to the very slightly higher level $t_0 = t_1^N + \varepsilon$. This has a zero first-order effect for the welfare of country 1, as $W_1(t_1^N, t_2^N)$ has a slope of zero at N. But it induces an equilibrium reaction by country 2, which increases its tax rate t_2 by ε times the slope of $t_2(t_1)$. This increase in t_2 does have a first-order marginal effect for country 1's welfare, and it is beneficial. Thus agreement on a minimum tax rate that is above but sufficiently close to the lower of the unconstrained Nash equilibrium rates t_1^N is Pareto improving. In Figure 8, both countries gain if N_0, on the upper right of N, is to the left of the tax rate $\hat{t}$ at which $t_2(t_1)$ and $W_1(t_1^N, t_2^N)$ intersect: any minimum rate $t_0 \in (t_1^N, \hat{t})$ induces an increase in both countries' welfare, whereas lower bounds in the higher range $t_0 \in (\hat{t}, t_2^N)$ make the low tax country 1 worse off.[41]

Matters are quite different when countries choose sequentially. Wang (1999) addresses this case in the KK model, but the same insights can be seen using the linear model illustrated in Figure 9. Focusing on the asymmetric case and taking the larger country 1 to be the Stackelberg leader, the initial equilibrium in the absence of any minimum taxes is at

---

[41] Peralta and van Ypersele (2006) show, however, that this result need not hold more generally in related models. In their framework with three countries, a minimum tax rate may not make all countries better off, whereas a combination of a lower and an upper bound might.

S^1, the point of tangency between country 1's iso-welfare curve $W_1(t_1^s, t_2^s)$ and country 2's reply function, which has $t_1^s > t_2^s$. Now imposing a minimum tax rate t_0 between the two initial equilibrium rates $(t_1^s > t_0 > t_2^s)$ may cause the tax rate of the Stackelberg leader to fall and, for a broad range of parameters and under quite general conditions, lead to higher welfare for the leader and lower welfare for the follower. Figure 9 illustrates. Here a minimum tax t_0 that is slightly higher than t_2^s leads to kinked reply functions $\hat{t}_1(t_2)$ and $\hat{t}_2(t_1)$, just as above. When country 1 chooses its most preferred point (t_1, t_2) along the reply function $\hat{t}_2(t_1)$ of country 2, subject to the constraint $t_1 \geq t_0$, it selects $\hat{S}$. The Stackelberg leader thus chooses a tax rate that is considerably lower than its choice in the initial equilibrium t_1^s, with the effect, as Figure 9 suggests, that the leader is better-off, but the follower may be worse off, than in the unconstrained Stackelberg equilibrium. Setting such a low rate was not attractive to the leader in the absence of the minimum tax rate, because the follower would react to such a choice by an even lower tax. The minimum tax prevents such a reaction, making $t_1 = t_0$ attractive for the Stackelberg leader. Had the Ruding Committee proposal of a 30% minimum tax rate been adopted, for instance, EU members setting a higher rate could have reduced their rate secure in the knowledge that no other country would undercut them by going below 30%.

Konrad (2009) goes one step further and considers a minimum rate $t_0 < t_2^s$: a minimum, that is, below the lower of the two tax rates chosen in the unconstrained equilibrium. One might expect this to have no effect. But, in the Stackelberg case, even such seemingly unconstraining floors change the nature of the equilibrium and may induce all countries to reduce their tax rates. The reason for this can be seen in Figure 10, which is similar to Figure 9. With a lower bound of t_0, the reply functions $\hat{t}_1(t_2)$ and $\hat{t}_2(t_1)$

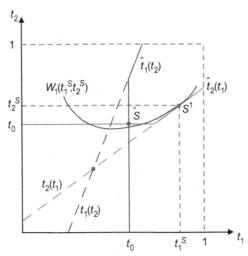

Figure 10 Effects of a minimum tax that is lower than the lowest equilibrium tax rate in the Stackelberg equilibrium.

are drawn as closed lines, kinked as above at this very low minimum. Now $\hat{S}$ is the new equilibrium, yielding an increased payoff for country 1 and a reduced payoff for country 2. Both countries thus switch to setting their rate at the minimum permissible level even though, in the initial equilibrium, both rates were higher than that. The intuition is essentially as above: without a floor, the leader refrains from setting $\hat{t}_1 = t_0$ because this would induce the follower to choose a very low tax rate chosen by country 2 in the unconstrained situation, but the imposition of the minimum cuts off this possibility. What is striking is that the same intuition continues to apply even for non-binding minima.

These are surprising results. But they also call for some caution in drawing policy conclusions, showing that such a straightforward and central policy idea as imposing a minimum rate can (but need not) lead to a Pareto improvement depending on the precise nature of the strategic interaction in tax-setting.

3.3. Coordination Among a Subset of Countries

A simultaneous coordination of all countries is hard to envisage if there is no supra-national agency that could enforce such an agreement. However, supra-national structures such as the European Union may enable their members to commit to joint action. But is it in the interest of subsets of countries to coordinate only among themselves? Non-participating countries' equilibrium tax rates may then well be different from those they set in the fully non-cooperative Nash equilibrium. So even though participating countries can benefit from joint action in the absence of such strategic effects on non-participants (they can at least not do worse), it is not clear whether or not, once those effects come into play, the overall outcome of this coordinated action will be beneficial for them. The issue, it should be stressed, is a very real one for the several regional blocs facing the question of whether some degree of coordination toward higher taxation would be to their advantage or would simply make them more vulnerable to tax competition from non-participating countries.[42]

This problem has been addressed formally by Burbidge et al. (1997) and Konrad and Schjelderup (1999). The latter addressed the general question in a modified version of the reaction curve figure above, now with three countries. Suppose that the symmetric Nash equilibrium in pure strategies exists and denote the uniform equilibrium tax rate $t_1 = t_2 = t_3 = t^N$. Could countries 1 and 2 gain if, rather than maximizing their own welfare individually and finding themselves in this Nash equilibrium, they join forces and credibly and publicly agree on choosing a common tax rate $t_1 = t_2 \equiv t_A$ that maximizes their joint welfare $W_A \equiv W_1 + W_2$, where W_i is as in (4) above?

---

[42] Related issues emerge in the context of customs unions and in the literature on coalition formation more generally. The members of a customs union can choose their tariffs and compensation payments in order to improve their joint welfare. However, the formation of the customs union affects trade relationships with non-members (see Panagariya (2000) for a survey).

A first question is whether they can increase their welfare by both choosing a slightly higher tax rate, assuming first that country 3 still chooses $t_3 = t^N$. That they can follows on differentiating their aggregate welfare at $(t_1, t_2, t_3) = (t^N, t^N, t^N)$ to find

$$\frac{\partial(W_1 + W_2)}{\partial t_A} = \frac{\partial(W_1 + W_2)}{\partial t_1} + \frac{\partial(W_1 + W_2)}{\partial t_2} = \frac{\partial W_2}{\partial t_1} + \frac{\partial W_1}{\partial t_2} > 0, \qquad (36)$$

where use is made of the first-order conditions $\partial W_i / \partial t_i = 0$. Intuitively, if both countries 1 and 2 slightly increase their tax rate starting at the non-cooperative Nash equilibrium, the direct first-order effect of the increase in their own tax rate on their own welfare is zero because the deviation occurs at the local optimum. However, each country enjoys a first-order gain from the increase in the other's tax rate, due to the tax-base effect. The non-participating country 3 gains even more, since it benefits from the base effect from the increased tax rates in two countries, not just one.

But country 3 is unlikely to continue to set $t_3 = t^N$ given the higher rate set elsewhere. The new equilibrium is obtained as a set of taxes (t_A, t_A, t_3) that fulfills two conditions. First, given country 3's Nash conjecture that countries 1 and 2 both choose t_A, country 3 chooses the t_3 that maximizes $W_3(t_A, t_A, t)$. Second, the joint tax rate t_A is the argument $t \in (0, 1)$ that maximizes the sum of $W_1(t, t, t_3) + W_2(t, t, t_3)$ given the Nash conjecture about t_3. Whether or not the coordinated choice of countries 1 and 2 improves their joint welfare in the new equilibrium will crucially depend on the new equilibrium value of t_3. However, if tax rates are strategic complements, the optimal reply of country 3 to the conjectured $t_1 = t_2 = t_A > t^N$ is a choice of $t_3 > t^N$. This higher tax rate typically benefits countries 1 and 2, so that the overall welfare effect for countries 1 and 2 of their coordinated tax increase is positive in this case. Indeed it is greater with the strategic response of country 3 than it would be without. This analysis can easily be extended to more than three symmetric countries, with a subset of these partially coordinating.

These implications of regional cooperation have a parallel in work on the merger of m firms in an oligopoly with $n > m$ firms and price competition (see Deneckere & Davidson, 1985). Merger of firms in this context means that they maximize their joint profits by a coordinated choice of their prices. If the prices of all firms are strategic complements, the merging firms typically choose higher prices. The strategic effect of this increase on bystanding firms is that they also increase their prices. Overall, the merger increases the profits of all firms.

Aspects of regional tax coordination are explored in several other studies. Conconi, Perroni, and Riezman (2008) essentially analyze coordination by subsets of countries in a context combining downward pressure on tax rates from tax competition and upward pressure due to time consistent confiscatory taxation. Coordination by a suitably chosen subgroup may be used to find the right balance for this trade-off. Haufler and Wooton (2006) apply a related logic in a competition for direct investment. Sørensen (2004a) explores a similar logic (as do Burbidge et al., 1997), focusing on the amount of redistributive taxation, rather than on the provision of public goods and providing numerical simulations of the welfare effects (compared to fully uncoordinated tax competition) of regional (subgroup) rather than global coordination. These suggest that the beneficial effect of coordination among a subset of all countries is small relative to the benefit for the country that is not part of the coordinating subgroup. Simulation results with a similar flavor which allow for asymmetries between the countries are presented in Parry (2003), Brochner et al. (2007), and Vrijburg and de Mooij (2010) highlight the importance of asymmetries between countries. Strategic complementarity of tax rates cannot be taken for granted in this case, and it is then no longer certain that the alliance partners 1 and 2 benefit from their cooperation.

Burbidge et al. (1997) also address the question of which subgroup of countries may enter into a tax alliance if this choice is endogenous. If there are $n > 2$ symmetric countries, for instance, the formation of a subgroup of 2 typically is a Pareto improvement relative to no group formation at all. But the gains to those in the subgroup are typically smaller than those of outsiders—so which countries, if any, would voluntarily join such a subgroup? Moreover, an enlargement of the participating group from $n - 1$ to n, or what could be called the "grand tax alliance," is typically not a Pareto improvement. Understanding how and which subgroups might form becomes a challenging theoretical question. In the case of Europe and potentially other supra-national entities, the set of candidate countries that may enter into a regional coordination agreement is given exogenously or has been determined by other factors outside the context of the tax competition problem.

3.4. Coordination Across a Subset of Instruments

As stressed earlier, countries generally have more than one tax instrument to deploy. Partial coordination in such contexts can mean that all countries agree on restrictions as regards some but not all of their instruments. Keen and Marchand (1997), for instance, consider coordination of tax rates in a framework in which countries can continue to compete along another dimension, which is their decision about infrastructure investment, and which works like an input subsidy; and Fuest and Huber (1999) consider a framework with multiple tax or subsidy instruments.

The key lessons in such contexts are straightforward. When countries have several policy instruments, some may be redundant, in that coordinated action that fixes the value of one instrument at some level can be undone by changes in the other instruments. And if the instruments available are only imperfect substitutes, coordinated action that constrains the value of one may lead to a substitute instrument being used more aggressively as a tool of competition. In Keen and Marchand (1997), for instance, coordination on higher capital tax rates may lead countries to distort their public spending patterns towards infrastructure and other items that raise the productivity of, and so tend to attract, mobile capital, and away from items that contribute directly to private welfare. The final effect of such distortions may be a Pareto-worsening relative to the non-cooperative outcome. Cremer and Gavhari (2000), for instance, consider a KK-type setting in which welfare-maximizing governments choose both a statutory rate of tax and the intensity with which it is enforced by auditing firms to detect evasion: a lower audit probability then has effects very similar to a reduction in the statutory rate (a possibility not without echoes in actual practice). Setting a common tax rate may—but need not (this depends on values of parameters and the harmonized tax rate)—lead to such a reduction in enforcement activities that, ultimately, both countries are worse off.

3.5. Dynamic Aspects

Tax competition takes place, in practice, in a dynamic framework. This has several implications. Where there is an unknown, possibly unending series of choices, the theory of infinitely repeated games becomes relevant. A second aspect of these dynamics is that decisions are made sequentially. Some early decisions may generate stock effects that determine the environment in which later decisions take place. Today's capital stock is the result of earlier decisions on savings and consumption, and this may generate time consistency problems for the optimal tax policy that interact with the effects of tax competition. A third aspect is the relationship between stocks and flows and the trade-off between taxing stocks and attracting an inflow of new capital. We consider these three aspects in turn.

3.5.1. Infinitely Repeated Interaction

Tax laws change from time to time, and there is no reason for an end to this process. This makes the folk theorems of infinitely repeated games potentially relevant in thinking about tax competition. One question is whether the benefits of coordination or tax harmonization can be obtained in a fully non-cooperative game due to the infinite repetition. Analyses of this problem are given in Cardarelli, Taugourdeau, and Vidal (2002), Catenaro and Vidal (2006), Kessing, Konrad, and Kotsogiannis (2006), and Kiss (2012). The last of these considers a symmetric setup with n countries and uses simple trigger strategies to generate efficient tax harmonization as a non-cooperative equilibrium outcome. The most striking point that emerges, however, is that in this setting introducing a minimum tax rate that is higher than that in the static Nash equilibrium may destabilize an existing efficient equilibrium.

The following multiperiod version of the workhorse model with two countries illustrates why. Generalizing it to an infinitely repeated game with the static game as a state game, the local strategies of countries in a given period $h = 0, 1, \ldots$ are their tax rate choices t_1^h and t_2^h which may generally be functions of the whole history. Let $W_i(t_1^h, t_2^h)$ be the period payoff of country i in period h if the tax rates are t_1^h and t_2^h in that period, and let

$$\sum_{h=k}^{\infty} \delta^h W_i(t_1^h, t_2^h) \tag{37}$$

be the discounted present value of payoffs for all periods from period k on that emerge from a series of tax rate choices $(t_1^k, t_2^k), (t_1^{k+1}, t_2^{k+1}), \ldots$, with δ a discount factor that is invariant over time and the same for both countries. Further, denote by (t^N, t^N) the static symmetric Nash equilibrium tax rates, and by (t^0, t^0) the efficient tax rates that implement the symmetric first-best Pareto optimum. Suppose both countries follow the simple local strategy of choosing t^0 in the first period and then, for all further periods, choosing t^0 if both players chose t^0 in the previous period but t^N if one did not. These strategies constitute an equilibrium with $(t_1^h, t_2^h) = (t^0, t^0)$ for all $h = 0, 1, \ldots$, if the condition

$$\sum_{h=0}^{\infty} \delta^h W_i(t^0, t^0) \geq W_i(t_i(t^0), t^0) + \sum_{h=1}^{\infty} \delta^h W_i(t^N, t^N) \tag{38}$$

is fulfilled, where $t_i(t^0)$ is the tax rate that maximizes i's period payoff given the choice of t^0 by the other country. The left-hand side of (38) is the present value of the sum of all payoffs of country i if both countries choose the efficient taxes t^0 forever. The right-hand side consists of two terms. The first is the period payoff if country i chooses the optimal deviation tax rate $t_i(t^0)$ that maximizes its period payoff. The second term is the present value of the sum of all payoffs from all future periods, in which both countries choose the tax t^N that characterizes the static non-cooperative Nash equilibrium. So if (38) holds, both countries prefer to stick to t^0 rather than to defect; this will be the case if they are sufficiently patient, in the sense that the discount factor δ is above some critical value. Note that in this equilibrium $t^N < t_i(t^0) < t^0$, which is a consequence of the assumed strategic complementarity of the tax rates.

Suppose now that countries enter into a binding agreement in period 0 which states that none of them will ever set a tax rate lower than some t_{min}, with $t_{min} \in (t^N, t_i(t^0))$. This changes the equilibrium of the static game, since the Nash equilibrium (t^N, t^N) is no longer feasible. Instead, reversion to the static non-cooperative Nash equilibrium will imply that the countries both choose t_{min}. The condition for an equilibrium with sustained cooperation thus becomes

$$\sum_{h=0}^{\infty} \delta^h W_i(t^0, t^0) \geq W_i(t_i(t^0), t^0) + \sum_{h=1}^{\infty} \delta^h W_i(t_{min}, t_{min}). \tag{39}$$

All that has changed, compared to (38), is that reversion to the static Nash equilibrium is now less harmful for the two countries since it yields a present value of the discounted sum of period payoffs $W_i(t_{min}, t_{min}) > W_i(t^N, t^N)$. Accordingly, if a country deviates from

t^0, its immediate gain is the same as without a minimum tax, but the present value of future payoffs does not drop by as much. With the costs of deviating reduced by adoption of the minimum, sustaining the efficient outcome becomes less likely: the critical level of the discount factor above which it can be sustained is increased.

This result is an application of the "topsy-turvy principle" from industrial organization: an institutional change that causes an improvement for the static non-cooperative Nash equilibrium may be harmful for the stabilization of collusive outcomes in infinitely repeated games. This is because such a change reduces the punishment that players experience in future periods if they defect from the collusive path.

3.5.2. Endogenous Savings and Time Consistent Taxation

So far, we have considered the world capital stock to be exogenous. In a dynamic perspective, however, the current capital stock is the outcome of consumption and savings choices made in earlier periods. The implications for international capital taxation have been explored (Gordon, 1986). A simple strategic setting can be used to analyze optimal and time consistent tax choices of symmetric, equally sized countries $i = 1, 2, \ldots, n$ in a dynamic framework with two periods, 0 and 1. This is a natural extension of the workhorse model and a simplified version of the two-period framework analyzed by Huizinga (1995). In each country, a (representative) individual is born in period 0 with an endowment κ and decides how much to save ($\bar{k}_i$, this becoming, as the notation suggests, the endowment of the next period) and how much to consume ($\kappa - \bar{k}_i$) in that period. At the beginning of period 1, the sum of these savings $\sum_i \bar{k}_i$ determines the world capital stock; the period 1 economy is very similar to that in the static workhorse model. International capital market clearing requires

$$\sum_i \bar{k}_i = \sum_i k_i \tag{40}$$

and, as before,

$$\rho = f'(k_i) - t_i \text{ for all } \quad i = 1, \ldots, n. \tag{41}$$

The public good is produced and used only in period 1. Assuming additively separable period utilities with increasing and concave consumption utility $u(\kappa - \bar{k}_i)$ in period 0, the objective function of a welfarist government is

$$W_i = u(\kappa - \bar{k}_i) + f(k_i) - f'(k_i)k_i + \rho\bar{k}_i + G_i(t_i k_i). \tag{42}$$

The first component here is the utility of period 0 consumption of private goods. The second is the utility of private consumption in period 1, the assumed quasi-linearity sterilizing the analysis with respect to income effects. This private consumption is equal to output net of the remuneration of capital used in the country plus citizens' net-of-tax capital income. The third component is $G_i(t_i k_i)$, utility from the public good that is produced from the tax revenue $t_i k_i$; this is assumed to take the same linear form as in (17) above.

Before analyzing the equilibrium outcome for $n > 1$, we discuss two benchmark outcomes for $n = 1$. This reduces the problem to a special case of the analysis of Kydland and Prescott (1980) which they used to show the pitfalls of time consistent capital taxation. Suppose first that the government can commit to the tax rate it will set in period 1. Taking as given the tax rate credibly announced by the government in period 0, the representative individual chooses savings according to

$$u'(\kappa - \bar{k}_1) = f'(\bar{k}_1) - t_1, \tag{43}$$

use being made here of $k_1 = \bar{k}_1$ for $n = 1$. This first-order condition implies that $\bar{k}_1$ is a decreasing function of t_1. The government takes this relationship $\bar{k}_1(t_1)$ into consideration when choosing the t_1 that it will commit to, the first-order condition for which leads to

$$1 + \lambda = \frac{1}{1 + \frac{t_1}{\bar{k}_1} \frac{\partial \bar{k}_1}{\partial t_1}}, \tag{44}$$

an elasticity rule that just balances the benefit of additional public good against the marginal excess burden from the distortion of the consumption-savings decision. Typically, this condition singles out one tax rate that induces the second-best optimal amount of savings.

Difficulty arises, however, if the government cannot commit to the tax rate. For once the individual savings decisions have been made, $\bar{k}_1$ becomes exogenous and fixed, so that the marginal welfare cost of taxing capital is no longer $1 + \lambda$ but is instead unity: taxing the fixed capital as lump sum. A welfare-maximizing government able to set whatever tax rate it likes in period 1 will find, assuming that a unit tax exceeding full expropriation is not feasible, that the welfare optimum is attained either at $t_1 = 1$ if $\bar{k}_1 < \bar{G}$, or at t_1 that solves $t_1 \bar{k}_1 = \bar{G}$ if $\bar{k}_1 > \bar{G}$. But this high tax rate will be anticipated by the individuals already in period 0 and its anticipation will generally discourage savings. Even though the ex-post optimal tax does not change the capital stock when it is introduced, its anticipation imposes an excess burden. In particular, in an economy in which aggregate savings are formed by many individuals, there is typically an equilibrium in which $\bar{k}_1 = 0$. Ex-post optimal taxation leads to excessive taxation in the single economy.

Return now to $n > 1$. As has been shown in the benchmark analysis, tax competition has a tendency to drive down tax rate levels. Kehoe (1989) argued that this effect may be desirable when the government cannot credibly commit on a capital tax early on, and suffers from the Kydland and Prescott (1980) time consistency just described. If we open up tax competition between a set of such identical economies of the kind just described, this will drive equilibrium tax rates below these excessive levels. But can tax competition without commitment lead to the same equilibrium outcome as the optimal ex-ante program of capital taxation with commitment?[43]

The answer is: possibly, but the outcome is generically still inefficient. To see that efficiency may be restored, consider first the downward sloping function $\bar{k}_1(t_1)$. For the solitary economy, denote the ex-ante optimal tax rate with commitment by t^p, and the corresponding savings by $\bar{k}^p$. Now turn to the case of n symmetric, identical countries with tax competition and tax rates chosen at the beginning of period 1. Suppose that the citizens in each of these countries expect the tax rate that will be chosen at the beginning of period 1 will be t^p. Then, there is indeed an equilibrium in which the individually optimal consumption choices in period 0 induce savings in each country equal to $\bar{k}^p$.

But is there a symmetric Nash equilibrium in the tax competition game that really induces t^p as the tax rate? Note that the situation in period 1 is essentially the same as in the static tax competition problem that has been solved in the benchmark case, with capital endowments $\bar{k}_i = \bar{k}^p$ in each of the n countries. For this $\bar{k}^p$ to be induced by optimal ex-post taxation, the elasticity formula (13) (replacing G' by $(1 + \lambda)$) implies that the corresponding tax rate t^N must satisfy

$$1 + \lambda = \frac{1}{1 + \dfrac{t^N}{\bar{k}^p}\left(\dfrac{n-1}{n}\right)\dfrac{1}{f''(\bar{k}^p)}}. \tag{45}$$

This typically has one solution $t^N(\bar{k}^p, n)$. If it so happens that $t^N = t^p$, then the expectations of the individuals that induced their savings of $\bar{k}^p$ were justified and tax competition can indeed implement the ex-ante efficient outcome with t^p and $\bar{k}^p$. For $n = 1$, we return to the case of excessive ex-post efficient taxation for the case of the solitary economy, with $t^N > t^p$. However, $t^N(\bar{k}^p, n)$ is a downward sloping function of n. Assuming away the indivisibility problem for n, and depending on the shape of the production function f, for sufficiently large n the solution to (45) may just be equal to t^p. In this case the forces of tax competition happen to exactly compensate for the ex-post inefficiently high incentives to confiscate capital. In general, however, this will not be so, though it remains the case that the pressure of tax competition allows the country to credibly commit to a tax rate that is lower than the high tax rate on capital that would be the time consistent solution in the solitary economy.

Kehoe's (1989) result is in the tradition of Lipsey and Lancaster (1956): distortions can reinforce or offset each other. It is only fortuitously, however, that a combination of some degree of tax competition and of time consistent capital taxation will lead to fully efficient taxation. Generically, the outcome will be inefficient. If, moreover, countries are asymmetric, it will typically be the case that the degree of tax competition that is just

---

[43] Ways to moderate this problem, other than tax competition, have also been discussed. Boadway and Keen (1998), for instance, show that commitment to a lax audit policy can reduce the ex-post tax rate that is optimal and can thereby mitigate the time consistency problem.

desirable from the perspective of one country will be suboptimal for other countries. And there is one further problem with the notion that tax competition can ease the time consistency problem in taxing capital income. It relies on the idea that the world capital stock is fixed once savings decisions are made, but this capital remains mobile internationally once it has been formed and can be shifted between the countries as a reaction to the tax rate choices. It is true that single investors can sell their assets in one country and purchase assets in another country. Capital is, hence, mobile at the level of the individual. At the aggregate country level, however, most tangible capital assets are essentially immobile and can be taxed at source.[44] (Even so, it might be argued that profit-shifting devices make taxable profits mobile, especially in relation to intangibles; as seen earlier, this though calls for a different type of analysis).

An analysis that develops a more credible mechanism but remains in the spirit of Kehoe (1989) is that of Janeba (2000), who considers a hold-up problem that essentially resembles the problem of time consistent taxation. A firm faces an exogenously given block demand. It can sell up to m units of a homogenous product for a given unit price (normalized to unity). Any additional output can be sold only at a price of zero. The firm's production technology is characterized by a capacity cost of $\gamma \in (0, 1/2)$ per unit of capacity, and zero variable cost up to the capacity limit. Suppose the firm can invest only in one location, say, country A, and let μ_A be the capacity that it chooses to build up in this country at a cost of $\gamma \mu_A$. The government of A, interested, suppose, only in tax—can levy a unit tax t_A on goods produced inside the country. It has to choose t_A at a time when the capacity investment is made, but prior to the firm's output choice. In this case the following hold-up problem emerges. The firm's quasi-rent (ignoring capacity costs), net of taxes, is $x(1 - t_A)$ for any x up to the block demand m, and $m(1 - t_A)$ at any higher output. Anticipating that the firm will maximize this quasi-rent, the government optimally chooses a t_A that equals, or is just an epsilon below, the selling price, reducing the net producer rent to zero. Anticipating this, however, the firm will not invest in capacity since it will then make a loss equal to its investment cost $\gamma \mu_A$.

Suppose now that this firm can also build up capacity μ_B in country B, also with a marginal capacity cost of γ. Governments in A and B must decide on their tax rates t_A and t_B on each unit produced in their country, and they must do so after the capacity investment is made but before the production decision. Janeba (2000) shows that the firm would then be wise to build capacity of m in both countries, giving it twice the capacity needed to cover the block demand: for then it becomes evident to each government that the firm will produce the whole quantity m in whichever country has the lower tax and nothing in the other. Countries face cutthroat competition from each other, and the

---

[44] Andersson and Konrad (2003) explore a similar approach in the context of human capital investments, and argue that the international mobility of human capital can cure the problems created by time consistent taxation of human capital that emerged in a closed economy. Unlike physical capital, human capital is mobile ex-post. It is embodied in persons, but the persons are mobile.

equilibrium tax rates they choose are $t_A = t_B = 0$. Tax competition thus removes the hold-up problem—but this does not come for free, as the firm incurs additional costs from the excess capacity it holds. And without excess capacity, the firm's threat of relocating production is empty.

3.5.3. Stock Effects and Agglomeration

In a dynamic framework there is a critical distinction between the stock of capital invested in a country, which is typically embodied in physical capital and very expensive or impossible to relocate, and the flow of additional net investment in a given period. Countries must then distinguish between two effects of raising their tax rate. A higher tax rate will generate potentially considerable revenue from the existing "old" stock of capital. But it may also discourage investors from building up new capital (Wildasin, 2003). Conversely, the choice of a low tax rate makes a country an attractive location for new investment but brings in little tax revenue in the short term.

This is the trade-off faced by a government that would like to generate a large present value of revenue from the taxation of the stock of capital in a sequence of periods. In a strategic environment, a large stock of old capital can be a disadvantage for a country that competes for new capital with other countries: it has a higher opportunity cost from a reduction in its tax rate in the ongoing period than does a country with less old capital (Janeba & Peters, 1999; Marceau, Mongrain, & Wilson, 2010). For this reason, some countries may decide to extract as much as possible from the given stock of capital invested there and leave it to other countries to attract the new investment; this can lead to capital-rich countries with high taxes and a lack of investment dynamics and young emerging countries with low taxes and dynamic investment.

There is an important countervailing force to this divergence in tax rates, however, if a large installed capital base has positive externalities for new investors. Such agglomeration advantages may make it attractive for new investment to locate in the country with the larger capital base, even if the tax rates are higher there. Baldwin and Krugman (2004) analyze the tax competition outcome in a framework with such agglomeration advantages. They show that an optimal tax policy of the country with large agglomeration advantages can be "limit taxation" (in analogy to limit pricing in competition policy): setting a tax rate that puts a strictly positive net fiscal burden on new investors but is sufficiently low such that this burden is smaller than or just equal to the benefits from joining the agglomeration, rather than investing in a competitor country without such agglomeration advantages, even if this competitor country chooses a zero tax. If this equilibrium exists, it can perpetuate agglomeration advantages.

Whether such a perpetuated equilibrium with limit taxation exists, and under which conditions the equilibrium is one with capital-rich high tax countries that exploit their existing capital and suffer from lack of new investment on the one hand and capital-poor low tax countries with strong growth on the other, is analyzed by Konrad and

Kovenock (2009). They show that both outcomes are possible and which emerges in equilibrium depends on the size of the agglomeration benefit for newly attracted capital and on the quantity of newly attracted capital compared to the stock of existing capital that cannot escape taxation. They also consider the case in which existing capital and new capital can be taxed at different rates or in which newly attracted capital receives tax holidays. In this case the agglomeration is more stable, but tax revenue is very low in the long run as there is strong competition for the newly attracted capital. Empirically, asymmetric equilibria in which one country or region chooses a high tax strategy and extracts from the existing immobile capital base while another competes for new investments have been the motivation for the analysis by Cai and Treisman (2005), who study this type of asymmetric equilibrium in Russia.

4. BROADENING THE PERSPECTIVE

The benchmark ZMW model of tax competition considers a tax base "capital" as a continuously divisible quantity that flows between countries, with these flows affecting the marginal product of capital in all of them. It describes changes in capital use at the intensive margin and assumes a perfectly competitive market for capital inside each country. From the perspective of industrial economics, countries operate much like companies that are price setters and compete with each other for aggregate demand, where this demand may be fixed (as in an oligopoly with block demand) or where aggregate demand may also react to the prices offered. From the point of view of formal structure, the main difference is the different objective function of governments which do not simply maximize tax revenue, but rather a more complex notion of national welfare. This does not exhaust all practically relevant models of competition, and some of these alternative concepts also matter in the context of tax competition. What follows discusses several other concepts. Governments may make bids for lumpy investment, trying to attract firms much like in an auction. Governments may apply the concept of "third-order tax discrimination" when they compete for tax bases with different mobility. Information exchange between countries can also be an important element of tax competition and coordination. Also geography, and proximity in particular, may play a role in shaping tax competition. All these concepts play a role in understanding the phenomenon of tax havens, which we address at the end of this section.

4.1. Bidding for Firms

Where countries compete for foreign direct investment, this is often not a competition for additional capital that is then used at the intensive margin, but for individual firms or projects: that is, it is competition at the extensive margin and makes the taxed subjects strategic players.

A number of contributions consider the bidding for firms by governments that stand to benefit from attracting them to their country. Ferrett and Wooton (2010a) provide a simple and fairly general framework of two countries bidding for one firm. They consider two countries A and B who can make bids y_A and y_B to attract a firm from the rest of the world. Let π_A and π_B be the gross profits of the firm when locating in A and B, respectively, and $\pi_A - \pi_B \geq 0$ the difference between them. Further, let w_A and w_B be some additional benefits that accrue to countries A and B, respectively, should the firm locate there. This captures the idea, commonplace among policy makers, that inward foreign direct investment conveys external benefits to the wider economy. Possible channels by which this may happen include a reduction in the per-capita cost of provision of public goods or inputs[45], increases in wage income[46], technological spillovers, and other external effects. Denoting by σ_A and σ_B the shares in the firm owned by citizens of country A and B, welfare in country i is then

$$\sigma_i(\pi_i + y_i) - y_i + w_i \text{ if the firm locates in } i \text{ and} \tag{46}$$

$$\sigma_i(\pi_{-i} + y_{-i}) \text{ if it does not.}$$

Assuming a suitable tie-breaking rule for the case in which a firm is just indifferent, one can characterize the equilibrium (y_A^*, y_B^*) as follows: The country i that loses makes a bid such that it is indifferent to losing or winning, which, from (46), is the case if

$$y_i^* = \sigma_i(\pi_i - \pi_j + y_i^* - y_j^*) + w_i. \tag{47}$$

The winning country j makes a bid that is just large enough to win against this bid, and thus bids $y_j^* = \pi_i + y_i^* - \pi_j$. Note that this latter condition implies $\pi_i - \pi_j + y_i^* - y_j^* = 0$ and hence, from (47), $y_i^* = w_i$, whereas $y_j^* = \pi_i - \pi_j + w_i$. This equilibrium has attractive features. First, it can be shown, by way of contradiction, that $\pi_j + w_j \geq \pi_i + w_i$ if country j wins the bid in this equilibrium, so that the firm allocates where it generates the higher social surplus. Second, both the bids and the equilibrium allocation are independent of the ownership shares in the firm. The reason for this is that by making a bid that is just large enough to attract the firm, that is for which $\pi_i - \pi_j + y_i - y_j = 0$, the winning country ensures that the firm's owners are just indifferent to locating the firm in A or B.

Allocative efficiency of the bidding equilibrium can be destroyed, however, by additional considerations. Kessing et al. (2009), for instance, apply a very similar auction framework with two countries making bids for a foreign direct investment. One is a unitary country with a government that has essentially the same objective function as above. The other is a federal union in which several layers of government share the tax revenue that can be collected if the investment occurs in this country. As discussed in Section 2.2, this may create a vertical fiscal externality that may lead to an excessively high tax burden

---

[45] See, for instance, Black and Hoyt (1989).
[46] Among these contributions is Haaparanta (1996).

and taxation on the downward sloping part of the Laffer curve. In addition, while the governments at the different layers share a common interest in the bidding process, they face a collective good problem when making their contributions to the country's overall bid. Vertical fiscal externalities and free-riding problems within the federal union generate a disadvantage for the federal union in a bidding competition with a unitary country.

Another set of effects derive from the dynamic nature of investments, particularly in a multiperiod framework. The analysis of King, McAfee, and Welling (1993) addresses some of these. First, the location choice of a firm may involve sunk costs and may reduce the firm's mobility, thus exposing it to a host government that may then be tempted to extract from this firm. (This is true not only if the firm becomes fully immobile, but even if some capital investment is made that is immobile or that may lose some of its value if it is relocated.) As a result, and unless there are other means to overcome this hold-up problem, governments may compensate firms for the later extraction of tax revenue by making upfront subsidies. Also, a government may invest in infrastructure in order to increase the profitability of a firm should it locate in this country. If countries cannot coordinate on such investment choices, the result may be a non-cooperative equilibrium with asymmetric investment choices in which one country invests a lot and the other country little.[47]

Bidding for firms occurs in a setup in which foreign direct investment may have a number of externalities. In similar spirit, Haufler and Wooton (1999) analyze the competition between two countries for a foreign owned monopolist and show that a large home market is advantageous if there are trade costs. The role of trade cost and market size is also important in the context of other types of imperfect competition, making this paper the starting point of a large literature exploring these effects.[48]

4.2. Preferential Regimes

In its report on Harmful Tax Competition, the OECD (1998) pays particular attention to practices by which countries may apply different tax rules to different types of business activity, typically setting a lower tax rate for more mobile activities. The presumption in the OECD work was that such "preferential regimes" aggravate the inefficiencies associated with international tax competition. But this may not be right.

To see why, broaden the benchmark two-country ZMW model to allow for two capital tax bases rather than just one. Denote the tax bases that locate in country i as k_i and κ_i, respectively, and let t_i and τ_i be the unit source-based taxes applied to each. Generally, these quantities are functions $k_i(t_i; t_{-i})$ and $\kappa_i(\tau_i; \tau_{-i})$ where, as before, $-i$ denotes the corresponding tax rate in the other country. Tax revenue in country i is thus

$$T_i = t_i k_i(t_i; t_{-i}) + \tau_i \kappa_i(\tau_i; \tau_{-i}). \tag{48}$$

---

[47] An elegant way to overcome the problem of opportunistic behavior of the host government ex-post is offered by Janeba (2000), as discussed above.

[48] That literature includes Raff (2004), Bjorvatn and Eckel (2006), Ferrett and Wooton (2010b), Becker and Fuest (2010b), and Haufler and Wooton (2010).

A first and straightforward observation is that if the (semi-) elasticities of the two bases differ then, given any fixed tax policy of the other country, it is always possible to strictly increase tax revenue by appropriate rate differentiation. To see this, focusing on situations in which first-order conditions describe optimized choices and there is an interior equilibrium, note that if country i must tax both tax bases at the same uniform rate $t_i = \tau_i = z_i$ then, maximizing in (48), it will choose that rate so that

$$k_i + z_i \frac{\partial k_i}{\partial t_i} + \kappa_i + z_i \frac{\partial \kappa_i}{\partial \tau_i} = 0, \tag{49}$$

where the optimal uniform rate is thus the inverse of a weighted average of the semi-elasticities of the two bases. When the two bases can be taxed differentially, however, the first-order conditions become

$$k_i + t_i \frac{\partial k_i}{\partial t_i} = 0 \text{ and } \kappa_i + \tau_i \frac{\partial \kappa_i}{\partial \tau_i} = 0, \tag{50}$$

and thus the rate on each base will be set to the inverse of its own semi-elasticity. Since the ability to differentiate can never reduce revenue, optimal differentiation strictly increases revenue whenever the semi-elasticities differ. All this, of course, is well known from the theory of third-degree price discrimination in monopolies.

In the context of competition between countries, however, the strategic response of the other country cannot be ignored. How does a world in which all countries may apply a preferential regime differ from one in which they are constrained to apply a uniform regime? Are preferential regimes, in that sense, necessarily a harmful form of tax competition?

When preferential treatment is permitted, (50) implies that equilibrium tax revenues are

$$T_i^P = -k_i^2 / (\partial k_i / \partial t_i) - \kappa_i^2 / (\partial \kappa_i / \partial \tau_i). \tag{51}$$

If on the other hand both countries apply uniform taxation, maximization of tax revenue in country i, as in (49), yields

$$T_i^U = -(k_i + \kappa_i)^2 / \left(\frac{\partial k_i}{\partial t_i} + \frac{\partial \kappa_i}{\partial \tau_i} \right). \tag{52}$$

Keen (2001) compares the implied equilibrium tax revenues in these two cases when countries are symmetric, assuming also that $k_i(t_i, t_{-i}) = k_i(t_i - t_{-i})$, and $\kappa_i(\tau_i, \tau_{-i}) = \kappa_i(\tau_i - \tau_{-i})$; the base in each country is thus assumed to depend solely on the difference in tax rates between them, essentially removing from the picture any effect of the general tax level on the aggregate tax base. The difference in each country's tax revenues between the Nash equilibrium in which all countries are constrained to applying uniform taxation (T^U) and that in which they may deploy preferential regimes (T^P) is

$$T_i^U - T_i^P = \frac{k_i^2 \kappa_i^2}{k_i' \kappa_i' (k_i' + \kappa_i')} \left(\frac{k_i'}{k_i} - \frac{\kappa_i'}{\kappa_i} \right)^2 \leq 0, \tag{53}$$

with $k_i' \equiv \partial k_i(0)/\partial t_i$ and $\kappa_i' \equiv \partial \kappa_i(0)/\partial \tau_i$. Equality only holds if $k_i'/k_i = \kappa_i'/\kappa_i$, that is, only if there is no difference in elasticities in the two tax bases. In the general case, in which elasticities differ, however, revenue is now unambiguously *higher* when preferential regimes may be deployed. In that sense, preferential regimes actually make tax competition less harmful. The intuitive attraction of imposing uniformity as a coordination measure is in making it more costly for countries to tax mobile capital by ensuring that this implies a revenue loss from less mobile capital. But differentiation, while increasing the scope for competition for mobile capital, protects the revenue from the less mobile base. In the setting of Keen (2001), this latter effect always dominates.

This result, running exactly counter to the commonplace presumption against preferential regimes of various kinds has triggered much further consideration—see, for instance, Bucovetsky and Haufler (2007), Haupt and Peters (2005), Janeba and Peters (1999), and Janeba and Smart (2003)—exploring the robustness of this result. The variant of the benchmark model which yields the largest divergence maintains the assumption of symmetry between countries and two tax bases, but assumes that one of them is completely immobile and inelastic up to a maximum tax rate of $\bar{\tau}$ in each of the countries. Above this rate, the owners of the tax base make use of a disposal option and the tax base vanishes. The other type of capital has a perfectly elastic tax base of $2k$ that floats freely between the two countries and locates in whichever has the lower tax rate, and locates symmetrically between them if they tax it at the same rate. In this case, the equilibrium with preferential taxation is characterized by $t_1 = t_2 = 0$ and $\tau_1 = \tau_2 = \bar{\tau}$: both countries make full use of their monopoly power as regards their immobile tax base, but face cutthroat competition as regards the fully mobile tax base. In case of uniform taxation, an equilibrium in pure strategies typically does not exist. However, an equilibrium in mixed strategies does. For symmetric countries, applying the logic of Narasimhan (1988), this mixed strategy equilibrium is characterized by uniform tax rates z_1 and z_2 that are random draws from a distribution that is defined by a cumulative distribution function $F(z) = 1 + \frac{\kappa}{2k} - \frac{\kappa \bar{\tau}}{2kz}$ and supports $\left[\frac{\kappa \bar{\tau}}{2k+\kappa}, \bar{\tau} \right]$. The expected tax revenue in this equilibrium is equal to $\kappa \bar{\tau}$ for each of the two countries. Accordingly, preferential treatment generates exactly the same tax revenue as uniform taxation in the equilibrium.[49]

---

[49] The results on preferential tax regimes are reminiscent of those on third-degree price discrimination in interfirm competition. This literature first concentrated on third-degree price discrimination of a monopolist who serves several distinguishable customer groups (see, for instance, Schmalensee, 1981). Here, price discrimination never yields monopoly profits that are lower than with uniform pricing, and as Holmes (1989) discusses, this carries over to collusive duopoly. This structural similarity is noted by Janeba and Smart (2003).

4.3. Information Exchange and Implementation of the Residence Principle

As noted in Section 2.1, it is the residence principle—not the source principle, which most of the formal literature reviewed here presumes—that is the international norm for personal-level taxation of capital income,[50] and which continues to be important at corporate level too. Its implementation, however, can be problematic, for two reasons. One is that residence country taxes are generally not imposed until income is repatriated there, so that the real liability can be reduced by retaining funds abroad. A number of countries seek to address this at corporate level through "controlled foreign corporation" (CFC) legislation, which enables them to tax income remaining abroad—albeit generally only income that is "passive" in the sense of not arising from immediate business activities. Deferral, nonetheless, remains a key instrument of international tax planning (though not the only one, of course). The second difficulty, which arises primarily at the individual level, is simply the risk that taxpayers will not reveal to their home authorities income arising abroad. The most obvious remedy for this is for the tax authorities to provide their counterparts abroad with information on the income arising in their country to residents of others. Fostering such information sharing has been the focus of considerable (indeed unprecedented) action in recent years,[51] as is described in the next subsection, and has attracted some theoretical interest.

Much of the literature on information exchange has focused on the question of whether or not countries might choose to provide such information voluntarily.[52] At first sight, it might seem that those which are net recipients of income undeclared to the investors' home authorities would not, since by providing information they would enable the residence country to levy additional taxation and so make themselves less attractive a location for such funds. Strategic considerations, however, again come into play, a point first stressed by Bacchetta and Espinosa (1995). For if it can commit to providing such information—and double tax treaties and tax information exchange agreements may provide a vehicle for doing so—a low tax country enables the residence country to charge a higher tax rate than would otherwise be the case, which in itself tends to increase the inflow of capital that it receives—an effect that counteracts and may outweigh the directly harmful impact.[53]

---

[50] There are some exceptions: Capital gains related to real estate, for instance, are generally taxable only where that real estate is located.

[51] The practicalities of information sharing are outlined in Keen and Ligthart (2006), though this predates the recent expansion of information agreements.

[52] Some papers compare information exchange in this setting with the imposition of withholding taxes by the low tax country, following Huizinga and Nielsen (2003). This is motivated largely by particularities of the EU Savings Directive, under which countries may either provide information or impose a withholding tax. In practice, many countries do both (double tax agreements for instance, typically providing for both information exchange and withholding taxes).

[53] Eggert and Kolmar (2002) consider the case in which tax rates and the extent of information sharing are chosen simultaneously, showing that the equilibrium degree of information sharing is then indeterminate.

To see this, consider again a world of just two countries, with $t_2 > t_1 > 0$. In the high tax country 2, there is a fixed amount of savings S that can be invested in either country, in amounts s_1 and s_2; the former incurring expected (non tax-deductible) costs of $C(s_1)$, with C increasing and strictly convex. There are no savings in the low tax country (to avoid the complication of cross-hauling of savings). The authorities in low tax country 1 collect taxes at the rate t_1 on all savings located there, and will provide information to the authorities in country 2 only on some proportion λ of their residents' savings there. These are then liable to additional taxation in country 2 at $t_2 - t_1$ (credit being given for taxes paid abroad). Assuming the gross rate of return to be the same in both countries (and normalizing it to unity), country 2's investors will allocate their savings in order to minimize the sum of taxes paid and transaction costs incurred, which is given by

$$t_2(S - s_1) + (1 - \lambda)t_1 s_1 + \lambda t_2 s_1 + C(s_1), \tag{54}$$

with the first term being the tax paid on savings retained at home, the second that paid on income abroad that is successfully concealed, and the third being total tax paid on income abroad that is reported and so ultimately subject to the full home rate. Maximizing this to trade off the tax advantage of saving abroad against the transactions cost of doing so, savings allocated abroad, $s_1(\lambda, t_1, t_2)$, are an increasing function $h[\beta(\lambda, t_1, t_2)]$ of the tax saved by doing so, per unit of saving, given by $\beta \equiv (1 - \lambda)(t_2 - t_1)$. Thus

$$\frac{\partial s_1}{\partial t_2} = (1 - \lambda)h'(\beta) > 0 \tag{55}$$

so that, as one would expect, the amount saved abroad increases with the tax rate at home. Similarly, it decreases with both the foreign tax rate and (at constant tax rates) the extent of information sharing. For simplicity, assume that revenue rather than welfare is the object of policy-making. In country 1, this is simply

$$r_1 = t_1 s_1(\lambda, t_1, t_2), \tag{56}$$

while in country 2 it is

$$r_2 = t_2 s_2 + \lambda(t_2 - t_1)s_1 = t_2 S - \{\lambda t_1 + (1 - \lambda)t_2\}s_1(\lambda, t_1, t_2). \tag{57}$$

With the degree of information sharing assumed to be determined at the first stage of the game (being more in the nature of a long-term commitment, perhaps embodied in a treaty), each country chooses its tax rate taking as given both λ and the tax rate of the other country. The tax rate chosen in the high tax country, in particular, is thus $t_2(\lambda, t_1)$. Suppose then that the low tax country commits to a small increase in the extent of information sharing λ. From (57), the revenue impact in the high tax country, given that the effect of any induced change in its own tax rate vanishes as an envelope property, is

$$\frac{dr_2}{d\lambda} = (t_2 - t_1)s_1 - \{\lambda t_1 + (1 - \lambda)t_2\}\frac{\partial s_1}{\partial \lambda} \tag{58}$$

and so is unambiguously positive: there is a gain from both the increased taxation of any income invested abroad and the reduction in the extent of such investments. For the low tax country 1, matters are more complex. With revenue being $t_1 s_1[\lambda, t_1, t_2(\lambda, t_1)]$, the effect is given by

$$\frac{dr_1}{d\lambda} = t_1 \left\{ \frac{\partial s_1}{\partial \lambda} + \frac{\partial s_1}{\partial t_2} \frac{\partial t_2}{\partial \lambda} \right\}. \tag{59}$$

Here the first term is the direct, adverse effect on the low tax country: it becomes less attractive as a venue for tax evasion. The second is the strategic effect: to the extent that the fuller information induces the high tax country to increase its tax rate—as is plausible, but not assured without further restriction of functional forms—this leads to more evasion into the low tax country. The overall impact of the low tax country is thus, in principle, unclear.

It is possible, however, that the strategic effect dominates. Indeed, in the simple structure above, this is, under plausible conditions, sure to be the case. To see why, suppose that the high tax country 2 reacts to increased information sharing by raising its own tax rate just enough to leave the tax saved by investing abroad, β, unchanged in the face of the higher λ. This means that the amount of savings allocated abroad is also unchanged, and hence revenue in the low tax country remains as it initially was. Recalling (55), however, the higher λ means that savings invested abroad are now less responsive than they were to the tax set by the high tax country 2, which tips the balance of country 2's considerations towards increasing its tax rate further—pushing savings further in country 1's direction, and implying that it too is ultimately better off.[54]

This, of course, is a strong and quite special result. Fuller treatments allow also for the adjustment of country 1's tax rate and endogenize the choice of tax rates (relating them in particular to country size, with the standard conclusion that rates tend to be lower in smaller countries). They allow too for cross-hauling of savings, and explore the implications of differential tax treatment of residents and non-residents. Importantly, the strategic effect clearly becomes much less powerful when there is more than one low tax country: greater information sharing by one will then be met in part by a shifting of savings to other low tax countries, so that the impact on the tax-setting decisions of the high tax country will be greatly muted. The most robust result is probably the most obvious: there can be a sharp divergence of interests, with high tax countries being much more certain to gain from mutual information exchange than are low tax countries.[55]

[54] The result follows more formally by noting, from (57), that

$$\partial r_2 / \partial t_2 = S - (1 - \lambda) s_1(\beta) - (1 - \lambda)(\beta + t_1) h'(\beta)$$

from which, for given t_1 and β, satisfaction of the necessary condition $\partial r_2 / \partial t_2 = 0$ in the initial position implies that $\partial r_2 / \partial t_2 > 0$ if country 2 were to hold β unchanged in the face of the increased λ. So long as r_2 is convex in t_2 (as is the case, for example, if the cost function $C(s)$ is quadratic), the higher λ must therefore be associated with a higher choice of t_2.

[55] The last observation perhaps suggests it might be Pareto-improving for the low tax jurisdiction to receive some of the proceeds of the additional revenue raised as a consequence of the information it provides. Keen and Ligthart (2006)

4.4. Tax Havens

Though widely used, the precise meaning of the term "tax haven" is elusive, and even in the practical world of policy there is no agreed definition. A low or zero tax rate on some activities or forms of income is clearly a necessary ingredient, but is not enough to capture common usage: Very resource-rich countries, for example, may simply not need tax rates at the same levels found elsewhere, and have little interest in how that affects capital or other cross-border flows. Beyond low taxation, the term carries the connotations that it is paper rather than real economic activity that is being attracted, and moreover that these are jurisdictions which encourage, or at least do not adequately discourage, tax avoidance or evasion that undermines tax revenues of other countries, perhaps by providing secrecy laws or other restrictions that preclude their sharing of information.[56] Quite what the standard of adequacy should be is, of course, by no means clear. Where the line lies that defines a tax haven remains hazy, but three features seem to capture the essence: low taxation that is not a reflection of high revenue, relative to needs, from other sources; the attraction of profit-shifting and other tax arbitrage activities more than real activity; and imperfect sharing of information.

4.4.1. Which Countries Become Tax Havens?

The theory set out above carries the strong prediction that it is smaller countries which are more likely to become, in this broad sense, tax havens. They are more likely to set low tax rates that encourage profit-shifting and tax arbitrage, as seen in Section 2.1.2, and, by having low tax rates, they are likely, as was seen in the preceding section, to have the least to gain from information sharing.

The empirical evidence broadly matches this prediction. Dharmapala and Hines (2009) identify 41 countries as "tax havens" and compare these with nonhavens. Their descriptive statistics suggest that, relative to nonhavens, tax havens are small as regards population and area, are more likely to be islands, and provide an institutional framework that is characterized, in broad terms, by good governance. These descriptive results are supported by their multivariate analysis, which suggests a strong positive correlation with governance quality, and a negative correlation with population size. These findings are in line with those of Slemrod (2008), who offers an explanation based on the concept of commercialization of a country's sovereignty. Such commercialization for the purpose of tax haven activities has benefits that are not closely related to population size. However, the status as tax haven may have a cost in terms of "integrity" or "reputation," and this

---

show that this can indeed be the case, if the countries concerned are sufficiently asymmetric, even though such transfers may, perhaps surprisingly, reduce total revenue collected (by increasing the incentive for the low tax country to attract would-be evaders, since they then have less to fear if the evaders are caught).

[56] Dharmapala and Hines (2009), for example, define a tax haven as "a state or a country or territory where certain taxes are levied at a low rate or not at all while offering due process, good governance and a low corruption rate." But many would argue that it is bad governance—in the form of unwillingness to share tax information—that is a hallmark of tax havens.

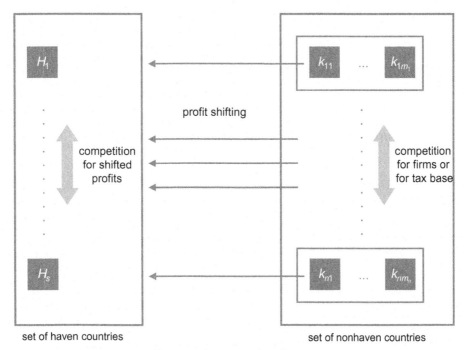

Figure 11 Interactions within and between havens and nonhavens.

may be strongly correlated with population size, or with the size of regular economic activity in the respective country.

4.4.2. Are Tax Havens Good or Bad?

The term "tax haven" has clear pejorative overtones—one reason why policy makers have found an agreed definition so hard to find—but the recent literature has begun to focus on whether their existence and activities might not have beneficial effects. The question is closely related to the wider one of whether tax competition itself can be welfare-improving (political economy aspects of which are taken up in Section 4.6): After all, in any asymmetric equilibrium, some country will have the lowest tax rate and in that sense look like a tax haven. The importance of pure arbitrage activities in the tax haven context does, however, raise distinct issues.[57]

The structure mapped in Figure 11 provides a constructive way of looking at tax havens as specific players in the context of tax competition rather than as especially small but otherwise ordinary countries. This shows a number of "nonhaven" countries on the right-hand side. These provide an environment for real sector activity and host production facilities for firms. Some firms are fully immobile and locate their business

---

[57] Dharmapala (2008) provides an overview of the theoretical and empirical literature that analyzed the consequences and existence of tax haven countries.

completely in nonhaven countries. Others are mobile and make a location decision, choosing where and how much capital to locate. The right-hand side of the diagram can then be interpreted as corresponding to the benchmark ZMW model. Apart from "real" production decisions, firms may use other means to relocate accounting profits from one country to another. This may also happen between the nonhaven countries, but this is the point where haven countries enter into the picture. As they typically have a real sector that is negligible in comparison to the financial business they host, or have means to separate these two types of activities, they have an interest in firms shifting their taxable profits from nonhaven countries in return for low tax payments or small fees.[58] Tax havens compete with each other regarding the quality of their concealment or profit-shifting services and in how much they charge for them. Some firms in the nonhaven countries—presumably the larger and more international—then have a choice along a second dimension. They must determine how much of their tax base to shift, bearing in mind the various costs potentially associated with this: taxes or "fees" charged by the haven, the cost of setting up the appropriate international firm structure, and potentially some economic cost from adjustments required for the actual business operations. There may also be an indirect cost, given that nonhaven countries may take countermeasures to such shifting activities.[59] It is in this broader framework that work has identified several partial but important effects, some detrimental but others possibly beneficial.

Slemrod and Wilson (2009) adopt this perspective and identify several reasons why the provision of tax reduction services by haven countries can be undesirable. Most obviously, it involves some resource cost: as with tax avoidance activities in a standard tax compliance model that are pursued with the help of tax consultants, tax payers should be willing to expend up to 99 cents to avoid an additional $1 in taxes, meaning social waste of 99 cents at the margin. A further insight of this paper is on the role of the direct shifting cost. An increase of this cost (for instance, due to relaxed competition between tax havens) generally reduces the amount of shifting and may even reduce the total amount of associated cost. Less shifting implies a broadening of the tax base and, thereby, reduces the marginal cost of public funds. An element that adds to the analysis of the relationship between the tax office, tax payers, and a sector of tax consultants in this analysis is the role of competition between "ordinary" countries that may take place along the lines of tax rates or the intensity of enforcement effort.

Hong and Smart (2010) highlight a different effect by which, to the contrary, profit shifting to zero-tax jurisdictions can have beneficial consequences. In their framework, the nonhaven country has a mobile and an immobile sector, with a single tax rate applied

---

[58] As pointed out in Schön (2005), a tax haven may successfully raise revenue even if the nominal tax rate on profits is zero, through registration fees or levies and charges on the financial service industry that facilitates multinational companies' operations in the tax haven.

[59] This perspective makes tax havens similar or comparable to tax consultancy companies which offer legal means to reduce the tax burden, charge a fee for this service, and compete among themselves.

to taxable profits in each. Profits in the immobile sector are fully taxed. The mobile sector, however, can use debt operations to shift some of its taxable profits to a zero-tax jurisdiction by borrowing from a related company in the latter. A key assumption is that the amount of profit that can be shifted is proportional to the capital invested in the nonhaven country, reflecting such potential constraints as thin-capitalization rules (denying the interest deductibility underlying the arbitrage if debt levels are high relative to assets employed). Firms that can engage in such profit shifting thus face a lower effective tax rate than those that cannot. If the government of the small open economy they consider can perfectly and costlessly control the amount of profit shifting through the severity of its thin-capitalization rules, it has two independent fiscal instruments at its disposal which is very similar to having two independent corporate tax rates, one for mobile and one for immobile capital—as analyzed in Section 4.2 above. Desai, Foley, and Hines (2006a) conclude that the effect of profit shifting in reducing the effective corporate tax rates for firms, and so increasing the net-of-tax marginal return on real investment in nonhaven countries, may dominate other, possibly detrimental effects of tax havens for investment in nonhaven countries. Their companion paper Desai, Foley, and Hines (2006b) shows that there is indeed a positive relationship between firms' international investment activities in nonhaven countries and their activities in haven countries.

Johannesen (2010) explores another way in which the existence of tax havens changes the nature of international tax competition. He starts with an analysis of tax competition between n countries, with a representative multinational firm that can relocate a given amount of physical capital between them and also, at some cost, shift accounting profits. There emerge from these asymmetric equilibria in which some countries charge high taxes and lose some tax base through profit shifting while others set low taxes that attract a considerable amount of shifted profits. Equilibrium tax rates are not zero, however, even in the low-tax countries. Now introduce a set of haven countries defined to be such that they choose zero taxes and do not allow for real production. If these have a sufficient capacity, they absorb all the profit shifting and essentially make the low tax strategy unprofitable for those countries that would otherwise be low tax countries in the asymmetric equilibrium, leading to symmetric behavior among the nonhaven countries. The tax havens deflect competition that took place between nonhaven countries toward competition between nonhaven and haven countries. And this, it turns out, can yield higher equilibrium tax revenue for the nonhaven countries.

4.4.3. Closing Down Tax Havens

Although few drew any strong links between the activities of tax havens and the 2009 financial crisis, at their London summit that year, G20 leaders put substantial new vigor into the OECD work on encouraging widespread information exchange. Much of this effort has focused on encouraging tax havens to sign information exchange agreements (TIEAs), in order to make the concealment of taxable income more difficult, with peer reviews to ensure both that the legal mechanisms to do this are in place and that these arrangements are implemented in practice. Johannesen and Zucman (2012) survey these events and use data from the Bank of International Settlements on total deposits held by residents from one country at banks in 14 tax havens, to measure the impact of TIEAs on deposit holdings. They find that signing an agreement between a nonhaven and a haven tends to reduce the deposits from the nonhaven in this haven country—but also that these deposits tend to shift to other havens.

Elsayyad and Konrad (2012) study a competition framework in which attempts are made to convince tax havens to close down their operations, for instance, by exchanging information with nonhaven governments. They show that this process may work well, initially, in a framework with a large number of tax havens. In this early stage, what each tax haven can earn from offering these concealment services is low, due to intense competition from the large number of other havens. However, once a large number of tax havens have exited from this business, the rents that accrue to those that remain increase. It then becomes ever more difficult to convince those remaining tax havens to exit. The outcome may be one in which a smaller set of havens is operative, charging higher fees and acquiring a larger share of the accounting profits that are generated from business activities in nonhaven countries. Using Zucman's (2011) estimate for total world financial wealth located in tax havens and applying their static competition model straightforwardly, Elsayyad and Konrad (2012) estimate that the profit losses of the last of the 35 tax havens listed by the OECD (2000) is 17 times as high as for each of the 34 havens that may exit previously. If the process stops short of completion, the outcome can be worse, from a welfare perspective, for the nonhaven countries than it would be in the initial state, with much competitive pressure among haven countries.

4.5. Formula Apportionment

The incentive for companies to use transfer pricing and other devices to shift profits between jurisdictions—and for governments to design their tax systems to affect that incentive—would be removed if, instead of seeking to identify profits earned in particular jurisdictions, taxes were simply levied on the aggregate of a multinational's profits over all jurisdictions.[60] "Formula apportionment" is an alternative to either residence or source principles that goes some way in this direction, by using indicators of the extent of a company's activities in particular countries ("apportionment factors") to attribute to each a share of those aggregate profits, which it may then tax at whatever rate it chooses. This is the norm for state-level corporate taxation in the US and Canada, for instance (generally using as apportionment factors some combination of the shares of sales, payroll,

---

[60] Nielsen, Raimondos-Møller, and Schjelderup (2003) show, however, that formula apportionment may not eliminate transfer pricing incentives when subsidiaries of a controlling parent compete in oligopolistic markets. An additional motive which may reinforce tax considerations then comes into play: if the subsidiary takes that transfer price as the basis for its decision making, the center may manipulate it as a commitment device to improve product market outcome.

and assets located in each state), and has been proposed by the European Commission, as a "common consolidated corporate tax base" (CCCTB) for the EU.[61]

Consider the simple case in which there is a single apportionment factor, so that with some α_i indicating the extent of a multinational's activity in country i and n countries, the total tax payable on a multinational's groupwide profit of $\pi(\alpha_1, \ldots, \alpha_n)$ is

$$\pi(\alpha_1, \ldots, \alpha_n) \sum_{i=1}^{n} \left(\frac{\alpha_i}{\sum_{h=1}^{n} \alpha_h} \right) t_i. \tag{60}$$

The attraction of this approach is that, for given decisions α there is no gain in simply reallocating paper profits across jurisdictions, even though they may charge different tax rates. There is, however, a potential distortion to those decisions. Assuming Π to be strictly concave in the α_i, these would be chosen in the absence of taxation (or with tax levied directly on aggregate profit) so that $\partial \Pi / \partial \alpha_i = 0$, for all i. Under formula apportionment, however, cross-country differences in tax rates distort these choices, it being straightforward to show that maximization of net profits implies $\partial \Pi / \partial \alpha_i < 0$ if the tax rate in country i is below the α-weighted average and the converse where it is above: broadly speaking, whatever the factor in the apportionment, it will tend to be reallocated from high to low tax countries.[62]

Of particular interest here is that revenue-seeking governments will generally have an incentive to set tax rates with the intention of manipulating the multinational's choice of the α_i.[63] Suppose, for instance, that capital is used as the sole apportionment factor α_i, and consider a multinational with some fixed amount of capital 2κ to allocate between just two identical countries. Then the multinational will maximize after-tax profits

$$[\Pi(k_1) + \Pi(2\kappa - k_1)](1 - T(t_1, t_2, k_1)), \tag{61}$$

where we assume that "true" profits can meaningfully be ascribed to countries (that earned in each depending only on the capital located there), and where the average tax rate

$$T(t_1, t_2, k_1) \equiv \frac{t_1 k_1 + t_2(2\kappa - k_1)}{2\kappa} \tag{62}$$

is endogenous to the investment decision. The solution to the firm's optimization problem leads to an allocation of capital $k_1(t_1, t_2)$ with the property that, where $t_1 = t_2 = t$,

$$\frac{\partial k_1}{\partial t_1} = \frac{\Pi(\kappa)}{(1 - t) 2\kappa \Pi''(\kappa)}. \tag{63}$$

---

[61] Adoption would be optional by country and by company. On the CCCTB debate, see Sørensen (2004b) and Bettendorf et al. (2011).

[62] Gordon and Wilson (1986) provide a detailed analysis of how formula apportionment can affect firm behavior, including through incentives to merge or dissolve. The analysis here follows Keen (1999).

[63] On other aspects of and practical experience with formula apportionment, see Weiner (2005).

Supposing revenue to be the governments' sole concern, that in country 1 (say) then chooses t_1 to maximize $t_1(\Pi(k_1) + \Pi(2\kappa - k_1))k_1$; the necessary condition for which, using (63), implies that in symmetric equilibrium where $k_1 = k_2 = \kappa$,

$$\frac{t^{FA}}{1 - t^{FA}} = -\frac{(2\kappa)^2 \Pi''(\kappa)}{2\Pi(\kappa)} \equiv \Delta^{FA}, \tag{64}$$

where "FA" stands for formula apportionment. This outcome is clearly inefficient, since any higher common tax rate would yield both countries greater revenue.

More striking, however, is the comparison with the non-cooperative outcome under source taxation. In this case, the total tax paid by the multinational is $t_1\Pi(k_1) + t_2\Pi(2\kappa - k_1)$, and, by steps analogous to those leading to (64), the symmetric equilibrium tax rate has a tax rate in each country of

$$\frac{t^{ST}}{1 - t^{ST}} = -\frac{2\Pi(\kappa)\Pi''(\kappa)}{(\Pi'(\kappa))^2}, \tag{65}$$

where "ST" refers to source taxation. Comparing this with (64) gives

$$\frac{t^{FA}}{1 - t^{FA}} - \frac{t^{ST}}{1 - t^{ST}} = \frac{2\Pi''}{(\Pi')^2\Pi}[\Pi(\kappa)^2 - (\Pi'(\kappa))^2\kappa^2] < 0, \tag{66}$$

the inequality being from the strict concavity of Π. Tax competition thus leads to an unambiguously lower equilibrium tax rate under formula apportionment than under source taxation, and so, in that sense, to unambiguously more intense tax competition. To see the intuition for this, suppose that initially both countries charge the same tax rate. Under source taxation, attracting an additional unit of capital raises revenue of $t_1\Pi'(\kappa)$, reflecting the marginal product of that capital; under formula apportionment, however, it raises additional revenue of $t_1\Pi(\kappa)/2\kappa$, reflecting—because the country is taking a share in aggregate profits, wherever earned—the average profit rate $\Pi(\kappa)/\kappa$. So long as the average rate of return exceeds the marginal rate, the incentive to attract capital is thus greater under formula apportionment.

This comparison of regimes is somewhat unnatural in that there is assumed to be no scope for manipulating liability under the source regime other than by relocating real activities: the profit-shifting to which formula apportionment is seen as a possible response is thus absent. What the result does suggest, nonetheless, is that formula apportionment can be preferred only if the distortions to firms' and governments' behavior that profit-shifting leads to are sufficiently large to outweigh what would otherwise be an adverse strategic effect. Introducing the possibility of transfer pricing, at some cost to the multinational, into a framework similar to that above, Nielsen, Raimondos-Møller, and Schjelderup (2010) provide a fuller treatment of the issue, elaborating on the circumstances, which turn on the level of profitability and the ease of transfer pricing, under which profit-shifting concerns dominate and formula apportionment consequently leads to a Pareto-superior non-cooperative outcome.

4.6. Political Economy and Agency Issues

There has long been debate as to whether international tax competition is good or bad from a welfare perspective. In the workhorse model, tax competition is (almost) certainly bad, in the sense that (leaving aside the time consistency issue discussed in Section 3.5.2) a central planner could implement any tax rates that can emerge in a decentralized equilibrium but could also choose the potentially many other tax rate combinations that cannot. Hence, coordinated tax rate choices—complemented as need be with international transfers of tax revenue—are at least as good, in a Pareto sense, as decentralized choices, and, since there are several externalities at work, will generally be Pareto-superior.[64]

But comparing a decentralized tax competition equilibrium outcome with the centrally coordinated solution brought about by a fully benevolent government is not a very satisfying exercise. If there were no more to say, then for the same reason all private market economies should be transformed into centrally planned ones. The aim in this section is to review the implications for tax competition and coordination of richer views of policy-making.

Both centralized and decentralized political decision making suffer from problems other than the possible externalities between decentralized decision makers. One can doubt, in particular, if policy decisions are well described as those of a benevolent dictator who maximizes the utility of a representative citizen. Political decision making reflects distributional conflicts, with the electoral process, perhaps giving the median voter a key role, and special interest groups may lobby for their preferred tax policy.[65] And, perhaps most importantly, power is delegated to governments which generates a number of accountability problems between the government and its constituency. We focus on these problems.

4.6.1. Tax Competition and Leviathan

There is a long-standing tradition in the public choice literature to the effect that tax competition is not, as the analysis and arguments above suggest, a source of inefficiency. On the contrary, when other limits on their actions are weak, tax competition in this view serves a valuable social purpose in constraining leviathans; that is, policy makers who are inherently inclined to raise public revenue to serve their own rather than society's wide interests. To Brennan and Buchanan (1980, p. 186), for instance, "... tax competition

---

[64] This reasoning is also in line with Sinn's (1997) selection principle, which argues that the government is ideally involved in tasks which are performed poorly in the private sector, and with the financing of public goods as a classical example. With intergovernmental competition, inefficiencies may return, now on the intergovernmental level, and this may suggest centralization of these tasks on the supra-national level.

[65] Lobbying activities by powerful groups can affect the outcome of tax competition. Citizens who own above-average quantities of capital, for instance, may lobby in the political process, trying to shift the reply function "downward" toward lower capital taxes. Chirinko and Wilson (2010) report evidence suggesting that business campaign contributions may indeed affect the tax reaction function and so influence tax policy.

among separate units ... is an objective to be sought in its own right." The view that policy makers divert all revenue to their own use is, of course, extreme. So too, however, is the assumption in the preceding sections that they are concerned only with the general social good.

Edwards and Keen (1996) set out a variant of the ZMW model that blends the two views. Everything remains as in the symmetric version of the model analyzed in Section 2.1, except that now policymakers are assumed to maximize some function $V(W, B)$ that reflects both the amount of tax revenue that they are able to divert to their own use, B, and, perhaps through concerns of re-election or revolt, the welfare W of the taxpayer (all non-policy makers being assumed identical, and as described in Section 2.1). The problem of the policy maker in country i can then be broken down into two stages. At the first, B_i is taken as given and the tax rate t_i chosen so as to maximize the citizen's welfare

$$W_i = f_i(k_i) - f_i'(k_i)k_i + \rho \bar{k}_i + G_i(t_i k_i - B_i). \tag{67}$$

The solution to this gives $W(B_i)$, and the second stage of the problem is then that of choosing B_i to maximize the policy maker's welfare $V(W(B_i), B_i)$.

Consider then the effects of a coordinated small increase in the tax rate charged by each country, starting from the Nash equilibrium. This evidently makes the policy makers in each country better off. But what of the citizens? For this, note first that with B_i fixed the first stage of the policy maker's problems is formally the same as that in Section 2.1.1, so that (13) will again hold in the symmetric equilibrium:

$$G'(t\bar{k}) = \frac{1}{1 + E_k} < 1. \tag{13}$$

Along the same lines as before Eq. (9), the welfare impact of this coordinated reform is $dW = -\bar{k}dt + dG$, but now dG is less than $G'\bar{k}dt$ to the extent that part of the additional revenue that this reform yields is spent on B instead. So:

$$dW = \left(G'(t\bar{k})\bar{k}\left(1 - \frac{dB}{d(t\bar{k})}\right) - \bar{k}\right)dt \tag{68}$$

and hence, using (13) in (68), the citizen's welfare increases if and only if

$$\frac{dB}{d(t\bar{k})} < E_k, \tag{69}$$

meaning that the policy makers' marginal propensity to consume on the item that benefits only themselves is less than the (absolute value of) the elasticity of the tax base with respect to its own tax rate. The former is essentially an aspect of policy makers' preferences, and the latter can be thought of as increasing in the intensity of tax competition. One implication of (69) is, thus, that a coordinated tax increase is more likely to benefit the citizenry, all else equal, the more intense is tax competition.

A limitation of the Edwards-Keen model is that the form of policy makers' preferences and the nature of "wasteful" spending B are left unspecified: one person's waste is another's socially worthwhile spending. The fundamental issue ultimately is one of distributional politics. This aspect is pursued further by Eggert and Sørensen (2008), who take B to be rents paid to public sector workers by politicians anxious to secure their support in a probabilistic voting setting. An appealing feature of this framework is that there is in principle an optimal degree of tax competition: too little and rents are excessive, too much and underprovision of a beneficial public good dominates the gain from rent destruction. Interestingly, their simulations suggest that this optimal degree of tax competition may be fairly low, leading them to conclude that: "… tax competition … seems a badly targeted remedy against political distortions, compared to domestic institutional reform such as restrictions on campaign contributions by lobby groups."[66]

4.6.2. Voters' Choices

Several of the approaches used to describe democratic decision making have been applied to tax rate choices in a framework with tax competition. Persson and Tabellini (1992), Brückner (2001), and Fuest and Huber (2001) consider a median voter framework, while Ihori and Yang (2009) consider a citizen-candidate model. A general insight from these models is that the political process may distort the intrajurisdictional tax rate choice away from that which a benevolent planner would have chosen, and this political distortion has to be compared with those that are introduced through the various fiscal externalities associated with tax competition. To illustrate this in the context of the linearized framework of Section 2.1.1, suppose that voters differ only in their shares in the ownership of capital. Suppose further that, as one would expect, the median voter in each country has less than the mean ownership of capital: $\bar{k}_m < \bar{k}$. Recalling (22), with decision reflecting the capital ownership of the median voter rather than the average in the population, yields $t_i^m(t_j)$ that are obtained from $t_i(t_j)$ by an upward shift, leading to an equilibrium with higher taxes: tax competition becomes less aggressive.

An alternative view of electoral politics, one that also captures the self-interest of policy makers that motivates the Edward-Keen model, is explored by Besley and Smart (2007). They consider a world in which there are two types of politicians—some pure Leviathans, concerned only with the surplus B that they can extract from themselves, and some wholly benevolent—competing for office in a world with a two-period term limit. Voters do not directly observe politicians' types, and while they can observe the taxes they pay and the public services they enjoy, they cannot observe the cost of providing those services or, hence, the surplus that the incumbent policy maker extracts for himself. There are then two broad types of outcome, depending on the parameters of the model. One possibility is a separating equilibrium in which leviathan incumbents "go for broke," extracting as

[66] Eggert and Sørensen (2008, p. 1154).

much revenue as they can when in office, accepting that in doing so they will reveal their identity as leviathans and consequently not be re-elected. The other possibility is a pooling equilibrium in which leviathan incumbents will restrain the amount of revenue they raise so as to mimic the behavior of a benevolent policy maker faced with an adverse cost shock, so improving their chances of being re-elected and extracting as much surplus as they can in a final period of office.

Though it is not cast as a model of international taxation, Besley and Smart (2007) directly address in this framework the question of interest here: might an increase in the efficiency of the tax system—such as a coordinated increase in the tax rate in circumstances of international tax competition—reduce voter welfare (evaluated before the type of the first-period incumbent is known)? They show that it could, if it causes a shift from a separating to a pooling equilibrium. Such an increase in efficiency makes it more attractive for a leviathan to mimic a benevolent policy maker—the latter would now choose a higher level of public good provision, which enables the former to extract more rent by pretending that cost has proved to be high—so that the electoral process becomes less effective at removing leviathans, thereby creating more risk of abuse in the final term of office. This source of loss is greater the more likely it is that a candidate with no record of office would prove to be benevolent, since then the shift to a pooling equilibrium involves a greater loss of electoral effectiveness.[67] For this reason—and counter, perhaps, to simple intuition—a coordinated increase in tax rates is more likely to reduce voter welfare the *fewer* the number of politicians that are potential Leviathans.

5. CONCLUDING REMARKS

Thirty years ago, at the time of the first *Handbook*, there was almost no formal literature on international tax competition and coordination. Its growth since then has been spectacular, and it has produced a range of elegant, and in some cases powerful, results. These suggest, for instance, that agreement on minimum tax rates at levels somewhat above the lowest in the observed outcome is likely to be a more fruitful path to coordinating away from inefficient outcomes than is agreeing on common rates.[68] It would be too much to expect conclusions to be unqualified—we do not expect this in other areas—and they are not: it has also been seen, for instance, that the adoption of a minimum rate has less clear-cut effects in a Stackelberg game and can even undermine "good" equilibria in a repeated game context. The literature does, nonetheless, provide a coherent basis for contributing to and perhaps also shaping policy debates.

The literature does a much better job, however, in explaining why concerted action may be difficult than in suggesting with great precision or confidence which actions might

[67] It is also greater the lower the voter's discount rate is, since then the greater is the present value cost of a future unrestrained leviathan.
[68] Effective or statutory, depending on the context, and assuming agreement on a common base.

be both desirable and feasible. Empirical work can of course help policy navigate through the various possibilities that the theory identifies, and already is—as, for instance, in tending to confirm that strategic complementarity of tax rates across jurisdictions, though not a theoretical necessity, does indeed seem to be the norm. But deeper conceptual issues remain. Perhaps most fundamentally, the literature has not answered the basic question that has loomed over policy debates since OECD (1998): How can one distinguish tax competition that is "harmful" from that which is not? Progress has been made, but not yet enough to confidently determine whether, for instance, the presumption should be against or in favor of preferential regimes.

Further advance may require not only deeper empirical understanding and perhaps more use of calibrated simulations, but less simplistic views of the international tax regime itself. Much of the practical policy debate takes place not at the grand level of the models reviewed here but over details of international taxation of quite extraordinary complexity: relating for instance, to cross-country mismatches in the treatment of corporate forms or financial instruments, and the pricing of intangibles. This disconnect between the theory (and much of the empirics) and the details of practical concerns is perhaps greater in this area of public economics than most, and it may be growing. Models are no more than metaphors, but closer attention to detail might enable both the development of more informative ones—less rooted, for instance, in the view of a now vanishing word in which investment is essentially about large amounts of tangible capital and more rooted in one in which much corporate income is "stateless"[69]—and a more direct contribution on issues where real change seems most possible. While much of the theory in this area predated the greatly increased policy importance of the issues, the risk now is that the world will move more quickly than the theory.

ACKNOWLEDGMENTS

We are grateful to David R. Agrawal, Alan Auerbach, Johannes Becker, Bob Chirinko, May Elsayyad, Luisa Herbst, Grégoire Rota Graziosi, Hans-Werner Sinn, Joann Weiner, David Wildasin, and participants in the *Handbook* Conference at Berkeley for helpful comments on an earlier draft. Views expressed here are those of the authors and should not be attributed to the IMF, its Executive Board, or its management.

REFERENCES

Agrawal, D. (2011). The tax gradient: Do local sales taxes reduce tax differentials at state borders? University of Michigan: Mimeo.

Agrawal, D. (2012). Games within borders: Are geographically differentiated taxes optimal? *International Tax and Public Finance, 19*(4), 574–597.

Altshuler, R., & Goodspeed, T.J. (2002). Follow the leader? Evidence on European and US tax competition. *Departmental working paper*, No. 200226, Department of Economics, Rutgers University.

Amir, R. (2005). Supermodularity and complementarity in economics: An elementary survey. *Southern Economic Journal, 71*(3), 636–660.

[69] The apt term is due to Kleinbard (2011).

Andersson, F., & Konrad, K. A. (2003). Human capital investment and globalization in extortionary states. *Journal of Public Economics, 87*(7–8), 1539–1555.

Bacchetta, P., & Espinosa, M. P. (1995). Information sharing and tax competition among governments. *Journal of International Economics, 39*(1–2), 103–121.

Baldwin, R. E., & Krugman, P. (2004). Agglomeration, integration and tax harmonisation. *European Economic Review, 48*(1), 1–23.

Becker, J., & Fuest, C. (2010a). Taxing foreign profits with international mergers and acquisitions. *International Economic Review, 51*(1), 171–186.

Becker, J., & Fuest, C. (2010b). EU regional policy and tax competition. *European Economic Review, 54*(1), 150–161.

Becker, J., & Fuest, C. (2011). Source versus residence based taxation with international mergers and acquisitions. *Journal of Public Economics, 95*(1–2), 28–40.

Besley, T. J., & Smart, M. (2007). Fiscal restraints and voter welfare. *Journal of Public Economics, 91*(3–4), 755–773.

Bettendorf, L., Devereux, M., van der Horst, A., & Loretz, S. (2011). *Corporate tax reform in the EU: Weighing pros and cons, policy briefing.* Centre for Business Taxation, University of Oxford.

Binet, M.-E. (2003). Testing for fiscal competition among French municipalities: Granger causality evidence in a dynamic panel data model. *Papers in Regional Science, 82*(2), 277–289.

Bjorvatn, K., & Eckel, C. (2006). Policy competition for foreign direct investment between asymmetric countries. *European Economic Review, 50*(7), 1891–1907.

Black, D. A., & Hoyt, W. H. (1989). Bidding for firms. *American Economic Review, 79*(5), 1249–1256.

Blonigen, B. A., & Davies, R. B. (2004). Do bilateral tax treaties promote foreign direct investment? In J. Hartigan (Ed.), *Handbook of international trade. Economic and legal aspects of trade policy and institutions* (Vol. II, pp. 526–546). Boston: Blackwell Publishers.

Boadway, R. W., & Hayashi, M. (2001). An empirical analysis of intergovernmental tax interaction: The case of business taxes in Canada. *Canadian Journal of Economics, 34*(2), 481–503.

Boadway, R. W., & Keen, M. (1998). Evasion and time consistency in the taxation of capital income. *International Economic Review, 39*(2), 461–476.

Boadway, R. W., & Tremblay, J.-F. (2012). Reassessment of the Tiebout model. *Journal of Public Economics, 96*(11-12), 1063–1078.

Brennan, G., & Buchanan, J. M. (1980). *The power to tax: Analytical foundations of a fiscal constitution.* Cambridge: Cambridge University Press.

Brochner, J., Jensen, J., Svensson, P., & Sørensen, P. B. (2007). The dilemmas of tax coordination in the enlarged European Union. *CESifo Economic Studies, 53*(4), 561–595.

Broner, F., Martin, A., & Ventura, J. (2010). Sovereign risk and secondary markets. *American Economic Review, 100*(4), 1523–1555.

Brückner, M. (2001). Strategic delegation and international capital taxation. *ZEI working paper B*, No. 22-2001, University of Bonn, ZEI.

Brueckner, J. K. (2003). Strategic interaction among governments: An overview of empirical studies. *International Regional Science Review, 26*(2), 175–188.

Bucovetsky, S. (1991). Asymmetric tax competition. *Journal of Urban Economics, 30*(2), 167–181.

Bucovetsky, S. (2009). An index of capital tax competition. *International Tax and Public Finance, 16*(6), 727–752.

Bucovetsky, S., & Haufler, A. (2007). Preferential tax regimes with asymmetric countries. *National Tax Journal, 60*(4), 789–795.

Bucovetsky, S., & Wilson, J. D. (1991). Tax competition with two tax instruments. *Regional Science and Urban Economics, 21*, 333–350.

Burbidge, J. B., DePater, J. A., Myers, G. M., & Sengupta, A. (1997). A coalition-formation approach to equilibrium federations and trading blocs. *American Economic Review, 87*(5), 940–956.

Büttner, T. (2003). Tax base effect and fiscal externalities of local capital taxation: evidence from a panel of German jurisdictions. *Journal of Urban Economics, 54*(1), 110–128.

Cai, H., & Treisman, D. (2005). Does competition for capital discipline governments? Decentralization, globalization, and public policy. *American Economic Review, 95*(3), 817–830.

Cardarelli, R., Taugourdeau, E., & Vidal, J.-P. (2002). A repeated interactions model of tax competition. *Journal of Public Economic Theory, 4*(1), 19–38.

Carlsen, F., Langset, B., & Rattsø, J. (2005). The relationship between firm mobility and tax level: Empirical evidence of fiscal competition between local governments. *Journal of Urban Economics, 58*(2), 273–288.

Catenaro, M., & Vidal, J.-P. (2006). Implicit tax co-ordination under repeated policy interactions. *Louvain Economic Review, 72*(1), 5–17.

Chirinko, R. S., & Wilson, D. J. (2010). Can lower tax rates be bought? Business rent-seeking and tax competition among US states. *National Tax Journal, 63*(4), 967–994.

Conconi, P., Perroni, C., & Riezman, R. (2008). Is partial tax harmonization desirable? *Journal of Public Economics, 92*(1–2), 254–267.

Cremer, H., & Gavhari, F. (2000). Tax evasion, fiscal competition and economic integration. *European Economic Review, 44*, 1633–1657.

Deneckere, R., & Davidson, C. (1985). Incentives to form coalitions with Bertrand competition. *RAND Journal of Economics, 16*(4), 473–486.

Desai, M. A., Foley, C. F., & Hines, J. R., Jr. (2006a). Do tax havens divert economic activity? *Economics Letters, 90*(2), 219–224.

Desai, M. A., Foley, C. F., & Hines, J. R., Jr. (2006b). The demand for tax haven operations. *Journal of Public Economics, 90*(3), 513–531.

Devereux, M. P. (1992). The ruding committee report: An economic assessment. *Fiscal Studies, 13*(2), 96–107.

Devereux, M. P., Lockwood, B., & Redoano, M. (2008). Do countries compete over corporate tax rates? *Journal of Public Economics, 92*(5–6), 1210–1235.

Dharmapala, D. (2008). What problems and opportunities are created by tax havens? *Oxford Review of Economic Policy, 24*(4), 661–679.

Dharmapala, D., & Hines, J. R., Jr. (2009). Which countries become tax havens? *Journal of Public Economics, 93*, 1058–1068.

Dhrymes, P. J. (1978). *Mathematics for econometrics.* New York: Springer.

Dick, A. R. (1993). Strategic trade-policy and welfare—The empirical consequences of cross-ownership. *Journal of International Economics, 35*(3–4), 227–249.

Eaton, B. C. (2004). The elementary economics of social dilemmas. *Canadian Journal of Economics, 37*(4), 805–829.

Edwards, J., & Keen, M. (1996). Tax competition and Leviathan. *European Economic Review, 40*(1), 113–134.

Eggert, W., & Kolmar, M. (2002). Residence-based capital taxation in a small open economy: Why information is voluntarily exchanged and why it is not. *International Tax and Public Finance, 9*(4), 465–482.

Eggert, W., & Sørensen, P. B. (2008). The effects of tax competition when politicians create rents to buy votes. *Journal of Public Economics, 92*(5–6), 1142–1163.

Elsayyad, M., & Konrad, K. A. (2012). Fighting multiple tax havens. *Journal of International Economics, 86*(2), 295–305.

Feeney, J., & Hillman, A. L. (2001). Privatization and the political economy of strategic trade policy. *International Economic Review, 42*(2), 535–556.

Fenge, R., & Wrede, M. (2007). EU financing and regional policy: Vertical fiscal externalities when capital is mobile. *FinanzArchiv, 63*(4), 457–476.

Ferrett, B., & Wooton, I. (2010a). Tax competition and the international distribution of firm ownership: An invariance result. *International Tax and Public Finance, 17*(5), 518–531.

Ferrett, B., & Wooton, I. (2010b). Competing for a duopoly: International trade and tax competition. *Canadian Journal of Economics, 43*(3), 776–794.

Flowers, M. R. (1988). Shared tax sources in a leviathan model of federalism. *Public Finance Quarterly, 16*(1), 67–77.

Fuest, C. (2005). Economic integration and tax policy with endogenous foreign firm ownership. *Journal of Public Economics, 89*(9–10), 1823–1840.

Fuest, C., & Huber, B. (1999). Can tax coordination work? *Finanzarchiv, 56*(3–4), 443–458.

Fuest, C., & Huber, B. (2001). Tax competition and tax coordination in a median voter model. *Public Choice, 107*(1–2), 97–113.

Fuest, C., Huber, B., & Mintz, J. (2005). Capital mobility and tax competition: A survey. *Foundations and Trends in Microeconomics, 1*(1), 1–62.

Genschel, P., & Schwarz, P. (2011). Tax competition: A literature review. *Socio-Economic Review, 9*(2), 339–370.

Gérard, M., Jayet, H., & Paty, S. (2010). Tax interaction among Belgian municipalities: Do interregional differences matter? *Regional Science and Urban Economics, 40*(5), 336–342.

Gordon, R. H. (1986). Taxation of investment and savings in a world-economy. *American Economic Review, 76*(5), 1086–1102.

Gordon, R.H., & Hines, J.R., Jr. (2002). International taxation. In A.J. Auerbach, & M. Feldstein, (Eds.), *Handbook of Public Economics* (Vol. 4, pp. 1935–1995). Amsterdam: Elsevier.

Gordon, R. H., & Wilson, J. D. (1986). An examination of multijurisdictional corporate income taxation under formula apportionment. *Econometrica, 54*(6), 1357–1373.

Gresik, T. A. (2001). The taxing task of taxing transnationals. *Journal of Economic Literature, 39*(3), 800–838.

Haaparanta, P. (1996). Competition for foreign direct investment. *Journal of Public Economics, 63*(1), 141–153.

Hamilton, J. H., & Slutsky, S. M. (1990). Endogenous timing in duopoly games: Stackelberg or Cournot equilibria. *Games and Economic Behavior, 2*(1), 29–46.

Haufler, A., & Schulte, C. (2011). Merger policy and tax competition: the role of foreign firm ownership. *International Tax and Public Finance, 18*(2), 121–145.

Haufler, A., & Wooton, I. (1999). Country size and tax competition for foreign direct investment. *Journal of Public Economics, 71*(1), 121–139.

Haufler, A., & Wooton, I. (2006). The effects of regional tax and subsidy coordination on foreign direct investment. *European Economic Review, 50*(2), 285–305.

Haufler, A., & Wooton, I. (2010). Competition for firms in an oligopolistic industry: The impact of economic integration. *Journal of International Economics, 80*(2), 239–248.

Haupt, A., & Peters, W. (2005). Restricting preferential tax regimes to avoid harmful tax competition. *Regional Science and Urban Economics, 35*(5), 493–507.

Hayashi, M., & Boadway, R. W. (2001). An empirical analysis of intergovernmental tax interaction: The case of business income taxes in Canada. *Canadian Journal of Economics, 34*(2), 481–503.

Holmes, T. J. (1989). The effects of third-degree price discrimination in oligopoly. *American Economic Review, 79*(1), 244–250.

Hong, Q., & Smart, M. (2010). In praise of tax havens: International tax planning and foreign direct investment. *European Economic Review, 54*(1), 82–95.

Huck, S., & Konrad, K. A. (2003). Strategic trade policy and the home bias in firm ownership structure. *Japan and the World Economy, 15*(3), 299–305.

Huck, S., & Konrad, K. A. (2004). Merger profitability and trade policy. *Scandinavian Journal of Economics, 106*(1), 107–122.

Huizinga, H. (1995). The optimal taxation of savings and investment in an open economy. *Economics Letters, 47*(1), 59–62.

Huizinga, H., & Nicodème, G. (2006). Foreign ownership and corporate income taxation: an empirical evaluation. *European Economic Review, 50*(5), 1223–1244.

Huizinga, H., & Nielsen, S. B. (1997). Capital income and profit taxation with foreign ownership of firms. *Journal of International Economics, 42*(1–2), 149–165.

Huizinga, H., & Nielsen, S. B. (2002). The coordination of capital income and profit taxation with cross-ownership of firms. *Regional Science and Urban Economics, 32*(1), 1–26.

Huizinga, H., & Nielsen, S. B. (2003). Withholding taxes or information exchange: The taxation of international interest flows. *Journal of Public Economics, 87*(1), 39–72.

Huizinga, H., & Nielsen, S. B. (2008). Must losing taxes on saving be harmful? *Journal of Public Economics, 92*(5–6), 1183–1192.

Ihori, T., & Yang, C. C. (2009). Interregional tax competition and intraregional political competition: the optimal provision of public goods under representative democracy. *Journal of Urban Economics, 66*(3), 210–217.

Jacobs, J. P. A. M., Ligthart, J. E., & Vrijburg, H. (2010). Consumption tax competition among governments: Evidence from the United States. *International Tax and Public Finance, 17*(3), 271–294.

Janeba, E. (2000). Tax competition when governments lack commitment: Excess capacity as a countervailing threat. *American Economic Review, 90*(5), 1508–1519.

Janeba, E., & Osterloh, S. (2012). Tax and the city: A theory of local tax competition and evidence for Germany. *ZEW discussion papers*, No. 12-005, ZEW, Mannheim.

Janeba, E., & Peters, W. (1999). Tax evasion, tax competition and the gains from nondiscrimination: The case of interest taxation in Europe. *Economic Journal, 109*(452), 93–101.

Janeba, E., & Smart, M. (2003). Is targeted tax competition less harmful than its remedies? *International Tax and Public Finance, 10*(3), 259–280.

Johannesen, N. (2010). Imperfect tax competition for profits, asymmetric equilibrium and beneficial tax havens. *Journal of International Economics, 81*(2), 253–264.

Johannesen, N., & Zucman, G. (2012). The end of bank secrecy? An evaluation of the G20 tax haven crackdown. *Working paper*, No. 2012-04, Paris School of Economics, Paris.

Kanbur, R., & Keen, M. (1993). Jeux sans frontières: Tax competition and tax coordination when countries differ in size. *American Economic Review, 83*(4), 877–892.

Karkalakos, S., & Kotsogiannis, C. (2007). A spatial analysis of provincial corporate income tax responses: Evidence from Canada. *Canadian Journal of Economics, 40*(3), 782–811.

Keen, M. (1999). *EMU and tax competition.* International Monetary Fund, Mimeo, Washington, DC.

Keen, M. (2001). Preferential regimes can make tax competition less harmful. *National Tax Journal, 54*(4), 757–762.

Keen, M. (2002). Some international issues in commodity taxation. *Swedish Economic Policy Review, 9*(2002), 9–45.

Keen, M., & Kotsogiannis, C. (2002). Does federalism lead to excessively high taxes? *American Economic Review, 92*(1), 363–370.

Keen, M., & Kotsogiannis, C. (2004). Tax competition in federations and the welfare consequences of decentralization. *Journal of Urban Economics, 56*(3), 397–407.

Keen, M., & Ligthart, J. E. (2006). Information sharing and international taxation: A primer. *International Tax and Public Finance, 13*(1), 81–110.

Keen, M., & Marchand, M. (1997). Fiscal competition and the pattern of public spending. *Journal of Public Economics, 66*(1), 33–53.

Keen, M., & Wildasin, D. (2004). Pareto-efficient international taxation. *American Economic Review, 94*(1), 259–275.

Kehoe, P. J. (1989). Policy cooperation among benevolent governments may be undesirable. *Review of Economic Studies, 56*(2), 289–296.

Kelders, C., & Koethenbuerger, M. (2010). Tax incentives in fiscal federalism: An integrated perspective. *Canadian Journal of Economics, 43*(2), 683–703.

Kempf, H., & Rota Graziosi, G. (2010). Endogenizing leadership in tax competition. *Journal of Public Economics, 94*(9–10), 768–776.

Kempf, H., & Rota Graziosi, G. (2012). Further analysis on leadership in tax competition: The role of capital ownership. A reply.

Kessing, S. G., Konrad, K. A., & Kotsogiannis, C. (2006). Federal tax autonomy and the limits of cooperation. *Journal of Urban Economics, 59*(2), 317–329.

Kessing, S. G., Konrad, K. A., & Kotsogiannis, C. (2009). Federalism, weak institutions and the competition for foreign direct investment. *International Tax and Public Finance, 16*(1), 105–123.

King, I., McAfee, P. R., & Welling, L. A. (1993). Industrial blackmail: Dynamic tax competition and public investment. *Canadian Journal of Economics, 26*(3), 590–608.

Kiss, Á. (2012). Minimum taxes and repeated tax competition. *International Tax and Public Finance, 19*(5), 641–649.

Kleinbard, E. D. (2011). Stateless income. *Florida Tax Review, 11*(9), 699–773.

Konrad, K. A. (2009). Non-binding minimum taxes may foster tax competition. *Economics Letters, 102*(2), 109–111.

Konrad, K. A., & Kovenock, D. (2009). Competition for FDI with vintage investment and agglomeration advantages. *Journal of International Economics, 79*(2), 230–237.

Konrad, K. A., & Lommerud, K. E. (2001). Foreign direct investment, intra-firm trade and ownership structure. *European Economic Review, 45*(3), 475–494.

Konrad, K. A., & Schjelderup, G. (1999). Fortress building in global tax competition. *Journal of Urban Economics, 46*(1), 156–167.

Kotsogiannis, C. (2010). Federal tax competition and the efficiency consequences for local taxation of revenue equalization. *International Tax and Public Finance, 17*(1), 1–14.

Kydland, F. E., & Prescott, E. C. (1980). Dynamic optimal taxation, rational-expectations and optimal control. *Journal of Economic Dynamics and Control, 2*(1), 79–91.

Laussel, D., & Le Breton, M. (1998). Existence of Nash equilibria in fiscal competition models. *Regional Science and Urban Economics, 28*(2), 283–296.

Lipsey, R. G., & Lancaster, K. (1956). The general theory of second best. *Review of Economic Studies, 24*(1), 11–32.

Lockwood, B. (1997). Can international commodity tax harmonisation be Pareto-improving when governments supply public goods? *Journal of International Economics, 43*(3–4), 387–408.

Lockwood, B. (2004). Competition in unit vs. ad valorem taxes. *International Tax and Public Finance, 11*(6), 763–772.

Marceau, N., Mongrain, S., & Wilson, J. D. (2010). Why do most countries set high tax rates on capital? *Journal of International Economics, 80*(2), 249–259.

Mintz, J., & Smart, M. (2004). Income shifting, investment, and tax competition: Theory and evidence from provincial taxation in Canada. *Journal of Public Economics, 88*(6), 1149–1168.

Mintz, J., & Tulkens, H. (1986). Commodity tax competition between members of a federation: Equilibrium and efficiency. *Journal of Public Economics, 29*(2), 133–172.

Mintz, J., & Tulkens, H. (1996). Optimality properties of alternative systems of taxation of foreign capital income. *Journal of Public Economics, 60*(2), 373–399.

Mintz, J., & Weichenrieder, A. (2010). *The indirect side of direct investment: Multinational company finance and taxation.* Cambridge, MA: MIT Press.

Musgrave, P. B. (1963). *Taxation of foreign investment income: An economic analysis.* Baltimore, MD: Johns Hopkins Press.

Narasimhan, C. (1988). Competitive promotional strategies. *Journal of Business, 61*(4), 427–449.

Nielsen, S. B. (2001). A simple model of commodity taxation and cross-border shopping. *Scandinavian Journal of Economics, 103*(4), 599–623.

Nielsen, S. B., Raimondos-Møller, P., & Schjelderup, G. (2003). Formula apportionment and transfer pricing under oligopolistic competition. *Journal of Public Economic Theory, 5*(2), 419–437.

Nielsen, S. B., Raimondos-Møller, P., & Schjelderup, G. (2010). Company taxation and tax spillovers: Separate accounting versus formula apportionment. *European Economic Review, 54*(1), 121–132.

Norbäck, P. J., & Persson, L. (2005). Privatization policy in an international oligopoly. *Economica, 72*(288), 635–653.

Ogawa, H. (2013). Further analysis on leadership in tax competition: The role of capital ownership. *International Tax and Public Finance, 20*(3), 474–484.

Ohsawa, Y. (1999). Cross-border shopping and commodity tax competition among governments. *Regional Science and Urban Economics, 29*(1), 33–51.

Organisation for Economic Cooperation and Development (1998). *Harmful tax competition: An emerging global issue.* Paris: OECD.

Organisation for Economic Cooperation and Development (2000). *Towards global tax cooperation: Progress in identifying and eliminating harmful tax practices.* Paris: OECD.

Overesch, M., & Rincke, J. (2009). Competition from low-wage countries and the decline of corporate tax rates: evidence from European integration. *World Economy, 32*(9), 1348–1364.

Panagariya, A. (2000). Preferential trade liberalization: The traditional theory and new developments. *Journal of Economic Literature, 38*(2), 287–331.

Parry, I. W. H. (2003). How large are the welfare costs of tax competition? *Journal of Urban Economics, 54*(1), 39–60.

Peralta, S., & van Ypersele, T. (2005). Factor endowments and welfare levels in an asymmetric tax competition game. *Journal of Urban Economics, 57*(2), 258–274.

Peralta, S., & van Ypersele, T. (2006). Coordination of capital taxation among asymmetric countries. *Regional Science and Urban Economics, 36*(6), 708–726.

Persson, T., & Tabellini, G. (1992). The politics of 1992: Fiscal policy and European integration. *Review of Economic Studies, 59*(4), 689–701.

Raff, H. (2004). Preferential trade agreements and tax competition for foreign direct investment. *Journal of Public Economics, 88*(12), 2745–2763.

Revelli, F. (2003). Reaction or interaction? Spatial process identification in multi-tiered government structures. *Journal of Urban Economics, 53*(1), 29–53.

Rota Graziosi, G. (2013). On the supermodularity of the tax competition game. International Monetary Fund, Washington, DC, Mimeo.

Ruding, O. (1992). *Conclusions and recommendations of the committee of independent experts on company taxation.* Report of the committee of independent experts on company taxation, Commission of the European communities, Official Publications of the EC, Commission of the European communities, Brussels.

Schmalensee, R. (1981). Output and welfare implications for monopolistic third-degree price discrimination. *American Economic Review, 71*(1), 242–247.

Schön, W. (2005). Playing different games? Regulatory competition in tax and company law compared. *Common Market Law Review, 42*(2), 331–365.

Schön, W., & Konrad, K. A. (Eds.), (2012). *Fundamentals of international transfer pricing in law and economics.* Heidelberg: Springer.

Sinn, H.-W. (1997). The selection principle and market failure in systems competition. *Journal of Public Economics, 66*(2), 247–274.

Slemrod, J. (2008). Why is Elvis on Burkina Faso postage stamps? Cross-country evidence on the commercialization of state sovereignty. *Journal of Empirical Legal Studies, 5*(4), 683–712.

Slemrod, J., & Wilson, J. D. (2009). Tax competition with parasitic tax havens. *Journal of Public Economics, 93*(11–12), 1261–1270.

Sørensen, P. B. (2004a). International tax coordination: Regionalism versus globalism. *Journal of Public Economics, 88*(6), 1187–1214.

Sørensen, P. B. (2004b). Company tax reform in the European Union. *International Tax and Public Finance, 11*(1), 91–115.

Taugourdeau, E., & Ziad, A. (2011). On the existence of Nash equilibria in an asymmetric tax competition game. *Regional Science and Urban Economics, 41*(5), 439–445.

Vanistendael, F. (1992). The Ruding committee report: A personal view. *Fiscal Studies, 13*(2), 85–95.

Vrijburg, H., & de Mooij, R. A. (2010), Enhanced cooperation in an asymmetric model of tax competition. *CESifo Working Paper* No. 2915, CESifo, Munich.

Wang, Y.-Q. (1999). Commodity taxes under fiscal competition: Stackelberg equilibrium and optimality. *American Economic Review, 89*(4), 974–981.

Weightman, G. (2007). *The Industrial revolutionaries.* New York: Grove Press.

Weiner, J. (2005). Formulary apportionment and group taxation in the European Union: Insights from the United States and Canada. *Taxation paper* 8/2005, Commission of the European communities, Brussels.

Wildasin, D. E. (1988). Nash equilibria in models of fiscal competition. *Journal of Public Economics, 35*(2), 229–240.

Wildasin, D. E. (1991a). Some rudimentary duopolity theory. *Regional Science and Urban Economics, 21*(3), 393–421.

Wildasin, D. E. (1991b). Income distribution in a common labor market. *American Economic Review, 81*(4), 757–774.

Wildasin, D. E. (2003). Fiscal competition in space and time. *Journal of Public Economics, 87*(11), 2571–2588.

Wildasin, D. E., & Wilson, J. D. (1998). Risky local tax bases: Risk-pooling vs. rent-capture. *Journal of Public Economics, 69*(82), 229–247.

Wilson, J. D. (1986). A theory of interregional tax competition. *Journal of Urban Economics, 19*(3), 296–315.

Wilson, J. D. (1991). Tax competition with interregional differences in factor endowments. *Regional Science and Urban Economics, 21*(3), 423–451.

Wilson, J. D. (1999). Theories of tax competition. *National Tax Journal, 52*(2), 269–304.

Wilson, J. D., & Janeba, E. (2005). Decentralization and international tax competition. *Journal of Public Economics, 89*(7), 1211–1229.

Wilson, J. D., & Wildasin, D. E. (2004). Capital tax competition: Bane or boon. *Journal of Public Economics, 88*(6), 1065–1091.

Winner, H. (2005). Has tax competition emerged in OECD countries? Evidence from panel data. *International Tax and Public Finance, 12*(5), 667–687.

Wrede, M. (1999). Tragedy of the fiscal common? Fiscal stock externalities in a leviathan model of federalism. *Public Choice, 101*(3–4), 177–193.

Zodrow, G. R. (2003). Tax competition and tax coordination in the European Union. *International Tax and Public Finance, 10*(6), 651–671.

Zodrow, G. R. (2010). Capital mobility and capital tax competition. *National Tax Journal, 63*(4), 865–902.

Zodrow, G. R., & Mieszkowski, P. (1986). Pigou, Tiebout, property taxation, and the underprovision of local public goods. *Journal of Urban Economics, 19*(3), 356–370.

Zucman, G. (2011), The missing wealth of nations: Are Europe and the US net debtors or net creditors? *Working paper,* 2011-07, Paris School of Economics, Paris.

Taxation of Intergenerational Transfers and Wealth

Wojciech Kopczuk
Department of Economics and School of International and Public Affairs and National Bureau of Economic Research, Columbia University

Contents

Handbook of Public Economics, Volume 5
ISSN 1573-4420, http://dx.doi.org/10.1016/B978-0-444-53759-1.00006-6

1. INTRODUCTION

The objective of this chapter is to provide an introduction to and review of economic literature related to taxation of transfers and wealth. As will become clear in what follows, the focus will be primarily on taxes imposed on intergenerational transfers. Such taxes take many different forms. Transfers that occur at death may be taxed in the form of estate taxation, i.e., the tax may be imposed on the total amount of wealth left by the decedent. They may take the form of an inheritance tax, in which case the base is defined on the level of the donee, and reflects the transfers to that particular individual.[1] If taxes were imposed only at death, the simplest form of avoidance would be to transfer resources inter vivos (during lifetime). Hence transfer taxation systems usually include a tax on gifts as well.[2] Taxes on estates are a form of a tax on wealth and, although it is rare, some countries (e.g., France and Norway) impose annual taxes of that kind.

Transfer and wealth taxes have unique features that make them different than other types of direct taxation. First of all, they inherently affect two-related parties so that the distortion affects a transaction (transfer) that is not arms-length and that may involve externalities. This makes understanding and assumptions about transfer motives central to both positive and normative analysis. Second, they are infrequent (at the extreme, occurring just at death), thereby allowing for a long period of planning, making expectations about future tax policy critical and empirical identification of the effect of incentives particularly hard. Potentially large amounts of money at stake make investment in tax avoidance worthwhile in the presence of fixed costs and incentives to do so are potentially quite salient. Third, in practice, this type of taxation often applies only to a small but important group of individuals—those with sufficiently high wealth at the time of taxation—and thus plays a potentially important role in overall distributional implications of taxation, both in the short and in the long term.

There are many dimensions of differences in the implementation of transfer taxation across countries, states, and over time. On the basic design level, the estate tax may treat preferentially transfers to the spouse or charity, inheritance tax may vary depending on the relationship to the donor, gifts may be taxed on annual or lifetime basis, they may be integrated (or not) with taxation at death, details of interaction with capital gains taxation regime may vary. Many features of implementation of the tax may matter greatly—some examples are valuation rules, preferences for particular types of assets, treatment of transfers shortly before death, treatment of marital assets, implications of

[1] Inheritance taxation may in principle be integrated with personal income taxation, see Batchelder (2009) for a discussion and a proposal for the reform of the US transfer tax system along these lines.

[2] The actual implementation does vary though. For example, in the US, the estate tax operated without a gift tax from 1916 until 1932, and since then gifts made within three years of death may be subject to different treatment than those made earlier (if made in "contemplation of death"; they were automatically included in estate between 1976 and 1981, see Luckey (2008) for the history of provisions). In the UK, there is no tax on gifts made more than seven years before death (though there was one between 1975 and 1984, see Boadway, Chamberlain, and Emmerson (2010b) for the discussion of changes).

joint vs community property, treatment of charity, and treatment of transfers that skip generations. The purpose of this chapter is not to discuss all of these issues, although in Section 2, I will provide a short overview of history of the estate tax in the United States and international differences in transfer tax systems. Instead, my objective is to focus on the economics of transfer taxation and to offer a critical review of related theoretical and empirical research. This research is of course largely motivated by the existing forms of taxation. In particular, empirical work naturally relies on what can be observed in practice and some of it is directly motivated by important current policy questions. Most, though not all, of research on these topics took place in the United States and hence the "bias" toward evidence (and salient policy questions) from the US will be present. However, the focus of the chapter is on taxation of transfers in general, with the US being just a (prominent) example. I will discuss taxation of wealth briefly, to the extent that it relates to taxation of transfers (rather than being a form of tax on capital incomes that is discussed elsewhere in this Handbook).

This is not the first survey of literature related to transfers and their taxation. Gale and Slemrod (2001) and Boadway, Chamberlain, and Emmerson (2010a) provide useful background to the issues surrounding the design of transfer taxation. Cremer and Pestieau (2006, chap. 16) discuss some theoretical contributions to the literature on taxation of bequests. Laitner (1997), Laferrère and Wolff (2006, chap. 13), and Arrondel and Masson (2006, chap. 14) discuss theoretical and empirical work on intergenerational linkages. Davies and Shorrocks (2000) and Cagetti and De Nardi (2008) cover work on wealth distribution. Luckey (2008) and Joulfaian (2011) provide excellent overviews of the history of estate tax legislations in the United States.

Before dwelling into details, it is worth emphasizing the structure, major themes, and conclusions of this review.

I will begin in the next section with a brief overview of how taxation of this kind works and varies in practice—across countries, across states in the United States, and over time.

In Section 3, I discuss evidence on bequest motives and basic normative implications of different motives for thinking about taxation. Bequest motives are the key building block for theoretical analysis of taxation of transfers, but the empirical literature has not settled on a clear answer to the question about the nature of bequest motivations. I emphasize heterogeneity of two different kinds. First, search for *the* bequest motive is unlikely to be fruitful—saving plays dual role of protecting against lifetime risk and increasing transfers to others. Different motivations for transfers are not mutually exclusive—the same person may be altruistic and yet interested in controlling wealth or engaged in strategic interactions with children. Second, I emphasize the evidence suggesting that preferences are heterogeneous and do not necessarily cut across predictable lines (such as having kids). The primary conclusion of this section is that theoretical work should either be somewhat agnostic (general) about the nature of the bequest motive or it should explicitly account for heterogeneity.

In Section 4, I focus on the main theoretical framework for analyzing bequests taxation that builds on Mirrlees (1971) and Atkinson and Stiglitz (1976) approach to taxation of commodities in the presence of non-linear income taxation, adapted to transfer context by Kaplow (1998, 2001). This approach of course incorporates redistributive preferences for a policy maker. The basic insight is that transfers can be modeled as a form of consumption, albeit one with two unusual but related features. First, transfers directly benefit someone else besides the donor. Second, the presence of such a benefit may generate a form of externality from giving. An externality from giving is natural to consider in this context and provides a reason for subsidizing rather than taxing bequests. I discuss the logic of corrective taxation of externalities in a context with individualized rather than atmospheric externality and conclude that externalities from giving are not important for thinking about taxation at the top of the distribution: that is, they are irrelevant precisely where taxation of transfers is important in practice. Furthermore, I point out that theoretical implications of inequality in received inheritances are not yet fully understood and are likely to lead to arguments for positive taxation of bequests. I then discuss work on capital income taxation more generally and point out its relationship to transfer taxation.

In Section 5, I begin to review empirical evidence on the effects of taxation of transfers. The focus of that section is on "real" responses—changes in the volume and timing of actual transfers, effect on labor supply, capital gains realizations, charity and transfer and survival of businesses. I follow up in Section 6 with the discussion of responses that fall along the avoidance margin. That section is focused primarily on evidence that applies to people with significant net worth and the key message of this discussion is that transfer tax planning involves a trade-off between tax minimization and control over wealth.

Section 7 is devoted to a few other topics that do not naturally fit elsewhere. I elaborate further on the relationship of estate taxation and the shape of wealth distribution, discuss empirical work related to charitable bequests, and briefly comment on research on marital bequests, tax competition, and political economy of this type of taxation. The final section concludes.

The main message of this chapter may be summarized as follows. Empirical evidence on bequest motivations and responses to estate taxation is spotty and much remains be done, but what we know points in the direction of (1) mixed motives, (2) heterogeneity of preferences, and (3) importance of retaining control over wealth. Incorporating these components of empirical evidence into theoretical analysis is crucial, and especially so when thinking about taxation toward the top of the distribution. Theoretical work should further focus on understanding implications of inequality of inherited wealth: the topic that has been neglected in the past, even though it is closely related to—more carefully studied but arguably much less important in practice—externalities from giving. Finally, potential negative externalities from wealth accumulation and concentration are yet to be seriously addressed.

2. OVERVIEW OF WEALTH AND ESTATE TAXATION IN PRACTICE

Taxation at death is administratively convenient: this is the time when assets change hands and need to be valued anyway, thereby increasing tax administration's ability to observe them. Wealth is arguably easier to observe than income, and taxes on wealth—most importantly on land but also on successions—have historically preceded taxation of income. Following the development of modern forms of income and consumption taxation, estate and wealth taxes are rarely a major source of revenue. However, they remain an unusually progressive component of the tax code. Limited revenue makes elimination of such taxes a realistic policy proposal and, indeed, a number of developed countries (for example, Canada, Sweden, and Australia and some states in the United States) repealed such taxes. Large financial stakes for a limited number of wealthy taxpayers make politics surrounding these issues contentious and subject to massive lobbying (Graetz & Shapiro, 2005).

Luckey (2008) and Joulfaian (2011) provide excellent and detailed overviews of the history of estate and inheritance taxation in the United States. A reader interested in state provisions should consult Bakija (2007) and sources referenced there. Gale and Slemrod (2001), Boadway et al. (2010b), and Scheve and Stasavage (2012) provide international comparison of transfer tax systems and rates for a few developed countries. An older discussion by Bird (1991) provides a comparison of inheritance taxes and annual wealth taxation for both developed and developing countries. Able reviews of economic aspects of inheritance tax systems exist for a number of other countries—for example, Boadway et al. (2010a, chap. 8) present detailed overview of inheritance taxation in the UK, Ohlsson (2011) does so for Sweden and Piketty (2011) describes the French system.

The United States instituted a number of short-lived inheritance or estates taxes[3] in the eighteenth and nineteenth century: the Death Stamp Tax was in place between 1789 and 1802, an inheritance tax during the Civil War, and an estate tax during the Spanish-American War.[4] A number of states had estate or inheritance taxes before the turn of the 20th century. The modern estate tax was enacted in 1916 with initial rates ranging from 1% to 10% and exemption of $50,000. The rates changed often before the top rate reached its peak of 77% by 1941, where it stayed until 1977. The estate tax was supplemented by a cumulative gift tax starting in 1932[5] in an effort to combat tax avoidance.[6]

The base of the tax was subject to numerous changes over the years. Tax treatment of marital transfers used to be a controversial issue in the early years of the estate tax, in

---

[3] This summary of the US provisions follows Luckey (2008) and Joulfaian (2011).

[4] See Scheve and Stasavage (2012) for exploration of the potential link between wars and transfer taxation.

[5] A short-lived and retroactively repealed gift tax was in place between 1924 and 1926.

[6] Nominal gift rates were set lower than estate tax rates apparently in deliberate effort to accelerate revenue flow (Joulfaian, 2011). This practice continues to date: even though tax rates are nominally the same, gift and estate taxes are calculated differently—gifts are taxed on a tax exclusive basis while estate tax applies to tax-inclusive base, resulting in higher effective marginal tax rates for estates than for gifts (see footnote 39).

part due to different marital property regimes in place in different states: in community property states half of property acquired during marriage belongs to each spouse and thus was automatically excluded from the estate, while in the remaining states such property originally could be excluded only to the extent that the surviving spouse could be shown to have contributed to its acquisition. This was perceived as inequitable and in 1942 the Congress attempted to address it by extending non-community property treatment to the community property states; this solution was considered complex and was replaced by marital deduction in 1948. Initially, half of adjusted gross estate was eligible for marital deduction (but community property was not); this was modified to allow for the marital deduction equal to the adjusted gross estate or $250,000 (whichever was greater) in 1977, and then unlimited marital deduction as of 1982.

Until 1976, gift and estate taxes were separate. The Tax Reform Act of 1976 introduced a uniform tax with a single tax schedule applying to the sum of cumulative lifetime taxable gifts and the estate; allowing, in particular, for a *unified* estate and gift tax credit (equivalent to a lifetime exemption). The same act also introduced a Generation Skipping Transfer Tax that imposes an additional layer of tax liability for certain transfers to grandchildren and related transactions. The effective exemption was increased at the same time from $60,000 (where it was since 1942) to $120,667 stopping the process of inflation-driven "bracket creep" that pushed the number of taxable tax returns to its all-time maximum of 7.65% of all deaths by 1976 (in contrast, the tax affected fewer than 2% of decedents in other periods). At the same time, the top tax rate was reduced to 70%. The additional rate reductions and increases in exemption level were enacted in 1981 and phased in over the number of following years, bringing the top rate to 55% and the exemption to $600,000 by 1987 where it stayed for more than a decade.

A number of other changes took place in the 1970s, 1980s, and 1990s. The 1976 reform attempted to introduce a carryover basis for capital gains. Capital gains that are not realized at the time of death are subject to the estate tax but escape capital gains taxation due to step-up provision that modifies the tax basis of the asset to its value at the time of death of the original owner. The carryover approach was intended to eliminate such resetting of the basis so that capital gains tax would still be due on full accumulation when a beneficiary ultimately sells the asset. This provision had, however, been delayed first and then repealed before it became effective. The same reform also changed treatment of gifts shortly before death by requiring that any gifts within three years of death be included in the estate (rather than relying on gifts in "contemplation of death"). During the 1980s, a number of changes benefiting closely-held businesses and farms were introduced, including alternate valuation rules, installment payments, and special rules applying to qualified family businesses.

In 2001, the estate tax was "repealed"—the Economic Growth and Tax Relief Reconciliation Act of 2001 enacted a 10-year schedule of reductions in rates and increases in exemption of the tax that was supposed to culminate in a repeal in 2010. The whole legislation was scheduled to sunset at the end of 2010 so that, absent additional action, the repeal would last one year only, at which point the schedule would return to their 2001 shape. Few, if any, observers expected this sequence of events to play itself out and yet this is almost exactly what happened: for most of 2010 there was no estate tax on the books, for the first time since 1916. At the end of 2010, the Tax Relief, Unemployment Insurance Reauthorization, and Job Creation Act of 2010 reinstated the estate tax in a modified form. While this provision was retroactive, estates for decedents who died in 2010 had an option of electing out of the estate tax. Such decision was not without trade-offs—assets passed in that way will not benefit from the step-up in basis at death and instead will effectively be subject to carryover basis treatment for capital gains purposes—but it is expected that few estates will choose to pay the estate tax in 2010 (data is not available yet). The provisions enacted in 2010 were temporary and applied to 2011 and 2012. They were made permanent for 2013 and beyond as part of the Taxpayer Relief Act of 2012 passed on January 1st 2013.

Even prior to the"repeal," changes in the 2000s were substantial—the exemption increased from $675,000 in 2001 to $3.5 million in 2009 and the maximum rate fell from 55% to 45%. The reinstated tax features an even larger exemption ($5 million) and lower top rate (35%). The implications of the 2010 repeal are yet to be studied (or even observed given the lags involved in filing and publication of statistics). Over that period, the number of estate tax returns filed (the date-of-death numbers are not yet available for most recent years) declined from over 108,000 in 2001 to 15,000 in 2010; and the number of taxable returns fell from over 50,000 to 6700; however the reduction in net estate tax liability was much smaller than these numbers and tax reductions might suggest: it fell from $23 billion to $13 billion, primarily reflecting skewness of the wealth distribution.[7] Changes in rates that applied to estates, applied also to gifts. The sole exception was the 2010 repeal: the gift tax remained in place throughout that year. As of 2013, the marginal tax rate is set at 40% and the exemption, $5.25 million in 2013, will be indexed for inflation.

There are many differences in how transfer taxation could be implemented in prac-tice. The United States federal tax is a tax on estates—the overall value of wealth left by a decedent. Somewhat similar structure is present in the UK and other English-speaking countries (or was present before the tax was repealed—as in the case of Canada). An alternative approach—in place in some US states (for example, Indiana, Maryland, Penn-sylvania, New Jersey) and in many continental European countries—is to impose a tax on inheritances, that is to shift the base to the recipient. This has two noteworthy implications: the overall tax liability depends on how estate is distributed and tax payments may be made dependent on the relationship to the donee in a straightforward way. Indeed, it is common for inheritance tax systems to vary tax liability depending on the relationship, usually with

---

[7] IRS Statistics of Income Division, Tax Stats, available online at http://www.irs.gov/taxstats/indtaxstats/article/0,,id=210646,00.html, accessed on 3/20/2012.

preferences for close relatives.[8] Yet another possibility—rarely in place in practice—is to integrate transfer tax within income tax system so that inheritances increase income tax base.[9]

Taxation of transfers is not the only way of imposing a general tax on wealth. Mintz (1991) and Auerbach (2008) discuss many different forms such taxes can take. Obviously, many types of taxation of income from wealth (interests, capital gains, dividends, etc.) are common. Taxation of particular forms of wealth—property, land, certain durable goods—is also often in place. Taxation of capital income is discussed in a separate chapter of the Handbook and taxes imposed on particular goods raise many interesting issues related to these specific markets but are not the focus of this chapter. Some countries— for example, France and Norway—also impose a net worth tax (usually annual). Brown (1991) carefully analyzes administrative difficulties in implementing an annual net wealth tax and concludes that practical problems are intractable. Adam et al. (2011, chap. 14) assert that practical difficulties and actual experience of the implementation in countries that tried to do it have been discouraging. Defining base in a comprehensive manner is difficult—it requires costly and sometimes impractical valuation, especially in the case of business assets. Naturally, taxation of "human capital" in this way is not a realistic option. Deviating from the comprehensive basis, as is done in practice, allows for tax avoidance opportunities. A regular tax on wealth is closely related to a tax on capital income. As Adam et al. (2011, chap. 14) point out though, net worth tax predominantly taxes the normal rate of return rather than excess return. In particular, under wealth taxation exempting the normal rate of return is not a realistic option, thereby making it a less desirable form of taxation than direct taxes on capital income.[10] The main advantage of this form of taxation over capital income taxation is its ability to tax assets that do not generate income (in particular, due to tax avoidance). Transfer taxation, on which this chapter mostly focuses, retains this property and takes advantage of the administratively convenient (even if unpopular) timing—death—when assets change hands anyway so that they are more easily observable and when difficult valuation issues often would need to be addressed anyway, thereby easing tax compliance burden.

[8] Estate tax systems do allow for some adjustments to the overall tax liability depending on the recipient through deductions—for example, in the US transfers to a spouse or to a charity are fully deductible. In principle, one could also imagine introducing variation in rates through tax credits for gifts to specific recipients; naturally though inheritance taxation makes such adjustments much less complex.

[9] See Batchelder (2009) for an extensive discussion of this possibility. In particular, she reports that a few countries (Denmark, Iceland, Lithuania, and Russia) include gifts in the income tax base. A short-lived (struck down as unconstitutional) 1894 the US income and inheritance tax was supposed to include inheritances as part of the income tax base.

[10] Using Adam et al. (2011, chap. 14) example, assume that the normal rate of return is 5%. A 20% capital income tax is equivalent to upfront 1% wealth tax. Both systems discourage saving, but under capital income tax excess return is taxed at 20%, while wealth tax exempts it. Shifting the net worth tax in this example to the second period makes only minor difference by taxing excess returns lightly (at 1% if keeping the present value of revenue constant). Exempting the normal rate of return under net worth tax would effectively wipe out tax liability, while doing so under capital income taxation is conceivable. Such an approach (rate-of-return allowance, RRA) has in fact been implemented in Norway.

3. BEQUEST MOTIVES AND TAXATION

3.1. Single Generation

In order to systematize the discussion of theoretical arguments related to transfer taxation, it is instructive to start with a single individual utility maximization problem. Consider an individual maximizing utility $u(C, B)$ defined over consumption (C) and transfers to a beneficiary (B), subject to the budget constraint $C + pB = y$ where y is income, p is the relative price of transfers and the price of consumption is normalized to one. Individuals will naturally set $u_B/u_C = p$ and changes in p and y will give rise to price and substitution responses.

Let's denote the pre-tax relative price of bequests by R (absent taxation we have $p = R$; one natural interpretation is as $R = (1 + r)^{-1}$ where r is the rate of return). The base for the estate tax is $y - C$ and, denoting the estate tax rate by t, the budget constraint is $(1 - t)C + RB = (1 - t)y$ or, equivalently, $C + \frac{R}{1-t}B = y$. The estate tax increases relative price of bequests and stimulates negative substitution response and further reduction of bequests via income effect (unless bequests are an inferior good). Imposing a tax on the basis of the amount received by the beneficiary (as is done in the case of gift taxation in the US) would instead correspond to the tax liability of $t^G B$, the budget constraint of $C + R(1 + t^G)B = y$ and identical predictions about the direction of the response.

This simple formulation is an example of a particular type of bequest motive—the "joy-of-giving" or "warm-glow"—and is the baseline reduced-form approach used in analyzing implications of taxation of bequests or charitable contributions when the focus is on the donor only (Andreoni, 1990).

The assumption here is that bequests are just as any other consumption good in that they deliver utility to the giver and correspondingly respond to price incentives. This is an assumption that may not hold in practice. The simplest alternative is to consider a situation in which a taxpayer does not care about the amount received by the recipient but is instead concerned with the amount of wealth W that she contributes. Using the linear estate-tax formulation, $B = (1 - t)W/R$. The simplest wealth-in-utility formulation $u(C, W)$ is observationally equivalent to the joy-of-giving motive, except for the implications of taxation: the budget constraint remains $C + W = y$ in the presence of taxation and changes in taxation have no implications for individual behavior. Hence, these two very similar formulations—joy-of-giving and wealth-in-utility—have very different implications when considering responses to and efficiency cost of taxation.

This approach (also referred to as "capitalistic spirit," following Weber, 1958) has been advocated in the literature modeling the top end of wealth distribution as a suitable way of representing motives of high net worth individuals (Carroll, 2000; Francis, 2009; Reiter, 2004), the topic to which we will return in Section 7.1. Some possible justifications for considering wealth-in-utility are either as an intrinsic utility from accumulating wealth or as a proxy for unmodeled benefits of wealth holding—power that it allows to exert over others, relaxing of borrowing constraints, precautionary benefits, or using wealth as a measure of relative status (e.g. due to positional externalities as in Frank, 2008).

An alternative model of bequests that do not yield utility to the donor is the "accidental" bequest approach. In the life-cycle framework with uncertain lifespan (Yaari, 1965), individuals save for future consumption but, except for the last possible period of life, may die with positive wealth holdings. Whether that occurs depends on actuarial fairness of the market for annuities: if annuities are fairly priced, all consumption should be effectively annuitized and bequests would not occur (instead, insurance company would gain *ex post* in case of early death). If the annuity market is imperfect, as the empirical evidence suggests (Friedman & Warshawsky, 1990; Mitchell, Poterba, Warshawsky, & Brown, 1999), people die with positive wealth. Hence, bequests are unintended and stochastic. As with wealth-in-utility approach, taxation has no effect on the size of bequests.

One often-repeated statement about taxation of accidental bequests is that 100% tax is efficient because it elicits no response. While the latter part of this statement is true, the former requires qualifications (Kopczuk, 2003b). The tax on accidental bequests in a representative individual context indeed has the benefit of reducing "waste"—bequests would otherwise not be available for consumption purposes. Naturally this argument does not survive considering a more realistic context when bequests instead flow to some other party and hence are not assumed to be wasted. In that case, the tax on accidental bequests becomes simply equivalent to lump-sum taxation on the beneficiary. More subtly, accidental bequests reflect the presence of underlying imperfections in the market for annuities. A taxpayer would clearly be better off by selling the right to (unintended) bequest conditional on dying at some time t (that has no value to him) and using proceeds for consumption in any other period. While confiscating a bequest of this kind yields no harm, it also does not directly address the underlying market failure. The first-best policy would instead allow for complete consumption smoothing via annuities and imply no accidental bequest.

Kopczuk (2003b) shows that the estate tax itself may play an annuity role: the insight is that given interest rate r and sequence of effective tax liabilities T_i conditional on dying in period i, surviving from period i to period $i + 1$ implies a reduction of lifetime tax liability by $T_i - \frac{T_{i+1}}{1+r}$. The presence of this implicit annuity increases the value of the tax on accidental bequests—by using confiscatory tax on bequests, one reduces tax payments relative to the alternative of unconditional lifetime taxation with the same present value— but it becomes of more interest when individuals have additionally an explicit bequest motive where it can be shown that (1) a small estate tax is welfare improving because of its annuity role and (2) under strong enough bequest motive, sufficiently flexible estate tax can implement the first-best solution.[11]

---

[11] Even more generally, one can think of the estate tax as serving insurance role against other types of risks—such as investment risk—that would affect the value of estate at death.

3.2. Intergenerational Links

The discussion so far abstracted from the recipients of transfers. From the point of view of understanding bequest behavior the recipients may matter because the donor may respond to their characteristics or behavior. Furthermore, transfers—actual or expected—may also change the behavior of a recipient. For normative analysis, understanding implications of transfers for welfare of the recipient is important.

The most influential way of modeling intergenerational linkages is by introducing altruistic preferences la Barro (1974). It is assumed that prior generation cares directly about welfare of the following generation(s). With just two generations (parents and children) to begin with, preferences of the parents can be expressed as $u^P(C^P, C^K) = v^P(C^P) + \rho u^K(C^K)$ where C^P is a vector of consumption goods of the parent, C^K is a vector of consumption goods of the child, v^P is utility of the parent from own consumption and u^K is the utility of a child from own consumption. The parent is assumed to care about welfare of a child but discount it at some rate ρ (presumably with $\rho < 1$). Of course, this is a workhorse model used in hundreds of papers with many variants and extensions that are beyond the scope of this chapter (Laitner (1997) provides a good survey of theoretical aspects of altruistic preferences). In its simplest variant, one abstracts from overlap between generations (C^P occurs now, C^K in the future) and considers maximization subject to the common resource constraint

$$y^P + Ry^K = C^P + RC^K, \qquad (1)$$

where y^P is income of parents and y^K is income of children. In this formulation, bequests are equal to the unconsumed resources of the parent $y^P - C^P$.[12] The standard result is that re-allocating resources in a lump-sum fashion between period P and period C has no effect on the budget constraint (1)—the Ricardian equivalence result—with bequests adjusting to offset. This implication has been tested in the context of bequests (Altonji, Fumio, & Kotlikoff, 1992, 1997; Laitner & Ohlsson, 2001; Wilhelm, 1996) and soundly rejected. Another way of describing the implication is by noting that it calls for smoothing of marginal utility profile $v^P_C = \rho R u^K_C$. With multiple potential beneficiaries (e.g., multiple children), this condition should hold for *any* beneficiary—a conclusion that is not consistent with the pattern of equal bequest splitting documented in the literature (Light & McGarry, 2004; Menchik, 1980; Menchik & David, 1983).[13]

To understand implications for bequests, it is useful to explicitly consider a single period of life so that C^P and C^K are scalars and the parent's optimization problem is

[12] Perhaps augmented by investment returns R^{-1}, depending on the assumed convention about whether transfer occurs at the end of period when P generation is alive or the beginning of period when the C generation is active.

[13] Bernheim and Severinov (2003) propose an explanation for equal splitting that is based on the assumption that children care about altruistic parent's affection and infer it based in part on observable bequests. Severinov (2006) shows that this model can generate transfer patterns that are very similar to those under standard altruism but does not imply Ricardian equivalence. Dunn and Phillips (1997) and McGarry (1999) provide evidence that (presumably harder to observe) inter vivos gifts are compensatory while bequests are split equally.

$\max_{B,C^P} v^P(C^P) + \rho u^K(y^K + B)$ subject to the constraint $C^P + pB = y$, where $p = \frac{R}{1-t}$ is the after-tax cost of a dollar transfer to the beneficiary. This formulation makes it clear that when the focus is on donors' behavior only, there is a close connection between this model and the warm-glow one: parents care about their own consumption and bequests, except that the marginal value of bequests depends on the income of a child. Abel and Warshawsky (1988) build on this argument to show how intensity of altruism relates to the strength of the joy-of-giving bequest motive in a model with infinite horizon (although the relationship that they establish is not invariant to changes in taxation).

An alternative approach to bequests treats them as a transaction between parents and children with bequests compensating children for services that they provide to their parents, such as direct help, attention, access to grandchildren, etc. (Bernheim, Shleifer, & Summers, 1985; Cox, 1987; Perozek, 1998).[14] As with altruism, evidence in support of the exchange motive is mixed, see Arrondel and Masson (2006, chap. 14) and Laferrère and Wolff (2006, chap. 13) for recent surveys.

The conclusion that arises in the most recent work on bequest motives is that searching for *the* bequest motive is unlikely to be successful. This is for two reasons. First, different motives are not exclusive—in the presence of uncertainty, the precautionary/accidental and intentional motives naturally co-exist (Dynan, Skinner, & Zeldes, 2002, 2004); a person may also have a mix of altruistic and exchange motivations, or simultaneously put weight on both wealth and bequests for example.

Second, different individuals may have different motives. For example, Light and McGarry (2004) document heterogeneity in preference for leaving bequests based on verbatim answers given to a question about reasons for planning not to split bequests equally in National Longitudinal Surveys of Young Women and Mature Women. Laitner and Juster (1996), based on a survey of TIAA-Cref participants, show that the intention to leave a bequest is not universal and, in fact, does not seem to be even remotely close to being well explained by having children—45% of people with children consider bequests important relative to 21% of the childless ones.

Hurd (1987) shows that wealth profiles of people with and without children are similar. Using cross-sectional AHEAD/HRS data and a structural approach to modeling wealth profiles, Hurd (1989) allows for accidental and intended (joy-of-giving) bequests and tests for the presence of a bequest motive by assuming that people with kids have one and those without them do not. Given similarity of wealth profiles for those with and without children, he rejects that a bequest motive is present. Noting evidence in Laitner and Juster (1996) suggesting that children are unlikely to be a deterministic indicator of the presence of a bequest motive, Kopczuk and Lupton (2007) extend this approach to exploit longitudinal information and allow kids to be just one of the many potential (but non-deterministic) indicators of the presence of the motive in a switching

---

[14] Exchange motives give rise to "strategic" interactions between parents and children, but strategic interactions naturally arise in the multi-period altruistic context as well (Bruce & Waldman, 1991; Coate, 1995).

regression framework with unknown sample separation. They conclude that bequest motive is present (in fact, their parameters indicate that 3/4 of the population has one), but only weakly related to having children. Ameriks, Caplin, Laufer, and Van Nieuwerburgh (2011) model saving for long-term care and bequest motives; they use very similar switching regression strategy as Kopczuk and Lupton (2007) to conclude that both public long-term care aversion and bequest motives are important. Both of these papers find evidence supporting heterogeneity of the *presence* of the motive and they both find that bequests are a mix of accidental and intentional ones. The intentional bequests are effectively modeled as a luxury good. The results indicate that intentional bequest motive is not operational for much of the distribution where accidental bequest dominates. However, both type of motives become quantitatively important at higher levels of wealth.

Using estate tax data for filers in 1977, Kopczuk (2007) shows that wealth accumulation for the very wealthy continues until the onset of a terminal illness but that tax avoidance is responsive to that event, supporting the notion that people value both lifetime wealth and bequests. In the survey of literature on bequest motives, Arrondel and Masson (2006, chap. 14) advocate a mix of altruistic and strategic motives. The literature on the determinants of savings and wealth distribution grappled with this question as well (it will be discussed in more detail in Section 7.1). A strand of this literature assumes away the presence of a bequest motive (Hubbard, Skinner, & Zeldes, 1994, 1995; Scholz, Seshadri, & Khitatrakun, 2006), but it has problems explaining the very top of the wealth distribution. Adding an explicit bequest motive helps (Cagetti & De Nardi, 2008; De Nardi, 2004; Reiter, 2004), but the standard in the literature approach of assuming altruism is not able to generate sufficient skewness within the top 1% or so. Hence, researchers are often resorting to reduced-form specifications of the wealth-in-utility or warm-glow kind (though, as mentioned before, the choice between the two is not innocuous when considering implications of tax policy).

3.3. Normative Issues

The lack of consensus about the nature of bequest motives makes reaching definitive theoretical conclusions about the impact of taxation difficult and it makes normative analysis hard because it (often) requires taking a stand on the unknown nature of the bequest motive.[15]

Before engaging in a normative analysis, it is worthwhile to pause to understand what role taxation might play. To do so, consider a parent with utility of $u^P(C, W, B, X)$ where W is wealth, B is effective bequest, X are other variables describing interaction with the child (attention, services, non-monetary transfers); and a child with a reduced-form utility of $u^K(B, X)$. Suppose that the social planner is interested in maximizing the weighted

---

[15] Kopczuk (2001) and Cremer and Pestieau (2006, chap. 16) analyze bequest taxation using models that have different types of bequest motives as special cases.

sum of utilities

$$u^P + \beta u^K \tag{2}$$

subject to the relevant resource constraint. The nature of the transfer motive, details of the household bargaining problems, strategic interactions between parents and children influence the value of the objective. The outcome need not be efficient in general— for example, addressing the Samaritan's dilemma problem may require commitment on the part of the parents. The outcome need not also be fair—in the exchange context, the market power may be on the side of the parent or on the side of the child and need not reflect social preferences. Hence, there may be a conceivable justification of an intervention to address the potential inefficiency or redistribute resources within family. While not dismissing the relevance of such concerns, tax treatment of bequests or gifts is a blunt instrument for addressing them. In what follows, I will abstract from the issues that would call for the government intervention into family problem unless they explicitly relate to bequests. In particular, I will assume that the government respects the outcome of the family problem as efficient, unless explicitly stated otherwise.

The main reasons for a departure of government objective from respecting the maximization of family objective function considered in the literature has to do with the potential presence of externalities from giving (Kaplow, 1995, 1998). A dollar of bequests provides utility to both parents and children. From the social point of view, the benefit of a bequest is given by $u_B^P + \rho u_B^K$, but when maximizing her own utility the parent is only taking into account her own marginal benefit u_B^P and ignores the ρu_B^K component giving rise to an interpersonal externality. This externality is there regardless of the bequest motive *if* one accounts for welfare of a child beyond its effect on parent's utility. In many cases, this is a natural approach. For example, when the bequest motive has the warm-glow structure, the parent does not care about the utility of a child and instead is assumed to derive the utility from the value of a gift itself. Naturally then, one is inclined to consider bequests as being under-provided: the benefit that they deliver to the donee is not taken into account by the donor.

Selecting the normative criterion under altruistic model is more controversial, because parent's preferences already explicitly depend on child's utility. Writing, as before, the parental utility as $u^P(C^P, C^K) = v^P(C^P) + \rho u^K(C^K)$, the social planner's objective that accounts for both utility of the parent and the child becomes $u^P + \beta u^K = v^P + (\rho + \beta) u^K$. In the special case when $\beta = 0$, the social planner simply maximizes parental welfare. This is of course the standard approach of focusing on dynastic welfare. If instead $\beta > 0$, it corresponds to social planner putting an extra weight on welfare of children beyond what parents do.[16]

The key thing to observe is that normative analysis requires taking a stand on the presence of such an externality. In standard cases such as altruistic preferences or joy-of-giving

---

[16] One could also imagine $\beta < 0$—social planner discounting welfare of children more than parents do—the case that has been considered in political economy models.

bequest motive, the externality is caused by bequests and it is positive. As the result, its presence calls for corrective policies that would address the external effect. The Pigouvian subsidy to bequests that corrects the parental incentive to internalize the externality is the optimal policy in the first-best. In the second-best Ramsey commodity tax problems, it calls for adjustments to the tax structure but, as Sandmo (1975) shows, these adjustments should be targeted to the source of the externality—i.e., lead to a subsidy to bequests. Kopczuk (2003a) shows that the "targeting principle" logic applies to general tax problems with atmospheric externality (i.e., an externality that is generated by aggregate consumption) as long as the source of the externality can be taxed directly.

Considering an externality from giving is a normative assumption. Showing that it gives rise to subsidies to bequests is a straightforward consequence to keep in mind when evaluating normative tax exercises even when analytics of obtaining that conclusion is complicated. Having said that, the externality of that kind does come up naturally. Diamond (2006) provides a normative discussion of arguments for including the warm-glow motive in the social welfare function. In other words, the question he poses is not whether the benefit to the donee should be explicitly counted (as arises when one considers the altruistic case), but rather whether the benefit to the donor from the act of giving should be accounted for. The main argument for accounting for the warm glow is obviously that warm-glow preferences are presumed to determine behavior and hence should be accounted for by the social planner just as preferences for any other good. The main counter-arguments have to do with reduced-form of such preferences that may miss other benefits or costs, and with consequences of accounting for the utility from the process (giving) rather than consumption of resources. For example, under a naive interpretation, two parties exchanging gifts of the same value would increase the utility of both parties with no change in ultimate consumption. Hence, a policy subsidizing such gifts might increase welfare. Alternatively, a policy that would substitute one-for-one bequests for direct government transfers to donees would reduce welfare by depriving donors of the warm glow.

Phelan (2006) and Farhi and Werning (2007) explicitly analyze placing an extra weight on future generations in an altruistic context. Considering altruism has an advantage over reduced-form motives for bequests in that it avoids placing f value on the act of giving and instead focuses squarely on the final allocation of resources. The disadvantage is weak empirical support for these types of preferences especially when considering the very top of the distribution that estate taxation in practice is about.

Assuming that a form of an externality from giving is to be considered, there are a few additional things to note.

First, as mentioned before, targeting prescription for dealing with externalities relies on the presence of an instrument that can target the source of an externality directly. The standard case is an "atmospheric externality" when the identity of the person taking action generating the externality is irrelevant. More generally, the social planner should target directly any source of the externality in proportion to the damage. Since with an atmospheric externality every source has the same impact on the social welfare, the tax does not need to be differentiated. This is not the case with bequest externality: the externality is interpersonal and, with sufficient heterogeneity, marginal social welfare impact of bequests by different individuals will be different. This would then call for differentiating subsidies to bequests and whether it is feasible depends on available tax instruments.

Second, and relatedly, the importance of accounting for the giving externality may vary with the context considered. For example, one may place a high value on welfare of low-income children but correcting for inadequate gifts by wealthy parents to their wealthy children does not sound as an important policy objective. We will return to this issue when considering estate taxation in a redistributive context.

To conclude, externality due to giving is often a component of the normative analysis of estate taxation. Its presence tilts the policy in the direction of subsidies to giving. The assumed type of a bequest motive influences the presence and nature of this externality. Still, a normative choice may often be explicitly made: for example, one can ignore the warm-glow or make a decision about the extra weight, if any, to be put on welfare of future generations. The best theoretical practice is to be explicit about the presence of such an externality and its precise consequences; in particular about the consequences of varying its strength or its complete elimination.

4. REDISTRIBUTION

In the previous section, I abstracted from redistributive motives. Taxation of estates in practice is about closely connected with redistribution. For example, according to the Piketty and Saez (2007) assessment of the overall progressivity of the US tax code in 1970,[17] the estate, gift, and wealth taxes contributed 23.4 percentage points to the overall 74.6% average effective tax rate applying to the top 0.01% of the distribution, while by 2004 contribution of these taxes fell to just 2.5 points out of the 34.7% total—according to that study, the decline in this type of taxation accounted for half of the change in effective tax burden of the wealthiest over that period. Clearly, analyzing taxes that apply predominantly to those with high net worth and have the potential to make such a difference in the overall progressivity cannot ignore redistributional issues.

Building on the standard optimal income tax model of Mirrlees (1971) and Kaplow (2001) provides the starting point for thinking about redistribution and estate taxation. Focusing on the donors, consider a society consisting of individuals maximizing utility given by $u(C, L, B)$ where C is consumption, L is labor supply, and B is bequest. As in

---

[17] The study assigns (cross-sectional) realized tax liability to groups defined by their gross income reported on tax returns. In the case of the estate tax, they assign the current tax liability for a given group of decedents (e.g., top 0.01% ranked by the size of estate) to the corresponding group of living taxpayers (top 0.01%, ranked by gross income). There are many limitations to this procedure—in particular, it assumes that top income and top estate taxpayers are the same group, it assumes that the current law will continue and it makes no attempt to adjust for the expected differences in terminal wealth of the decedents and that of current high income taxpayers.

optimal income tax literature, assume that every individual is characterized by skill level w that remains private information. The planner can observe income wL and bequests B and can impose tax liability based on that information so that individuals are maximizing utility subject to the budget constraint $C + B \leq wL - T(wL, B)$. Denoting by $w(\cdot)$ a concave welfare function, one is interested in finding the tax schedule $T(\cdot)$ that maximizes welfare $\int w(u(C, L, B))$ subject to the revenue and incentive compatibility constraints.

This basic framework assumes that bequests are just like any other good. It also assumes that skills are the only source of heterogeneity. It implies that bequests are deterministic function of labor income. It also assumes away heterogeneity in tastes that led McCaffery (1994) to argue against estate taxation on the basis of its horizontally inequitable treatment of savers vs spenders.

This framework is of course a special case of Atkinson and Stiglitz (1976) and leads to the classic result that tax on commodities—bequests in this case—is redundant when utility has weakly separable structure $u(v(C, B), L)$.[18] The intuition for this result can be seen by appealing to the informational content of potential tax base. The unobservable piece of information is w. Under weak separability, one can consider a subproblem of maximizing utility from regular consumption and bequests given labor income wL : $\max_{C,B} v(C, B)$ subject to $C + B \leq wL - T(wL, B)$ that yields a solution $(C(wL), B(wL))$: consumption and bequests are a function of labor income and do not depend on wage rate directly. In other words, individuals with different wages will select the same level of consumption and bequests *if* their incomes are the same. As the result, distorting the price of bequests does not provide any additional information about wages beyond that already contained in income. Hence, such a distortion is redundant.

There are many limitations of this exercise of course, some of which we will cover below (see also Kaplow, 2001, for an extensive discussion), but it illustrates one of the components of the analysis of the estate tax: its interaction with lifetime redistribution. Viewed in this way, analysis of bequest taxation is analogous to analyzing desirability of capital taxation. That literature focused on understanding implications of preference heterogeneity (Diamond & Spinnewijn, 2010; Golosov, Tsyvinski, & Weinzierl, 2010; Saez, 2002b) and shows that uniform tax on capital income may be desirable even under the weak separability assumption if higher ability individuals have a lower discount rate,[19,20] while the tax on savings of just high ability individuals may be optimal under

---

[18] Laroque (2005) and Kaplow (2006) show that commodity taxation is redundant even when income tax is not optimally selected. Kaplow (2008) builds on the Atkinson-Stiglitz framework to analyze a wide range of tax policy issues.

[19] Banks and Diamond (2010, chap. 6) discuss empirical evidence consistent with this pattern, while Gordon and Kopczuk (2010) test directly for a weaker condition necessary for deviation from the Atkinson-Stiglitz result—ability of capital income to predict wages conditional on labor income—and find empirical support for it.

[20] Cremer and Pestieau (2001) show in the appendix desirability of bequest taxation in a two-type model that violates the Atkinson-Stiglitz assumption. See also Cremer, Pestieau, and Rochet (2003) who consider the context where inheritance is not observable and show desirability of using an additional instrument (a tax on capital income) that is informative about the unobserved inheritances.

weaker assumption. Treating bequests as a form of saving and allowing for heterogeneity of preference for bequests would be a natural extension of this framework.

The natural next step is to explicitly consider multiple generations. Let us consider first the case when generations are altruistically linked, since this is the most common specification in the literature. The simplest approach builds on the Atkinson-Stiglitz framework and continues to abstract from decisions of children, instead assuming that there are two generations with parents choosing labor supply and consumption, and children selecting consumption level given the transfer. The dynastic utility is given by

$$u_P(C^P, L) + \rho u_K(C^K). \tag{3}$$

I will use this formulation in what follows. Note that bequests are present here as $B = C^K$, because bequests are the only source of income for the young generation. Denoting the pre-tax estate as $E = wL - C^P$, the general budget constraint of the parents (and the dynasty) may be written without loss of generality as

$$C^P + B/R = wL - T(wL, E) \iff C^P + C^K/R = wL - T(wL, wL - C^P), \tag{4}$$

where $T(\cdot, \cdot)$ is a general tax function that depends on the two observable pieces of information wL and E. In particular, observing C^P and C^K is redundant since they can be recovered based on the values of wL and E.

When welfare is based on aggregating dynastic utilities, this model is again an example of the standard Atkinson-Stiglitz framework with two consumption goods C^P and C^K. Further assuming additive separability $u_P(C^P, L) = u_p(C^P) - v(L)$ to guarantee the weak separability assumption (as does the paper of Farhi and Werning (2010) discussed in more details below), the model implies no tax distortions beyond income tax at the optimum, the point previously made by Kaplow (2001).

One might argue that the social planner should separately account for both utility of parents and children. One way to introduce it is by putting an extra weight $\nu \geq 0$ on a child's utility when evaluating welfare of a given dynasty

$$u_P(C^P, L) + (\rho + \nu)u_K(C^K). \tag{5}$$

This approach may be interpreted as social planner disagreeing with dynastic preferences. Farhi and Werning (2010) consider a planner that puts an extra weight on the future generation but they take a slightly different tack. They set up their problem in terms of maximization of the welfare of the first period generation

$$\int u_p(C^P) - v(L) + \rho u_K(C^K) \tag{6}$$

subject to the lower bound on welfare of the second generation

$$\int u_K(C^K) \geq \underline{V} \tag{7}$$

with $\underline{V}$ indexing the problem. When $\underline{V}$ is low enough, the constraint is not binding and the standard Atkinson-Stiglitz no-estate-tax result applies. When the constraint is binding, the problem is equivalent to maximizing $\int u_p(C^P) - v(L) + \rho u_K(C^K) + v u_K(C^K)$ as in Eq. (5) where (with some abuse of the notation) v is the optimum value of the multiplier on the welfare constraint for the second generation.

Whether the problem is set up by appealing to an externality from giving on the individual level or whether it introduces it on the generational level, makes no difference in the utilitarian case. The two approaches depart from each other when applying a non-linear welfare function—in one case, the welfare should be evaluated as

$$\int W(u_P(C^P, L) + (\rho + v)u_K(C^K)), \tag{8}$$

while in the other the welfare function is applied to parent's and child's utility separately, possibly using different welfare criteria: $W_1(u_p(C^P) - v(L) + \rho u_K(C^K))$. As the result, given the multiplier v on the constraint (7), the planner's objective is

$$\int W_1(u_p(C^P) - v(L) + \rho u_K(C^K)) + v W_2(u_K(C^K)). \tag{9}$$

While objective functions (8) and (9) represent slightly different problems, we will see shortly that the difference in the welfare criterion has no implications for qualitative solutions.

The objective function of the social planner does not coincide here with that of the parent generation. Instead, it puts an extra weight on the utility of the next generation. From the point of view of evaluating social welfare, there is a *positive* externality associated with children consumption. Since in this model bequests play the sole role of determining consumption of children, there is then a positive externality associated with bequests.

4.1. Estate Taxation with Externalities from Giving—Intuition

To gain the intuition for implications of externalities from giving note the following.

First, as has been known since (Pigou, 1920), the presence of externalities in the first-best world calls for internalizing the externality via the Pigouvian tax. Writing the dynastic budget constraint as $C^P + C^K/R = wL - T(wL, wL - C^P)$, individuals set $\rho R u'_K = (1 - T_2)u'_P$. The social optimum needs to satisfy $\left(\frac{W'_2}{W'_1}v + \rho\right) R u'_K = u'_P$ and setting the marginal bequest tax rate to the value of $T_2 \equiv \frac{W'_2}{W'_1}\frac{u'_K}{u'_P}$ (with the right-hand side evaluated at the social optimum) brings incentives in line. With sufficiently flexible instruments (ability to pursue individualized lump-sum taxation and to set the marginal tax rates on bequests for each individual at the corresponding Pigouvian level) to address the underlying heterogeneity, it allows for implementing the first-best allocation.

Second, the prescription for dealing with *atmospheric* externalities i.e., externalities stemming from aggregate consumption of some dirty good $\int D$ when first-best taxation is not available but a tax on D is possible if only a slight modification of the Pigouvian taxation. For simplicity, suppose that the effect of externality on social welfare is additive and given by $g(\int D)$. The logic of the targeting principle (Cremer, Gahvari, & Ladoux, 1998; Kopczuk, 2003a; Sandmo, 1975) is straightforward. The problem with an externality is equivalent to the one without any externalities, but with (1) the price of a dirty good adjusted (via the marginal tax rate τ) to internalize the otherwise ignored social cost of increasing $\int D$, and (2) the revenue requirement modified by the amount collected by that tax ($\tau \int D^*$) at the allocation one wishes to implement. As the result, the presence of an externality modifies the qualitative structure of the solution only through the tax on the dirty good.[21]

This result calls for a linear tax at the rate that internalizes the externality. It is easy to see that with an atmospheric externality the marginal social damage due to anyone's consumption of D is the same and given by $g'(\int D)$ so that the rate is indeed expected to be constant. What is that rate? The social planner weighs the resource cost of $\int D$ against any other uses and the shadow price reflects the multiplier on the resource constraint μ. As the result, the corrective rate can be shown to be equal to $\tau = g'/\mu$. The multiplier μ reflects the cost of public funds and its value need not be equal to u_p for any particular individual, so that the correction departs from person-by-person Pigouvian correction of externality and, in fact, it will usually depart on average because μ also reflects the distortionary cost of taxation.[22]

Third, it is not important that the externality is aggregate, rather what is important is that there is an instrument that can target it directly. In particular, if the dirty good is consumed by a subset of individuals $\tilde{D}$, so that it's given by $g\left(\int_{\tilde{D}} D\right)$, the optimal correction remains g'/μ. This applies even when there is a single individual consuming the good: the correction of an externality weighs on one hand its social cost and on the other hand revenue implications. Furthermore, multiple externalities need not be a problem if each of them can be targeted independently (or, if they are linked in a way that allows restricted instruments to work as well as independent targeting).[23]

---

[21] See Kopczuk (2003a) for the precise statement and a proof.

[22] The second-best Pigouvian rate can also be written as $\tau = \frac{1}{MCF}\frac{g'}{\lambda}$ where λ is some weighted average of individual utilities and $MCF = \frac{\mu}{\lambda}$ is the marginal cost of public funds. Writing the optimal tax schedule from the standard optimal income tax model as $T(y) - G$ (with $T(0) = 0$ as the normalization), the perturbation argument with respect to a small change in the demogrant component dG (an increase in the lump-sum transfer for everyone) implies $\int \frac{\partial u}{\partial G} = \mu\left(1 - \int T'\frac{\partial y}{\partial G}\right)$ and defining $\lambda = \int \frac{\partial u}{\partial G}$ yields $MCF = \frac{1}{1-\int T'\frac{\partial y}{\partial G}}$. Interestingly, as shown by Sandmo (1998), when $T' > 0$ and income is a normal good this means that $MCF < 1$—raising funds can be accomplished more cheaply than using a lump-sum tax. This is because lump-sum taxation is a potential instrument here, but it is revealed to have an interior solution at the optimum due to redistributive considerations. Consequently, the optimal way of collecting revenue on the margin relies on a mix of lump-sum tax and distortionary taxation.

[23] See for example Green and Sheshinsky (1976) and Micheletto (2008) for explorations of corrective taxation when externalities are not uniform and cannot be targeted using independent instruments.

Coming back to the externalities from transfers, the complication is that there is not a single atmospheric externality here and instead one can think of the problem as involving a *continuum* of externalities given by $vW_1\left(u_K(C^K)\right)$ for each dynasty. The straightforward application of the targeting principle would then call for a *continuum* of taxes targeting each of these externalities separately at the rate of $-R\frac{vW_1'u_K'}{\mu}$ (with the minus sign, because it is a positive rather than a negative externality and with R reflecting the price of C^K relative to the numeraire C^P). If it is possible to implement such a scheme that would force each individual to internalize the giving externalities that she causes, and if the externality does not interact with other considerations (most importantly, with incentive constraints), the optimal prescription follows the principle of targeting: forcing individuals to internalize the externality turns the problem into the standard one without an externality present. In such a case, adding the giving externality on top of the Atkinson-Stiglitz setup should yield a tax targeting its source (if feasible to implement) with no qualitative modifications to the optimal tax schedule implications otherwise. In particular, under weak separability assumption, the sole role of distortions to bequest decisions would then stem from internalization of the externality.

4.2. Estate Taxation with Giving Externalities—Results

The intuition described in the previous section applies directly to the analysis of Farhi and Werning (2010) who allow for imposing an extra weight on the welfare of future generations and embed the analysis in the optimal income/consumption tax problem. Their central result is indeed that the optimal "implicit" marginal estate tax rate is given by $t^E = -R\frac{vW_1'u_K'}{\mu}$ or, reinterpreting, it is equal to the optimal estate tax rate when the externality is not present (trivially, equal to zero because of the weak separability assumption) plus the Pigouvian correction. Under their assumptions, the marginal estate tax rate t^E is only a function of bequest (or child's consumption):

$$t^E(B) = -\frac{Rv}{\mu}W_1'(u_K(B))u_K'(B) \tag{10}$$

(obviously, R, μ, and v are constant). They show that the size of bequests (B) and the estate ($wL - C^P$) are increasing function of wages, so that this desired marginal incentive may be implemented using either a tax on estates or a tax on inheritances that is separable from the income tax. This can be seen by integrating $t^E(B)$ over B to obtain the tax liability that a person who at the optimum leaves the bequest of B should face:

$$\tilde{T}(w) = \tilde{c} - \frac{Rv}{\mu}\int_0^{B(w)} W_1'(u_K(x))u_K'(x)\,dx = c - \frac{Rv}{\mu}W_1(u_k(B(w))), \tag{11}$$

where $B(w)$ is bequest left by person w and c is an arbitrary constant. Finally, denoting estate of person w as $\tilde{E}(w)$ yields the estate tax schedule implementing the correct marginal incentives of $T(E) = \tilde{T}(\tilde{E}^{-1}(E))$. Implementing such a scheme requires an adjustment to the optimal income tax schedule as well, but again this is feasible to implement.

While imposing continuum of corrective taxes to deal with continuum of interpersonal externalities from giving may have seemed like a daunting task, it turns out feasible under the assumptions of one-dimensional heterogeneity that implies that estates and bequests increase with the type. Furthermore, in this case, the implementation takes a form of estate taxation.

There are a few interesting features of this result. First, it is an explicit characterization of the optimal estate tax structure. Second, the rates are negative everywhere—$t^E(B) < 0$. This should not come as a surprise because the sole role that the tax plays here is addressing the externality from giving. Third, quite unusually in the optimal tax literature, there is a clear result about the profile of the marginal tax rates: the tax wedge that individuals are facing—characterized by Eq. (10)—is decreasing with the size of bequest (and, by implication, also with the type and with the size of estate because all three are monotonically related). This is because the marginal tax rate is a function of $W_1'(u_K(B))u_K'(B)$ that is declining due to concavity of welfare function and utility (a slightly weaker assumption of $W_1(u(\cdot))$ being concave would also be sufficient).

Farhi and Werning (2010) describe this result as demonstrating progressivity of the optimal estate tax schedule. Progressive subsidies are not the first thing that comes to mind when thinking about treatment of estate taxation for redistributive purposes. As should be clear from the discussion above, this result is purely driven by the assumed externality from giving. Effectively, the role of the estate tax is to facilitate redistribution across generations within the same dynasty, rather than within generations—the latter role is played by income taxation. Hence, the message does not fall far from the basic Atkinson-Stiglitz logic—redistribution across members of the same generation or across dynasties does not call for estate taxation.

There is one important feature of the solution that should be pointed out: asymptotically, the marginal estate tax rate goes to zero, because the marginal utility tends to zero as wages and bequests increase. As Kopczuk (2009) suggested and Kaplow (2009) further elaborates, for the purpose of evaluating marginal tax rates at the top of the distribution, externalities from giving are irrelevant. The intuition is simply that even if such an externality is present and recognized by the social planner, it involves transfers between wealthy parents and wealthy children. Hence, the marginal impact on overall welfare is negligible when bequests are large but, as seen before, the cost of addressing externalities is driven by the overall cost of public funds and hence non-negligible.

This analysis could be easily extended to incorporate other types of bequest motives. For example, analysis with the joy-of-giving motive is almost identical. Consider using $u(C^P, L) + v(B)$ rather than preferences in (3) and continue to assume that the utility of the child is $u(C^K)$. In this formulation, $B = C^K$, so that the objective of the planner that puts weight v on the next generation can be expressed as $u(C^P, L) + v(C^K) + vu(C^K)$: the only difference relative to objective under altruism (formula 5) is the joy-of-giving component replacing $u(C^K)$. In particular, the externality term remains exactly the same, and exactly the same analysis as before goes through.

4.3. Accounting for Inheritance Received

The model considered so far involved two generations—parents and children only.

Kopczuk (2001) and Piketty and Saez (2012a,2012b) consider a different extension of the Mirrlees model by allowing for both bequest decisions and heterogeneity in inheritance received by those who make bequests themselves and imposing the steady-state restriction that the distribution of bequests received should be the same as that of bequests left. Kopczuk (2001) makes the simplifying assumption of perfect correlation in skills across generation, which implies that on the individual level bequest received and left should be the same.

There are important limitations of such an approach. In particular, it ignores the issue of whether an economy can converge to the "optimal" allocation from an arbitrary initial point. Very importantly, it also ignores welfare implications of the transition by placing no weight on welfare of generations during the transition. For many questions such as, for example, analyzing consumption vs income tax or pay-as-you-go Social Security systems, the impact on the initial generation and transitional issues are of foremost importance and the approach along these lines is not suitable. The focus on the long-term welfare is inherent to this type of steady-state analysis, and simplifications that it introduces help in clarifying implications of the dual role of inheritance (it is both given and received). Piketty and Saez (2012a) argue that this kind of approach is more suitable for normative analysis. In part, this is so by making it possible to abstract from the ability of government to go after the initial wealth that plays an important role in the Judd–Chamley framework. Focusing on the steady state makes it also more straightforward to express the results in terms of empirically observable parameters.

The main result of Kopczuk (2001) may be seen by considering a special case of the more general utility that he considers: the joy-of-giving formulation of the form $u(C) + v(L) + g(B)$ where C is consumption, L is labor supply, B is bequest left. Denoting by X the bequest received, the budget constraint is of the form $X + wL - T(B, wL) = C + RB$.[24] The bequest received, X, is taken as given by an individual but the planner's problem imposes the steady-state constraint that $B = X$ for all individuals. Changing variables as $D = C - X$, the individual problem may be expressed as $u(D + X) + v(L) + g(B)$ subject to $wL - T(B, wL) = D + RB$. In this (equivalent to

---

[24] R is endogenized by considering constant returns to scale technology in aggregate bequests and aggregate labor.

the original one) formulation, B, L, and D are the choice variables and the externality acts through the utility rather than the budget constraint.

As before, this is a modification of the Atkinson-Stiglitz setup with an externality from bequests. However, contrary to the cases previously considered, the external effect has a very specific form: its strength depends on the level of consumption. Absent externality, labor income tax would be sufficient here, because the Atkinson-Stiglitz separability assumption holds. The targeting principle discussed previously calls for the corrective subsidy of $-\frac{Ru'(X+D)}{\mu}$. Contrary to the two period model exemplified by the analysis of Farhi and Werning (2010), the Pigouvian tax rate is not just a function of X but rather it interacts with the level of consumption. For the same reason, X also interacts with incentive constraints.[25] It turns out that it is important: the optimal formula for estate taxation includes three additive components: an aggregate term,[26] Pigouvian correction (that can be negative) and a term proportional to the product of the multiplier on the incentive constraint and $\frac{\partial}{\partial X}\left\{\frac{g'(B)}{u'(D+X)}\right\} > 0$ that gives rise to a positive contribution to the tax rate. Kopczuk (2001) suggests that one way of thinking about it is that in the presence of an externality from giving, bequests are a form of "income" that carries informational content about individual skill level and therefore should be taxed. This is obviously a very stylized model, in particular it ignores dynamics that is considered in the next section and instead focuses on the question of the properties of a "golden rule" steady state without accounting for the transition to it. However, it allows for incorporating the dual role of bequests in a very tractable way.

The key points so far are applicability of the Atkinson-Stiglitz logic to bequests and clarifying the role of externalities from giving. Externalities from giving tend to imply subsidies to bequests, while the baseline Atkinson-Stiglitz case implies no tax on bequests. Combining the two in the intergenerational context that does allow for the inheritance received to be partially "exogenous" seems to point in the direction of estate taxation playing a role.

In two recent papers, Piketty and Saez (2012a,2012b) follow the approach of focusing on the welfare of a steady state generation to characterizing the optimal Mirleesian policy and further stress the effect of receiving an inheritance. They consider a model that allows for imperfect correlation of abilities across generations. In doing so, they relax the assumption of one-dimensional differences between individuals that was made in the

---

[25] Interestingly, all specifications considered by Farhi and Werning (2010) do not have this feature. They consider a two period model with perfect correlation of skills so that the steady-state interaction between bequests received and left is not present. They also consider (discussed later) an infinite horizon model with i.i.d. skills. In that case, the externality from giving is present and the steady-state distributions of bequests left and received have to coincide, but each bequest is distributed over the whole population so that the externality is a function of X and aggregates: $-\frac{RE[u'(X+D)|X]}{\mu}$ and does not affect incentive constraints either.

[26] In the presence of a positive externality from giving, there is an incentive to increase the flow of bequests in aggregate.

papers discussed so far. They find the role for bequest taxation and argue that it is driven by multi-dimensionality of the steady-state distribution: both labor income and inheritances are (partially) independent sources of information about individual circumstances. In Piketty and Saez (2012b), they consider multiple extensions that show robustness of their conclusions to relaxing the focus on steady state.

In an attempt to isolate the key mechanism behind optimality of estate taxes in these frameworks, Kopczuk (2013) considers a model with two generations and the joy-of-giving bequest motive. He explicitly derives the optimal tax formula. He shows that beyond correction of the externality from giving, the optimal formula includes an additional term that reflects fiscal externality due to the income effect of bequests on effort of children. He argues that this is reflecting the key trade-off in this context: between encouraging generosity and reducing inequality in the subsequent generations. The sign of the optimal tax in this case is theoretically ambiguous due to this trade-off but the rates are likely to be positive toward the top of the distribution where the externality from giving is no longer of interest.

A few extensions of this basic framework have been considered in the literature. Blumkin and Sadka (2004) assume altruistic parents, introduce mortality risk and assume away the existence of annuity markets; they also allow for double-counting of children utility. They analyze linear (income, capital, and estate) taxation only. As discussed before, as long as the estate tax declines with age at death, estate taxation provides insurance benefit and a small estate tax is welfare improving (Kopczuk, 2003b). This is true in the model of Blumkin and Sadka (2004). Bequests in their model are a mix of accidental and intentional and the estate tax can be shown to decline with the strength of the bequest motive reflecting the trade-off between distortions to intentional bequests and insurance benefit.[27] They also consider shutting down the altruism of parents in the model and investigate optimality of 100% tax on purely accidental bequests and argue that it rests on the effect on aggregate labor supply of the second generation: if (on the margin), revenue neutral reduction in the estate tax coupled with an increase in the lump-sum tax on the second generation results in higher aggregate labor supply, the 100% tax need not be optimal. Note that the bequests are lump-sum income from the young generation's point of view so that this exercise is effectively about tweaking the distribution of lump-sum transfers to the young generation—the lump-sum tax adjustment is a uniform tax, while the impact of the estate tax adjustment varies with the size and timing of accidental bequests. It is these distributional differences that are key for the result. Blumkin and Sadka (2004) provide a numerical example in which the effect is strong enough to make 100% estate tax not optimal. It remains unclear whether this mechanism would survive in the non-linear income tax context.

---

[27] This result is shown assuming logarithmic preferences.

Farhi and Werning (2010) also consider a number of extensions of their basic frame-work. Variation in the number of children requires the estate tax schedule to vary with the number of children to restore the equivalence between inheritance and estate taxation. They also consider imposing a non-negativeness restriction on the estate tax rate and allowing the rate of return to be endogenous. In that case, they show that the positive estate tax rate above a threshold is optimal: the intuition for this result is that reduction in bequests raises the rate of return and this effect serves as a substitute for an explicit bequest subsidy.

4.4. Dynamic Issues and Relationship to Optimal Capital Taxation

Taxation of wealth and bequests is a form of a tax on capital. In this section, I briefly review the main results about capital income and wealth taxation in general. Models of capital taxation in finite or infinite setting with altruistically linked individuals can usually be interpreted as very simplified models of taxation of bequests, with each period corresponding to a different generation. I do not review here work on capital taxation with overlapping generations that are not explicitly linked by some form of bequest considerations or work on capital income taxation that is explicitly within the lifetime (e.g., focusing on age-dependent features).

Literature on optimal capital income taxation in the long run is vast. Chari and Kehoe (1999) provide an able survey of the older work on the topic that considered capital income taxation in a growth framework with linear restrictions on available instruments and redistributive issues ignored.[28] The key result (Chamley, 1986; Judd, 1985) is that the optimal capital income tax rates (or, more generally, tax rates on any accumulated factors including human capital, see Milesi-Ferretti & Roubini, 1998) should converge asymptotically to zero. The intuition for this result is that any non-zero capital income tax imposes a distortion between consumption in different periods that is increasing with the distance and that cannot be optimal. Atkeson, Chari, and Kehoe (1999) provide an excellent exposition of this argument.

Another key contribution is due to Aiyagari (1995) who introduced non-trivial het-erogeneity. He assumes that markets are incomplete and allows for uninsured idiosyncratic risk and borrowing constraints. In this context, he showed that there is a role for cap-ital income taxation. The intuition for this result can be seen by considering the Euler equation for an unconstrained individual:

$$u'(C_i) = \rho(1 + r(K_i))\mathrm{E}[u'(C_{i+1})], \tag{12}$$

where $r(K_i)$ is the rate of return rate in period i, expressed as a function of the level of capital stock.

---

[28] This is referred to as Ramsey taxation—it builds on Ramsey growth model framework *and* is an extension of the Ramsey commodity taxation problem.

In the ergodic steady state, the distribution of consumption in each period is the same. Suppose then that we integrate Eq. (12) over the whole population: this would result in the population expectation of $u'(C)$ on both sides and yield $\rho(1 + r(K_i)) = 1$ if that expectation was finite. It cannot be finite however. To see it note that $u'(C_i) = E[u'(C_{i+1})]$ implies $u'(C_{i+1}) = u'(C_i) + \varepsilon_i$ where $\varepsilon_{i+1} \perp u'(C_i)$ and $E[\varepsilon_{i+1}^2] > 0$, so that $\text{var}(u'(C_{i+1})) > \text{var}(u'(C_i))$ which violates the ergodicity assumption. As Atkeson and Lucas (1992) demonstrate, efficiency in fact requires immiseration so that inequality is ever increasing and $E[u'(C_i)]$ grows over time. By allowing for liquidity constraints, Aiyagari (1995) breaks the Euler equation for some individuals:

$$u'(C_i) \geq \rho(1 + r(K_i))E[u'(C_{i+1})] \tag{13}$$

with strict inequality for individuals whose borrowing is constrained. As the result, he demonstrates that a stationary steady state exists but that it implies $\rho(1 + r(K_i)) < 1$ so that the rate of return is below and the capital stock is above the golden rule level. Intuitively, precautionary saving motive acts to increase saving on the individual level and leads to overaccumulation of capital and Aiyagari (1995) shows that positive capital income tax is welfare improving.

Saez (2002a) introduces heterogeneity in the Ramsey model in a different way. He assumes that dynasties differ permanently with respect to their initial wealth (and assumes away other heterogeneity) and considers the capital income tax that applies above a certain threshold—mimicking the structure of the US estate tax. He shows that the optimal tax of that kind has a finite threshold under reasonable assumptions about the shape of wealth distribution (sufficiently thick tail) and intertemporal elasticity that guarantee that tax distortions are not too strong.[29] Interestingly, a policy of this kind reduces wealth accumulation of high wealth holders to the threshold level but does not distort long-run capital accumulation (Piketty, 2001) because asymptotically all remaining wealth is untaxed.

Work in this tradition has an important flaw: it imposes ad hoc restrictions on the set of available tax instruments. Most obviously, linearity of capital income and labor income taxation is unrealistic. More subtly, assumptions about tax treatment of initial resources, government commitment and its ability to save play an important role.

The new dynamic public finance literature initiated by Golosov, Kocherlakota, and Tsyvinski (2003) seeks to remedy the first concern by embedding dynamic capital income taxation questions in the Mirrleesian framework. It considers individuals with unobserved and stochastically evolving ability. One way of thinking about the standard Mirrlees model is that the undistorted allocation is efficient but inequitable and the planner's problem is to address such an inequity. Another is to interpret income taxation as insurance against

---

[29] As in optimal income tax literature, raising marginal tax rates for high income population has mostly inframarginal effect (Diamond, 1998; Saez, 2001) when the tail of the distribution is thick.

lifetime risk: such insurance does not result in the full information first-best allocation because inability to observe state of the world (individual skill type) generates the moral hazard problem (reduced effort). In a way, there is a market failure in the standard Mirrleesian framework too—asymmetric information does not allow for implementing the first-best lifetime insurance scheme—but interpretation of this framework as insurance rather than redistribution is very stylized. Some extensions of this framework as lifetime income insurance have been considered in the literature (see e.g., Eaton & Rosen, 1980).

The new dynamic public finance literature adds to the picture dynamics so that incompleteness of insurance markets explicitly kicks in within the time frame of the model rather than behind the veil of ignorance. The role of the policy is to insure, the cost is moral hazard due to reduced incentives to exert costly effort in the presence of insurance. It turns out that intertemporal distortions are required to mitigate that disincentive effect. The basic result builds on insights of Diamond and Mirrlees (1978) and Rogerson (1985) and can be illustrated as follows. Consider a single individual and two period model. Suppose that the utility is additively separable in consumption and effort (e)

$$u(C_0) + \rho E[u(C_1) - v(e)] \tag{14}$$

and that the overall resource constraint is given by $(1 + r)C_0 + E[C_1(\theta)] = E[\theta e(\theta)]$, where the rate of return is given by r and neither effort e nor θ (state of the world, interpreted as skills) are observable (though their product is). The person consumes in the two periods and provides effort in the second period, however the return to effort is not observable. The objective of policy is to provide insurance in the second period, while accounting for disincentive effects.

The new dynamic public finance adopts the mechanism design approach to characterizing Pareto efficient allocations by proposing schedules $C_1(\theta)$ and $y(\theta) = \theta e(\theta)$. Suppose that an individual chooses to report its type as θ'. A change in reported type from θ' to θ'' results in a change in utility from consumption by $u(C_1(\theta'')) - u(C_1(\theta'))$. The key result can be derived by considering the following variation to the optimal policy. If we modify the profile C_1 to $\tilde{C}_1$ so that utility in every state of the world changes by exactly the same amount ε, $u(\tilde{C}_1(\theta)) \stackrel{\text{df}}{=} u(C_1(\theta)) + \varepsilon$, it will not change the report of the individual because $u(C_1(\theta'')) - u(C_1(\theta')) = u(\tilde{C}_1(\theta'')) - u(\tilde{C}_1(\theta'))$ for all θ' and θ''. In other words, the incentive compatibility constraint is unaffected by such a modification: the gain in utility from consumption due to a change in report is unaffected and hence there is no reason to change the original level of effort ($y(\theta')/\theta$, where θ is the true type).

Put differently, we are considering a change in second period tax-and-transfer scheme that results in no behavioral response—a uniform lump-sum adjustment would distort labor supply decisions but a transfer combined with offsetting marginal rate adjustment can keep it intact. Expressed explicitly in consumption terms, the necessary modification for small values of ε is given by $\tilde{C}_1(\theta) - C_1(\theta) = \frac{\varepsilon}{u'(C_1(\theta))}$. At the optimum, shifting consumption from period 0 to period 1 in an incentive compatible way should have no impact on welfare so that, accounting for the storage technology that allows for transferring consumption between periods at the rate of $1 + r$, implementing this variation implies

$$u'(C_0)\mathrm{E}\left[\frac{\varepsilon}{u'(C_1(\theta))}\right] - (1+r)\rho\mathrm{E}\left[u'(C_1) \cdot \frac{\varepsilon}{u'(C_1(\theta))}\right] = 0$$

and this equation can be simplified as

$$\frac{(1+r)\rho}{u'(C_0)} = \mathrm{E}\left[\frac{1}{u'(C_1(\theta))}\right]. \tag{15}$$

This is the inverse Euler equation formula. It represents a necessary condition for the allocation to be Pareto efficient given incentive constraints—it was obtained by appealing to a shift from consumption in period zero to consumption in period one in a way that implies no resource cost and has no effect on relative utility comparisons between states of the world in period 1 thereby leaving incentive constraints intact. This formula differs subtly but importantly from the standard Euler equation (12), that can be written as $\frac{(1+r)\rho}{u'(C_0)} = \frac{1}{\mathrm{E}[u'(C_1(\theta))]}$—the expectations in Eq. (15) are of $1/u'$ rather than u'. The concavity of $1/x$ implies that $\frac{1}{\mathrm{E}[u'(C_1(\theta))]} \leq \mathrm{E}\left[\frac{1}{u'(C_1(\theta))}\right]$ (with equality if and only if there is no uncertainty), so that the inverse Euler equation implies that consumption should be distorted toward period 0. In particular, it implies that individuals should not be allowed to invest at the rate r but rather should face a positive "wedge" between current and future consumption, hence introducing a rationale for capital taxation.

The inverse Euler equation is a necessary condition for the constrained Pareto efficient allocation in a dynamic setting: it describes the optimal program in the presence of private information. There is a trade-off between insurance and incentives to provide effort: provision of insurance (equalizing marginal utility across states) weakens incentives to provide effort. The way to (partially) restore work incentives is to discourage saving.[30] The lesson carries over to multiple periods and infinite horizon settings with arbitrary data-generating process for skills (Golosov et al., 2003).

Applied in the bequest context, the model would call for discouraging bequests in order to stimulate effort of the younger generation (note though that this is a different mechanism that considered by Kopczuk (2013), where uncertainty is not present but instead incentives of parents and children are not aligned)—it seems, though it has not been seriously explored, that the case for the importance of this channel should hinge on the empirical effect of inheritance on labor supply of children. We will discuss such evidence in Section 5.4.

[30] The model builds in normality of second-period leisure via the assumption of additive separability.

The implementation of the optimum turns out to be more complex than simply coming up with the deterministic marginal capital income tax rate t that would make the solution to the standard Euler equation governing individual choice, $\frac{(1+r(1-t))\rho}{u'(C_0)} = \frac{1}{E[u'(C_1(\theta))]}$, satisfy the inverse Euler formula, Eq. (15). In the stochastic setting, there are in principle more ways to impose the wedge because the tax rate may vary depending on the state in the second period. In terms of implementation, it means that the tax rate on saving may depend on (current and past) labor income and, in fact, it turns out that this is optimal.

One lesson from this line of work is that there are many ways to implement the optimal allocation. Of course, this is also true without uncertainty and/or dynamics: for example, Fullerton (1997) considers implications of various normalizations in the context of taxation of externalities and large literature analyzes relationship between income and consumption taxation (see e.g., Auerbach, 2009). The dynamic context allows for a rich set of instruments that includes current labor and capital income, assets, as well as history of these tax bases. Uncertainty adds richness of interactions, so that the quest is for a "simple" and realistic implementation. For example, Kocherlakota (2005) proposes an implementation that has zero wealth tax rate on *average*, but that rate depends in general on the history of labor income reports (the wealth tax in each state of the world can be linear in wealth). Albanesi and Sleet (2006) propose an implementation that depends on current assets and income only but it applies only in a setting with shocks that are i.i.d., i.e., it rules out persistence of productivity over time. Golosov and Tsyvinski (2006) highlight the importance of asset testing in the empirical implementation.

As discussed by Kocherlakota (2010) and Salanié (2011, chap. 6), the implementation requires intertemporal distortion to be negatively correlated with the level of labor income or, in other words, the marginal tax rate on capital or assets to decline with labor income. This has two noteworthy implications for thinking about estate or wealth taxation. First, the optimal taxes are non-trivially joint functions of income and assets, possibly involving the full history of these variables. This is in contrast to the actual estate and gift taxation in the United States that operates independently from income taxation. It is also in contrast to the important types of capital taxation such as capital gains and (currently) dividend tax that impose linear tax rates with relatively minor interactions with the rest of the tax system. It is also in contrast to corporate taxation that, while complex and to some extent nonlinear, does not account for other taxes paid by shareholders. Second, all proposed implementations feature capital or wealth distortions that either explicitly or on average fall with the current income/productivity.[31] As the result, this line of work

---

[31] The exception is a recent paper by Werning (2011) that proposes an implementation that features history-dependent labor taxation and savings tax that is independent of the current shock (though history-dependent, although sufficient conditions for history independence are discussed). The unique feature of this implementation is that savings are always set at *zero* and the role of the savings tax is to implement that as an optimum with transfer of resources across periods taking instead the form of adjustments to the labor income tax schedule.

appears to provide arguments for capital taxation at the bottom of the distribution—for example, asset testing in the context of disability/welfare programs—rather than lessons for understanding potential optimality of capital taxation at high income levels.

This vibrant literature delivers new and interesting insight but has remained somewhat stylized in its empirical applications. In particular, there were no attempts to express the results in terms of empirically estimable quantities along the lines of Saez (2001) (in the context of optimal income tax). This approach relies on the presence of private information but also on individuals placing value on insurance. Indeed, trivially, there would be no inefficiency due to the presence of private information and no role for taxation if individuals were risk neutral. More subtly, the literature has not (yet?) attempted to carefully disentangle the implications of uncertainty, risk attitudes, and incentives for the shape of the optimal tax schedule in this context. The absolute utility gains from insurance are high when marginal utility is high so that the planner's objective should be to deliver utility in those case *and*, by the logic of the inverse Euler equation, distort accumulation decisions in situations that are correlated with experiencing high marginal utility. In the contexts considered by the new dynamic public finance literature, this implies little role for distorting intertemporal margin in states of the world that correspond to experiencing low marginal utility from consumption. As the result, as of now, this literature provides little constructive insight for thinking about tax policy toward the top of the distribution.

The only contribution in the new dynamic public finance that explicitly incorporates bequests is again Farhi and Werning (2010) who consider an infinite horizon version of their model basic model with the externality from giving, allowing for abilities uncorrelated across generations. They show that the presence of the giving externality modifies the inverse elasticity rule familiar from this literature precisely by the additive component reflecting the externality as before. Adapting the implementation of the optimal allocation in terms of linear (but history dependent) taxes on inherited wealth as in Kocherlakota (2005), they show that the average inheritance tax rate (that would be zero absent externality from giving) has exactly the same structure as given in Eq. (10) thereby preserving their conclusions about negativity and "progressivity."

5. BEHAVIORAL RESPONSES TO TRANSFER TAXATION

Empirical work on effects of estate taxation on taxpayers' decisions is marred with practical difficulties. On the conceptual side, the question is how to identify the effect of the tax that will apply at the time of death—which is uncertain and, *in expectations*, many years away—on current behavior. Alternatively, one might wonder how what is observed at the time of death might have been impacted by tax policy regime (s) earlier in life. Potentially long lag between behavioral response and the ultimate taxation,[32] makes it difficult to

---

[32] In one of the most famous examples of effective estate tax planning, Sam Walton set up a family limited partnership that allowed for great majority of his estate to pass tax free to his wife and children in 1953, 39 years before his death.

credibly establish the causal link between estate taxation and behavior. Still, certain aspects of taxpayer behavior can be studied over shorter-term. In particular, studying the effect of gift taxation and behavior very late in life can be more conclusively related to tax incentives.

The second important issue has to do with availability of data. With some exceptions, estate tax returns are not public information and, because the estate tax applies to high net worth population, standard surveys that do not focus on high net worth population are of limited use. Surveys that oversample high net worth population (such as Survey of Consumer Finance), probate records and administrative datasets are potential sources of data.

Despite these difficulties, the literature has made some strides into understanding the impact of transfer taxation on behavior.

Perhaps the most basic question is about the effect of estate taxation on wealth accumulation. The simplest approach is to consider a certainty framework that ignores dynamic dimension, with individual maximizing utility $u(C, L, B)$ subject to the constraint $C + RB = y - T(E)$, where $E = wL - C$ is the size of the estate. Following the approach of Feldstein (1995,1999), the literature on responsiveness to income taxation (recently surveyed by Saez, Slemrod, & Giertz, 2012) focused on the "sufficient statistic" for behavioral response—the responsiveness of taxable income. A similar sufficient statistic argument can be applied in the estate tax context. While the estate tax can affect behavior on many possible margins (even in this simple formulation, labor supply and bequests may both respond), the welfare impact of the estate tax should be summarized by the impact of the tax on taxable base—in this case, the size of the estate. This would be so even when we add other margins of response such as, for example, tax avoidance. This argument relies on considering a small change in the marginal estate tax rate dt above some threshold $\bar{E}$ (so that the tax is $T(E) + dt \cdot (E - \bar{E})$). By the envelope theorem, the effect of that change on the overall level of utility is $-u_C \cdot (E - \bar{E}) \cdot dt$, while the impact on revenue reflects the effect of a change in the tax rate on the size of estate: $T'(E) \cdot dE + dt \cdot (E - \bar{E})$. In either case, it is the level and responsiveness of the overall estate rather than the composition of the response that matters. Hence, by extension, focusing on the effect of estate taxation on the size of estate at the time of death is a natural starting point for understanding the efficiency cost of estate taxation.

It is obvious that this simple framework misses a lot of things. Comprehensively applying Feldstein's argument requires understanding the effect on *overall* tax liability. Even within the simplest framework, it calls for estimating the effect not just on estates but also on gifts, as well as that on another main source of tax revenue—income taxation. Reducing labor supply is one obvious margin that the donor can respond on but by far not the only one. Investment decisions and occupational choice might respond to taxation and have implications for income and corporate tax base. Delaying capital gains realization due to step-up in basis at death reduces capital gains tax revenue. Taxpayers who might respond to the estate tax by increasing their charitable contributions, might do so via giving in life with income tax consequences. Avoidance strategies that rely on freezing the value of estate and transferring ownership to beneficiaries might shift taxable income (not just estate) to other individuals. The natural margins of interest for understanding tax consequences of changes in transfer taxation are responsiveness of inter vivos gifts, and life-time taxes such as due to the impact on income, capital gains or corporate tax base. Response of transfers also naturally has implications for behavior and tax liabilities of beneficiaries.

Similarly as in the case of taxable income, focusing on the tax base has limitations. In the presence of tax evasion or other situations where revenue or welfare spillovers are present, decomposing the response into "real" and "shifting" component is important as pointed out by Slemrod (1998) and elaborated by Chetty (2009). Additionally, response of the tax base to tax incentives is informative about implications of narrow reforms modifying tax rate structure but not about implications of reforms that might affect the base or other non-rate aspects of the system that may themselves affect the magnitude of the behavioral response (Slemrod & Kopczuk, 2002). Last, but certainly not least, the effect of taxation on real quantities is the relevant parameter to know for many non-tax related questions.

In what follows, I review empirical evidence on major types of responses to transfer taxation, but begin with clarifying magnitude of distortions that are caused by such taxation.

5.1. Magnitude of Distortions

Taxes on transfers are related to other forms of taxation. Most obviously, a tax on estates or bequests is a form of a tax on wealth. To see that, consider first the following asset accumulation equation:

$$A_{k+1} = (1 - t^w)(1 + (1 - t^k)r)(A_k + S_k), \tag{16}$$

where A_k represents assets in period k, t^w is an annual wealth tax, t^k is a tax imposed on return to savings, r is in the interest rate and S_k is net new saving as of the end of period k. I am going to assume that $A_i \geq 0$ for all i.

In the event of death at the beginning of period $t + 1$, after tax bequests are given by $B_{k+1} = (1 - t)A_{k+1}$. Iterating Eq. (16), yields

$$B_{k+1} = (1 - t)\left(R^{k+1}A_0 + \sum_{i=0}^{k} R^{k-i}S_i\right) \quad \text{where} \quad R = (1 - t^w)(1 + (1 - t^k)r). \tag{17}$$

Assuming first no saving, $S_i = 0$ for all i, the tax on estate is equivalent to an annual wealth tax given by $1 - t^w = (1 - t)^{1/(k+1)}$. For example, assuming $k + 1 = 50$ and

$t = 0.35$ implies $t^w = 0.0086$: obviously, the longer the horizon the lower the equivalent wealth tax. Similarly, there is equivalence here between capital income tax and the estate tax: $1 + (1 - t^k)r = (1 + r)(1 - t)^{1/(k+1)}$. Again, as an example, additionally assuming 5% rate of return, one obtains $t^k = 0.18$. It is straightforward to show that the equivalent capital income tax rate is a decreasing function of the rate of return: the return on the taxed amount does not accrue to the taxpayer and this effect is more important when the rate of return is higher.

Adding saving to the picture complicates the analysis: the equivalent (resulting in the same bequest holding behavior constant) wealth or capital income tax rate depends on when saving takes place—the shorter the horizon, the lower the rates. The main point here is that the horizon and rate of return matter: the estate tax is an infrequent tax so that it is mechanically less burdensome (as measured by equivalent tax rates) relative to annual taxes as horizon increases and it provides a deferral advantage that grows with the horizon and the rate of return.

This discussion illustrates how one might compare the effective tax rate under the estate tax to that under other types of capital taxation, but it does not appropriately describe the distortion induced by the tax. As one example, the 35% estate tax rate from the example above has different incentive effects than annual capital income tax rate of 18%: holding bequest constant, estate tax does not distort lifetime consumption profile while capital income tax does.

Evaluating the marginal estate tax rate that applies at the time of death is a reasonably well-defined exercise although even that is not always straightforward. The actual tax liability is affected by many factors including reliance on marital and other types of deductions, valuation discounts, interaction with state taxation and deferred payment schedule among other things.[33] We will delay talking about such complications until reviewing related empirical papers.

The actual marginal tax rate at the time of death is directly relevant for decisions that take place around that time—deathbed estate tax planning or choices made by the executor of the estate. However, decision of the donor earlier in life should be governed by *expectations* of the estate tax rate at the time of death rather than its actual value.

Poterba (2000b) asks how the marginal investment decisions are affected by the presence of estate taxation. He points out that saving rate of return between period i and $i+1$ is not affected by the presence of the estate tax if there is no mortality risk. Denoting mortality rate by m_i, the expected rate of return is given by $(1 - m_i)(1 + (1 - t^k)r) + m_i(1 - t)(1 + (1 - t^k)r) = (1 - m_i t)(1 + (1 - t^k)r)$: on the margin, the estate tax is equivalent to a wealth tax at the rate of $m_i t$. Equivalently, the rate of return is $1 + (1 - t^k)r - m_i t(1 + (1 - t^k)r)$. Closer inspection of this formula reveals that the effect of the estate tax on the marginal rate of return increases with mortality rate, but

---

[33] The estate tax liability attributable to a qualified business may be eligible for payment in installments over a 10 year period.

otherwise is not very sensitive to the rate of return because $1 + (1 - t^k)r \approx 1$. The estate tax is relatively more important than capital income taxation when the rate of return is low and less important when the rate of return is high.

Note though that this is marginal analysis that applies to investments over short horizon. Suppose that the taxpayer is saving with the purpose of leaving a bequest. In that case, as the first pass, mortality risk does not matter. To see it, consider period N that is sufficiently distant to guarantee that a taxpayer dies by then. The future value of a marginal dollar of current saving as of period N is given by $(1 - t)(1 + r(1 - t^k))^N$: regardless of the timing of death, the estate tax will be paid once before period N. As long as the marginal increase in tax liability is neutral with respect to the timing of death and the utility from bequest is not a function of age at death, the mortality risk should not enter. Neither of these assumptions are automatic: the timing of capital gains step-up matters and welfare neutrality of the timing of bequests would depend on the presence of liquidity constraints and precise assumptions about the nature of the bequest motive. Ultimately, the extent to which mortality risk interacts with estate taxation is an empirical (and, as of now, unresolved) question.

Saving/investment decision is just one of the many margins that may be distorted by the estate tax. In particular, taxpayers might choose to make transfers in life instead of making them at death. This has nuanced tax consequences under the US (and other countries') tax law. Marginal tax rates applying to gifts and estates are usually different. Denote the gift tax rate by t^G and continue to denote the estate tax rate as t. For simplicity of the exposition, I assume here that they are applied to the same base—the total amount of the transfer. Let's continue to assume that taxpayers are interested in maximizing the total after tax amount of transfers. In the certainty, one shot context, one should select the mode of transfer that corresponds to the lower marginal tax rate. In practice, usually $t^G < t$,[34] so that there is a presumption that gifts are advantageous. Now consider the same decision but instead assume that the transfer at death will take place n years from now (for now assumed certain) and the asset accumulates at the rate of return r.[35] Denoting by G is the value of the transfer considered, the value of tax at period n is $(1 + r)^n t^G G$ or $(1 + r)^n t G$ so that the comparison is unchanged.

However, in practice, the tax schedule is often non-linear. Using T and T^G to represent the two tax schedules, the correct comparison of net ex-post tax liabilities is between $T(B^E) + (1 + r)^n T^G(B^G + G)$ and $T(B^E + (1 + r)^n G) + (1 + r)^n T^G(B^G)$ where B^E and B^G are bases for gift and estate tax, respectively. A gift changes the base for the gift tax by its pre-accumulation value while it changes the base for the estate tax by its (higher) after-accumulation value. The effect will depend on the relationship between the two schedules, but in practice it is likely to make gift taxation further preferred when

[34] In the US, gifts are taxed on tax exclusive basis that implies lower marginal tax rate; see footnote 39.
[35] This assumption is not necessarily correct—it is possible that the donor may have access to different investment opportunities than the donee.

the two schedules are closely related and the nominal rate of return is high or the horizon is long. In particular, in the US case, B^E and B^G are (imperfectly) tied to each other via unified credit (lifetime exemption). Ignoring for simplicity the difference in how gift and estate tax is calculated and writing the tax as a single schedule, on the margin the taxpayer should be comparing $(1 + r)^n T' \left(B^E + B^G + G \right)$ in the case when an inter vivos gift is made to $(1 + r)^n T' \left(B^E + B^G + (1 + r)^n G \right)$ when it is delayed until death, providing the strong case for pre-paying the estate tax via gift taxation as long as the marginal tax rate increases with the base without even appealing to the difference in statutory marginal tax rate schedules. The key point here is that early gifts remove future appreciation from the tax base and this effect is beneficial in the presence of progressivity. The effect is especially strong when assets are expected to appreciate (even if just in nominal terms) or horizon is long.

Another wrinkle influencing the choice between gifts and bequests relates to tax treatment of capital gains. Suppose that fraction β of the asset to be transferred corresponds to appreciated taxable gain to be taxed at realization at some rate t^K (assume that this is the rate that accounts for the benefits of the deferral). In the US, capital gains transferred at death benefit from step-up in basis but gifts do not. Hence, the cost consequences of the bequest are unaffected by this modification but those of the gift are. The tax basis of an asset is adjusted for gift taxes paid that are attributable to the capital gains liability so that there is an incremental tax liability of $(\beta - \beta t^G) t^K$. One can go further by modeling benefits of deferral and implications of various liquidation strategies. There are additional complications in case of gifts shortly (3 years) before death that may be treated as bequests and further opportunities to benefit from step-up by first transferring the asset to a surviving spouse. See Joulfaian (2005a) for further discussion and illustrative calculations. Another aspect that has not been accounted for here are differences in marginal tax rates of donors and donees that create additional opportunities for tax arbitrage (Agell & Persson, 2000; Stiglitz, 1985). It has been argued that it has important implications in the context of the estate tax (Bernheim, 1987).

5.2. Effect on Wealth Accumulation and Reported Estates

A number of papers attempted to relate estate taxation to wealth or estates at death. Kopczuk and Slemrod (2001) use estate tax returns covering selected years between 1916 and 1996.[36] They first pursue aggregate and micro-based analysis using aggregate time-series variation in top marginal tax rate and marginal tax rates evaluated at 40 or 100 times average wealth as instruments for the individual marginal tax rate at death. This is not a particularly convincing identification strategy and, unsurprisingly, the results are not particularly robust. They subsequently attempt to exploit cross-sectional variation.

---

[36] The IRS has complete micro data for period 1916–1945 and samples for 1962, 1965, 1969, 1972, 1976 and annually starting from 1982 (though with varying coverage and design). See McCubbin (1994) for a description of the pre-1945 data and Johnson (1994) for the discussion of post-1982 datasets.

To do so, they note that it is expected taxation over individual lifetime that should matter and they propose using the imputed marginal tax rate at age 45 as a proxy (instrumented using tax rates at the fixed point of the distribution as before). This approach introduces variation in the marginal tax rate at any particular point in time that is driven by variation in age of decedents, and this variable turns out to dominate other measures of tax burden in "horse-race" specifications. This strategy yields significant net-of-tax elasticity of net worth at death of about 0.16.

Holtz-Eakin and Marples (2001) use Health and Retirement Survey to estimate the effect of estate taxation on wealth of the *living* population. They primarily rely on cross-sectional variation in state inheritance and estate tax rates to identify the effect. In principle, this could be a more credible source of variation than age-variation considered by Kopczuk and Slemrod (2001) and focusing on the living individuals allows for interpreting the results as the response to estate taxation expected in the future (under the assumption that current rates are a good proxy for future tax rates). However, the HRS data contains few high net worth individuals, and cross-sectional variation may not deal adequately with location-based heterogeneity and endogeneity of location decisions. Joulfaian (2006b) pursues a systematic attempt to exploit time variation to explain the size of estates. Rather than using marginal tax rates at death, he uses an ("representative") equivalent marginal tax rate 10 years before death. That rate is constructed using a stylized procedure that follows the insight of Poterba (2000b): that rate is obtained by solving for t^k the equation given by $(1 + r)^n(1 - t) = (1 + r(1 - t^k))^n$, where t is the tax rate that applies 10 years before death, r is linked to the growth rate of S&P 500 and constant life-expectancy of $n = 15$ or $n = 20$ years is assumed.

As can be inferred from this brief summary, as of yet, the literature has not been able to come up with a fully convincing empirical strategy to estimate this key dimension of the response. It is worth noting though that all these papers estimate similar baseline elasticity of net worth/reported estate estimates with respect to the net-of-tax rate of between 0.1 and 0.2.[37] The baseline specifications in each case attempt to shed a light on the response to incentives over the lifetime (rather than marginal tax rates at death), but use different dependent variables: in Holtz-Eakin and Marples (2001) it is wealth at some point while alive measured in survey data, while the other two papers focus on estate at death as reported on tax returns. Taken at face value, these results would be consistent with the notion that tax avoidance is not the main driver of the response, the topic to which we will return below.[38]

---

[37] Both Holtz-Eakin and Marples (2001) and Joulfaian (2006b) do not estimate the elasticity directly but discuss converting their estimates to those obtained from the "standard" log-log specification used by Kopczuk and Slemrod (2001).

[38] In a very recent paper, Seim (2012) finds evidence of significant responses of reported wealth to marginal tax rate incentives under the Swedish annual wealth tax that he attributes to tax evasion.

5.3. Inter Vivos Giving

In contrast to the work on responsiveness of wealth and estates, the literature has made more significant strides in estimating the effect of taxation on giving while alive. The US and many other countries tax gifts and estates in ways that create opportunities for tax avoidance (see Nordblom & Ohlsson, 2006, for a theoretical analysis). In the US, estate and gift taxes have operated completely independently since 1932 (when the gift tax was introduced) until 1976. Since 1977, gift and estate taxation have been integrated, that is gifts reduce the size of exemption available at the time of death. Since the very beginning, the gift tax applies to lifetime gifts, that is gifts made in the past are accumulated to provide a lifetime basis. Also, since the beginning of its existence, the gift tax rates have been lower than estate tax rates: explicitly initially and through the distinction between tax-inclusive and tax-exclusive basis since.[39] Gift taxation allows for annual exemptions[40] and interacts in non-trivial way with step-up in basis at death. The final component of the system in the United States is the Generation-Skipping Transfer Tax that's imposed on transfers that skip a generation.[41] See Joulfaian (2004) for the history of changes in gift tax provisions.

The tax advantaged nature of gifts usually provides an incentive to transfer inter vivos rather than at death. This incentive is particularly strong in the case of assets that are expected to appreciate. On the other hand, gifts generally do not benefit from the step-up in basis and hence may trigger capital gains tax liability.

Joulfaian (2004) focuses on aggregate gift tax revenue and documents massive spikes corresponding to changes in gift tax rates. In particular, gifts in 1976—in anticipation of integration of gifts and estates and, simultaneously, an increase in the top gift rate from 57.5% to 70%—quadrupled compared to the previous year, only to decline to well below pre-1976 levels for another decade or so. This is further supported by more formal aggregate time-series econometric specifications that convert striking salient features of the time series into large and very significant estimates of elasticity to current and anticipated tax rates. The aggregate evidence strongly indicates that some (presumably large) gifts are very responsive. Ohlsson (2011) documents similar dynamics in Sweden in 1948 just before Sweden instituted a temporary estate tax on top of existing inheritance and gift taxation.

Bernheim, Lemke, and Scholz (2004) provide micro-based evidence. They use data from the Survey of Consumer Finances between 1989 and 2001 and focus on the impact of increases in estate tax exemption. The increase should have no effect on people who

[39] The estate tax applies on the tax inclusive basis, so that a dollar of estate yields the tax liability of T' and the gift of $1 - T'$. The gift tax applies on the tax exclusive basis so that the gift of a dollar entails additional liability of T'. As the result, a one dollar expense (to be comparable to estate) results in an after tax gift of $\frac{1}{1+T'}$ and the tax liability of $\frac{T'}{1+T'}$ (which is obviously smaller than T').

[40] $13,000 in 2011, for each donee separately.

[41] In particular, it applies to related individuals who are more than one generation apart (such as grandchildren) and to unrelated parties that are younger by 37.5 or more years.

never expected to be above the exemption, it should discourage gifts for those who are phased out of the tax reach and it could possibly increase gifts for very high net worth individuals via wealth effect.[42] They crudely classify individuals into groups that may fall into each category based on their current net worth and do find patterns of gift-giving that are very supportive of the presence of response: gifts for the middle category decline relative to others while gifts for the top category (insignificantly) increase. Page (2003) relies on cross-sectional variation in state estate tax rates and shows relationship between marginal tax rates and the size of gifts in the SCF. Joulfaian (2005a) revisits the same question but focuses more carefully on the role of capital gains taxation. The capital gains tax applies to gifts but not to estates that benefit from the step-up at death. This matters more when appreciated assets constitute a large part of the estate and when the planning horizon is short. He shows the magnitude of this effect and demonstrates that the advantage of gifts over estates is not universal. Using the relative tax price that accounts for the capital gains considerations and relying on state tax variation, he also finds that gifts are responsive to tax considerations. Arrondel and Laferrère (2001) also document that gifts in France responded to major changes in fiscal incentives.

A number of papers (Joulfaian & McGarry, 2004; McGarry, 2000, 2001; Poterba, 2001) focused on a different outcome: reliance of taxpayers on the annual gift tax exclusion. This is estate tax planning 101: taxpayers are allowed to transfer tax free up to $13,000 (in 2011) per donee annually, to as many people as they wish. For example, a married couple with two children can make four such transfers every year (each spouse can make a gift to each child) so that, let's say over 20 year horizon, they could transfer over $1 million tax free (even before adjusting for the rate of return). Before 2000, which is the period that these studies used, the exclusion was $10,000 and the estate tax threshold $600,000 so that the potential for reliance on this strategy to effectively eliminate tax liability for many otherwise taxable taxpayers was very high. Even with higher exemptions, this continues to be the basic planning strategy. Yet, the key finding in these studies is that this strategy is significantly underutilized by potential estate taxpayers.[43] Poterba (2001) concludes that the results imply that taxpayers fail to minimize tax liability.[44]

Joulfaian and McGarry (2004) report, based on linked estate and gift tax data for 1992 decedents, that relatively few (1/3) ultimate estate taxpayers make taxable gifts over their

---

[42] There were other changes, such as the decline in the capital gains rate, that may have increased the advantage of making gifts by taxable individuals. They argue that the effect is likely small and otherwise would work against finding an effect for the most interesting middle group.

[43] Poterba (2001) uses SCF that oversamples high net-worth population and shows that relatively weak gift giving strategy extends to individuals with net worth several times the exemption limit. McGarry (2000, 2001) relies on HRS/AHEAD data that focuses on elderly population and reaches similar conclusion for elderly households that are on average closer to the estate threshold than the SCF sample.

[44] This is in contrast to predictions from a stylized frictionless model that has been used as a benchmark elsewhere in the literature. A small literature considered that question previously using aggregate information and illustrative marginal tax rate calculations (Adams, 1978; Kuehlwein, 1994).

lifetime and that such gifts are infrequent; ultimately the volume of lifetime taxable gifts is of the order of 10% of the estate.

Hence, the literature does find that gifts are very responsive to tax considerations but it also finds that, despite responsiveness, gifts appear to be significantly underutilized as a tax planning tool. These patterns are consistent with previously mentioned results of Kopczuk (2007) who concluded that avoidance is particularly pronounced shortly before death and, when coupled with robustly increasing wealth profiles, it reveals that tax minimization is not by itself a complete description of the objective of estate tax payers. As the result, evidence on gift-giving is consistent with the notion stressed previously in this chapter that some motive going beyond consumption value for holding onto wealth until late in life is necessary. I will return to this theme in Section 6.1.

5.4. Labor Supply of Recipients

A number of papers have considered the effect of receiving inheritance on labor supply of recipients. This is one of the important dimensions necessary for understanding the efficiency cost of transfer taxation. It is of relevance because it represents an incentive effect and has revenue consequences: one needs to be able to trace the effect of changes in the tax on all sources of revenue in order to understand its efficiency cost. It is also the response that is potentially linked to externalities from bequests.

At its simplest form, inheritance is the type of exogenous, non-wage, income for the donee. Express the utility of the donee as $u^K(C, L)$ and the budget constraint as $C = y + B(t) + wL$, where $B(t)$ is the bequest received given donor's tax rate t and y represents income from other exogenous sources. Labor supply may be written as $L(w, y + B(t))$, making it clear that when B is taken as given by the donee, the receipt of inheritance should generate income effect response of labor supply. Under the standard assumption that leisure is a normal good, receiving inheritance should then lead to a reduction in labor supply.

An increase in the estate tax should (other things constant) generate a response in labor supply proportional to the effect that the tax has on the size of inheritance. In this simple framework, knowledge of the effect of taxation on the size of inheritance ($B'(t)$) and an estimate of the income effect on labor supply coming from elsewhere would be sufficient for evaluating the effect of taxation on labor supply of the donees. As we have seen though, estimating the effect of taxation on inheritance is not trivial (and credible direct estimates of income elasticity of labor supply are not abound either). Furthermore, this simple reasoning requires at least three important qualifications.

First, the assumption that inheritance is "exogenous" need not be correct. In particular, the basic prediction of the altruistic model is that the size of inheritance should respond to individual characteristics. In that case, using the simple labor supply framework as before, the bequest itself should be a function of individual characteristics such as the recipients' wage rate, $B(t, w)$. When this is the case, simply regressing donee's labor supply on the size of inheritance is not necessarily informative about tax implications because bequests are correlated with individual characteristics. Tax induced variation remains necessary for the purpose of identifying the labor supply response.

The second qualification to the basic view of inheritance as an exogenous income effect is that bequests are not unexpected (although their timing often might be). Individuals who anticipate a bequest may respond before the actual receipt of inheritance, making it difficult to estimate the effect of inheritance itself. Additionally, a natural concern is the potential presence of strategic interactions. When that is the case, bequests and labor supply of the donee are jointly determined. In particular, labor supply may be affected by characteristics of the donor beyond the size of the bequest itself. The natural way of considering this issue is to do so in the context of a dynamic framework along the lines considered in the Samaritan's dilemma (Bruce & Waldman, 1991; Coate, 1995) results that break Becker's "rotten kid" theorem (Becker, 1974; Bergstrom, 2008; Bruce & Waldman, 1990).[45] Casting it in an empirical framework, labor supply may be written as $L(w, w^P, \gamma + B(t, w, w^P))$, where w^P is the strategic effect of wage (or other characteristics) of the parent and it is assumed that upon the receipt of inheritance the source of income does not matter. Considering strategic considerations further complicates interpretation of any estimated effect of inheritance, but variation in tax incentives remains a natural source of identification and the reduced form effect of tax on labor supply is in principle the parameter of interest for understanding revenue consequences. However, since the behavior of a family can no longer be assumed to be efficient, understanding the strength of strategic interactions is of relevance too for thinking about policy implications.

Thirdly, the effect of inheritance may vary with characteristics and circumstances of the recipient. In particular, potential presence of liquidity constraints is of natural interest for thinking about implications of taxation, because in that case estate taxation interacts with other market imperfections.[46]

Holtz-Eakin, Joulfaian, and Rosen (1993) framed the question about the effect of inheritance on labor supply as "Carnegie conjecture." Famously, Andrew Carnegie suggested that inheritance makes donees less productive members of society. Anecdotal evidence abound of course and labor supply is not the only margin that may be considered as being "less productive," but it is certainly one with important economic consequences.[47] Holtz-Eakin et al. (1993) used information from income tax returns of

---

[45] The "rotten kid" results clarify conditions under which a benevolent household head can use transfers to guarantee that self-interested household members will act to maximize family income/utility. See Bergstrom (2008) for discussion. In particular, when parents cannot commit not to help their children in the future ("Samaritan's dilemma"), it creates a strategic incentive for children to take actions that will increase such transfers (such as overconsumption/underinvesting) and may lead to an inefficient allocation for the family as a whole.

[46] Presumably by aggravating them, although recall the result of Aiyagari (1995) that calls for capital taxation in the presence of liquidity constraints due to general equilibrium implications of "excessive" precautionary saving.

[47] A conceptually different but fascinating channel that wealthy parents invest in preference for leisure for their children has been analyzed theoretically by Doepke and Zilibotti (2008).

inheritance recipients to study the effect on their labor force participation and earnings and found robust negative effect on participation and some evidence suggesting earnings declines. Joulfaian and Wilhelm (1994) study the same question using PSID and find smaller participation responses in that sample.

Brown, Coile, and Weisbenner (2010) focus on an older population using Health and Retirement Survey. This older sample is more likely to receive inheritance than the general public. The nature of this sample allows them to focus on retirement decision rather than hours response—this is important, because evidence suggests that labor supply responses are much stronger on the extensive margin in general and on retirement in particular. Importantly, HRS includes questions about expected inheritance and, by relying on the first wave of the survey, they construct measures of whether the inheritance was expected and how its actual size compares to prior expectations. They confirm the finding of negative participation effect and further show that the effect is stronger for unexpected inheritances.[48]

Elinder, Erixson, and Ohlsson (2011) use Swedish tax register data and confirm that the receipt of inheritance reduces labor income (they do not decompose the response into extensive and intensive margins).[49] They also find a short-lived increase in capital income, possibly suggesting temporary consumption increases. This is also consistent with findings of Joulfaian and Wilhelm (1994) who document small consumption increases following receipt of inheritance and Joulfaian (2006a) who documents that wealth responds much less than one for one to the receipt of inheritance.

There are other estimates of the effect of unearned income on labor supply and consumption, using variation in lottery winnings (Imbens, Rubin, & Sacerdote, 2001; Kuhn, Kooreman, Soetevent, & Kapteyn, 2011) and stock market wealth (e.g., Coile & Levine, 2006; Poterba, 2000a), although the results do not paint a fully consistent picture. As discussed before, their applicability in the context of bequests requires the strong assumption of inheritance being equivalent to exogenous income so that direct studies of the impact of inheritance remain of independent interest (and they can be also viewed as identifying the effect of an unearned income shock). The literature on the effect of wealth shocks has provided evidence suggestive of negative effects on labor supply of donors, though much remains to be done. None of this work has provided evidence derived from tax variation so that the tax policy relevant effect—the impact of the transfer tax on labor supply of the donee that requires accounting for the effect of the tax on the size of inheritance—has not yet been carefully studied.

---

[48] They also argue that the effect is not driven by grieving—the labor supply estimate is unaffected by inclusion of the dummy for death of one's parent (rather than the parent of the spouse).

[49] They provide weak evidence of potential anticipation effect. This is not necessarily evidence of a strategic response though: reduction in labor supply prior to inheritance receipt may be due to devoting time to taking care of an ill family member.

5.5. Entrepreneurship, Family Firms, and Inherited Control

Going beyond simple labor supply responses, Holtz-Eakin, Joulfaian, and Rosen (1994a, 1994b) focus on the effect of inheritance receipt on entrepreneurship and survival of existing small businesses. They find that inheritance matters for both and conclude that liquidity constraints are important. This suggests that the impact of taxation on behavior of the next generation may be substantially more nuanced than negative labor supply effects would suggest. If negative labor supply effects reflect the presence of liquidity constraints, welfare implications of increasing estate taxation would need to account for exacerbating the distortion on this margin. Additionally, positive effects on entrepreneurship may not have immediate revenue consequences so that estimates of short-term revenue impact may not be informative about longer term effects. Evidence on the link between inheritance and lifting liquidity constraints is mixed. Tsoutsoura (2011) uses 2002 repeal of inheritance taxation in Greece to show the positive effect of the tax on investment in transferred firms and provides some evidence consistent with the importance of financial constraints in driving this effect. Hurst and Lusardi (2004) show that both past and future inheritances predict entrepreneurship suggesting that they may capture either anticipation effects (inconsistent with liquidity constraints) or other factors correlated with both entrepreneurship and inheritance such as preferences or habits (Charles & Hurst, 2003).

While recipients of inheritance may set up a new business, continuing a family firm is another possible and common outcome. It is popularly claimed that forcing beneficiaries to sell a business is an undesirable effect of estate taxation. The economic evidence on this topic is much less clear: a number of papers found that inheritance of control in family firms reduces performance (Bloom & Van Reenen, 2007; Pérez-González, 2006; Villalonga & Amit, 2006).[50] Evidence on whether the estate tax has any effect on transfer of control is scarce. Brunetti (2006) uses probate records from San Francisco in 1980–1982 in order to study the effect of reduction in federal and state estate tax rates on the likelihood that decedent's business is sold and finds small positive effects of the tax on the likelihood of selling a business. The results are based on a small sample and variety of imperfect diff-in-diff strategies, but are intriguing. However, if this effect is there and is undesirable, entrepreneurs should pursue strategies to reduce the likelihood that the business will have to be sold. Holtz-Eakin, Phillips, and Rosen (2001) study life insurance purchases of entrepreneurs and conclude that they do not take full advantage of opportunities to protect their firms from being sold in order to meet the estate tax liability.

---

[50] Grossmann and Strulik (2010) analyze theoretically whether family firms should face preferential transfer tax treatment. The trade-off they consider is between the cost of firm dissolution and lower management quality. In their model, preferential taxation can induce a pooling equilibrium in which low ability children (inefficiently) continue a firm.

6. TAX AVOIDANCE RESPONSES

6.1. Trade-Off Between Tax Minimization and Control

The discussion so far made no serious distinction between responses that involve "real" behavior—wealth accumulation, labor supply, lifetime transfers—and those that are solely intended to reduce tax liability with no real consequences.

As usual in tax-related contexts, drawing a line between "real" and "avoidance" responses is difficult. Consider for example an extreme type of response that has been discussed in the literature: Kopczuk and Slemrod (2003a) show that during two weeks before/after major estate tax changes, the likelihood of dying in the low tax regime is positively correlated with the magnitude of tax savings; Gans and Leigh (2006) and Eliason and Ohlsson (2008) show similar evidence surrounding the repeals of transfer taxes in Australia and Sweden respectively. The response may be real—the will to live may be strengthened by the benefits to one's beneficiaries (or dislike of the government). Another possible explanation is tax evasion—perhaps death certificate can be forged (possibly more likely with pre-1945 reforms studied by Kopczuk and Slemrod (2003a), than in recent years in Australia or Sweden). The response may also be due to avoidance: there may be some control over the timing of disconnecting life support. Sorting out these possibilities is very hard in practice.

It does not require much convincing that estate tax planning does take place in practice and taxpayers are in fact interested in reducing their tax liability—the existence of estate tax planning industry is a prima facie evidence of that. How effective can tax planning be?

In a very influential paper, Cooper (1979) dubbed the estate tax a "voluntary tax." His argument was that with sufficient planning, taxpayers can significantly reduce and perhaps even eliminate tax liability. Some of the strategies he described are no longer available but estate tax planning remains an active arena. The extent of tax avoidance is controversial and naturally hard to estimate.

Schmalbeck (2001) argues that the "voluntary" nature of the estate tax ignores an important consequence of all strategies identified by Cooper (1979) (and many others): in order to reduce the estate, the taxpayer has to give up control over assets. Hence, the right framework for thinking about tax planning is not as tax minimization but rather as a trade-off between reducing tax liability and losing control over assets. A taxpayer who does not value control may be able to significantly reduce tax liability, while taxpayers with significant preference for retaining control will choose not to do so.

Perhaps the most direct evidence in favor of this trade-off is provided by Kopczuk (2007). Relying on (publicly available) estate tax returns filed in 1977, he first shows that the size of estate at death in this very wealthy elderly sample is strongly correlated with age, indicating that wealth accumulation continues until very old age (there is sufficient data to show cross-sectional upward sloping wealth profile extending to people in the 1990s). However, since the estate tax return form used to include (reported by the executor of the estate) information about the length of terminal illness, it is possible to evaluate the effect of terminal illness on the size of the estate. It turns out that the effect is very strong—15–20% drop with an illness lasting "months to years." After evaluating alternative explanations, he concludes that the most likely one is tax avoidance. In particular, composition of assets and deductions reported on tax returns changes in a way indicating tax avoidance and a very strong response is present for "lifetime transfers"— gifts that need to be included on the estate tax return because they were made shortly before or in anticipation of death (and hence are "unsuccessful" in obtaining preferential gift tax treatment), but that are likely fingerprints of tax avoidance.[51] Taken together, it suggests that despite continuing accumulation, wealthy taxpayers underinvest in tax planning until the onset of a terminal illness, but they still reveal by their actions at the end of life that they value tax reductions. Because tax planning is much more effective when done early, it implies that taxpayers also forgo significant tax savings. This pattern of behavior requires a combination of the desire to leave a bequest and some form of a reason not to part with wealth while alive. Some notion of benefits from controlling wealth is a natural candidate here.

The desire to retain control is also consistent with previously discussed evidence about strong responsiveness of gifts to tax incentives, even though the level of giving is grossly insufficient for the purpose of minimizing tax liability. Such behavior could be naturally explained by simultaneous desire to reduce taxation coupled with some control motive.

An alternative explanation, not yet seriously explored in this context, is the possibility of inattention—taxpayers may not be paying attention to tax consequences. While possible, this is also a population that is financially sophisticated and one that in most cases has professional assistance in place. Still, inadequate life insurance holdings by business owners (Holtz-Eakin et al., 2001) could potentially be explained by this motivation.[52]

While the literature has been exploring explanation for wealth accumulation due to precautionary motives—longevity, health care costs, long-term care insurance—such evidence does not appear as applicable for thinking about very high net worth individuals

[51] Such transfers are reported on Schedule G of the estate tax form. They may correspond to attempts at tax avoidance that were not successful because of premature death but they may also correspond to successful tax avoidance strategies. For example, many trust instruments involve a transfer from the taxpayer to the trust. A popular example is an irrevocable life insurance trust that is intended to exclude the proceeds of a policy from the estate (incidentally, popularity of gifts of life insurance might possibly be partially explained by the desire to postpone giving control over assets to children). Private annuities discussed by Cooper (1979) may involve a transfer if not fairly priced. Disposing of stocks by a majority shareholder at or before death, in order to reduce holdings to a minority position and therefore qualify for a minority discount may involve a direct transfer. A transfer of an asset to a family limited partnership in exchange for a minority interest (with associated minority discount, see Schmalbeck, 2001 p. 133, for an example) and retained right to interest or use would be included on Schedule G. Proceeds of buy-out agreements to be executed at death popular at that time may also have been reported on Schedule G. A non-estate tax reason for Schedule G transfers may be an attempt to avoid probate.

[52] Motivated by Becker (1973) and Kopczuk and Slemrod (2005) model theoretically the "denial of death" behavior with agents rationally repressing information (as in Carrillo & Mariotti, 2000; Bénabou & Tirole, 2002) about their mortality in order to reduce the psychological cost due to high mortality risk.

who are subject to the estate tax and who, one might think, have sufficient wealth for such precautionary considerations not to be important. As discussed previously, some form of utility from holding onto wealth appears necessary for successfully explaining the upper tail of wealth distribution and direct microeconomic evidence on this topic remains limited.

6.2. Tax Avoidance and Evasion

There were some attempts to estimate the overall extent of tax avoidance and evasion in this context. Wolff (1996) and Poterba (2000b) proposed an approach that is based on comparing estate tax returns to wealth of the living population (in practice, the data from Survey of Consumer Finances). In order to make this comparison, wealth of the living is *weighted by mortality risk*, and the difference between such mortality risk weighted wealth and observed estates is interpreted as reflecting the extent of tax evasion (and forms of tax avoidance that would give rise to the difference in wealth during lifetime and at death). This procedure needs to take a stand on the appropriate mortality rates to use (mortality experience of high net worth individuals is unlikely to be well proxied by mortality rates for the general public) and cannot account for adjustments shortly before death discussed before. As the result, as Eller, Erard, and Ho (2001) elaborate, different assumptions about mortality assumptions lead to estimates varying from 70% of tax loss to the very small amount. Furthermore, this procedure is sensitive to assumptions about mortality differences between married and single individuals and about the distribution of charitable bequests.

An alternative approach is to rely on audits. Audit-based studies estimate the extent of non-compliance at 8–13% of the overall tax liability (Eller & Johnson, 1999; Erard, 1999) but they cannot identify legal or unchallenged types of responses. Audits of estate tax returns used to be fairly common—Eller et al. (2001) report that they applied to 19% of estates overall and almost 50% of returns with gross estate over $5 million—so that the scope for easily detectable and obviously illegal tax evasion is arguably not large. Instead, responses likely take the form of plausibly legal but often legally uncertain strategies. Somewhat surprisingly, Eller et al. (2001) find that almost 20% of estates had their tax liability *reduced*. At the same time, in 60% of cases the assessed tax increased indicating an important role for enforcement. Changes primarily involved revaluation of assets, with non-compliance spread out over most categories of assets. Mortgages and notes and insurance featured the largest percentage revaluation, adjustments to closely held stock were most important in aggregate and there were only small adjustments for stocks and mutual funds. These patterns are consistent with the presence of opportunities for tax evasion and tax avoidance motivated by legal uncertainty surrounding valuation of assets that result in aggressive tax planning.

A small number of papers looked at particular types of legal avoidance-related responses. Johnson, Mikow, and Eller (2001) and Schmalbeck (2001) discuss the most important avenues for tax avoidance. Valuation of assets is one of the key issues. Estates have an option of valuing assets either as of time of death or using alternative valuation as of six months after death. For assets that are easily marketable, IRS regulations specify that they should be valued using market prices in the case of stocks or using comparative sales in case of real estate. Assets such as pieces of art should be valued by experts. Valuation tables taking into account life expectancy and market rates of returns exist for valuing annuities and partial interest—some tax avoidance strategies are designed by arbitraging the tables and personal circumstances (e.g., when mortality risk is known to deviate from that assumed by the IRS).

Valuing closely-held businesses is notoriously difficult. This is aggravated by existence of additional rules applying in this context. Special use valuation applies to particular types of businesses and family farms that, if they qualify, can be valued at actual rather than market use. Minority and marketability discounts are a particularly important avenue for reducing tax liability. They allow for a reduction in taxable value of assets if the taxpayer does not hold a controlling interest or when there is no easily available market for the particular asset. Johnson et al. (2001) found that approximately 6% of returns used minority or lack-of-marketability discounts that were on average 10% of the gross estate (conditional on use). Poterba and Weisbenner (2003) compare asset information from the Survey of Consumer Finances, weighted by mortality rates, to the asset composition on estate tax returns reported by the IRS. They find patterns consistent with significant use of minority discounts for non-marketable assets. Their results raise the possibility that the opportunities for valuation discounts present in the estate tax system induce important inter-asset distortions.

6.3. Unrealized Capital Gains

One of the important features of the US capital gains tax is the step-up in basis at death. Consider an asset with the basis of p that by the time of death of the owner is worth $p \cdot (1 + r)$. If sold just before taxpayer's death, proceeds would be subject to the capital gains tax t^G and then to the estate tax τ, resulting in the overall bequest of $p \cdot (1 + r \cdot (1 - t^G)) \cdot (1 - \tau)$. If held until death without realizing the gain, the basis of the asset is reset to its value at the time of death and the overall value of a transfer is $p \cdot (1 + r) \cdot (1 - \tau)$. In particular, this is the liquidation value of the bequest if the recipient/estate chooses to realize the gain immediately after taxpayer's death.

This feature of the tax system gives rise to a strong incentive to hold capital gains until death. The distortion to the holding period is present even in the absence of step-up in basis, reflecting benefits from deferral of taxation on realized capital gains,[53] but the step-up in basis introduces a particularly strong form of the associated lock-in effect.

---

[53] See Auerbach (1991) and Auerbach and Bradford (2004) for a theoretical proposals of a realization-based tax system that would eliminate holding period distortions.

The literature on capital gains realizations (for example, Auerbach, Burman, & Siegel, 2000; Burman & Randolph, 1994; Burman, 1999; Dai, Maydew, Shackelford, & Zhang, 2008) focused on distortions to the holding period and related tax avoidance strategies.

A small number of papers analyzed the interaction of estate tax and capital gains taxation. Poterba (2001) shows that taxpayers with larger unrealized capital gains are less likely to make inter vivos gifts, thereby providing indirect evidence of the lock-in effect being present in practice. On the other hand, Auten and Joulfaian (2001) present evidence that higher estate tax weakens the magnitude of the lock-in effect by encouraging capital gains realizations earlier in life. One possible channel is via the estate tax encouraging consumption or charitable bequests; another theoretical possibility is that in the presence of the estate tax, the effective capital gains marginal tax rates associated with rebalancing of taxpayer's portfolio are smaller than otherwise because they reduce taxable estate and hence tax liability. Finally, taxpayers may want to realize capital gains early as part of their tax avoidance strategy.

Poterba and Weisbenner (2001) use the SCF data to analyze distributional implications of replacing the estate tax by constructive realization of capital gains at death. While revenue estimates are dated, because of changes in rates and exemptions since then, the paper documents significant heterogeneity in the importance of unrealized gains and hence distributional implications of such a policy switch. Indeed, the 2010 "repeal" highlighted some of these issues in practice. The elimination of the estate tax was associated with basis carryover (rather than constructive realization that Poterba and Weisbenner (2001), assumed).[54] Reduction in tax liability generated by differences in marginal tax rates under capital gains and estate taxation was not uniform, because (among other reasons) the distribution of unrealized capital gains is not uniform. Naturally, many taxpayers dying with capital gains are not subject to the estate tax but they still do benefit from step-up. Hence, the replacement of carryover provision could actually increase their tax burden relative to the estate tax. This has been mitigated by allowing for up to $1.3 million of assets to continue to benefit from the step-up. Still, given the 2009 exemption of $3.5 million and availability of deductions for marital bequests (among other things) that change would have resulted in an increase in tax burden for some otherwise non-taxable taxpayers.[55] While the retroactive repeal made this issue moot for 2010, distributional implications of the relative estate tax vs capital gains treatment will continue to be an important issue in considering future reform proposals.

---

[54] Under the constructive realization regime, capital gains would be subject to the tax at the time of death with the step-up basis for the recipient reset to the value at death. Under carryover basis, the recipient assumes the basis of the original owner and the tax is not due until the asset is sold. Hence, under the carryover basis capital gains are taxed later and realization may continue to be distorted due to the presence of locked-in gains that accrued to the original owner.

[55] Many commentators and practitioners also worry about administrative complexity of implementing a carryover regime that requires recipients to keep track of the basis of the original owner—potentially for generations. Presumed complexity was one the main reasons why the 1976 provision to introduce carryover basis has never gone into effect.

7. OTHER TOPICS

7.1. Implications for Wealth Distribution and Intergenerational Transmission of Inequality

A large literature has focused on the role of transfers and, sometimes, their taxation in understanding wealth accumulation. Prominently, Kotlikoff and Summers (1981) and Modigliani (1988) reached dramatically different conclusions about the importance of intergenerational transfers in overall wealth accumulation; methodological issues and findings of the resulting literature are summarized in Davies and Shorrocks (2000) who conclude that inheritances are responsible for approximately 35–45% of current wealth. More interestingly, the literature—recently reviewed by Cagetti and De Nardi (2008)—has firmly concluded that while realistic life-cycle framework may account for much of wealth accumulation (for example, Hubbard et al., 1994, 1995; Scholz et al., 2006), understanding the full distribution of wealth requires incorporating some form of a bequest motive (De Nardi, 2004; Dynan et al., 2002, 2004; Gale & Scholz, 1994). A small number of papers analyzed implications of changes in estate taxation for the wealth distribution. The long-term implications are ambiguous in general. Stiglitz (1978) highlights general equilibrium implications of the estate tax: an increase in the estate tax leads to a reduction in capital accumulation and an increase in return to capital; depending on the elasticity of substitution between labor and capital, it may then result in overall increase in the share of capital income. Since capital income is more unequally distributed than labor income, this may result in overall increase in inequality of income and consumption. Using dynamic models augmented to account for, respectively, idiosyncratic labor endowment risk and entrepreneurial risk and calibrated to match selected moments of income and wealth distribution, Castaneda, Diaz-Gimenez, and Rios-Rull (2003) and Cagetti and De Nardi (2009) conclude that long-term implications of repealing the estate tax for wealth inequality are small, although distributional implications depend on the source of revenue used to replace the estate tax and efficiency improves. Benhabib, Bisin, and Zhu (2011) instead allow for capital income risk and, in their policy experiment, find that implications of changes in estate taxation for inequality of wealth are quantitatively large. They argue that the strong effect of estate taxation on wealth inequality in their framework is driven by its effect on capital income dispersion.

Papers in this strand of the literature are routinely calibrated to (static) moments of income and wealth distribution. However, such analysis has not yet incorporated empirical evidence on behavioral responses to estate taxation or bequest motives, hence quantitative implications are likely to be model-dependent. It also treats tax systems in a very stylized manner. Consequently, the results that are supposed to pertain to changes in estate taxation have to be treated very cautiously. In particular, as mentioned when discussing bequest motives, observational implications of the joy-of-giving and wealth-in-utility models are identical except for the consequences of changes in inheritance taxation. Hence, in a model calibrated to the empirical moments of wealth and income distribution for a particular estate tax structure (the standard procedure in this literature), implications of changing the estate tax are driven by assumptions about bequest motives that are completely arbitrary: because the commonly assumed[56] joy-of-giving motive and wealth-in-utility can generate the same distribution of wealth, calibration procedure pins down the implicit strength of behavioral response to taxation using the assumption about the form of a bequest motive rather than by appealing to any observable quantities. As the result, predictions about the impact of changes in estate taxation in this kind of framework are to a large (but unknown) extent driven by modeling assumptions. One could imagine calibrating a model of this kind to the empirical elasticities of bequests to marginal tax rates, perhaps simply by allowing for a mix of the joy-of-giving and wealth-in-utility motivations in order to gain an extra degree of freedom, but it has not been done yet (and neither are the implied micro elasticities explicitly reported in these papers). This approach has, however, the advantage of considering general equilibrium and long-term implications.

Calibration of either initial or steady state of the economy to a distribution at a point in time is convenient but likely to miss first-order features of the actual practical experience. Recent work of Piketty, Postel-Vinay, and Rosenthal (2003), Kopczuk and Saez (2004a), and Roine and Waldenström (2009) documents long-term evolution of wealth concentration.[57] The key point is that wealth concentration has significantly evolved over time. Piketty (2011) shows that the overall annual flow of bequests in France exceeded 20% in the 19th century, fell to 5% by the 1950s and increased to 15% by the early 21st century. These changes highlight that modeling long-term steady-state distribution of wealth, as much of literature has done, is likely to miss first-order facts about historical and future experience. Piketty (2011) shows that these patterns can be accounted by changes in the relationship of growth rate and private rate of return and, hence, as that relationship changes, the role of inheritance in generating inequality changes as well. Piketty and Saez (2012a) build on this insight to study the role of capital and inheritance taxation in a framework that allows for both labor and inheritance inequality to influence welfare objectives and find a role for inheritance taxation that varies with the overall share of inheritances.

The US evidence on changes in wealth concentration is somewhat inconclusive. In an influential paper, Piketty and Saez (2003) documented dramatic changes in *income* shares at the very top of the distribution (see Atkinson, Piketty & Saez, 2011, for a recent review of this literature) since the 1970s. These changes were to a large extent labor income phenomena. A number of papers attempted to document the corresponding trends in wealth concentration but found no or only small increase in wealth accruing to the very

---

[56] Altruistic motive is not sufficient to generate a thick upper tail of the wealth distribution.

[57] This line of research generally relies on estate multiplier technique, building on older work of Mallet (1908), Atkinson and Harrison (1978), and Lampman (1962). See Piketty (2011) for additional references and appendices in Kopczuk and Saez (2004b) for the discussion of the limitations of this approach.

richest (see Kennickell (2006) and Scholz (2003) using Survey of Consumer Finances data and Kopczuk and Saez (2004a) using estate multiplier technique). Edlund and Kopczuk (2009) show that the composition of the top wealth holders has dramatically changed over the last 30 years, shifting from inheritors to self-made—these patterns are visible explicitly in the Forbes list of the richest Americans and can be indirectly corroborated based on the gender composition of top estate taxpayers relying on the assumption that self-made wealth is more male-biased than inheritances. They argue that this change in composition—new wealth building up and old (presumably, in large part dating back to the early 20th century) wealth declining—are consistent with both income inequality increases and relative stability of wealth concentration.

7.2. Charity

Deduction for charitable contributions is the second largest deduction (after marital deduction) used by estate taxpayers and the largest one for unmarried decedents. By exempting charitable bequests from taxation, the estate tax provides price incentives to contribute to charity rather than to other beneficiaries. The presence of the estate tax also has wealth effect that should reduce overall charitable bequests (assuming that they are a normal good). A strand of literature tried to understand how these incentives affect charitable contributions; in particular, attempting to separate price and wealth effects and attempting to evaluate the overall impact of taxation on the flow of charity. Cross-sectional evidence (Auten & Joulfaian, 1996; Boskin, 1976; Joulfaian, 1991,1998; McNees, 1973) has problems separately identifying the direct of wealth from the effect of tax price because wealth and tax price are in practice correlated. Joulfaian (2000) uses cross-sectional state-level variation that improves on earlier identification strategies but continues to be subject to concerns about endogeneity of state tax policy and taxpayers' mobility. Barthold and Plotnick (1984) use data from probate records in Connecticut in the 1930s and 1940s. Brunetti (2005) studied effect of the repeal of the California estate tax in 1982 using 1980–1982 probate records from San Francisco. Kopczuk and Slemrod (2003b) rely instead of time series evidence using current and lagged marginal tax rates. Bakija, Gale and Slemrod (2003) rely on repeated cross-sectional tabulations based on IRS estate tax return data and state-level variation in tax rates. Joulfaian (2005b) uses microdata for estate taxpayers in 1976 and 1982 and exploits variation generated by changes in marginal tax rates and exemption that took place in between.

The literature generally finds that charitable bequests are very sensitive to both their tax price and to wealth, with the first effect dominating so that eliminating the estate tax would likely lead to reduction in charitable bequests. A number of papers additionally recognized that incentives to give at death are also affected by other taxes. For example, a taxpayer making lifetime gifts could additionally benefit from income tax deduction. Alternatively, giving in life and at death may be complements, so that high income tax rates may increase charitable bequests. Bakija, Gale, and Slemrod (2005) and Joulfaian

(2001) account for lifetime incentives and find that they matter but that bequests remain very sensitive to tax rates at death.

A channel that the literature acknowledges (e.g., Bernheim, 1987; Kopczuk & Slemrod, 2003b) but that has not been extensively studied empirically is the interaction of charitable bequests with tax avoidance. Indeed, some of the prominent tax avoidance techniques have charitable contribution components or, conditional on making legitimate charitable gift, there may be additional tax opportunities depending on how the gift is structured (Schmalbeck, 2001). This is an interesting area for future work.

7.3. Other Issues

An important consideration in tax planning is the treatment of marital bequests. Before 2011, taxpayers with a surviving spouse had an incentive to limit the bequest to the surviving spouse in order to take advantage of the exemption. More generally, there is an incentive (quantitatively important, at least at low estate levels) to go through the progressive tax schedule twice by splitting the bequest between the spouse and other potential beneficiaries. Empirically, heavy reliance on the marital deduction is very common but, as recognized by estate tax planners, it raises difficult issues related to the conflict of interest between spouses—preferences about the ultimate disposition of bequest may differ and hence the transfer to the spouse may result in the ultimate disposition of bequests that is inconsistent with preferences of the first-to-die spouse. While this could potentially be evidence in support of a unitary household model, Johnson et al. (2001) document widespread use and Kopczuk and Slemrod (2003b) analyze implications of the so-called Qualified Terminable Interest Property (QTIP) trusts that can resolve this tension: introduced in 1982, such trusts are transferred to the widow or widower who gains access to earnings but at her death the principal is transferred to the beneficiaries indicated by the first-to-die spouse's will. Hence, they qualify for a marital deduction but allow for addressing the conflict of interest.

A few papers considered the issues related to jurisdictional-level estate taxes. Bakija and Slemrod (2004) and Conway and Rork (2006) focus on impact of state-level taxes on elderly mobility using longitudinal variation in state tax rates. Bakija and Slemrod (2004) find significant but modest effects, while Conway and Rork (2006) find no impact and instead argue for the reverse causality with mobility affecting tax rate setting. Conway and Rork (2004) find some evidence of tax competition between US estates in this dimension, while Brülhart and Parchet (2011) do not find competitive effects for the Swiss cantons.

Several papers attempted to provide explanations for introduction and elimination of estate taxes. Bertocchi (2011) attempted to link evolution of estate taxation to the dynamics of wealth accumulation induced by the process of industrialization. Scheve and Stasavage (2012) focus on the role of wars. Graetz and Shapiro (2005) discuss politics surrounding estate tax changes in the United States in the 2000s.

8. SUMMARY AND CONCLUSIONS

In this chapter, I reviewed theoretical and empirical literature on taxation of intergenerational transfers. As signaled in the introduction, the conclusions are mixed and pointing to the need for further research. The normative analysis has overemphasized the importance of externalities from giving, while not adequately accounting for the importance of inherited wealth. When taking an *ex ante* perspective, inherited wealth is endogenous and does not constitute a reason for redistribution per se. While this is consistent with the logic of that model, it does not reflect the possibility that policy makers may be instead focused on redistribution within a generation. The steady-state approaches (Kopczuk, 2001; Piketty & Saez, 2012a,2012b) find a positive role for capital taxation but it imposes restrictive assumptions.

The key empirical observation that should feed into theoretical work is the presence of heterogeneity. The literature on bequest motives has failed to identify the single motive and instead points to both mixed motives present at the same time for a given person and to heterogeneity in preferences in the population. In particular, the first-order fact in understanding behavior of the very wealthy is the importance of control over wealth. The presence of such a motive is consistent with relative scarcity of giving during lifetime coupled with significant tax avoidance and increasing age-wealth profiles. Some direct preference for wealth (rather than consumption or welfare of children) is necessary to account for the extent of wealth concentration.

The empirical work has focused on many dimensions of distortions due to the estate tax and generally has found evidence that a number of decisions are sensitive to the tax rates—estates at death, tax avoidance, inter vivos giving, charitable contributions. It has also identified interesting and adverse effects on labor supply of donors and performance of family businesses. At the same time, the identification issues in this context are difficult and rarely satisfactorily addressed. In particular, the estate tax incentives operate over a long period of time and relating such incentives to wealth accumulation (which is perhaps the most interesting dimension of responsiveness) is notoriously difficult. The literature has been more successful in analyzing decisions where focusing on short-term incentives is appropriate, such as the inter vivos giving.

Tax avoidance is believed to be very important in practice but precise econometric evidence is scarce. In particular, issues related to separating response of wealth accumulation from tax avoidance (both of which affect reported estates), the interaction of charity and tax avoidance, impact of cross-asset differences in effective tax rates, the role of family structure and conflicts of interest, use of family-related partnerships, valuation issues for closely-held business and other types of assets have all received only limited attention from economists.

Finally, the topic that has not yet been incorporated in the formal models of intergenerational transfers are potential negative externalities from wealth concentration. Examples are positional externalities (Frank, 2008), the impact of corporate power on the political process (Morck, Wolfenzon, & Yeung, 2005) and previously discussed evidence of inheritance of control resulting in mis-allocation of entrepreneurial skills. Recently, a number of papers started considering implications of negative externalities associated with income inequality—primarily rent-seeking—for optimal taxation (Rothschild & Scheuer, 2011; Piketty, Saez, & Stantcheva, 2011). Incorporating such considerations in the analysis of intergenerational transfers is long overdue.

ACKNOWLEDGMENTS

I am grateful to Alan Auerbach, Louis Kaplow, László Sándor and participants in the Handbook of Public Economics conference in Berkeley for helpful comments.

REFERENCES

Abel, A. B., & Warshawsky, M. (1988). Specification of the joy of giving: Insights from altruism. *Review of Economics and Statistics, 70*(1), 145–149.
Adam, S., Besley, T., Blundell, R., Bond, S., Chote, R., Gammie, M., et al. (2011). Taxes on wealth transfers. In *Tax by design. The mirrlees review* (pp. 347–367). Oxford University Press.
Adams, J. D. (1978). Equalization of true gift and estate tax rates. *Journal of Public Economics, 9*(1), 59–71.
Agell, J., Persson, M. (2000). Tax arbitrage and labor supply. *Journal of Public Economics, 78*(1–2), 3–24.
Aiyagari, S. R. (1995). Optimal capital income taxation with incomplete markets, borrowing constraints and constant discounting. *Quarterly Journal of Economics, 103*(6), 1158–1175.
Albanesi, S., & Sleet, C. (2006). Dynamic optimal taxation with private information. *Review of Economic Studies, 73*(1), 1–30.
Altonji, J. G., Hayashi, F., & Kotlikoff, L. J. (1992). Is the extended family altruistically linked? Direct tests using micro data. *American Economic Review, 82*(5), 1177–1198.
Altonji, J. G., Hayashi, F., & Kotlikoff, L. J. (1997). Parental altruism and inter vivos transfers: Theory and evidence. *Journal of Political Economy, 105*(6), 1121–66.
Ameriks, J., Caplin, A., Laufer, S., & Van Nieuwerburgh, S. (2011). The joy of giving or assisted living? Using strategic surveys to separate public care aversion from bequest motives. *Journal of Finance, 66*(2), 519–561.
Andreoni, J. (1990). Impure altruism and donations to public goods: A theory of warm-glow giving. *Economic Journal, 100*(401), 464–477.
Arrondel, L., & Masson, A. (2006). Altruism, exchange or indirect reciprocity: What do the data on family transfers show? In S. -C. Kolm, & J. M. Ythier (Eds.), *Handbook on the economics of giving, reciprocity and altruism, Vol. 2* (pp. 971–1053). Elsevier.
Arrondel, L., & Laferrère, A. (2001). Taxation and wealth transmission in France. *Journal of Public Economics, 79*(1), 3–33. ISPE 1998: Bequests and Wealth Taxation.
Atkeson, A., & Lucas, R. E., Jr. (1992). On efficient distribution with private information. *Review of Economic Studies, 59*(3), 427–453.
Atkeson, Andrew, Chari, V. V., & Kehoe, Patrick J. (1999). Taxing capital income: A bad idea. *Federal Reserve Bank of Minneapolis Quarterly Review, 23*(3), 3–17.
Atkinson, A. B., & Harrison, A. J. (1978). *Distribution of personal wealth in Britain.* Cambridge: Cambridge University Press.
Atkinson, A. B., & Stiglitz, J. E. (1976). The design of tax structure: Direct versus indirect taxation. *Journal of Public Economics, 6*(1–2), 55–75.
Atkinson, A. B., Piketty, T., & Saez, E. (2011). Top incomes in the long run of history. *Journal of Economic Literature, 49*(1), 3–71.

Auerbach, A. J. (1991). Retrospective capital gains taxation. *American Economic Review, 81*(1), 167–178.

Auerbach, A. J. (2008). Taxation of wealth. In S. N. Durlauf, & L. E. Blume (Eds.), *The new palgrave dictionary of economics* (second ed.). Palgrave Macmillan.

Auerbach, A. J. (2009). The choice between income and consumption taxes: A primer. In A. J. Auerbach, & D. N. Shavior (Eds.), *Institutional foundations of public finance: Economic and legal perspectives* (pp. 13–46). Harvard University Press.

Auerbach, A. J., & Bradford, D. F. (2004). Generalized cash flow taxation. *Journal of Public Economics, 88*(5), 957–80.

Auerbach, A. J., Burman, L. E., & Siegel, J. M. (2000). Capital gains taxation and tax avoidance: New evidence from panel data. In J. Slemrod (Ed.), *Does atlas shrug? The economic consequences of taxing the rich.* New York: Harvard University Press and Russell Sage Foundation.

Auten, G., Joulfaian, D. (1996). Charitable contributions and intergenerational transfers. *Journal of Public Economics, 59*(1), 55–68.

Auten, G., & Joulfaian, D. (2001). Bequest taxes and capital gains realizations. *Journal of Public Economics, 81*(2), 213–229.

Bakija, J. (2007). *Documentation for a federal and state inheritance and estate tax calculator.* Williams College: Mimeo.

Bakija, J., & Slemrod, J. (2004). Do the rich flee from high tax states? Evidence from federal estate tax returns. *Working paper* 10645, National Bureau of Economic Research.

Bakija, J., Gale, W. G., & Slemrod, J. B. (2003). Charitable bequests and taxes on inheritances and estates: Aggregate evidence from across states and time. *American Economic Review Papers and Proceedings, 93*(2), 366–370.

Bakija, J., Gale, W., & Slemrod, J. (2005). *New evidence on the effect of taxes on charitable bequests.* Williams College, Brookings and University of Michigan: Mimeo.

Banks, J., & Diamond, P. A. (2010). The Base for direct taxation. In J. A. Mirrlees, S. Adam, T. Besley, R. Blundell, S. Bond, R. Chote, M. Gammie, P. Johnson, G. D. Myles, & J. Poterba (Eds.), *Dimensions of tax design: The mirrlees review.* Oxford University Press.

Barro, R. J. (1974). Are government bonds net wealth? *Journal of Political Economy, 82*(6), 1095–1117.

Barthold, T., & Plotnick, R. (1984). Estate taxation and other determinants of charitable bequests. *ntj, 37*(2), 225–37.

Batchelder, L. L. (2009). What should society expect from heirs? A proposal for a comprexensive inheritance tax. *Tax Law Review, 63*(1), 1–111.

Becker, E. (1973). *The denial of death.* New York: The Free Press.

Becker, G. S. (1974). A theory of social interactions. *Journal of Political Economy, 82*(6), 1063–1093.

Bénabou, R., & Tirole, J. (2002). Self-confidence and personal motivation. *Quarterly Journal of Economics, 117*(3), 871–915.

Benhabib, J., Bisin, A., & Zhu, S. (2011). The distribution of wealth and fiscal policy in economies with finitely lived agents. *Econometrica, 79*(1), 123–157.

Bergstrom, T. C. (2008). Rotten kid theorem. In S. N. Durlauf & L. E. Blume (Eds.), *The new palgrave dictionary of economics.* Basingstoke: Palgrave Macmillan.

Bernheim, B. D. (1987). Does the estate tax raise revenue? In L. H. Summers (Ed.), *Tax policy and the economy, Vol. 1* (pp. 113–138). Chicago: National Bureau of Economic Research; Cambridge, Mass: MIT Press.

Bernheim, B. D., & Severinov, S. (2003). Bequests as signals: An explanation for the equal division puzzle. *Journal of Political Economy, 111*(4), 733–764.

Bernheim, B. D., Shleifer, A., & Summers, L. H. (1985). The strategic bequest motive. *Journal of Political Economy, 93*(6), 1045–76.

Bernheim, B. D., Lemke, R. J., & Scholz, J. K. (2004). Do estate and gift taxes affect the timing of private transfers? *Journal of Public Economics, 88*(12), 2617–34.

Bertocchi, G. (2011). The vanishing bequest tax: The comparative evolution of bequest taxation in historical perspective. *Economics & Politics, 23,* 107–131.

Bird, R. M. (1991). The taxation of personal wealth in international perspective. *Canadian Public Policy andsang Analyse de Politiques, 17*(3), 322–334.

Bloom, N., & Van Reenen, J. (2007). Measuring and explaining management practices across firms and countries. *Quarterly Journal of Economics, 122*(4), 1351–1408.

Blumkin, T., & Sadka, E. (2004). Estate taxation with intended and accidental bequests. *Journal of Public Economics, 88*(1–22), 1–21.

Boadway, R., Chamberlain, E., & Emmerson, C. (2010a). Taxation of wealth and wealth transfers. In J. A. Mirrlees, S. Adam, T. Besley, R. Blundell, S. Bond, R. Chote, M. Gammie, P. Johnson, G. D. Myles, & J. Poterba (Eds.), *Dimensions of tax design: The mirrlees review.* Oxford University Press.

Boadway, R., Chamberlain, E., & Emmerson, C. (2010b). Taxation of wealth and wealth transfers. Online Appendix, <http://www.ifs.org.uk/mirrleesreview/reports/wealthtransfersapps.pdf>

Boskin, M. (1976). Estate taxation and charitable bequests. *Journal of Public Economics, 5*(1–2), 27–56.

Brown, J. R., Coile, C. C., & Weisbenner, S. J. (2010). The Effect of inheritance receipt on retirement. *Review of Economics and Statistics, 92*(2), 425–434.

Brown, R. D. (1991). A primer on the implementation of wealth taxes. *Canadian Public Policy / Analyse de Politiques, 17*(3), 335–50.

Bruce, N., & Waldman, M. (1990). The rotten-kid theorem meets the Samaritan's dilemma. *Quarterly Journal of Economics, 105*(1), 155–165.

Bruce, N., & Waldman, M. (1991). Transfers in kind: Why they can be efficient and nonpaternalistic. *American Economic Review, 81*(5), 1345–1351.

Brülhart, M., & Parchet, R. (2011). *Alleged tax competition: The mysterious death of bequest tax in Switzerland.* University of Lausanne: Mimeo.

Brunetti, M. J. (2005). The estate tax and charitable bequests: Elasticity estimates using probate records. *National Tax Journal, 58*(2), 165–188.

Brunetti, M. J. (2006). The estate tax and the demise of the family business. *Journal of Public Economics, 90*(10–11), 1975–93.

Burman, L. E. (1999). *The labirynth of capital gains tax policy.* Washington, D.C.: Brookings Institution Press.

Burman, L. E., & Randolph, W. C. (1994). Measuring permanent responses to capital-gains tax changes in panel data. *American Economic Review, 84*(4), 794–809.

Cagetti, M., & De Nardi, M. (2008). Wealth inequality: Data and models. *Macroeconomic Dynamics, 12,* 285–313.

Cagetti, M., & De Nardi, M. (2009). Estate taxation, entrepreneurship, and wealth. *American Economic Review, 99*(1), 85–111.

Carrillo, J. D., & Mariotti, T. (2000). Strategic ignorance as a self-disciplining device. *Review of Economic Studies, 67,* 529–544.

Carroll, C. D. (2000). Why do the rich save so much? In J. Slemrod (Ed.), *Does atlas shrug? The economic consequences of taxing the rich.* New York: Harvard University Press and Russell Sage Foundation.

Castaneda, A., Diaz-Gimenez, J., & Rios-Rull, J.-V. (2003). Accounting for the U.S. earnings and wealth inequality. *Journal of Political Economy, 111*(4), 818–857.

Chamley, C. (1986). Optimal taxation of capital income in general equilibrium with infinite lives. *Econometrica, 54*(3), 607–22.

Chari, V. V., & Kehoe, P. J. (1999). Optimal fiscal and monetary policy. In J. B. Taylor & M. Woodford (Eds.), *Handbook of macroeconomics* (pp. 1671–1745). Number 1C: Elsevier.

Charles, K. K., & Hurst, E. (2003). The correlation of wealth accross generations. *Journal of Political Economy, 6*(111), 1155–1182.

Chetty, R. (2009). Is the taxable income elasticity sufficient to calculate deadweight loss? The implications of evasion and avoidance. *American Economic Journal: Economic Policy, 1* (2), 31–52.

Coate, S. (1995). Altruism, the Samaritan's dilemma, and government transfer policy. *American Economic Review, 85*(1), 46–57.

Coile, C. C., & Levine, P. B. (2006). Bulls, bears, and retirement behavior. *Industrial and Labor Relations Review, 59*(3), 408–429.

Conway, K. S., & Rork, J. C. (2004). Diagnosis murder: The death of state death taxes. *Economic Inquiry, 42*(4), 537–559.

Conway, K. S., & Rork, J. C. (2006). State 'death' taxes and elderly migration—the chicken or the egg? *National Tax Journal, 59*(1), 97–128.

Cooper, G. (1979). *A voluntary tax? New perspectives on sophisticated tax avoidance.* Studies of Government Finance, Washington D.C.: The Brookings Institution.

Cox, D. (1987). Motives for private income transfers. *Journal of Political Economy, 95*(3), 508–546.

Cremer, H., & Pestieau, P. (2001). Non-linear taxation of bequests, equal sharing rules and the tradeoff between intar- and inter-family inequalities. *Journal of Public Economics, 79*(1), 35–54.

Cremer, H., & Pestieau, P. (2006). Wealth transfer taxation: A survey of the theoretical literature. In S.-C. Kolm & J. M. Ythier (Eds.), *Handbook on the economics of giving, reciprocity and altruism, Vol. 2* (pp. 1107–1134). Elsevier.

Cremer, H., Gahvari, F., & Ladoux, N. (1998). Externalities and optimal taxation. *Journal of Public Economics, 70*(3), 343–364.

Cremer, H., Pestieau, P., & Rochet, J. -C. (2003). Capital income taxation when inherited wealth is not observable. *Journal of Public Economics, 87*(11), 2475–2490.

Dai, Z., Maydew, E. L., Shackelford, D. A., & Zhang, H. H. (2008). Capital gains taxes and asset prices: Capitalization or lock-in? *Journal of Finance, 63*(2), 709–742.

Davies, J. B., & Shorrocks, A. F. (2000). The distribution of wealth. In A. B. Atkinson & F. Bourguignon (Eds.), *Handbook of income distribution*. Amsterdam, New York: Elsevier.

De Nardi, M. (2004). Wealth inequality and intergenerational links. *Review of Economic Studies, 71*(3), 743–768.

Diamond, P. (1998). Optimal income taxation: An example with u-shaped pattern of optimal tax rates. *American Economic Review, 88*(1), 83–95.

Diamond, P. (2006). Optimal tax treatment of private contributions for public goods with and without warm glow preferences. *Journal of Public Economics, 90*(4–5), 897–919.

Diamond, P. A., & Mirrlees, J. A. (1978). A model of social insurance with variable retirement. *Journal of Public Economics, 10*(3), 295–336.

Diamond, P., & Spinnewijn, J. (2010). *Capital income taxes with heterogeneous discount rates*. MIT and LSE: Mimeo.

Doepke, M., & Zilibotti, F. (2008). Occupational choice and the spirit of capitalism. *Quarterly Journal of Economics, 123*(2), 747–793.

Dunn, T. A., & Phillips, J. W. (1997). The timing and division of parental transfers to children. *Economics Letters, 54*(2), 135–137.

Dynan, K. E., Skinner, J., & Zeldes, S. P. (2002). The importance of bequests and life-cycle saving in capital accumulation: A new answer. *American Economic Review, 92*(2), 274–78.

Dynan, K. E., Skinner, J., & Zeldes, S. P. (2004). Do the rich save more? *Journal of Political Economy, 112*(2), 397–444.

Eaton, J., & Rosen, H. S. (1980). Taxation, human capital and uncertainty. *American Economic Review, 70*(4), 705–715.

Edlund, L., & Kopczuk, W. (2009). Women, wealth and mobility. *American Economic Review, 99*(1), 146–78.

Eliason, M., & Ohlsson, H. (2008). Living to save taxes. *Economics Letters, 100*(3), 340–343.

Elinder, M., Erixson, O., & Ohlsson, H. (2011). Carnegie visits nobel: Do inheritances affect labor and capital income? *Working paper* 2011:5. Department of Economics: Uppsala University.

Eller, M., & Johnson, B. W., (1999). Using a sample of federal estate returns to examine the effects of audit revaluation on pre-audit estimates. In: *Proceedings of the 1999 meeting of the American statistical association, section on government statistics*.

Eller, M., Erard, B., & Ho, C. -C. (2001). The magnitude and determinants of federal estate tax noncompliance. In W. G. Gale, J. R. Hines, Jr., & J. Slemrod (Eds.), *Rethinking estate and gift taxation* (pp. 375–410) Brookings Institution Press.

Erard, B. (1999). *Estate tax underreporting gap study: A report prepared for the internal revenue service economic analysis and modeling group*. TIRNO-98-P-00406, Internal Revenue Service.

Farhi, E., & Werning, I. (2007). Inequality and social discounting. *Journal of Political Economy, 115*(3), 365–402.

Farhi, E., & Werning, I. (2010). Progressive estate taxation. *Quarterly Journal of Economics, 125*(2), 635–73.

Feldstein, M. S. (1995). The effect of marginal tax rates on taxable income: A panel study of the 1986 tax reform act. *Journal of Political Economy, 103*(3), 551–572.

Feldstein, M. S. (1999). Tax avoidance and the deadweight loss of the income tax. *Review of Economics and Statistics, 4*(81), 674–680.

Francis, J. L. (2009). Wealth and the capitalist spirit. *Journal of Macroeconomics, 31*(3), 394–408.

Frank, R. H. (2008). Should public policy respond to positional externalities?. *Journal of Public Economics, 92*(8–9), 1777–1786. (Special Issue: Happiness and Public Economics.)

Friedman, B. M., & Warshawsky, M. (1990). The cost of annuities: Implications for saving behavior and bequests. *Quarterly Journal of Economics, 105*(1), 135–54.

Fullerton, D. (1997). Environmental levies and distortionary taxes: Comment. *American Economic Review, 87*(1), 245–51.

Gale, W. G., Slemrod, J. (2001). Rethinking the estate and gift tax: Overview. In W. G. Gale, J. R. Hines, Jr., & J. Slemrod (Eds.), *Rethinking estate and gift taxation*. Brookings Institution Press.

Gale, W. G., & Scholz, J. K. (1994). Intergenerational transfers and the accumulation of wealth. *Journal of Economic Perspectives, 8*(4), 145–160.

Gans, J. S., & Leigh, A. (2006). Did the death of Australian inheritance taxes affect deaths? *B.E. Journal of Economic Analysis and Policy: Topics in Economic Analysis and Policy, 6*(1), 1–7.

Golosov, M., Tsyvinski, A., & Weinzierl, M. (2010). *Preference heterogeneity and optimal commodity taxation.* Yale and Harvard: Mimeo.

Golosov, M., & Tsyvinski, A. (2006). Designing optimal disability insurance: A case for asset testing. *Journal of Political Economy, 114*(2), 257–279.

Golosov, M., Kocherlakota, N., & Tsyvinski, A. (2003). Optimal indirect and capital taxation. *Review of Economic Studies, 70*(244), 569–587.

Gordon, R., & Kopczuk, W. (2010). *The choice of personal income tax base.* UC-San Diego and Columbia, preliminary draft: Mimeo. <http://www.columbia.edu/~wk2110/bin/choiceBase.pdf>.

Graetz, M. J., & Shapiro, I. (2005). *Death by a thousand cuts: The fight over taxing inherited wealth* (1st ed.). Princeton University Press.

Green, J., & Sheshinsky, E. (1976). Direct versus indirect remedies for externalities. *Journal of Political Economy, 84*(4), 797–808.

Grossmann, V., & Strulik, H. (2010). Should continued family firms face lower taxes than other estates? *Journal of Public Economics, 94*(1–2), 87–101.

Holtz-Eakin, D., & Marples, D. (2001). Distortion costs of taxing wealth accumulation: Income versus estate taxes. *Working paper* 8261, National Bureau of Economic Research.

Holtz-Eakin, D., Joulfaian, D., & Rosen, H. S. (1993). The carnegie conjecture: Some empirical evidence. *Quarterly Journal of Economics, 108*(2), 413–435.

Holtz-Eakin, D., Joulfaian, D., & Rosen, H. S. (1994a). Entrepreneurial decisions and liquidity constraints. *RAND Journal of Economics, 25*(2), 334–347.

Holtz-Eakin, D., Joulfaian, D., & Rosen, H. S. (1994b). Sticking it out: Entrepreneurial survival and liquidity constraints. *Journal of Political Economy, 102*(1), 53–75.

Holtz-Eakin, D., Phillips, J. W., & Rosen, H. S. (2001). Estate taxes, life insurance, and small business. *Review of Economics and Statistics, 83*(1), 52–63.

Hubbard, R. G., Skinner, J., & Zeldes, S. P. (1994). The importance of precautionary motives in explaining individual and aggregate saving. *Carnegie-Rochester Conference Series on Public Policy, 40*, 59–125.

Hubbard, R. G., Skinner, J., & Zeldes, S. (1995). Precautionary saving and social insurance. *Journal of Political Economy, 103*(2), 360–399.

Hurd, M. D. (1987). Savings of the elderly and desired bequests. *American Economic Review, 77*(3), 298–312.

Hurd, M. D. (1989). Mortality risk and bequests. *Econometrica, 57*(4), 779–813.

Hurst, E., Lusardi, A. (2004). Liquidity constraints, household wealth, and entrepreneurship. *Journal of Political Economy, 112* (2), 319–347.

Imbens, G. W., Rubin, D. B., & Sacerdote, B. I. (2001). Estimating the effect of unearned income on labor earnings, savings, and consumption: Evidence from a survey of lottery players. *American Economic Review, 91*(4), 778–794.

Johnson, B. W. (Ed.). (1994). Compendium of federal estate tax and personal wealth studies. Department of Treasury, *Internal Revenue Service, Pub., 1773*(4–94), 1994.

Johnson, B. W., Mikow, J. M., & Eller, M. B. (2001). Elements of federal estate taxation. In W. G. Gale, J. R. Hines, Jr., & J. Slemrod (Eds.), *Rethinking estate and gift taxation*. Brookings Institution Press.

Joulfaian, D. (1991). Charitable bequests and estate taxes. *National Tax Journal, 44*(2), 169–180.

Joulfaian, D. (1998). *Charitable bequests and estate taxes: Another look at the evidence.* Office of Tax Analysis, US Department of Treasury: Mimeo.

Joulfaian, D. (2000). Estate taxes and charitable bequests by the wealthy. *Working paper* 7663, National Bureau of Economic Research.

Joulfaian, D. (2001). Charitable giving in life and death. In W. G. Gale, J. R. Hines, Jr., & J. Slemrod (Eds.), *Rethinking estate and gift taxation* (pp. 350–69). Brookings Institution Press.

Joulfaian, D. (2004). Gift taxes and lifetime transfers: Time series evidence. *Journal of Public Economics, 88*(9–10), 1917–1929.

Joulfaian, D. (2005a). Choosing between gifts and bequests: How taxes affect the timing of wealth transfers. *Journal of Public Economics, 89*(11–12), 2069–2091.

Joulfaian, D. (2005b). Estate taxes and charitable bequests. Evidence from two tax regimes. *Office of tax policy analysis working paper 92*, US Department of Treasury 2005.

Joulfaian, D. (2006a). *Inheritance and saving.* WP 12569, National Bureau of Economic Research October 2006.

Joulfaian, D. (2006b). The behavioral response of wealth accumulation to estate taxation: Time series evidence. *National Tax Journal, 59*(2), 253–68.

Joulfaian, D. (2011). *The federal estate tax: History, law, and economics.* Office of Tax Analysis, US Department of Treasury. Available at SSRN: <http://ssrn.com/abstract=1579829>.

Joulfaian, D., & McGarry, K. (2004). Estate and gift tax incentives and inter vivos giving. *National Tax Journal, 57*(2 (part 2)), 429–444.

Joulfaian, D., & Wilhelm, M. O. (1994). Inheritance and labor supply. *Journal of Human Resources, 29*(4), 1205–1234.

Judd, K. L. (1985). Redistributive taxation in a simple perfect foresight model. *Journal of Public Economics, 28*(1), 59–83.

Kaplow, L. (1995). A note on subsidizing gifts. *Journal of Public Economics, 58*(3), 496–77.

Kaplow, L. (1998). Tax policy and gifts. *American Economic Review Papers and Proceedings, 88*(2), 283–88.

Kaplow, L. (2001). A framework for assessing estate and gift taxation. In W. G. Gale, J. R. Hines, Jr., & J. Slemrod (Eds.), *Rethinking estate and gift taxation.* Brookings Institution Press.

Kaplow, L. (2006). On the undesirability of commodity taxation even when income taxation is not optimal. *Journal of Public Economics, 90*(6–7), 1235–50.

Kaplow, L. (2008). *The theory of taxation and public economics.* Princeton and Oxford: Princeton University Press.

Kaplow, L. (2009). On the taxation of private transfers. *Tax Law Review, 63*(1), 159–188.

Kennickell, A. B. (2006). Currents and undercurrents: Changes in the distribution of wealth, 1989–2004. *Discussion paper 2006–13*, Federal Reserve Board.

Kocherlakota, N. R. (2005). Zero expected wealth taxes: A mirrlees approach to dynamic optimal taxation. *Econometrica, 73*(5), 1587–1622.

Kocherlakota, N. R. (2010). *The new dynamic public finance.* Princeton and Oxford: Princeton University Press.

Kopczuk, W. (2001). *Optimal estate taxation in the steady state.* University of Michigan: Mimeo.

Kopczuk, W. (2003a). A note on optimal taxation in the presence of externalities. *Economics Letters, 80*(1), 81–86.

Kopczuk, W. (2003b). The trick is to live: Is the estate tax social security for the rich? *Journal of Political Economy, 111*(6), 1318–1341.

Kopczuk, W. (2007). Bequest and tax planning: Evidence from estate tax returns. *Quarterly Journal of Economics, 122*(4), 1801–1854.

Kopczuk, W. (2009). Economics of estate taxation: A brief review of theory and evidence. *Tax Law Review, 63*(1), 139–157.

Kopczuk, W. (2013). Incentive effects of inheritances and optimal estate taxation. *American Economic Review Papers and Proceedings, 103*(3).

Kopczuk, W., & Saez, E. (2004a). Top wealth shares in the united states, 1916–2000: Evidence from estate tax returns. *National Tax Journal, 57* (2 (part 2)), 445–488.

Kopczuk, W., & Saez, E. (2004b). Top wealth shares in the united states, 1916–2000: Evidence from estate tax returns. *Working paper* 10399, National Bureau of Economic Research 2004.

Kopczuk, W., & Slemrod, J. (2001). The impact of the estate tax on the wealth accumulation and avoidance behavior of donors. In W. G. Gale, J. R. Hines, Jr., & J. Slemrod (Eds.), *Rethinking estate and gift taxation* (pp. 299–343). Brookings Institution Press.

Kopczuk, W., & Slemrod, J. (2003a). Dying to save taxes: Evidence from estate tax returns on the death elasticity. *Review of Economics and Statistics, 85*(2), 256–265.

Kopczuk, W., & Slemrod, J. (2003b). Tax consequences on wealth accumulation and transfers of the rich. In A. H. Munnell & A. Sundén (Eds.), *Death and dollars: The role of gifts and bequests in America* (pp. 213–249). Brookings Institution Press.

Kopczuk, W., & Slemrod, J. (2005). Denial of death and economic behavior. *Advances in Theoretical Economics, 5*(1), Article 5. <http://www.bepress.com/bejte/advances/vol5/iss1/art5>

Kopczuk, W., & Lupton, J. (2007). To leave or not to leave: An empirical investigation of the distribution of bequest motives. *Review of Economic Studies, 74*(1), 207–235.

Kotlikoff, L. J., & Summers, L. H. (1981). The role of intergenerational transfers in aggregate capital accumulation. *Journal of Political Economy, 89*(4), 706–732.

Kuehlwein, M. (1994). The non-equalization of true gift and estate tax rates. *Journal of Public Economics, 53*(2), 319–323.

Kuhn, P., Kooreman, P., Soetevent, A., & Kapteyn, A. (2011). The effects of lottery prizes on winners and their neighbors: Evidence from the Dutch postcode lottery. *American Economic Review, 101*(5), 2226–2247.

Laferrère, A., & Wolff, F. -C. (2006). Microeconomic models of family transfers. In: S. -C. Kolm & J. M. Ythier (Eds.), *Handbook on the economics of giving, reciprocity and altruism, Vol. 2* (pp. 889–969). Elsevier.

Laitner, J. (1997). Intergenerational and interhousehold economic links. In M. K. Rosenzweig & O. Stark (Eds.), *Handbook of population and family economics, Vol. 1A*. Amsterdam, New York: Elsevier/North Holland.

Laitner, J., & Juster, F. T. (1996). New evidence on altruism: A study of TIAA-CREF retirees. *American Economic Review, 86*(4), 893–908.

Laitner, J., & Ohlsson, H. (2001). Bequest motives: A comparison of Sweden and the United States. *Journal of Public Economics, 79*(1), 205–236. ISPE 1998: Bequests and Wealth Taxation.

Lampman, R. J. (1962). *The share of top wealth-holders in national wealth, 1922–56*, Princeton, NJ: Princeton University Press.

Laroque, G. (2005). Indirect taxation is superfluous under separability and taste homogeneity: A simple proof. *Economics Letters, 87*(1), 141–44.

Light, A., McGarry, K. (2004). Why parents play favorites: Explanations for unequal bequests. *American Economic Review, 94*(5), 1669–81.

Luckey, J. R. (2008). A history of federal estate, gift and generation-skipping taxes, *CRS Report for Congress 95-444*, Congressional Research Service January 2008.

Mallet, B. (1908). A method of estimating capital wealth from estate duty statistics. *Journal of the Royal Statistical Society, 71*, 65–101.

McCaffery, E. J. (1994). The uneasy case for wealth transfer taxation. *Yale Law Journal, 104*(2), 283–365.

McCubbin, J. G. (1994). Improving wealth estimates derived from estate tax data. In Johnson (Ed.), 363–369.

McGarry, K. (1999). Inter vivos transfers and intended bequests. *Journal of Public Economics, 73*(3), 321–51.

McGarry, K. (2000). Inter vivos transfers or bequests? Estate taxes and the timing of parental giving. *Tax Policy and the Economy, 14*, 93–121.

McGarry, K. (2001). The cost of equality: Unequal bequests and tax avoidance. *Journal of Public Economics, 79*(1), 179–204.

McNees, S. (1973). Deductibility of charitable bequests. *National Tax Journal, 26*(1), 79–98.

Menchik, P. L. (1980). Primogeniture, equal sharing, and the U.S. distribution of wealth. *Quarterly Journal of Economics, 94*(2), 299–316.

Menchik, P. L., & David, M. (1983). Income, distribution, lifetime savings, and bequests. *American Economic Review, 73*(4), 672–690.

Micheletto, L. (2008). Redistribution and optimal mixed taxation in the presence of consumption externalities. *Journal of Public Economics, 92*(10–11), 2262–2274.

Milesi-Ferretti, G. M., & Roubini, N. (1998). On the taxation of human and physical capital in models of endogenous growth. *Journal of Public Economics, 70*(2), 237–54.

Mintz, J. M. (1991). The role of wealth taxation in the overall tax system. *Canadian Public Policy/ Analyse de Politiques, 17*(3), 248–63.

Mirrlees, J. A. (1971). An exploration in the theory of optimum income taxation. *Review of Economic Studies, 38*(114), 175–208.

Mitchell, O. S., Poterba, J. M., Warshawsky, M. J., & Brown, J. R. (1999). New evidence on the money's worth of individual annuities. *American Economic Review, 89*(5), 1299–1317.

Modigliani, F. (1988). The role of intergenerational transfers and life cycle saving in the accumulation of wealth. *Journal of Economic Perspectives, 2*(2), 15–40.

Morck, R., Wolfenzon, D., & Yeung, B. (2005). Corporate governance, economic entrenchment, and growth. *Journal of Economic Literature, 43*(3), 655–720.

Nordblom, K., & Ohlsson, H. (2006). Tax avoidance and intra-family transfers. *Journal of Public Economics, 90*(8–9), 1669–1680.

Ohlsson, H. (2011). The legacy of the Swedish gift and inheritance tax, 1884–2004. *European Review of Economic History, 15*(3), 539–69.

Page, B. R. (2003). Bequest taxes, inter vivos gifts, and the bequest motive. *Journal of Public Economics, 87*(5–6), 1219–1229.

Pérez-González, F. (2006). Inherited control and firm performance. *American Economic Review, 96*(5), 1559–1588.

Perozek, M. G. (1998). Comment: A reexamination of the strategic bequest motive. *Journal of Political Economy, 106*(2), 423–445.

Phelan, C. (2006). Opportunity and social mobility. *Review of Economic Studies, 72*(2), 487–504.

Pigou, A. C. (1920). *Economics of welfare.* London: Macmillan and Co.

Piketty, T. (2001). Income inequality in France 1901–98. *DP 2876,* CEPR 2001.

Piketty, T. (2011). On the long-run evolution of inheritance: France 1820–2050. *Quarterly Journal of Economics, 126*(3), 1071–1131.

Piketty, T., & Saez, E. (2003). Income inequality in the United States, 1913–1998. *Quarterly Journal of Economics, 118,* 1–39.

Piketty, T., & Saez, E. (2007). How progressive is the U.S. federal tax system? A historical and international perspective. *Journal of Economic Perspectives, 21*(1), 3–24.

Piketty, T., & Saez, E. (2012a). A theory of capital income taxation. *Working paper* 17989, NBER April 2012.

Piketty, T., & Saez, E. (2012b). *A theory of optimal inheritance taxation.* Paris School of Economics and UC Berkeley: Mimeo.

Piketty, T., Saez, E., & Stantcheva, S. (2011). Optimal taxation of labor incomes: A tale of three elasticities. *Working paper* 17616, National Bureau of Economic Research November 2011.

Piketty, T., Postel-Vinay, G., & Rosenthal, J. -L. (2003). *Wealth concentration in a developing economy: Paris and France, 1807–1994.* EHESS and UCLA: Mimeo.

Poterba, J. M. (2000a). Stock market wealth and consumption. *Journal of Economic Perspectives, 14*(2), 99–118.

Poterba, J. M. (2000b). The estate tax and after-tax investment returns. In J. Slemrod (Ed.), *Does atlas shrug? The economic consequences of taxing the rich* (pp. 329–349). New York: Harvard University Press and Russell Sage Foundation.

Poterba, J. M. (2001). Estate and gift taxes and incentives for inter vivos giving in the U.S. *Journal of Public Economics, 79*(1), 237–64.

Poterba, J. M., & Weisbenner, S. (2001). The distributional burden of taxing estates and unrealized capital gains at the time of death. In W. G. Gale, J. R. Hines, Jr., & J. Slemrod (Eds.), *Rethinking estate and gift taxation.* Brookings Institution Press.

Poterba, J. M., & Weisbenner, S. (2003). Inter-asset differences in effective estate-tax burdens. *American Economic Review, 93*(2), 360–365.

Reiter, M. (2004). *Do the rich save too much? How to explain the top tail of the wealth distribution.* Universitat Pompeu Fabra: Mimeo.

Rogerson, W. P. (1985). Repeated moral hazard. *Econometrica, 53*(1), 69–76.

Roine, J., & Waldenström, D. (2009). Wealth concentration over the path of development: Sweden, 1873–2006. *Scandinavian Journal of Economics, 111*(1), 151–187.

Rothschild, C., & Scheuer, F. (2011). Optimal taxation with rent-seeking. *Working paper* 17035, National Bureau of Economic Research May 2011.

Saez, E. (2001). Using elasticities to derive optimal income tax rates. *Review of Economic Studies, 68*(1), 205–29.

Saez, E. (2002a). Optimal progressive capital income taxes in the infinite horizon model. *Working paper* 9046, National Bureau of Economic Research July 2002.

Saez, E. (2002b). The desirability of commodity taxation under non-linear income taxation and heteroge-neous tastes. *Journal of Public Economics, 83*(2), 217–320.

Saez, E., Slemrod, J. B., & Giertz, S. H. (2012). The elasticity of taxable income with respect to marginal tax rates: A critical review. *Journal of Economic Literature, 50*(1), 3–50.

Salanié, B. (2011). *The economics of taxation* (2nd ed.). Cambrige, MA and London, England: The MIT Press.

Sandmo, A. (1975). Optimal taxation in the presence of externalities. *Swedish Journal of Economics, 77*(1), 86–98.

Sandmo, A. (1998). Redistribution and the marginal cost of public funds. *Journal of Public Economics, 70*(3), 365–382.

Scheve, K., & Stasavage, D. (2012). Democracy, war and wealth: Evidence from two centuries of inheritance taxation. *American Political Science Review, 106*(1), 81–102. Yale and NYU, mimeo.

Schmalbeck, R. (2001). Avoiding federal wealth transfer taxes. In W. G. Gale, J. R. Hines, Jr., & J. Slemrod (Eds.), *Rethinking estate and gift taxation*. Brookings Institution Press.

Scholz, J. K. (2003). *Wealth inequality and the wealth of cohorts*. University of Wisconsin: Mimeo.

Scholz, J. K., Seshadri, A., & Khitatrakun, S. (2006). Are americans saving optimally for retirement? *Journal of Political Economy, 114*(4), 607–643.

Seim, D. (2012). *Smart enough to evade?* On the Incidence of a Wealth Tax, Mimeo.

Severinov, S. (2006). Bequests as signals: Implications for fiscal policy. *Journal of Public Economics, 90*(10–11), 1995–2008.

Slemrod, J. (1998). Methodological issues in measuring and interpreting taxable income elasticities. *National Tax Journal, 51*(4), 773–788.

Slemrod, J., & Kopczuk, W. (2002). The optimal elasticity of taxable income. *Journal of Public Economics, 84*(1), 91–112.

Stiglitz, J. E. (1978). Notes on estate taxes, redistribution, and the concept of balanced growth path incidence. *Journal of Political Economy, 86*(2), S137–S150.

Stiglitz, J. E. (1985). The general theory of tax avoidance. *National Tax Journal, 38*(3), 325–37.

Tsoutsoura, M. (2011). *The effect of succession taxes on family firm investment: Evidence from a natural experiment.* Chicago Booth: Mimeo.

Villalonga, B., & Amit, R. (2006). How do family ownership, control and management affect firm value? *Journal of Financial Economics, 80*(2), 385–417.

Weber, M. (1958). *The Protestant ethic and the spirit of capitalism.* New York: Scribner. (Translated by Talcott Parsons; with a foreword by R.H. Tawney.)

Werning, I. (2011). *Nonlinear capital taxation.* MIT: Mimeo.

Wilhelm, M. O. (1996). Bequest behavior and the effect of heirs' earnings: Testing the altruistic model of bequests. *American Economic Review, 86*(4), 874–892.

Wolff, E. N. (1996). Discussant's comments on Douglas Holtz-Eakin, The uneasy case for abolishing the estate tax. *Tax Law Review, 51*(3), 517–22.

Yaari, M. E. (1965). Uncertain lifetime, life insurance, and the theory of the consumer. *Review of Economic Studies, 32*(2), 137–150.

CHAPTER 7

Optimal Labor Income Taxation

Thomas Piketty[*] and Emmanuel Saez[†,‡]

[*]Paris School of Economics, Paris, France
[†]Department of Economics, University of California, 530 Evans Hall #3880, Berkeley, CA 94720, USA
[‡]National Bureau of Economic Research, USA

Contents

Handbook of Public Economics, Volume 5
ISSN 1573-4420, http://dx.doi.org/10.1016/B978-0-444-53759-1.00007-8

1. INTRODUCTION

This handbook chapter considers optimal labor income taxation, that is, the fair and efficient distribution of the tax burden across individuals with different earnings. A large academic literature has developed models of optimal tax theory to cast light on this issue. Models in optimal tax theory typically posit that the tax system should maximize a social welfare function subject to a government budget constraint, taking into account how individuals respond to taxes and transfers. Social welfare is larger when resources are more equally distributed, but redistributive taxes and transfers can negatively affect incentives to work and earn income in the first place. This creates the classical trade-off between equity and efficiency which is at the core of the optimal labor income tax problem.

In this chapter, we present recent developments in the theory of optimal labor income taxation. We emphasize connections between theory and empirical work that were previously largely absent from the optimal income tax literature. Therefore, throughout the chapter, we focus less on formal modeling and rigorous derivations than was done in previous surveys on this topic (Atkinson & Stiglitz, 1980; Kaplow, 2008; Mirrlees (1976, 1986, chap. 24); Stiglitz, 1987, chap. 15; Tuomala, 1990) and we try to systematically connect the theory to both real policy debates and empirical work on behavioral responses to taxation.[1] This chapter limits itself to the analysis of optimal *labor income* taxation and related means-tested transfers.[2]

First, we provide historical and international background on labor income taxation and transfers. In our view, knowing actual tax systems and understanding their history and the key policy debates driving their evolution is critical to guide theoretical modeling and successfully capture the first order aspects of the optimal tax problem. We also briefly review the history of the field of optimal labor income taxation to place our chapter in its academic context.

Second, we review the theoretical underpinnings of the standard optimal income tax approach, such as the social welfare function, the fallacy of the second welfare theorem, and hence the necessity of tackling the equity-efficiency trade off. We also present the

---

[1] Boadway (2012) also provides a recent, longer, and broader survey that aims at connecting theory to practice.

[2] The analysis of optimal *capital income* taxation naturally involves dynamic considerations and is covered in the chapter by Kopczuk in this volume.

key parameters capturing labor supply responses as they determine the efficiency costs of taxation and hence play a crucial role in optimal tax formulas.

Third, we present the simple model of optimal linear taxation. Considering linear labor income taxation simplifies considerably the exposition but still captures the key equity-efficiency trade-off. The derivation and the formula for the optimal linear tax rate are also closely related to the more complex nonlinear case, showing the tight connection between the two problems. The linear tax model also allows us to consider extensions such as tax avoidance and income shifting, random earnings, and median voter tax equilibria in a simpler way.

Fourth, we consider optimal nonlinear income taxation with particular emphasis on the optimal top tax rate and the optimal profile of means-tested transfers at the bottom. We consider several extensions including extensive labor supply responses, international migration, or rent-seeking models where pay differs from productivity.

Fifth, we consider additional deeper extensions of the standard model including tagging (i.e., conditioning taxes and transfers on characteristics correlated with ability to earn), the use of differential commodity taxation to supplement the income tax, the use of in-kind transfers (instead of cash transfers), the treatment of couples and children in tax and transfer systems, or models with relative income concerns. Many of those extensions cannot be satisfactorily treated within the standard utilitarian social welfare approach. Hence, in a number of cases, we present the issues only heuristically and leave formal full-fledged modeling to future research.

Sixth and finally, we come back to the limitations of the standard utilitarian approach that have appeared throughout the chapter. We briefly review the most promising alternatives. While many recent contributions use general Pareto weights to avoid the strong assumptions of the standard utilitarian approach, the Pareto weight approach is too general to deliver practical policy prescriptions in most cases. Hence, it is important to make progress both on normative theories of justice stating how social welfare weights should be set and on positive analysis of how individual views and beliefs about redistribution are formed.

Methodologically, a central goal of optimal tax analysis should be to cast light on actual tax policy issues and help design better tax systems. Theory and technical derivations are very valuable to rigorously model the problem at hand. A key aim of this chapter is to show how to make such theoretical findings applicable. As argued in Diamond and Saez (2011), theoretical results in optimal tax analysis are most useful for policy recommendations when three conditions are met. (1) Results should be based on economic mechanisms that are empirically relevant and first order to the problem at hand. (2) Results should be reasonably robust to modeling assumptions and in particular to the presence of heterogeneity in individual preferences. (3) The tax policy prescription needs to be implementable—that is, the tax policy needs to be relatively easy to explain and discuss publicly, and not too complex to administer relative to actual practice.[3] Those conditions lead us to adopt two methodological choices.

First, we use the "sufficient statistics" approach whereby optimal tax formulas are derived and expressed in terms of estimable statistics including social marginal welfare weights capturing society's value for redistribution and labor supply elasticities capturing the efficiency costs of taxation (see Chetty, 2009a for a recent survey of the "sufficient statistics" approach in public economics). This approach allows us to understand the key economic mechanisms behind the formulas, helping meet condition (1). The "sufficient statistics" formulas are also often robust to change the primitives of the model, which satisfies condition (2).

Second, we tend to focus on simple tax structures—e.g., a linear income tax—without systematically trying to derive the most general tax system possible. This helps meet condition (3) as the tax structures we obtain will by definition be within the realm of existing tax structures.[4] This is in contrast to the "mechanism design" approach that derives the most general optimum tax compatible with the informational structure. This "mechanism design" approach tends to generate tax structures that are highly complex and results that are sensitive to the exact primitives of the model. The mechanism design approach has received renewed interest in the new dynamic public finance literature that focuses primarily on dynamic aspects of taxation.[5]

The chapter is organized as follows. Section 2 provides historical and international background on labor income taxation and means-tested transfers, and a short review of the field of optimal labor income taxation. Section 3 presents the key concepts: the standard utilitarian social welfare approach, the fallacy of the second welfare theorem, and the key labor supply concepts. Section 4 discusses the optimal linear income tax problem. Section 5 presents the optimal nonlinear income taxation problem with particular emphasis on the optimal top tax rate and the optimal profile of means-tested transfers. Section 6 considers a number of extensions. Section 7 discusses limits of the standard utilitarian approach.

2. BACKGROUND ON ACTUAL TAX SYSTEMS AND OPTIMAL TAX THEORY

2.1. Actual Tax Systems

Taxes. Most advanced economies in the OECD raise between 35% and 50% of national income (GNP net of capital depreciation) in taxes. As a first approximation, the share

---

[3] Naturally, the set of possible tax systems evolves overtime with technological progress. If more complex tax innovations become feasible and can realistically generate large welfare gains, they are certainly worth considering.
[4] The simple tax structure approach also helps with conditions (1) and (2) as the economic trade-offs are simpler and more transparent, and the formulas for simple tax structures tend to easily generalize to heterogeneous populations.
[5] See Golosov, Tsyvinski, and Werning (2006) and Kocherlakota (2010) for recent surveys of the new dynamic public finance literature. Piketty and Saez (2012a,b) analyze the problem optimal taxation of capital and inheritances in a dynamic model but using a sufficient statistics approach and focusing on simple tax structures.

of total tax burden falling on capital income roughly corresponds to the share of capital income in national income (i.e., about 25%).[6] The remaining 75% of taxes falls on labor income (OECD 2011a),[7] which is the part we are concerned with in this chapter.

Historically, the overall tax to national income ratio has increased substantially during the first part of the 20th century in OECD countries from about 10% on average around 1900 to around 40% by 1970 (see e.g., Flora, 1983 for long time series up to 1975 for a number of Western European countries and OECD, *Revenue Statistics*, OECD, 2011a for statistics since 1965). Since the late 1970s, the tax burden in OECD countries has been roughly stable. The share of taxes falling on capital income has declined slightly in Europe and has been approximately stable in the United States.[8] Similar to the historical evolution, tax revenue to national income ratios increase with GDP per capita when looking at the current cross-section of countries. Tax to national income ratios are smaller in less developed and developing countries and higher on average among the most advanced economies.

To a first approximation, the tax burden is distributed proportionally to income. Indeed, the historical rise in the tax burden has been made possible by the ability of the government to monitor income flows in the modern economy and hence impose payroll taxes, profits taxes, income taxes, and value-added-taxes, based on the corresponding income and consumption flows. Before the 20th century, the government was largely limited to property and presumptive taxes, and taxes on a few specific goods for which transactions were observable. Such archaic taxes severely limited the tax capacity of the government and tax to national income ratios were low (see Ardant, 1971 and Webber & Wildavsky, 1986 for a detailed history of taxation). The transition from archaic to broad-based taxes involves complex political and administrative processes and may occur at various speeds in different countries.[9]

In general, actual tax systems achieve some tax progressivity, i.e., tax rates rising with income, through the individual income tax. Most individual income tax systems have brackets with increasing marginal tax rates. In contrast, payroll taxes or consumption taxes tend to have flat rates. Most OECD countries had very progressive individual income

[6] This is defining taxes on capital as the sum of property and wealth taxes, inheritance and gift taxes, taxes of corporate and business profits, individual income taxes on individual capital income, and the share of consumption taxes falling on capital income. Naturally, there are important variations over time and across countries in the relative importance of these various capital tax instruments. See e.g., Piketty and Saez (2012a).

[7] Including payroll taxes, individual income tax on labor income, and the share of consumption taxes falling on labor income.

[8] Again, there are important variations in capital taxes which fall beyond the scope of this chapter. In particular, corporate tax rates have declined significantly in Europe since the early 1990s (due to tax competition), but tax revenues have dropped only slightly, due to a global rise in the capital share, the causes of which are still debated. See e.g., Eurostat (2012).

[9] See e.g., Piketty and Qian (2009) for a contrast between China (where the income tax is about to become a mass tax, like in developed countries) and India (where the income tax is still very much an elite tax raising limited revenue). Cagé and Gadenne (2012) provide a comprehensive empirical analysis of the extent to which low- and middle-income countries were able to replace declining trade tax revenues by modern broad based taxes since the 1970s. See Kleven, Kreiner and Saez (2009b) for a theoretical model of the fiscal modernization process.

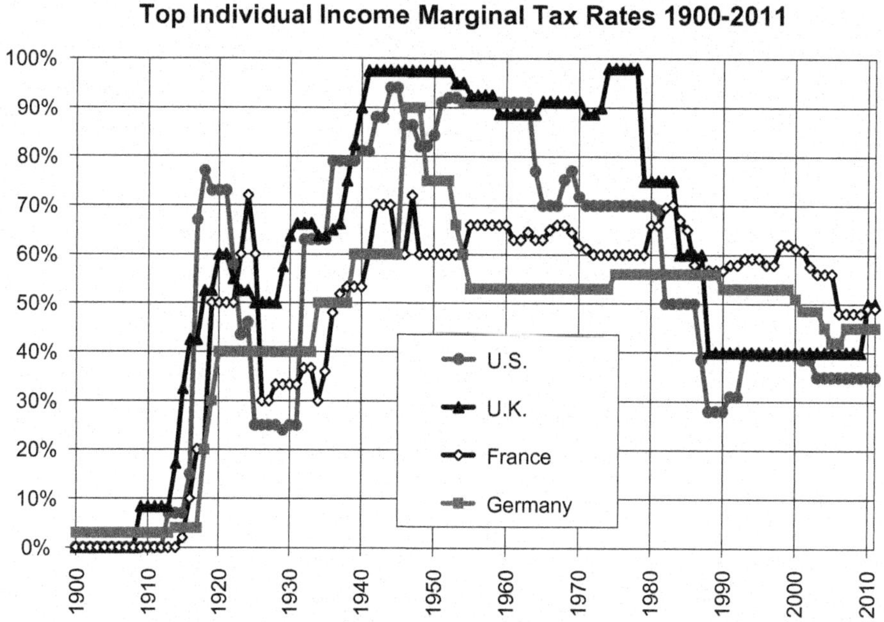

Top Individual Income Marginal Tax Rates 1900-2011

Figure 1 Top Marginal income tax rates in the US, UK, France, Germany. This figure, taken from Piketty et al. (2011), depicts the top marginal individual income tax rate in the US, UK, France, Germany since 1900. The tax rate includes only the top statutory individual income tax rate applying to ordinary income with no tax preference. State income taxes are not included in the case of the United States. For France, we include both the progressive individual income tax and the flat rate tax "Contribution Sociale Généralisée."

taxes in the post-World War II decades with a large number of tax brackets and high top tax rates (see e.g., OECD, 1986). Figure 1 depicts top marginal income tax rate in the United States, the United Kingdom, France, and Germany since 1900. When progressive income taxes were instituted—around 1900–1920 in most developed countries, top rates were very small—typically less than 10%. They rose very sharply in the 1920–1940s, particularly in the US and in the UK. Since the late 1970s, top tax rates on upper income earners have declined significantly in many OECD countries, again particularly in English speaking countries. For example, the US top marginal federal individual tax rate stood at an astonishingly high 91% in the 1950–1960s but is only 35% today (Figure 1). Progressivity at the very top is often counter balanced by the fact that a substantial fraction of capital income receives preferential tax treatment under most income tax rules.[10]

---

[10] For example, (Landais, Piketty, and Saez (2011)) show that tax rates decline at the very top of the French income distribution because of such preferential tax treatment and of various tax loopholes and fiscal optimization strategies. In the United States as well, income tax rates decline at the very top due to the preferential treatment of realized capital gains which constitute a large fraction of top incomes (US Treasury, 2012). See Piketty and Saez (2007) for an analysis of progressivity of the federal tax system since 1960. Note that preferential treatment for capital income did not exist when modern income taxes were created in 1900–1920. Preferential treatment was developed mostly in the

Table 1 Public Spending in OECD Countries (2000–2010, Percent of GDP)

	US (1)	Germany (2)	France (3)	UK (4)	Total OECD (5)
Total public spending	35.4%	44.1%	51.0%	42.1%	38.7%
Social public spending	22.4%	30.6%	34.3%	26.2%	25.1%
Education	4.7%	4.4%	5.2%	4.8%	4.9%
Health	7.7%	7.8%	7.1%	6.1%	5.6%
Pensions	6.0%	10.1%	12.2%	4.8%	6.5%
Income support to working age	2.7%	3.9%	4.8%	4.9%	4.4%
Other social public spending	1.3%	4.4%	5.1%	5.7%	3.7%
Other public spending	13.0%	13.5%	16.7%	15.9%	13.6%

Notes and sources: OECD Economic Outlook 2012, Annex Tables 25–31; Adema et al., 2011, Table 1.2; Education at a Glance, OECD 2011, Table B4.1. Total public spending includes all government outlays (except net debt interest payments). Other social public spending includes social services to the elderly and the disabled, family services, housing and other social policy areas (see Adema et al., 2011, p.21). We report 2000–2010 averages so as to smooth business cycle variations. Note that tax to GDP ratios are a little bit lower than spending to GDP ratios for two reasons: (a) governments typically run budget deficits (which can be large, around 5–8 GDP points during recessions), (b) governments get revenue from non-tax sources (such as user fees, profits from government owned firms, etc.).

As we shall see, optimal nonlinear labor income tax theory derives a simple formula for the optimal tax rate at the top of the earnings distribution. We will not deal however with the dynamic redistributive impact of tax progressivity through capital and wealth taxation, which might well have been larger historically than its static impact, as suggested by the recent literature on the long run evolution of top income shares.[11]

Transfers. The secular rise in taxes has been used primarily to fund growing public goods and social transfers in four broad areas: education, health care, retirement and disability, and income security (see Table 1). Indeed, aside from those four areas, government spending (as a fraction of GDP) has not grown substantially since 1900. All advanced economies provide free public education at the primary and secondary level, and heavily subsidized (and often almost free) higher education.[12] All advanced economies except the United States provide universal public health care (the United States provides public health care

postwar period in order to favor savings and reconstruction, and then extended since the 1980–1990s in the context of financial globalization and tax competition. For a detailed history in the case of France, see Piketty (2001).

[11] See Atkinson, Piketty and Saez (2011) for a recent survey. One of the main findings of this literature is that the historical decline in top income shares that occurred in most countries during the first half of the twentieth century has little to do with a Kuznets-type process. It was largely due to the fall of top capital incomes, which apparently never fully recovered from the 1914–1945 shocks, possibly because of the rise of progressive income and estate taxes and their dynamic impact of savings, capital accumulation and wealth concentration.

[12] Family benefits can also be considered as part of education spending. Note that the boundaries between the various social spending categories reported on Table 1 are not entirely homogenous across OECD countries (e.g., family benefits are split between "Income support to the working age" and "Other social public spending"). Also differences

to the old and the poor through the Medicare and Medicaid programs respectively, which taken together happen to be more expensive than most universal health care systems), as well as public retirement and disability benefits. Income security programs include unemployment benefits, as well as an array of means-tested transfers (both cash and in-kind). They are a relatively small fraction of total transfers (typically less than 5% of GDP, out of a total around 25–35% of GDP for social spending as a whole; see Table 1).

Education, family benefits, and health care government spending are approximately a demogrant, that is, a transfer of equal value for all individuals in expectation over a life-time.[13] In contrast, retirement benefits are approximately proportional to lifetime labor income in most countries.[14] Finally, income security programs are targeted to lower income individuals. This is therefore the most redistributive component of the transfer system. Income security programs often take the form of in-kind benefits such as subsidized housing, subsidized food purchases (e.g., food stamps and free lunches at school in the United States), or subsidized health care (e.g., Medicaid in the United States). They are also often targeted to special groups such as the unemployed (unemployment insurance), the elderly or disabled with no resources (for example Supplemental Security Income in the United States). Means-tested cash transfer programs for "able bodied" individuals are only a small fraction of total transfers. To a large extent, the rise of the modern welfare state is the rise of universal access to "basic goods" (education, health, retirement and social insurance), and not the rise of cash transfers (see e.g., Lindert, 2004).[15]

In recent years, traditional means-tested cash welfare programs have been partly replaced by in-work benefits. The shift has been particularly large in the United States and the United Kingdom. Traditional means-tested programs are L-shaped with income. They provide the largest benefits to those with no income and those benefits are then phased-out at high rates for those with low earnings. Such a structure concentrates benefits among those who need them most. At the same time and as we shall see, these phase-outs discourage work as they create large implicit taxes for low earners. In contrast, in-work benefits are inversely U-shaped, first rising and then declining with earnings. Benefits are nil for those with no earnings and concentrated among low earners before being phased-out. Such a structure encourages work but fails to provide support to those with no earnings, arguably those most in need of support.

---

in tax treatment of transfers further complicate cross country comparisons. Here we simply care about the broad orders of magnitude. For a detailed cross-country analysis, see Adema, Fron, and Ladaique (2011).

[13] Naturally, higher income individuals are often better able to navigate the public education and health care systems and hence tend to get a better value out of those benefits than lower income individuals. However, the value of those benefits certainly grows less than proportionally to income.

[14] In most countries, benefits are proportional to payroll tax contributions. Some countries—such as the United Kingdom—provide a minimum pension that is closer to a demogrant.

[15] It should be noted that the motivation behind the historical rise of these public services has to do not only with redistributive objectives, but also with the perceived failure of competitive markets in these areas (e.g., regarding the provision of health insurance or education). We discuss issues of individual and market failures in Section 6 below.

Overall, all transfers taken together are fairly close to a demogrant, i.e., are about constant with income. Hence, the optimal linear tax model with a demogrant is a reasonable first order approximation of actual tax systems and is useful to understand how the level of taxes and transfers should be set. At a finer level, there is variation in the profile of transfers. Such a profile can be analyzed using the more complex nonlinear optimal tax models.

Budget Set. The budget set relating pre-tax and pre-transfers earnings to post-tax post-transfer disposable income summarizes the net impact of the tax and transfer system.

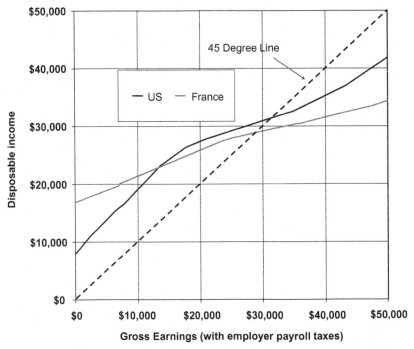

Figure 2 Tax/transfer system in the US and France, 2010, single parent with two children. The figure depicts the budget set for a single parent with two children in France and the United States (exchange rate 1 Euro = $1.3). The figure includes payroll taxes and income taxes on the tax side. It includes means-tested transfer programs (TANF and Food stamps in the United States, and the minimum income–RSA for France) and tax credits (the Earned Income Tax Credit and the Child Tax Credit in the United States, in-work benefit Prime pour l'Emploi and cash family benefits in France). Note that this graph ignores important elements. First, the health insurance Medicaid program in the United States is means tested and adds a significant layer of implicit taxation on low income work. France offers universal health insurance which does not create any additional implicit tax on work. Second, the graph ignores in-kind benefits for children such as subsidized child care and free pre-school kindergarten in France that have significant value for working single parents. Such programs barely exist in the United States. Third, the graph ignores temporary unemployment insurance benefits which depend on previous earnings for those who have become recently unemployed and which are significantly more generous in France both in level and duration.

The slope of the budget set captures the marginal incentive to work. Figure 2 depicts the budget set for a single parent with two children in France and the United States. The figure includes all payroll taxes and the income tax, on the tax side. It includes means-tested transfer programs (TANF and Food Stamps in the United States, and the minimum income—RSA for France) and tax credits (the Earned Income Tax Credit and the Child Tax Credit in the United States, in-work benefit Prime pour l'Emploi and cash family benefits in France). France offers more generous support to single parents with no earnings but the French tax and transfer system imposes higher implicit taxes on work.[16] As mentioned above, optimal nonlinear income tax theory precisely tries to assess what is the most desirable profile for taxes and transfers.

Policy Debate. At the center of the political debate on labor income taxation and transfers is the equity-efficiency trade off. The key argument in favor of redistribution through progressive taxation and generous transfers is that social justice requires the most successful to contribute to the economic well being of the less fortunate. The reasons why society values such redistribution from high to low incomes are many. As we shall see, the standard utilitarian approach posits that marginal utility of consumption decreases with income so that a more equal distribution generates higher social welfare. Another and perhaps more realistic reason is that differences in earnings arise not only from differences in work behavior (over which individuals have control) but also from differences in innate ability or family background or sheer luck (over which individuals have little control). The key argument against redistribution through taxes and transfers is efficiency. Taxing the rich to fund means-tested programs for the poor reduces the incentives to work both among the rich and among transfer recipients. In the standard optimal tax theory, such responses to taxes and transfers are costly solely because of their effect on government finances.

Do Economists Matter? The academic literature in economics does play a role, although often an indirect one, in shaping the debate on tax and transfer policy. In the 1900–1910s, when modern progressive income taxes were created, economists appear to have played a role, albeit a modest one. Utilitarian economists like Jevons, Edgeworth, and Marshall had long argued that the principles of marginal utility and equal sacrifice push in favor of progressive tax rates (see e.g., Edgeworth, 1897)—but such theoretical results had little impact on the public debate. Applied economists like Seligman wrote widely translated and read

---

[16] Note that this graph ignores important elements. First, the health insurance Medicaid program in the United States is means-tested and adds a significant layer of implicit taxation on low income work. France offers universal health insurance which does not create any additional implicit tax on work. Second, the graph ignores in-kind benefits for children such as subsidized child care and free pre-school kindergarten in France that have significant value for working single parents. Such programs barely exist in the United States. Third, the graph ignores housing benefits, which are substantial in France. Fourth, the graph ignores temporary unemployment insurance benefits which depend on previous earnings for those who have become recently unemployed and which are significantly more generous in France both in level and duration. Finally, this graph ignores consumption taxes, implying that the cutoff income level below which transfers exceed taxes is significantly overestimated. This cutoff also greatly varies with the family structure (e.g., able bodied single individuals with no dependent receive zero cash transfers in the US but significant transfers in France).

books and reports (see e.g., Seligman, 1911) arguing that progressive income taxation was not only fair but also economically efficient and administratively manageable.[17] Such arguments expressed in terms of practical economic and administrative rationality helped to convince reluctant mainstream economists in many countries that progressive income taxation was worth considering.[18]

In the 1920–1940s, the rise of top tax rates seems to have been the product of public debate and political conflict—in the context of chaotic political, financial, and social situations—rather than the outcome of academic arguments. It is worth noting, however, that a number of US economists of the time, e.g., Irving Fisher, then president of the American Economic Association, repeatedly argued that concentration of income and wealth was becoming as dangerously excessive in America as it had been for a long time in Europe, and called for steep tax progressivity (see e.g., Fisher, 1919). It is equally difficult to know whether economists had a major impact on the great reversal in top tax rates that occurred in the 1970–1980s during the Thatcher and Reagan conservative revolutions in Anglo-Saxon countries. The influential literature showing that top tax rate cuts can generate large responses of reported taxable income came after top tax rate cuts (e.g., Feldstein, 1995).

Today, most governments also draw on the work of commissions, panels, or reviews to justify tax and transfer reforms. Such reviews often play a big role in the public debate. They are sometimes commissioned by the government itself (e.g., the President's Advisory Panel on Federal Tax Reform in the United States, US Treasury, 2005), by independent policy research institutes (e.g., the Mirrlees review on Reforming the Tax System for the 21st Century in the United Kingdom, Mirrlees (2010,2011)), or proposed by independent academics (e.g., Landais et al., 2011 for France). Such reviews always involve tax scholars who draw on the academic economic literature to shape their recommendations.[19] The press also consults tax scholars to judge the merits of reforms proposed by politicians, and tax scholars naturally use findings from the academic literature when voicing their views.

2.2. History of the Field of Optimal Income Taxation

We offer here only a brief overview covering solely optimal income taxation.[20] The modern analysis of optimal income taxation started with Mirrlees (1971) who rigorously posed and solved the problem. He considered the maximization of a social welfare function based on individual utilities subject to a government budget constraint and

---

[17] See e.g., Mehrotra (2005) for a longer discussion of the role of Seligman on US tax policy at the beginning of the 20th century.

[18] This is particularly true in countries like France where mainstream laissez-faire economists had little sympathy for Anglo-Saxon utilitarian arguments, and were originally very hostile to tax progressivity, which they associated with radical utopia and with the French Revolution. See e.g., Delalande (2011a,b, pp. 166-170).

[19] Boadway (2012), Chapter 1 provides a longer discussion of the role played by such reviews.

[20] For a survey of historical fiscal doctrine in general see Musgrave (1985, chap. 1). For a more complete overview of modern optimal Boadway (2012), chapter 2.

incentive constraints arising from individuals' labor supply responses to the tax system.[21] Formally, in the Mirrlees model, people differ solely through their skill (i.e., their wage rate). The government wants to redistribute from high skill to low skill individuals but can only observe earnings (and not skills). Hence, taxes and transfers are based on earnings, leading to a non-degenerate equity-efficiency trade off.

Mirrlees (1971) had an enormous theoretical influence in the development of contract and information theory, but little influence in actual policy making as the general lessons for optimal tax policy were few. The most striking and discussed result was the famous zero marginal tax rate at the top. This zero-top result was established by Sadka (1976) and Seade (1977). In addition, if the minimum earnings level is positive with no bunching of individuals at the bottom, the marginal tax rate is also zero at the bottom (Seade, 1977). A third result obtained by Mirrlees (1971) and Seade (1982) was that the optimal marginal tax rate is never negative if the government values redistribution from high to low earners.

Stiglitz (1982) developed the discrete version of the Mirrlees (1971) model with just two skills. In this discrete case, the marginal tax rate on the top skill is zero making the zero-top result loom even larger than in the continuous model of Mirrlees (1971). That likely contributed to the saliency of the zero-top result. The discrete model is useful to understand the problem of optimal taxation as an information problem generating an incentive compatibility constraint for the government. Namely, the tax system must be set up so that the high skill type does not want to work less and mimic the low skill type. This discrete model is also widely used in contract theory and industrial organization. However, this discrete model has limited use for actual tax policy recommendations because it is much harder to obtain formulas expressed in terms of sufficient statistics or put realistic numbers in the discrete two skill model than in the continuous model.[22]

Atkinson and Stiglitz (1976) derived the very important and influential result that under separability and homogeneity assumptions on preferences, differentiated commodity taxation is not useful when earnings can be taxed nonlinearly. This famous result was influential both for shaping the field of optimal tax theory and in tax policy debates. Theoretically, it contributed greatly to shift the theoretical focus toward optimal nonlinear taxation and away from the earlier Diamond and Mirrlees (1971) model of differentiated commodity taxation (itself based on the original Ramsey (1927) contribution). Practically, it gave a strong rationale for eliminating preferential taxation of necessities on redistributive grounds, and using instead a uniform value-added-tax combined with income-based transfers and progressive income taxation. Even more importantly, the

---

[21] Vickrey (1945) had proposed an earlier formalization of the problem but without solving explicitly for optimal tax formulas.

[22] Stiglitz (1987, chap. 15) handbook chapter on optimal taxation provides a comprehensive optimal tax survey using the Stiglitz (1982) discrete model. In this chapter, we will not use the Stiglitz (1982) discrete model and present instead an alternative discrete model, first developed by Piketty (1997) which generates optimal tax formulas very close to those of the continuous model, and much easier to calibrate meaningfully.

Atkinson and Stiglitz (1976) result has been used to argue against the taxation of capital income and in favor of taxing solely earnings or consumption.

The optimal linear tax problem is technically simpler and it was known since at least Ramsey (1927) that the optimum tax rate can be expressed in terms of elasticities. Sheshinski (1972) is the first modern treatment of the optimal linear income tax problem. It was recognized early that labor supply elasticities play a key role in the optimal linear income tax rate. However, because of the disconnect between the nonlinear income tax analysis and the linear tax analysis, no systematic attempt was made to express nonlinear tax formulas in terms of estimable "sufficient statistics" until relatively recently.

Atkinson (1995), Diamond (1998), Piketty (1997), Saez (2001) showed that the optimal nonlinear tax formulas can also be expressed relatively simply in terms of elasticities.[23] This made it possible to connect optimal income tax theory to the large empirical literature estimating behavioral responses to taxation.

Diamond (1980) considered an optimal tax model with participation labor supply responses, the so-called extensive margin (instead of the intensive margin of the Mirrlees, 1971). He showed that the optimal marginal tax rate can actually be negative in that case. As we shall see, this model with extensive margins has received renewed attention in the last decade. Saez (2002a) developed simple elasticity-based formulas showing that a negative marginal tax rate (i.e., a subsidy for work) is optimal at the bottom in such an extensive labor supply model.

With hindsight, it may seem obvious that the quest for theoretical results in optimal income tax theory with broad applicability was doomed to yield only limited results. We know that the efficiency costs of taxation depend on the size of behavioral responses to taxes and hence that optimal tax systems are going to be heavily dependent on the size of those empirical parameters.

In this handbook chapter, in addition to emphasizing connections between theory and practical recommendations, we also want to flag clearly areas, where we feel that the theory fails to provide useful practical policy guidance. Those failures arise both because of limitations of empirical work and limitations of the theoretical framework. We discuss limitations of the standard utilitarian framework in Section 7. Another theoretical limitation arises because of behavioral considerations, i.e., the fact that individuals do not behave according to the standard utility maximization model, due to psychological effects and cognitive limitations. Such behavioral effects naturally affect the analysis and have generated an active literature both theoretical and empirical that we do not cover here (see e.g., Congdon, Mullainathan, & Schwartzstein, 2012 and the chapter by Chetty and Finkelstein in this volume for applications of behavioral economics to public economics).

---

[23] In the field of nonlinear pricing in industrial organization, the use of elasticity-based formulas came earlier (see e.g., Wilson, 1993).

3. CONCEPTUAL BACKGROUND

3.1. Utilitarian Social Welfare Objective

The dominant approach in normative public economics is to base social welfare on individual utilities. The simplest objective is to maximize the sum of individual utilities, the so-called utilitarian (or Benthamite) objective.[24]

Fixed Earnings. To illustrate the key ideas, consider a simple economy with a population normalized to one and an exogenous pre-tax earnings distribution with cumulative distribution function $H(z)$, i.e., $H(z)$ is the fraction of the population with pre-tax earnings below z. Let us assume that all individuals have the same utility function $u(c)$ increasing and concave in disposable income c (since there is only one period, disposable income is equal to consumption). Disposable income is pre-tax earnings minus taxes on earnings so that $c = z - T(z)$. The government chooses the tax function $T(z)$ to maximize the utilitarian social welfare function:

$$SWF = \int_0^\infty u(z - T(z))dH(z) \quad \text{subject to} \quad \int_0^\infty T(z)dH(z) \geq E\ (p),$$

where E is an exogenous revenue requirement for the government and p is the Lagrange multiplier of the government budget constraint. As incomes z are fixed, this is a point-wise maximization problem and the first order condition in $T(z)$ is simply:

$$u'(z - T(z)) = p \Rightarrow c = z - T(z) = \text{constant across } z.$$

Hence, utilitarianism with fixed earnings and concave utility implies full redistribution of incomes. The government confiscates 100% of earnings, funds its revenue requirement, and redistributes the remaining tax revenue equally across individuals. This result was first established by Edgeworth (1897). The intuition for this strong result is straightforward. With concave utilities, marginal utility $u'(c)$ is decreasing with c. Hence, if $c_1 < c_2$ then $u'(c_1) > u'(c_2)$ and it is desirable to transfer resources from the person consuming c_2 to the person consuming c_1.

Generalized social welfare functions of the form $\int G(u(c))dH(z)$ where $G(\cdot)$ is increasing and concave are also often considered. The limiting case where $G(\cdot)$ is infinitely concave is the *Rawlsian* (or *maxi-min*) criterion where the government's objective is to maximize the utility of the most disadvantaged person, i.e., maximize the minimum utility (maxi-min). In this simple context with fixed incomes, all those objectives also leads to 100% redistribution as in the standard utilitarian case.

Finally, with heterogeneous utility functions $u_i(c)$ across individuals, the utilitarian optimum is such that $u_i'(c)$ is constant over the population. Comparing the levels of marginal utility of consumption conditional on disposable income $z - T(z)$ across people with different preferences raises difficult issues of interpersonal utility comparisons.

[24] Utilitarianism as a social justice criterion was developed by the English philosopher Bentham in the late 18th century (Bentham, 1791).

There might be legitimate reasons, such as required health expenses due to medical conditions, that make marginal utility of consumption higher for some people than for others even conditional on after-tax income $z - T(z)$. Another legitimate reason would be the number of dependent children. Absent such need-based legitimate reasons, it does not seem feasible nor reasonable for society to discriminate in favor of those with high marginal utility of consumption (e.g., those who really enjoy consumption) against those with low marginal utility of consumption (e.g., those less able to enjoy consumption). This is not feasible because marginal utility of consumption cannot be observed and compared across individuals. Even if marginal utility were observable, it is unlikely that such discrimination would be acceptable to society (see our discussion in Section 6).

Therefore, it seems fair for the government to consider social welfare functions such that social marginal utility of consumption is the same across individuals conditional on disposable income. In the fixed earnings case, this means that the government can actually ignore individual utilities and use a "universal" social utility function $u(c)$ to evaluate social welfare. The concavity of $u(c)$ then reflects society's value for redistribution rather than directly individual marginal utility of consumption.[25] We will come back to this important point later on.

Endogenous Earnings. Naturally, the result of complete redistribution with concave utility depends strongly on the assumption of fixed earnings. In the real world, complete redistribution would certainly greatly diminish incentives to work and lead to a decrease in pre-tax earnings. Indeed, the goal of optimal income tax theory has been precisely to extend the basic model to the case with endogenous earnings (Vickrey, 1945 and Mirrlees, 1971). Taxation then generates efficiency costs as it reduces earnings, and the optimal tax problem becomes a non-trivial equity-efficiency trade off. Hence, with utilitarianism, behavioral responses are the sole factor preventing complete redistribution. In reality, society might also oppose complete redistribution on fairness grounds even setting aside the issue of behavioral responses. We come back to this limitation of utilitarianism in Section 6.

Let us therefore now assume that earnings are determined by labor supply and that individuals derive disutility from work. Individual i has utility $u^i(c, z)$ increasing in c but decreasing with earnings z. In that world, 100% taxation would lead everybody to completely stop working, and hence is not desirable.

Let us consider general social welfare functions of the type:

$$SWF = \int \omega_i G(u^i(c, z)) dv(i),$$

where $\omega_i \geq 0$ are *Pareto weights* independent of individual choices (c, z) and $G(\cdot)$ an increasing transformation of utilities, and $dv(i)$ is the distribution of individuals.

---

[25] Naturally, the two concepts are not independent. If individuals have very concave utilities, they will naturally support more redistribution under the "veil of ignorance," and the government choice for $u(c)$ will reflect those views.

The combination of arbitrary Pareto weights ω_i and a social welfare function $G(\cdot)$ allows us to be fully general for the moment. We denote by

$$g_i = \frac{\omega_i G'(u^i) u_c^i}{p}$$

the *social marginal welfare weight* on individual i, with p the multiplier of the government budget constraint.

Intuitively, g_i measures the dollar value (in terms of public funds) of increasing consumption of individual i by \$1. With fixed earnings, any discrepancy in the g_i's across individuals calls for redistribution as it increases social welfare to transfer resources from those with lower g_i's toward those with higher g_i's. Hence, absent efficiency concerns, the government should equalize all the g_i's.[26] With endogenous earnings, the g_i's will no longer be equalized at the optimum. As we shall see, social preferences for redistribution enter optimal tax formulas solely through the g_i weights.

Under the utilitarian objective, $g_i = u_c^i/p$ is directly proportional to the marginal utility of consumption. Under the Rawlsian criterion, all the g_i are zero, except for the most disadvantaged.

In the simpler case with no income effects on labor supply, i.e., where utility functions take the quasi-linear form $u^i(c, z) = v^i(c - h^i(z))$ with $v^i(\cdot)$ increasing and concave and $h^i(z)$ increasing and convex, the labor supply decision does not depend on non-labor income (see Section 3.3) and the average of g_i across all individuals is equal to one. This can be seen as follows. The government is indifferent between one more dollar of tax revenue and redistributing \$1 to everybody (as giving one extra dollar lump-sum does not generate any behavioral response). The value of giving \$1 extra to person i, in terms of public funds, is g_i so that the value of redistributing \$1 to everybody is $\int g_i dv(i)$.

3.2. Fallacy of the Second Welfare Theorem

The second welfare theorem seems to provide a strikingly simple theoretical solution to the equity-efficiency trade off. Under standard perfect market assumptions, the second welfare theorem states that any Pareto efficient outcome can be reached through a suitable set of lump-sum taxes that depend on exogenous characteristics of each individual (e.g., intrinsic abilities or other endowments or random shocks), and the subsequent free functioning of markets with no additional government interference. The logic is very simple. If some individuals have better earnings ability than others and the government wants to equalize disposable income, it is most efficient to impose a tax (or a transfer) based on earnings ability and then let people keep 100% of their actual earnings at the margin.[27]

---

[26] As we saw, under utilitarianism and concave and uniform utility functions across individuals, this implies complete equalization of post-tax incomes.

[27] In the model above, the government would impose taxes T_i based on the intrinsic characteristics of individual i but independent of the behavior of individual i so as to equalize all the g_i's across individuals (in the equilibrium where each individual chooses labor supply optimally given T_i).

In standard models, it is assumed that the government cannot observe earnings abilities but only realized earnings. Hence, the government has to base taxes and transfers on actual earnings only, which distort earnings and create efficiency costs. This generates an equity-efficiency trade off. This informational structure puts optimal tax analysis on sound theoretical grounds and connects it to mechanism design. While this is a theoretically appealing reason for the failure of the second welfare theorem, in our view, there must be a much deeper reason for governments to systematically use actual earnings rather than proxies for ability in real tax systems.

Indeed, standard welfare theory implies that taxes and transfers should depend on any characteristic correlated with earnings ability in the optimal tax system. If the characteristic is immutable, then average social marginal utilities across groups with different characteristics should be perfectly equalized. Even if the characteristic is manipulable, it should still be used in the optimal system (see Section 6.1). In reality, actual income tax or transfer systems depend on very few other characteristics than income. Those characteristics, essentially family situation or disability status, seem limited to factors clearly related to need.[28]

The traditional way to resolve this puzzle has been to argue that there are additional horizontal equity concerns that prevent the government from using non-income characteristics for tax purposes (see e.g., Atkinson and Stiglitz (1980) pp. 354–5). Recently, Mankiw and Weinzierl (2010) argue that this represents a major failure of the standard social welfare approach. This shows that informational concerns and observability is not the overwhelming reason for basing taxes and transfers almost exclusively on income. This has two important consequences.

First, finding the most general mechanism compatible with the informational set of the government—as advocated for example in the New Dynamic Public Finance literature (see Kocherlakota, 2010 for a survey)—might not be very useful for understanding actual tax problems. Such an approach can provide valuable theoretical insights and results but is likely to generate optimal tax systems that are so fundamentally different from actual tax systems that they are not implementable in practice. It seems more fruitful practically to assume instead exogenously that the government can only use a limited set of tax tools, precisely those that are used in practice, and consider the optimum within the set of real tax systems actually used. In most of this chapter, we therefore pursue this "simple tax structure" approach.[29]

Second, it would certainly be useful to make progress on understanding what concepts of justice[l] or fairness could lead the government to use only a specific subset of taxes

[28] When incomes were not observable, archaic tax systems did rely on quasi-exogenous characteristics such as nobility titles, or land taxes based on rarely updated cadasters (Ardant, 1971). Ironically, when incomes become observable, such quasi-first best taxes were replaced by second-best income-based taxes.

[29] As mentioned above, the set of tools available changes over time. For example, individual incomes become observable only in modern economies.

and deliberately ignore other tools—such as taxes based on non-income characteristics correlated with ability—that would be useful to maximize standard utilitarian social welfare functions. We will come back to those important issues in Section 6.1 where we study tagging and in Section 7 where we consider alternatives to utilitarianism.

3.3. Labor Supply Concepts

In this chapter, we always consider a population of measure one of individuals. In most sections, individuals have heterogeneous preferences over consumption and earnings. Individual i utility is denoted by $u^i(c, z)$ and is increasing in consumption c and decreasing in earnings z as earnings require labor supply. Following Mirrlees (1971), in most models, heterogeneity in preferences is due solely to differences in wage rates w^i where utility functions take the form $u(c, z/w^i)$ where $l = z/w^i$ is labor supply needed to earn z. Our formulation $u^i(c, z)$ is more general and can capture both heterogeneity in ability as well as heterogeneity in preferences. As mentioned earlier, we believe that heterogeneity is an important element of the real world and optimal tax results should be reasonably robust to it.

To derive labor supply concepts, we consider a linear tax system with a tax rate τ combined with a lump sum demogrant R so that the budget constraint of each individual is $c = (1 - \tau)z + R$.

Intensive Margin. Let us focus first on the intensive labor supply margin, that is on the choice of how much to earn conditional on working. Individual i chooses z to maximize $u^i((1 - \tau)z + R, z)$ which leads to the first order condition

$$(1 - \tau)\frac{\partial u^i}{\partial c} + \frac{\partial u^i}{\partial z} = 0,$$

which defines implicitly the individual uncompensated (also called Marshallian) earnings supply function $z_u^i(1 - \tau, R)$.

The effect of $1 - \tau$ on z^i defines the *uncompensated elasticity* $e_u^i = \frac{1-\tau}{z_u^i}\frac{\partial z_u^i}{\partial(1-\tau)}$ of earnings with respect to the *net-of-tax rate* $1 - \tau$. The effect of R on z_u^i defines the *income effect* $\eta^i = (1 - \tau)\frac{\partial z^i}{\partial R}$. If leisure is a normal good, an assumption we make from now on, then $\eta^i \leq 0$ as receiving extra non-labor income induces the individual to consume both more goods and more leisure.

Finally, one can also define the compensated (also called Hicksian) earnings supply function $z_c^i(1 - \tau, u)$ as the earnings level that minimizes the cost necessary to reach utility u.[30] The effect of $1 - \tau$ on z^i keeping u constant defines the *compensated elasticity* $e_c^i = \frac{1-\tau}{z^i}\frac{\partial z_c^i}{\partial(1-\tau)}$ of earnings with respect to the *net-of-tax rate* $1 - \tau$. The compensated elasticity is always positive.

---

[30] Formally $z_c^i(1 - \tau, u)$ solves the problem $\min_z c - (1 - \tau)z$ subject to $u(c, z) \geq u$.

The *Slutsky equation* relates those parameters $e_c^i = e_u^i - \eta^i$. To summarize we have:

$$e_u^i = \frac{1-\tau}{z_u^i}\frac{\partial z_u^i}{\partial(1-\tau)} \lessgtr 0, \quad \eta^i = (1-\tau)\frac{\partial z_u^i}{\partial R} \leq 0, \quad e_c^i = \frac{1-\tau}{z_c^i}\frac{\partial z_c^i}{\partial(1-\tau)} > 0,$$

$$\text{and} \quad e_c^i = e_u^i - \eta^i. \tag{1}$$

In the long-run process of development over the last century in the richest countries, wage rates have increased by a factor of five. Labor supply measured in hours of work has declined only very slightly (Ramey & Francis, 2009). If preferences for consumption and leisure have not changed, this implies that the uncompensated elasticity is close to zero. This does not mean however that taxes would have no effect on labor supply as a large fraction of taxes are rebated as transfers (see our discussion in Section 2). Therefore, on average, taxes are more similar to a compensated wage rate decrease than an uncompensated wage rate decrease. If income effects are large, government taxes and transfers could still have a large impact on labor supply.

Importantly, although we have defined those labor supply concepts for a linear tax system, they continue to apply in the case of a nonlinear tax system by considering the linearized budget at the utility maximizing point. In that case, we replace τ by the marginal tax rate $T'(z)$ and we replace R by virtual income defined as the non-labor income that the individual would get if her earnings were zero and she could stay on the virtual linearized budget. Formally $R = z - T(z) - (1 - T'(z)) \cdot z$.

Hence, the marginal tax rate $T'(z)$ reduces the marginal benefit of earning an extra dollar and reduces labor supply through *substitution* effects, conditional on the tax level $T(z)$. The income tax level $T(z)$ increases labor supply through *income* effects. In net, taxes (with $T'(z) > 0$ and $T(z) > 0$) hence have an ambiguous effect on labor supply while transfers (with $T'(z) > 0$ and $T(z) < 0$) have an unambiguously negative effect on labor supply.

Extensive Margin. In practice, there are fixed costs of work (e.g., searching for a job, finding alternative child care for parents, loss of home production, transportation costs, etc.). This can be captured in the basic model by assuming that choosing $z > 0$ (as opposed to $z = 0$) involves a discrete cost d_i.

It is possible to consider a pure extensive margin model by assuming that individual i can either not work (and earn zero) or work and earn z_i where z_i is fixed to individual i and reflects her earning potential. Assume that utility is linear, i.e., $u_i = c_i - d_i \cdot l_i$ where c_i is net-of-tax income, d_i is the cost of work and $l_i = 0, 1$ is a work dummy. In that case, individual i works if and only if $z_i - T(z_i) - d_i \geq -T(0)$, i.e., if $d_i \leq z_i - T(z_i) + T(0) = z_i \cdot (1 - \tau_p)$ where $\tau_p = [T(z_i) - T(0)]/z_i$. τ_p is the participation tax rate, defined as the fraction of earnings taxed when the individual goes from not working and earning zero to working and earning z_i. Therefore, the decision to work depends on the net-of-tax participation tax rate $1 - \tau_p$.

To summarize, there are three key concepts for any tax and transfer system $T(z)$. First, the transfer benefit with zero earnings $-T(0)$, sometimes called demogrant or lump-sum grant. Second, the marginal tax rate (or phasing-out rate) $T'(z)$: The individual keeps $1 - T'(z)$ for an additional \$1 of earnings. $1 - T'(z)$ is the key concept for the intensive labor supply choice. Third, the participation tax rate $\tau_p = [T(z) - T(0)]/z$: The individual keeps a fraction $1 - \tau_p$ of his earnings when going from zero earnings to earnings z. $1 - \tau_p$ is the key concept for the extensive labor supply choice. Finally, note that $T(z)$ integrates both the means-tested transfer program and the income tax that funds such transfers and other government spending. In practice transfer programs and taxes are often administered separately. The break even earnings point z^* is the point at which $T(z^*) = 0$. Above the break even point, $T(z) > 0$ which encourages labor supply through income effects. Below the break even point, $T(z) < 0$ which discourages labor supply through income effects.

Tax Reform Welfare Effects and Envelope Theorem. A key element of optimal tax analysis is the evaluation of the welfare effects of small tax reforms. Consider a nonlinear tax $T(z)$. Individual i chooses z to maximize $u^i(z - T(z), z)$, leading to the first order condition $u_c^i \cdot (1 - T'(z)) + u_z^i = 0$. Consider now a small reform $dT(z)$ of the nonlinear tax schedule. The effect on individual utility u^i is

$$du^i = u_c^i \cdot [-dT(z)] + u_c^i \cdot [1 - T'(z)]dz + u_z^i \cdot dz = u_c^i \cdot [-dT(z)],$$

where dz is the behavioral response of the individual to the tax reform and the second equality is obtained because of the first order condition $u_c^i \cdot (1 - T'(z)) + u_z^i = 0$. This is a standard application of the envelope theorem. As z maximizes utility, any small change dz has no first order effect on individual utility. As a result, behavioral responses can be ignored and the change in individual welfare is simply given by the *mechanical effect* of the tax reform on the individual budget multiplied by the marginal utility of consumption.

4. OPTIMAL LINEAR TAXATION

4.1. Basic Model

Linear labor income taxation simplifies considerably the exposition but captures the key equity-efficiency trade off. Sheshinski (1972) offered the first modern treatment of optimal linear income taxation following the nonlinear income tax analysis of Mirrlees (1971). Both the derivation and the optimal formulas are also closely related to the more complex nonlinear case. It is therefore pedagogically useful to start with the linear case where the government uses a linear tax at rate τ to fund a demogrant R (and additional non-transfer spending E taken as exogenous).[31]

---

[31] In terms of informational constraints, the government would be constrained to use linear taxation (instead of the more general nonlinear taxation) if it can only observe the amount of each earnings transaction but cannot observe the identity of individual earners. This could happen for example if the government can only observe the total payroll paid by each employer but cannot observe individual earnings perhaps because there is no identity number system for individuals.

Summing the Marshallian individual earnings functions $z_u^i(1-\tau, R)$, we obtain aggregate earnings which depend upon $1 - \tau$ and R and can be denoted by $Z_u(1 - \tau, R)$. The government's budget constraint is $R + E = \tau Z_u(1 - \tau, R)$, which defines implicitly R as a function of τ only (as we assume that E is fixed exogenously). Hence, we can express aggregate earnings as a sole function of $1 - \tau : Z(1 - \tau) = Z_u(1 - \tau, R(\tau))$. The tax revenue function $\tau \rightarrow \tau Z(1 - \tau)$ has an inverted U-shape. It is equal to zero both when $\tau = 0$ (no taxation) and when $\tau = 1$ (complete taxation) as 100% taxation entirely discourages labor supply. This curve is popularly called the Laffer curve although the concept of the revenue curve has been known since at least Dupuit (1844). Let us denote by $e = \frac{1-\tau}{Z} \frac{dZ}{d(1-\tau)}$ the elasticity of aggregate earnings with respect to the net-of-tax rate. The tax rate τ^* maximizing tax revenue is such that $Z(1 - \tau) - \tau \frac{dZ}{d(1-\tau)} = 0$, i.e., $\frac{\tau}{1-\tau} e = 1$. Hence, we can express τ^* as a sole function of e:

Revenue maximizing linear tax rate: $\dfrac{\tau^*}{1 - \tau^*} = \dfrac{1}{e}$ or $\tau^* = \dfrac{1}{1 + e}.$ (2)

Let us now consider the maximization of a general social welfare function. The demogrant R evenly distributed to everybody is equal to $\tau Z(1 - \tau) - E$ and hence disposable income for individual i is $c^i = (1 - \tau)z^i + \tau Z(1 - \tau) - E$ (recall that population size is normalized to one). Therefore, the government chooses τ to maximize

$$SWF = \int_i \omega^i G[u^i((1 - \tau)z^i + \tau Z(1 - \tau) - E, z^i)]d\nu(i).$$

Using the envelope theorem from the choice of z^i in the utility maximization problem of individual i, the first order condition for the government is simply

$$0 = \frac{dSWF}{d\tau} = \int_i \omega^i G'(u^i)u_c^i \cdot \left[Z - z^i - \tau \frac{dZ}{d(1 - \tau)} \right] d\nu(i),$$

The first term in the square brackets $Z - z^i$ reflects the mechanical effect of increasing taxes (and the demogrant) absent any behavioral response. This effect is positive when individual income z^i is less than average income Z. The second term $-\tau \, dZ/d(1 - \tau)$ reflects the efficiency cost of increasing taxes due to the aggregate behavioral response. This is an efficiency cost because such behavioral responses have no first order positive welfare effect on individuals but have a first order negative effect on tax revenue.

Introducing the aggregate elasticity e and the "normalized" social marginal welfare weight $g^i = \omega^i G'(u^i)u_c^i / \int \omega^j G'(u^j)u_c^j d\nu(j)$, we can rewrite the first order condition as:

$$Z \cdot \left[1 - \frac{\tau}{1 - \tau} e \right] = \int_i g_i z_i d\nu(i).$$

Hence, we have the following optimal linear income tax formula

Optimal linear tax rate: $\tau = \dfrac{1 - \bar{g}}{1 - \bar{g} + e}$ with $\bar{g} = \dfrac{\int g_i z_i d\nu(i)}{Z}.$ (3)

$\bar{g}$ is the average "normalized" social marginal welfare weight weighted by pre-tax incomes z_i. $\bar{g}$ is also the ratio of the average income weighted by individual social welfare weights g_i to the actual average income Z. Hence, $\bar{g}$ measures where social welfare weights are concentrated on average over the distribution of earnings. An alternative form for formula (3) often presented in the literature takes the form $\tau = -cov(g_i, z_i/Z)/[-cov(g_i, z_i/Z) + e]$ where $cov(g_i, z_i/Z)$ is the covariance between social marginal welfare weights g_i and normalized earnings z_i/Z. As long as the correlation between g_i and z_i is negative, i.e., those with higher incomes have lower social marginal welfare weights, the optimum τ is positive. Five points are worth noting about formula (3).

First, the optimal tax rate decreases with the aggregate elasticity e. This elasticity is a mix of substitution and income effects as an increase in the tax rate τ is associated with an increase in the demogrant $R = \tau Z(1-\tau) - E$. Formally, one can show that $e = [\bar{e}_u - \bar{\eta}]/[1 - \bar{\eta}\tau/(1-\tau)]$ where $\bar{e}_u = \frac{1-\tau}{Z_u}\frac{\partial Z_u}{\partial(1-\tau)}$ is the average of the individual uncompensated elasticities e_u^i weighted by income z^i and $\bar{\eta} = (1-\tau)\frac{\partial Z_u}{\partial R}$ is the unweighted average of individual income effects η^i.[32] This allows us to rewrite the optimal tax formula (3) in a slightly more structural form as $\tau = (1-\bar{g})/(1-\bar{g} - \bar{g}\cdot\bar{\eta} + \bar{e}_u)$.

When the tax rate maximizes tax revenue, we have $\tau = 1/(1+e)$ and then $e = \bar{e}_u$ is a pure uncompensated elasticity (as the tax rate does not raise any extra revenue at the margin). When the tax rate is zero, e is conceptually close to a compensated elasticity as taxes raised are fully rebated with no efficiency loss.[33]

Second, the optimal tax rate naturally decreases with $\bar{g}$ which measures the redistributive tastes of the government. In the extreme case where the government does not value redistribution at all, $g_i \equiv 1$ and hence $\bar{g} = 1$ and $\tau = 0$ is optimal.[34] In the polar opposite case where the government is Rawlsian and maximizes the lump sum demogrant (assuming the worst-off individual has zero earnings), then $\bar{g} = 0$ and $\tau = 1/(1+e)$, which is the revenue maximizing tax rate from Eq. (2). As mentioned above, in that case $e = \bar{e}_u$ is an uncompensated elasticity.

Third and related, for a given profile of social welfare weights (or for a given degree of concavity of the utility function in the homogeneous utilitarian case), the higher the pre-tax inequality at a given τ, the lower $\bar{g}$, and hence the higher the optimal tax rate. If there is no inequality, then $\bar{g} = 1$ and $\tau = 0$ with a lump-sum tax $-R = E$ is optimal. If inequality is maximal, i.e., nobody earns anything except for a single person who earns everything and has a social marginal welfare weight of zero, then $\tau = 1/(1+e)$, again equal to the revenue maximizing tax rate.

Fourth, it is important to note that, as is usual in optimal tax theory, formula (3) is an implicit formula for τ as both e and especially $\bar{g}$ vary with τ. Under a standard utilitarian

---

[32] To see this, recall that $Z(1-\tau) = Z_u(1-\tau, \tau Z(1-\tau) - E)$ so that $\frac{dZ}{d(1-\tau)}\left[1 - \tau\frac{\partial Z_u}{\partial R}\right] = \frac{\partial Z_u}{\partial(1-\tau)} - Z\frac{\partial Z_u}{\partial R}$.

[33] It is not exactly a compensated elasticity as $\bar{e}_u$ is income weighted while $\bar{\eta}$ is not.

[34] This assumes that a lump sum tax E is feasible to fund government spending. If lump sum taxes are not feasible, for example because it is impossible to set taxes higher than earnings at the bottom, then the optimal tax in that case is the smallest τ such that $\tau Z(1-\tau) = E$, i.e., the level of tax required to fund government spending E.

social welfare criterion with concave utility of consumption, $\bar{g}$ increases with τ as the need for redistribution (i.e., the variation of the g_i with z_i) decreases with the level of taxation τ. This ensures that formula (3) generates a unique equilibrium for τ.

Fifth, formula (3) can also be used to assess tax reform. Starting from the current τ, the current estimated elasticity e, and the current welfare weight parameter $\bar{g}$, if $\tau < (1 - \bar{g})/(1 - \bar{g} + e)$ then increasing τ increases social welfare (and conversely). The tax reform approach has the advantage that it does not require knowing how e and $\bar{g}$ change with τ, since it only considers local variations.

Generality of the Formula. The optimal linear tax formula is very general as it applies to many alternative models for the income generating process. All that matters is the aggregate elasticity e and how the government sets normalized marginal welfare weights g^i. First, if the population is discrete, the same derivation and formula obviously apply. Second, if labor supply responses are (partly or fully) along the extensive margin, the same formula applies. Third, the same formula also applies in the long run when educational and human capital decisions are potentially affected by the tax rate as those responses are reflected in the long-run aggregate elasticity e (see e.g., Best & Kleven, 2012).[35]

Random Earnings. If earnings are generated by a partly random process involving luck in addition to ability and effort, as in Varian (1980) and Eaton and Rosen (1980), formula (3) still applies as long as the social welfare objective is defined over individual expected utilities.

To see this, suppose that pre-tax income for individual i is a random function of labor supply l^i and an idiosyncratic luck shock ε (with distribution dF^i) with $z^i = l^i + \varepsilon$ for simplicity. Individual i chooses l^i to maximize expected utility

$$EU^i = \int u^i((l^i + \varepsilon) \cdot (1 - \tau) + R, l^i)dF^i(\varepsilon),$$

so that l^i is function of $1 - \tau$ and R. The government budget implies again that $R = \tau Z - E$ so that Z is also a function of $1 - \tau$ as in the standard model (recall that $R = \tau Z(1 - \tau) - E$ is an implicit function of τ). The government then chooses τ to maximize $SWF = \int \omega^i G(EU^i)d\nu(i)$. This again leads to formula (3) with $\bar{g}$ the "normalized" average of $g^i = \omega^i G'(EU^i)u_c^i$ weighted by incomes z^i where now the average is taken as a double integral over both $dF^i(\varepsilon)$ and $d\nu(i)$.

Therefore, the random earnings model generates both the same equity-efficiency trade-off and the same type of optimal tax formula. This shows the robustness of the optimal linear tax approach. This robustness was not clearly apparent in the literature because of the focus on the nonlinear income tax case where the two models no longer deliver identical formulas.[36]

---

[35] Naturally, such long-run responses are challenging to estimate empirically as short-term comparisons around a tax reform cannot capture them.

[36] Varian (1980) analyzes the optimal nonlinear tax with random earnings.

Political Economy and Median Voter. The most popular model for policy decisions among economists is the median voter model. As is well known, the median voter theorem applies for unidimensional policies and where individual preferences are single-peaked with respect to this unidimensional policy. In our framework, the unidimensional policy is the tax rate τ (as the demogrant R is a function of τ). Each individual has single-peaked preferences about the tax rate τ as $\tau \to u^i((1-\tau)z_i(1-\tau) + \tau Z(1-\tau), z_i(1-\tau))$ is single-peaked with a peak such that $-z_i + Z - \tau \, dZ/d(1-\tau) = 0$, i.e., $\tau_i = (1 - z_i/Z)/(1 - z_i/Z + e)$. Hence, the median voter is the voter with median income z_m. Recall that with single-peaked preferences, the median voter preferred tax rate is a Condorcet winner, i.e., wins in majority voting against any other alternative tax rate.[37] Therefore, the median voter equilibrium has:

$$\textbf{Median voter optimal tax rate:} \quad \tau_m = \frac{1 - z_m/Z}{1 - z_m/Z + e}. \tag{4}$$

The formula implies that when the median z_m is close to the average Z, the optimal tax rate is low because a linear tax rate achieves little redistribution (toward the median) and hence a lump-sum tax is more efficient.[38] In contrast, when the median z_m is small relative to the average, the tax rate τ_m gets close to the revenue maximizing tax rate $\tau^* = 1/(1 + e)$ from Eq. (2).

Formula (4) is a particular case of formula (3) where social welfare weights are concentrated at the median so that $\bar{g} = z_m/Z$. This shows that there is a tight connection between optimal tax theory and political economy. Political economy uses social welfare weights coming out of the political game process rather than derived from marginal utility of consumption as in the standard utilitarian tax theory but the structure of resulting tax formulas is the same (see Persson & Tabellini, 2002, chap. 24 for a comprehensive survey of political economy applied to public finance). We come back to the determination of social welfare weights in Section 6.

Finally and as caveats, note that the median voter theory applies only to unidimensional policies so that those results do not carry over to the nonlinear income tax case. The political economy literature has also shown that real world outcomes differ substantially from median voter predictions.

4.2. Accounting for Actual Tax Rates

As we saw in Section 2, tax to GDP ratios in OECD countries are between 30% and 45% and the more economically meaningful tax to national income ratios between 35% and 50%. Quantitatively, most estimates of aggregate elasticities of taxable income are

---

[37] To see this, if the alternative is $\tau' < \tau_m$, everybody below and including the median prefers τ_m to τ' so that τ_m wins. Conversely, if $\tau' > \tau_m$, everybody above and including the median prefers τ_m to τ' and τ_m still wins.

[38] Formula (4) shows that if $z_m > Z$, then a negative tax rate is actually optimal. Empirically however, it is always the case that $z_m < Z$.

between .1 and .4 with .25 perhaps being a reasonable estimate (see Saez, Slemrod, & Giertz, 2012 for a recent survey), although there remains considerable uncertainty about these magnitudes.[39]

Table 2 proposes simple illustrative calculations using the optimal linear tax rate formula (3). It reports combinations of τ and $\bar{g}$ in various situations corresponding to different elasticities e (across columns) and different social objectives (across rows). We consider three elasticity scenarios. The first one has $e = .25$ which is a realistic mid-range estimate (Saez et al., 2012, Chetty, 2012). The second has $e = .5$, a high range elasticity scenario. We add a third scenario with $e = 1$, an extreme case well above the current average empirical estimates.

Panel A considers the standard case where $\bar{g}$ is pinned down by a given social objective criterion and τ is then given by the optimal tax formula. The first row is the Rawlsian criterion (or revenue maximizing tax rate) with $\bar{g} = 0$. The second row is a utilitarian criterion with coefficient of relative risk aversion (CRRA) equal to one (social marginal welfare weights are proportional to $u_c = 1/c$ where $c = (1 - \tau)z + R$ is disposable income).[40] Chetty (2006) shows that a CRRA equal to one is consistent with empirical labor supply behavior and hence a reasonable benchmark. The third row is the median voter optimum with a median to average earnings ratio of 70% (corresponding approximately to the current US distribution based on individual adult earnings from the Current Population Survey in 2010). Panel B considers the inverse problem of determining the social preference parameter $\bar{g}$ for a given tax rate τ. The first row uses $\tau = 35\%$, corresponding to a low tax country such as the United States. The second row uses $\tau = 50\%$, corresponding to a high tax country such as a typical country from the European Union. Three points should be noted.

First, panel A shows that an empirically realistic elasticity $e = .25$ implies a revenue maximizing tax rate of 80% which is considerably higher than any actual average tax rate, even in the countries with the highest tax to GDP ratios, around 50%. The optimal tax rate under the utilitarian criterion with CRRA coefficient equal to one is 61%. The optimal tax rate for the median earner is $\tau = 55\%$ which corresponds to average tax rates in high tax countries. Correspondingly as shown in panel B, with $e = .25$, a tax rate of 35%, such as current US tax rates, would be optimal in a situation where $\bar{g} = 87\%$, i.e., with low redistributive tastes. A tax rate of 50% (as in a high tax country) would be optimal with $\bar{g} = 75\%$.

Second, a fairly high elasticity estimate of $e = .5$ would still generate a revenue maximizing tax rate of 67%, above current rates in any country. The median voter optimum tax

[39] Note however that the tax base tends to be smaller than national income as some forms of income (or consumption) are excluded from the tax base. Therefore, with existing tax bases, the tax rate needed to raise say 40% of national income, will typically be somewhat higher, perhaps around 50%.

[40] $\bar{g}$ is endogenously determined using the actual US earnings distribution and assuming that government required spending E (outside transfers) is 10% of total actual earnings. The distribution is for earnings of individuals aged 25 to 64 from the 2011 Current Population Survey for 2010 earnings.

Table 2 Optimal Linear Tax Rate Formula $\tau = (1 - g)/(1 - g + e)$

	Elasticity $e = .25$ (empirically realistic)		Elasticity $e = .5$ (high)		Elasticity $e = 1$ (extreme)	
	Parameter g (%) (1)	Tax rate τ (2)	Parameter g (%) (3)	Tax rate τ (4)	Parameter g (%) (5)	Tax rate τ (6)
A. Optimal linear tax rate τ						
Rawlsian revenue maximizing rate	0	80	0	67	0	50
Utilitarian (CRRA $= 1$, $u_c = 1/c$)	61	61	54	48	44	36
Median voter optimum ($z_{median}/z_{average} = 70\%$)	70	55	70	38	70	23
B. Revealed preferences g for redistribution						
Low tax country (US): Tax rate $\tau = 35\%$	87	35	73	35	46	35
High tax country (EU): Tax rate $\tau = 50\%$	75	50	50	50	0	50

Notes: This table illustrates the use of the optimal linear tax rate formula $\tau = (1 - g)/(1 - g + e)$ derived in the main text. It reports combinations of τ and g in various situations corresponding to different elasticities e (across columns) and different social objectives (across rows). Panel A considers the standard case where g is pinned down by a given social objective criterion and τ is then given by the optimal tax formula. The first row is the Rawlsian criterion (or revenue maximizing tax rate) with $g = 0$. The second row is a utilitarian criterion with coefficient of relative risk aversion (CRRA) equal to one (social marginal welfare weights are proportional to $u_c = 1/c$ where $c = (1 - \tau)z + R$ is disposable income), g is endogenously determined using the actual US earnings distribution and assuming that government required spending (outside transfers) is 10% of total earnings. The third row is the median voter optimum with a median to average earnings ratio of 70% (corresponding approximately to the current US situation). Panel B considers the inverse problem of determining the social preference parameter g for a given tax rate τ. The first row uses $\tau = 35\%$, corresponding to a low tax country such as the United States. The second row uses $\tau = 50\%$, corresponding to a high tax country such as a typical country from the European Union.

rate of 38% would actually be close to the current US tax rate in that situation. A high tax rate of 50% would be rationalized by $\bar{g} = .5$, i.e., fairly strong redistributive tastes. The utilitarian criterion also generates an optimal tax rate close to 50% in that elasticity scenario.

Third, in the unrealistically high elasticity scenario $e = 1$, the revenue maximizing rate is 50%, about the current tax rate in countries with the highest tax to GDP ratios. Hence, only in that case would social preferences for redistribution be approaching the polar Rawlsian case.

4.3. Tax Avoidance

As shown by many empirical studies (see Saez et al., 2012 for a recent survey), responses to tax rates can also take the form of tax avoidance. We can define tax avoidance as changes in reported income due to changes in the form of compensation but not in the total level of compensation. Tax avoidance opportunities typically arise when taxpayers can shift part of their taxable income into another form of income or another time period that receives a more favorable tax treatment.[41]

The key distinction between real and tax avoidance responses is that real responses reflect underlying, deep individual preferences for work and consumption while tax avoidance responses depend critically on the design of the tax system and the avoidance opportunities it offers. While the government cannot change underlying deep individual preferences and hence the size of the real elasticity, it can change the tax system to reduce avoidance opportunities.

A number of papers incorporate avoidance effects for optimal tax design. In this chapter, we adapt the simple modeling of Piketty, Saez, and Stantcheva (2011) to the linear tax case so as to capture the key tradeoffs as simply and transparently as possible.[42]

We can extend the original model as follows to incorporate tax avoidance. Let us denote by y real income and by x sheltered income so that taxable income is $z = y - x$. Taxable income z is taxed at linear tax rate τ, while sheltered income x is taxed at a constant and linear tax rate t lower than τ. Individual i's utility takes the form:

$$u_i(c, y, x) = c - h_i(y) - d_i(x),$$

where $c = y - \tau z - tx + R = (1-\tau)y + (\tau - t)x + R$ is disposable after tax-income. $h_i(y)$ is the utility cost of earning real income y, and $d_i(x)$ is the cost of sheltering an amount of income x. We assume a quasi-linear utility to simplify the derivations and eliminate cross-elasticity effects in real labor supply and sheltering decisions. We assume that both

---

[41] Examples of such avoidance/evasion are (a) reductions in current cash compensation for increased fringe benefits or deferred compensation such as stock-options or future pensions, (b) increased consumption within the firm such as better offices, vacation disguised as business travel, private use of corporate jets, etc., (c) re-characterization of ordinary income into tax favored capital income, and (d) outright tax evasion such as using off-shore accounts.

[42] Slemrod and Kopczuk (2002) endogenize avoidance opportunities in a multi-good model where the government selects the tax base. Finally, a large literature (surveyed in Slemrod and Yitzhaki (2002)) analyzes optimal policy design in the presence of tax evasion.

$h_i(\cdot)$ and $d_i(\cdot)$ are increasing and convex, and normalized so that $h_i'(0) = d_i'(0) = 0$. Individual utility maximization implies that

$$h_i'(y_i) = 1 - \tau \quad \text{and} \quad d_i'(x_i) = \tau - t,$$

so that y_i is an increasing function of $1 - \tau$ and x_i is an increasing function of the tax differential $\tau - t$. Aggregating over all individuals, we have $Y = Y(1 - \tau) = \int y_i(1 - \tau) \, dv(i)$ with real elasticity $e_Y = [(1 - \tau)/Y] dY/d(1 - \tau) > 0$ and $X = X(\tau - t) = \int x_i(\tau - t) dv(i)$ increasing in $\tau - t$. Note that $X(\tau - t = 0) = 0$ as there is sheltering only when $\tau > t$.

Hence aggregate taxable income $Z = Z(1 - \tau, t) = Y(1 - \tau) - X(\tau - t)$ is increasing in $1 - \tau$ and t. We denote by $e = [(1 - \tau)/Z] \partial Z / \partial(1 - \tau) > 0$ the total elasticity of taxable income Z with respect to $1 - \tau$ when keeping t constant. Note that $e = (Y/Z)e_Y + ((1 - \tau)/Z) dX/d(\tau - t) > (Y/Z)e_Y$. We immediately obtain the following optimal formulas.

Partial Optimum. For a given t, the tax rate τ maximizing tax revenue $\tau Z(1 - \tau, t) + tX(\tau - t)$ is

$$\tau = \frac{1 + t \cdot (e - (Y/Z)e_Y)}{1 + e}. \tag{5}$$

General Optimum. Absent any cost of enforcement, the optimal global tax policy (τ, t) maximizing tax revenue $\tau[Y(1 - \tau) - X(\tau - t)] + tX(\tau - t)$ is

$$t = \tau = \frac{1}{1 + e_Y}. \tag{6}$$

Four elements are worth noting about formulas (5) and (6).

First, if $t = 0$ then Eq. (5) becomes $\tau = 1/(1 + e)$ as in the standard model, Eq. (2). In the narrow framework where the tax system is taken as given (i.e., there is nothing the government can do about tax evasion and income shifting), and where sheltered income is totally untaxed, it is irrelevant whether the elasticity e arises from real responses or avoidance responses, a point made by Feldstein (1999).

Second however, if $t > 0$, then sheltering creates a "fiscal externality," as the shifted income generates tax revenue. In that case, Eq. (5) implies that τ is above the standard revenue maximization rate $1/(1 + e)$. As discussed earlier and as shown in the empirical literature (Saez et al., 2012), it is almost always the case that large short-term behavioral responses generated by tax changes are due to some form of income shifting or income retiming that generates fiscal externalities.

Third and most important, the government can improve efficiency and its ability to tax by closing tax avoidance opportunities (setting $t = \tau$ in our model), in which case the tax avoidance response becomes irrelevant and the real elasticity e_Y is the only factor limiting tax revenue.[43] This strong result is obtained under the assumption that the tax avoidance opportunity arises solely from a poorly designed tax system that can be fixed at no cost.

Fourth and related, actual tax avoidance opportunities come in two varieties. Some are indeed pure creations of the tax system—such as the exemption of fringe benefits or tax exempt local government bonds—and hence could be entirely eliminated by reforming the tax system. In that case, t is a free parameter that the government can change at no cost as in our model. Yet other tax avoidance opportunities reflect real enforcement constraints that are costly—sometimes even impossible—for the government to eliminate. For example, it is very difficult for the government to tax income from informal businesses using only cash transactions, monitor perfectly consumption inside informal businesses, or fight offshore tax evasion.[44] The important policy question is then what fraction of the tax avoidance elasticity can be eliminated by tax redesign and tax enforcement effort.[45]

4.4. Income Shifting

The previous avoidance model assumed that shifting was entirely wasteful so that there was no reason for the government to set t lower than τ to start with. In reality, there are sometimes legitimate efficiency or distributional reasons why a government would want to tax different forms of income differently. On efficiency grounds, the classic Ramsey theory of optimal taxation indeed recommends lower tax rates on the most elastic goods or factors (Ramsey, 1927 and Diamond & Mirrlees, 1971).

Let us therefore extend our previous model by considering that there are two sources of income that we will call labor income and capital income for simplicity.[46] We follow again the simple modeling presented in Piketty et al. (2011). In this chapter, we focus solely on the static equilibrium and abstract from explicit dynamic considerations.[47] Labor income and capital income may respond to taxes differently and individuals can at some cost shift income from one form to the other. For example, small business owners can choose to pay themselves in the form of salary or business profits.

We assume that labor income z_L is taxed linearly at rate τ_L, while capital income z_K is taxed linearly at rate τ_K. True labor (respectively, capital) income is denoted by y_L, (respectively, y_K) while reported labor (respectively, capital) income is $z_L = y_L - x$

---

[43] Kopczuk (2005) shows that the Tax Reform Act of 1986 in the United States, which broadened the tax base and closed loopholes did reduce the elasticity of reported income with respect to the net-of-tax rate.

[44] Offshore tax evasion is very difficult to fight from a single country's perspective but can be overcome with international coordination. This shows again that whether a tax avoidance/evasion opportunity can be eliminated depends on the institutional framework.

[45] Slemrod and Kopczuk (2002) present a model with costs of enforcement, where the government can adopt a broader tax base but where expanding the tax base is costly, to capture this trade-off theoretically.

[46] Other examples could be individual income vs. corporate income, or realized capital gains vs. ordinary income, or self-employment earnings vs. employee earnings.

[47] Chiappori (2008) propose an optimal tax analysis with shifting between capital and labor income in an OLG model.

(respectively, $z_K = y_K + x$) where x represents the amount of income shifting between the tax bases. Individual i has utility function:

$$u_i(c, y_L, y_K, x) = c - h_{Li}(y_L) - h_{Ki}(y_K) - d_i(x),$$

with $c = R + (1 - \tau_L)z_L + (1 - \tau_K)z_K = R + (1 - \tau_L)y_L + (1 - \tau_K)y_K + (\tau_L - \tau_K)x$,

where $h_{Li}(y_L)$ is the cost of producing labor income y_L, $h_{Ki}(y_K)$ is the cost of producing capital income y_K, and $d_i(x)$ is the cost of shifting income from the labor to the capital base. We assume that h_{Li}, h_{Ki}, and d_i are all convex. Note that $d_i(x) \geq 0$ is defined for both positive and negative x. We assume that $d_i(0) = 0$ and $d_i'(0) = 0$ and that $d_i'(x) \gtreqless 0$ if and only if $x \gtreqless 0$.[48] Individual utility maximization implies that

$$h_{Li}'(y_{Li}) = 1 - \tau_L, \quad h_{Ki}'(y_{Ki}) = 1 - \tau_K, \quad \text{and} \quad d_i'(x) = \tau_L - \tau_K,$$

so that y_{Li} is an increasing function of $1 - \tau_L$, y_{Ki} is an increasing function of $1 - \tau_K$, and x_i is an increasing function of the tax differential $\tau_L - \tau_K$. Aggregating over all individuals, we have $Y_L(1 - \tau_L) = \int y_{Li}dv(i)$ with real elasticity $e_L > 0$, $Y_K(1 - \tau_K) = \int y_{Ki}dv(i)$ with real elasticity $e_K > 0$, and $X(\tau_L - \tau_K) = \int x_i dv(i)$ increasing in $\Delta \tau = \tau_L - \tau_K$ with $X(0) = 0$. We can derive the revenue maximizing tax rates τ_L and τ_K in the following three cases:

No Income Shifting. If $X \equiv 0$, then $\tau_L = 1/(1 + e_L)$ and $\tau_K = 1/(1 + e_K)$.

Finite Shifting Elasticity. If $e_L < e_K$, we have: $1/(1 + e_L) \geq \tau_L > \tau_K \geq 1/(1 + e_K)$ (and conversely if $e_L > e_K$).

Infinite Shifting Elasticity. In the limit where X' is very large and real responses have finite elasticities e_L and e_K, then $\tau_L = \tau_K = 1/(1 + \bar{e})$ where $\bar{e} = (Y_L e_L + Y_K e_K)/(Y_L + Y_K)$ is the average real elasticity (weighted by income).

Those results have four notable implications. First, absent any shifting elasticity, there is no cross elasticity and we obtain the standard Ramsey inverse elasticity rule for each income factor.[49]

Second, the presence of shifting opportunities brings the optimal tax rates τ_L and τ_K closer together (relative to those arising under the inverse elasticity rule). When the shifting elasticity is large, optimal tax rates τ_L and τ_K should be close—even if the real elasticities e_L and e_K are quite different. Importantly, the presence of shifting does not necessarily reduce the ability of the government to tax but only alters the relative mix of tax rates. For example, in the case with infinite shifting, the optimum tax rates on labor and capital are equal and should be based on the average of the real elasticities.

---

[48] This model nests the pure tax avoidance model of the previous section in the case where $y_K \equiv 0$, i.e., there is no intrinsic capital income.

[49] As we have no income effects, the elasticities are also compensated elasticities.

Third, in this simple model, deciding whether labor or capital income should be taxed more requires comparing the elasticities e_L and e_K of *real* labor and capital income, and not the elasticities of reported labor and capital income. Empirically, this would require changing simultaneously and equally both τ_L and τ_K to determine which factor responds most keeping the level of income shifting $x(\Delta\tau)$ constant. Concretely, if shifting elasticities are large, a cut in τ_K will produce a large response of reported capital income but at the expense of labor income. It would be wrong to conclude that τ_K should be reduced. It should instead be brought closer to τ_L.

Fourth, it is possible to consider a standard social welfare maximization objective. In that case, optimal tax rates depend also on the distribution of each form of income. For example, under a standard utilitarian criterion with concave social marginal utility of consumption, if capital income is more concentrated than labor income, it should be taxed more (everything else equal). Those distributive effects in optimal tax formulas are well known from the theory of optimal commodity taxation (Diamond, 1975; Diamond & Mirrlees, 1971).[50]

5. OPTIMAL NONLINEAR TAXATION

Formally, the optimal nonlinear tax problem is easy to pose. It is the same as the linear tax problem except that the government can now choose any nonlinear tax schedule $T(z)$ instead of a single linear tax rate τ with a demogrant R. Therefore, the government chooses $T(z)$ to maximize

$$SWF = \int_i \omega^i G(u^i(z^i - T(z^i), z^i))d\nu(i) \quad \text{subject to} \quad \int_i T(z^i)d\nu(i) \geq E\ (p),$$

and the fact that z^i is chosen by individual i to maximize her utility $u^i(z^i - T(z^i), z^i)$. Note that transfers and taxes are fully integrated. Those with no earnings receive a transfer $-T(0)$. We start the analysis with the optimal top tax rate. Next, we derive the optimal marginal tax rate at any income level z. Finally, we focus on the bottom of the income distribution to discuss the optimal profile of transfers.

In this chapter, we purposefully focus on intuitive derivations using small reforms around the optimum. This allows us to understand the key economic mechanisms and obtain formulas directly expressed in terms of estimable "sufficient statistics" (Chetty, 2009a; Saez, 2001). Hence, we will omit discussions of technical issues about regularity conditions needed for the optimal tax formulas.[51]

---

[50] Note that there also exists dynamic reasons—e.g., the relative importance of inheritance and life-cycle saving in aggregate wealth accumulation—explaining why one might want to tax capital income more than labor income. See Piketty and Saez (2012a).

[51] The optimal income tax theory following Mirrlees (1971) has devoted substantial effort studying those issues thoroughly (see e.g., Mirrlees (1976,1986, chap. 24) for extensive surveys). The formal derivations are gathered in the appendix.

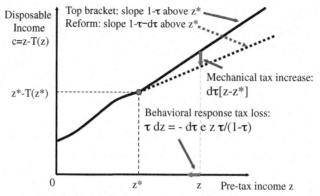

Figure 3 Optimal top tax rate derivation. The figure adapted from Diamond and Saez (2011), depicts the derivation of the optimal top tax rate $\tau = 1/(1 + ae)$ by considering a small reform around the optimum which increases the top marginal tax rate τ by $d\tau$ above z^*. A taxpayer with income z mechanically pays $d\tau[z - z^*]$ extra taxes but, by definition of the elasticity e of earnings with respect to the net-of-tax rate $1 - \tau$, also reduces his income by $dz = -d\tau ez/(1 - \tau)$ leading to a loss in tax revenue equal to $d\tau ez\tau/(1 - \tau)$. Summing across all top bracket taxpayers and denoting by z the average income above z^* and $a = z/(z - z^*)$, we obtain the revenue maximizing tax rate $\tau = 1/(1 + ae)$. This is the optimum tax rate when the government sets zero marginal welfare weights on top income earners.

5.1. Optimal Top Tax Rate

As discussed extensively in Section 2, the taxation of high income earners is a very important aspect of the tax policy debate. Initial progressive income tax systems were typically limited to the top of the distribution. Today, because of large increases in income concentration in a number of countries and particularly the United States (Piketty & Saez, 2003), the level of taxation of top incomes (e.g., the top 1%) matters not only for symbolic equity reasons but also for quantitatively for revenue raising needs.

5.1.1. Standard Model

Let us assume that the top tax rate above a fixed income level z^* is constant and equal to τ as illustrated on Figure 3. Let us assume that a fraction q of individuals are in the top bracket. To obtain the optimal τ, we consider a small variation $d\tau$ as depicted on Figure 3. Individual i earning z^i above z^*, mechanically pays $[z^i - z^*]d\tau$ extra in taxes. This extra tax payment creates a social welfare loss (expressed in terms of government public funds) equal to $-g^i \cdot [z^i - z^*]d\tau$ where $g^i = \omega_i G'(u^i)u_c^i/p$ is the social marginal welfare weight on individual i. [52] Finally, the tax change triggers a behavioral response dz^i leading to an additional change in taxes τdz^i. Using the elasticity of reported income z^i with respect to the net-of-tax rate $1 - \tau$, we have $dz^i = -e^i z^i d\tau/(1 - \tau)$. Hence, the

---

[52] Because the individual chooses z^i to maximize utility, the money-metric welfare effect of the reform on individual i is given by $[z^i - z^*]d\tau$ using the standard envelope theorem argument (see the end of Section 3.3).

net effect of the small reform on individual i is:

$$\left[(1 - g^i)(z^i - z^*) - e^i z^i \frac{\tau}{1 - \tau}\right] d\tau.$$

To obtain the total effect on social welfare, we simply aggregate the welfare effects across all top bracket taxpayers so that we have:

$$dSWF = \left[(1 - g)(z - z^*) - ez \frac{\tau}{1 - \tau}\right] q \, d\tau,$$

where q is the fraction of individuals in the top bracket, z is average income in the top bracket, g is the average social marginal welfare weight (weighted by income in the top bracket $z^i - z^*$) of top bracket individuals, and e is the average elasticity (weighted by income z^i) of top bracket individuals. We can introduce the tail-parameter $a = z/(z - z^*)$ to rewrite $dSWF$ as

$$dSWF = \left[1 - g - a \cdot e \frac{\tau}{1 - \tau}\right] (z - z^*) q \, d\tau.$$

At the optimum, $dSWF = 0$, leading to the following optimal top rate formula.

Optimal top tax rate: $\tau = \dfrac{1 - g}{1 - g + a \cdot e}.$ (7)

Formula (7) expresses the optimal top tax rate in terms of three parameters: a parameter g for social preferences, a parameter e for behavioral responses to taxes, and a parameter a for the shape of the income distribution.[53] Five points are worth noting about formula (7).

First, the optimal tax rate decreases with g, the social marginal welfare weight on top bracket earners. In the limit case where society does not put any value on the marginal consumption of top earners, the formula simplifies to $\tau = 1/(1 + a \cdot e)$ which is the revenue maximizing top tax rate. A utilitarian social welfare criterion with marginal utility of consumption declining to zero, the most commonly used specification in optimal tax models following Mirrlees (1971), has the implication that g converges to zero when z^* grows to infinity.

Second, the optimal tax rate decreases with the elasticity e as a higher elasticity leads to larger efficiency costs. Note that this elasticity is a mixture of substitution and income effects as an increase in the top tax rate generates both substitution and income effects.[54] Importantly, for a given compensated elasticity, the presence of income effects *increases* the optimal top tax rate as raising the tax rate reduces disposable income and hence increases labor supply.

---

[53] Note that the derivation and formula are virtually the same as for the optimal linear rate by simply multiplying e by the factor $a > 1$. Indeed, when $z^* = 0$, $a = z/(z - z^*) = 1$ and the problem boils down to the optimal linear tax problem.

[54] Saez (2001) provides a decomposition and shows that $e = \bar{e}^u + \bar{\eta} \cdot (a - 1)/a$ with $\bar{e}^u$ the average (income weighted) uncompensated elasticity and $\bar{\eta}$ the (unweighted) average income effect.

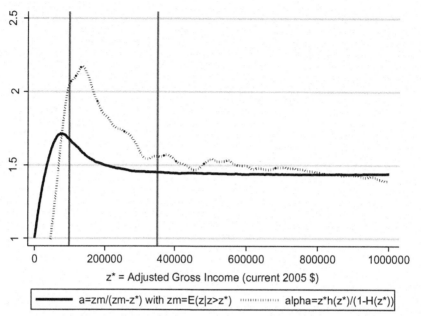

Figure 4 Empirical Pareto coefficients in the United States, 2005. The figure, from Diamond and Saez (2011), depicts in solid line the ratio $a = z_m/(z_m - z^*)$ with z^* ranging from $0 to $1,000,000 annual income and z_m the average income above z^* using US tax return micro data for 2005. Income is defined as Adjusted Gross Income reported on tax returns and is expressed in current 2005 dollars. Vertical lines depict the 90th percentile ($99,200) and 99th percentile ($350,500) nominal thresholds as of 2005. The ratio a is equal to one at $z^* = 0$, and is almost constant above the 99th percentile and slightly below 1.5, showing that the top of the distribution is extremely well approximated by a Pareto distribution for purposes of implementing the optimal top tax rate formula $\tau = 1/(1 + ae)$. Denoting by $h(z)$ the density and by $H(z)$ the cdf of the income distribution, the figure also displays in dotted line the ratio $\alpha(z^*) = z^*h(z^*)/(1-H(z^*))$ which is also approximately constant, around 1.5, above the top percentile. A decreasing (or constant) $\alpha(z)$ combined with a decreasing $g^+(z)$ and a constant $e(z)$ implies that the optimal marginal tax rate $T'(z) = [1 - g^+(z)]/[1 - g^+(z) + \alpha(z)e(z)]$ increases with z.

Third, the optimal tax rate decreases with the parameter $a \geq 1$ which measures the thinness of the top tail of the income distribution. Empirically, $a = z/(z - z^*)$ is almost constant as z^* varies in the top tail of the earnings distribution. Figure 4 depicts a (as a function of z^*) for the case of the US pre-tax income distribution and shows that it is extremely stable above $z^* = \$400,000$, approximately the top 1% threshold.[55] This is due to the well-known fact—since at least Pareto (1896)—that the top tail is very closely approximated by a Pareto distribution.[56]

---

[55] This graph is taken from Diamond and Saez (2011) who use the 2005 distribution of total pre-tax family income (including capital income and realized capital gains) based on tax return data.

[56] A Pareto distribution with parameter a has a distribution of the form $H(z) = 1 - k/z^a$ and density $h(z) = ka/z^{1+a}$ (with k a constant parameter). For any z^*, the average income above z^* is equal to $z^* \cdot a/(a - 1)$.

Fourth and related, the formula shows the limited relevance of the zero-top tax rate result. Formally, z/z^* reaches 1 when z^* reaches the level of income of the single highest income earner, in which case $a = z/(z - z^*)$ is infinite and indeed $\tau = 0$, which is the famous zero-top rate result first demonstrated by Sadka (1976) and Seade (1977). However, notice that this result applies only to the very top income earner. Its lack of wider applicability can be verified empirically using distributional income tax statistics as we did in Figure 4 (see Saez, 2001 for an extensive analysis). Furthermore, under the reasonable assumption that the level of top earnings is not known in advance and where potential earnings are drawn randomly from an underlying Pareto distribution then, with the budget constraint satisfied in expectation, formula (7) remains the natural optimum tax rate (Diamond & Saez, 2011). This finding implies that the zero-top rate result and its corollary that marginal tax rates should decline at the top have no policy relevance.

Fifth, the optimal top tax rate formula is fairly general and applies equally to populations with heterogeneous preferences, discrete populations, or continuous populations. Although the optimal formula does not require the strong homogeneity assumptions of the Mirrlees (1971) problem, it is also the asymptotic limit of the optimal marginal tax rate of the fully nonlinear tax problem of Mirrlees (1971) as we shall see below.

5.1.2. Rent-Seeking Effects

Pay may not be equal to the marginal economic product for top income earners. In particular, executives can be overpaid if they are entrenched and can use their power to influence compensation committees. Indeed, a large literature in corporate finance has made those points (see for instance Bebchuk and Fried (2004) for an overview).[57]

There is relatively little work in optimal taxation that uses models where pay differs from marginal product.[58] Here we adapt the very basic model of Piketty et al. (2011) to illustrate the key issues created by rent seeking effects. Rothschild and Scheuer (2011) consider a more elaborate model with rent-seeking and earnings heterogeneity with two sectors where rent-seeking activities prone to congestion are limited to a single sector.[59]

Let us assume that individual i receives a fraction η of her actual product y. Individual i can exert productive effort to increase y or bargaining effort to increase η. Both types

---

[57] In principle, executives could also be underpaid relative to their marginal product if there is social outrage about high levels of compensation. In that case, a company might find it more profitable to under-pay its executives than face the wrath of its other employees, customers, or the public in general.

[58] A few studies have analyzed optimal taxation in models with labor market imperfections such as search models, union models, efficiency wages models (see Sorensen, 1999 for a survey). Few papers have addressed redistributive optimal tax policy in models with imperfect labor markets. Hungerbuhler, Lehmann, Parmentier Der Linden, and Bruno (2006) analyze a search model with heterogeneous productivity, and Stantcheva (2011) considers contracting models where firms cannot observe perfectly the productivity of their employees.

[59] In their model (and in contrast to the simple model we use here), when rent-seekers "steal" only from other rent-seekers, it is not optimal to impose high top tax rates because low top tax rates stimulate rent-seeking efforts, thereby congesting the rent-seeking sector and discouraging further entry.

of effort are costly to the individual. Hence, individual i utility is given by

$$u^i(c, \eta, y) = c - h_i(y) - k_i(\eta),$$

where c is disposable after-tax income, $h_i(y)$ is the cost of producing output y as in the standard model, and $k_i(\eta)$ is the cost of bargaining to get a share η of the product. Both h_i and k_i are increasing and convex.

Let $b = (\eta - 1)y$ be bargained earnings defined as the gap between received earnings ηy and actual product y. Note that the model allows both overpay (when $\eta > 1$ and hence $b > 0$) and underpay (when $\eta < 1$ and hence $b < 0$). Let us denote by $E(b)$ the average bargained earnings in the economy. In the aggregate, it must be the case that aggregate product must be equal to aggregate compensation. Hence, if $E(b) > 0$, average overpay $E(b)$ must come at the expense of somebody. Symmetrically, if $E(b) < 0$, average underpay $-E(b)$ must benefit somebody. For simplicity, we assume that any gain made through bargaining comes at the expense of everybody else in the economy uniformly. Hence, individual incomes are all reduced by the same amount $E(b)$ (or increased by $-E(b)$ if $E(b) < 0$).[60]

Because the government uses a nonlinear income tax schedule, it can adjust the demogrant intercept $-T(0)$ to fully offset $E(b)$. Effectively, the government can always tax (or subsidize) $E(b)$ at 100% before applying its nonlinear income tax. Hence, we can assume without loss of generality that the government absorbs one-for-one any change in $E(b)$. Therefore, we can simply define earnings as $z = \eta y = y + b$ and assume that those earnings are taxed nonlinearly.

Individual i chooses y and η to maximize:

$$u^i(c, \eta, y) = \eta \cdot y - T(\eta \cdot y) - h_i(y) - k_i(\eta),$$

which leads to the first order conditions

$$(1 - \tau)\eta = h_i'(y) \quad \text{and} \quad (1 - \tau)y = k_i'(\eta),$$

where $\tau = T'$ is the marginal tax rate. This naturally defines y_i, η_i as *increasing* functions of the net-of-tax rate $1 - \tau$. Hence $z_i = \eta_i \cdot y_i$ and $b_i = (\eta_i - 1) \cdot y_i$ are also functions of $1 - \tau$.

Let us consider as in the previous section the optimal top tax rate τ above income level z^*. We assume again that there is a fraction q of top bracket taxpayers. Let us denote by $z(1 - \tau)$, $y(1 - \tau)$, $b(1 - \tau)$ average reported income, productive earnings, and bargained earnings across all taxpayers in the top bracket. We can then define the real labor supply elasticity e_y and the total compensation elasticity e as:

$$e_y = \frac{1 - \tau}{y} \frac{dy}{d(1 - \tau)} \geq 0 \quad \text{and} \quad e = \frac{1 - \tau}{z} \frac{dz}{d(1 - \tau)} \geq 0.$$

[60] Piketty et al. (2011) show that this assumption can be relaxed without affecting the substance of the results.

We define s as the fraction of the marginal behavioral response due to bargaining and let $e_b = s \cdot e$ be the *bargaining elasticity component*:

$$s = \frac{db/d(1-\tau)}{dz/d(1-\tau)} = \frac{db/d(1-\tau)}{db/d(1-\tau) + dy/d(1-\tau)} \quad \text{and} \quad e_b = s \cdot e = \frac{1-\tau}{z} \frac{db}{d(1-\tau)}.$$

This definition immediately implies that $(y/z)e_b = (1-s) \cdot e$. By construction, $e = (y/z)e_y + e_b$. Importantly, s (and hence e_b) can be either positive or negative but it is always positive if individuals are overpaid (i.e., if $\eta > 1$). If individuals are underpaid (i.e., $\eta < 1$) then s (and hence e_b) may be negative.

For simplicity, let us assume that bargaining effects are limited to individuals in the top bracket. As there is a fraction q of top brackets individuals, we hence have $E(b) = qb(1-\tau)$. We assume that the government wants to maximize tax revenue collected from top bracket earners, taking into account bargaining effects:

$$T = \tau[y(1-\tau) + b(1-\tau) - z^*]q - E(b) = \tau[y(1-\tau) + b(1-\tau) - z^*]q - qb(1-\tau).$$

The second term $-E(b)$ arises because we assume that average underpay $-E(b)$ due to rent-seeking at the top is fully absorbed by the government budget as discussed above.

In this model, the top tax rate maximizing tax revenue satisfies the first order condition

$$0 = \frac{dT}{d\tau} = [y + b - z^*]q - q\tau \frac{dy}{d(1-\tau)} - q\tau \frac{db}{d(1-\tau)} + q\frac{db}{d(1-\tau)}.$$

The last term reflects the rent-seeking externality. Any decrease in top incomes due to a reduction in b creates a positive externality on all individuals, which can be recouped by the government by adjusting the demogrant. The optimal top tax rate can then be rewritten as follows:

Optimal top tax rate with rent-seeking: $\quad \tau^* = \dfrac{1 + a \cdot e_b}{1 + a \cdot e} = 1 - \dfrac{a(y/z)e_y}{1 + a \cdot e}, \quad$ (8)

τ^* decreases with the total e (keeping the bargaining component e_b constant) and increases with e_b (keeping e constant). It also decreases with the real elasticity e_y (keeping e and y/z constant) and increases with the level of overpayment $\eta = z/y$ (keeping e_y and e constant). If $e_y = 0$ then $\tau^* = 1$. Two scenarios are theoretically possible.

Trickle-Up. In the case where top earners are overpaid relative to their productivity ($z > y$), then $s > 0$ and hence $e_b > 0$ and the optimal top tax rate is higher than in the standard model (i.e., $\tau^* > 1/(1+a \cdot e)$). This corresponds to a "trickle-up" situation where a tax cut on upper incomes shifts economic resources away from the bottom and toward the top. Those effects can have a large quantitative impact on optimal top tax rates. In the extreme case where all behavioral responses at the top are due to rent-seeking effects ($e_b = e$ and $e_y = 0$) then $\tau^* = 1$.

Trickle-Down. In the case where top earners are underpaid relative to their productivity ($z < y$) it is possible to have $s < 0$ and hence $e_b < 0$, in which case the optimal top tax rate is lower than in the standard model (i.e., $\tau^* < 1/(1 + a \cdot e)$). This corresponds to a "trickle-down" situation where a tax cut on upper incomes also shifts economic resources toward the bottom, as upper incomes are underpaid and hence work in part for the benefit of lower incomes.

Implementing formula (8) requires knowing not only how compensation responds to tax changes but also how real economic product responds to tax changes, which is considerably more difficult than estimating the standard taxable income elasticity e (see Piketty et al., 2011 for such an attempt). The issue of whether top earners deserve their incomes or are rent-seekers certainly looms large in the debate on top income taxation. Yet little empirical evidence can bear on the issue. This illustrates the limits of the theory of optimal taxation. Realistic departures from the standard economic model might be difficult to measure and yet can affect optimal tax rates in substantial ways.[61]

Finally, note that the model with rent-seeking is also related to the derivation of the optimal tax rates in the presence of externalities due to charitable giving responses (see e.g., Saez, 2004a) or the presence of transfers across agents (Chetty, 2009b).

5.1.3. International Migration

Taxes and transfers might affect migration in or out of the country. For example, high top tax rates might induce highly skilled workers to emigrate to low top tax rate countries.[62]

We consider a simplified version of the migration model of Mirrlees (1982) in order to obtain a simple formula.[63]

Let us assume that the only behavioral response to taxes is migration so that individual earnings z conditional on residence are fixed. Let us denote by $P(c|z)$ the number of resident individuals earning z when disposable domestic income is c. With the income tax, we have $c = z - T(z)$. We assume that $P(c|z)$ increases with c due to migration responses.

We can consider a small reform which increases taxes by dT for those earning z. The mechanical effect net of welfare is $dM + dW = (1 - g(z))P(c|z)dT$ where $g(z)$ is the social marginal welfare weight on individuals with earnings z. The net fiscal cost of somebody earning z emigrating is $T(z)$. We can define an elasticity of migration with respect to disposable income $\eta_m = [(z - T(z))/P(c|z)] \cdot \partial P/\partial c$. Hence the fiscal cost is $dB = -T(z) \cdot P(c|z) \cdot \eta_m/(z - T(z))$. Marginal emigrants are indifferent between emigrating or staying and hence the welfare cost is second order in this case as well. At the

---

[61] The same issue arises with optimal Ramsey taxation in the presence of imperfect competition, which has been explored in depth in the traditional optimal tax literature (see e.g., Auerbach and James (2002), Section 7 for a survey).

[62] The government can use other tools, such as immigration policy, to affect migration. Those other tools are taken here as given. Note that democracies typically do not control emigration but can control to some extent immigration. In the European Union context, emigration and immigration across EU countries is almost completely deregulated and hence our analysis is relevant in this context.

[63] Simula and Trannoy (2010) also derive optimal income tax formulas in a model including both migration and standard labor supply responses.

optimum, we have $dM + dW + dB = 0$, which implies:

Optimal tax with migration only: $\quad \dfrac{T(z)}{z - T(z)} = \dfrac{1}{\eta_m} \cdot (1 - g(z)).$ (9)

In the EU context, the most interesting application of the tax induced migration model is at the high income end. Indeed, there have been heated discussions of brain drain issues across EU countries due to differential tax rates at the top across countries. If we assume that high incomes respond both along the intensive margin as in Section 5.1.1 with elasticity e, and along the migration margin with elasticity η_m, then, it is possible to show that the optimal top rate maximizing tax revenue becomes (see Brewer, Shephard, & Saez, 2010):

Optimal top tax rate adding migration effects: $\quad \tau^* = \dfrac{1}{1 + a \cdot e + \eta_m}.$ (10)

For example if $a = 2, e = 0.25$, the optimal tax rate with no migration is $\tau^* = 1/(1 + 2 \cdot 0.25) = 2/3$. If there is migration with elasticity $\eta_m = 0.5$, then the optimal tax rate decreases to $\tau^* = 1/(1 + 2 \cdot 0.25 + 0.5) = 1/2$. Thus, large migration elasticities could indeed decrease significantly the ability of European countries to tax high incomes.

Two important additional points should be made. First, the size of the migration elasticity η_m depends not only on individual preferences but also on the size of the jurisdiction. Small jurisdictions—such as a town—typically have large elasticities as individuals can relocate outside the jurisdiction at low costs, for example without having to change jobs, etc. (see the chapter in this volume by Glaeser on urban public finance for a detailed discussion). The elasticity becomes infinite in the case of very small jurisdictions. Conversely, very large jurisdictions—such as a large country—have lower elasticities as it is costly to relocate. In the limit case of the full world, the migration elasticity is naturally zero. Therefore and as is well known, it is harder for small jurisdictions to implement redistributive taxation and indeed most redistributive tax and transfer programs tend to be carried out at the country level rather than the regional or city level.

Second and related, a single jurisdiction does not recognize the external cost it might impose on others by cutting its top tax rate. In that case, fiscal coordination across jurisdictions (e.g., European countries) could be mutually beneficial to internalize the externality. With complete fiscal coordination, the migration elasticity again becomes irrelevant for optimal tax policy (see the chapter by Keen and Konrad in this volume for an complete treatment of tax competition issues). When making policy recommendations, economists should try to be as clear as possible as to whether they are concerned with a single country optimum or with a global welfare perspective.[64]

---

[64] E.g. the Mirrlees Report is sometimes ambiguous as to whether the objective is to maximize social welfare at the global level or to find the tax system maximizing UK welfare.

5.1.4. Empirical Evidence on Top Incomes and Top Tax Rates

Micro-Level Tax Reform Studies. A very large literature has used tax reforms and micro-level tax return data to identify the elasticity of reported incomes with respect to the net-of-tax marginal rate. Those studies typically compare changes in pre-tax incomes of groups affected by a tax reform to changes in pre-tax incomes of groups unaffected by the reform. Hence, such tax reform-based analysis can only estimate short-term responses (typically 1–5 years) to tax changes. This literature, surveyed in Saez, Slemrod, and Giertz (2012), obtains three key conclusions that we briefly summarize here. First, there is substantial heterogeneity in the estimates: Many studies finding relatively small elasticity estimates (below 0.25), but some have found that tax reform episodes do generate large short-term behavioral responses, which imply large elasticities, particularly at the top of the income distribution. Second however, all the cases with large behavioral responses are due to tax avoidance such as retiming or income shifting. To our knowledge, none of the empirical tax reform studies to date have shown large responses due to changes in real economic behavior such as labor supply or business creation.[65] Furthermore, "anatomy analysis" shows that the large tax avoidance responses obtained are always the consequence of poorly designed tax systems offering arbitrage opportunities[66] or income retiming opportunities in anticipation of or just after-tax reforms.[67] When the tax system offers few tax avoidance opportunities, short-term responses to changes in tax rates are fairly modest with elasticities typically below 0.25.[68] Therefore, the results from this literature fit well with the tax avoidance model presented above with fairly small real elasticities and potentially large avoidance elasticities that can be sharply reduced through better tax design.

International Mobility. Mobility responses to taxation often loom larger in the policy debate on tax progressivity than traditional within country labor supply responses.[69] A large literature has shown that capital income mobility is a substantial concern (see e.g. the chapter by Keen and Konrad in this volume). However, there is much less empirical work on the effect of taxation on the spatial mobility of individuals, especially among high-skilled workers. A small literature has considered the mobility of people across local

---

[65] For example, the US Tax Reform Act of 1986 which cut the top marginal tax rate from 50% down to 28% led to a surge in reported top incomes but no effect on hours of work of top income earners (Moffitt & Wilhelm, 2000).

[66] For example, Slemrod (1996), Gordon and Slemrod (2000), and Saez (2004c) showed that part of the surge in top incomes immediately following the US tax cuts of the 1980s was due to income shifting from the corporate toward the individual sector.

[67] Auerbach (1988) showed that realized capital gains surged in 1986, in anticipation of the increase in the tax rate on realized capital gains starting in 1987. Goolsbee (2000) showed that stock-option realizations surged in 1992, in anticipation of the 1993 increase in top tax rates.

[68] For example, Kleven and Schultz (2012) provide very compelling estimates of modest—but not zero—elasticities around large tax reforms in Denmark, where the tax system offers few avoidance opportunities.

[69] For example, most of the objections in the popular and political debate to the recently proposed top marginal income tax rate of 75% in France are centered around mobility concerns: Will top talented workers (and top fortunes) leave France?

jurisdictions *within* countries.[70] While mobility costs within a country may be small, within country variations in taxes also tend to be modest. Therefore, it is difficult to extrapolate from those studies to international migration where both tax differentials and mobility costs are much higher. There is very little empirical work on the effect of taxation on international mobility partly due to lack of micro data with citizenship information and challenges in identifying causal tax effects on migration. In recent decades however, many countries, particularly in Europe, have introduced preferential tax rates for specific groups of foreign workers, and often highly paid foreign workers (see OECD, 2011c, chap. 4, Table 4.1, p. 138 for a summary of all such existing schemes). Such preferential tax schemes offer a promising route to identify tax induced mobility effects, recently exploited in two studies.

Kleven, Landais, and Saez (2013) study the tax induced mobility of professional football players in Europe and find substantial mobility elasticities. The mobility elasticity of the number of domestic players with respect to the domestic net-of-tax rate is relatively small, around .15. However, the mobility elasticity of the number of foreign players with respect to the net-of-tax rate that applies to foreign players is much larger, around 1. This difference is due to the fact that most players still play in their home country. Kleven et al. (in press) confirm that this latter result applies to the broader market of highly skilled foreign workers and not only football players. They show, in the case study of Denmark, that the preferential tax scheme for highly paid foreigners introduced in 1991 doubled the number of high earning foreigners in Denmark. This translates again into an elasticity of the number of foreign workers with respect to the net-of-tax rate above one.

Those results imply that, from a single country's perspective, as the number of foreigners at the top is still relatively small, the migration elasticity η_m of all top earners with respect to a single net-of-tax top rate is still relatively small, likely below .25 for most countries. This is the relevant elasticity to use in formula (10). Hence, the top income tax rate calculation is unlikely to be drastically affected by migration effects. However, this elasticity is likely to grow overtime as labor markets become better integrated and the fraction of foreign workers grows. Nevertheless, because the elasticity of the number of foreign workers with respect to the net-of-tax rate applying to foreign workers is so large, it is indeed advantageous from a single country perspective to offer such preferential tax schemes. This could explain why such schemes have proliferated in Europe in recent years. Such schemes are typical beggar-thy-neighbor policies which reduce the collective ability of countries to tax top earners. Hence, regulating such schemes at a supranational level (for example at the European Union level for European countries) is likely to become a key element in tax coordination policy debates.

---

[70] See Kirchgassner and Pommerehne (1996) on mobility across Swiss Cantons in response to Canton taxes or Young and Varner (2011) on mobility across US states in response to state income taxes.

Cross Country and Time Series Evidence. The simplest way to obtain evidence on the long-term behavioral responses of top incomes to tax rates is to use long time series analysis within a country or across countries. Data on top incomes overtime and across countries have been compiled by a number of recent studies (see Atkinson et al., 2011 for a survey) and gathered in the *World Top Incomes Database* (Alvaredo, Atkinson, Piketty & Saez 2011. A few recent studies have analyzed the link between top income shares and top tax rates (Atkinson & Leigh, 2010; Roine, Vlachos, & Waldenstrom, 2009; Piketty et al., 2011).

There is a strong negative correlation between top tax rates and top income shares, such as the fraction of total income going to the top 1% of the distribution. This long-run correlation is present overtime within countries as well as across countries. As an important caveat, the correlation between top tax rates and top income shares may not be causal as other policies potentially affecting top income shares, such as financial or industrial regulation or policies affecting Unions, may be correlated with top tax rate policy, creating an omitted variable bias. Alternatively and in reverse causality, higher top income shares may increase the political influence of top earners leading to lower top tax rates.[71]

Panel A in Figure 5 illustrates the cross-country evidence. It plots the change in top income shares from 1960–1964 to 2004–2009 (on the y-axis) against the change in the top marginal tax rate (on the x-axis) for 18 OECD countries. The figure shows a very clear and strong correlation between the cut in top tax rates and the increase in the top 1% income share with interesting heterogeneity. Countries such as France, Germany, Spain, Denmark, or Switzerland which did not experience any significant top rate tax cut did not experience large changes in top 1% income shares. Among the countries which experienced significant top rate cuts, some experience a large increase in top income shares (all five English speaking countries but also Norway and Finland) while others experience only modest increases in top income shares (Japan, Italy, Sweden, Portugal, and the Netherlands). Interestingly, no country experiences a significant increase in top income shares without implementing significant top rate tax cuts. Overall, the elasticity implied by this correlation is large, above 0.5. However, this evidence cannot tell whether the elasticity is due to real effects, tax evasion, or rent-seeking effects.

Panel B in Figure 5 illustrates the time series evidence for the case of the United States. It depicts the top 1% income shares including realized capital gains (pictured with full diamonds) and excluding realized capital gains (the empty diamonds) since 1913, which marks the introduction of the US federal income tax. Both top income shares, whether including or excluding realized capital gains, display an overall U-shape over the century. Panel A also displays (on the right y-axis) the federal individual income top marginal tax rate for ordinary income (dashed line), and for long-term realized capital gains (dotted line). Two important lessons emerge from this panel. Considering first the top income share excluding realized capital gains which corresponds roughly

[71] Analyzing the data in first differences can alleviate omitted variable bias but can only capture short-term effects of tax rates on top incomes, which might differ from long-term effects.

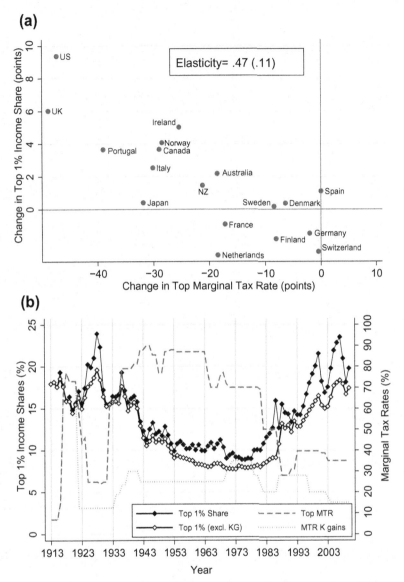

Figure 5 Top marginal tax rates and top incomes shares. This figure is from Piketty, Saez, and Stantcheva (2011). Panel A depicts the change in pre-tax top income shares against the change in pre-tax top income tax rate from 1960–1964 to 2005–2009 based on data for 18 OECD countries (exact years depend on availability of top income share data in the World Top Incomes Database (Alvaredo et al., 2011). Panel B depicts the pre-tax top 1% US income shares including realized capital gains in full diamonds and excluding realized capital gains in empty diamonds from 1913 to 2010. Computations are based on family market cash income. Income excludes government transfers and is before individual taxes (source is Piketty and Saez (2003), series updated to 2010). Panel B also depicts the top marginal tax rate on ordinary income and on realized long-term capital gains.

to income taxed according to the regular progressive schedule, there is a clear negative overall correlation between the top 1% income share and the top marginal tax rate, showing again that the elasticity of reported income with respect to the net-of-tax rate is large in the long run. Second, the correlation between the top 1% income share and the top tax rate also holds for the series including capital gains. Realized capital gains have been traditionally tax favored (as illustrated by the gap between the top tax rate and the tax rate on realized capital gains in the figure) and have constituted the main channel for tax avoidance of upper incomes.[72] This suggests that, in contrast to short-run tax reform analysis, income shifting responses cannot be the main channel creating the long-run correlation between top income shares and top tax rates.[73]

If the long-term correlation between top income shares and top tax rates is not driven by tax avoidance, the key question is whether it is driven by real supply side responses or whether it reflects rent-seeking effects whereby top earners can gain at the expense of others when top rates are low. In principle, the two types of behavioral responses can be distinguished by looking at economic growth as supply-side responses affect economic growth while rent-seeking responses do not. Piketty et al. (2011) analyze cross-country time series for OECD countries since 1960 and do not find any evidence that cuts in top tax rates stimulate growth. This suggests that rent-seeking effects likely play a role in the correlation between top tax rates and top incomes, and therefore that optimal top tax rates might be substantially larger than what it commonly assumed (say, above 80% rather than 50–60%). In our view, this is the right model to account for the quasi-confiscatory top tax rates during large parts of the 20th century (particularly in the US and in the UK; see Figure 1 above). Needless to say, more compelling empirical identification would be very useful to cast further light on this key issue for the optimal taxation of top earners.[74]

5.2. Optimal Nonlinear Schedule
5.2.1. Continuous Model of Mirrlees
It is possible to obtain the formula for the optimal marginal tax rate $T'(z)$ at income level z for the fully general nonlinear income tax using a similar variational method as the one used to derive the top income tax rate. To simplify the exposition, we consider the case with no income effects, where labor supply depends solely on the net-of-tax

---

[72] When individual top tax rates are high (relative to corporate and realized capital gains tax rates), it becomes more advantageous for upper incomes to organize their business activity using the corporate form and retain profits in the corporation. Profits only show up on individual returns as realized capital gains when the corporate stock is eventually sold (see Gordon and Slemrod, 2000 for a detailed empirical analysis).

[73] If top income share variations were due solely to tax avoidance, taxable income subject to the progressive tax schedule should be much more elastic than a broader income definition that also includes forms of income that are tax favored. Indeed, in the pure tax avoidance scenario, total real income of top earners should be completely inelastic to tax rates.

[74] Piketty et al. (2011) provide suggestive micro-level evidence. They show that CEO pay sensitivity to outcomes outside CEOs' control (such as industry wide shocks) is higher when top rates are low, both in the US time series and across countries.

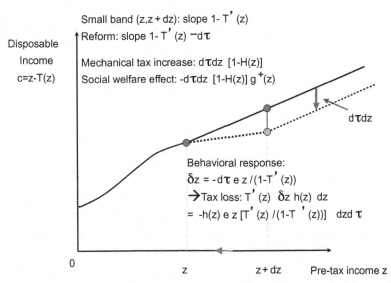

Figure 6 Derivation of the optimal marginal tax rate at income level z. The figure, adapted from Diamond and Saez (2011), depicts the optimal marginal tax rate derivation at income level z by considering a small reform around the optimum, whereby the marginal tax rate in the small band $(z, z + dz)$ is increased by $d\tau$. This reform mechanically increases taxes by $d\tau dz$ for all taxpayers above the small band, leading to a mechanical tax increase $d\tau dz[1 - H(z)]$ and a social welfare cost of $-d\tau dz[1 - H(z)]g^+(z)$. Assuming away income effects, the only behavioral response is a substitution effect in the small band: The $h(z)dz$ taxpayers in the band reduce their income by $\delta z = -d\tau ez/(1 - T'(z))$ leading to a tax loss equal to $-d\tau dzh(z)ezT'(z)/(1 - T'(z))$. At the optimum, the three effects cancel out leading to the optimal tax formula $T'(z)/(1 - T'(z)) = (1/e)(1 - g^+(z))(1 - H(z))/(zh(z))$, or equivalently $T'(z) = [1 - g^+(z)]/[1 - g^+(z) + \alpha(z)e]$ after introducing $\alpha(z) = zh(z)/(1 - H(z))$.

rate $1 - T'(z)$.[75] We present in the text a graphical proof adapted from Saez (2001) and Diamond and Saez (2011) and we relegate to the appendix the formal presentation and derivation in the standard Mirrlees model with no income effects (as in the analysis of Diamond, 1998).

Figure 6 depicts the optimal marginal tax rate derivation at income level z. Again, the horizontal axis in Figure 6 shows pre-tax income, while the vertical axis shows disposable income. Consider a situation in which the marginal tax rate is increased by $d\tau$ in the small band from z to $z + dz$, but left unchanged anywhere else. The tax reform has three effects.

First, the mechanical tax increase, leaving aside behavioral responses, will be the gap between the solid and dashed lines, shown by the vertical arrow equal to $dz\, d\tau$. The total mechanical tax increase is $dM = dz\, d\tau[1 - H(z)]$ as there are $1 - H(z)$ individuals above z.

---

[75] Atkinson (1995) and Diamond (1998) showed that this case generates simpler formulas. Saez (2001) considers the case with income effects.

Second, this tax increase creates a social welfare cost of $dW = -dz\, d\tau[1-H(z)]g^+(z)$ where $g^+(z)$ is defined as the average (unweighted) social marginal welfare weight for individuals with income above z.

Third, there is a behavioral response to the tax change. Those in the income range from z to $z + dz$ have a behavioral response to the higher marginal tax rate, shown by the horizontal line pointing left. Assuming away income effects, this is the only behavioral response; those with income levels above $z + dz$ face no change in marginal tax rates and hence have no behavioral response. A taxpayer in the small band reduces her income by $\delta z = -ez\, d\tau/(1 - T'(z))$ where e is the elasticity of earnings z with respect to the net-of-tax rate $1 - T'$. As there are $h(z)dz$ taxpayers in the band, those behavioral responses lead to a tax loss equal to $dB = -dz\, d\tau\, h(z)ezT'(z)/(1 - T'(z))$.[76]

At the optimum, the three effects should cancel out so that $dM + dW + dB = 0$. Define the local Pareto parameter as $\alpha(z) = zh(z)/(1 - H(z))$.[77] This leads to the following optimal tax formula

Optimal nonlinear marginal tax rate: $\quad T'(z) = \dfrac{1 - g^+(z)}{1 - g^+(z) + \alpha(z) \cdot e}$ $\qquad$ (11)

Formula (11) has essentially the same form as (7). Five further points are worth noting.

First, the simple graphical proof shows that the formula does not depend on the strong homogeneity assumptions of the standard Mirrlees model where individuals differ solely through a skill parameter. This implies that the formula actually carries over to heterogeneous populations as is the case of the basic linear tax rate formula (3).[78]

Second, the optimal tax rate naturally decreases with $g^+(z)$, the average social marginal welfare weight above z. Under standard assumptions where social marginal welfare weights decrease with income, $g^+(z)$ is decreasing in z. With no income effects, the average social marginal welfare weight is equal to one (see Section 3.1) so that $g^+(0) = 1$ and $g^+(z) < 1$ for $z > 0$. This immediately implies that $T'(z) \geq 0$ for any z, one of the few general results coming out of the Mirrlees model and first demonstrated by Mirrlees (1971) and Seade (1982).[79] A decreasing $g^+(z)$ tends to make the tax system

---

[76] This derivation has ignored the fact that the tax schedule is locally nonlinear. Saez (2001) shows that, in the exact formula for dB, the density $h(z)$ should be replaced by the "virtual density" $h^*(z)$ defined as the density at z that would arise if the nonlinear tax system were replaced by the linearized tax system at point z (see the appendix for a formal treatment).

[77] We call $\alpha(z)$ a local Pareto parameter because for an exact Pareto distribution, $\alpha(z)$ is constant and equal to the Pareto parameter a.

[78] This point does not seem to have been formally established in the case of optimal tax theory but is well known in the mathematically equivalent optimal nonlinear pricing problem in the Industrial Organization literature (see e.g., Wilson, 1993, Section 8.4).

[79] $T'(z) < 0$ is never optimal in the Mirrlees model when marginal welfare weights decrease with z. This is because increasing $T'(z)$ locally (as depicted on Figure 6) would raise more revenue from everybody above z which is desirable for redistribution. The behavioral response δz in the small band would further increase tax revenue (as $T'(z) < 0$) making the reform desirable.

more progressive. Note that the extreme Rawlsian case has $g^+(z) = 0$ for all z except at $z = 0$ (assuming realistically that the most disadvantaged are those with no earnings). In that case, the formula simplifies to $T'(z) = 1/(1 + \alpha(z) \cdot e)$ and the optimal tax system maximizes tax revenue raised to make the lump sum demogrant $-T(0)$ as large as possible.

Third, the optimal tax rate decreases with the elasticity e at income level z as a higher elasticity leads to larger efficiency costs in the small band $(z, z + dz)$. Note that this elasticity remains a pure substitution elasticity even in the presence of income effects.[80]

Fourth, the optimal tax rate decreases with the local Pareto parameter $\alpha(z) = zh(z)/[1 - H(z)]$ which reflects the ratio of the total income of those affected by the marginal tax rate at z relative to the number of people at higher income levels. The intuition for this follows the derivation from Figure 6. Increasing $T'(z)$ creates efficiency costs proportional to the number of people at income level z times the income level z while it raises more taxes (with no distortion) from everybody above z. As shown on Figure 4 for the US case, empirically $\alpha(z)$ first increases and then decreases before being approximately constant in the top tail. Hence, when z is large, formula (11) converges to the optimal top rate formula (7) that we derived earlier.

Fifth, suppose the government has no taste for redistribution and wants to raise an exogenous amount of revenue while minimizing efficiency costs. If lump sum taxes are realistically ruled out because those with no earnings could not possibly pay them, then the optimal tax system is still given by (11) with constant social marginal welfare weights and hence constant $g^+(z)$ set to exactly raise the needed amount of exogenous revenue (Saez, 1999, chap. 3).

Increasing Marginal Tax Rates at the Top. With an elasticity e constant across income groups, as $g^+(z)$ decreases with z and $\alpha(z)$ also decreases with z in the upper part of the distribution (approximately the top 5% in the US case, see Figure 4), formula (11) implies that the optimal marginal tax rate should increase with z at the upper end, i.e., the income tax should be progressive at the top. Diamond (1998) provides formal theoretical results in the Mirrlees model with no income effects.

Numerical Simulations. For low z, $g^+(z)$ decreases but $\alpha(z)$ increases. Numerical simulations calibrated using the actual US earnings distribution presented in Saez (2001) show that the $\alpha(z)$ effect dominates at the bottom so that the marginal tax rate is high and decreasing for low z. We come back to this important issue when we discuss the optimal profile of transfers below. Therefore, assuming that the elasticity is constant with z, the optimal marginal tax rate in the Mirrlees model is U-shaped with income, first decreasing with income and then increasing with income before converging to its limit value given by formula (7).

---

[80] Income effects positively affect labor supply above z so that the mechanical tax revenue increase is actually higher than $dz\,d\tau[1 - H(z)]$ and the optimal tax rate is correspondingly higher (see Saez, 2001).

5.2.2. Discrete Models

Stiglitz (1982) developed the 2 skill-type discrete version of the Mirrlees (1971) model where individuals can have either a low or a high wage rate. This discrete model has been used widely in the subsequent literature because it has long been perceived as more tractable than the continuous model of Mirrlees. However, the discrete model is perhaps deceiving when it comes to understanding optimal tax progressivity. Indeed, the zero top marginal tax rate result implies that the marginal tax rate on the highest skill is zero and hence lower than the marginal tax rate on the lowest skill, suggesting that the marginal tax rate should decrease with earnings. Furthermore, it is impossible to express optimal tax formulas in the Stiglitz (1982) model in terms of estimable statistics and hence to quantitatively calibrate the model.

More recently, Piketty (1997) introduced and Saez (2002a) further developed an alternative form of discrete Mirrlees model with a finite number of possible earnings levels $z_0 = 0 < z_1 < ... < z_N$ (corresponding for example to different possible jobs) but a continuum of individual types so that the fraction of individuals at each earnings level is a smooth function of the tax system. This model generates formulas close to the continuum case, and can also be easily extended to incorporate extensive labor supply responses, as we shall see.

Formally, individual i has a utility function $u^i(c_n, n)$ defined on after-tax income $c_n \geq 0$ and job choice $n = 0, ..., N$. Each individual chooses n to maximize $u^i(c_n, n)$ where $c_n = z_n - T_n$ is the after-tax reward in occupation n. For a given tax and transfer schedule $(c_0, ..., c_N)$, a fraction $h_n(c_0, ..., c_N)$ of individuals choose occupation n. It is assumed that the tastes for work embodied in the individual utilities are smoothly distributed so that the aggregate functions h_n are differentiable. Denoting by $n(i)$ the occupational choice of individual i, the government chooses $(T_0, ..., T_N)$ so as to maximize welfare

$$SWF = \int_i \omega_i G[u^i(z_{n(i)} - T_{n(i)}, n(i))]dv(i) \quad \text{s.t.} \quad \sum_n h_n T_n \geq E(p).$$

Even though the population is potentially very heterogeneous, as possible work outcomes are in finite number, the maximization problem is a simple finite dimensional maximization problem. The first order condition with respect to T_n is

$$(1 - g_n)h_n = \sum_{m=0}^{N} T_n \frac{\partial h_m}{\partial c_n} \quad \text{with} \quad g_n = \frac{1}{p \, h_n} \int_{i \in \text{job } n} \omega^i \, G'(u^i)u_c^i(c_n, n)dv(i). \quad (12)$$

Hence, g_n is the average social marginal welfare weight among individuals in occupation n.[81]

---

[81] When obtaining (12), it is important to note that, because of the envelope theorem, the effect of an infinitesimal change in c_n has no discrete effect on welfare for individuals moving in or out of occupation n. Hence, the welfare effects on movers is second order. See Saez (2002a), appendix for complete details.

This model allows for any type of behavioral responses. Two special cases are of particular interest: pure intensive responses as in the standard Mirrlees (1971) model and pure extensive responses. We consider in this section the intensive model case and defer to Section 5.3.2 the extensive model case.

The intensive model. The intensive model with no income effects (first developed by Piketty, 1997) can be obtained by assuming that the population is partitioned into N groups. An individual in group $n \in (0, \ldots, N-1)$ can only work in two adjacent occupations n and $n+1$. For example, with no effort the individual can hold job n and with some effort the individual can obtain job $n+1$.[82] This implies that the function h_n depends only on c_{n+1}, c_n, and c_{n-1}. Assuming no income effects, with a slight abuse of notation, h_n can be expressed as $h_n(c_{n+1} - c_n, c_n - c_{n-1})$. In that context, we can denote by $\tau_n = (T_n - T_{n-1})/(z_n - z_{n-1})$ the marginal tax rate between earnings levels z_{n-1} and z_n and by $e_n = \frac{1-\tau_n}{h_n} \frac{\partial h_n}{\partial(1-\tau_n)}$ the elasticity of the fraction of individuals in occupation n with respect to the net-of-tax rate $1 - \tau_n$. The optimal tax formula (12) can be rearranged as:

Optimal marginal tax rate, discrete model:
$$\frac{\tau_n}{1-\tau_n} = \frac{1}{e_n}\left[\frac{\sum_{m \geq n}(1-g_m)h_m}{h_n}\right].$$
(13)

The proof is presented in Saez (2002a). Note that the form of the optimal formula is actually very close the continuum case where the marginal tax rate from Eq. (11) can also be written as: $T'(z)/[1 - T'(z)] = (1/e)[\int_z^\infty (1 - g(z'))dH(z')/(zh(z))]$.

5.3. Optimal Profile of Transfers

5.3.1. Intensive Margin Responses

It is possible to obtain a formula for the optimal phase-out rate of the demogrant in the optimal income tax model of Mirrlees (1971) where labor supply responds only through the intensive margin.

Recall first that when the minimum income z_0 is positive, the optimal marginal tax rate at the very bottom is zero (this result was first proved by Seade, 1977). This can be seen from formula (11) as $G(z_0) = 1$.[83]

However, the empirically relevant case is $z_0 = 0$ with a non-zero fraction $h_0 > 0$ of the population not working and earning zero. In that case, the optimal phase-out rate τ_1

---

[82] Those preferences are embodied in the individual utility functions u^i. In the case just described, we would have $u^i(c, n) = c$, $u^i(c, n+1) = c - \theta_i$ with θ_i cost of effort to get job $n+1$, and $u^i(c, m) = -\infty$ if $m \notin \{n, n+1\}$.

[83] This result can be seen as the symmetric counterpart of the zero-top result. At the top, it is straightforward to show that the optimum marginal tax rate cannot be positive (if it were, set it to zero above z_{top}, the top earner works more, is better off, and pays the same taxes). However, it is not as easy to show that the top rate cannot be negative (this requires the more sophisticated argument presented in comments of formula (11)). At the bottom symmetrically, it is straightforward to show that the optimum marginal tax rate cannot be negative (if it were, set it to zero below z_{bottom}, the bottom earner works less, is better off, and pays the same taxes). However, it is not as easy to show that the bottom rate cannot be positive (this again requires a symmetric argument to the one presented in comments of formula (11).)

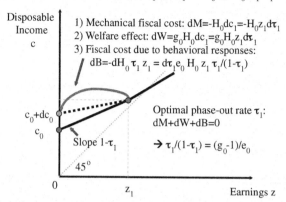

Figure 7 Optimal bottom marginal tax rate with only intensive labor supply responses. The figure, adapted from Diamond and Saez (2011), depicts the derivation of the optimal marginal tax rate at the bottom in the discrete Mirrlees (1971) model with labor supply responses along the intensive margin only. Let H_0 be the fraction of the population not working. This is a function of $1 - \tau_1$, the net-of-tax rate at the bottom, with elasticity e_0. We consider a small reform around the optimum: The government increases the maximum transfer by c_0 by increasing the phase-out rate by $d\tau_1$ leaving the tax schedule unchanged for those with income above z_1. This creates three effects which cancel out at the optimum. At the optimum, we have $\tau_1/(1 - \tau_1) = (g_0 - 1)/e_0$ or $\tau_1 = (g_0 - 1)/(g_0 - 1 + e_0)$. Under standard redistributive preferences, g_0 is large implying that τ_1 is large.

at the bottom can be written as:

Optimal bottom marginal tax rate in Mirrlees model: $\quad \tau_1 = \dfrac{g_0 - 1}{g_0 - 1 + e_0},$

$$(14)$$

where g_0 is the average social marginal welfare weight on zero earners and $e_0 = -[(1 - \tau_1)/h_0]dh_0/d(1 - \tau_1)$ is the elasticity of the fraction non-working h_0 with respect to the bottom net-of-tax rate $1 - \tau_1$ with a minus sign so that $e_0 > 0$.[84] This formula is proved by Saez (2002a) in the discrete model presented above.[85]

The formula also applies in the standard Mirrlees model although it does not seem to have been ever noticed and formally presented. We present the proof in the standard Mirrlees model in the appendix. In the text, we present a simple graphical proof adapted from Diamond and Saez (2011) using the discrete model with intensive margin responses presented above.

As illustrated on Figure 7, suppose that low ability individuals can choose either to work and earn z_1 or not work and earn zero ($z_0 = 0$). The government offers a transfer $c_0 = -T(0)$ to those not working phased-out at rate τ_1 so that those working receive

[84] This elasticity e_0 reflects substitution effects only, as income effects are second order when the marginal tax rate is changed only on a small band of income at the bottom.

[85] It can be obtained from Eq. (13) noting that the average social marginal welfare weight is equal to one so that $\sum_{m\geq0} (1 - g_m)h_m = 0$. Therefore, $\tau_1/(1 - \tau_1) = (1/e_1)(g_0 - 1)h_0/h_1$. Finally, note that $h_1 e_1 = h_0 e_0$.

on net $c_1 = (1 - \tau_1)z_1 + c_0$. In words, non-workers keep a fraction $1 - \tau_1$ of their earnings should they work and earn z_1. Therefore, increasing τ_1 discourages some low income workers from working. Suppose now that the government increases both the c_0 by dc_0 and the phase-out rate by $d\tau_1$ leaving the tax schedule unchanged for those with income equal to or above z_1 so that $dc_0 = z_1 d\tau_1$ as depicted on Figure 7. The fiscal cost is $-h_0 dc_0$ but the welfare benefit is $h_0 g_0 dc_0$ where g_0 is the social welfare weight on non-workers. Because behavioral responses take place along the intensive margin only in the Mirrlees model, with no income change above z_1, the labor supply of those above z_1 is not affected by the reform. By definition of e_0, a number $dh_0 = d\tau_1 e_0 h_0/(1 - \tau_1)$ of low income workers stop working creating a revenue loss of $-\tau_1 z_1 dh_0 = -dc_0 h_0 e_0 \tau_1/(1-\tau_1)$. At the optimum, the three effects sum to zero leading to the optimal bottom rate formula (14). Three points are worth noting about formula (14).

First, if society values redistribution toward zero earners, then g_0 is likely to be large (relative to 1). In that case, τ_1 is going to be high even if the elasticity e_0 is large. For example, if $g_0 = 3$ and $e_0 = .5$ then $\tau_1 = 80\%$, a very high phase-out rate. The intuition is simple: increasing transfers by increasing the phase-out rate is valuable if g_0 is large, the fiscal cost due to the behavioral response is relatively modest as those dropping out of the labor force would have had very modest earnings anyway. The phase-out rate is highest in the Rawlsian case where all the social welfare weight is concentrated at the bottom.[86]

Second and conversely, if society considers that non-workers are primarily free-loaders taking advantage of transfers, then $g_0 < 1$ is conceivable. In that case, the optimal phase-out rate is negative and the government provides higher transfers for low income earners rather than those out-of-work. Naturally, this cannot happen under the standard assumption where social marginal welfare weights decrease with income.

Finally, note that it is not possible to obtain an explicit formula for the optimal demogrant $-T(0)$ as the demogrant is determined in general equilibrium. This is a general feature of optimal tax problems (in the optimal linear tax rate, the demogrant was also deduced from the optimal tax rate τ using the government budget constraint).

5.3.2. Extensive Margin Responses

The optimality of a traditional means-tested transfer program with a high phase-out rate depends critically on the assumption of intensive labor supply responses. Empirically however, there is substantial evidence that labor supply responses, particularly among low income earners, are also substantial along the extensive margin with less compelling evidence of intensive marginal labor supply response.[87] In that case, it is optimal to give

---

[86] In the Rawlsian case, $g_0 = 1/h_0$ and the optimum phase-out rate is almost 100% when the fraction non-working h_0 is small.

[87] Chetty (2012) argues that intensive elasticities are more affected by frictions or inattention issues than extensive elasticities. This makes it more challenging to identify long-run intensive elasticities. For example, Chetty, Friedman, and Saez (2012) show that intensive responses to the EITC can also be substantial in the long-run in places where knowledge about the EITC is high.

higher transfers to low income workers rather than non-workers, which amounts to a negative phase-out rate, as with the current Earned Income Tax Credit (Diamond, 1980; Saez, 2002a).

To see this, consider now a model where behavioral responses of low- and mid-income earners take place through the extensive elasticity only, i.e., whether or not to work, and that earnings when working do not respond to marginal tax rates. Within the general discrete model developed in Section 5.2.2, the extensive model can be obtained by assuming that each individual can only work in one occupation or be unemployed. This can be embodied in the individual utility functions by assuming that $u^i(c_n, n) = -\infty$ for all occupations $n \geq 1$ except the one corresponding to the skill of the individual. This structure implies that the fraction of the population h_n working in occupation n depends only on c_0 and c_n for $n \geq 1$. As a result, and using the fact that $\partial h_n/\partial c_n + \partial h_0/\partial c_n = 0$, and defining the elasticity of participation $e_n = [(1 - \tau_n)/h_n]dh_n/d(1 - \tau_n)$, Eq. (12) becomes,

Optimal tax rate with extensive responses only: $\dfrac{\tau_n}{1 - \tau_n} = \dfrac{1}{e_n}(1 - g_n).$ (15)

To obtain this result, as depicted on Figure 8, suppose the government starts from a transfer scheme with a positive phase-out rate $\tau_1 > 0$ and introduces an additional small in-work

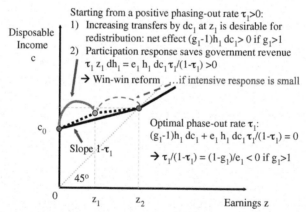

Figure 8 Optimal bottom marginal tax rate with extensive labor supply responses. The figure, adapted from Diamond and Saez (2011), depicts the derivation of the optimal marginal tax rate at the bottom in the discrete model with labor supply responses along the extensive margin only. Starting with a positive phase-out rate $\tau_1 > 0$, the government introduces a small in-work benefit dc_1. Let h_1 be the fraction of low income workers with earnings z_1, and let e_1 be the elasticity of h_1 with respect to the participation net-of-tax rate $1 - \tau_1$. The reform has three standard effects: mechanical fiscal cost $dM = -h_1 dc_1$, social welfare gain, $dW = g_1 h_1 dc_1$, and tax revenue gain due to behavioral responses $dB = \tau_1 z_1 dh_1 = e_1 h_1 dc_1 \tau_1/(1 - \tau_1)$. If $g_1 > 1$, then $dW + dM > 0$. If $\tau_1 > 0$, then $dB > 0$ implying that $\tau_1 > 0$ cannot be optimal. The optimal τ_1 is such that $dM + dW + dB = 0$ implying that $\tau_1/(1 - \tau_1) = (1 - g_1)/e_1$.

benefit dc_1 that increases net transfers to low income workers earning z_1. Let h_1 be the fraction of low income workers with earnings z_1. The reform has again three effects.

First, the reform has a mechanical fiscal cost $dM = -h_1 dc_1$ for the government. Second, it generates a social welfare gain, $dW = g_1 h_1 dc_1$ where g_1 is the marginal social welfare weight on low income workers with earnings z_1. Third, there is a tax revenue gain due to behavioral responses $dB = \tau_1 z_1 dh_1 = e_1[\tau_1/(1-\tau_1)]h_1 dc_1$. If $g_1 > 1$, then $dW + dM > 0$. In that case, if $\tau_1 > 0$, then $dB > 0$, implying that $\tau_1 > 0$ cannot be optimal. The optimal τ_1 is such that

$$0 = dM + dW + dB = h_1 dc_1 \left[g_1 - 1 + e_1 \frac{\tau_1}{1 - \tau_1} \right],$$

implying that the optimal phase-out rate at the bottom is given by:

Optimal bottom tax rate, extensive model: $\tau_1 = \dfrac{1 - g_1}{1 - g_1 + e_1}$,

$$\tau_1 < 0 \quad \text{if} \quad g_1 > 1, \quad (16)$$

Intuitively, starting with a transfer system with a positive phase-out rate as depicted on Figure 8 and ignoring behavioral responses, an in-work benefit reform depicted on Figure 8 is desirable if the government values redistribution to low income earners. If behavioral responses are solely along the extensive margin, this reform induces some non-workers to start working to take advantage of the in-work benefit. However, because we start from a situation with a positive phase-out rate, this behavioral response increases tax revenue as low income workers still end up receiving a smaller transfer than non-workers. Hence, the in-work benefit increases social welfare implying that a positive phase-out rate cannot be optimal.[88] Another way to see this is the following. Increasing c_0 distorts the labor supply decision of all types of workers who might quit working. In contrast, increasing c_1 distorts labor supply of low-skilled workers only. Hence an in-work benefit is less distortionary than an out-of-work benefit in the pure extensive model.

5.3.3. Policy Practice

In practice, both extensive and intensive elasticities are present. An intensive margin response would induce those earning slightly more than the minimum to reduce labor supply to take advantage of the in-work benefit, thus reducing tax revenue. Therefore,

---

[88] At the optimum, it is always the case that $g_1 < 1 + e_1$ so that the denominator in formula (16) is always positive. To see this, suppose $g_1 \geq 1 + e_1$, then $g_1 - 1 + e_1 \frac{\tau_1}{1-\tau_1} \geq e_1/(1-\tau_1) > 0$ as $\tau_1 < 1$, implying that the reform dc_1 described above is always welfare improving. This result can be understood as follows. Suppose we start from an initial tax system (not optimal) where $g_1 > 1 + e_1$, i.e., low-skilled workers are deserving and their elasticity e_1 is not too high. In such a configuration, it is always desirable to increase in-work benefits for low-skilled workers. Increasing in-work benefits reduces g_1 as low-skilled workers become less and less in need of additional support. At the optimum where (16) holds, $g_1 < 1 + e_1$. In the extreme case with no behavioral responses, τ_1 should be set so that $g_1 = 1$. Conversely, when the elasticity e_1 is very large, the optimal bottom tax rate goes to zero.

the government has to trade off the two effects. If, as empirical studies show (see e.g., Blundell & MaCurdy, 1999 for a survey), the extensive elasticity of choosing whether to participate in the labor market is large relative to the intensive elasticity of choosing how many hours to work, initially low (or even negative) phase-out rates combined with high positive phase-out rates further up the distribution would be the optimal profile.

In recent decades in most OECD countries, a concern arose that traditional welfare programs overly discouraged work and there has been a marked shift toward lowering the marginal tax rate for low earners through a combination of: (a) introduction and then expansion of in-work benefits such as the Earned Income Tax Credit in the United States or the Family Credit in the United Kingdom,[89] (b) reduction of the statutory phase-out rates in transfer programs for earned income as under the U.S. welfare reform; and (c) reduction of payroll taxes for low income earners.[90] Those reforms are consistent with the logic of the optimal tax model we have outlined, as they both encourage labor force participation and provide transfers to low income workers seen as a deserving group. As we saw on Figure 2, the current US system imposes marginal tax rates close to zero on the first $15,000 of earnings but significantly higher marginal rates between $15,000 and $30,000.

How can we explain however that means-tested social welfare programs with high phase-out rates were widely used in prior decades? Historically, most means-tested transfer programs started as narrow programs targeting specific groups deemed unable to earn enough such as widows with children, the elderly, or the disabled. For example, the ancestor of the traditional US welfare program (Aid for Families with Dependent Children, renamed Temporary Aid for Needy Families after the 1996 welfare reform) were "mothers' pensions" state programs providing help primarily to widows with children and no resources (Katz, 1996). If beneficiaries cannot work but differ in terms of unearned income (for example, the presence of a private pension), then the optimal redistribution scheme is indeed a transfer combined with a 100% phasing-out rate. As governments expanded the scope of transfers, a larger fraction of beneficiaries were potentially able to work. The actual tax policy response to this moral hazard problem over the last few decades has been remarkably close to the lessons from optimal tax theory we have outlined.

Note that following the Reagan and Thatcher conservative revolutions two other elements likely played a role in the shift from traditional means-tested programs toward in-work benefits. First, it is conceivable that society has less tolerance for non-workers living off government transfers because it believes, rightly or wrongly, that most of such non-workers could actually work and earn a living on their own absent government transfers. This means that the social welfare weights on non-workers has fallen relative to the social welfare weights on workers, and especially low income workers. This effect can be captured in our model simply assuming that social welfare weights change (see Section 7 for a discussion of how social welfare weights could be formed in non-utilitarian

---

[89] See OECD (2005, chap. 3) for a review of all the in-work benefits introduced in OECD countries up to year 2004.
[90] See OECD 2011b for a summary of such payroll tax reductions in OECD countries.

contexts). Second and related, the perception that relying on transfers generates negative externalities on children or neighbors through a "culture of welfare dependency" might have increased. Such externalities are not incorporated in our basic model but could conceivably be added. In both cases, perceptions of the public and actual facts do not necessarily align (see e.g., Bane & Ellwood, 1994 for a detailed empirical analysis).

6. EXTENSIONS

6.1. Tagging

We have assumed that $T(z)$ depends only on earnings z. In reality, the government can observe many other characteristics (denoted by vector X) also correlated with ability (and hence social welfare weights), such as gender, race, age, disability, family structure, height, etc. Hence, the government could set $T(z, X)$ and use the characteristic X as a "tag" in the tax system. There are two noteworthy theoretical results.

First, if characteristic X is *immutable* then there should be full redistribution across groups with different X. This can be seen as follows. Suppose X is a binary 0–1 variable. If the average social marginal welfare weight for group 1 is higher than for group 0, a lump sum tax on group 0 funding a lump sum transfer on group 1 will increase total social welfare.

Second, if characteristic X is not *immutable*, i.e., it can be manipulated through cheating,[91] then it is still desirable to make taxes depend on X (in addition to z). At the optimum however, the redistribution across the X groups will not be complete. To see this, suppose again that X is a binary 0–1 variable and that we start from a pure income tax $T(z)$. As X is correlated with ability, the average social marginal welfare weight for group 1 is different from the one for group 0. Let us assume it is higher. In that case, a small lump sum transfer from group 0 to group 1 increases social welfare, absent any behavioral response. As X is no longer immutable, this small transfer might induce some individuals to switch from group 0 to group 1. However, because we start from a unified tax system, at the margin those who switch do not create any first order fiscal cost (nor any welfare cost through the standard envelope theorem argument).[92]

Those points on tagging have been well known in the literature for decades following the analysis of Akerlof (1978) and Nichols and Zeckhauser (1982) for tagging disadvantaged groups for welfare benefits. It has received recent attention in Mankiw and Weinzierl (2010) and Weinzierl (2011) who use the examples of height and age respectively to argue

[91] A good example would be disability status that can only be imperfectly observed and that individuals can fake to some extent.
[92] Note that this derivation assumes that labor supply choices z are independent of X. This assumption is reasonable when X is manipulated through cheating only but would not necessarily hold if X was manipulated through real choices (e.g., hurting oneself to becoming truly disabled).

that the standard utilitarian maximization framework fails to incorporate important elements of real tax policy design.

Indeed, in reality, actual tax systems depend on a very limited set of characteristics besides income. Those characteristics are primarily family structure (in particular the number of dependent children), disability status (for permanent and temporary disability programs). Hence, characteristics used reflect direct "need" (for example, the size of the household relative to income), or direct "ability-to-earn" (as is the case with disability status). To the best of our knowledge, the case for using indirect tags correlated with ability in the tax or transfer system has never been made in practice in the policy debate, implying that society does have a strong aversion for using indirect tags. We come back to this issue in Section 7 when we discuss the limits of utilitarianism.

6.2. Supplementary Commodity Taxation

The government can also implement differentiated commodity taxation in addition to nonlinear income taxes and transfers. The usual hypothesis is that commodity taxes have to be linear because of retrading (see e.g., Guesnerie, 1995, Chapter 1). The most common form of commodity taxation, value added taxes and general sales taxes, do display some variation in rates across goods, with exemptions for specific goods, such as food or housing. Such exemptions are in general justified on redistributive grounds. The government also imposes additional taxes on specific goods such as gasoline, tobacco, alcohol, airplane tickets, or motor vehicles.[93] Here, we want to analyze whether it is desirable to supplement the optimal nonlinear labor income tax with differentiated linear commodity taxation.

Consider a model with K consumption goods $c = (c_1, \ldots, c_K)$ with pre-tax prices $p = (p_1, \ldots, p_K)$. Individual i derives utility from the K consumption goods and earnings supply according to a utility function $u^i(c_1, \ldots, c_K, z)$. The question we want to address is whether the government can increase social welfare using differentiated commodity taxation $t = (t_1, \ldots, t_K)$ in addition to nonlinear optimal income tax on earnings z. Naturally, adding fiscal tools cannot reduce social welfare. However, Atkinson and Stiglitz (1976) demonstrated the following.

Atkinson-Stiglitz Theorem. Commodity taxes cannot increase social welfare if utility functions are weakly separable in consumption goods vs. leisure and the subutility of consumption goods is the same across individuals, i.e., $u^i(c_1, \ldots, c_K, z) = U^i(v(c_1, \ldots, c_K), z)$ with the subutility function $v(c_1, \ldots, c_K)$ homogenous across individuals.

The original proof by Atkinson and Stiglitz (1976) was based on optimum conditions and not intuitive. Recently, Laroque (2005) and Kaplow (2006) have simultaneously and independently proposed a much simpler and intuitive proof that we present here.

---

[93] Traditionally, excise taxes have been used on goods where transactions were relatively easy for the government to monitor. In modern times, current excise taxes are often justified because of externalities (e.g., gasoline taxes because of pollution or global warming), or "internalities" (e.g., tobacco and addiction in models with self-control issues). We assume away such effects in what follows. Externalities are covered in the handbook chapter by Bovenberg and Goulder (2002).

Proof. The idea of the proof is that a tax system $(T(\cdot), t)$ that includes both a nonlinear income tax and a vector of commodity taxes can be replaced by a pure income tax $(\overline{T}(\cdot), t = 0)$ that keeps all individual utilities constant and raises at least as much tax revenue.

Let $V(p + t, y) = \max_c v(c_1, \ldots, c_K)$ subject to $(p + t) \cdot c \leq y$ be the indirect utility of consumption goods common to all individuals. Consider replacing $(T(\cdot), t)$ with $(\overline{T}(\cdot), t = 0)$ where $\overline{T}(z)$ is defined such that $V(p + t, z - T(z)) = V(p, z - \overline{T}(z))$. Such a $\overline{T}(z)$ naturally exists (and is unique) as $V(p, y)$ is strictly increasing in y. This implies that $U^i(V(p + t, z - T(z)), z) = U^i(V(p, z - \overline{T}(z)), z)$ for all z. Hence, both the utility and the labor supply choice are unchanged for each individual i.

By definition of an indirect utility, attaining utility of consumption $V(p, z - \overline{T}(z))$ at price p costs at least $z - \overline{T}(z)$. Let c^i be the consumer choice of individual i under the initial tax system $(T(\cdot), t)$. Individual i attains utility $V(p, z - \overline{T}(z)) = V(p + t, z - T(z))$ when choosing c^i. Hence $p \cdot c^i \geq z - \overline{T}(z)$. As $(p + t) \cdot c^i = z - T(z)$, we have $\overline{T}(z) \geq T(z) + t \cdot c^i$, i.e., the government collects more taxes with $(\overline{T}(\cdot), t = 0)$ which completes the proof. QED.

Intuitively, with separability and homogeneity, conditional on earnings z, the consumption choices $c = (c_1, \ldots, c_K)$ do not provide any information on ability. Hence, differentiated commodity taxes $t_1, \ldots, t_K$ create a tax distortion with no benefit and it is better to do all the redistribution with the individual nonlinear income tax. With the weaker linear income taxation tool, stronger assumptions on preferences, namely linear Engel curves uniform across individuals, are needed to obtain the commodity tax result (Deaton 1979).[94] Intuitively, in the linear tax case, unless Engel curves are linear, commodity taxation can be useful to "non-linearize" the tax system.

Heterogeneous Preferences. Saez (2002b) shows that the Atkinson-Stiglitz theorem can be naturally generalized to cases with heterogeneous preferences. No tax on commodity k is desirable under three assumptions: (a) conditional on income z, social marginal welfare weights are uncorrelated with the levels of consumption of good k, (b) conditional on income z, the behavioral elasticities of earnings are uncorrelated with the consumption of good k, and (c) at any income level z, the average individual variation in consumption of good k with z is identical to the cross-sectional variation in consumption of good k with z.

Assumption (a) is clearly necessary and might fail when earnings z is no longer a sufficient statistic for measuring welfare. For example, if some individuals face high

---

[94] The Laroque-Kaplow method can be easily adapted to the linear earnings tax case. Consider a linear earnings tax with tax rate τ and demogrant R. The same proof carries over if any tax system (τ, R, t) can be replaced by a pure income tax $(\overline{\tau}, \overline{R}, t = 0)$ such that $V((1 - \tau)z + E, p + t) = V((1 - \overline{\tau})z + \overline{E}, p)$ for all z. This is possible if and only if $V(y, p)$ takes the linear form $\phi(p) \cdot y + \psi(p)$ (up to an increasing transformation). This in turn is equivalent to having a direct subutility of consumption of the form $v(c_1 - c_1^0(q), \ldots, c_K - c_K^0(q))$ homogeneous of degree 1 (up to an increasing transformation) which delivers affine Engel curves of the form $c_k(y, q) = c_k^0(q) + d_k(q)y$. Importantly, the subutility has to be uniform across individuals.

uninsured medical expenses due to poor health, then this assumption would not hold, and it would be desirable to subsidize health expenditures.[95] However, when heterogeneity in consumption reflects heterogeneity in preferences and not in need, assumption (a) is a natural assumption.

Assumption (b) is a technical assumption required to ensure that consumption of specific goods is not a tag for low responsiveness of labor supply to taxation. For example, if consumers of luxury cars happened to have much lower labor supply elasticities than average, it would become efficient to tax luxury cars as a way to indirectly tax more the earnings of those less responsive individuals. In practice, too little is known about the heterogeneity in labor supply across individuals to exploit such possibilities. Hence, assumption (b) is also a natural assumption.

Assumption (c) is the critical assumption. When it fails, the thought experiment to decide on whether commodity k ought to be taxed is the following. Suppose high ability individuals are forced to work less and earn only as much as lower ability individuals. In that scenario, if higher ability individuals consume more of good k than lower ability individuals, then taxing good k is desirable. This can happen for two reasons. First, high ability people may have a relatively higher taste for good k (independently of income) in which case taxing good k is a form of indirect tagging of high ability. Second, good k is positively related to leisure, i.e., consumption of good k increases when leisure increases keeping after-tax income constant. This suggests taxing more holiday-related expenses and subsidizing work-related expenses such as child care.

In general the Atkinson-Stiglitz assumption is a good starting place for most goods. This implies that lower or zero VAT rates on some goods for redistribution purposes is inefficient (in addition to being administratively burdensome). Under those assumptions, eliminating such preferential rates and replacing them with a more redistributive income tax and transfer system would increase social welfare.[96]

6.3. In-Kind Transfers

As we discussed in Section 3, the largest transfer programs are in-kind rather than cash. OECD countries in general provide universal public health care benefits and public education. They also often provide in-kind housing or nutrition benefits on a means-tested basis.

As is well known, from a rational individual perspective, if the in-kind benefit is tradable, it is equivalent to cash. Most in-kind benefits however are not tradable. In that

[95] It also fails in the case with bequests as earnings are no longer a sufficient statistic for lifetime resources in that case. This implies that positive bequest taxes are desirable when the redistributive tastes of the government are strong enough (Piketty and Saez (2012a,2012b)).

[96] This is one of the main recommendations of the recent Mirrlees review (Mirrlees, 2011). The political issue is that it would be difficult in practice to ensure that the VAT reform would indeed by accompanied by truly compensating changes on the income tax and transfer side. Boadway (2012) provides a comprehensive summary of the discussions and applications of the Atkinson and Stiglitz theorem in the literature.

case, recipients may be forced to overconsume the good provided in-kind and would instead prefer to receive the cash equivalent value of the in-kind transfer. Therefore, from a narrow rational individual perspective, cash transfers dominate in-kind transfers. From a social perspective, three broad lines of justification have been provided in favor of in-kind benefits.[97]

1. *Commodity Egalitarianism:* A number of goods, such as education or health care are seen as rights everybody in society is entitled to.[98] Those goods are hence put in the same category as other rights that democratic governments offer to all citizens without distinction such as protection under the law, free speech, right to vote, etc. The difficulty with this view is that it does not say which level of education or health care should be seen as a right.

2. *Paternalism:* The government might want to impose its preferences on transfer recipients. For example, voters might support providing free shelter and free meals to the homeless but would oppose giving them cash that might be used for alcohol or tobacco consumption. In that case, recipients would rather get the cash equivalent value of the non-cash transfers they get but society's paternalistic views prevail upon recipients' preferences. Those arguments have been developed mostly by libertarians to criticize in-kind benefits (e.g., Milton Friedman was favorable to basic redistribution through a negative income tax cash transfer rather than in-kind benefits).

3. *Individual Failures:* Related, recipients could themselves realize that, if provided with only cash, they might choose too little health care, education, or retirement savings for their long-term well being, perhaps because of lack of information or self-control problems (e.g., hyperbolic discounting is an elegant way to model such self-control issues). In this case, recipients understand that non-cash benefits are in their best interest. Hence, recipients would actually support getting such non-cash benefits instead of the equivalent cash value. This type of rationalization for non-cash transfers hence differs drastically from the paternalistic view. The fact that all advanced economies systematically provide large amounts of non-cash benefits universally (retirement, health, education) through a democratic process is more consistent with the "individual failures" scenario than the "paternalism" scenario. The case of education, and especially primary education, is particularly important. Children cannot be expected to have fully forward looking rational preferences. Parents make educational choices on behalf of their children and most—but not all—parents have the best interests of their children at heart. Compulsory and free public education is a simple way for the government to ensure that all children get a minimum level of education regardless of how caring their parents are.

---

[97] The traditional externality and public good justification, analyzed extensively, may also apply to some although not all types of non-cash benefits and is left aside here.

[98] Retirement benefits, although not strictly speaking in-kind benefits, can also be seen as non-cash benefits because they are not transferrable over time, i.e., a young worker typically cannot borrow against her future retirement benefits.

4. *Second-best Efficiency:* A number of studies have shown that, with limited information and limited policy tools, non-cash benefits can actually be desirable in a "second-best" equilibrium. In-kind benefits can be used by the government to relax the incentive constraint created by the optimal tax problem. This point was first noted by Nichols and Zeckhauser (1982) and later developed in a number of studies (see Currie & Gahvari, 2008 and Boadway, 2012, Chapter 4 for detailed surveys). Those results are closely related to the Atkinson and Stiglitz (1976) theorem presented above. If the utility function is not separable between consumption goods and leisure, then we know that commodity taxation is useful to supplement optimal nonlinear earnings taxation. By the same token, it can be shown that providing an in-kind transfer of a good complementary with work is desirable because it makes it relatively more costly for high skill people to work less. Although such "second-best" arguments have attracted the most attention in the optimal tax literature, they are second order in the public debate which focuses primarily on the other justifications we discussed above.

6.4. Family Taxation

In practice, the treatment of families raises important issues. Any tax and transfer system must make a choice on how to treat singles vs. married households and how to make taxes and transfers depend on the number of children. There is relatively little normative work on those questions, in large part because the standard utilitarian framework is not successful at capturing the key trade offs. Kaplow (2008), Chapter 8 provides a detailed review.

Couples. Any income tax system needs to decide how to treat couples vs. single individuals. As couples typically share resources, welfare is best measured by family income rather than individual income. There are two main treatments of the family in actual tax (or transfer) systems. (a) The individual system where every person is taxed separately based on her individual income. In that case, couples are treated as two separate individuals. As a result, an individual system does not impose any tax or subsidy on marriage as tax liability is independent of living arrangements. At the same time, it taxes in the same way a person married to a wealthy spouse vs. a person married to a spouse with no income. (b) The family system where the income tax is based on total family income, i.e., the sum of the income of both spouses in case of married couples. The family system can naturally modulate the tax burden based on total family resources, which best measures welfare under complete sharing within families. However and as a result, a family tax system with progressive tax brackets cannot be neutral with respect to living arrangements, creating either a marriage tax or a marriage subsidy. Under progressive taxation, if the tax brackets for married couples are the same as for individuals, the family system typically creates a marriage tax. If the tax brackets for married couple are twice as wide as for individuals, the family system typically creates a marriage subsidy.[99]

---

[99] The US system creates marriage subsidies for low to middle income families and marriage taxes for high income families with two earners.

Hence and as is well known, it is impossible to have a tax system that simultaneously meets three desirable properties: (1) the tax burden is based on family income, (2) the tax system is marriage neutral, and (3) the tax system is progressive (i.e., the tax system is not strictly linear). Although those properties clearly matter in the public debate, it is not possible to formalize their trade off within the traditional utilitarian framework as the utilitarian principle cannot put a weight on the marriage neutrality principle.

If marriage responds strongly to any tax penalty or subsidy, it is better to reduce the marriage penalty/subsidy and move toward an individualized system. This issue might be particularly important in countries (such as Scandinavian countries for example), where many couples cohabit without being formally married and as it is difficult (and intrusive) for the government to observe (and monitor) cohabitation status.

Traditionally, the labor supply of secondary earners—typically married women—has been found to be more elastic than the labor supply of primary earners—typically married men (see Blundell & MaCurdy, 1999 for a survey). Under the standard Ramsey taxation logic, this implies that it is more efficient to tax secondary earners less (Boskin & Sheshinski, 1983). If the tax system is progressive, this goal is naturally achieved under an individual-based system as secondary earners are taxed on their sole earnings. Note however that the difference in labor supply elasticities between primary and secondary earners has likely declined over time as more and more married women work (Blau & Kahn, 2007).

In practice, most OECD countries have switched from family based to individual-based income taxation. In contrast, transfer systems remain based on family income. It is therefore acceptable to the public that a spouse with modest earnings would face a low tax rate, no matter how high the earnings of her/his spouse are.[100] In contrast, it appears unacceptable to the public that a spouse with modest earnings should receive means-tested transfers if the earnings of his or her spouse are high. A potential explanation could be framing effects as direct transfers might be more salient than an equivalent reduction in taxes. Kleven, Kreiner, and Saez (2009b) offer a potential explanation in a standard utilitarian model with labor supply where they show that the optimal joint tax system is to have transfers for non-working spouses (or equivalently taxes on secondary earnings) that *decrease* with primary earnings. The intuition is the following. With concave utilities, the presence of secondary earnings make a bigger difference in welfare when primary earnings are low than when primary earnings are large. Hence, it is more valuable to compensate one earner couples (relative to two earner couples) when primary earnings are low. This translates into an implicit tax on secondary earnings that decreases with primary earnings. Such negative jointness in the tax system is approximately achieved by having family based means-tested transfers along with individually based income taxation.

---

[100] Note that under a progressive and individual based tax system, only small earnings of secondary earners face low tax rates. As secondary earnings increase, they get taxed at progressively higher rates.

Children. Most tax and transfer systems offer tax reductions for children or increases in benefits for children. The rationale for such transfers is simply that, conditional on income z, families with more children are more in need of transfers and have less ability to pay taxes. The interesting question that arises is how the net transfer (additional child benefits or reduction in taxes) per additional child should vary with income z. On the one hand, the need for children related transfers is highest for families with very small incomes. On the other hand, the cost of children is higher for families with higher incomes particularly when parents work and need to purchase childcare.

Actual tax and transfers do seem to take both considerations into account. Means-tested transfers tend to offer child benefits that are phased-out with earnings. Income taxes tend to offer child benefits that increase with income for two reasons. First, the lowest income earners do not have taxable income and hence do not benefit from child-related tax reductions. Second, child-related tax reductions are typically a fixed deduction from taxable income which is more valuable in upper income tax brackets. Hence, the level of child benefits tends to be U-shaped as a function of earnings. Two important qualifications should be made.

First, as mentioned in Section 5.3.3, a number of countries have introduced in-work benefits that are tied to work and presence of children. This tends to make child benefits less decreasing with income at the low income end. In the United States, because of the large EITC and child tax credits and small traditional means-tested transfers, the benefit per child is actually increasing with family earnings at the bottom. Second, another large child benefit often subsidized or government provided is pre-school child care (infant child care, kindergarten starting at age 2 or 3, etc.). Such child care benefits are quantitatively large and most valuable when both parents work or for single working parents. Hence, economically, they are a form of in-kind in-work benefit which also promotes labor force participation (see OECD, 2006, chap. 4, Figure 4.1, p.129 for an empirical analysis). It is perhaps not a coincidence that cash in-work benefits for children are highest in the US and the UK, countries which provide minimal child care public benefits. Understanding in that context whether a cash transfer or an in-kind child care benefit is preferable is an interesting research question that has received little attention.

Child-related benefits raise two additional interesting issues.

First, families do not take decisions as a single unit (Chiappori, 1988). Interestingly, in the case of children, cash transfers to mothers (or grandmothers) have larger impacts on children's consumption than transfers to fathers. This has been shown in the UK context (Lundberg, Pollak, & Wales, 1997) when the administration of child tax benefits was changed from a reduction in tax withholdings of parents (often the father) to a direct check to the mother. Similar effects have been documented in the case of cash benefits for the elderly in South Africa (Duflo, 2003). This evidence suggests that in-kind benefits (such as child care or pre-school) might be preferable if the goal is to ensure that resources go toward children. As mentioned above, primary education is again the most important example of in-kind benefits designed so that children benefit regardless of how caring parents are.

Second, child benefits might promote fertility. A large empirical literature has found that child benefits have sometimes positive but in general quite modest effects on fertility (see Gauthier, 2007 for a survey). There can be externalities (both positive and negative) associated with children. For example, there can be congestion effects (such as global warming) associated with larger populations. Alternatively, declines in populations can have adverse effects on sustainability of pay-as-you-go pension arrangements. Such externalities should be factored into discussions of optimal child benefits.

6.5. Relative Income Concerns

Economists have long been interested in the possibility that individuals care not only about their absolute income but also their income relative to others. Recently, substantial evidence coming from observational studies (e.g., Luttmer, 2005), lab experiments (e.g., Fehr & Schmidt, 1999), and field experiments (Card, Mas, Moretti, & Saez 2012), provide support for relative income effects. A number of optimal tax studies have incorporated relative income in the analysis (Boskin & Sheshinski, 1978 analyze the linear income tax case and Oswald, 1983 and Tuomala, 1990, Chapter 8 consider the nonlinear income tax case). Those studies find that in general relative income concerns tend to increase optimal tax rates. Relative income effects can be modeled in a number of ways. The simplest way, which we consider here, is to posit that individual utility also depends on the utility of others.[101]

Relative income concerns affect optimal tax analysis in two ways. First, it changes the social marginal welfare weights as a decrease in the utility of others has a direct effect on one's utility (keeping one's work and income situation constant), creating externalities. In our view, the simplest way to capture this effect is to consider that those externalities affect the social welfare weights. If a decrease in a person's income increases others' utility, then the social welfare weight on this person ought to be reduced by this external effect. Whether such externalities should be factored in the social welfare function is a deep and difficult question. Surely, hurting somebody with higher taxes for the sole satisfaction of envy seems morally wrong, Hence, social welfare weights should not be allowed to be negative for anybody no matter how strong the envy effects. At the same, it seems to us that relative income concerns are a much more powerful and realistic way to justify social welfare weights decreasing with income than standard utilitarianism with concave utility of consumption.

Second, relative income concerns affect labor supply decisions. For example, if utility functions are such that $u(c/\bar{c}, z)$ with $\bar{c}$ average consumption in the economy, then a proportional tax on consumption affects c and $\bar{c}$ equally and hence has no impact on

---

[101] Alternatives could be to make individual utility depends on the earnings or consumption of others.

labor supply. This might be a simple explanation for why labor supply is relatively inelastic with respect to secular increases in wage rates over the long-term process of economic growth (Ramey and Francis, 2009).[102] This labor supply channel effect is fully captured by the behavioral response elasticity and hence does not change the optimal tax formulas.

As an illustration, let us go back to the optimal top tax rate analysis from Section 5.1 with a small variation $d\tau$ in the top tax rate. The key difference in the analysis is that the reduction in welfare for top bracket earners would now have a positive externality on the utility of lower income individuals. As long as this external effect is weakly separable from labor supply choices, i.e., $U^i(u^i(c, z), \bar{u}_{-i})$ where $u^i(c, z)$ is the standard utility function and $\bar{u}_{-i}$ is the vector of utilities of all other (non i) individuals, the individual earnings z^i decisions are not affected by the external effect. The external effect is proportional to the direct welfare effect on top bracket earners and the strength of the externality. Therefore, the external effect simply reduces the social marginal value of consumption of top bracket earners from g to $\hat{g}$. The optimal tax formula retains the same form as before $\tau = (1 - \hat{g})/(1 - \hat{g} + a \cdot e)$.

In sum, we think that relative income concerns are a useful way to interpret and justify optimal tax analysis and can be incorporated within standard optimal tax analysis.

6.6. Other Extensions

Endogenous Wages. The standard assumption in optimal labor income tax theory is that pre-tax wage rates are exogenous, i.e., that there is perfect substitutability between skills in production. Interestingly, in the discrete occupational models we have introduced in Section 5.2.2, this assumption can be relaxed without affecting the general optimal tax formula (12). To see this, consider a general production function $F(h_1, \ldots, h_N)$ of the consumption good with constant returns to scale.[103] In that case, wages are set by marginal product $z_n = \partial F/\partial h_n$. The maximization of the government can be rewritten as choosing $(c_0, \ldots, c_N)$ to maximize

$$SWF = \int_i \omega_i G(u^i(c_n(i), n(i))) dv(i) \quad \text{s.t.} \quad \sum_n h_n c_n + E \le F(h_1 \cdots h_N)(p).$$

Note that any explicit reference to wages z_n has disappeared from this maximization problem and the first order condition with respect to c_n immediately leads to the same optimal tax formula (12).

The intuition in a basic two skill model is the following. Suppose an increase in high skill taxes leads to a reduction in high skill labor supply and hence an increase in high skill wages (and a decrease in low skill wages) through demand effects. Because of the

---

[102] An alternative explanation is that income and substitution effects cancel out so that large uncompensated increases in wage rates have little effect on labor supply.

[103] If returns were not constant, there would be pure profits, the results would carry through assuming that pure profits can be taxed 100%.

absence of profits, those demand effects are a pure transfer from low to high skill workers. Therefore, the government can readjust the tax on high and low skills to offset those demand effects on the net consumption levels at no net fiscal cost, leaving the optimal tax formula unchanged.[104]

Theoretically, this result arises because the discrete occupational model is effectively mathematically identical to a Diamond and Mirrlees (1971), optimal commodity tax model where each occupation is a specific good taxed at a specific rate. As is well known from Diamond and Mirrlees (1971), optimal Ramsey tax formulas depend solely on consumers' demand and do not depend on production functions. This generates two important additional consequences. First, the production efficiency result of Diamond and Mirrlees (1971) carries over to the discrete occupational choice model, implying that distortions in the production process or tariffs (in the case of an open economy) are not desirable. Second, in an extended model with many consumption goods, the theorem of Atkinson and Stiglitz (1976) also carries over to the discrete occupational choice model. Namely, differentiated commodity taxation is not desirable to supplement optimal nonlinear earnings taxation under the standard separability assumption presented above. Those results are formally proven in Saez (2004b). They stand in sharp contrast to results obtained in the Stiglitz (1982) discrete model with endogenous wages where it is shown that the optimal tax formulas are affected by endogenous wages (Stiglitz, 1982), and where the production efficiency theorem and the Atkinson-Stiglitz theorem do not carry over (Naito, 1999). Saez (2004b) argues that the occupational model best captures the long-term when individuals choose their occupations while the Stiglitz (1982) model captures a short-term situation where individuals have fixed skills and only adjust hours of work.

Workfare, Take-Up Costs, and Screening. Workfare can be defined as requiring transfer beneficiaries to work, typically for a public project. In its extreme form, the work required has no productive value. In that case, workfare is similar to imposing an ordeal, such as time consuming take-up costs, on welfare beneficiaries. The literature has focused primarily on such "useless workfare requirements." Besley and Coate (1992) show that, if the government cares about poverty measured by net-income rather than individual utilities, it can be optimal to impose workfare. In their model, workfare screens away higher wage individuals who have a higher opportunity cost of time.[105]

Cuff (2000) shows, in a standard Stiglitz (1982) two-type discrete model that a useless workfare program is never desirable with a standard welfarist objective. Interestingly, Cuff

[104] The same result applies when considering differentiated linear taxation of capital and labor income. What matters for optimal tax formulas are the supply elasticities of labor (and capital) and the effects on the prices of factors are again irrelevant. Taxing labor more reduces labor supply, increases the wage rate, and reduces the return on capital, creating indirect redistribution from capital earners to labor earners. However, this indirect redistribution is irrelevant for optimal tax analysis as the government can adjust the capital and labor tax rates to fully offset it at no fiscal cost.

[105] Related, Kleven and Kopczuk (2011) show that imposing complex take-up rules that improve screening but reduce take-up is optimal when the government objective is poverty alleviation instead of standard welfare.

(2000) then extends the analysis to include heterogeneity in tastes for work (in addition to the standard wage rate heterogeneity). When there are lazy vs. hard working low skill workers and when society does not like to redistribute toward lazy low skill workers, workfare can become desirable. This is because work requirements are more costly to lazy types than hard working types.

In practice, finding ordeals which hurt more the undeserving beneficiaries than the deserving beneficiaries seems difficult. In particular, if society feels that welfare is too generous, it is more efficient to cut benefits directly rather than impose ordeals. Both reduce welfare benefits (and hence the incentives to become a recipient), but at least direct cuts save on government spending.

Screening mechanisms that also impose costs on recipients, (e.g., filing out forms, medical tests, etc.) can be desirable when they are successful in screening deserving recipients (e.g., the truly disabled) vs. undeserving recipients (e.g., those faking disability). Diamond and Sheshinski (1995) propose an analysis along those lines in the case of disability insurance (see also the chapter by Chetty and Finkelstein in this volume for more details on optimal social insurance). The key difference with useless workfare or ordeals is that such screening is directly designed at separating deserving vs. undeserving recipients. It is very unlikely that blanket ordeals can achieve this. Today, data driven screening (i.e., checking administrative databases for potential earnings, etc.) are far more powerful and efficient than direct in person screening (and a lot less intrusive for recipients).

Minimum Wages. The minimum wage is another policy tool that can be used for redistribution toward low skill workers. At the same time minimum wages can create unemployment among low skill workers, creating a trade off between equity and efficiency. A small literature has examined the desirability of minimum wages in addition to optimal taxes and transfers in the standard competitive labor market with endogenous wage rates (as in the model discussed above).[106]

Lee and Saez (2012) use the occupational model of Section 5.3.2 with endogenous wages and prove two results. First, they show that a binding minimum wage is desirable under the strong assumption that unemployment induced by the minimum wage hits the lowest surplus workers first. The intuition for this result is simple and can be understood using Figure 8. Suppose a minimum wage is set at level z_1 and that transfers to low-skilled workers earning z_1 are increased. The presence of the minimum wage at z_1 rations low skill work and effectively prevents the labor supply responses from taking place. Some non-workers would like to work and earn z_1 but cannot find jobs because those jobs are rationed by the minimum wage. Therefore, the minimum wage enhances the ability of the government to redistribute (via an EITC type benefit) toward low skill workers.

Second, when labor supply responses are along the extensive margin only, which is the empirically relevant case, the co-existence of a minimum wage with a positive tax rate on low-skilled work is always (second-best) Pareto inefficient. A Pareto improving policy consists of reducing the pre-tax minimum wage while keeping constant the post-tax minimum wage by increasing transfers to low-skilled workers, and financing this reform by increasing taxes on higher paid workers. Importantly, this result is true whether or not rationing induced by the minimum wage is efficient or not. This result can also rationalize policies adopted in many OECD countries in recent decades that have decreased the minimum wage while reducing the implicit tax on low skill work through a combination of reduced payroll taxes for low skill workers and in-work benefits of the EITC type for low skill workers.

Optimal Transfers in Recessions. In practice, some transfers (such as unemployment insurance in the United States) can be made more generous during recessions. Traditionally, optimal policy over the business cycle has been analyzed in the macro-economics literature rather than the public economics literature.[107] The macro-economics literature, however, rarely focuses on distributional issues. There are three channels through which recessions can affect the calculus of optimal transfers for those out-of-work.

First, recessions are a time of high unemployment where people want to work but cannot find jobs. This suggests that employment is limited by demand effects rather than the supply effects of the traditional optimal tax analysis. As a result, in recessions, unemployment is likely to be less sensitive to supply-side changes in search efforts and job search is likely to generate a negative externality on other job seekers in the queue. Landais, Michaillat, and Saez (2010) capture this effect in a search model where job rationing arises in recessions and show that unemployment insurance should be more generous during recessions. Crépon, Esther, Marc, Roland and Philippe (in press), using a large scale job placement aid randomized experiment in France, show that indeed there are negative externalities of job placement aid on other job seekers and that those externalities are larger when unemployment is high.

Second, in recessions, the ability to smooth consumption might be reduced, as the long-term unemployed might exhaust their buffer stock savings and might face credit constraints. This implies that the gap in social marginal utility of consumption between workers and non-workers might grow during recessions, further increasing the value of redistributing from workers to the unemployed (Chetty, 2008).

Third and related, individuals are less likely to be responsible for their unemployment status in a recession than in an expansion. In an expansion when jobs are easy to find, long unemployment spells are more likely to be due to low search efforts than in a recession when jobs are difficult to find even with large search efforts. If society wants to redistributive toward the hard-searching unemployed—i.e., those who would not have found jobs even absent unemployment benefits—then it seems desirable to have time

---

[107] Stabilization policy was one of the three pillars of public policy in the famous Musgrave terminology, the other two being the allocative and redistributive policies.

limited benefits during good times combined with expanded benefit durations in bad times. We will come back to such non-utilitarian social preferences in Section 7.

Education Policy. Education plays a critical role in generating labor market skills. All advanced economies provide free public education at the K-12 level and heavily subsidize higher education. As we have seen earlier, there is a strong rationale for providing K-12 public education to correct potential parenting failures. For higher education, the presence of credit constraints might lead to suboptimal educational levels, providing a strong rationale for government provision of loans (see e.g., Lochner and Monge, 2011).[108] However, governments in advanced economies not only provide loans but also direct subsidies to higher education. Direct subsidies could be justified by "behavioral considerations" if a significant fraction of young adults are not able to make wise educational choices on their own—due for example to informational or self-control issues.

A small literature in optimal taxation has examined the desirability of education subsidies in fully rational models. Higher education subsidies encourage skill acquisition but tend to benefit more the relatively skilled and hence are likely regressive. Absent any ability to observe educational choices, the total elasticity of earnings with respect to net-of-tax rates is due to both labor supply and education choices. If education choices are elastic, the corresponding optimal income tax should incorporate the full elasticity and not solely the labor supply elasticity. This naturally leads to lower optimal tax rates than those calibrated using solely the labor supply elasticity. Diamond and Mirrlees (Unpublished) develop this point, which they call the "Le Chatelier" principle.[109]

Suppose now that the government can observe educational choices and hence directly subsidize (or tax) them in addition to using income-based taxes and transfers. In that context, redistributive taxes and transfers discourage both labor supply and education investments as they reduce the net rewards from higher education. Bovenberg and Jacobs (2005) consider such a model and show that combining educational subsidies with redistributive income-based taxation is optimal—consistent with real policies.

In the simplest version of their model, education d increases the wage rate $w = n\phi(d)$ (with $\phi(d)$ increasing and concave and n being innate ability) at a cost d. Individuals choose d and l to maximize utility $c - h(l)$ subject to $c = (1 - \tau)n\phi(d) - (1 - s)d + R$ where τ is the income tax rate, s the subsidy rate on education expenses d, and R the demogrant. In this simple model, d is an intermediate good that does not directly enter the utility function which depends solely on c and l. The education choice is given by the first order condition $(1 - \tau)n\phi'(d) = 1 - s$. Hence, education is pure cost of production and individuals should be taxed on their earnings net of education costs $n\phi(d)l - d$. This implies that s should be set exactly equal to τ.

---

[108] The government has better ability than private lenders to enforce repayment of loans based on post-education earnings. For example, in the United States, it is much more difficult to default on (government provided) student loans than on private consumer credit loans.

[109] Related, Best and Kleven (2012) derive optimal tax formulas in a context where effort when young has positive effects on wages later in life.

7. LIMITS OF THE WELFARIST APPROACH AND ALTERNATIVES

7.1. Issues with the Welfarist Approach

All our analysis so far has followed the standard welfarist approach whereby the government objective is to maximize a weighted sum of individual utilities (or an increasing transformation of utilities). As we saw, all optimal tax formulas can be expressed in terms of the social marginal welfare weights attached to each individual which measure the social value of an extra dollar of consumption to each individual.

In standard optimal tax analysis, the utilitarian case (maximizing the unweighted sum of individual utilities) is by far the most widely used. In that case, social welfare weights are proportional to the marginal utility of consumption. As we have seen, this criterion generates a number of predictions at odds with actual tax systems and with people's intuitive sense of redistributive justice.

First, if individuals do not respond to taxes, i.e., if pre-tax incomes are fixed, and individual utilities are concave, then utilitarianism recommends a 100% tax, and full redistribution. In reality, even absent behavioral responses, many and perhaps even most people would still object to confiscatory taxation on the grounds that people deserve to keep part of the income they have created.

Second and related, views on taxes and redistribution seem largely shaped by views on whether the income generating process is fair and whether individual incomes are deserved or not. The public tends to dislike the redistribution of fairly earned income through one's effort but is in favor of redistributing income earned unfairly or due to pure luck (see Piketty, 1995 for a theoretical model and Alesina & Giuliano, 2011, chap. 4 for a recent survey). Such distinctions are irrelevant for utilitarianism.

Third, as we have seen in Section 6.1 on tagging, under utilitarianism, optimal taxes should depend on all observable characteristics which are correlated with intrinsic earning ability. In practice, taxes and transfers use very few of the potentially available tags. Society seems to have horizontal equity concerns and using tags to achieve indirect redistribution is hence perceived to be unfair.

Fourth, perceptions about recipients seem to matter a great deal for the public views on transfers. Most people support transfers for people really unable to work, such as the truly disabled but most people dislike transfers to people able to work and who would work absent transfers. In the standard model, behavioral responses matter for optimal taxes only through their effects on the government budget. In reality, the presence of behavioral responses also colors the public perceptions on how deserving transfer beneficiaries are.

7.2. Alternatives

A number of alternatives to welfarism have been proposed in the literature.

Pareto Principle. First, let us recall that the standard utilitarian criterion can be easily extended, as we have seen, by considering a weighted sum of individual utilities (instead of a simple sum). Those positive weights are called *Pareto weights*. By changing those weights, we can describe the set of all second-best Pareto efficient tax equilibria. It seems natural that any "optimal tax system" should be at least second-best Pareto efficient, i.e., no feasible tax reform can improve the welfare of everybody. Hence, the Pareto principle imposes a reasonable but weak condition on tax optima. Indeed, optimal tax analysis was particularly interested in finding properties that hold true for all such second-best optima.[110] Those properties are relatively few, an example being the Atkinson and Stiglitz theorem. Hence, considering arbitrary weights is not going to be enough to obtain definite conclusions in general. Hence, it is necessary to be able to put more structure on those Pareto weights so that we can select among the wide set of second-best Pareto optimal tax systems.

All the examples of alternatives to utilitarianism we describe next show that any criterion leads to a specific set of marginal social welfare weights.

Rawlsian Criterion. In the Rawlsian criterion, Pareto weights are concentrated solely on the most disadvantaged person in the economy. This amounts to maximizing the utility of the person with the minimum utility, hence this criterion is also called the *maxi-min* objective. A judgment needs to be made as to who is the most disadvantaged person. In models with homogeneous preferences and heterogeneous skills, the most disadvantaged person is naturally the person with the lowest skill and hence the lowest earnings. This criterion has the appealing feature that, once society agrees on who is the most disadvantaged person, the optimum is independent of the cardinal choice for individual utilities. The key weakness of this criterion is that it concentrates all social welfare on the most disadvantaged and hence represents extreme redistributive tastes. Intuitively, it seems clear that the political process will put weight on a broader set of voters than solely the most disadvantaged. Hence, the Rawlsian principle makes sense politically only if the most disadvantaged form a majority of the population. This is not a realistic assumption in the case of redistribution of labor income.[111] For example, we have seen in Section 4.1 that a standard median voter outcome puts all the weight on the median voter preferences.

Libertarianism and Benefits Principle. At the other extreme, libertarians argue that the government should not do any redistribution through taxes and transfers. Therefore, taxes should be set according to the benefits received from government spending, individual by individual. This is known as the *benefits principle* of taxation. Any redistribution over and above benefits is seen as unjust confiscation of individual incomes. Such a principle can be formally captured by assuming that social marginal welfare weights are

---

[110] Guesnerie (1995) studies the structure of Pareto optima in the Diamond and Mirrlees (1971) model of linear commodity taxation and Werning (2007) studies the structure of Pareto optima in the Mirrlees (1971) model of nonlinear optimal income taxation.

[111] It is a more realistic assumption in the case of inheritance taxation where indeed about half of the population receives negligible inheritances (see Piketty and Saez (2012a,b) for an analysis of optimal inheritance taxation along those lines).

identical across individuals (in the situation where taxes correspond to benefits). In that case, additional redistribution does not add to social welfare.[112] While some voters may hold libertarian views, as we discussed in Section 2.1, all OECD countries do accomplish very substantial redistribution across individuals, and hence depart very significantly from the benefits principle of taxation. This shows that the benefits principle cannot by itself account for actual tax systems.

Principles of Responsibility and Compensation. The general idea is that individuals should be compensated for circumstances affecting their welfare over which they have no control, such as their family background or disability at birth. This is the principle of compensation. In contrast, individuals should be held responsible for circumstances which they control such as how many hours they work. Hence, no redistribution should take place based on such choices. This is the principle of responsibility. These principles are presented and discussed in detail in Kolm (1996), Roemer (1998), Fleurbaey (2008), Fleurbaey and Maniquet (2011).

An example often presented in the literature is that of individuals differing by their wage rate which they do not control (for example because it is due to exogenous ability), and by their taste for leisure (some people prefer goods consumption, some people prefer leisure consumption). By the principle of compensation, it is fair to redistribute from high wage to low wage individuals. By the principle of responsibility, it is unfair to redistribute from goods lovers toward leisure lovers. When there is only one dimension of heterogeneity, those principles are easy to apply. For example, if individuals differ only according to their wage rate (and not in their tastes), then the principle of compensation boils down to a Rawlsian criterion whereby the tax and transfer system should provide as much compensation as possible to the lowest wage people. In terms of welfarism, social marginal welfare weights are fully concentrated on the lowest wage person. If individuals differ solely in taste for work, the principle of responsibility calls for no redistribution at all because everybody has the same time endowment that they can divide between work and leisure based on their relative tastes for goods consumption vs. leisure consumption. It would be unfair to redistribute based on tastes.[113] The standard welfarist approach cannot easily obtain this meaningful result, except through a renormalization of Pareto weights so that social marginal utilities of consumption are the same across individuals (absent transfers).[114]

---

[112] Weinzierl (2012) proposes a formalization of this principle and considers mixed utilitarian and libertarian objectives. Feldstein (2012) argues that it is "repugnant" to put zero asymptotic welfare weight on top earners (as implied by the utilitarian framework used in the Mirrlees Review), but does not propose an explicit model specifying how the proper welfare weights should be set.

[113] This becomes clear when one considers an equivalent model where everybody has the same money endowment to divide between two goods, say apples and oranges. In such an economy, there is no reason to discriminate in favor of or against apple lovers vs. orange lovers.

[114] Lockwood and Weinzierl (2012) explore the effects of taste heterogeneity for optimal income taxation and show that it can substantially affect optimal tax rates through its effects on social marginal welfare weights.

However, those two principles can conflict in situations where there is heterogeneity in both dimensions (skills and taste for leisure). Fleurbaey (2004) presents a simple example in a two skill, two levels of taste for leisure model showing that it is not possible to fulfill both the responsibility principle and the compensation principle at the same time. Therefore, some trade off needs to be made between the two principles. This trade-off needs to be specified through a social objective function. Fleurbaey (2008) reviews this literature and the many criteria that have been proposed.[115]

Equal Opportunity. One prominent example of how to trade-off the responsibility vs. the compensation principles is Roemer (1998) and Roemer et al. (2003) who propose an *Equal Opportunity* criterion. In the model of Roemer et al. (2003), individuals differ solely in their wage rate w but the wage rate depends in part on family background and in part on merit (i.e., personal effort in getting an education, getting ahead, etc.). The model uses quasi-linear utility functions $u = c - h(l)$ uniform across individuals. In the model, people are responsible for wage differences due to merit but not for wage differences due to family background. Suppose for simplicity there is a low and high family background. The distribution of wage rates is equal to $F_0(w)$ and $F_1(w)$ among those coming from low and high family backgrounds respectively. Assume that high family background provides an advantage so that $F_1(w)$ stochastically dominates $F_0(w)$. The government wants to redistribute from high to low family backgrounds but does not want to redistribute across individuals with different wages within a family background group because their position within the group is due to merit. The government can only observe earnings wl and cannot observe family background (nor the wage rate). Hence, the government is limited to using a nonlinear income tax $T(wl)$ and cannot discriminate directly based on family background. Individuals choose l to maximize their utility $u = wl - T(wl) - h(l)$.

By assumption, two individuals in the same wage percentile p within their family background group are equally deserving. Therefore, any discrepancy in the utility across family background conditional on wage percentile should be corrected. This can be captured by a local social welfare function at percentile p given by $\min_{i=0,1}[w_{p,i}l_{p,i} - T(w_{p,i}l_{p,i}) - h(l_{p,i})]$ where $w_{p,i}$ is the pth percentile wage rate in family background group i, and $l_{p,i}$ the labor supply choice of the pth percentile wage person in group i. Total social welfare is then obtained by summing across all percentiles. Hence, we have

$$SWF = \int_{p=0}^{p=1} \min_{i=0,1}[w_{p,i}l_{p,i} - T(w_{p,i}l_{p,i}) - h(l_{p,i})]dp.$$

Effectively, the social criterion is *locally Rawlsian* as it wants to redistribute across family background groups conditional on merit (percentile) to level the field as much as

---

[115] A number of those criteria can violate the Pareto principle, which is an unappealing feature. Hence, additional axioms have to be added to ensure that the Pareto principle is respected.

possible but does not value redistribution within a family background group (as utilities are quasi-linear).

Because high family background provides an advantage, we have $w_{p,1} > w_{p,0}$. Hence the pth percentile individual in the high family background has a higher utility than the pth percentile individual in the low family background. As a result, total social welfare can be rewritten as:

$$SWF = \int_{p=0}^{p=1} [w_{p,0} l_{p,0} - T(w_{p,0} l_{p,0}) - h(l_{p,0})] dp = \int_w [wl - T(wl) - h(l)] dF_0(w),$$

This criterion is equivalent to a standard welfarist objective $\int g(w)[wl - T(wl) - h(l)] dF(w)$ with the following social marginal welfare weights. The weights are equal to zero for those with high family background and equal and constant for those with low family background. Hence, the average social welfare weight at wage w is simply $g(w) = f_0(w)/(f_0(w) + f_1(w))$, i.e., the relative fraction of individuals at wage w coming from a low family background. Presumably, $g(w)$ decreases with w as it is harder to obtain (through merit) a high wage when coming from a low family background.

The standard Diamond (1998) optimal nonlinear tax theory of Section 5 applies in this case by simply substituting the standard welfarist weights by those weights. For example, the optimal top tax rate is given again by the simple formula $\tau = (1-g)/(1-g+a \cdot e)$ where g is the relative fraction of top earners coming from a low family background. If nobody coming from a low family background can make it to the top, then $g = 0$ and the optimal top tax rate is set to maximize tax revenue.

Generalized Social Welfare Weights. A systematic approach recently proposed by Saez and Stantcheva (2013) is to consider *generalized social marginal welfare weights* that are ex-ante specified to fit justice principles. Those social marginal welfare weights reflect the relative value of marginal consumption that society places on each individual. Hence, they can be used to evaluate the aggregate social gain or loss created by any revenue neutral tax reform. A tax system is "optimal" if no small revenue neutral reform yields a net gain when adding gains and losses across individuals weighted using those generalized social marginal welfare weights. Importantly, the optimum no longer necessarily maximizes an ex-ante social objective function. Naturally, the optimal tax system that arises is second-best Pareto efficient as long as the social marginal welfare weights are specified to be non-negative.

This framework is therefore general and contains as special cases virtually all the situations we have discussed before. The use of suitable generalized social welfare weights can resolve many of the puzzles of the traditional utilitarian approach and account for existing tax policy debates and structures.

First, if generalized social marginal welfare weights depend positively on net taxes paid, in addition to net disposable income, the optimal tax rate is no longer 100% even absent behavioral responses.

Second, generalized social welfare weights can also capture the fact that society prefers taxes on income due to luck rather than taxes on income due to work. As shown in the example above from Roemer et al. (2003), the social welfare weights can be set to zero for those who have an undue advantage because of family background or income due to luck. Such "locally Rawlsian" weights capture the intuition that it is fair to redistribute along some dimensions but not others. When redistribution is deemed fair, it should be as large as possible as long as it benefits those deem Roemer et al. (2003), Piketty and Saez (2012a,2012b) also use such weights in the context of inheritance taxation where weights are set to zero for all those who receive positive inheritances. In the context of inheritance taxation, this yields relatively robust outcomes, due to the fact that the bottom half of the population generally receives close to zero inheritance. We suspect that this approach could be fruitfully extended to the optimal taxation of top labor incomes. For example, if individuals whose parents were in the bottom half of the income distribution have small probabilities to reach the top 1% of the earnings distribution, then this probability could be used as the welfare weight for the top 1%. One key advantage of this approach-based upon transition probabilities and mobility matrices is that it provides an objective, non-ideological basis upon which welfare evaluations can be made.

Third and related, generalized social welfare weights can capture horizontal equity concerns as well. Weights can be set to zero on anybody who benefits from a favorable treatment based on a policy that creates horizontal inequity (such as, for instance, shorter people in a tax system based on height). In that case, tax policies creating horizontal inequities will arise only if they benefit the group that is being discriminated against, i.e., taxing the tall more is desirable only if the tall end up better off in this new tax system as well. This drastically reduces the scope for using additional characteristics in the tax and transfer system, consistent with the rare use of tags in real policies.

Fourth, generalized social welfare weights can be made dependent on what individuals would have done absent taxes and transfers. For example, social welfare weights can be set to zero on "free loaders" who would have worked absent means-tested transfers. This sharply reduces the desirability of transfers when behavioral responses are large for *fairness reasons* (in addition to the standard budgetary reason).

Naturally, the flexibility of generalized social weights begs the question of what social welfare weights ought to be and how they are formed. First, generalized welfare weights can be derived from social justice principles, leading to a normative theory of taxation. The most famous example is the Rawlsian theory where the generalized social marginal welfare weights are concentrated solely on the most disadvantaged members of society. As we discussed, "locally Rawlsian" weights as in Roemer (1998), Roemer et al. (2003), or Piketty and Saez (2012a,2012b) can also be normatively appealing to model preferences for redistribution based on some but not all characteristics. Second, generalized welfare weights could also be derived empirically, by estimating actual social preferences of the public, leading to a positive theory of taxation. There is indeed a small body of work trying to uncover perceptions of the public about various tax policies. Those approaches either start from the existing tax and transfers system and reverse engineer it to obtain the underlying social preferences (see e.g., Ahmad & Stern (1984) for commodity taxation and Bourguignon and Spadaro (2012) for nonlinear income taxation) or directly elicit preferences on various social issues in surveys (see e.g., Fong, 2001 and Frohlich & Oppenheimer, 1992). Social preferences of the public are shaped by beliefs about what drives disparities in individual economic outcomes (effort, luck, background, etc.) as in the model of Piketty (1995). In principle, economists can cast light on those mechanisms and hence enlighten public perceptions so as to move the debate back to higher level normative principles.

APPENDIX

A.1 Formal Derivation of the Optimal Nonlinear Tax Rate

We specialize the Mirrlees (1971) model to the case with no income effects, as in Diamond (1998). All individuals have the same quasi-linear utility function $u(c, l) = c - v(l)$ where c is disposable income and l is labor supply with $v(l)$ increasing and convex in l. Individuals differ only in their skill level, denoted by n, which measures their marginal productivity. Earnings are equal to $z = nl$. The population is normalized to one and the distribution of skills is $F(n)$, with density $f(n)$ and support $[0, \infty)$. The government cannot observe skills and thus is restricted to setting taxes as a function only of earnings, $c = z - T(z)$. Individual n chooses l_n to maximize utility $nl - T(nl) - v(l)$ leading to first order condition $n(1 - T'(nl)) = v'(l)$.

Under a linearized income tax system with constant marginal tax rate τ, the labor supply function $l \to l(n(1 - \tau))$ is implicitly defined by the equation $n(1 - \tau) = v'(l)$. Hence $dl/d(n(1 - \tau)) = 1/v''(l)$ and hence the elasticity of labor supply with respect to the net-of-tax rate $1 - \tau$ is $e = (n(1 - \tau)/l)dl/d(n(1 - \tau)) = v'(l)/lv''(l)$. As there are no income effects, this elasticity is both the compensated and the uncompensated elasticity.

Let c_n, $z_n = nl_n$, and u_n denote the consumption, earnings, and utility level of an individual with skill n. The government maximizes a social welfare function,

$$W = \int G(u_n) f(n) dn \quad \text{s.t.} \quad \int c_n f(n) dn \leq \int nl_n f(n) dn - E\,(p).$$

In the maximization program of the government, u_n is regarded as the state variable, l_n as the control variable, while $c_n = u_n + v(l_n)$ is a function of u_n and l_n. Using the envelope theorem and the individual first order condition, the utility u_n of individual n satisfies $du_n/dn = l_n v'(l_n)/n$.

Hence, the Hamiltonian is

$$H = [G(u_n) + p \cdot (nl_n - u_n - v(l_n))]f(n) + \phi(n) \cdot \frac{l_n v'(l_n)}{n},$$

where $\phi(n)$ is the multiplier of the state variable. The first order condition with respect to l is

$$p\left[n - v'(l_n)\right]f(n) + \frac{\phi(n)}{n} \cdot \left[v'(l_n) + l_n v''(l_n)\right] = 0.$$

The first order condition with respect to u is

$$-\frac{d\phi(n)}{dn} = \left[G'(u_n) - p\right]f(n),$$

which can be integrated to yield $-\phi(n) = \int_n^\infty [p - G'(u_m)]f(m)dm$ where we have used the transversality condition $\phi(\infty) = 0$. The other transversality condition $\phi(0) = 0$ yields $p = \int_0^\infty G'(u_m)f(m)dm$, i.e., social marginal welfare weights $G'(u_m)/p$ average to one.

Using this equation for $\phi(n)$, and noting that $n - v'(l_n) = nT'(z_n)$, and that $[v'(l_n) + l_n v''(l_n)]/n = [v'(l_n)/n][1 + 1/e] = [1 - T'(z_n)][1 + 1/e]$, we can rewrite the first order condition with respect to l_n as:

$$\frac{T'(z_n)}{1 - T'(z_n)} = \left(1 + \frac{1}{e}\right) \cdot \left(\frac{\int_n^\infty (1 - g_m)dF(m)}{nf(n)}\right), \tag{17}$$

where $g_m = G'(u_m)/p$ is the social marginal welfare weight on individual m. This formula is derived in Diamond (1998).

Under a linearized income tax system with marginal tax rate τ, we have $z_n = nl(n(1 - \tau))$ and hence $dz_n/dn = l + (1 - \tau)ndl/d(n(1 - \tau)) = l_n \cdot (1 + e)$. Therefore, denoting by $h(z_n)$ the density of earnings at z_n if the nonlinear tax were replaced by a linearized tax with marginal tax rate $\tau = T'(z_n)$, we have $h(z_n)dz_n = f(n)dn$ and hence $f(n) = h(z_n)l_n(1 + e)$. Therefore, $nf(n) = z_n h(z_n)(1 + e)$ and we can rewrite Eq. (17) as

$$\frac{T'(z_n)}{1 - T'(z_n)} = \frac{1}{e} \cdot \left(\frac{\int_n^\infty (1 - g_m)dF(m)}{z_n h(z_n)}\right) = \frac{1}{e} \cdot \left(\frac{1 - H(z_n)}{z_n h(z_n)}\right) \cdot (1 - G(z_n)), \tag{18}$$

where $G(z_n) = \int_n^\infty g_m dF(m)/(1 - F(n))$ is the average marginal social welfare weight on individuals above z_n. Changing variables from n to z_n, we have $G(z_n) = \int_{z_n}^\infty g_m dH(z_m))/(1 - H(z_n))$ where $H(z_n)$ is the actual (not virtual) cumulative distribution of earnings. This establishes Eq. (11) in the main text. Note that the transversality condition implies that $G(z_0 = 0) = 1$.

Equation (17) is particularly easy to use for numerical simulations calibrated to the actual income distribution. Using the specified utility function $u = c - v(l)$, the distribution $F(n)$ is calibrated so that, using the *actual* tax system, the resulting earnings distribution $H(z)$ match the actual earnings distribution. Once $F(n)$ is obtained, formula (17) can be used iteratively until a fixed point tax system $T'(z_n)$ is found. See e.g., Brewer et al. (2010) for an application to the UK case.

A.2 Optimal Bottom Tax Rate in the Mirrlees Model

In the Mirrlees (1971) model, all individuals have the same utility function $u(c, l)$ increasing in disposable income c and decreasing in labor supply l. Individuals differ only in their skill level, denoted by n, which measures their marginal productivity. Earnings are equal to $z = nl$. The population is normalized to one and the distribution of skills is $F(n)$, with density $f(n)$, and support $[0, \infty)$. The government cannot observe skills and thus is restricted to setting taxes as a function only of earnings, $c = z - T(z)$. Individual n chooses l_n to maximize utility $u(nl - T(nl), l)$ leading to first order condition $n(1 - T'(nl_n))u_c + u_l = 0$. Let c_n, $z_n = nl_n$, and u_n denote the consumption, earnings, and utility level of an individual with skill n. Note that $l_0 = 0$ and $c_0 = -T(0)$.

To have a fraction of non-workers, we assume that $u_l(c, l = 0) > 0$ for all $c \geq 0$. As a result, all individuals with skill n below n_0 defined as $n_0(1 - T'(0))u_c(c_0, 0) + u_l(c_0, 0) = 0$ will not work and choose the corner solution $l_n = 0$ and $c_n = c_0 = -T(0)$. Hence, the fraction non-working in the population is $F(n_0)$ and naturally depends on both $1 - T'(0)$ (substitution effects) and $-T(0)$ (income effects).

Using the envelope theorem, the utility u_n of individual n satisfies $du_n/dn = -l_n u_l/n$. Note that this equation remains true even for non-workers at the bottom as $u_n = u$ $(-c_0, 0)$ is constant with n and hence $du_n/dn = 0$ for $n \leq n_0$.

The government maximizes a social welfare function,

$$W = \int G(u_n)f(n)\,dn \quad \text{s.t.} \quad \int c_n f(n)\,dn \leq \int nl_n f(n)\,dn - E(p).$$

Following Mirrlees (1971), in the maximization program of the government, u_n is regarded as the state variable, l_n as the control variable, while c_n is determined implicitly as a function of u_n and l_n from the equation $u_n = u(c_n, l_n)$. The Hamiltonian is

$$H = [G(u_n) + p \cdot (nl_n - c_n)]f(n) + \phi(n) \cdot \frac{-l_n u_l(c_n, l_n)}{n},$$

where $\phi(n)$ is the multiplier of the state variable. As $\partial c/\partial l = -u_l/u_c$, the first order condition with respect to l is

$$p\left(n + \frac{u_l}{u_c}\right)f(n) + \frac{\phi(n)}{n} \cdot \left(-u_l - l_n u_{ll} + l_n u_{cl}\frac{u_l}{u_c}\right) = 0.$$

At $n = n_0$, $l = 0$, $n_0 + u_l/u_c = n_0 T'(0)$, and this first order condition becomes

$$pn_0 f(n_0) T'(0) = \frac{\phi(n_0)u_l}{n_0}.$$

As $\partial c/\partial u = 1/u_c$, the first order condition with respect to u is

$$-\frac{d\phi(n)}{dn} = \left[G'(u_n) - \frac{p}{u_c}\right]f(n) - \phi(n)\frac{l_n u_{cl}}{nu_c}.$$

For $n \leq n_0$, $l_n = 0$, $u_n = u(c_0, 0)$, $u_c = u_c(c_0, 0)$ are constant with n so that this equation simplifies to:

$$-\frac{d\phi(n)}{dn} = \left[G'(u_0) - \frac{p}{u_c} \right] f(n),$$

and can be integrated from $n = 0$ to $n = n_0$ to yield

$$\phi(n_0) = \frac{p}{u_c} \left[1 - \frac{G'(u_0)u_c}{p} \right] F(n_0),$$

where we have used the transversality condition $\phi(0) = 0$. Replacing this expression for $\phi(n_0)$ into the first order condition for l at $n = n_0$ yields

$$n_0 f(n_0) T'(0) = \frac{u_l}{u_c n_0} \left[1 - \frac{G'(u_0)u_c}{p} \right] F(n_0) = (1 - T'(0)) \left[\frac{G'(u_0)u_c}{p} - 1 \right] F(n_0),$$

which can be rewritten as

$$\frac{T'(0)}{1 - T'(0)} = (g_0 - 1) \cdot \frac{F(n_0)}{n_0 f(n_0)} \quad \text{or} \quad T'(0) = \frac{g_0 - 1}{g_0 - 1 + \frac{n_0 f(n_0)}{F(n_0)}}, \tag{19}$$

where $g_0 = G'(u_0)u_c/p$ is the social marginal welfare weight on non-workers.[116]

Recall that $n_0(1 - T'(0))u_c(c_0, 0) + u_l(c_0, 0) = 0$ which defines $n_0(1 - T'(0), c_0)$. Hence, the substitution effect of $1 - T'(0)$ on n_0 (keeping c_0 constant) is such that $\partial n_0 / \partial(1 - T'(0)) = -n_0/(1 - T'(0))$. Hence, the elasticity of the fraction non-working $F(n_0)$ with respect to $1 - T'(0)$ is

$$e_0 \equiv -\frac{1 - T'(0)}{F(n_0)} \frac{dF(n_0)}{d(1 - T'(0))}\bigg|_{c_0} = -\frac{1 - T'(0)}{F(n_0)} \cdot f(n_0) \cdot \frac{\partial n_0}{\partial(1 - T'(0))} = \frac{n_0 f(n_0)}{F(n_0)},$$

which allows us to rewrite (19) as

$$T'(0) = \frac{g_0 - 1}{g_0 - 1 + e_0},$$

exactly as in the discrete model formula (14) presented in the text.

Note that with quasi-linear iso-elastic preferences of the form $u(c, l) = c - l^{1+e}/(1+e)$, the individual first order condition is $[n(1 - T')]^e$ so that everybody with $n > 0$ works. If there is a positive fraction of individuals with zero skill (and hence not working), the formula above applies with $e_0 = 0$ so that $T'(0) = 1$. Intuitively, the fraction of individuals affected by a change in $T'(0)$ is negligible relative to the number of non-workers so that behavioral responses are negligible and hence $e_0 = 0$.

---

[116] Mirrlees (1971), Eq. (44), p. 185 came close to this equation but failed to note the key simplification for one of the terms (ψ_y in Mirrlees' notation) at the bottom when labor supply is zero.

ACKNOWLEDGMENTS

We thank Alan Auerbach, Raj Chetty, Peter Diamond, Laszlo Sandor, Joel Slemrod, Michael Stepner, Stefanie Stantcheva, Floris Zoutman, and numerous conference participants for useful discussions and comments. We acknowledge financial support from the Center for Equitable Growth at UC Berkeley, the MacArthur foundation, and NSF Grant SES-1156240.

REFERENCES

Adema, W., Fron, P., & Ladaique, M. (2011). Is the European welfare state really more expensive? Indicators on social spending, 1980–2012; and a manual to the OECD social expenditure database. *OECD social, employment and migration working papers*, No. 124.

Ahmad, E., & Stern, N. (1984). The theory of reform and Indian direct taxes. *Journal of Public Economics, 25*, 259–298.

Akerlof, G. (1978). The economics of "tagging" as applied to the optimal income tax, welfare programs, and manpower planning. *American Economic Review, 68*(1), 8–19.

Alesina, A., & Giuliano, P. (2011). Preferences for redistribution. In A. J. Bisin, Benhabib (Ed.). *Handbook of Social Economics* (pp. 93–132). Amsterdam: North Holland.

Alvaredo, F., Atkinson A., Piketty, T., & Saez, E. (2011). The World top incomes database. Online at http://g-mond.parisschoolofeconomics.eu/topincomes/.

Ardant, G. (1971). *Histoire de l'impôt (Vols. 1–2)* (p. 1971). Paris: Fayard.

Atkinson, A. (1995). *Public economics in action*. Oxford: Clarendon Press.

Atkinson, A. & Leigh, A. (2010). Understanding the distribution of top incomes in five Anglo-Saxon countries over the twentieth century. *IZA discussion paper*, No. 4937, May.

Atkinson, A., & Stiglitz, J. E. (1976). The design of tax structure: Direct versus indirect taxation. *Journal of Public Economics, 6*(1–2), 55–75.

Atkinson, A., & Stiglitz, J. E. (1980). *Lectures in public economics*. New York: McGraw Hill.

Atkinson, A., Piketty, T., & Saez, E. (2011). Top incomes in the long-run of history. *Journal of Economic Literature, 49*(1), 3–71.

Auerbach, A. (1988). Capital gains taxation in the United States. *Brookings Papers on Economic Activity, 2*, 595–631.

Auerbach, A., & James, H. (2002). Taxation and economic efficiency. In A. Auerbach, & M. Feldstein (Eds.), *Handbook of public economics (1st ed.). Vol. 3* (pp. 1347–1421). Amsterdam: North-Holland.

Bane, M. J., & Ellwood, D. T. (1994). *Welfare realities: From rhetoric to reform*. Cambridge: Harvard University Press.

Bebchuk, L., & Fried, J. (2004). *Pay without performance: The unfulfilled promise of executive compensation*. Cambridge: Harvard University Press.

Bentham, J. 1791. *Principles of morals and legislation*. London: Doubleday.

Besley, T., & Coate, S. (1992). Workfare versus welfare: Incentives arguments for work requirements in poverty-alleviation programs. *American Economic Review, 82*, 249–261.

Best, M. & Kleven, H. 2012. Optimal income taxation with career effects of work effort. *LSE working paper*.

Blau, F., & Kahn, L. (2007). Changes in the labor supply behavior of married women: 1980–2000. *Journal of Labor Economics, 25*, 393–438.

Blundell, R., & MaCurdy, T. (1999). Labor supply: A review of alternative approaches. In O. Ashenfelter, D. Card (Eds.), *Handbook of labor economics. Vol. 3*. Amsterdam: North-Holland.

Boadway, R. (2012). *From optimal tax theory to tax policy: Retrospective and prospective views*, 2009 Munich lectures in economics. Cambridge, MA: MIT Press.

Boskin, M. J., & Sheshinski, E. (1978). Optimal redistributive taxation when individual welfare depends upon relative income. *Quarterly Journal of Economics, 92*(4), 589–601.

Boskin, M. J., & Sheshinski, E. (1983). Optimal tax treatment of the family: Married couples. *Journal of Public Economics, 20*(3), 281–297.

Bourguignon, F., & Spadaro, A. (2012). Tax-benefit revealed social preferences. *Journal of Economic Inequality, 10*(1), 75–108.

Bovenberg, A. L., & Goulder, L. H. (2002). Environmental taxation and regulation. In A. Auerbach, M. Feldstein (Eds.), *Handbook of Public Economics (1st ed.). Vol. 3* (pp. 1471–1545). Amsterdam: North-Holland.

Brewer, M., Saez, E., & A. Shephard. 2010. Means-testing and tax rates on earnings. In *Dimension of tax design: The mirrlees review, institute for fiscal studies* (pp. 90–173). Oxford University Press.

Cagé, J., & Gadenne, L. (2012). The fiscal cost of trade liberalization. *working paper*, Harvard and PSE.

Card, D., Mas, A., Moretti, E., & Saez, E. (2012). Inequality at work: The effect of peers salary on job satisfaction. *American Economic Review, 102*(6), 2981–3003.

Chetty, R. (2006). A new method of estimating risk aversion. *American Economic Review, 96*(5), 1821–1834.

Chetty, R. (2008). Moral hazard vs. liquidity and optimal unemployment insurance. *Journal of Political Economy, 116*(2), 173–234.

Chetty, R. (2009a). Sufficient statistics for welfare analysis: A bridge between structural and reduced-form methods. *Annual Review of Economics, 1*, 451–488.

Chetty, R. (2009b). Is the taxable income elasticity sufficient to calculate deadweight loss? The implications of evasion and avoidance. *American Economic Journal: Economic Policy, 1*(2), 31–52.

Chetty, R. (2012). Bounds on elasticities with optimization frictions: A synthesis of micro and macro evidence on labor supply. *Econometrica, 80*(3), 969–1018.

Chetty, R., Friedman, J., & Saez, E. forthcoming. Using differences in knowledge across neighborhoods to uncover the impacts of the EITC on earnings. *NBER working paper*, No. 18232. *American Economic Review*.

Chiappori, P. (1988). Rational household labor supply. *Econometrica, 56*(1), 63–90.

Christiansen, V., & Tuomala, M. (2008). On taxing capital income with income shifting. *International Tax and Public Finance, 15*, 527–545.

Congdon, W., Mullainathan, S., & Schwartzstein, J. (2012). A reduced form approach to behavioral public finance. *Annual Review of Economics, 4*, 511–540.

Crépon, B., Duflo, E., Gurgand, M., Rathelot, R. & Zamora, P. (in press). Do labor market policies have displacement effect? Evidence from a clustered randomized experiment. *NBER working paper*, No. 18597. *Quarterly Journal of Economics*.

Cuff, K. (2000). Optimality of workfare with heterogeneous preferences. *Canadian Journal of Economics, 33*(1), 149–174.

Currie, J., & Gahvari, F. (2008). Transfers in cash and in-kind: Theory meets the data. *Journal of Economic Literature, 46*(2), 333–83.

Deaton, A. (1979). Optimally uniform commodity taxes. *Economic Letters, 2*, 357–361.

Delalande, N. (2011a). *Les Batailles de l'impôt. Consentement et résistances de 1789 à nos jours.* Paris Seuil, coll. L'Univers historique.

Delalande, N. (2011b). La Réforme Fiscale et l'Invention des Classes Moyennes–l'Exemple de la Création de l'Impôt sur le Revenu. In P. Bezes, A. Siné (Eds.), *Gouverner (par) les Finances Publiques.* Paris: Presses de Sciences Po.

Diamond, P. (1975). A many-person ramsey tax rule. *Journal of Public Economics, 4*(4), 335–342.

Diamond, P. (1980). Income taxation with fixed hours of work. *Journal of Public Economics, 13*, 101–110.

Diamond, P. (1998). Optimal income taxation: An example with a U-shaped pattern of optimal marginal tax rates. *American Economic Review, 88*, 83–95.

Diamond, P., & Mirrlees, J. (1971). Optimal taxation and public production I: Production efficiency and II: Tax rules. *American Economic Review, 61* 8–27 and 261–278.

Diamond, P. & Mirrlees, J. (Unpublished). *Optimal Taxation and the Le Chatelier Principle.* MIT working paper.

Diamond, P., & Saez, E. (2011). The case for a progressive tax: From basic research to policy recommendations. *Journal of Economic Perspectives, 25*(4), 165–190.

Diamond, P., & Sheshinski, E. (1995). Economic aspects of optimal disability benefits. *Journal of Public Economics, 57*, 1–23.

Duflo, E. (2003). Grandmothers and granddaughters: Old-age pensions and intra-household allocation in South Africa. *World Bank Economic Review, 17*, 1–25.

Dupuit, J. (1844). On the measurement of the utility of public works translated. In K. J. Arrow, T. Scitovsky (Eds.), *Readings in welfare economics* (1969), London: Allen and Unwin.

Eaton, J., & Rosen, H. S. (1980). Optimal redistributive taxation and uncertainty. *Quarterly Journal of Economics, 95*, 357–364.

Edgeworth, F. Y. (1897). The pure theory of taxation. *Economic Journal, 7*, 46–70, 226–238, and 550–571.

Eurostat (2012). *Taxation trends in the European union.* Luxembourg: Publications Office of the European Union.

Fehr, E., & Schmidt, K. M. (1999). A theory of fairness, competition, and cooperation. *Quarterly Journal of Economics, 114*(3), 817–868.

Feldstein, M. (1995). The effect of marginal tax rates on taxable income: A panel study of the 1986 tax reform act. *Journal of Political Economy, 103*(3), 551–572.

Feldstein, M. (1999). Tax avoidance and the deadweight loss of the income tax. *Review of Economics and Statistics, 81*(4), 674–680.

Feldstein, M. (2012). The mirrlees review. *Journal of Economic Literature, 50*(3), 781–790.

Fisher, I. (1919). Economists in public service: Annual address of the president. *American Economic Review, 9*(1), 5–21.

Fleurbaey, M. (2004). On fair compensation. *Theory and Decision, 36*, 277–307.

Fleurbaey, M. (2008). *Fairness, Responsability and Welfare*, Oxford: Oxford University Press.

Fleurbaey, M., & Maniquet, F. (2011). *A theory of fairness and social welfare.* Cambridge: Cambridge University Press.

Flora, P. (1983). *State, economy, and society in western Europe. Vol. I.* (pp. 1815–1975). London: Macmillan Press.

Fong, C. (2001). Social preferences, self-interest, and the demand for redistribution. *Journal of Public Economics, 82*(2), 225–246.

Frohlich, N., & Oppenheimer, J. A. 1992. *Choosing justice: An experimental approach to ethical theory.* Berkeley University of California Press, Berkeley: Berkeley University Press.

Gauthier, A. H. (2007). The impact of family policies on fertility in industrialized countries: A review of the literature. *Population Research and Policy Review, 26*(3), 323–346.

Golosov, Michael, Tsyvinski, Aleh, & Ivan Werning. 2006. New dynamic public finance: A user's guide. NBER Macroeconomics Annual. volume 21, chapter 5, 317–385, Cambridge, MA: MIT Press.

Goolsbee, A. (2000). What happens when you tax the rich? Evidence from executive compensation. *Journal of Political Economy, 108*(2), 352–378.

Gordon, R., & Slemrod, J. (2000). Are real responses to taxes simply income shifting between corporate and personal tax bases? In J. Slemrod (Ed.), *Does atlas shrug? The economic consequences of taxing the rich* (pp. 240–288). New York: Russell Sage Foundation and Harvard University Press.

Guesnerie, R. (1995). *A contribution to the pure theory of taxation.* Cambridge, MA: Cambridge University Press.

Hungerbuhler, M., Lehmann, E., Parmentier, A., Der Linden, V., & Bruno. (2006). Optimal redistributive taxation in a search equilibrium model. *Review of Economic Studies, 73*, 743–767.

Kaplow, L. (2006). On the undesirability of commodity taxation even when income taxation is not optimal. *Journal of Public Economics, 90*(6–7), 1235–50.

Kaplow, L. (2008). *The theory of taxation and public economics.* Princeton: Princeton University Press.

Katz, M. B. (1996). *In the shadow of the poorhouse: A social history of welfare in the United States. 2nd ed..* Basic Books: New York, NY.

Kirchgassner, G., & Pommerehne, W. (1996). Tax harmonization and tax competition in the European union: Lessons from Switzerland. *Journal of Public Economics, 60*, 351–371.

Kleven, H., & Kopczuk, W. (2011). Transfer program complexity and the take up of social benefits. *American Economic Journal: Economic Policy, 3*, 54–90.

Kleven, H., & Schultz, E. (2012). Estimating taxable income responses using danish tax reforms. *LSE working paper.*

Kleven, H., Kreiner, C., & Saez, E. (2009a). The optimal income taxation of couples. *Econometrica, 77*(2), 537–560.

Kleven, H., Kreiner, C., & Saez, E. (2009b). Why can modern governments tax so much? An agency model of firms as fiscal intermediaries. *NBER working paper*, No. 15218.

Kleven, H., Landais, C., Saez, E., & Schultz, E. (2013). Migration and wage effects of taxing top earners: Evidence from the foreigners' tax scheme in Denmark. *NBER working paper*, No. 18885.

Kleven, H., Landais, C., & Saez, E. (in press). Taxation and international mobility of superstars: Evidence from the European football market. *American Economic Review*.

Kocherlakota, N. R. (2010). *The new dynamic public finance*. Princeton: Princeton University Press.

Kolm, S.-C. (1996). *Modern theories of justice*. Cambridge: MIT Press.

Kopczuk, W. (2005). Tax bases, Tax rates and the elasticity of reported income. *Journal of Public Economics, 89*(11–12), 2093–2119.

Landais, C., Michaillat, P., & Saez, E. (2010). Optimal unemployment insurance over the business cycle. *NBER working paper*, No. 16526.

Landais, C., Piketty, T., & Saez, E. (2011). *Pour une révolution fiscale: Un impôt sur le revenu pour le XXIème siècle*. Paris: Le Seuil.

Laroque, G. R. (2005). Indirect taxation is superfluous under separability and taste homogeneity: A simple proof. *Economics Letters, 87*(1), 141–144.

Lee, D., & Saez, E. (2012). Optimal minimum wage in competitive labor markets. *Journal of Public Economics, 96*(9–10), 739–749.

Lindert, P. (2004). *Growing public: Social spending and economic growth since the eighteenth century*. [Two volumes]. Cambridge, MA: Cambridge University Press.

Lochner, L., & Monge-Naranjo, A. (2011). The nature of credit constraints and human capital. *American Economic Review, 101*(6), 2487–2529.

Lockwood, B. B., & Weinzierl, M. C. 2012. De Gustibus non est taxandum: Theory and evidence on preference heterogeneity and redistribution. *NBER working paper*, No. 17784.

Lundberg, S., Pollak, R., & Wales, T. (1997). Do husbands and wives pool their resources? Evidence from the United Kingdom child benefit. *Journal of Human Resources, 32*, 463–480.

Luttmer, E. (2005). Neighbors as negatives: Relative earnings and well-being. *Quarterly Journal of Economics, 120*(3), 963–1002.

Mankiw, N. G., & Weinzierl, M. (2010). The optimal taxation of height: A case study of utilitarian income redistribution. *American Economic Journal: Economic Policy, 2*(1), 155–176.

Mehrotra, A. K. (2005). Edwin R. A. Seligman and the beginnings of the US income tax. *Tax Notes* (pp. 933–950) [November 14].

Mirrlees, J. A. (1971). An exploration in the theory of optimal income taxation. *Review of Economic Studies, 38*, 175–208.

Mirrlees, J. A. (1976). Optimal tax theory: A synthesis. *Journal of Public Economics, 6*, 327–358.

Mirrlees, J. A. (1982). Migration and optimal income taxes. *Journal of Public Economics, 18*, 319–41.

Mirrlees, J. A. (1986). The theory of optimal taxation. In K. J. Arrow, M. D. Intriligator (Eds.), *Handbook of mathematical economics. Vol. 3* (pp. 1197–1249). Amsterdam: North-Holland.

Mirrlees, J. A. (Ed.). (2010). *Dimension of tax design: The mirrlees review*. Institute for Fiscal Studies. Oxford: Oxford University Press.

Mirrlees, J. A. (Ed.). (2011). *Tax by design: The mirrlees review*. Institute for Fiscal Studies, Oxford: Oxford University Press.

Moffitt, R., & Wilhelm, M. (2000). Taxation and the labor supply decisions of the affluent. In J. Slemrod (Ed.), *Does atlas shrug? The economic consequences of taxing the rich* (pp. 193–234). New York: Russell Sage Foundation and Harvard University Press.

Musgrave, R. (1985). A brief history of fiscal doctrine. In A. J. Auerbach, M. Feldstein (Eds.), *Handbook of Public Economics. Vol. 1* (pp. 1–59). Amsterdam: North-Holland.

Naito, H. (1999). Re-examination of uniform commodity taxes under a non-linear income tax system and its implication for production efficiency. *Journal of Public Economics, 71*, 165–188.

Nichols, A., & Zeckhauser, R. (1982). Targeting transfers through restrictions on recipients. *American Economic Review, 72*(2), 372–377.

OECD. (1986). *Personal income tax systems*. Paris: OECD.

OECD. (2005). Increasing financial incentives to work: The role of in-work benefits. In *OECD employment outlook*, OECD, Paris [2005 Edition].

OECD. (2006). Policies targeted at specific workforce groups or labour market segments. In *OECD employment outlook: Boosting jobs and incomes*, OECD, Paris [2006 Edition].

OECD. (2011a). *Revenue statistics*, 1965–2010. OECD, Paris [2011 Edition].

OECD. (2011b). The taxation of low-income workers. In *OECD tax policy study No. 21: Taxation and employment*, OECD, Paris.

OECD. (2011c). The taxation of mobile high-skilled workers. In *OECD Tax Policy Study No. 21: Taxation and employment*, OECD, Paris.

Oswald, A. J. (1983). Altruism, jealousy and the theory of optimal non-linear taxation. *Journal of Public Economics, 20*(1), 77–87.

Pareto, V. 1896. La courbe de la répartition de la richesse. *Ecrits sur la courbe de la répartition de la richesse* (pp. 1–15) [Writings by Pareto collected by G. Busino, Librairie Droz, 1965].

Persson, T., & Tabellini, G. (2002). Political economics and public finance. In A. J. Auerbach, M. Feldstein (Eds.), *Handbook of public economics. Vol. 3* (pp. 991–1042). Amsterdam: North-Holland.

Piketty, T. (1995). Social mobility and redistributive politics. *Quarterly Journal of Economics, 110*(3), 551–584.

Piketty, T. (1997). La redistribution fiscale face au Chômage. *Revue Française d'Economie, 12*, 157–201.

Piketty, T. (2001). Les hauts revenus en France au 20e siècle—Inégalités et redistributions 1901–1998 (p. 807). Paris: Grasset.

Piketty, T., & Nancy Q. (2009). Income inequality and progressive income taxation in China and India: 1986–2015. *American Economic Journal Applied Economics 1*(2), 53–63.

Piketty, T., & Saez, E. (2003). Income inequality in the United States, 1913–1998. *Quarterly Journal of Economics, 118*(1), 1–39.

Piketty, T., & Saez, E. (2007). How progressive is the US federal tax system? A historical and international perspective. *Journal of Economic Perspectives, 21*(1), 3–24.

Piketty, T., & Saez, E. (2012a). A theory of optimal capital taxation. *NBER Working Paper*, No. 17989.

Piketty, T., & Saez, E. (forthcoming). A theory of optimal inheritance taxation. *CEPR discussion paper*, No. 9241. *Econometrica*.

Piketty, T., Saez, E., & Stantcheva, S. (forthcoming). Optimal taxation of top labor incomes: A tale of three elasticities. *NBER working paper*. No. 17616. *American Economic Journal: Economic Policy*.

Ramey, V. A., & Francis, N. (2009). A century of work and leisure. *American Economic Journal: Macroeconomics, 1*(2), 189–224.

Ramsey, F. (1927). A contribution to the theory of taxation. *Economic Journal, 37*(145), 47–61.

Roemer, J. (1998). *Equality of opportunity*. Cambridge: Harvard University Press.

Roemer, J., et al. (2003). To what extent do fiscal systems equalize opportunities for income acquisition among citizens? *Journal of Public Economics, 87*, 539–565.

Roine, J., Vlachos, J., & Waldenstrom, D. (2009). The long-run determinants of inequality: what can we learn from top income data? *Journal of Public Economics, 93*(7–8), 974–988.

Rothschild, C., & Scheuer, F. (2011). Optimal taxation with rent-seeking. *NBER working paper*, No. 17035.

Sadka, E. (1976). On income distribution, incentive effects and optimal income taxation. *Review of Economic Studies, 43*(1), 261–268.

Saez, E. 1999. *A characterization of the income tax schedule minimizing deadweight burden*. MIT PhD thesis.

Saez, E. (2001). Using elasticities to derive optimal income tax rates. *Review of Economic Studies, 68*, 205–229.

Saez, E. (2002a). Optimal income transfer programs: Intensive versus extensive labour supply responses. *Quarterly Journal of Economics, 117*(2), 1039–73.

Saez, E. (2002b). The desirability of commodity taxation under non-linear income taxation and heterogeneous tastes. *Journal of Public Economics, 83*(2), 217–230.

Saez, E. (2004a). The optimal treatment of tax expenditures. *Journal of Public Economics, 88*(12), 2657–2684.

Saez, E. (2004b). Direct or indirect tax instruments for redistribution: Short-run versus long-run. *Journal of Public Economics, 88*(3–4), 503–518.

Saez, E. (2004c). Reported incomes and marginal tax rates, 1960–2000: Evidence and policy implications. In J. Poterba (Ed.), *Tax policy and the economy. Vol. 18* (pp. 117–174).

Saez, E. & Stantcheva, S. (2013). Generalized social marginal welfare weights for optimal tax theory. *NBER working paper*, No. 18835.

Saez, E., Slemrod, J., & Giertz, S. (2012). The elasticity of taxable income with respect to marginal tax rates: A critical review. *Journal of Economic Literature, 50*(1), 3–50.

Seade, J. K. (1977). On the shape of optimal tax schedules. *Journal of Public Economics, 7*(1), 203–236.

Seade, J. K. (1982). On the sign of the optimum marginal income tax. *Review of Economic Studies, 49*, 637–643.

Seligman, E. R. A. (1911). *The income tax: A study of the history, theory and practice of income taxation at home and abroad*. New York: Macmillan.

Sheshinski, E. (1972). The optimal linear income tax. *Review of Economic Studies, 39*(3), 297–302.

Simula, L., & Trannoy, A. (2010). Optimal income tax under the threat of migration by top-income earners. *Journal of Public Economics, 94*, 163–173.

Slemrod, J. (1996). High income families and the tax changes of the 1980s: The anatomy of behavioral response. In M. Feldstein, J. Poterba (Eds.), *Empirical foundations of household taxation* (pp. 169–192). Chicago: University of Chicago Press.

Slemrod, J., & Kopczuk, W. (2002). The optimal elasticity of taxable income. *Journal of Public Economics, 84*(1), 91–112.

Slemrod, J., & Yitzhaki, S. (2002). Tax avoidance, evasion and administration. In A. Auerbach, M. Feldstein (Eds.), *Handbook of public economics (1st ed.). Vol. 3* (pp. 1423–1470). Amsterdam: North-Holland.

Sorensen, P. B. (1999). Optimal tax progressivity in imperfect labour markets. *Labour Economics, 6*, 435–452.

Stantcheva, S. (2011). Optimal taxation with adverse selection in the labor market. *MIT working paper.*

Stiglitz, J. (1982). Self-selection and Pareto efficient taxation. *Journal of public economics, 17*, 213–240.

Stiglitz, J. (1987). Pareto efficient and optimal taxation and the new new welfare economics. In A. J. Auerbach, & M. Feldstein (Eds.), *Handbook of Public Economics. Vol. 2*, (pp. 991–1042). Amsterdam: North-Holland.

Treasury, US. (2005). *Simple, fair, and pro-growth: Proposals to fix America's tax system*. President's Advisory Panel on Federal Tax Reform: Washington, DC.

Tuomala, M. (1990). *Optimal income tax and redistribution*. Oxford: Clarendon Press.

US Treasury Department, Internal Revenue Service. (2012). Statistics of income: Individual statistical tables by tax rate and income percentile. Table 1 available online at http://www.irs.gov/taxstats/indtaxstats/article/0,id=133521,00.html.

Varian, H. R. (1980). Redistributive taxation as social insurance. *Journal of Public Economics, 14*(1) 49–68.

Vickrey, W. (1945). Measuring marginal utility by reactions to risk. *Econometrica, 13*, 319–333.

Webber, C., & Wildavsky, A. B. (1986). *A history of taxation and expenditure in the western world*. New York: Simon and Schuster.

Weinzierl, M. C. (2011). The surprising power of age-dependent taxes. *Review of Economic Studies, 78*(4), 1490–1518.

Weinzierl, M. C. (2012). Why do we redistribute so much but tag so little? The principle of equal sacrifice and optimal taxation. *Harvard business school working paper*, No: 12-64.

Werning, I. (2007). Pareto efficient income taxation. *MIT working paper.*

Wilson, R. B. (1993). *Nonlinear pricing*. Oxford: Oxford University Press.

Young, C., & Varner, C. (2011). Millionaire migration and state taxation of top incomes: Evidence from a natural experiment. *National Tax Journal, 64*, 255–284.

INDEX

A

Actual tax systems
  accounting methods, 414
  benefit principles, 460–461
  characteristics, 446
  first order approximation, 398–399
  individual incomes, 395–396
  of OECD countries, 394–395
  policy debates, 446
  vs. optimal tax system, 407, 459
Administration and compliance, 52, 54
Adverse selection
  vs. advantageous selection, 125–127
  annuity markets, 132
  defined, 128
  equilibrium, 118
  evidence of, 131–134
  key feature, 119, 121
  marginal cost, 120
  policy analysis, 123, 185
  private market and, 140–141, 168–169, 176
  tax subsidies, 121
  testing, assymmetric information, 128
  underinsurance and, 120
  welfare costs of, 115, 120–122, 134, 138
Agglomeration
  advantages, 301
  capital base, 301–302
  economies, 206–207, 216–217, 244
  stock effects, 301
Alternatives to welfarism
  compensation principles, 461
  equal opportunity principle, 462
  generalized social welfare weights, 463
  libertarianism, 460–461
  Pareto Principle, 459–460
  Rawlsian Criterion, 460
  responsibility principles, 461
Asking, for charity, power of, 32, 37
Atkinson-Stiglitz Theorem
  estate taxation, 352
  social welfare program, 446
  supplementary commodity taxation, 446
Audience effect

public broadcasting, 31
television commercial, 3–4

B

Bequest motives
  accidental, 340–341
  behavioral responses, 377–378
  empirical observation on, 381
  intentional, 340
  intergenerational links, 339
  normative issues, 341
  single generation, 337
  types, 350–351
Budget constraint
  for individual givers, 16
  utility function, 3
Bundled donation and consumption, 43

C

Capital gains taxation
  carryover basis, 334–335
  death and, 360–361, 364
  gifts and, 366–367
  implementation features, 330–331, 358–359
  timing of, 363
  unrealization of, 375
Carnegie conjecture, 369–370
Charitable foundations
  in Canada, 8
  Clinton Global Initiative (CGI) as, 9
  endowments of, 13
  share of giving, 7
  strategic interactions of, 3
  tax laws for, 8–9
  tax *versus* non-tax returns, 23, 25–26
  tax-deductible donations, 4
  total contributions in 2010, 6, 9–10
  in U.S., 8
Charitable giving
  adult habits, 42
  asking, avoidance of, 37
  by for-profit company, 43
  charity auctions, 39
  conscious and unconscious responses, 4

CPSIA information can be obtained
at www.ICGtesting.com
Printed in the USA
BVOW04*0711291217
503508BV00020B/91/P

9 780444 537591